P9-DEH-210

English Language Arts
Lesson Guide

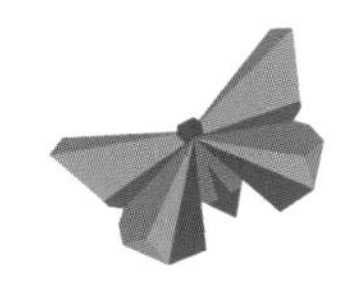

Book Staff and Contributors

Kristen Kinney-Haines *Director, English Language Arts*
Amy Rauen *Director, Instructional Design*
Allyson Jacob, Susan Raley *Text Editors*
Tricia Battipede *Senior Creative Manager*
Julie Jankowski *Senior Visual Designer*
Caitlin Gildrien *Visual Designer*
Sheila Smith *Cover Designer*
Robyn Campbell, Alane Gernon-Paulsen, Allyson Jacob, Tisha Ruibal *Writers*
Amy Eward *Content Specialist; Senior Manager, Writing and Editing*
Dan Smith *Senior Project Manager*

Doug McCollum *Senior Vice President, Product Development*
Kristin Morrison *Vice President, Design, Creative, and UX*
Kelly Engel *Senior Director, Curriculum*
Christopher Frescholtz *Senior Director, Program Management*
Erica Castle *Director, Creative Services*
Lisa Dimaio Iekel *Senior Production Manager*

Illustrations Credits

All illustrations © K12 unless otherwise noted.
Characters: Tommy DiGiovanni, Matt Fedor, Ben Gamache, Shannon Palmer
Cover: Spiral. © Silmen/iStock; Polygon. © LPETTET/iStock

About K12 Inc.
K12 Inc. (NYSE: LRN) drives innovation and advances the quality of education by delivering state-of-the-art digital learning platforms and technology to students and school districts around the world. K12 is a company of educators offering its online and blended curriculum to charter schools, public school districts, private schools, and directly to families. More information can be found at K12.com.

ISBN: 978-1-60153-604-4

Printed by Walsworth, Marceline, MO, USA, June 2020

Table of Contents

Folktales and Legends

Snowy Days

Ancient Greece

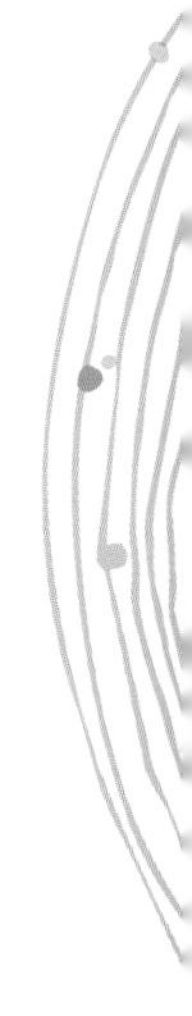

The Tale of Despereaux

Weather, Weather Everywhere

Lessons Learned

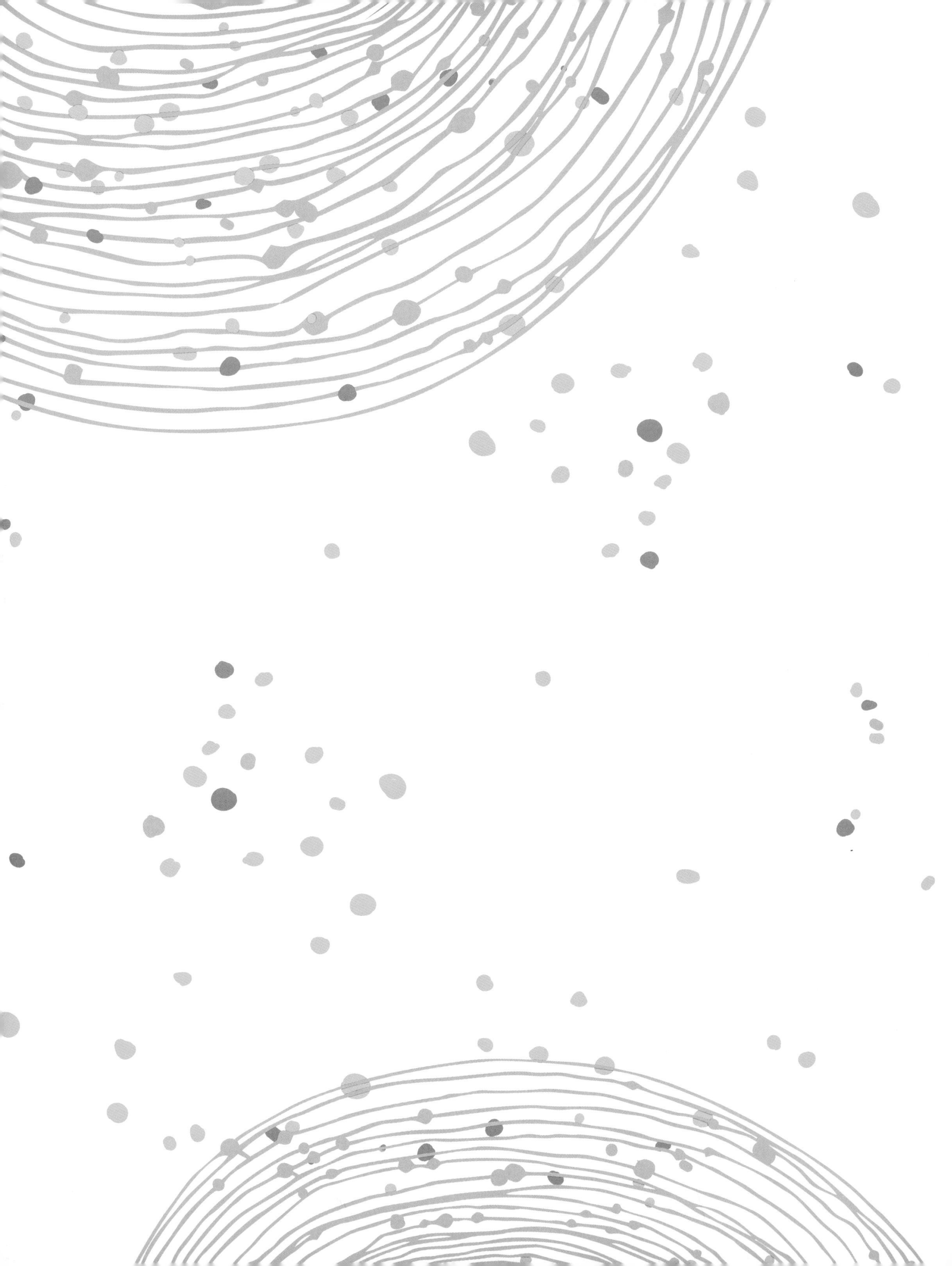

K12 Summit English Language Arts 3 Overview

Welcome to Summit English Language Arts 3. We are grateful for this opportunity to play a role in the English language arts education of your students. We offer this overview of the content and structure of the course as part of our effort to help you best support them. At any time, if you have questions or would like further clarification, please reach out to us. Let's begin.

Summit English Language Arts 3 encourages students to learn independently. As a Learning Coach, your role is to support and enhance the learning experience. Each lesson includes rich interactivity to ensure that students build the depth of understanding they need to succeed on state assessments. Online interactions provide a wealth of data, so teachers know exactly where students are struggling. Offline practice, during which students write directly in an activity book, offers variety. With rich content that engages and motivates students, and enough practice to reinforce each concept, this course includes the tools and technology that students need to succeed.

Course Components

Online Lessons

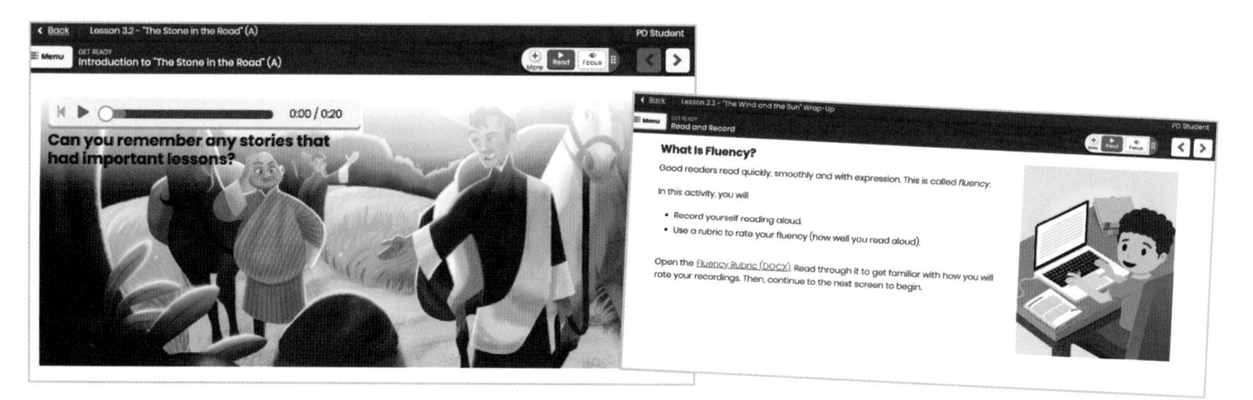

The online lessons make up the core instruction and multiple opportunities for practice in Summit ELA 3. These lessons include

- Instruction in reading, writing, word study, and spelling in a predictable lesson structure
- Interactive activities and assessments that challenge students to use higher-order thinking skills
- A carefully thought-out progression from guided to independent practice
- Computer-scored practice with instant and meaningful feedback

- Learning experiences that support struggling students
- Independent practice using Stride, an adaptive tool that offers individualized practice based on specific need
- Student-friendly learning goals
- Engaging games to review and practice skills
- Access to Big Universe, a digital library of thousands of fiction and nonfiction texts

Rich offline print materials support learning with ample opportunity for students to demonstrate mastery of concepts taught online. Contemporary literature, timely and engaging nonfiction, and a digital library give readers a variety of reading experiences.

Lesson Guide

The lesson guide that accompanies the course makes it quick and easy for Learning Coaches to understand each lesson at a glance—without logging in. The lesson guide provides an overview of a lesson's content, activities, and materials; answer keys for activity book pages; alerts when special Learning Coach attention is needed; and other features to aid the Learning Coach in supporting students.

Activity Book

Summit ELA 3 includes an activity book where students can put pencil to paper every instructional day. Key activity book features:

- Full color pages with sufficient space for students' answers
- Activities that require students to write explanations, analyze and reflect on readings through extended responses, and work through the writing process from brainstorming to publishing
- Custom drafting paper with built-in space for revising
- Spelling Pretest pages that double as study aids
- Spelling Activity Bank pages that offer students choice in how to practice their Spelling words
- A glossary of keywords from the course

Reading Materials

Summit ELA 3 offers students diverse perspectives through both classic and contemporary fiction and nonfiction texts. Print and digital formats are offered. The following materials are included.

***Expeditions in Reading*:** Fiction and nonfiction readings are brought to life through full-color illustrations and photographs. Select words and phrases are defined to support comprehension. While this collection is provided in both print and digital formats, K12 recommends that students read the print format whenever possible and use the digital format on those occasions when learning may need to take place on the go. Research continues to show that students are better able to comprehend their reading when holding a book in their hands.

Trade books: Students receive printed copies of contemporary, high-quality trade books that span genres.

Nonfiction magazine: A full-color magazine, in both print and digital formats, is included with the course and focuses on high-interest topics while teaching students important skills for comprehending a wide variety of text features.

Big Universe: Access to Big Universe, a leveled e-book library, is built into the course. In Big Universe students have at their fingertips over 14,000 fiction and nonfiction texts from more than forty publishers on countless topics.

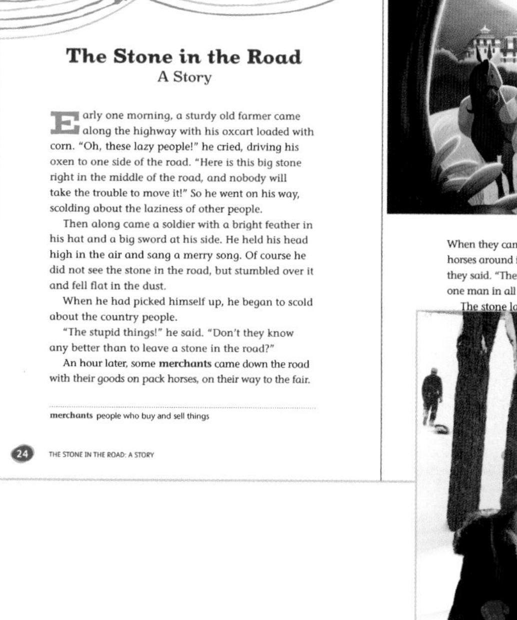

The Stone in the Road
A Story

Early one morning, a sturdy old farmer came along the highway with his oxcart loaded with corn. "Oh, these lazy people!" he cried, driving his oxen to one side of the road. "Here is this big stone right in the middle of the road, and nobody will take the trouble to move it!" So he went on his way, scolding about the laziness of other people.

Then along came a soldier with a bright feather in his hat and a big sword at his side. He held his head high in the air and sang a merry song. Of course he did not see the stone in the road, but stumbled over it and fell flat in the dust.

When he had picked himself up, he began to scold about the country people.

"The stupid things!" he said. "Don't they know any better than to leave a stone in the road?"

An hour later, some **merchants** came down the road with their goods on pack horses, on their way to the fair.

merchants people who buy and sell things

24 THE STONE IN THE ROAD: A STORY

When they came to the stone, they carefully drove their horses around it. "Did anyone ever see such a thing?" they said. "There is that big stone in the road, and not one man in all the country will pick it up!"

The stone lay in the road all that day until the sun

On a cold winter day, big white snowflakes float to the ground. What causes the snow?

When the water vapor in clouds freezes, it turns into tiny pieces of ice. These pieces, or crystals, come together to form snowflakes. If the air is cold all the way down to the ground, the flakes fall to earth as snow.

22 23

Course Structure

Summit ELA 3 uses a well-balanced approach to literacy that connects reading, writing, grammar, vocabulary, and spelling into one integrated course. Dedicated time for keyboarding practice is also included. The course is designed to lead students through concepts based on current state and national academic standards. The material is structured to fit a typical 180-day school year, but it can also be easily adapted to fit individual needs.

Summit ELA 3 is divided into **units**. Units are divided into a series of **workshops**, which are in turn divided into **daily lessons**. Each unit contains workshops, and a workshop centers on a major focus (reading, writing, or word study) and also includes spelling practice. Each workshop ends with time dedicated to review and a quiz or graded writing assignment. A separate **Big Ideas** lesson synthesizes the course content and occurs at the end of each unit.

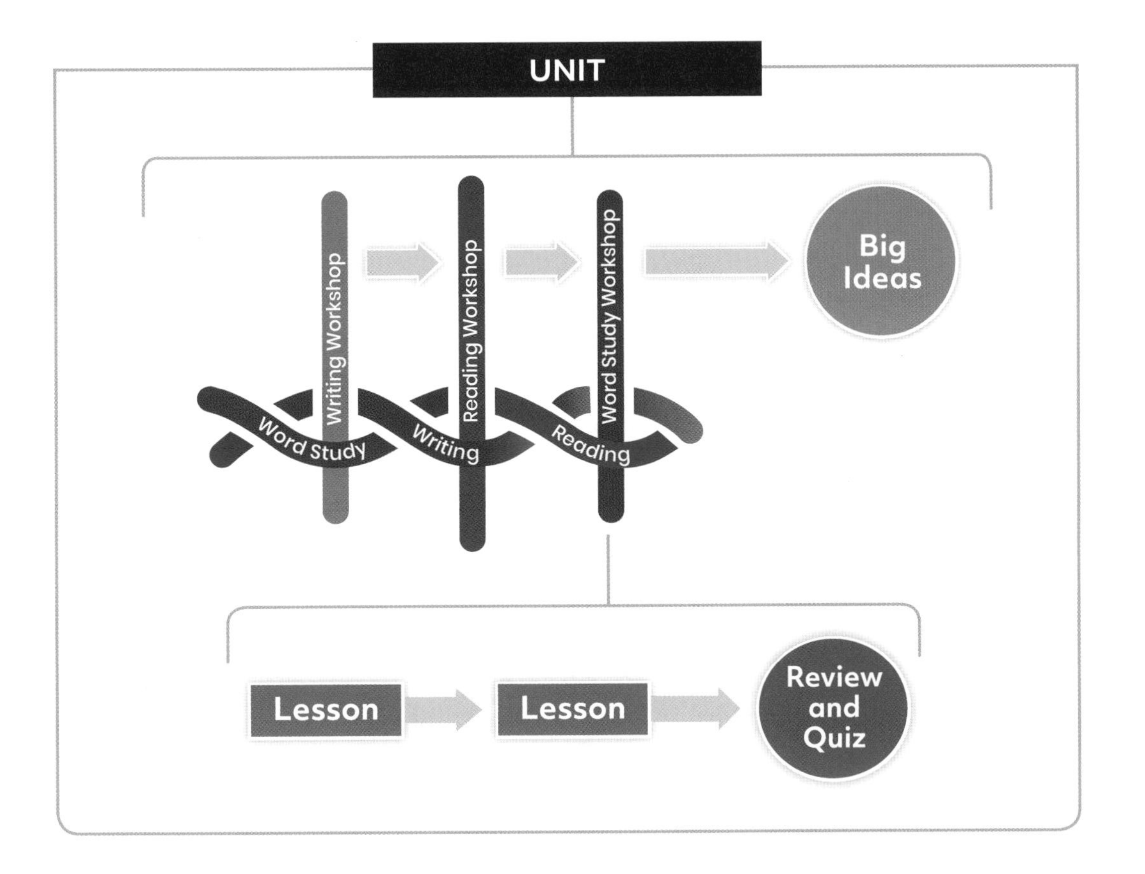

Lesson Model Overview

Reading and writing workshops in Summit ELA 3 follow a multiday learning cycle, consisting of an initial lesson, one or more middle lessons, and a final lesson. Word study workshops, however, are each made up of one lesson only. Regardless of length, each workshop follows a consistent, predictable instructional formula.

GET READY

Get Ready activities introduce and orient students to the lesson content. Spelling activities are also located in the Get Ready section.

LEARN AND TRY IT

Learn and Try It activities include one or more cycles of bite-size instruction coupled with guided practice, followed by opportunities to apply new skills. Reading workshops also contain a Read section, in which students read from the workshop text and answer comprehension questions.

WRAP-UP

Wrap-Up activities include one or two ungraded questions that serve to gauge students' understanding as they exit the lesson. These activities may also include independent practice in Stride, independent reading, and cursive handwriting practice. On the final day of each workshop, the Wrap-Up section is preceded by a graded quiz or graded written assignment.

Initial and Middle Days During the initial and middle days, students learn, practice, and apply the core content.

As students work through these lessons, they are asked to work more and more independently. They progress from explicit instruction, through guided practice, to independent practice and application.

Final Day In reading, word study, and writing skills workshops, the final day of the workshop includes a computer-graded quiz based on the workshop's key objectives. Activities in those lessons prepare students for the quiz. In most Planning and Drafting, and Revising and Publishing writing workshops, the final day includes a submitted writing assignment—either students' written drafts or their final published writing pieces.

Workshop	Section	INITIAL DAY	MIDDLE DAYS	FINAL DAY
READING WORKSHOP	GET READY	Lesson Introduction	Lesson Introduction	Lesson Introduction
		Spelling	Spelling	
		Read and Record (Semester A only)	Read and Record (Semester A only)	
		Reading Foundations or Look Back	Reading Foundations (Semester A only)	Read and Record
		Before You Read	Recall	
			Before You Read	
	READ	Read	Read	
		Check-In	Check-In	
	LEARN AND TRY IT	**LEARN**	**LEARN**	**TRY IT** Activity Book
		TRY IT Guided	**TRY IT** Guided	Review
		TRY IT Apply	**TRY IT** Apply	
		TRY IT Activity Book	**TRY IT** Activity Book	
		TRY IT Vocabulary	**TRY IT** Vocabulary	
	QUIZ			Reading Quiz
				Spelling Quiz
	WRAP-UP	Formative Assessment	Formative Assessment	Stride
		Handwriting	Handwriting	Handwriting
WRITING SKILLS WORKSHOP	GET READY	Lesson Introduction	Lesson Introduction	Lesson Introduction
		Spelling	Spelling	
		Look Back		
	LEARN AND TRY IT	**LEARN** Grammar, Usage, and Mechanics	**LEARN** Grammar, Usage, and Mechanics	**TRY IT** Activity Book
		TRY IT Grammar, Usage, and Mechanics	**TRY IT** Grammar, Usage, and Mechanics	Review: Grammar, Usage, and Mechanics
		LEARN Writing Skills	**LEARN** Writing Skills	
		TRY IT Writing Skills	**TRY IT** Writing Skills	
		LEARN Writing Skills	**TRY IT** Activity Book	
		TRY IT Activity Book		
	QUIZ			Writing & Grammar, Usage, and Mechanics Quiz
				Spelling Quiz
	WRAP-UP	Formative Assessment	Formative Assessment	Stride
		Handwriting	Handwriting	Handwriting
		Go Read!	Go Read!	Go Read!

		INITIAL DAY	MIDDLE DAYS	FINAL DAY
PLANNING AND DRAFTING WORKSHOP	GET READY	Lesson Introduction	Lesson Introduction	Lesson Introduction
		Spelling	Spelling	
		Look Back		
	LEARN AND TRY IT	**LEARN** Grammar, Usage, and Mechanics	**LEARN** Grammar, Usage, and Mechanics	Review: Grammar, Usage, and Mechanics
		TRY IT Grammar, Usage, and Mechanics	**TRY IT** Grammar, Usage, and Mechanics	
		LEARN Writing Skills	**LEARN** Writing Skills	
		TRY IT Writing Skills	**TRY IT** Activity Book	
		LEARN Writing Skills		
		TRY IT Activity Book		
	QUIZ			Grammar, Usage, and Mechanics Quiz
				Spelling Quiz
	WRAP-UP	Formative Assessment	Formative Assessment	Finish Drafting
		Handwriting	Handwriting	Submit Draft
		Go Read!	Go Read!	Stride
				Go Read!
REVISING AND PUBLISHING WORKSHOP	GET READY	Lesson Introduction	Lesson Introduction	Lesson Introduction
		Look Back	Look Back	
	LEARN AND TRY IT	**LEARN** Writing Skills	**LEARN** Writing Skills	**LEARN** Writing Skills
		TRY IT Activity Book	**TRY IT** Activity Book	**TRY IT** Writing Skills
	WRAP-UP	Formative Assessment	Formative Assessment	Publish Writing
		Handwriting	Handwriting	Submit Published Writing
		Go Read!	Go Read!	Stride
				Handwriting
				Go Read!

WORD STUDY WORKSHOP		SINGLE LESSON DAY
	GET READY	Lesson Introduction
		Look Back
	LEARN AND TRY IT	**LEARN**
		TRY IT Guided
		TRY IT Activity Book
		Review
	QUIZ	Word Study Quiz
	WRAP-UP	Stride
		Go Write!
		Go Read!

Activity Descriptions

This table describes each activity type in Summit ELA 3.

GET READY	Description
Unit Overview	The Unit Overview briefly introduces students to the content that will be covered in the unit.
Lesson Introduction	The Lesson Introduction introduces the content of each lesson within an engaging context. It also presents the objectives as student-friendly goals, defines new keywords that students will encounter in the lesson, and lists the key state standards covered in the lesson.
Spelling	Spelling activities include pretests, offline practice in the activity book, online practice activities or games, and graded quizzes.
Read and Record	Read and Record activities allow students to practice reading fluently. Students record themselves reading text aloud, listen to their recording, and evaluate their reading using a fluency checklist.
Reading Foundations	Reading Foundations activities serve to remind students of basic reading skills and reading behaviors mastered in earlier grades. The activities cover topics such as advanced decoding skills and various strategies for improving comprehension.
Before You Read	Before You Read activities introduce vocabulary from the reading by way of online flash cards, provide background information to set context for the upcoming reading, and ask guiding questions to help students set a purpose for reading.
Recall	Recall activities prepare students to continue reading by refreshing their knowledge of what they read in the previous lesson.
Look Back	Look Back activities provide a quick review of the prerequisite skills that are essential to understanding the new content. Students who struggle with the Look Back should seek additional help before proceeding.

LEARN AND TRY IT	Description
Read	Read activities direct students to complete an independent reading assignment.
Check-In	Check-In activities evaluate students' basic comprehension of what they just read. These activities are not graded, but results are visible to the teacher.
Learn	Learn activities are direct instruction. The format of this instruction varies, including guided exploration of a text or writing sample with narrated animation.
Try It	Learn activities are followed by a series of Try It activities. Try It activities differ depending on topic and specific purpose, but all share the purpose of allowing students to practice and apply what they've learned.
Review	Students review the workshop content either by answering questions or playing a game, after which they take a graded quiz.
WRAP-UP	**Description**
Formative Assessment	Formative assessments are those activities with "Questions About" in the activity title. These include 1–2 ungraded questions that gauge students' understanding at the end of the lesson. Although the questions are ungraded, the results are available to teachers.
Quiz	Final days of workshops include graded online quizzes, and/or graded writing assignments that students must submit.
Stride	Additional independent practice with ELA concepts is provided in Stride.
Handwriting	Students work at their own pace for 10 minutes in a handwriting workbook to learn and practice cursive handwriting.
Go Write!	Go Write! activities provide dedicated time for freewriting.
Go Read!	Go Read! activities allow for free reading time at the end of Writing and Word Study workshops.

A Balance of Online and Offline Time

Summit ELA 3 online activities make up about 60 percent of core lesson time. Equally critical to learning is that students spend time reading (for both instruction and pleasure), and put pencil to paper. Summit ELA 3 incorporates daily reading, and offline activities in a predictable place in each lesson sequence. After completing online practice in which instant feedback can help to address any misunderstandings, students complete an activity in their activity book or continue to work on a longer writing assignment.

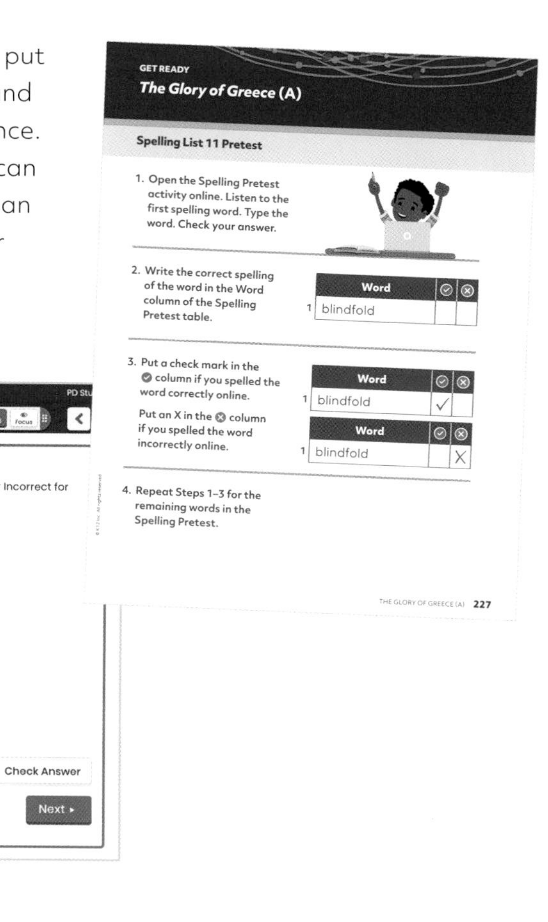

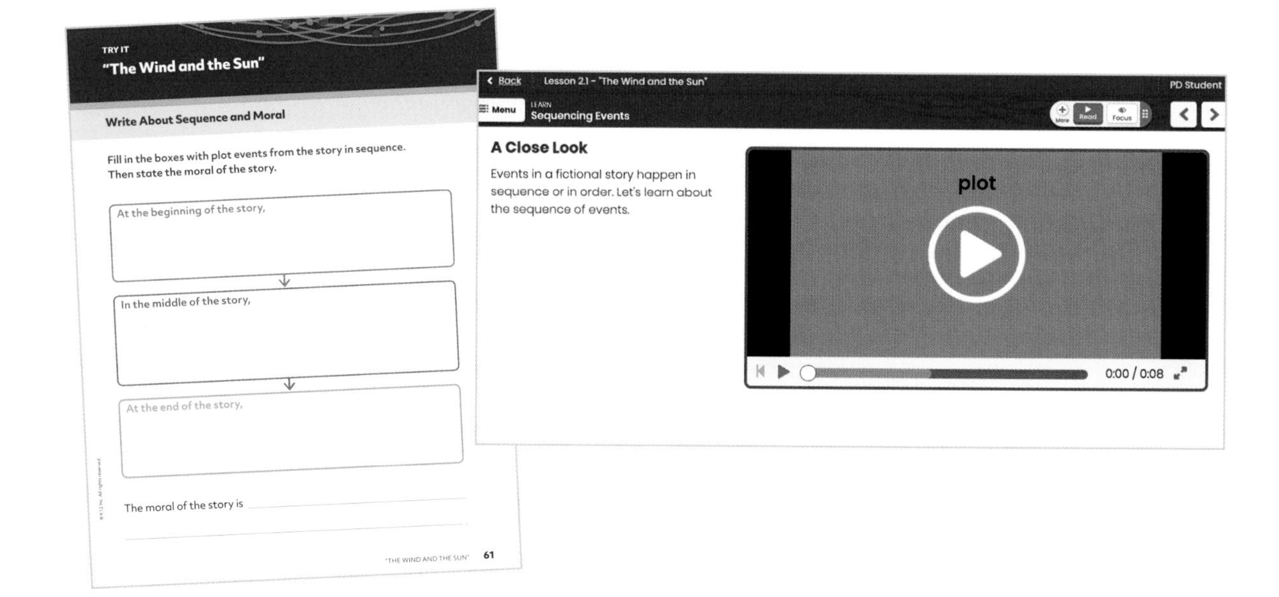

Special Features

In addition to the standard units and lessons, Summit ELA 3 has these special features.

Big Ideas Lessons

A Big Ideas lesson occurs at the end of each unit. In these lessons, students keep their skills fresh by reviewing prior content, practice answering the types of questions they will encounter on state assessments, and complete an assignment that allows them to connect and apply what they have learned. Note that some of these assignments are graded assessments.

Choice Reading Projects

Summit ELA 3 contains one Choice Reading Project unit. In this unit, students encounter a unique reading workshop designed to build their comprehension and critical-thinking skills as they read a work or works of their choice and complete a related project. Research indicates that opportunities for choice enhance student performance and motivate readers.

Students will select a project and corresponding book or books from a bank of options. Depending on the project, the book or books may be available in Big Universe, or you may need to acquire a book on your own. To help students make a choice, the online lessons include synopses of the books and descriptions of the related projects. Review the options with students well enough in advance so that, if selecting a project whose related reading is not in Big Universe, you can acquire the necessary book in time for students to begin the unit.

Embedded Keyboarding Practice

On Your Choice days, students will practice their keyboarding skills using an external website or program. You will need to work with students to select an appropriate keyboarding practice website or program; K12 does not specify which resource to use. A few suggestions are provided in the online activity, including a program that is navigable by keyboard and screen-reader accessible. Depending on which program is chosen, students may need to set up an account to save their progress. You should assist with this, if needed.

Assessment Overview

To ensure that students can show what they have learned and to support high academic outcomes, students need exposure to the types of questions they will see on state assessments.

Online Interactive Questions

Online interactive questions, similar in style and format to today's digital state assessments, provide powerful opportunities for students to demonstrate deep understanding. For this reason, a variety of online question types, including drag-and-drop and fill-in-the-blank, are used throughout Summit ELA 3.

Correctly fill in the blank.

I wouldn't have believed that a dog could surf, but I was at the beach this summer and I saw a collie catch a wave ______. It was one of the most incredible things I've ever witnessed.

dedicated | segregation | firsthand

Check Answer

1 2 3

Which word or phrase **best** completes the passage?

I was just waking up when I heard the [✓ Choose... / whoosh / slurp / squelch / pitter patter] of little feet outside in the hallway. Then came the gentle taps on my door and more so[...]huffling behind it, and I knew my youngest cousins had arrived.

Check Answer

1 2 3 4 5 6 7 8 9

Graded Assessments

Summit ELA 3 includes both online computer-scored quizzes and teacher-graded assignments.

Assessment Type	How Many?
Workshop Quizzes	44
Spelling Quizzes	27
Writing Assignments - Drafts	3
Writing Assignments - Published	4
Big-Ideas: Mini-Projects	4
Big Ideas: Critical Skills Assignments	4
Big Ideas: Responses to Prompts	4
Choice Reading Project	1
Mid-Year Assessment	1
End-of-Year Assessment	1

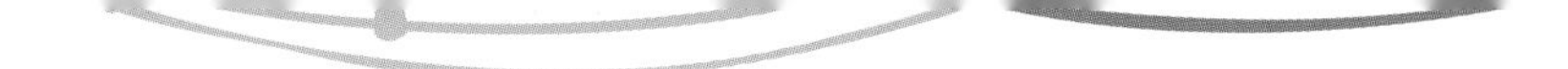

Instructional Approach: Reading Workshops

Close Reading and Textual Analysis

Summit ELA 3 uses a close-reading approach: students read first for comprehension and then reread to support further study of texts. Research shows that students who participate in repeated readings of instructional-level texts demonstrate better outcomes.

Back
Lesson 2.3 - "The Cruel Lion and the Clever Rabbit"
Menu
READ
"The Cruel Lion and the Clever Rabbit"
More
Read
Focus
Listen
Listen to the opening lines of "The Cruel Lion and the Clever Rabbit." Read along as you listen.
0:00 / 0:26
Once upon a time in the Indian forest of Gir lived a cruel lion named Bhaksuraka. Bhaksuraka was strong and mighty. He was also always hungry. Every night, Bhaksuraka would stalk the forest, looking for his dinner. The other animals scattered. They were afraid of the lion's huge teeth and enormous paws.

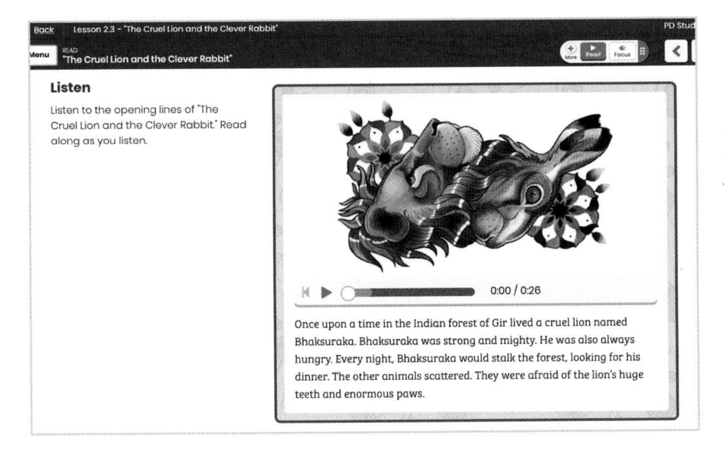

Students are first introduced to a reading selection by listening to a brief reading from it.

Lesson 2.3 - "The Cruel Lion and the Clever Rabbit"
READ
"The Cruel Lion and the Clever Rabbit"
More
Read
Focus
Instructions
It's time to go read.
Open your Expeditions in Reading book. Read "The Cruel Lion and the Clever Rabbit." As you read, pay special attention to text that helps you figure out what the characters are like. When you have finished reading, continue with the online lesson.

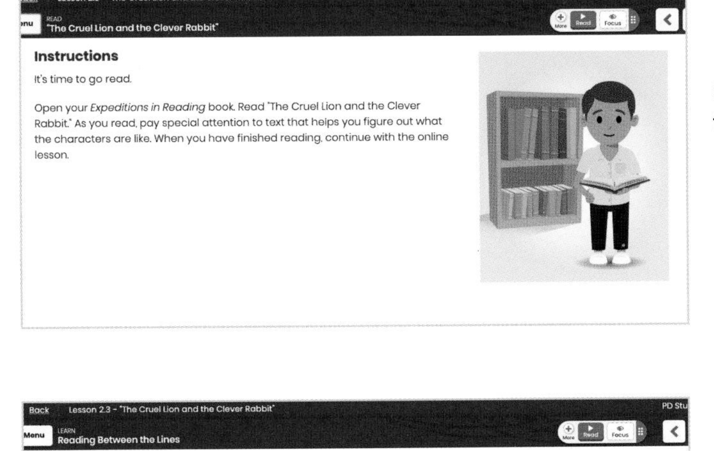

Students then spend dedicated time reading independently.

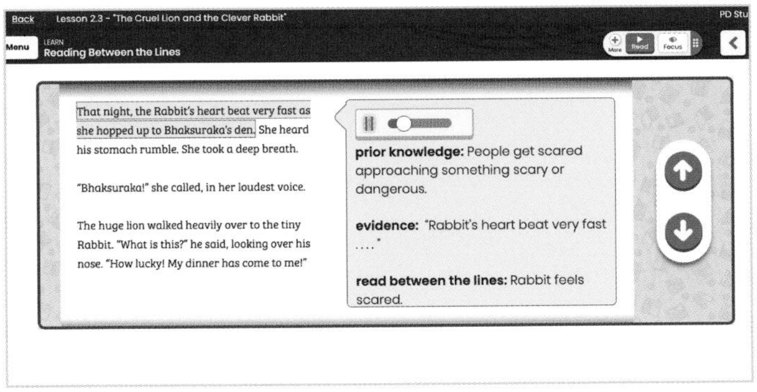

Back
Lesson 2.3 - "The Cruel Lion and the Clever Rabbit"
Menu
LEARN
Reading Between the Lines
More
Read
Focus
That night, the Rabbit's heart beat very fast as she hopped up to Bhaksuraka's den. She heard his stomach rumble. She took a deep breath.
"Bhaksuraka!" she called, in her loudest voice.
The huge lion walked heavily over to the tiny Rabbit. "What is this?" he said, looking over his nose. "How lucky! My dinner has come to me!"
prior knowledge: People get scared approaching something scary or dangerous.
evidence: "Rabbit's heart beat very fast . . . ."
read between the lines: Rabbit feels scared.

In the Learn activity, students engage in guided analysis of the text.

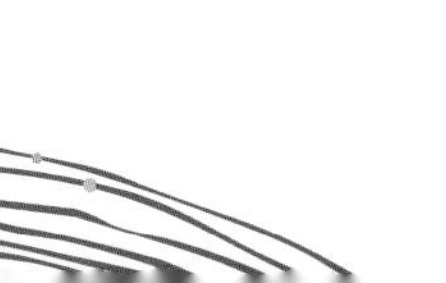

A Mix of Contemporary and Classic Literature and Engaging Informational Texts

The reading workshops engage students in works of literature and nonfiction texts from various genres. In grade 3, the program is an even split between fiction and nonfiction. The fiction selections provide students with contemporary novels to enjoy and picture books to savor, as well as classic tales retold in a new way. Nonfiction topics are wide and varied; students interact with magazines, biographical stories, websites, and even videos.

Reading List

TITLE	AUTHOR	DELIVERY	GENRE
Grandfather's Journey	Allen Say	trade book	fiction
Tea with Milk	Allen Say	trade book	fiction
The Sign Painter	Allen Say	trade book	fiction
"The Wind and the Sun"	adapted from a fable by Aesop	*Expeditions in Reading*	fiction
"The Cruel Lion and the Clever Rabbit"	K12	*Expeditions in Reading*	fiction
"Why the Larks Flew Away"	K12	*Expeditions in Reading*	fiction
"The Stone in the Road: A Story"	K12	*Expeditions in Reading*	fiction
"The Stone in the Road: A Play"	K12	*Expeditions in Reading*	drama
"The Tiger, the Brahman, and the Jackal"	K12	*Expeditions in Reading*	fiction
"Bruce and the Spider"	K12	*Expeditions in Reading*	fiction
Our Wonderful Weather: Snow	Valerie Bodden	trade book	nonfiction
Curious About Snow	Gina Shaw	trade book	nonfiction
Snowflake Bentley	Jacqueline Briggs Martin	trade book	nonfiction
Bear and Wolf	Daniel Salmieri	trade book	fiction
The Glory of Greece	Beth Zemble and John Holdren	K12 trade book	nonfiction
"Tangled Webs"	K12	*Expeditions in Reading*	fiction
"A Flight Through the Sky"	K12	*Expeditions in Reading*	fiction
"Repeat After Me, Me, Me…"	K12	*Expeditions in Reading*	fiction
"Roll, Roll, Roll That Rock"	K12	*Expeditions in Reading*	fiction
"Bury All Utility Wires"	K12	*Expeditions in Reading*	nonfiction
"Keep Our Wires High in the Sky"	K12	*Expeditions in Reading*	nonfiction
"In Favor of Fast Food"	K12	*Expeditions in Reading*	nonfiction
"Down with Fast Food"	K12	*Expeditions in Reading*	nonfiction
The Tale of Despereaux	Kate DiCamillo	trade book	fiction
"Forecasting the Weather"	K12	nonfiction magazine	nonfiction

Reading List (continued)

TITLE	AUTHOR	DELIVERY	GENRE
"Let It Rain"	K12	nonfiction magazine	nonfiction
"Winter Storms"	K12	nonfiction magazine	nonfiction
"Wind"	K12	nonfiction magazine	nonfiction
"Storm Chasers"	K12	nonfiction magazine	nonfiction
"The Secret"	Anonymous	*Expeditions in Reading*	poetry
"The Building of the Nest"	Margaret E. Sangster	*Expeditions in Reading*	poetry
"First Snow"	Mary Louise Allen	*Expeditions in Reading*	poetry
"Winter Jewels"	Mary F. Butts	*Expeditions in Reading*	poetry
"April Rain Song"	Langston Hughes	*Expeditions in Reading*	poetry
"The Raindrops' Ride"	Anonymous	*Expeditions in Reading*	poetry
Michelle Obama: First Lady, Going Higher	Shana Corey	trade book	nonfiction
I Dissent! Ruth Bader Ginsburg Makes Her Mark	Debbie Levy	trade book	nonfiction
Ben's Guide to the U.S. Government Website	U.S. Government Publishing Office	website	media
"Squirrel and Spider"	K12	*Expeditions in Reading*	fiction
"The Stone-Cutter"	K12	*Expeditions in Reading*	fiction
"The Bundle of Sticks"	adapted from a fable by Aesop	*Expeditions in Reading*	fiction
"The Necklace of Truth"	adapted from a story by Jean Mace	*Expeditions in Reading*	fiction

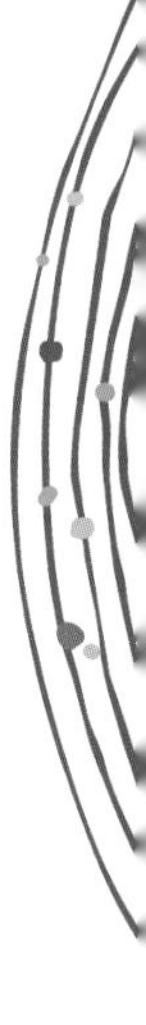

Instructional Approach: Writing Workshops

A Balance of Explicit Instruction and Authentic Writing Experiences

Summit ELA 3 writing workshops prepare students to express themselves as educated people in the twenty-first century. Students analyze model writing samples and then work through the writing process to develop original compositions of their own. An emphasis on thoughtful planning takes the fear out of writing as students learn tangible strategies to make the process manageable. Grammar, usage, and mechanics activities focus on grammatical terms, sentence construction, recognizing and fixing errors, punctuation, and using precise language. Students practice these skills in editing activities and apply them to their own writing assignments.

An Organized Approach to Teaching Process

Students will complete four major assignments by following the writing process: prewriting, drafting, revising, proofreading, and publishing. Assignments include a short story, research report, persuasive essay, and oral history presentation. Each assignment is completed over a series of two workshops, with both the rough draft and the final work submitted to the teacher. Additional writing skills workshops break down the skills needed using model writing samples and short writing assignments.

Research skills, including how to do research online ethically and effectively, are an integral part of the writing workshops. Students will conduct and incorporate research into their informative, opinion, and presentation writing.

UNITS 1–3	UNITS 4–6	UNITS 8–10	UNITS 11–13
NARRATIVE	INFORMATIVE	OPINION	PRESENTATION
Writing Skills	Writing Skills	Writing Skills	Writing Skills
Plan and Draft	Plan and Draft	Plan and Draft	Plan and Draft
Revise and Publish	Revise and Publish	Revise and Publish	Revise and Publish

Instructional Approach: Word Study Workshops

A Focus on Words and Strategies

Word study workshops expose students to a wide variety of vocabulary words, which in turn helps them with reading comprehension and writing. In each word study workshop, students are taught a set of vocabulary words and definitions while also learning about word relationships and using context clues to figure out unfamiliar words. Students look at synonyms, antonyms, and etymology to expand on the core word set. Workshop topics run from understanding nuance and shades of meaning to using Greek and Latin roots and affixes to determine word meanings. Several workshops are dedicated to domain-specific words, such as meteorology and judiciary words, providing a thorough word study experience that helps grow students' speaking, reading, listening, and writing vocabularies.

Instructional Approach: Spelling

A Focus on Patterns

In Summit ELA 3 students learn to spell words quickly by studying spelling patterns that are common to many words. Throughout the word lists, students develop an understanding of sound-symbol relationships and spelling patterns, identify affixes and how they affect the meaning of words, and recognize base words and roots in related words.

However, some words do not follow conventional spelling patterns. Spelling lists in Summit ELA 3 include words that follow the spelling pattern being studied.

Repetition, Variety, and Choice

In nearly all lessons, students are given opportunities to practice and master the spelling words. Each spelling list begins with a pretest, showing which words the student may already know and which require more practice. Pretests are followed by offline practice in which students complete an activity of their choice from a supplied bank. From there, students continue with online practice and a review game before wrapping up the spelling cycle with a graded quiz.

Individualized Learning

Summit ELA 3 is designed to help all students succeed.

Branching Pathways Particularly difficult concepts include practice with branching pathways for struggling students. These interactions are designed to uncover misconceptions and common errors to create a "tighter net" that catches struggling students at the point of instruction. Students receive feedback targeted to their individual responses and are then led through a reteaching activity that corrects the misconception or common error, if they need it.

Stride An engaging teaching tool that motivates students toward mastery and rewards learning with games, Stride offers students individualized practice. Following each workshop's quiz, students will practice related concepts based on their specific needs. Time to use Stride is integrated right into the course to ensure sufficient independent practice time.

Stride's adaptive technology guides students to practice where they need it most—and then serves up a variety of content that is lively and engaging. Stride's vast database of questions, video lessons, and printable resources delivers grade-level appropriate content aligned to the rigor of the Common Core and individual state standards. Stride's assessments identify where students are performing on specific grade-level standards throughout the year and help identify critical foundational gaps missed in prior grade levels. Test prep capabilities pinpoint student strengths and weaknesses for improved student outcomes on end-of-year assessments.

The Help Me Button Located on the lesson menu, this is an additional personalization feature that lets students opt into activities that are dynamically chosen based on the concept they are studying. Recommendations are powered by a sophisticated engine designed to serve up the activities most likely to be effective for the individual student.

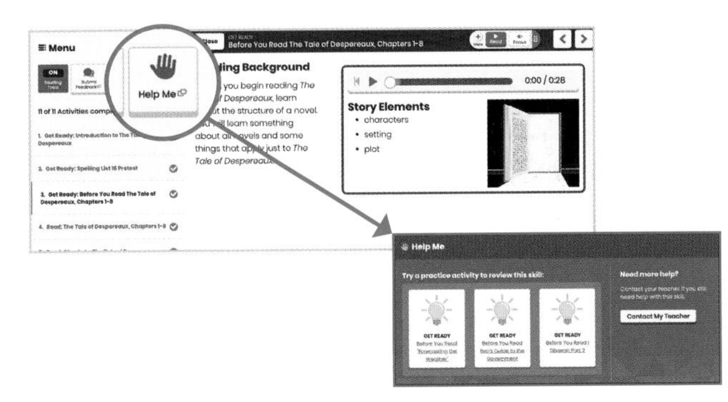

How to Use This Guide

This lesson guide contains information that will be helpful to you as you begin Summit English Language Arts 3 and daily as you work through the program. Here is what the lesson guide contains and how to use it.

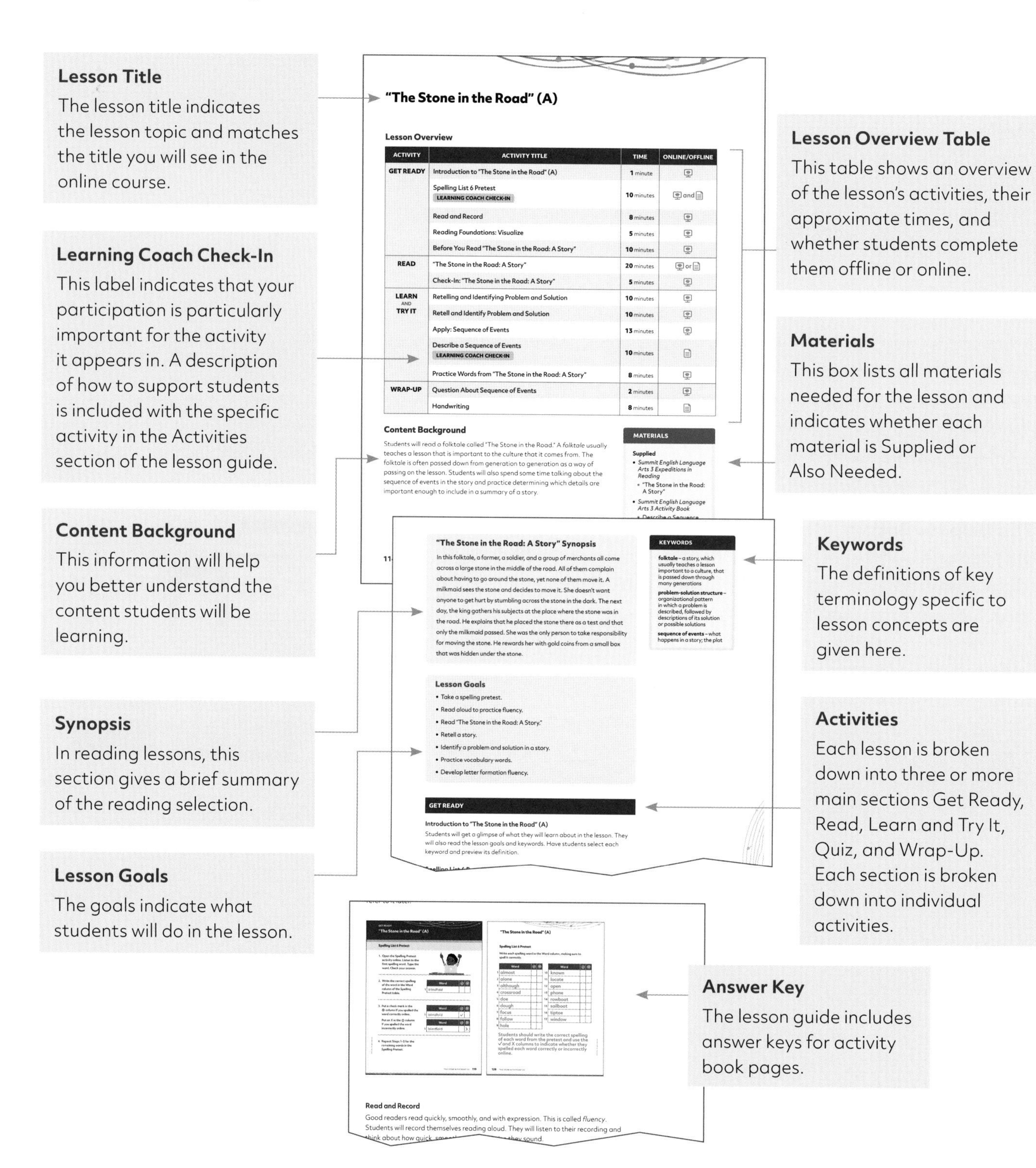

"The Stone in the Road" (A)

Lesson Overview

ACTIVITY	ACTIVITY TITLE	TIME	ONLINE/OFFLINE
GET READY	Introduction to "The Stone in the Road" (A)	1 minute	
	Spelling List 6 Pretest LEARNING COACH CHECK-IN	10 minutes	and
	Read and Record	8 minutes	
	Reading Foundations: Visualize	5 minutes	
	Before You Read "The Stone in the Road: A Story"	10 minutes	
READ	"The Stone in the Road: A Story"	20 minutes	or
	Check-In: "The Stone in the Road: A Story"	5 minutes	
LEARN AND TRY IT	Retelling and Identifying Problem and Solution	10 minutes	
	Retell and Identify Problem and Solution	10 minutes	
	Apply: Sequence of Events	13 minutes	
	Describe a Sequence of Events LEARNING COACH CHECK-IN	10 minutes	
	Practice Words from "The Stone in the Road: A Story"	8 minutes	
WRAP-UP	Question About Sequence of Events	2 minutes	
	Handwriting	8 minutes	

Content Background

Students will read a folktale called "The Stone in the Road." A *folktale* usually teaches a lesson that is important to the culture that it comes from. The folktale is often passed down from generation to generation as a way of passing on the lesson. Students will also spend some time talking about the sequence of events in the story and practice determining which details are important enough to include in a summary of a story.

MATERIALS

Supplied
- *Summit English Language Arts 3 Expeditions in Reading*
  - "The Stone in the Road: A Story"
- *Summit English Language Arts 3 Activity Book*

"The Stone in the Road: A Story" Synopsis

In this folktale, a farmer, a soldier, and a group of merchants all come across a large stone in the middle of the road. All of them complain about having to go around the stone, yet none of them move it. A milkmaid sees the stone and decides to move it. She doesn't want anyone to get hurt by stumbling across the stone in the dark. The next day, the king gathers his subjects at the place where the stone was in the road. He explains that he placed the stone there as a test and that only the milkmaid passed. She was the only person to take responsibility for moving the stone. He rewards her with gold coins from a small box that was hidden under the stone.

KEYWORDS

folktale – a story, which usually teaches a lesson important to a culture, that is passed down through many generations

problem-solution structure – organizational pattern in which a problem is described, followed by descriptions of its solution or possible solutions

sequence of events – what happens in a story; the plot

Lesson Goals
- Take a spelling pretest.
- Read aloud to practice fluency.
- Read "The Stone in the Road: A Story."
- Retell a story.
- Identify a problem and solution in a story.
- Practice vocabulary words.
- Develop letter formation fluency.

GET READY

Introduction to "The Stone in the Road" (A)

Students will get a glimpse of what they will learn about in the lesson. They will also read the lesson goals and keywords. Have students select each keyword and preview its definition.

Read and Record

Good readers read quickly, smoothly, and with expression. This is called *fluency*. Students will record themselves reading aloud. They will listen to their recording and think about how quick, ... they sound.

Lesson Title
The lesson title indicates the lesson topic and matches the title you will see in the online course.

Learning Coach Check-In
This label indicates that your participation is particularly important for the activity it appears in. A description of how to support students is included with the specific activity in the Activities section of the lesson guide.

Content Background
This information will help you better understand the content students will be learning.

Synopsis
In reading lessons, this section gives a brief summary of the reading selection.

Lesson Goals
The goals indicate what students will do in the lesson.

Lesson Overview Table
This table shows an overview of the lesson's activities, their approximate times, and whether students complete them offline or online.

Materials
This box lists all materials needed for the lesson and indicates whether each material is Supplied or Also Needed.

Keywords
The definitions of key terminology specific to lesson concepts are given here.

Activities
Each lesson is broken down into three or more main sections Get Ready, Read, Learn and Try It, Quiz, and Wrap-Up. Each section is broken down into individual activities.

Answer Key
The lesson guide includes answer keys for activity book pages.

Lessons with Graded Assessments

Check in with students when a lesson has a graded assessment.

- The final lesson of most workshops has a computer-scored quiz. Check to make sure students have completed and submitted this quiz.
- Teacher-graded assignments appear throughout the course. You may need to help students submit these assignments to their teacher. Discuss with the teacher the best method of turning in students' work.

Remember

Academic support at home is critical to student success. While Summit ELA 3 empowers students to work independently, this guide is designed help you support your students each day to help them maximize their learning.

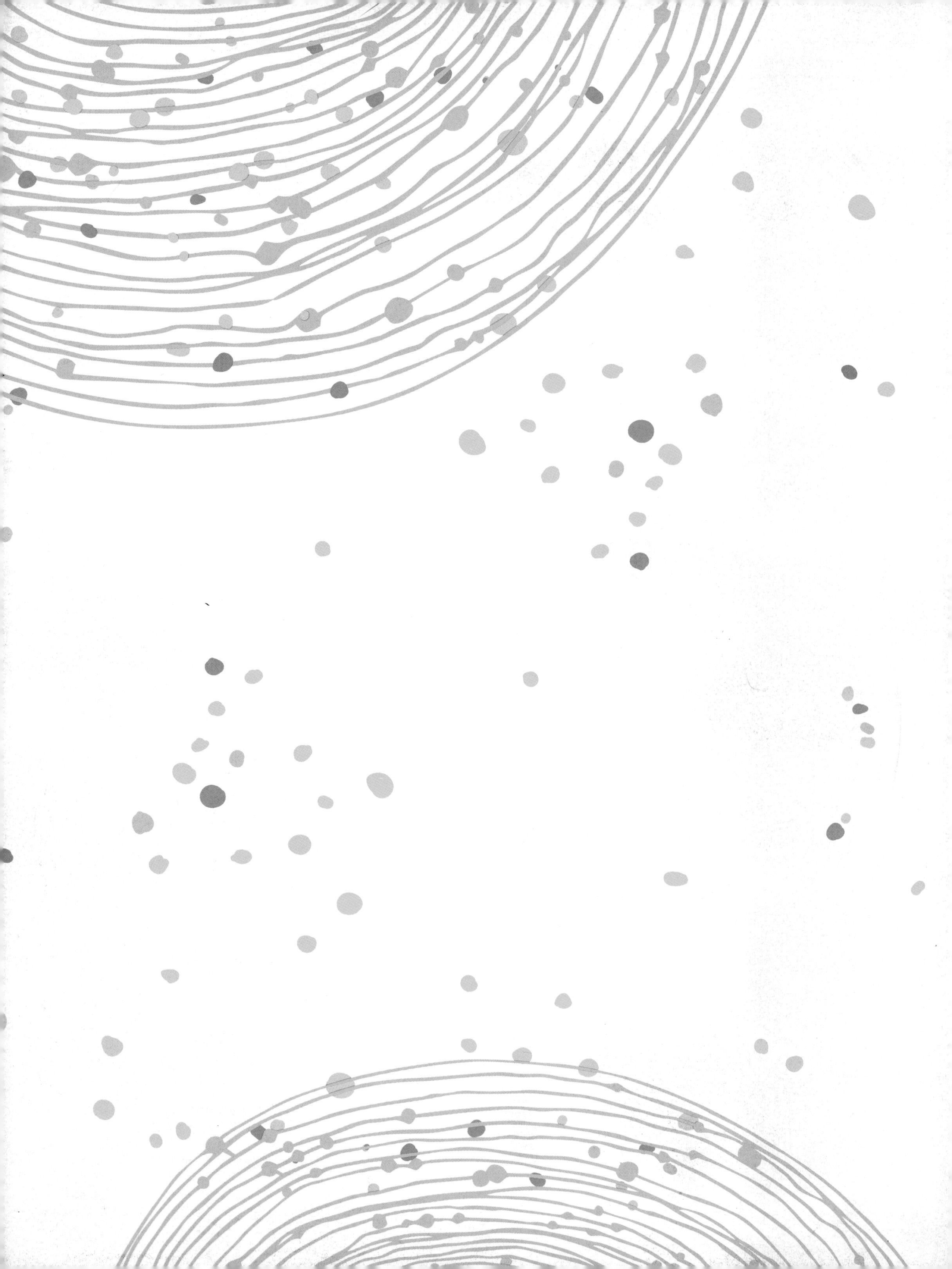

Author Study

Allen Say (A)

Lesson Overview

ACTIVITY	ACTIVITY TITLE	TIME	ONLINE/OFFLINE
GET READY	Introduction to Allen Say (A)	**2** minutes	online
	Spelling List 1 Pretest **LEARNING COACH CHECK-IN**	**10** minutes	online and offline
	Read and Record	**8** minutes	online
	Reading Foundations: Book Preview	**5** minutes	online
	Before You Read *Grandfather's Journey*	**10** minutes	online
READ	*Grandfather's Journey*	**15** minutes	offline
	Check-In: *Grandfather's Journey*	**5** minutes	online
LEARN AND TRY IT	Describing Characters, Setting, and Plot	**10** minutes	online
	Describe Characters, Setting, and Plot	**10** minutes	online
	Apply: Character's Actions	**10** minutes	online
	Sequence of Events in *Grandfather's Journey* **LEARNING COACH CHECK-IN**	**15** minutes	offline
	Practice Words from *Grandfather's Journey*	**8** minutes	online
WRAP-UP	Question About *Grandfather's Journey*	**2** minutes	online
	Handwriting	**9** minutes	offline

Content Background

Students will begin an author study on Allen Say, a Japanese American artist and writer. They will read three works by Allen Say: *Grandfather's Journey*, *Tea with Milk*, and *The Sign Painter*. All three are works of historical fiction. The times and global events that happen in historical fiction are real, but the characters and specific details about those characters may not be. The characters and events in *Grandfather's Journey* and *Tea with Milk* are related; Grandfather's daughter in the former becomes the protagonist in the latter.

In this lesson, students will read *Grandfather's Journey*. They will also spend some time reviewing elements of fiction such as characters, setting, and plot. Character traits and characters' actions often help advance a plot in fiction.

MATERIALS

Supplied

- *Grandfather's Journey* by Allen Say
- *Summit English Language Arts 3 Activity Book*
  - Spelling List 1 Pretest
  - Sequence of Events in *Grandfather's Journey*
- handwriting workbook

Grandfather's Journey Synopsis

Say's work of historical fiction *Grandfather's Journey* relates events from Say's grandfather's life. Grandfather, as the narrator of the book calls him, has a keen sense of adventure. As a young man, Grandfather leaves his homeland of Japan and takes a boat to North America. He explores the continent and eventually settles in California. He returns briefly to Japan to marry, and then he brings his wife back to California and settles in San Francisco. There they have a daughter. Grandfather feels pulled between his present in California and his past in Japan. When his daughter is grown, he moves his family back to Japan. His daughter is unhappy in his small village, so they move to a larger city. While in Japan, Grandfather misses San Francisco, so he makes plans to visit. Then World War II breaks out, and bombs level his home and the city where he lives. He is unable to visit California, but he tells his grandson (the narrator) all about his adventures there. Eventually, the narrator decides to visit and move to California. He also feels pulled between his two homes—Japan and California—and so feels closer than ever to his grandfather.

KEYWORDS

antonym – a word that means the opposite of another word

character – a person or animal in a story

character trait – a quality of a person or character; part of a personality

context clue – a word or phrase in a text that helps you figure out the meaning of an unknown word

historical fiction – a story set in a historical time period that includes facts about real people, places, and events, but also contains fictional elements that make the story exciting or interesting

illustration – a drawing

plot – what happens in a story; the sequence of events

setting – when and where a story takes place

synonym – a word that means the same, or almost the same, as another word

Lesson Goals

- Take a spelling pretest.
- Read aloud to practice fluency.
- Read and comprehend historical fiction.
- Read *Grandfather's Journey*.
- Identify and explain character traits and setting.
- Sequence plot events.
- Practice vocabulary words.
- Develop letter formation fluency.

GET READY

Introduction to Allen Say (A)

After a quick introductory activity, students will read the lesson goals and keywords. Have students select each keyword and preview its definition.

Spelling List 1 Pretest

Students will take a spelling pretest and learn a new spelling pattern.

LEARNING COACH CHECK-IN Have students turn to Spelling List 1 Pretest in *Summit English Language Arts 3 Activity Book* and open the online Spelling Pretest activity. Online, students will listen to the spelling word, type the word in the space indicated, and then check their answer. In the activity book, students will write the correct spelling of the word in the tables provided and indicate with a ✓ or an ✗ if they spelled the word correctly or incorrectly online. Students will repeat this process with the remaining words.

As needed, help students with the interaction between the online activity and the activity book page until they become comfortable with what they need to do. As students practice their spelling words throughout the workshop, they should pay special attention to words they spelled incorrectly on the pretest.

This is the complete list of words students will be tested on.

Words with Short Vowels		
children	finish	publish
difficult	happen	rabbit
establish	himself	sudden
exact	invent	ticket
expect	pocket	until
fantastic	problem	

NOTE Have students keep their completed activity page in a safe place so they can refer to it later.

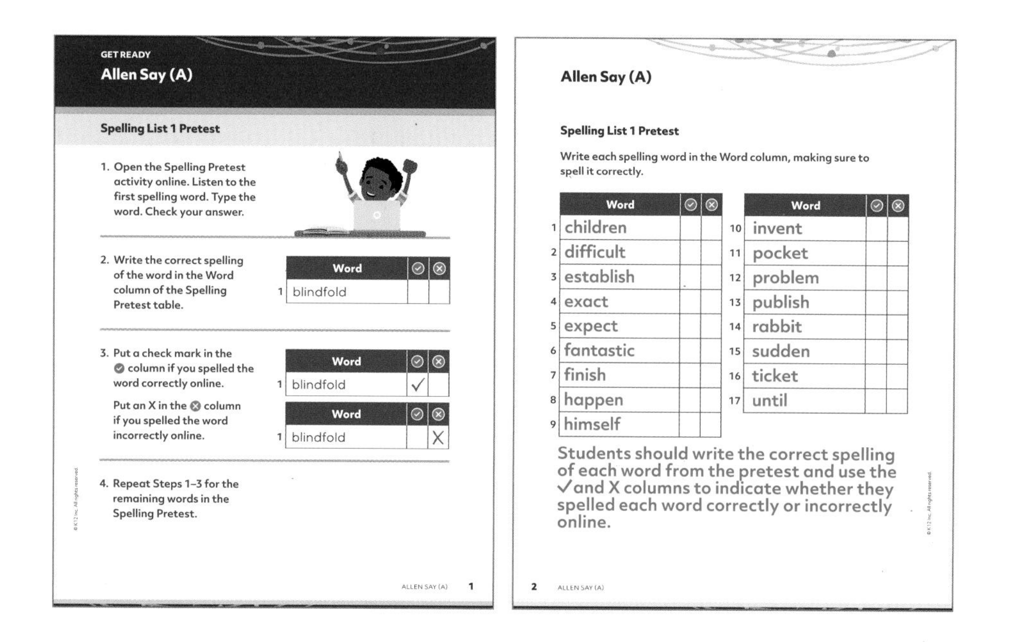

GET READY
Allen Say (A)

Spelling List 1 Pretest

1. Open the Spelling Pretest activity online. Listen to the first spelling word. Type the word. Check your answer.

2. Write the correct spelling of the word in the Word column of the Spelling Pretest table.

	Word	✓	✗
1	blindfold		

3. Put a check mark in the ✓ column if you spelled the word correctly online.

	Word	✓	✗
1	blindfold	✓	

Put an X in the ✗ column if you spelled the word incorrectly online.

	Word	✓	✗
1	blindfold		X

4. Repeat Steps 1–3 for the remaining words in the Spelling Pretest.

ALLEN SAY (A) 1

Allen Say (A)

Spelling List 1 Pretest

Write each spelling word in the Word column, making sure to spell it correctly.

	Word	✓	✗
1	children		
2	difficult		
3	establish		
4	exact		
5	expect		
6	fantastic		
7	finish		
8	happen		
9	himself		

	Word	✓	✗
10	invent		
11	pocket		
12	problem		
13	publish		
14	rabbit		
15	sudden		
16	ticket		
17	until		

Students should write the correct spelling of each word from the pretest and use the ✓ and X columns to indicate whether they spelled each word correctly or incorrectly online.

2 ALLEN SAY (A)

Read and Record

Good readers read quickly, smoothly, and with expression. This is called *fluency*. Students will record themselves reading aloud. They will listen to their recording and think about how quick, smooth, and expressive they sound.

TIP Encourage students to rerecord as needed.

Reading Foundations: Book Preview

Reading Foundations activities serve to remind students of basic reading skills and reading behaviors mastered in earlier grades. The activities cover topics such as advanced decoding skills and various strategies for improving comprehension.

Before You Read *Grandfather's Journey*

Students will be introduced to some key vocabulary words that they will encounter in the upcoming reading, learn some important historical background related to the reading, and answer questions to help them set a purpose for their reading.

READ

Grandfather's Journey

Students will read *Grandfather's Journey* by Allen Say.

Check-In: *Grandfather's Journey*

Students will answer several questions to demonstrate their comprehension of *Grandfather's Journey*.

LEARN AND TRY IT

LEARN Describing Characters, Setting, and Plot

Students will learn about three important elements of fiction: characters, setting, and plot. They will also learn that character traits and actions advance plot.

TRY IT Describe Characters, Setting, and Plot

Students will try identifying the characters and setting in the story. They will also practice putting events from the plot in chronological order.

TRY IT Apply: Character's Actions

Students will apply to a new work what they've learned about identifying and describing characters and setting and sequencing plot events.

TRY IT Sequence of Events in *Grandfather's Journey*

Students will complete Sequence of Events in *Grandfather's Journey* in *Summit English Language Arts 3 Activity Book*.

LEARNING COACH CHECK-IN If students have difficulty sequencing events, ask them which event came first, which came next, and so on.

TRY IT
Allen Say (A)

Sequence of Events in *Grandfather's Journey*

Number the events in the correct order. Use the text in *Grandfather's Journey* to help you. The first one has been done for you.

Events

War breaks out. Event 4

Grandfather explores North America. Event 1

Grandfather moves back to Japan. Event 3

Grandfather's daughter is born. Event 2

The narrator goes to California. Event 5

ALLEN SAY (A) 3

Use the information from the box to write the sequence of events in *Grandfather's Journey*. The first one has been done for you.

First, Grandfather explores North America.

Second, Grandfather's daughter is born.

Next, Grandfather moves back to Japan.

Then, war breaks out.

Finally, the narrator goes to California.

4 ALLEN SAY (A)

TRY IT Practice Words from *Grandfather's Journey*

Students will answer questions to demonstrate their understanding of the vocabulary words from the reading.

WRAP-UP

Question About *Grandfather's Journey*

Students will answer a question to show that they understand the element of setting in *Grandfather's Journey*.

Handwriting

Students should gather their handwriting workbook and a sharpened pencil. Begin by reviewing the table of contents with the students, and explain that they will work for 10 minutes to complete workbook pages on their own. Students should not race to complete lots of pages. Instead, they should take their time to form letters carefully and correctly. Students should work at their own pace, completing pages until 10 minutes have passed.

TIP Set a timer to help students stay focused during handwriting practice.

Allen Say (B)

Lesson Overview

ACTIVITY	ACTIVITY TITLE	TIME	ONLINE/OFFLINE
GET READY	Introduction to Allen Say (B)	**1** minute	
	Spelling List 1 Activity Bank	**10** minutes	
	Read and Record	**8** minutes	
	Reading Foundations: Predictions	**5** minutes	
	Recall *Grandfather's Journey*	**5** minutes	
	Before You Read *Tea with Milk*, Part 1	**8** minutes	
READ	*Tea with Milk*, Part 1	**17** minutes	
	Check-In: *Tea with Milk*, Part 1	**5** minutes	
LEARN AND **TRY IT**	Determining Mood	**10** minutes	
	Determine Mood	**8** minutes	
	Apply: Illustrations Create Mood	**10** minutes	
	Characters, Illustrations, and Mood **LEARNING COACH CHECK-IN**	**15** minutes	
	Practice Words from *Tea with Milk*, Part 1	**8** minutes	
WRAP-UP	Question About *Tea with Milk*, Part 1	**2** minutes	
	Handwriting	**8** minutes	

Content Background

Students will begin reading *Tea with Milk* by Allen Say. They will also spend time figuring out what mood Say conveys in the book's text and illustrations. They will find details in the text and illustrations to support the moods they identify.

Advance Preparation

Gather students' completed Spelling List 1 Pretest activity page from Allen Say (A). Students will refer to this page during Get Ready: Spelling List 1 Activity Bank.

Tea with Milk, Part 1 Synopsis

Tea with Milk by Allen Say follows a character introduced in *Grandfather's Journey* by the same author. May, or Masako as she is called throughout the book, is born in San Francisco. She is Grandfather's daughter. When she is in high school, her family moves from California back to the Japan, her parents' homeland. Masako has a difficult time adjusting to life in Japan, where wealthy women are expected to marry according to their parents' wishes and learn traditional arts such as calligraphy, flower arranging, and the tea service.

The first part of the text shows Masako's sadness. She already completed high school in California, but her mother wants her to attend the village high school to learn Japanese. Students laugh at her and call her *gaijin*, which means "foreigner." She has no friends and no patience for her parents' ideas on what to study and whom to marry. So she goes to Osaka, where she sees a department store and feels hopeful for the first time since leaving California.

MATERIALS

Supplied

- *Tea with Milk* by Allen Say
- *Summit English Language Arts 3 Activity Book*
  - Spelling List 1 Activity Bank
  - Characters, Illustrations, and Mood
- handwriting workbook

Also Needed

- completed Spelling List 1 Pretest activity page from Allen Say (A)

KEYWORDS

mood – the feeling that an author shows with words and pictures

Lesson Goals

- Practice all spelling words offline.
- Read aloud to practice fluency.
- Read and comprehend historical fiction.
- Read *Tea with Milk*.
- Use text and illustrations to determine mood in fiction.
- Practice vocabulary words.
- Develop letter formation fluency.

GET READY

Introduction to Allen Say (B)

Students will get a glimpse of what they will learn about in the lesson. They will also read the lesson goals and keywords. Have students select each keyword and preview its definition.

Spelling List 1 Activity Bank

Students will practice all spelling words from the workshop by completing Spelling List 1 Activity Bank from *Summit English Language Arts 3 Activity Book*. Make sure students have their completed Spelling List 1 Pretest activity page from Allen Say (A) to refer to during this activity.

Remind students to pay special attention to words they spelled incorrectly on the Spelling Pretest.

GET READY

Allen Say (B)

Spelling List 1 Activity Bank

Circle any words in the box that you did not spell correctly on your pretest. Choose one activity to do with your circled words. Do as much of the activity as you can in the time given.

Did you spell all the words on the pretest correctly? Do the one activity with as many spelling words as you can.

children	expect	himself	problem	sudden
difficult	fantastic	invent	publish	ticket
establish	finish	pocket	rabbit	until
exact	happen			

Spelling Activity Choices

Alphabetizing

1. In the left column, write your spelling words in alphabetical order.
2. Correct any spelling errors.

Vowel-Free Words

1. In the left column, write only the consonants in each of your spelling words. Put a dot where each vowel should be.
2. Spell each word aloud, stating which vowels should be in the places with dots.
3. In the right column, rewrite the entire spelling word.
4. Correct any spelling errors.

Rhymes

1. In the left column, write your spelling words.
2. In the right column, write a word that rhymes with each spelling word.
3. Correct any spelling errors.

Uppercase and Lowercase

1. In the left column, write each of your spelling words in all uppercase letters.
2. In the right column, write each of your spelling words in all lowercase letters.
3. Correct any spelling errors.

Complete the activity that you chose.

My chosen activity: ______

1. ______
2. ______
3. ______
4. ______
5. ______
6. ______
7. ______
8. ______
9. ______
10. ______
11. ______
12. ______
13. ______
14. ______
15. ______
16. ______
17. ______

Students should use this page to complete all steps in their chosen activity.

Read and Record

Good readers read quickly, smoothly, and with expression. This is called *fluency*. Students will record themselves reading aloud. They will listen to their recording and think about how quick, smooth, and expressive they sound.

TIP Encourage students to rerecord as needed.

Reading Foundations: Predictions

Reading Foundations activities serve to remind students of basic reading skills and reading behaviors mastered in earlier grades. The activities cover topics such as advanced decoding skills and various strategies for improving comprehension.

Recall *Grandfather's Journey*

Students will answer some questions to review the reading that they have already completed.

Before You Read *Tea with Milk*, Part 1

Students will be introduced to some key vocabulary words that they will encounter in the upcoming reading, learn some important historical background related to the reading, and answer questions to help them set a purpose for their reading.

READ

Tea with Milk, Part 1

Students will read Part 1 of *Tea with Milk* by Allen Say. Part 1 is the beginning of the book to the middle, when Masako first enters the department store in Osaka.

Check-In: *Tea with Milk*, Part 1

Students will answer several questions to demonstrate their comprehension of Part 1 of *Tea with Milk*.

LEARN AND TRY IT

LEARN Determining Mood

Students will learn about examining text and illustrations in a book to determine the mood a writer creates.

SUPPORT *Mood* can sometimes be a challenging idea for students. A good way to help them understand is to ask, *How does this text (or this picture) make you feel?* Then you can guide students to figure out what words or parts of a picture make them feel that way.

TRY IT Determine Mood

Students will examine text and illustrations in a book to determine the mood a writer creates.

TRY IT Apply: Illustrations Create Mood

Students will apply to a new work what they've learned about using text and illustrations to determine mood.

TRY IT Characters, Illustrations, and Mood

Students will complete Characters, Illustrations, and Mood in *Summit English Language Arts 3 Activity Book*.

LEARNING COACH CHECK-IN Review students' responses to ensure that they understand what mood is and how details from the text and illustrations can support their findings. Use the sample answers provided to guide you.

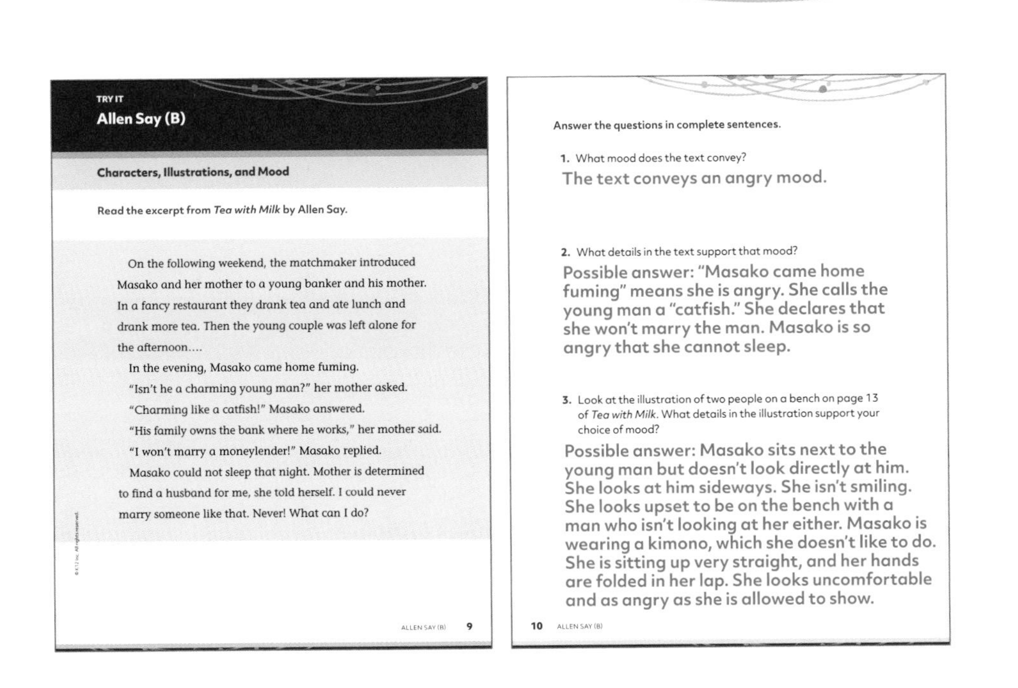
TRY IT
Allen Say (B)

Characters, Illustrations, and Mood

Read the excerpt from *Tea with Milk* by Allen Say.

On the following weekend, the matchmaker introduced Masako and her mother to a young banker and his mother. In a fancy restaurant they drank tea and ate lunch and drank more tea. Then the young couple was left alone for the afternoon....

In the evening, Masako came home fuming.

"Isn't he a charming young man?" her mother asked.

"Charming like a catfish!" Masako answered.

"His family owns the bank where he works," her mother said.

"I won't marry a moneylender!" Masako replied.

Masako could not sleep that night. Mother is determined to find a husband for me, she told herself. I could never marry someone like that. Never! What can I do?

ALLEN SAY (B) 9

Answer the questions in complete sentences.

1. What mood does the text convey?
The text conveys an angry mood.

2. What details in the text support that mood?
Possible answer: "Masako came home fuming" means she is angry. She calls the young man a "catfish." She declares that she won't marry the man. Masako is so angry that she cannot sleep.

3. Look at the illustration of two people on a bench on page 13 of *Tea with Milk*. What details in the illustration support your choice of mood?
Possible answer: Masako sits next to the young man but doesn't look directly at him. She looks at him sideways. She isn't smiling. She looks upset to be on the bench with a man who isn't looking at her either. Masako is wearing a kimono, which she doesn't like to do. She is sitting up very straight, and her hands are folded in her lap. She looks uncomfortable and as angry as she is allowed to show.

10 ALLEN SAY (B)

TRY IT Practice Words from *Tea with Milk*, Part 1

Students will answer questions to demonstrate their understanding of the vocabulary words from the reading.

WRAP-UP

Question About *Tea with Milk*, Part 1

Students will answer a question to show that they understand how an author shows mood with text and illustrations.

Handwriting

Students should gather their handwriting materials and begin where they left off. Remind students to form letters carefully and correctly.

TIP Set a timer to help students stay focused during handwriting practice.

Allen Say (C)

Lesson Overview

ACTIVITY	ACTIVITY TITLE	TIME	ONLINE/OFFLINE
GET READY	Introduction to Allen Say (C)	**1** minute	online
	Spelling List 1 Review Game	**10** minutes	online
	Read and Record	**8** minutes	online
	Reading Foundations: Purpose	**5** minutes	online
	Recall *Tea with Milk*, Part 1	**5** minutes	online
	Before You Read *Tea with Milk*, Part 2	**8** minutes	online
READ	*Tea with Milk*, Part 2	**17** minutes	offline
	Check-In: *Tea with Milk*, Part 2	**5** minutes	online
LEARN AND **TRY IT**	Explaining Theme and Supporting Details	**8** minutes	online
	Explain Theme and Supporting Details	**10** minutes	online
	Apply: Theme	**8** minutes	online
	Write About Supporting Details **LEARNING COACH CHECK-IN**	**15** minutes	offline
	Practice Words from *Tea with Milk*, Part 2	**10** minutes	online
WRAP-UP	Question About *Tea with Milk*, Part 2	**2** minutes	online
	Handwriting	**8** minutes	offline

Content Background

Students will finish reading *Tea with Milk*. They will spend some time learning about theme and supporting details. In this lesson, they will be given a theme and will have to find details that give more information about that theme.

MATERIALS

Supplied

- *Tea with Milk* by Allen Say
- *Summit English Language Arts 3 Activity Book*
  - Write About Supporting Details
- handwriting workbook

Tea with Milk, Part 2 Synopsis

In the second half of *Tea with Milk*, Masako asks for a job in a department store in Osaka. The store manager is surprised to learn that she can drive and gives her a job as an elevator operator. She sends word to her parents that she is staying in Osaka, and she rents a room to live in. At the department store, Masako overhears a family asking questions. When she responds in English and helps them, the store manager promotes her. She is now a guide for foreign businessmen. For three days, a young man joins her tour, and when she asks him why, he explains that he misses speaking English and invites her to tea. His name is Joseph. Masako and Joseph spend time together, and he eventually tells her that his company is transferring him to Yokohama. Neither of them is happy with this news, but Joseph believes that home isn't a place—it's a feeling that you can have in any place. He and Masako get married, move to Yokohama, and eventually have the narrator, who is the same narrator from *Grandfather's Journey*.

KEYWORDS

main idea – the most important point an author makes; it may be stated or unstated

supporting detail – a detail that gives more information about a main idea

theme – the author's message or big idea

Lesson Goals

- Practice all spelling words online.
- Read aloud to practice fluency.
- Read and comprehend historical fiction.
- Read *Tea with Milk*.
- Given a theme, identify supporting details.
- Practice vocabulary words.
- Develop letter formation fluency.

GET READY

Introduction to Allen Say (C)

Students will get a glimpse of what they will learn about in the lesson. They will also read the lesson goals and keywords. Have students select each keyword and preview its definition.

Spelling List 1 Review Game

Students will practice all spelling words from the workshop.

Read and Record

Good readers read quickly, smoothly, and with expression. This is called *fluency*. Students will record themselves reading aloud. They will listen to their recording and think about how quick, smooth, and expressive they sound.

TIP Encourage students to rerecord as needed.

Reading Foundations: Purpose

Reading Foundations activities serve to remind students of basic reading skills and reading behaviors mastered in earlier grades. The activities cover topics such as advanced decoding skills and various strategies for improving comprehension.

Recall *Tea with Milk*, Part 1

Students will answer some questions to review the reading that they have already completed.

Before You Read *Tea with Milk*, Part 2

Students will be introduced to some key vocabulary words that they will encounter in the upcoming reading, learn some important historical background related to the reading, and answer questions to help them set a purpose for their reading.

TIP Students may have questions about aspects of life in Japan before World War II, particularly for women. It may be helpful to point out that life for women in the United States then was also quite different than life for women in the United States today.

READ

Tea with Milk, Part 2

Students will read Part 2 of *Tea with Milk* by Allen Say. Part 2 is the middle of the book, when Masako becomes an elevator girl at the department store, to the end.

Check-In: *Tea with Milk*, Part 2

Students will answer several questions to demonstrate their comprehension of Part 2 of *Tea with Milk*.

LEARN AND TRY IT

LEARN Explaining Theme and Supporting Details

Students will learn what a theme is and how supporting details give more information about a theme in a text.

TRY IT Explain Theme and Supporting Details

Given a theme, students will practice identifying details that support that theme.

TRY IT Apply: Theme

Students will apply to a new work what they've learned about identifying details that support a theme.

TRY IT Write About Supporting Details

Students will complete Write About Supporting Details in *Summit English Language Arts 3 Activity Book*.

LEARNING COACH CHECK-IN This activity page contains open-ended questions, so it's important that you review students' responses. You may need to help students determine which details in the passage support the theme that determination leads to success.

TRY IT

Allen Say (C)

Write About Supporting Details

Read the excerpt from *Tea with Milk* by Allen Say.

The next morning, Masako returned to the department store office. No one had read her application yet, the clerk said. Masako asked to see the manager. She was very insistent. After a while, the supervisor interviewed her.

"Can you really drive a car?" he asked, looking at her application. "I've never seen a woman drive."

"Many women drive in America," she said.

"I see." He nodded and picked up his telephone.

Soon a girl appeared and took Masako to a changing room and gave her a uniform. An hour later, Masako was driving an elevator cage up and down, bowing to customers, and announcing the floors.

She rented a room in a rooming house for university students. Her parents were not happy, especially her mother. It was shameful for ladies to work, she said. Masako did not tell her she was an elevator girl.

One theme in *Tea with Milk* is that it takes determination to be successful. List at least two details from the excerpt that support this theme.

Students should list at least two details from the excerpt to support the theme that it takes determination to be successful. Examples of details include the following:

- Masako returns to the department store and follows up on the application she submitted.
- When she doesn't get a response, Masako doesn't back down. She is determined and asks to see the manager.
- Masako is insistent—she doesn't give up. Her determination pays off when the manager hires her.
- Masako is determined to stay in Osaka, even when her mother thinks she should come home. She rents a room for herself.

TRY IT Practice Words from *Tea with Milk*, Part 2

Students will answer questions to demonstrate their understanding of the vocabulary words from the reading.

WRAP-UP

Question About *Tea with Milk*, Part 2

Students will answer a question to show that they understand what a theme is.

Handwriting

Students should gather their handwriting materials and begin where they left off. Remind students to form letters carefully and correctly.

TIP Set a timer to help students stay focused during handwriting practice.

Allen Say (D)

Lesson Overview

ACTIVITY	ACTIVITY TITLE	TIME	ONLINE/OFFLINE
GET READY	Introduction to Allen Say (D)	**1** minute	online
	Read and Record	**8** minutes	online
	Recall *Tea with Milk*, Part 2	**5** minutes	online
	Before You Review	**8** minutes	online
READ	Review *Grandfather's Journey* and *Tea with Milk*	**5** minutes	offline
LEARN AND TRY IT	Comparing and Contrasting Texts	**15** minutes	online
	Compare and Contrast Texts	**18** minutes	online
	Apply: Compare or Contrast Theme	**15** minutes	online
	Explore a Model Comparison Paragraph	**10** minutes	online
	Write a Paragraph to Contrast Two Texts LEARNING COACH CHECK-IN	**15** minutes	offline
QUIZ	Spelling List 1	**10** minutes	online
WRAP-UP	Question About Comparing Texts	**2** minutes	online
	Handwriting	**8** minutes	offline

Content Background

Students will review *Grandfather's Journey* and *Tea with Milk* in preparation for comparing and contrasting the books' characters, settings, plots, and themes. They will be introduced to the ideas of skimming and scanning.

Students will also review a model paragraph in preparation for writing a paragraph themselves. The parts of a paragraph include the following:

- A topic sentence that states the main idea of the paragraph
- Several sentences that include details to support the main idea of the paragraph
- An ending sentence that restates the main idea in different words

MATERIALS

Supplied

- *Grandfather's Journey* by Allen Say
- *Tea with Milk* by Allen Say
- *Summit English Language Arts 3 Activity Book*
    - Write a Paragraph to Contrast Two Texts
- handwriting workbook

Lesson Goals

- Review *Grandfather's Journey* and *Tea with Milk*.
- Compare and contrast two texts.
- Write a comparison paragraph.
- Take a spelling quiz.
- Develop letter formation fluency.

KEYWORDS

character – a person or animal in a story

compare – to explain how two or more things are alike

contrast – to explain how two or more things are different

paragraph – a group of sentences about one topic or subject

setting – when and where a story takes place

theme – the author's message or big idea

topic sentence – the sentence that expresses the main idea of a paragraph

GET READY

Introduction to Allen Say (D)

Students will get a glimpse of what they will learn about in the lesson. They will also read the lesson goals and keywords. Have students select each keyword and preview its definition.

Read and Record

Good readers read quickly, smoothly, and with expression. This is called *fluency*. Students will record themselves reading aloud. They will listen to their recording and think about how quick, smooth, and expressive they sound.

TIP Encourage students to rerecord as needed.

Recall *Tea with Milk*, Part 2

Students will answer some questions to review the reading that they have already completed.

Before You Review

Before reviewing *Grandfather's Journey* and *Tea with Milk*, students will learn how to skim and scan to remind themselves of what they read.

READ

Review *Grandfather's Journey* and *Tea with Milk*

Students will review *Grandfather's Journey* and *Tea with Milk* by Allen Say.

TIP Remind students that reviewing a book does not mean rereading it from start to finish. They should look at the title and pictures and run their fingers over the words in the text to scan for words that will help them remember story details.

LEARN AND TRY IT

LEARN Comparing and Contrasting Texts

Students will compare the settings in *Grandfather's Journey* and *Tea with Milk*.

TRY IT Compare and Contrast Texts

Students will compare the characters, settings, and themes in *Grandfather's Journey* and *Tea with Milk*.

TRY IT Apply: Compare or Contrast Theme

Students will apply to a new work what they've learned about comparing texts.

LEARN Explore a Model Comparison Paragraph

Students will learn about the parts of a paragraph by exploring a model comparison paragraph.

TRY IT Write a Paragraph to Contrast Two Texts

Students will complete Write a Paragraph to Contrast Two Texts in *Summit English Language Arts 3 Activity Book*.

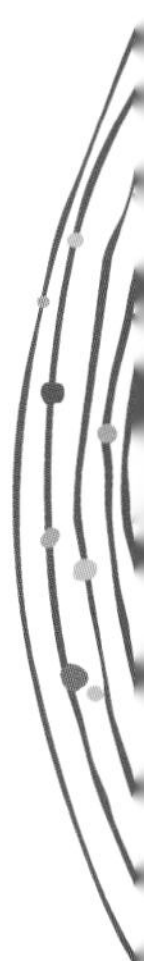

LEARNING COACH CHECK-IN This activity page contains open-ended questions, so it's important that you review students' responses. Use the sample paragraph provided to guide you.

TRY IT

Allen Say (D)

Write a Paragraph to Contrast Two Texts

Fill in the blanks to write a paragraph that contrasts Grandfather from *Grandfather's Journey* with Masako from *Tea with Milk*. Begin with a topic sentence that states the main idea of your paragraph.

Sample paragraph:

Grandfather and Masako are different in many ways. First, Grandfather was born in Japan, and Masako was born in San Francisco. Another difference is Grandfather felt at home in two places, and Masako learned that place is not important to make a home. Finally, Grandfather did not have a job in the story, and Masako worked in a department store. In conclusion, Grandfather and Masako may be from the same family, but they were born in different places and their ideas about home were different.

ALLEN SAY (D) 13

QUIZ

Spelling List 1

Students will complete the Spelling List 1 quiz.

WRAP-UP

Question About Comparing Texts

Students will answer a question to show that they understand one way that *Grandfather's Journey* and *Tea with Milk* are alike.

Handwriting

Students should gather their handwriting materials and begin where they left off. Remind students to form letters carefully and correctly.

TIP Set a timer to help students stay focused during handwriting practice.

Allen Say (E)

Lesson Overview

ACTIVITY	ACTIVITY TITLE	TIME	ONLINE/OFFLINE
GET READY	Introduction to Allen Say (E)	**1** minute	
	Spelling List 2 Pretest **LEARNING COACH CHECK-IN**	**10** minutes	and
	Read and Record	**8** minutes	
	Reading Foundations: Ask Questions—Fiction Text	**5** minutes	
	Before You Read *The Sign Painter*, Part 1	**13** minutes	
READ	*The Sign Painter*, Part 1	**20** minutes	
	Check-In: *The Sign Painter*, Part 1	**5** minutes	
LEARN AND **TRY IT**	Interpreting Words and Illustrations	**10** minutes	
	Interpret Words and Illustrations	**10** minutes	
	Apply: Illustrations Convey Setting	**10** minutes	
	Describe an Illustration **LEARNING COACH CHECK-IN**	**10** minutes	
	Practice Words from *The Sign Painter*, Part 1	**8** minutes	
WRAP-UP	Question About *The Sign Painter*, Part 1	**2** minutes	
	Handwriting	**8** minutes	

Content Background

Students will read the first half of *The Sign Painter* by Allen Say. They will spend some time thinking about mood in the text and how the illustrations contribute to the text's mood. Say's illustrations also help create the story's setting and lend insight into the characters. They will choose an illustration from either *The Sign Painter*, *Tea with Milk*, or *Grandfather's Journey* and brainstorm a list of sensory words and phrases that the illustration evokes. *Sensory language* includes words that evoke a sense—sight, hearing, touch, smell, and taste.

MATERIALS

Supplied

- *The Sign Painter* by Allen Say
- *Tea with Milk* by Allen Say
- *Grandfather's Journey* by Allen Say
- *Summit English Language Arts 3 Activity Book*
  - Spelling List 2 Pretest
  - Describe an Illustration
- handwriting workbook

The Sign Painter, Part 1 Synopsis

Allen Say's book begins with a young man stepping off a bus in a small town. It is early, and he is looking for a job. He sees a light in a shop and investigates. It is a sign painter's studio. The sign painter asks if he is lost, and the young man tells him he needs a job. He can paint, so the sign painter has the young man work on a billboard in a vacant lot.

The young man, who is called a boy from this point on, does well on the first billboard. A car approaches, and when the sign painter returns from talking to the driver, he asks the boy if he wants to work on a series of billboards for ArrowStar. The boy agrees, and the pair head to the desert to reproduce the same image on multiple billboards. Neither knows what ArrowStar is. Along the way, the boy asks a few questions and says that he wants to be an artist. The sign painter is more practical and says that one has to make a living.

KEYWORDS

dialogue – the words that characters say in a written work

mood – the feeling that an author shows with words and pictures

setting – when and where a story takes place

Lesson Goals

- Take a spelling pretest.
- Read aloud to practice fluency.
- Read *The Sign Painter*.
- Interpret and describe illustrations.
- Practice vocabulary words.
- Develop letter formation fluency.

GET READY

Introduction to Allen Say (E)

Students will get a glimpse of what they will learn about in the lesson. They will also read the lesson goals and keywords. Have students select each keyword and preview its definition.

Spelling List 2 Pretest

Students will take a spelling pretest and learn a new spelling pattern.

LEARNING COACH CHECK-IN Have students turn to Spelling List 2 Pretest in *Summit English Language Arts 3 Activity Book* and open the online Spelling Pretest activity. Online, students will listen to the spelling word, type the word

in the space indicated, and then check their answer. In the activity book, students will write the correct spelling of the word in the tables provided and indicate with a ✓ or an ✗ if they spelled the word correctly or incorrectly online. Students will repeat this process with the remaining words.

As needed, help students with the interaction between the online activity and the activity book page until they become comfortable with what they need to do. As students practice their spelling words throughout the workshop, they should pay special attention to words they spelled incorrectly on the pretest.

This is the complete list of words students will be tested on.

Words with Suffixes –s and –es		
facts	plants	gashes
hundreds	presidents	inches
insects	products	quizzes
napkins	systems	riches
numbers	dresses	sandwiches
objects	foxes	

NOTE Have students keep their completed activity page in a safe place so they can refer to it later.

GET READY

Allen Say (E)

Spelling List 2 Pretest

1. Open the Spelling Pretest activity online. Listen to the first spelling word. Type the word. Check your answer.
2. Write the correct spelling of the word in the Word column of the Spelling Pretest table.

	Word	✓	⊗
1	blindfold		

3. Put a check mark in the ✓ column if you spelled the word correctly online.

	Word	✓	⊗
1	blindfold	✓	

Put an X in the ⊗ column if you spelled the word incorrectly online.

	Word	✓	⊗
1	blindfold		X

4. Repeat Steps 1–3 for the remaining words in the Spelling Pretest.

ALLEN SAY (E) 15

Allen Say (E)

Spelling List 2 Pretest

Write each spelling word in the Word column, making sure to spell it correctly.

	Word	✓	⊗
1	facts		
2	hundreds		
3	insects		
4	napkins		
5	numbers		
6	objects		
7	plants		
8	presidents		
9	products		

	Word	✓	⊗
10	systems		
11	dresses		
12	foxes		
13	gashes		
14	inches		
15	quizzes		
16	riches		
17	sandwiches		

Students should write the correct spelling of each word from the pretest and use the ✓ and X columns to indicate whether they spelled each word correctly or incorrectly online.

16 ALLEN SAY (E)

Read and Record

Good readers read quickly, smoothly, and with expression. This is called *fluency*. Students will record themselves reading aloud. They will listen to their recording and think about how quick, smooth, and expressive they sound.

TIP Encourage students to rerecord as needed.

Reading Foundations: Ask Questions—Fiction Text

Reading Foundations activities serve to remind students of basic reading skills and reading behaviors mastered in earlier grades. The activities cover topics such as advanced decoding skills and various strategies for improving comprehension.

Before You Read *The Sign Painter*, Part 1

Students will be introduced to some key vocabulary words that they will encounter in the upcoming reading and learn some important historical background related to the reading.

READ

The Sign Painter, Part 1

Students will read Part 1 of *The Sign Painter* by Allen Say. Part 1 is the beginning of the book to the middle, when the boy tells the sign painter what's bothering him.

Check-In: *The Sign Painter*, Part 1

Students will answer several questions to demonstrate their comprehension of Part 1 of *The Sign Painter*.

LEARN AND TRY IT

LEARN Interpreting Words and Illustrations

Students will learn about mood and how illustrations contribute to the mood of a text. They will also learn that illustrations help create the setting and convey information about characters.

TIP If students are struggling with mood, encourage them to think about how the book makes them feel.

TRY IT Interpret Words and Illustrations

Students will try making connections between illustrations, mood, characters, and setting on their own. They will make these connections within a single text and among multiple texts by Allen Say.

TRY IT Apply: Illustrations Convey Setting

Students will apply to a new work what they've learned about how illustrations and text work together to evoke mood, setting, and characterization.

TRY IT Describe an Illustration

Students will complete Describe an Illustration in *Summit English Language Arts 3 Activity Book*.

LEARNING COACH CHECK-IN Students are asked to choose one of Allen Say's illustrations and brainstorm a list of words. They will use this list in a future activity. Give students feedback on their list.

SUPPORT Prompt students with questions such as, *If you were in this picture, what would you feel? Smell? Would you taste anything? What would you hear?* and so forth.

NOTE Have students keep their completed activity page in a safe place so they can refer to it later.

TRY IT
Allen Say (E)

Describe an Illustration

Read the writing prompt.

Prompt: **Write a paragraph that describes an illustration.**

Follow the instructions to brainstorm for your paragraph.

1. Choose an illustration from *Grandfather's Journey*, *Tea with Milk*, or *The Sign Painter*.

   Book I chose: ________

   Page number of illustration: ____

2. What sights, sounds, feeling, tastes, and smells does the illustration make you think of? List words and phrases that describe the illustration. Sample words that describe the illustration on page 13 of *The Sign Painter* are shown.

Sample words: hot, dry, dusty, empty, silent

Words and phrases will vary; students should include some words for sight, hearing, touch, smell, and taste.

ALLEN SAY (E) 17

TRY IT Practice Words from *The Sign Painter*, Part 1

Students will answer questions to demonstrate their understanding of the vocabulary words from the reading.

WRAP-UP

Question About *The Sign Painter*, Part 1

Students will answer a question to show that they understand mood in a story.

Handwriting

Students should gather their handwriting materials and begin where they left off. Remind students to form letters carefully and correctly.

TIP Set a timer to help students stay focused during handwriting practice.

Allen Say (F)

Lesson Overview

ACTIVITY	ACTIVITY TITLE	TIME	ONLINE/OFFLINE
GET READY	Introduction to Allen Say (F)	**1** minute	online
	Spelling List 2 Activity Bank	**10** minutes	offline
	Read and Record	**8** minutes	online
	Reading Foundations: Look at Pictures	**5** minutes	online
	Recall *The Sign Painter*, Part 1	**4** minutes	online
	Before You Read *The Sign Painter*, Part 2	**9** minutes	online
READ	*The Sign Painter*, Part 2	**15** minutes	offline
	Check-In: *The Sign Painter*, Part 2	**5** minutes	online
LEARN AND **TRY IT**	Thinking About an Author's Purpose and Connecting Texts	**10** minutes	online
	Think About an Author's Purpose and Connect Texts	**10** minutes	online
	Apply: Author's Purpose	**10** minutes	online
	Plan a Descriptive Paragraph **LEARNING COACH CHECK-IN**	**15** minutes	offline
	Practice Words from *The Sign Painter*, Part 2	**8** minutes	online
WRAP-UP	Question About Comparing Characters	**2** minutes	online
	Handwriting	**8** minutes	offline

Content Background

Students will finish reading *The Sign Painter* by Allen Say. They will spend some time working with illustrations in the book and thinking about how the illustrations contribute to mood, setting, and characters.

Students will also continue to work toward writing a descriptive paragraph. They will use the illustration they chose in Allen Say (E) and the Describe an Illustration activity page to plan a topic sentence, supporting details, and concluding sentence. This activity is a prewriting activity; students will not write an actual paragraph in this activity.

Advance Preparation

Gather students' completed Spelling List 2 Pretest activity page from Allen Say (E). Students will refer to this page during Get Ready: Spelling List 2 Activity Bank.

Gather students' completed Describe an Illustration activity page from Allen Say (E). Students will refer to this page during Try It: Plan a Descriptive Paragraph.

The Sign Painter, Part 2 Synopsis

The boy and the sign painter continue to paint billboards. They go to the final billboard and are caught in a dust storm. They stay in the car overnight. When the dust settles, they find that the panels in the last billboard were destroyed in the storm. The sign painter isn't sure what to do. While they are thinking about it, a woman driving a convertible nearly hits the sign painter.

The boy recognizes the driver as the woman from the ArrowStar billboards. The two turn their attention toward two towers in the desert and drive to them, eventually figuring out that the towers are part of a roller coaster. They see a cluster of houses on a mesa and a ramp leading down to the desert floor. They drive up the ramp to explore, find empty houses, and overhear a man on a phone call. He explains that the woman "couldn't wait" and that he had a dream about ArrowStar for years.

By listening to the conversation, the boy and the man realize that the billboards they have been painting are advertising the roller coaster and houses on the mesa. The pair leave and head back to the town where they began. They talk a little about dreams. When they return to the town, the boy says good-bye to the sign painter and, we assume, boards the bus toward a new destination.

MATERIALS

Supplied

- *The Sign Painter* by Allen Say
- *Tea with Milk* by Allen Say
- *Grandfather's Journey* by Allen Say
- *Summit English Language Arts 3 Activity Book*
  - Spelling List 2 Activity Bank
  - Plan a Descriptive Paragraph
- handwriting workbook

Also needed

- completed Spelling List 2 Pretest activity page from Allen Say (E)
- completed Describe an Illustration activity page from Allen Say (E)

KEYWORDS

author's purpose – the reason the author wrote a text: to entertain, to inform, to express an opinion, or to persuade

Lesson Goals

- Practice all spelling words offline.
- Read aloud to practice fluency.
- Read *The Sign Painter*.
- Interpret illustrations and connect texts.
- Plan to write a descriptive paragraph.
- Practice vocabulary words.
- Develop letter formation fluency.

GET READY

Introduction to Allen Say (F)

Students will get a glimpse of what they will learn about in the lesson. They will also read the lesson goals and keywords. Have students select each keyword and preview its definition.

Spelling List 2 Activity Bank

Students will practice all spelling words from the workshop by completing Spelling List 2 Activity Bank from *Summit English Language Arts 3 Activity Book*. Make sure students have their completed Spelling List 2 Pretest activity page from Allen Say (E) to refer to during this activity.

Remind students to pay special attention to words they spelled incorrectly on the Spelling Pretest.

GET READY
Allen Say (F)

Spelling List 2 Activity Bank

Circle any words in the box that you did not spell correctly on the pretest. Choose one activity to do with your circled words. Do as much of the activity as you can in the time given.

Did you spell all the words on the pretest correctly? Do the one activity with as many spelling words as you can.

facts	numbers	products	foxes	quizzes
hundreds	objects	systems	gashes	riches
insects	plants	dresses	inches	sandwiches
napkins	presidents			

Spelling Activity Choices

Silly Sentences

1. Write a silly sentence for each of your spelling words.
2. Underline the spelling word in each sentence.
   Example: The dog was driving a car.
3. Correct any spelling errors.

ALLEN SAY (F) 19

Spelling Story

1. Write a very short story using each of your spelling words.
2. Underline the spelling words in the story.
3. Correct any spelling errors.

Riddle Me This

1. Write a riddle for each of your spelling words.
   Example: "I have a trunk, but it's not on my car."
2. Write the answer, which is your word, for each riddle.
   Example: Answer: elephant
3. Correct any spelling errors.

RunOnWord

1. Gather some crayons, colored pencils, or markers. Use a different color to write each of your spelling words. Write the words end to end as one long word.
   Example: dogcat**birdfishturtle**
2. Rewrite the words correctly and with proper spacing.
3. Correct any spelling errors.

20 ALLEN SAY (F)

Complete the activity that you chose.

My chosen activity: ____________

Students should use this page to complete all steps in their chosen activity.

ALLEN SAY (F) 21

Read and Record

Good readers read quickly, smoothly, and with expression. This is called *fluency*. Students will record themselves reading aloud. They will listen to their recording and think about how quick, smooth, and expressive they sound.

TIP Encourage students to rerecord as needed.

Reading Foundations: Look at Pictures

Reading Foundations activities serve to remind students of basic reading skills and reading behaviors mastered in earlier grades. The activities cover topics such as advanced decoding skills and various strategies for improving comprehension.

Recall *The Sign Painter*, Part 1

Students will answer some questions to review the reading that they have already completed.

Before You Read *The Sign Painter*, Part 2

Students will be introduced to some key vocabulary words that they will encounter in the upcoming reading and answer questions to help them set a purpose for their reading.

READ

The Sign Painter, Part 2

Students will read Part 2 of *The Sign Painter* by Allen Say. Part 2 is the middle of the book, when the sign painter and the boy are caught in a dust storm, to the end.

NOTE The events at the end of the book are somewhat vague and open to interpretation. That's okay. Encourage students to draw their own conclusions, using the details in the text to support their ideas.

Check-In: *The Sign Painter*, Part 2

Students will answer several questions to demonstrate their comprehension of Part 2 of *The Sign Painter*.

LEARN AND TRY IT

LEARN Thinking About an Author's Purpose and Connecting Texts

Students will learn different reasons authors write books and think about why Allen Say wrote *The Sign Painter*.

TRY IT Think About an Author's Purpose and Connect Texts

Students will identify Allen's Say's reason for writing *Grandfather's Journey*, *Tea with Milk*, and *The Sign Painter*. They will also explore similarities among the three texts.

TRY IT Apply: Author's Purpose

Students will apply to a new work what they've learned about determining an author's purpose in writing a text.

TRY IT Plan a Descriptive Paragraph

Students will complete Plan a Descriptive Paragraph in *Summit English Language Arts 3 Activity Book*. Make sure students have their completed Describe an Illustration activity page from Allen Say (E) to refer to during this activity.

LEARNING COACH CHECK-IN This activity page contains open-ended questions, so it's important that you review students' responses. Remind students that a topic sentence is supported by details that come from the text.

NOTE Have students keep their completed activity page in a safe place so they can refer to it later.

TRY IT
Allen Say (F)

Plan a Descriptive Paragraph

Read the writing prompt.

Prompt: **Write a paragraph that describes an illustration.**

Follow the instructions to plan your paragraph. Use complete sentences.

1. State the **purpose** of your paragraph.
   Students should respond that they are writing a descriptive paragraph to describe the illustration they chose.

Purpose is another word for "reason." My purpose for writing is to create something beautiful!

ALLEN SAY (F) 23

2. Complete the graphic organizer to plan your descriptive paragraph. Use the sensory words that you brainstormed to help you. Sample answers are shown.

Topic Sentence
Sample answer: The illustration shows two people looking at a billboard in the desert.
Students should write the main idea of their paragraph.

First Detail
Sample answer: The desert looks sandy and dry.
Students should write a detail about the illustration.

24 ALLEN SAY (F)

Second Detail
Sample answer: It is very sunny and bright. The metal car is shiny in the sun.
Students should write a detail about the illustration.

Third Detail
Sample answer: It feels hot because there is no shade.
Students should write a detail about the illustration.

Conclusion
Sample answer: In the illustration, there are two people in the middle of the desert.
Students should restate the main idea of the paragraph in different words.

ALLEN SAY (F) 25

TRY IT Practice Words from *The Sign Painter*, Part 2

Students will answer questions to demonstrate their understanding of the vocabulary words from the reading.

WRAP-UP

Question About Comparing Characters

Students will answer a question to show that they understand the similarities among characters in the three books by Allen Say that they have read.

Handwriting

Students should gather their handwriting materials and begin where they left off. Remind students to form letters carefully and correctly.

TIP Set a timer to help students stay focused during handwriting practice.

Allen Say (G)

Lesson Overview

ACTIVITY	ACTIVITY TITLE	TIME	ONLINE/OFFLINE
GET READY	Introduction to Allen Say (G)	**1** minute	online
	Spelling List 2 Review Game	**10** minutes	online
	Read and Record	**8** minutes	online
	Recall *The Sign Painter*, Part 2	**6** minutes	online
LEARN AND TRY IT	Comparing and Contrasting Plot	**10** minutes	online
	Compare and Contrast Plot	**10** minutes	online
	History and Culture Influence Plot	**10** minutes	online
	Determine How History and Culture Influence Plot	**15** minutes	online
	Apply: Compare or Contrast Plot	**15** minutes	online
	Write a Descriptive Paragraph LEARNING COACH CHECK-IN	**25** minutes	offline
WRAP-UP	Question About Plot Influences	**2** minutes	online
	Handwriting	**8** minutes	offline

Content Background

Students will review the second half of *The Sign Painter* by Allen Say. They will learn how to compare and contrast the plots of all three books by Say: *Grandfather's Journey*, *Tea with Milk*, and *The Sign Painter*.

Students will also spend time learning how the historical era in which a story is set and the culture in which the characters exist have a strong influence on a story's characters and plot. For example, Masako in *Tea with Milk* has to learn calligraphy and flower painting because in her culture at the time, the most important thing was for a woman to find a good husband. Being skilled in traditional arts was seen as a way to signify to potential mates that a woman was well bred, would be obedient, and would make a good home for future children. Masako rejects these ideas and leaves home to forge her own life in the big city. This example shows how cultural expectations play a role in the plot and characters of a story.

Advance Preparation

Gather students' completed Describe an Illustration activity page from Allen Say (E) and Plan a Descriptive Paragraph activity page from Allen Say (F). Students will refer to these pages during Try It: Write a Descriptive Paragraph.

Lesson Goals

- Practice all spelling words online.
- Read aloud to practice fluency.
- Compare and contrast two texts.
- Determine how history and culture influence texts.
- Develop letter formation fluency.

MATERIALS

Supplied

- *The Sign Painter* by Allen Say
- *Tea with Milk* by Allen Say
- *Grandfather's Journey* by Allen Say
- *Summit English Language Arts 3 Activity Book*
    - Write a Descriptive Paragraph
- handwriting workbook

Also needed

- completed Describe an Illustration activity page from Allen Say (E)
- completed Plan a Descriptive Paragraph activity page from Allen Say (F)

KEYWORDS

plot – what happens in a story; the sequence of events

supporting detail – a detail that gives more information about a main idea

topic sentence – the sentence that expresses the main idea of a paragraph

GET READY

Introduction to Allen Say (G)

Students will get a glimpse of what they will learn about in the lesson. They will also read the lesson goals and keywords. Have students select each keyword and preview its definition.

Spelling List 2 Review Game

Students will practice all spelling words from the workshop.

Read and Record

Good readers read quickly, smoothly, and with expression. This is called *fluency*. Students will record themselves reading aloud. They will listen to their recording and think about how quick, smooth, and expressive they sound.

TIP Encourage students to rerecord as needed.

Recall *The Sign Painter*, Part 2

Students will answer some questions to review the reading that they have already completed.

LEARN AND TRY IT

LEARN Comparing and Contrasting Plot

Students will learn about the journeys the characters take in the three books by Allen Say that they have read: *Grandfather's Journey*, *Tea with Milk*, and *The Sign Painter*.

TRY IT Compare and Contrast Plot

Students will identify how an author uses characters to develop plot and theme in the three books by Allen Say that they have read.

LEARN History and Culture Influence Plot

Students will learn that history and culture influence a story's sequence of events.

TRY IT Determine How History and Culture Influence Plot

Students will identify that history and culture influence a character's actions in a story.

TRY IT Apply: Compare or Contrast Plot

Students will apply to a new work what they've learned about how history and culture influence plot or sequence of events in a story.

TRY IT Write a Descriptive Paragraph

Students will complete Write a Descriptive Paragraph in *Summit English Language Arts 3 Activity Book*. Make sure students have their completed Describe an Illustration activity page from Allen Say (E) and Plan a Descriptive Paragraph activity page from Allen Say (F) to refer to during this activity.

LEARNING COACH CHECK-IN This activity page contains an open-ended writing prompt, so it's important that you review students' responses. Give students feedback, using the sample answer provided to guide you.

NOTE Have students keep their completed activity page in a safe place so they can refer to it later.

TRY IT

Allen Say (G)

Write a Descriptive Paragraph

Read the writing prompt.

Prompt: **Write a paragraph that describes an illustration.**

Respond to the writing prompt. Use your prewriting work to help you. Indent your paragraph. Write a topic sentence, supporting details, and a concluding sentence.

Students should use their notes and their graphic organizer to write a descriptive paragraph.

Sample answer:

The illustration shows two people looking at a billboard in the desert. The desert looks dry and sandy. The weather is very bright and sunny, and the metal car is shining in the sun. The people in the illustration are probably feeling hot, since there is no shade in the picture. In conclusion, this is a beautiful picture of two people in the middle of the desert.

ALLEN SAY (G) 27

28 ALLEN SAY (G)

WRAP-UP

Question About Plot Influences

Students will answer a question to show that they understand how history and culture influence the plot of a story.

Handwriting

Students should gather their handwriting materials and begin where they left off. Remind students to form letters carefully and correctly.

TIP Set a timer to help students stay focused during handwriting practice.

Allen Say Wrap-Up

Lesson Overview

ACTIVITY	ACTIVITY TITLE	TIME	ONLINE/OFFLINE
GET READY	Introduction to Allen Say Wrap-Up	**1** minute	online
	Read and Record	**8** minutes	online
TRY IT	Revise and Proofread a Descriptive Paragraph LEARNING COACH CHECK-IN	**20** minutes	offline
	Review Allen Say	**20** minutes	online
QUIZ	Allen Say	**30** minutes	online
	Spelling List 2	**10** minutes	online
WRAP-UP	More Language Arts Practice	**23** minutes	online
	Handwriting	**8** minutes	offline

Advance Preparation

Gather students' completed Write a Descriptive Paragraph activity page from Allen Say (G). Students will refer to this page during Try It: Revise and Proofread a Descriptive Paragraph.

MATERIALS

Supplied

- *Summit English Language Arts 3 Activity Book*
    - Revise and Proofread a Descriptive Paragraph
- handwriting workbook

Also needed

- completed Write a Descriptive Paragraph activity page from Allen Say (G)

Lesson Goals

- Read aloud to practice fluency.
- Proofread your writing.
- Review what you learned.
- Take a reading quiz.
- Take a spelling quiz.
- Develop letter formation fluency.

GET READY

Introduction to Allen Say Wrap-Up

Students will read the lesson goals.

Read and Record

Good readers read quickly, smoothly, and with expression. This is called *fluency*. Students will record themselves reading aloud. They will listen to their recording and think about how quick, smooth, and expressive they sound.

TIP Encourage students to rerecord as needed.

TRY IT

Revise and Proofread a Descriptive Paragraph

Students will complete Revise and Proofread a Descriptive Paragraph in *Summit English Language Arts 3 Activity Book*. Make sure students have their completed Write a Descriptive Paragraph activity page from Allen Say (G) to refer to during this activity.

LEARNING COACH CHECK-IN This activity page is a revision and proofreading checklist. Assist students in looking over their descriptive paragraph from Allen Say (G) and checking for each item on the list.

TIP Remind students to focus on the checklist questions. They should not worry about any other proofreading tasks at this time.

TRY IT

Allen Say Wrap-Up

Revise and Proofread a Descriptive Paragraph

Read your descriptive paragraph. Use the checklist to revise and proofread your paragraph.

Ideas

- ☑ Did I include a topic sentence that states the main idea of the paragraph?
- ☑ Did I include sensory details?
- ☑ Did I include a concluding sentence?

Grammar

- ☑ Are all sentences complete and correct?
- ☑ Does every sentence begin with a capital letter?
- ☑ Does every sentence end with the correct punctuation?
- ☑ Did I indent the first sentence in the paragraph?

Students should check off each item after they make any necessary changes to their descriptive paragraph.

ALLEN SAY WRAP-UP 29

Review Allen Say

Students will answer questions to review what they have learned about *Grandfather's Journey, Tea with Milk, The Sign Painter*, characters, setting, theme, and sequence of events.

QUIZ

Allen Say

Students will complete the Allen Say quiz.

Spelling List 2

Students will complete the Spelling List 2 quiz.

WRAP-UP

More Language Arts Practice

Students will practice skills according to their individual needs.

Handwriting

Students should gather their handwriting materials and begin where they left off. Remind students to form letters carefully and correctly.

TIP Set a timer to help students stay focused during handwriting practice.

Word Relationships and Context Clues

Lesson Overview

ACTIVITY	ACTIVITY TITLE	TIME	ONLINE/OFFLINE
GET READY	Introduction to Word Relationships and Context Clues	**1** minute	
	Look Back at Context	**4** minutes	
LEARN AND **TRY IT**	Word Relationships and Context Clues	**10** minutes	
	Practice Using Word Relationships and Context Clues	**10** minutes	
	Apply: Word Relationships and Context Clues **LEARNING COACH CHECK-IN**	**15** minutes	
	Review Word Relationships and Context Clues	**15** minutes	
QUIZ	Word Relationships and Context Clues	**15** minutes	
WRAP-UP	More Language Arts Practice	**15** minutes	
	Go Write! Who Are You?	**15** minutes	
	Go Read!	**20** minutes	or

Content Background

In this lesson, students will learn several words that they will typically encounter in testing situations. They will learn how to use context clues to help define unknown words. They will learn that words are related through synonyms, which are words with the same or similar meanings, and antonyms, which are words with opposite meanings. Students will learn that synonyms and antonyms are types of context clues that can help unlock the meanings of unknown words.

For example, in the following sentences *look up* is a synonym for *refer*, which can help students determine the meaning of *refer*.

> **Example:** That way she could refer to the rules when she explained the game to her friends. She could look up the rules and wouldn't forget the details.

MATERIALS

Supplied
- *Summit English Language Arts 3 Activity Book*
  - Apply: Word Relationships and Context Clues
  - Go Write! Who Are You?

Also Needed
- dictionary
- thesaurus
- reading material for Go Read!

Advance Preparation

During the Go Read! activity, students will have the option of using the digital library. Allow extra time for students to make their reading selection, or have students make a selection before beginning the lesson.

Lesson Goals

- Practice vocabulary words.
- Use context clues to determine the meaning of unknown words.
- Use synonyms and antonyms to understand the meaning of words.
- Use words that are commonly found on assessments.
- Take the Word Relationships and Context Clues quiz.
- Freewrite about a topic to develop writing fluency and practice letter formation.
- Read independently to develop fluency.

GET READY

Introduction to Word Relationships and Context Clues

Students will get a glimpse of what they will learn about in the lesson. They will also read the lesson goals.

Look Back at Context

Students will practice the prerequisite skill of using synonyms and antonyms for context.

LEARN AND TRY IT

LEARN Word Relationships and Context Clues

Students will be introduced to the vocabulary words for the lesson. Then they will learn how to use word relationships like synonyms and context clues to determine the meaning of new vocabulary words.

TRY IT Practice Using Word Relationships and Context Clues

Students will work along with the character Maria to practice using synonyms and other context clues to determine the meaning of new vocabulary words.

TRY IT Apply: Word Relationships and Context Clues

Students will complete Apply: Word Relationships and Context Clues from *Summit English Language Arts 3 Activity Book*. First students will use a dictionary or thesaurus to find synonyms and antonyms for some of their vocabulary words. Then they will apply

what they learned about word relationships and context clues by using the synonyms and antonyms they found to add a context clue to a sentence, defining the vocabulary word.

OPTIONAL Have students look up synonyms and antonyms and write sentences with context clues for the remainder of the vocabulary words.

LEARNING COACH CHECK-IN This activity page requires the use of a dictionary or thesaurus, which you might assist students with. It also contains open-ended responses, so it's important that you review students' responses. Give students feedback, using the sample answers provided to guide you.

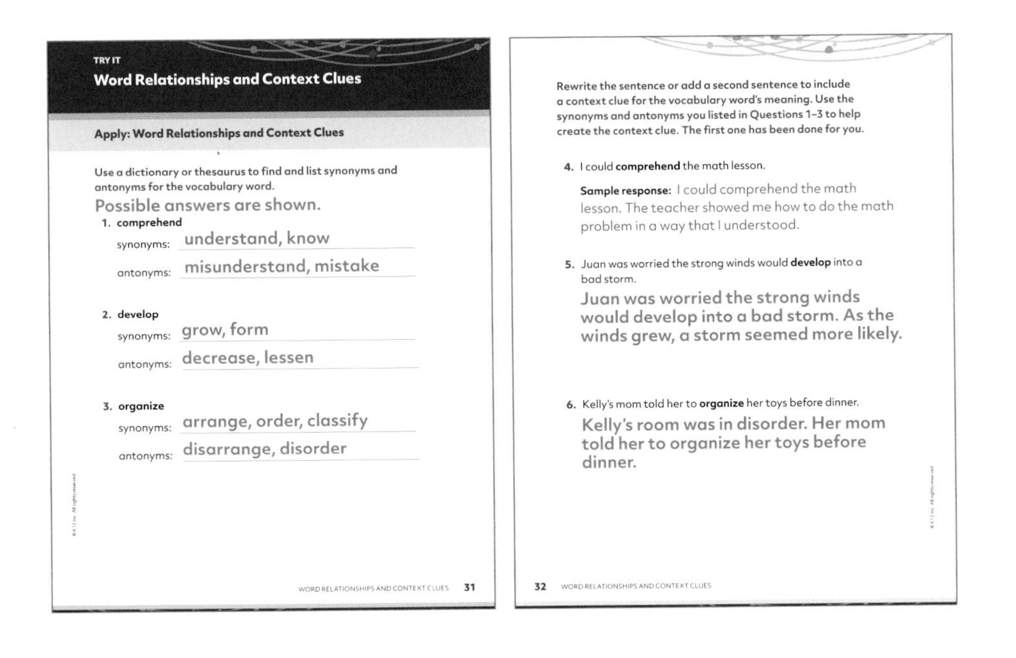

TRY IT
Word Relationships and Context Clues

Apply: Word Relationships and Context Clues

Use a dictionary or thesaurus to find and list synonyms and antonyms for the vocabulary word.

Possible answers are shown.

1. **comprehend**
   synonyms: understand, know
   antonyms: misunderstand, mistake
2. **develop**
   synonyms: grow, form
   antonyms: decrease, lessen
3. **organize**
   synonyms: arrange, order, classify
   antonyms: disarrange, disorder

WORD RELATIONSHIPS AND CONTEXT CLUES 31

Rewrite the sentence or add a second sentence to include a context clue for the vocabulary word's meaning. Use the synonyms and antonyms you listed in Questions 1–3 to help create the context clue. The first one has been done for you.

4. I could **comprehend** the math lesson.
   Sample response: I could comprehend the math lesson. The teacher showed me how to do the math problem in a way that I understood.
5. Juan was worried the strong winds would **develop** into a bad storm.
   Juan was worried the strong winds would develop into a bad storm. As the winds grew, a storm seemed more likely.
6. Kelly's mom told her to **organize** her toys before dinner.
   Kelly's room was in disorder. Her mom told her to organize her toys before dinner.

32 WORD RELATIONSHIPS AND CONTEXT CLUES

TRY IT Review Word Relationships and Context Clues

Students will answer questions to review what they have learned about word relationships and context clues.

QUIZ

Word Relationships and Context Clues

Students will complete the Word Relationships and Context Clues quiz.

WRAP-UP

More Language Arts Practice

Students will practice skills according to their individual needs.

Go Write! Who Are You?

Students will complete Go Write! Who Are You? in *Summit English Language Arts 3 Activity Book*. They will have the option to either respond to a prompt or write about a topic of their choice.

NOTE This activity is intended to build writing fluency. Students should write for the entire allotted time.

SUPPORT If students have trouble writing for the allotted time, prompt them with questions. For example, *Can you tell me more about this? How did you feel when this happened?*

OPTIONAL Have students decorate a folder and use it to store their freewriting pages throughout the course.

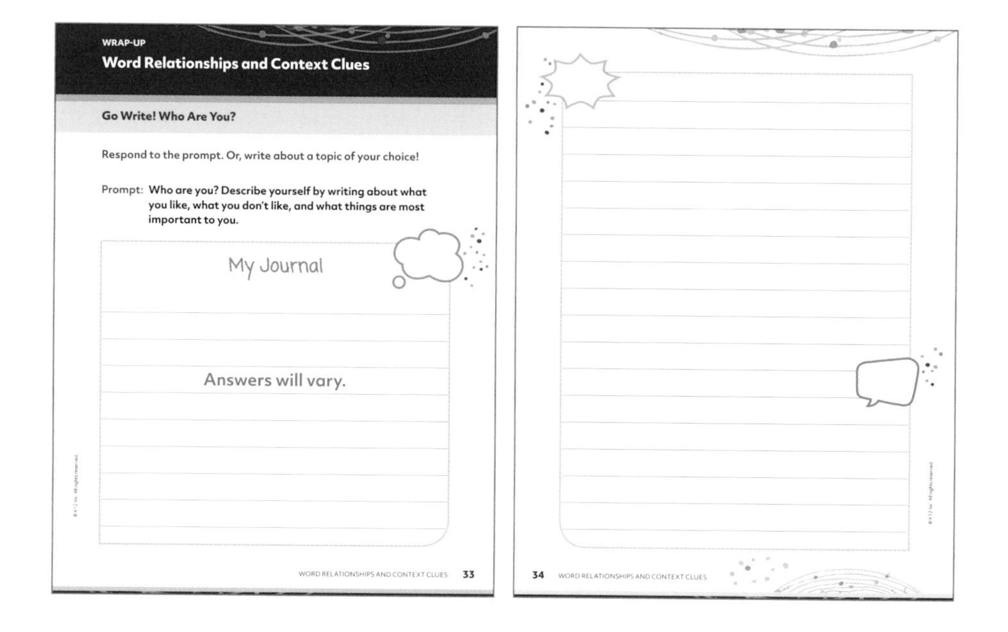
WRAP-UP

Word Relationships and Context Clues

Go Write! Who Are You?

Respond to the prompt. Or, write about a topic of your choice!

Prompt: **Who are you? Describe yourself by writing about what you like, what you don't like, and what things are most important to you.**

My Journal

Answers will vary.

WORD RELATIONSHIPS AND CONTEXT CLUES 33

34 WORD RELATIONSHIPS AND CONTEXT CLUES

Go Read!

Students will read for pleasure. They should choose a book or a magazine that interests them, or they may choose a selection from the digital library, linked in the online lesson.

- Have students read aloud a few paragraphs of their selection.
- Then have students read silently for the rest of the time.

SUPPORT Students should make no more than five errors in decoding when they read aloud a few paragraphs of their Go Read! selection. If students struggle or make more than five errors, they need to select a different (and easier) text for the Go Read! activity.

TIP Have students select something to read ahead of time to help them stay focused.

Narrative Writing Skills (A)

Lesson Overview

ACTIVITY	ACTIVITY TITLE	TIME	ONLINE/OFFLINE
GET READY	Introduction to Narrative Writing Skills (A)	**1** minute	
	Spelling List 3 Pretest **LEARNING COACH CHECK-IN**	**10** minutes	and
	Look Back at Parts of a Sentence	**5** minutes	
LEARN AND **TRY IT**	Simple Sentences	**10** minutes	
	Write Simple Sentences	**10** minutes	
	Explore a Model Personal Story	**10** minutes	
	Respond to a Personal Story	**5** minutes	
	Plan a Personal Story	**10** minutes	
	Plan Your Personal Story **LEARNING COACH CHECK-IN**	**25** minutes	
WRAP-UP	Questions About Simple Sentences and Chronological Order	**4** minutes	
	Handwriting	**8** minutes	
	Go Read!	**22** minutes	or

Content Background

A *narrative* is a story—it can be either fiction or nonfiction. Throughout this workshop, students will build narrative writing skills by analyzing a model personal story and writing their own personal story. In this lesson, students will focus on how writers organize events in a personal story.

While there are different ways to organize events in a narrative, students will learn and be expected to use one organizational strategy—chronological order. *Chronological order* is time order. The events are recounted in the order in which they occurred. There are no flashbacks or flash forwards in a narrative that is organized chronologically.

The personal story is a relatively short piece of writing, so students will follow an abbreviated version of the writing process. In this lesson, they will *prewrite* by choosing a topic and organizing their ideas.

MATERIALS

Supplied

- *Summit English Language Arts 3 Activity Book*
  - Spelling List 3 Pretest
  - Model Personal Story
  - Plan Your Personal Story
- handwriting workbook

Also Needed

- folder for organizing personal story assignment pages
- reading material for Go Read!

Grammar, Usage, and Mechanics A simple sentence tells one complete thought. It has exactly one subject and one predicate. In the following examples, subjects are underlined once, and predicates are underlined twice.

Simple sentence: Ralph plays the piano.

Not a simple sentence: Kendra plays the guitar, but her sister doesn't.

Advance Preparation

Gather a folder that students can use to keep all notes and activity pages related to their personal story.

During the Go Read! activity, students will have the option of using the digital library. Allow extra time for students to make their reading selection, or have students make a selection before beginning the lesson.

KEYWORDS

chronological order – a way to organize that puts details in time order

narrative – a kind of writing that tells a story

predicate – tells what the subject of a sentence is or does

sentence – a group of words that tells a complete thought

subject – a word or words that tell whom or what the sentence is about

Lesson Goals

- Take a spelling pretest.
- Write a simple sentence.
- Read a model personal story, and start planning your own.
- Develop letter formation fluency.
- Read independently to develop fluency.

GET READY

Introduction to Narrative Writing Skills (A)

Students will get a glimpse of what they will learn about in the lesson. They will also read the lesson goals and keywords. Have students select each keyword and preview its definition.

Spelling List 3 Pretest

Students will take a spelling pretest and learn a new spelling pattern.

LEARNING COACH CHECK-IN Have students turn to Spelling List 3 Pretest in *Summit English Language Arts 3 Activity Book* and open the online Spelling Pretest activity. Online, students will listen to the spelling word, type the word in the space indicated, and then check their answer. In the activity book, students will write the correct spelling of the word in the tables provided and indicate with a ✓ or an ✗ if they spelled the word correctly or incorrectly online. Students will repeat this process with the remaining words.

As needed, help students with the interaction between the online activity and the activity book page until they become comfortable with what they need to do. As students practice their spelling words throughout the workshop, they should pay special attention to words they spelled incorrectly on the pretest.

This is the complete list of words students will be tested on.

Words with /nk/ and /ng/ Sounds		
chunk	cling	something
drink	hangs	string
honk	lungs	strong
shrink	mustang	thing
think	nothing	wings
yanking	singing	

NOTE Have students keep their completed activity page in a safe place so they can refer to it later.

GET READY

Narrative Writing Skills (A)

Spelling List 3 Pretest

1. Open the Spelling Pretest activity online. Listen to the first spelling word. Type the word. Check your answer.

2. Write the correct spelling of the word in the Word column of the Spelling Pretest table.

	Word	✓	✗
1	blindfold		

3. Put a check mark in the ✓ column if you spelled the word correctly online.

	Word	✓	✗
1	blindfold	✓	

Put an X in the ✗ column if you spelled the word incorrectly online.

	Word	✓	✗
1	blindfold		X

4. Repeat Steps 1–3 for the remaining words in the Spelling Pretest.

NARRATIVE WRITING SKILLS (A) 35

Narrative Writing Skills (A)

Spelling List 3 Pretest

Write each spelling word in the Word column, making sure to spell it correctly.

	Word	✓	✗
1	chunk		
2	drink		
3	honk		
4	shrink		
5	think		
6	yanking		
7	cling		
8	hangs		
9	lungs		

	Word	✓	✗
10	mustang		
11	nothing		
12	singing		
13	something		
14	string		
15	strong		
16	thing		
17	wings		

Students should write the correct spelling of each word from the pretest and use the ✓and X columns to indicate whether they spelled each word correctly or incorrectly online.

36 NARRATIVE WRITING SKILLS (A)

Look Back at Parts of a Sentence

Students will practice the prerequisite skill of identifying the subject and the predicate of a sentence.

LEARN AND TRY IT

LEARN Simple Sentences

Students will learn that a simple sentence tells one complete idea. They will learn how to identify a simple sentence.

TRY IT Write Simple Sentences

Students will practice identifying and completing simple sentences. They will also write simple sentences of their own by responding to prompts and using mentor sentences.

LEARN Explore a Model Personal Story

By reading and exploring a model personal story, students will learn what a personal story is and how it is organized.

TIP The model personal story that students read in the online activity is the same story on the Model Personal Story activity page. Students may wish to reference and make notes on the activity page as they complete the online activity.

TRY IT Respond to a Personal Story

Students will answer questions to check and expand their understanding of chronological order and the author's purpose in writing a personal story.

LEARN Plan a Personal Story

Students will learn how to choose a topic and organize their ideas in preparation to begin writing their own personal story.

TRY IT Plan Your Personal Story

Students will complete Plan Your Personal Story in *Summit English Language Arts 3 Activity Book*. They should have the Model Personal Story activity page to refer to as they work.

SUPPORT Choosing a topic for a personal story may seem monumental for some students. To help these students, have them name times they experienced big feelings, such as pride, joy, fear, or frustration. Help students narrow their experiences into small moments that they can realistically tackle in a three-paragraph story. Point out that in the Model Personal Story, Winnie did not write about her entire trip to the amusement park; she wrote about a single ride.

LEARNING COACH CHECK-IN This activity page contains open-ended questions, so it's important that you review students' responses.

NOTE Have students add the Model Personal Story and their completed Plan Your Personal Story activity page to the folder they are using to store their personal story assignment pages.

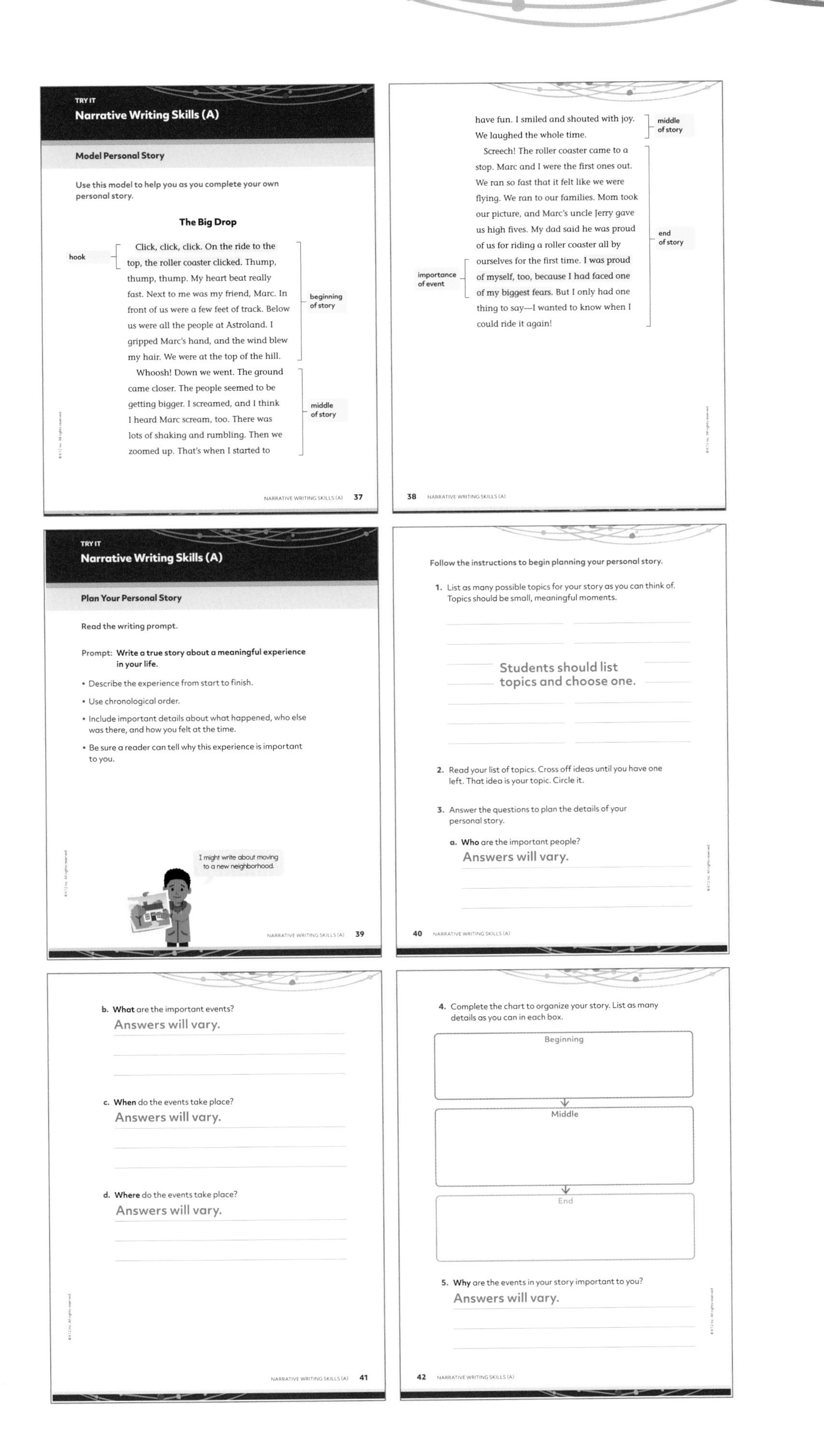
TRY IT

Narrative Writing Skills (A)

Model Personal Story

Use this model to help you as you complete your own personal story.

The Big Drop

Click, click, click. On the ride to the top, the roller coaster clicked. Thump, thump, thump. My heart beat really fast. Next to me was my friend, Marc. In front of us were a few feet of track. Below us were all the people at Astroland. I gripped Marc's hand, and the wind blew my hair. We were at the top of the hill.

Whoosh! Down we went. The ground came closer. The people seemed to be getting bigger. I screamed, and I think I heard Marc scream, too. There was lots of shaking and rumbling. Then we zoomed up. That's when I started to have fun. I smiled and shouted with joy. We laughed the whole time.

Screech! The roller coaster came to a stop. Marc and I were the first ones out. We ran so fast that it felt like we were flying. We ran to our families. Mom took our picture, and Marc's uncle Jerry gave us high fives. My dad said he was proud of us for riding a roller coaster all by ourselves for the first time. I was proud of myself, too, because I had faced one of my biggest fears. But I only had one thing to say—I wanted to know when I could ride it again!

NARRATIVE WRITING SKILLS (A) 37

38 NARRATIVE WRITING SKILLS (A)

TRY IT

Narrative Writing Skills (A)

Plan Your Personal Story

Read the writing prompt.

Prompt: **Write a true story about a meaningful experience in your life.**

- Describe the experience from start to finish.
- Use chronological order.
- Include important details about what happened, who else was there, and how you felt at the time.
- Be sure a reader can tell why this experience is important to you.

NARRATIVE WRITING SKILLS (A) 39

Follow the instructions to begin planning your personal story.

1. List as many possible topics for your story as you can think of. Topics should be small, meaningful moments.

   Students should list topics and choose one.

2. Read your list of topics. Cross off ideas until you have one left. That idea is your topic. Circle it.

3. Answer the questions to plan the details of your personal story.

   a. **Who** are the important people?

   Answers will vary.

40 NARRATIVE WRITING SKILLS (A)

   b. **What** are the important events?

   Answers will vary.

   c. **When** do the events take place?

   Answers will vary.

   d. **Where** do the events take place?

   Answers will vary.

NARRATIVE WRITING SKILLS (A) 41

4. Complete the chart to organize your story. List as many details as you can in each box.

Beginning
Middle
End

5. **Why** are the events in your story important to you?

   Answers will vary.

42 NARRATIVE WRITING SKILLS (A)

WRAP-UP

Questions About Simple Sentences and Chronological Order

Students will answer questions to show that they understand how to form a simple sentence and how to organize ideas in chronological order.

Handwriting

Students should gather their handwriting materials and begin where they left off. Remind students to form letters carefully and correctly.

TIP Set a timer to help students stay focused during handwriting practice.

Go Read!

Students will read for pleasure. They should choose a book or a magazine that interests them, or they may choose a selection from the digital library, linked in the online lesson.

- Have students read aloud a few paragraphs of their selection.
- Then have students read silently for the rest of the time.

SUPPORT Students should make no more than five errors in decoding when they read aloud a few paragraphs of their Go Read! selection. If students struggle or make more than five errors, they need to select a different (and easier) text for the Go Read! activity.

TIP Have students select something to read ahead of time to help them stay focused.

Narrative Writing Skills (B)

Lesson Overview

ACTIVITY	ACTIVITY TITLE	TIME	ONLINE/OFFLINE
GET READY	Introduction to Narrative Writing Skills (B)	**1** minute	
	Spelling List 3 Activity Bank	**10** minutes	
LEARN AND **TRY IT**	Simple Sentences with Compound Parts	**10** minutes	
	Write Simple Sentences with Compound Parts	**15** minutes	
	Explore the Introduction and Description	**10** minutes	
	Respond to Description in a Personal Story	**5** minutes	
	Show What Happened **LEARNING COACH CHECK-IN**	**35** minutes	
WRAP-UP	Questions About Simple Sentences and Description	**4** minutes	
	Handwriting	**8** minutes	
	Go Read!	**22** minutes	or

Content Background

Students will learn about introductions and description in narrative writing. Strong narrative pieces begin with an introduction that grabs readers' attention with a hook and reveals the setting, situation, and main characters. Throughout a narrative piece, good writers include sensory words, or description, to bring their story to life.

Students will continue working on their personal story. In this lesson, they will continue prewriting by planning how they can incorporate sensory details throughout their story, including the introduction.

Grammar, Usage, and Mechanics A simple sentence expresses one complete idea. When the subject of a sentence names more than one person, place, or thing, it has a **compound subject**. When the predicate of a sentence tells about more than one action, the sentence has a **compound predicate**.

Simple sentence with compound subject: Tom and Sue ran to the book store.

Simple sentence with compound predicate: Joe ate an apple and drank milk.

MATERIALS

Supplied

- *Summit English Language Arts 3 Activity Book*
  - Spelling List 3 Activity Bank
  - Show What Happened
- handwriting workbook

Also Needed

- completed Spelling List 3 Pretest activity page from Narrative Writing Skills (A)
- folder in which students are storing personal story assignment pages
- reading material for Go Read!

Advance Preparation

Gather students' completed Spelling List 3 Pretest activity page from Narrative Writing Skills (A). Students will refer to this page during Get Ready: Spelling List 3 Activity Bank.

Gather the folder that students are using to store the activity pages related to their personal story. The folder should contain the following:

- Model Personal Story activity page from Narrative Writing Skills (A)
- Students' completed Plan Your Personal Story activity page from Narrative Writing Skills (A)

During the Go Read! activity, students will have the option of using the digital library. Allow extra time for students to make their reading selection, or have students make a selection before beginning the lesson.

KEYWORDS

compound predicate – two or more predicates that have the same subject

compound subject – two or more subjects that have the same predicate

narrative – a kind of writing that tells a story

sensory detail – descriptive detail that appeals to any of the five senses—sight, hearing, touch, smell, or taste

Lesson Goals

- Practice all spelling words offline.
- Write simple sentences with compound parts.
- Explore the introduction and description of a model personal story.
- Develop description in your personal story.
- Develop letter formation fluency.
- Read independently to develop fluency.

GET READY

Introduction to Narrative Writing Skills (B)

Students will get a glimpse of what they will learn about in the lesson. They will also read the lesson goals and keywords. Have students select each keyword and preview its definition.

Spelling List 3 Activity Bank

Students will practice all spelling words from the workshop by completing Spelling List 3 Activity Bank from *Summit English Language Arts 3 Activity Book*. Make sure students have their completed Spelling List 3 Pretest activity page from Narrative Writing Skills (A) to refer to during this activity.

Remind students to pay special attention to words they spelled incorrectly on the Spelling Pretest.

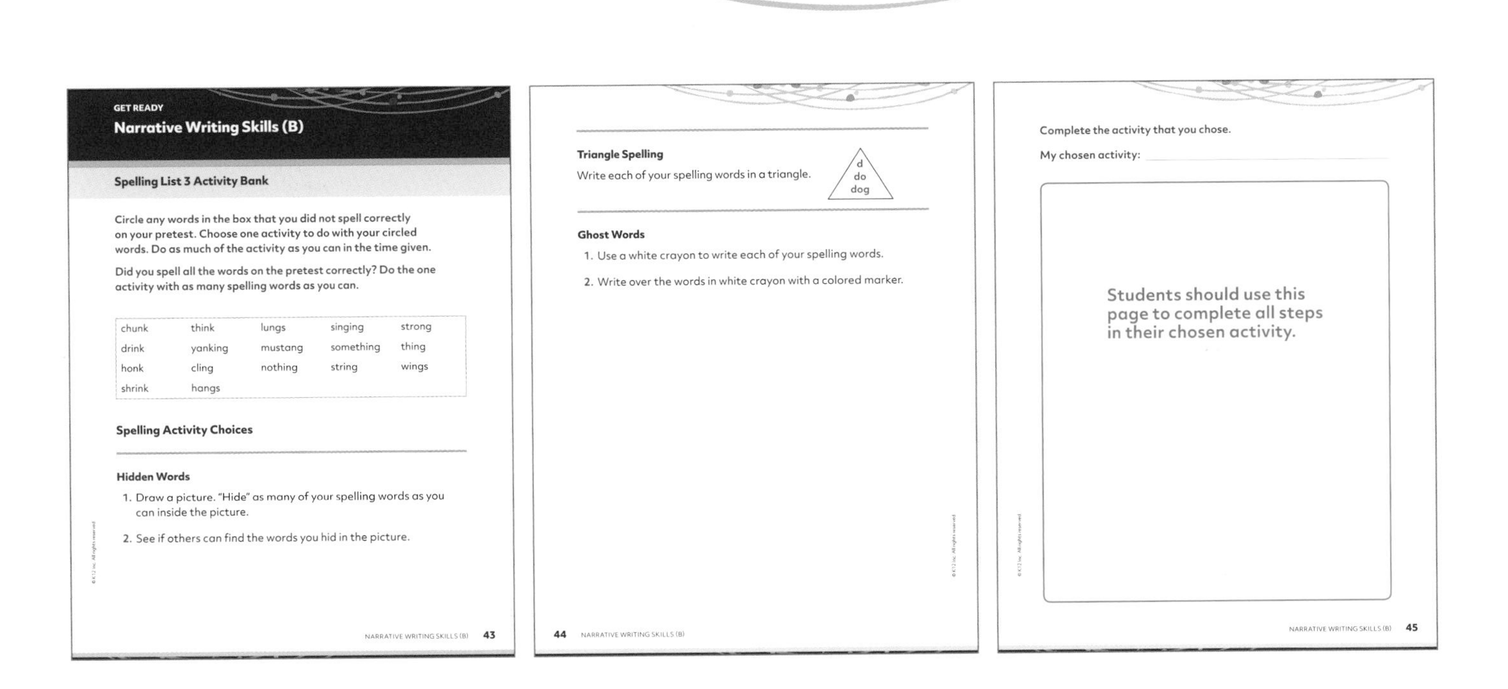
GET READY

Narrative Writing Skills (B)

Spelling List 3 Activity Bank

Circle any words in the box that you did not spell correctly on your pretest. Choose one activity to do with your circled words. Do as much of the activity as you can in the time given.

Did you spell all the words on the pretest correctly? Do the one activity with as many spelling words as you can.

chunk	think	lungs	singing	strong
drink	yanking	mustang	something	thing
honk	cling	nothing	string	wings
shrink	hangs			

Spelling Activity Choices

Hidden Words

1. Draw a picture. "Hide" as many of your spelling words as you can inside the picture.
2. See if others can find the words you hid in the picture.

NARRATIVE WRITING SKILLS (B) 43

Triangle Spelling

Write each of your spelling words in a triangle.

d
do
dog

Ghost Words

1. Use a white crayon to write each of your spelling words.
2. Write over the words in white crayon with a colored marker.

44 NARRATIVE WRITING SKILLS (B)

Complete the activity that you chose.

My chosen activity: ______

Students should use this page to complete all steps in their chosen activity.

NARRATIVE WRITING SKILLS (B) 45

LEARN AND TRY IT

LEARN Simple Sentences with Compound Parts

Students will learn that a simple sentence may have a compound subject or predicate. They will learn how to identify a simple sentence with compound parts.

TIP A simple sentence with a compound part is not the same as a compound sentence. Students will learn about compound sentences in Narrative Writing Skills (C).

TRY IT Write Simple Sentences with Compound Parts

Students will practice identifying and completing simple sentences with compound parts. They will also write simple sentences with compound parts of their own by responding to prompts and using mentor sentences.

LEARN Explore the Introduction and Description

Students will read and explore the introduction and description in a model personal story. They will learn that sensory details strengthen narrative writing.

TIP Students often focus on visual description, but description can evoke all five senses: sight, hearing, touch, smell, and taste.

TRY IT Respond to Description in a Personal Story

Students will answer questions about the introduction and description in a model personal story.

TRY IT Show What Happened

Students will complete Show What Happened in *Summit English Language Arts 3 Activity Book*. They should have their completed Plan Your Personal Story activity page and Model Personal Story from Narrative Writing Skills (A) to refer to as they work.

LEARNING COACH CHECK-IN This activity page contains open-ended questions, so it's important that you review students' responses. Give students feedback about the sensory details they have used to describe the events and characters of their personal story.

SUPPORT Some students may find it easier to say their answers aloud before writing them down.

NOTE Have students add their completed Show What Happened activity page to the folder they are using to store their personal story assignment pages.

TRY IT

Narrative Writing Skills (B)

Show What Happened

Read the writing prompt.

Prompt: **Tell a true story about a meaningful experience in your life.**

- Describe the experience from start to finish.
- Use chronological order.
- Include important details about what happened, who else was there, and how you felt at the time.
- Be sure a reader can tell why this experience is important to you.

Follow the instructions to plan how you will describe the events in your story.

Answers will vary.

1. Draw an important part of your meaningful experience.

2. Describe your drawing. Use words that will help readers imagine what was happening.

   Example from "The Big Drop": Whoosh! Down we went. The ground came closer. The people seemed to be getting bigger.

Follow the instructions to plan how you will describe your feelings in your story.

Answers will vary.

3. Complete the chart to show how you felt during your meaningful experience. A sample answer is shown.

Tell How You Felt	Show How You Felt
Sample answer: I felt nervous.	**Sample answer:** My hands started to shake.

Follow the instructions to plan the hook for your story.

Answers will vary.

4. Think about your meaningful experience.

   a. What does the reader need to know right away about the setting?

   b. What does the reader need to know right away about the situation?

5. Use your answers to Question 4 to draft the first few sentences of your personal story. Write sentences that *show* instead of tell.

   Example from "The Big Drop": Click, click, click. On the ride to the top, the roller coaster clicked.

WRAP-UP

Questions About Simple Sentences and Description

Students will answer questions to show that they understand how to form a simple sentence with compound parts and how to include sensory details in writing.

Handwriting

Students should gather their handwriting materials and begin where they left off. Remind students to form letters carefully and correctly.

TIP Set a timer to help students stay focused during handwriting practice.

Go Read!

Students will read for pleasure. They should choose a book or a magazine that interests them, or they may choose a selection from the digital library, linked in the online lesson.

- Have students read aloud a few paragraphs of their selection.
- Then have students read silently for the rest of the time.

SUPPORT Students should make no more than five errors in decoding when they read aloud a few paragraphs of their Go Read! selection. If students struggle or make more than five errors, they need to select a different (and easier) text for the Go Read! activity.

TIP Have students select something to read ahead of time to help them stay focused.

Narrative Writing Skills (C)

Lesson Overview

ACTIVITY	ACTIVITY TITLE	TIME	ONLINE/OFFLINE
GET READY	Introduction to Narrative Writing Skills (C)	1 minute	online
	Spelling List 3 Review Game	10 minutes	online
LEARN AND TRY IT	Compound Sentences	10 minutes	online
	Write Compound Sentences	15 minutes	online
	Explore Transitions and a Conclusion	10 minutes	online
	Respond to Transitions and the Conclusion of a Personal Story	5 minutes	online
	Write Your Personal Story LEARNING COACH CHECK-IN	40 minutes	offline
WRAP-UP	Questions About Compound Sentences and Transitions	4 minutes	online
	Handwriting	8 minutes	offline
	Go Read!	17 minutes	online or offline

Content Background

Students will learn about transitions and conclusions in narrative writing. *Transitions* show how the ideas and events within a piece of writing are related. Students will learn specifically about transitions that clarify the order of events. Examples of these transitions include *first*, *then*, and *finally*.

The *conclusion* is the end of a piece of writing. Strong narrative pieces end with a conclusion that logically wraps up the writing. The conclusion should also make it clear why the events in the narrative are important to the writer.

Students will continue working on their personal story. In this lesson, they will *draft* their story, writing it from beginning to end. Note that students will not be revising or proofreading their personal story in this course.

Grammar, Usage, and Mechanics A **compound sentence** expresses two complete and different ideas. A compound sentence needs a *coordinating conjunction*, or joining word, to join the two complete ideas. *And*, *but*, *yet*, *or*, *nor*, *for*, and *so* are coordinating conjunctions. In compound sentences, a comma comes before the conjunction.

MATERIALS

Supplied

- *Summit English Language Arts 3 Activity Book*
    - Write Your Personal Story
- handwriting workbook

Also Needed

- folder in which students are storing personal story assignment pages
- reading material for Go Read!

Simple sentence: Dogs bark.

Simple sentence: Cats purr.

Compound sentence: Dogs bark, and cats purr.

Advance Preparation

Gather the folder that students are using to store the activity pages related to their personal story. The folder should contain the following:

- Model Personal Story activity page from Narrative Writing Skills (A)
- Students' completed Plan Your Personal Story activity page from Narrative Writing Skills (A)
- Students' completed Show What Happened activity page from Narrative Writing Skills (B)

During the Go Read! activity, students will have the option of using the digital library. Allow extra time for students to make their reading selection, or have students make a selection before beginning the lesson.

KEYWORDS

compound sentence – a sentence that has at least two independent parts

conclusion – the final paragraph of a written work

coordinating conjunction – one of seven words—*and*, *but*, *yet*, *or*, *nor*, *for*, *so*—that connects words, phrases, or independent clauses

narrative – a kind of writing that tells a story

transition – a word, phrase, or clause that connects ideas

Lesson Goals

- Practice all spelling words online.
- Write compound sentences.
- Explore the transitions and conclusion of a model personal story.
- Write your personal story.
- Develop letter formation fluency.
- Read independently to develop fluency.

GET READY

Introduction to Narrative Writing Skills (C)

Students will get a glimpse of what they will learn about in the lesson. They will also read the lesson goals and keywords. Have students select each keyword and preview its definition.

Spelling List 3 Review Game

Students will practice all spelling words from the workshop.

LEARN AND TRY IT

LEARN Compound Sentences

Students will learn that a compound sentence expresses two complete and different ideas, and they will learn how to identify a compound sentence.

TIP Make sure students understand the difference between compound sentences and simple sentences with compound parts.

TRY IT Write Compound Sentences

Students will practice identifying and completing compound sentences. They will also write compound sentences of their own by responding to prompts and using mentor sentences.

SUPPORT Go on a hunt for compound sentences in a favorite book or magazine. Share what you notice about the sentences you find. For example, "I notice that this sentence uses the conjunction *and*. I notice that the two ideas in the sentence are similar." You can discuss anything students notice about the sentence.

LEARN Explore Transitions and a Conclusion

Students will read and explore the transitions and conclusion in a model personal story.

TIP There are many types of transitions. In this activity, students will focus only on transitions that show order.

TRY IT Respond to Transitions and the Conclusion of a Personal Story

Students will answer questions about the introduction and description in a model personal story.

TRY IT Write Your Personal Story

Students will complete Write Your Personal Story in *Summit English Language Arts 3 Activity Book*. They should have their completed Plan Your Personal Story activity page from Narrative Writing Skills (A) and Show What Happened activity page from Narrative Writing Skills (B) to refer to as they write.

LEARNING COACH CHECK-IN Students will write their entire personal story in this activity. They should use the prewriting work they have done to guide them as they write. Give students feedback on the introduction, description, transitions, and conclusion of their writing. Most importantly of all, encourage students to keep writing!

NOTE Have students add their completed Write Your Personal Story activity page to the folder they are using to store their personal story assignment pages.

TRY IT

Narrative Writing Skills (C)

Write Your Personal Story

Read the writing prompt.

Prompt: **Tell a true story about a meaningful experience in your life.**

- Describe the experience from start to finish.
- Use chronological order.
- Include important details about what happened, who else was there, and how you felt at the time.
- Be sure a reader can tell why this experience is important to you.

Respond to the writing prompt. Use your prewriting work to help you.

Students should write their personal story from beginning to end. Students' story should meet the requirements listed in the prompt and be at least three paragraphs long.

NARRATIVE WRITING SKILLS (C) 51

52 NARRATIVE WRITING SKILLS (C)

NARRATIVE WRITING SKILLS (C) 53

If you wish, draw a picture of an important part of your story.

54 NARRATIVE WRITING SKILLS (C)

WRAP-UP

Questions About Compound Sentences and Transitions

Students will answer questions to show that they understand how to form a compound sentence and how to use transitions that show order in writing.

Handwriting

Students should gather their handwriting materials and begin where they left off. Remind students to form letters carefully and correctly.

TIP Set a timer to help students stay focused during handwriting practice.

Go Read!

Students will read for pleasure. They should choose a book or a magazine that interests them, or they may choose a selection from the digital library, linked in the online lesson.

- Have students read aloud a few paragraphs of their selection.
- Then have students read silently for the rest of the time.

SUPPORT Students should make no more than five errors in decoding when they read aloud a few paragraphs of their Go Read! selection. If students struggle or make more than five errors, they need to select a different (and easier) text for the Go Read! activity.

TIP Have students select something to read ahead of time to help them stay focused.

Narrative Writing Skills Wrap-Up

Lesson Overview

ACTIVITY	ACTIVITY TITLE	TIME	ONLINE/OFFLINE
GET READY	Introduction to Narrative Writing Skills Wrap-Up	**1** minute	
TRY IT	Reflect on Your Personal Story LEARNING COACH CHECK-IN	**30** minutes	
	Review Simple and Compound Sentences	**15** minutes	
QUIZ	Simple and Compound Sentences and Narrative Writing Skills	**20** minutes	
	Spelling List 3	**10** minutes	
WRAP-UP	More Language Arts Practice	**20** minutes	
	Handwriting	**8** minutes	
	Go Read!	**16** minutes	or

Advance Preparation

Gather the folder that students are using to store the activity pages related to their personal story. The folder should contain the following:

- Model Personal Story activity page from Narrative Writing Skills (A)
- Students' completed Plan Your Personal Story activity page from Narrative Writing Skills (A)
- Students' completed Show What Happened activity page from Narrative Writing Skills (B)
- Students' completed Write Your Personal Story activity page from Narrative Writing Skills (C)

During the Go Read! activity, students will have the option of using the digital library. Allow extra time for students to make their reading selection, or have students make a selection before beginning the lesson.

MATERIALS

Supplied

- *Summit English Language Arts 3 Activity Book*
  - Reflect on Your Personal Story
- handwriting workbook

Also needed

- folder in which students are storing personal story assignment pages
- reading material for Go Read!

Lesson Goals

- Reflect on your personal story.
- Review simple and compound sentences.
- Take a quiz on simple and compound sentences and narrative writing skills.
- Take a spelling quiz.
- Develop letter formation fluency.
- Read independently to develop fluency.

GET READY

Introduction to Narrative Writing Skills Wrap-Up

Students will read the lesson goals.

TRY IT

Reflect on Your Personal Story

Students will complete Reflect on Your Personal Story in *Summit English Language Arts 3 Activity Book*. They should have their completed Write Your Personal Story activity page from Narrative Writing Skills (C) to refer to as they work.

LEARNING COACH CHECK-IN This activity page contains open-ended questions, so it's important that you review students' responses and give them feedback. Be sure to point out things students did well in their personal story as well as offer a few suggestions for improvement.

TRY IT

Narrative Writing Skills Wrap-Up

Reflect on Your Personal Story

Read your personal story. Then, answer the questions in complete sentences.

Possible answers are shown.

1. A strong narrative begins with a strong introduction.
   a. What do you think you did well in your introduction?
   Answer may include reflection on introducing the setting, characters, and problem of the story.
   b. What do you think you could improve?
   Answers will vary.

NARRATIVE WRITING SKILLS WRAP-UP 55

2. Good writers use sensory details to describe events and show how characters feel.
   a. List two examples of sentences that *show* instead of *tell*.
   Sentences listed should include sensory details that describe sights, sounds, feelings, smells, or tastes.
   b. Rewrite one sentence that you could improve with descriptive writing.
   Answers will vary.
3. Good writers use transitions to show order.
   a. List one sentence that includes a transition.
   Answers will vary.

56 NARRATIVE WRITING SKILLS WRAP-UP

   b. Rewrite one sentence that you could clarify by adding a transition.
   First, *Next*, *Then*, and *Later* are examples of transitions students could add to connect ideas and show the order of events in their story.
4. A strong narrative ends with a strong conclusion.
   a. Does your conclusion explain why the event in your story is important to you? Explain.
   Answers will vary.
   b. If not, what could you add to let readers know why the event is important?
   Answers will vary.

NARRATIVE WRITING SKILLS WRAP-UP 57

Review Simple and Compound Sentences

Students will answer questions to review what they have learned about simple and compound sentences.

QUIZ

Simple and Compound Sentences and Narrative Writing Skills

Students will complete the Simple and Compound Sentences and Narrative Writing Skills quiz.

Spelling List 3

Students will complete the Spelling List 3 quiz.

WRAP-UP

More Language Arts Practice

Students will practice skills according to their individual needs.

Handwriting

Students should gather their handwriting materials and begin where they left off. Remind students to form letters carefully and correctly.

TIP Set a timer to help students stay focused during handwriting practice.

Go Read!

Students will read for pleasure. They should choose a book or a magazine that interests them, or they may choose a selection from the digital library, linked in the online lesson.

- Have students read aloud a few paragraphs of their selection.
- Then have students read silently for the rest of the time.

SUPPORT Students should make no more than five errors in decoding when they read aloud a few paragraphs of their Go Read! selection. If students struggle or make more than five errors, they need to select a different (and easier) text for the Go Read! activity.

TIP Have students select something to read ahead of time to help them stay focused.

Big Ideas: Critical Skills Assignment

Lesson Overview

Big Ideas lessons provide students the opportunity to further apply the knowledge acquired and skills learned throughout the unit workshops. Each Big Ideas lesson consists of these parts:

1. **Cumulative Review:** Students keep their skills fresh by reviewing prior content.
2. **Preview:** Students practice answering the types of questions they will commonly find on standardized tests.
3. **Synthesis:** Students complete an assignment that allows them to connect and apply what they have learned. Synthesis assignments vary throughout the course.

   In the Synthesis portion of this Big Ideas lesson, students will read new selections. They will answer literal and inferential comprehension questions and complete writing questions that ask for short responses about the reading selections. Students should refer to the selections while answering the questions, because the questions emphasize using textual evidence. The questions call for students to demonstrate critical thinking, reading, and writing skills.

   LEARNING COACH CHECK-IN This is a graded assessment. Make sure students complete, review, and submit the assignment to their teacher.

All materials needed for this lesson are linked online and not provided in the activity book.

MATERIALS

Supplied

- Critical Skills Assignment (printout)

Fables

"The Wind and the Sun"

Lesson Overview

ACTIVITY	ACTIVITY TITLE	TIME	ONLINE/OFFLINE
GET READY	Introduction to "The Wind and the Sun"	**2** minutes	online
	Spelling List 4 Pretest **LEARNING COACH CHECK-IN**	**10** minutes	online and offline
	Read and Record	**5** minutes	online
	Reading Foundations: Words and Sounds	**5** minutes	online
	Before You Read "The Wind and the Sun"	**13** minutes	online
READ	"The Wind and the Sun"	**10** minutes	offline
	Check-In: "The Wind and the Sun"	**5** minutes	online
LEARN AND **TRY IT**	Sequencing Events	**10** minutes	online
	Sequence of Events	**5** minutes	online
	Finding the Moral of the Story	**10** minutes	online
	Moral of the Story	**5** minutes	online
	Apply: Moral of the Story	**15** minutes	online
	Write About Sequence and Moral **LEARNING COACH CHECK-IN**	**10** minutes	offline
	Practice Words from "The Wind and the Sun"	**5** minutes	online
WRAP-UP	Question About "The Wind and the Sun"	**2** minutes	online
	Handwriting	**8** minutes	offline

Content Background

In this lesson, students will begin to explore characteristics of fables. They will learn that fables typically have nonhuman characters that act like people. An example of this is the fable "The Tortoise and the Hare" in which animals act like people. In this lesson, students will read "The Wind and the Sun" in which the main characters, the Wind and the Sun, act like people. Students will also learn that a fable conveys a lesson that can be applied to life called a *moral*. The moral is usually included at the end of the fable.

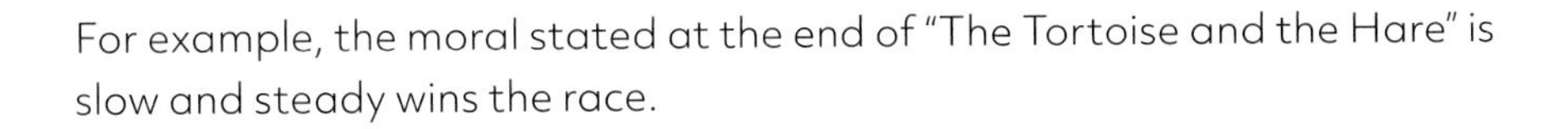

For example, the moral stated at the end of "The Tortoise and the Hare" is slow and steady wins the race.

"The Wind and the Sun" Synopsis

The fierce Wind and the gentle Sun decide to have a contest to determine which is stronger. The winner of the contest will be the one who can make a man take off his coat. The Wind blows hard on a man trying to make him take off his coat. When this does not work, the Sun shines gently on the man. The man becomes warm and removes his coat.

Lesson Goals

- Take a spelling pretest.
- Read aloud to practice fluency.
- Listen for parts of sentences and words.
- Read "The Wind and the Sun."
- Determine the sequence of events and moral of a fable.
- Practice vocabulary words.
- Develop letter formation fluency.

MATERIALS

Supplied

- *Summit English Language Arts 3 Expeditions in Reading*
  - "The Wind and the Sun"
- *Summit English Language Arts 3 Activity Book*
  - Spelling List 4 Pretest
  - Write About Sequence and Moral
- handwriting workbook

KEYWORDS

moral – the lesson of a story, particularly a fable

sequence – the order in which things happen

GET READY

Introduction to "The Wind and the Sun"

After a quick introductory activity, students will read the lesson goals and keywords. Have students select each keyword and preview its definition.

Spelling List 4 Pretest

Students will take a spelling pretest and learn a new spelling pattern.

LEARNING COACH CHECK-IN Have students turn to Spelling List 4 Pretest in *Summit English Language Arts 3 Activity Book* and open the online Spelling Pretest activity. Online, students will listen to the spelling word, type the word in the space indicated, and then check their answer. In the activity book, students will write the correct spelling of the word in the tables provided and indicate with a ✓ or an ✗ if they spelled the word correctly or incorrectly online. Students will repeat this process with the remaining words.

As needed, help students with the interaction between the online activity and the activity book page until they become comfortable with what they need to do. As students practice their spelling words throughout the workshop, they should pay special attention to words they spelled incorrectly on the pretest.

This is the complete list of words students will be tested on.

Words with Long *a* Sounds				
able	cupcake	flare	label	sleigh
always	decade	freight	ladle	snail
away	dictate	glare	maintain	Sunday
basic	eight	gravy	neighbor	training
claim	explain	holiday	payment	weight

NOTE Have students keep their completed activity page in a safe place so they can refer to it later.

GET READY
"The Wind and the Sun"

Spelling List 4 Pretest

1. Open the Spelling Pretest activity online. Listen to the first spelling word. Type the word. Check your answer.
2. Write the correct spelling of the word in the Word column of the Spelling Pretest table.

	Word	✓	✗
1	blindfold		

3. Put a check mark in the ✓ column if you spelled the word correctly online.

	Word	✓	✗
1	blindfold	✓	

Put an X in the ✗ column if you spelled the word incorrectly online.

	Word	✓	✗
1	blindfold		X

4. Repeat Steps 1–3 for the remaining words in the Spelling Pretest.

"THE WIND AND THE SUN" 59

"The Wind and the Sun"

Spelling List 4 Pretest

Write each spelling word in the Word column, making sure to spell it correctly.

	Word	✓	✗		Word	✓	✗
1	able			14	gravy		
2	always			15	holiday		
3	away			16	label		
4	basic			17	ladle		
5	claim			18	maintain		
6	cupcake			19	neighbor		
7	decade			20	payment		
8	dictate			21	sleigh		
9	eight			22	snail		
10	explain			23	Sunday		
11	flare			24	training		
12	freight			25	weight		
13	glare						

Students should write the correct spelling of each word from the pretest and use the ✓ and X columns to indicate whether they spelled each word correctly or incorrectly online.

60

Read and Record

Good readers read quickly, smoothly, and with expression. This is called *fluency*. Students will record themselves reading aloud. They will listen to their recording and think about how quick, smooth, and expressive they sound.

TIP Encourage students to rerecord as needed.

Reading Foundations: Words and Sounds

Reading Foundations activities serve to remind students of basic reading skills and reading behaviors mastered in earlier grades. The activities cover topics such as advanced decoding skills and various strategies for improving comprehension.

Before You Read "The Wind and the Sun"

Students will be introduced to some key vocabulary words that they will encounter in the upcoming reading and answer questions to help them set a purpose for their reading.

READ

"The Wind and the Sun"

Students will read "The Wind and the Sun" in *Expeditions in Reading*.

Check-In: "The Wind and the Sun"

Students will answer questions to demonstrate their comprehension of "The Wind and the Sun."

LEARN AND TRY IT

LEARN Sequencing Events

Students will learn that events in a story can be organized according to when they happen: at the beginning, middle, or end of the story.

TRY IT Sequence of Events

Students will organize events from "The Wind and the Sun" in the order in which they happen.

SUPPORT For students having difficulty determining the order of events, try the following task. Print a copy of "The Wind and the Sun." Have students highlight the events listed in the question item that must be put in order. Then, have them number the highlighted events in order so they can clearly identify the sequence of events. Have them place the events in the question item in order according to how they numbered the events in the story.

LEARN Finding the Moral of the Story

Students will learn that a fable teaches a lesson called a *moral*. The moral is usually stated at the end of the story. They will also learn that the characters' actions convey the moral of the story.

TRY IT Moral of the Story

Students will determine which story excerpts state the moral and convey details that develop the moral.

TRY IT **Apply: Moral of the Story**

Students will apply to a new work what they've learned about finding the moral of a story.

TRY IT **Write About Sequence and Moral**

Students will complete Write About Sequence and Moral in *Summit English Language Arts 3 Activity Book*.

LEARNING COACH CHECK-IN If students have difficulty sequencing events, ask them which event came first, which came next, and so on.

TRY IT

"The Wind and the Sun"

Write About Sequence and Moral

Fill in the boxes with plot events from the story in sequence. Then, state the moral of the story.

At the beginning of the story,
the Wind says it is stronger than the Sun. They have a contest to prove who is stronger and see who can make a man take off his coat.

In the middle of the story,
the Wind blows hard on the man. The man pulls his coat on tighter.

At the end of the story,
the Sun shines down its gentle rays. The man gets hot and takes off his coat. The Sun wins the contest.

The moral of the story is
sometimes gentle ways are stronger than fierce ways.

"THE WIND AND THE SUN" 61

TRY IT **Practice Words from "The Wind and the Sun"**

Students will answer questions to demonstrate their understanding of the vocabulary words from the reading.

WRAP-UP

Question About "The Wind and the Sun"

Students will answer a question to show that they understand how a character's actions affect the plot of a story.

Handwriting

Students should gather their handwriting materials and begin where they left off. Remind students to form letters carefully and correctly.

TIP Set a timer to help students stay focused during handwriting practice.

"The Wind and the Sun" Wrap-Up

Lesson Overview

ACTIVITY	ACTIVITY TITLE	TIME	ONLINE/OFFLINE
GET READY	Introduction to "The Wind and the Sun" Wrap-Up	**1** minute	online
	Spelling List 4 Activity Bank	**10** minutes	offline
	Read and Record	**8** minutes	online
TRY IT	Write About a New Fable LEARNING COACH CHECK-IN	**30** minutes	offline
	Review "The Wind and the Sun"	**15** minutes	online
QUIZ	"The Wind and the Sun"	**30** minutes	online
WRAP-UP	More Language Arts Practice	**18** minutes	online
	Handwriting	**8** minutes	offline

Advance Preparation

Gather students' completed Spelling List 4 Pretest activity page from "The Wind and the Sun." Students will refer to this page during Try It: Spelling List 4 Activity Bank.

MATERIALS

Supplied

- *Summit English Language Arts 3 Activity Book*
  - Spelling List 4 Activity Bank
  - Write About a New Fable
- handwriting workbook

Also Needed

- completed Spelling List 4 Pretest activity page from "The Wind and the Sun"

Lesson Goals

- Practice all spelling words offline.
- Read aloud to practice fluency.
- Write about the sequence of events and characters in a fable.
- Review the moral and characters and their actions in a fable.
- Take a reading quiz.
- Develop letter formation fluency.

GET READY

Introduction to "The Wind and the Sun" Wrap-Up

Students will read the lesson goals.

Spelling List 4 Activity Bank

Students will practice all spelling words from the workshop by completing Spelling List 4 Activity Bank from *Summit English Language Arts 3 Activity Book*. Make sure students have their completed Spelling List 4 Pretest activity page from "The Wind and the Sun" to refer to during this activity.

Remind students to pay special attention to words they spelled incorrectly on the Spelling Pretest.

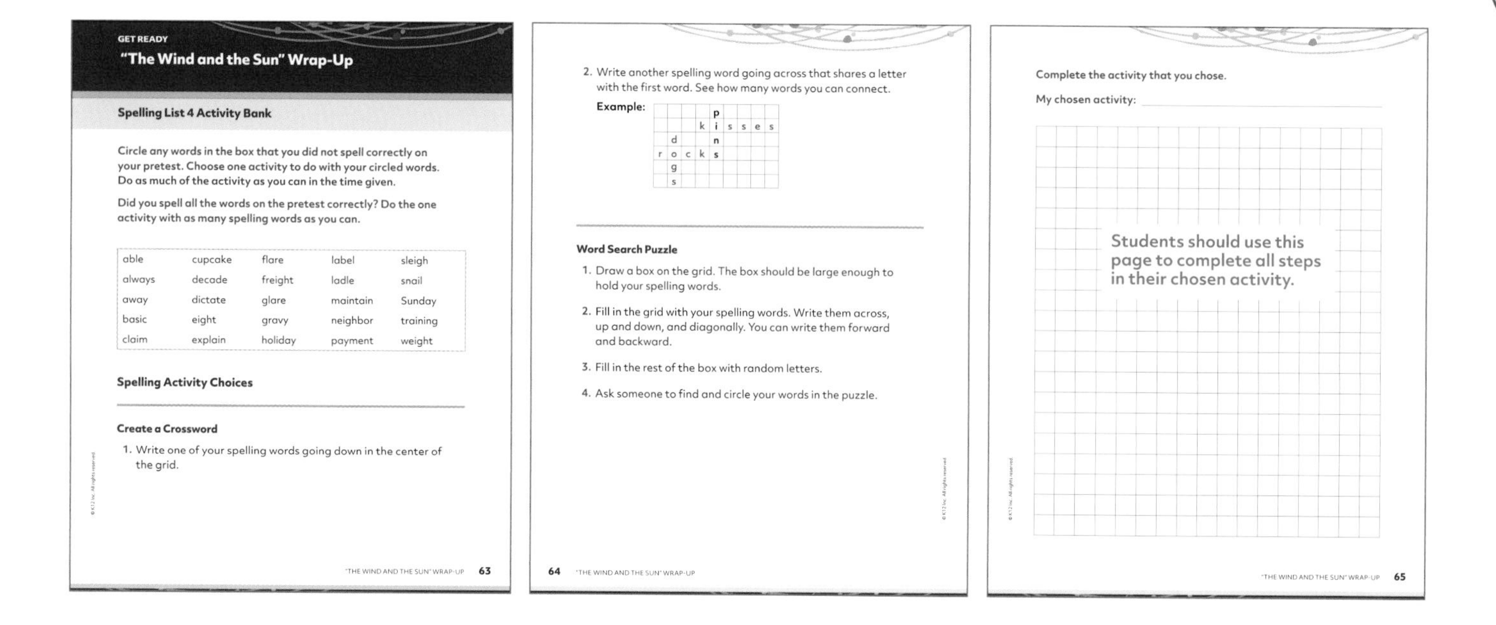
GET READY

"The Wind and the Sun" Wrap-Up

Spelling List 4 Activity Bank

Circle any words in the box that you did not spell correctly on your pretest. Choose one activity to do with your circled words. Do as much of the activity as you can in the time given.

Did you spell all the words on the pretest correctly? Do the one activity with as many spelling words as you can.

able	cupcake	flare	label	sleigh
always	decade	freight	ladle	snail
away	dictate	glare	maintain	Sunday
basic	eight	gravy	neighbor	training
claim	explain	holiday	payment	weight

Spelling Activity Choices

Create a Crossword

1. Write one of your spelling words going down in the center of the grid.

"THE WIND AND THE SUN" WRAP-UP 63

2. Write another spelling word going across that shares a letter with the first word. See how many words you can connect.

Example:

Word Search Puzzle

1. Draw a box on the grid. The box should be large enough to hold your spelling words.
2. Fill in the grid with your spelling words. Write them across, up and down, and diagonally. You can write them forward and backward.
3. Fill in the rest of the box with random letters.
4. Ask someone to find and circle your words in the puzzle.

64 "THE WIND AND THE SUN" WRAP-UP

Complete the activity that you chose.

My chosen activity:

Students should use this page to complete all steps in their chosen activity.

"THE WIND AND THE SUN" WRAP-UP 65

Read and Record

Good readers read quickly, smoothly, and with expression. This is called *fluency*. Students will record themselves reading aloud. They will listen to their recording and think about how quick, smooth, and expressive they sound.

TIP Encourage students to rerecord as needed.

TRY IT

Write About a New Fable

Students will complete Write About a New Fable in *Summit English Language Arts 3 Activity Book*. This activity page requires students to apply what they have learned about sequence of events and moral to a new fable.

LEARNING COACH CHECK-IN Ask students to give a brief retelling of the new fable to confirm that they understand the story before they begin writing.

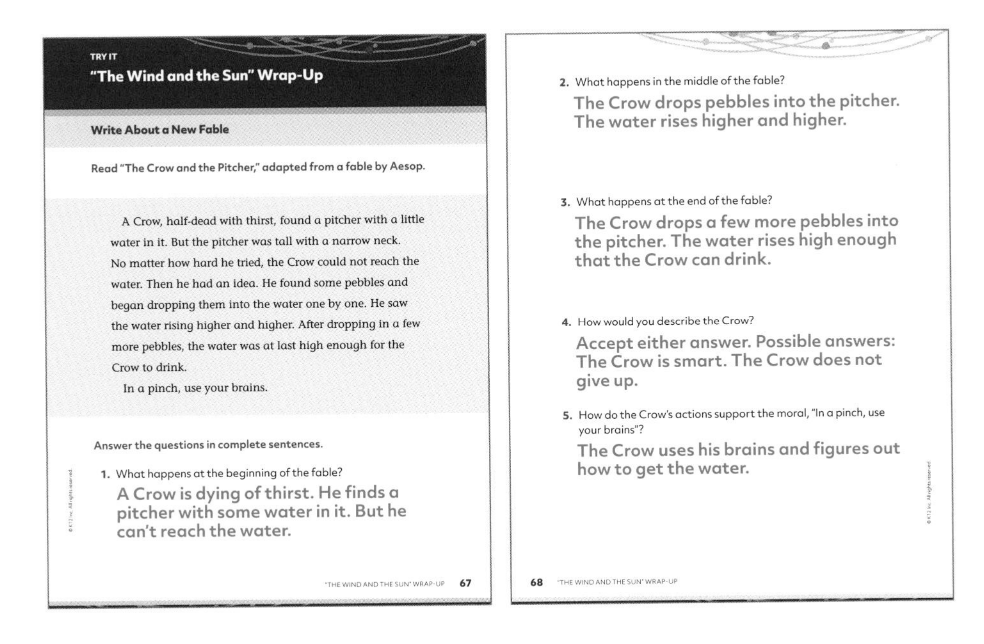

TRY IT

"The Wind and the Sun" Wrap-Up

Write About a New Fable

Read "The Crow and the Pitcher," adapted from a fable by Aesop.

A Crow, half-dead with thirst, found a pitcher with a little water in it. But the pitcher was tall with a narrow neck. No matter how hard he tried, the Crow could not reach the water. Then he had an idea. He found some pebbles and began dropping them into the water one by one. He saw the water rising higher and higher. After dropping in a few more pebbles, the water was at last high enough for the Crow to drink.

In a pinch, use your brains.

Answer the questions in complete sentences.

1. What happens at the beginning of the fable?
   A Crow is dying of thirst. He finds a pitcher with some water in it. But he can't reach the water.

"THE WIND AND THE SUN" WRAP-UP 67

2. What happens in the middle of the fable?
   The Crow drops pebbles into the pitcher. The water rises higher and higher.

3. What happens at the end of the fable?
   The Crow drops a few more pebbles into the pitcher. The water rises high enough that the Crow can drink.

4. How would you describe the Crow?
   Accept either answer. Possible answers: The Crow is smart. The Crow does not give up.

5. How do the Crow's actions support the moral, "In a pinch, use your brains"?
   The Crow uses his brains and figures out how to get the water.

68 "THE WIND AND THE SUN" WRAP-UP

Review "The Wind and the Sun"

Students will answer questions to review what they have learned about identifying the moral of a fable and describing characters and how their actions convey the moral.

QUIZ

"The Wind and the Sun"

Students will complete the "The Wind and the Sun" quiz.

WRAP-UP

More Language Arts Practice

Students will practice skills according to their individual needs.

Handwriting

Students should gather their handwriting materials and begin where they left off. Remind students to form letters carefully and correctly.

TIP Set a timer to help students stay focused during handwriting practice.

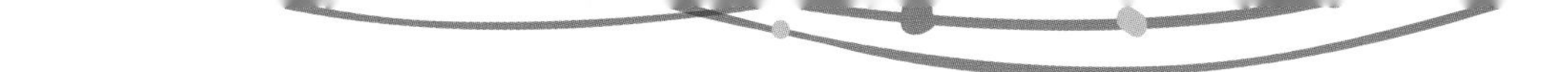

"The Cruel Lion and the Clever Rabbit"

Lesson Overview

ACTIVITY	ACTIVITY TITLE	TIME	ONLINE/OFFLINE
GET READY	Introduction to "The Cruel Lion and the Clever Rabbit"	**1** minute	online
	Spelling List 4 Practice	**10** minutes	online
	Read and Record	**8** minutes	online
	Reading Foundations: Words Within Words	**5** minutes	online
	Before You Read "The Cruel Lion and the Clever Rabbit"	**8** minutes	online
READ	"The Cruel Lion and the Clever Rabbit"	**20** minutes	offline
	Check-In: "The Cruel Lion and the Clever Rabbit"	**5** minutes	online
LEARN AND TRY IT	Reading Between the Lines	**10** minutes	online
	Read Between the Lines	**10** minutes	online
	Apply: Character Traits	**15** minutes	online
	Write About Characters and Evidence LEARNING COACH CHECK-IN	**10** minutes	offline
	Practice Words from "The Cruel Lion and the Clever Rabbit"	**8** minutes	online
WRAP-UP	Question About "The Cruel Lion and the Clever Rabbit"	**2** minutes	online
	Handwriting	**8** minutes	offline

Content Background

In this lesson, students will learn how to support answers to comprehension questions with text-based evidence. Text-based evidence would be a quotation directly from a story that supports, or proves, an inference, conclusion, or answer to a comprehension question. For example, one can infer that in "The Cruel Lion and the Clever Rabbit," the lion is hungry. This inference is supported by the quotation, "She heard Bhaksuraka's stomach rumble before the lion appeared."

MATERIALS

Supplied

- *Summit English Language Arts 3 Expeditions in Reading*
  - "The Cruel Lion and the Clever Rabbit"
- *Summit English Language Arts 3 Activity Book*
  - Write About Characters and Evidence
- handwriting workbook

"The Cruel Lion and the Clever Rabbit" Synopsis

Night after night, the animals of the forest are terrorized by the hungry lion Bhaksuraka as he hunts for his next meal. But clever Rabbit decides that the lion's bullying must stop. The Rabbit forms a plan and tells Bhaksuraka that there is a stronger, mightier lion in the forest. Bhaksuraka demands that Rabbit take him to this lion. Rabbit leads him to a deep well. Upon looking in the well, Bhaksuraka sees the new lion. He jumps into the well to attack the lion and discovers that Rabbit has tricked him. It was only Bhaksuraka's reflection. Trapped in the well, Bhaksuraka is no longer a threat to the forest animals.

Lesson Goals

- Practice all spelling words online.
- Read aloud to practice fluency.
- Read small words within longer words.
- Read "The Cruel Lion and the Clever Rabbit."
- Use evidence from text to support answers to questions.
- Describe characters and support descriptions with evidence from text.
- Practice vocabulary words.
- Develop letter formation fluency.

GET READY

Introduction to "The Cruel Lion and the Clever Rabbit"

Students will get a glimpse of what they will learn about in the lesson. They will also read the lesson goals.

Spelling List 4 Practice

Students will practice all spelling words from the workshop.

OPTIONAL Students may do an activity from Spelling List 4 Activity Bank instead of the online practice activity.

Read and Record

Good readers read quickly, smoothly, and with expression. This is called *fluency*. Students will record themselves reading aloud. They will listen to their recording and think about how quick, smooth, and expressive they sound.

TIP Encourage students to rerecord as needed.

Reading Foundations: Words Within Words

Reading Foundations activities serve to remind students of basic reading skills and reading behaviors mastered in earlier grades. The activities cover topics such as advanced decoding skills and various strategies for improving comprehension.

Before You Read "The Cruel Lion and the Clever Rabbit"

Students will be introduced to some key vocabulary words that they will encounter in the upcoming reading and answer a question to help them activate background knowledge about fables.

READ

"The Cruel Lion and the Clever Rabbit"

Students will read "The Cruel Lion and the Clever Rabbit" in *Expeditions in Reading*.

Check-In: "The Cruel Lion and the Clever Rabbit"

Students will answer several questions to demonstrate their comprehension of "The Cruel Lion and the Clever Rabbit."

LEARN AND TRY IT

LEARN Reading Between the Lines

Students will learn about "reading between the lines," which means figuring out things about a story that are not directly stated in the text. An emphasis will be placed on using text-based evidence to support students' thinking.

SUPPORT For students having difficulty recognizing text evidence to support their thinking, help them practice with a simple fairy tale such as "Goldilocks and the Three Bears." For example, ask them how they can tell that somebody sat in Baby Bear's chair. Use the prompt, *How do you know that?* Then help them locate the text that states that the chair is broken.

TRY IT Read Between the Lines

Students will practice figuring out things that are not directly stated in a story. They will also use text-based evidence to support their thinking.

TRY IT Apply: Character Traits

Students will apply to a new work what they've learned about describing characters.

TRY IT Write About Characters and Evidence

Students will complete Write About Characters and Evidence in *Summit English Language Arts 3 Activity Book*. Students should include a direct quotation from the story "The Cruel Lion and the Clever Rabbit" in their response.

LEARNING COACH CHECK-IN This activity page contains a question that offers students a choice for response, so it's important that you review students' responses. Give students feedback, using the sample answer provided to guide you.

NOTE Have students keep their completed activity page in a safe place so they can refer to it later.

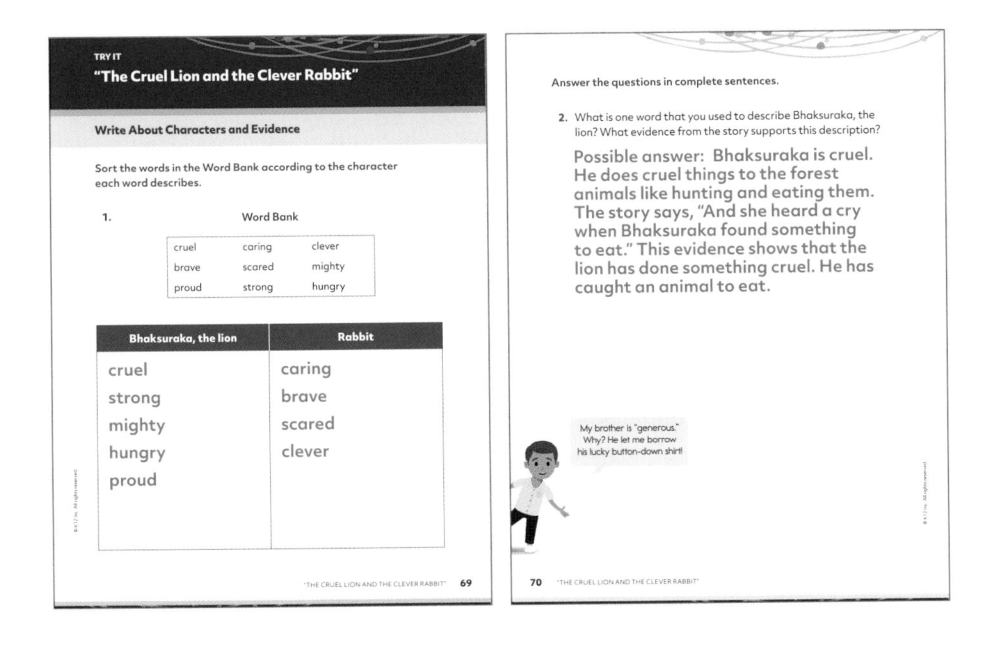

TRY IT
"The Cruel Lion and the Clever Rabbit"

Write About Characters and Evidence

Sort the words in the Word Bank according to the character each word describes.

1. Word Bank

cruel	caring	clever
brave	scared	mighty
proud	strong	hungry

Bhaksuraka, the lion	Rabbit
cruel	caring
strong	brave
mighty	scared
hungry	clever
proud	

"THE CRUEL LION AND THE CLEVER RABBIT" 69

Answer the questions in complete sentences.

2. What is one word that you used to describe Bhaksuraka, the lion? What evidence from the story supports this description?

Possible answer: Bhaksuraka is cruel. He does cruel things to the forest animals like hunting and eating them. The story says, "And she heard a cry when Bhaksuraka found something to eat." This evidence shows that the lion has done something cruel. He has caught an animal to eat.

70 "THE CRUEL LION AND THE CLEVER RABBIT"

TRY IT Practice Words from "The Cruel Lion and the Clever Rabbit"

Students will answer questions to demonstrate their understanding of the vocabulary words from the reading.

WRAP-UP

Question About "The Cruel Lion and the Clever Rabbit"

Students will answer a question to show that they understand the ending of "The Cruel Lion and the Clever Rabbit."

Handwriting

Students should gather their handwriting materials and begin where they left off. Remind students to form letters carefully and correctly.

TIP Set a timer to help students stay focused during handwriting practice.

"The Cruel Lion and the Clever Rabbit" Wrap-Up

Lesson Overview

ACTIVITY	ACTIVITY TITLE	TIME	ONLINE/OFFLINE
GET READY	Introduction to "The Cruel Lion and the Clever Rabbit" Wrap-Up	**1** minute	online
	Spelling List 4 More Practice	**10** minutes	online
	Read and Record	**8** minutes	online
TRY IT	Write More About Characters and Evidence LEARNING COACH CHECK-IN	**20** minutes	offline
	Review "The Cruel Lion and the Clever Rabbit"	**20** minutes	online
QUIZ	"The Cruel Lion and the Clever Rabbit"	**30** minutes	online
WRAP-UP	More Language Arts Practice	**23** minutes	online
	Handwriting	**8** minutes	offline

Advance Preparation

Gather students' completed Write About Characters and Evidence activity page from "The Cruel Lion and the Clever Rabbit." Students will refer to this page during Try It: Write More About Characters and Evidence.

MATERIALS

Supplied

- *Summit English Language Arts 3 Activity Book*
  - Write More About Characters and Evidence
- handwriting workbook

Also Needed

- completed Write About Characters and Evidence activity page from "The Cruel Lion and the Clever Rabbit"

Lesson Goals

- Practice all spelling words online.
- Read aloud to practices fluency.
- Describe a character and support descriptions with evidence from text.
- Review what you learned.
- Take a reading quiz.
- Develop letter formation fluency.

GET READY

Introduction to "The Cruel Lion and the Clever Rabbit" Wrap-Up

Students will read the lesson goals.

Spelling List 4 More Practice

Students will practice all spelling words from the workshop.

OPTIONAL Students may do an activity from Spelling List 4 Activity Bank instead of the online practice activity.

Read and Record

Good readers read quickly, smoothly, and with expression. This is called *fluency*. Students will record themselves reading aloud. They will listen to their recording and think about how quick, smooth, and expressive they sound.

TIP Encourage students to rerecord as needed.

TRY IT

Write More About Characters and Evidence

Students will complete Write More About Characters and Evidence in *Summit English Language Arts 3 Activity Book*. Students should include a direct quotation from the story "The Cruel Lion and the Clever Rabbit" in each of their responses. Make sure students have their completed Write About Characters and Evidence activity page from "The Cruel Lion and the Clever Rabbit" to refer to during this activity.

LEARNING COACH CHECK-IN This activity page contains questions that offer students choices for response, so it's important that you review students' responses. Give students feedback, using the sample answers provided to guide you.

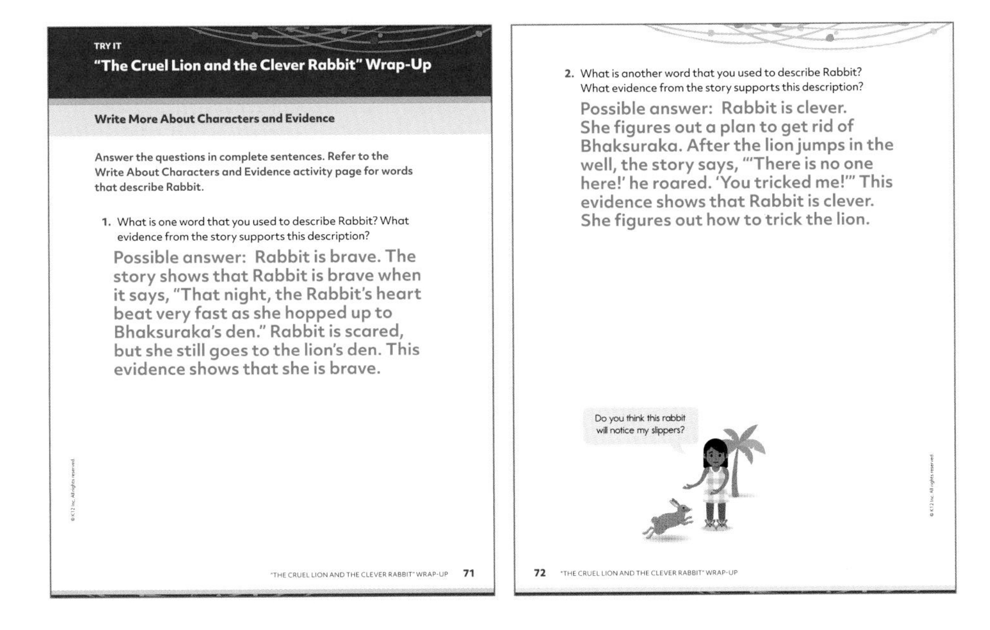

TRY IT

"The Cruel Lion and the Clever Rabbit" Wrap-Up

Write More About Characters and Evidence

Answer the questions in complete sentences. Refer to the Write About Characters and Evidence activity page for words that describe Rabbit.

1. What is one word that you used to describe Rabbit? What evidence from the story supports this description?

Possible answer: Rabbit is brave. The story shows that Rabbit is brave when it says, "That night, the Rabbit's heart beat very fast as she hopped up to Bhaksuraka's den." Rabbit is scared, but she still goes to the lion's den. This evidence shows that she is brave.

"THE CRUEL LION AND THE CLEVER RABBIT" WRAP-UP 71

2. What is another word that you used to describe Rabbit? What evidence from the story supports this description?

Possible answer: Rabbit is clever. She figures out a plan to get rid of Bhaksuraka. After the lion jumps in the well, the story says, "'There is no one here!' he roared. 'You tricked me!'" This evidence shows that Rabbit is clever. She figures out how to trick the lion.

72 "THE CRUEL LION AND THE CLEVER RABBIT" WRAP-UP

Review "The Cruel Lion and the Clever Rabbit"

Students will answer questions to review what they have learned about "The Cruel Lion and the Clever Rabbit."

QUIZ

"The Cruel Lion and the Clever Rabbit"

Students will complete "The Cruel Lion and the Clever Rabbit" quiz.

WRAP-UP

More Language Arts Practice

Students will practice skills according to their individual needs.

Handwriting

Students should gather their handwriting materials and begin where they left off. Remind students to form letters carefully and correctly.

TIP Set a timer to help students stay focused during handwriting practice.

"Why the Larks Flew Away"

Lesson Overview

ACTIVITY	ACTIVITY TITLE	TIME	ONLINE/OFFLINE
GET READY	Introduction to "Why the Larks Flew Away"	**1** minute	
	Spelling List 4 Review Game	**10** minutes	
	Read and Record	**8** minutes	
	Reading Foundations: Decoding and Multisyllabic Words	**5** minutes	
	Before You Read "Why the Larks Flew Away"	**8** minutes	
READ	"Why the Larks Flew Away"	**25** minutes	
	Check-In: "Why the Larks Flew Away"	**5** minutes	
LEARN AND TRY IT	Summarizing and Sequencing	**10** minutes	
	Summarize and Sequence	**10** minutes	
	Apply: Characters and Their Actions	**10** minutes	
	Compare Two Stories LEARNING COACH CHECK-IN	**10** minutes	
	Practice Words from "Why the Larks Flew Away"	**8** minutes	
WRAP-UP	Question About "Why the Larks Flew Away"	**2** minutes	
	Handwriting	**8** minutes	

Content Background

In this lesson, students will learn that summarizing a story's events in sequence is a good way to check that they understand what they have read. A *summary* is a short retelling of a text. A retelling should include a story's most important details in sequence, which means students should retell the events and details in the order in which they appear in the story.

MATERIALS

Supplied

- *Summit English Language Arts 3 Expeditions in Reading*
  - "Why the Larks Flew Away"
- *Summit English Language Arts 3 Activity Book*
  - Compare Two Stories
- handwriting workbook

"Why the Larks Flew Away" Synopsis

A mother lark and her babies live in a wheat field, but they must leave as soon as the farmer comes to cut the grain. For two mornings, the mother lark says it isn't time to leave because the farmer has asked others to help cut the wheat. When the baby larks finally hear the farmer say he and his son must do the work themselves, the mother lark says it is truly time to leave.

KEYWORDS

sequence – the order in which things happen

summarize – to tell in order the most important ideas or events of a text

summary – a short retelling that includes only the most important ideas or events of a text

Lesson Goals

- Practice all spelling words online.
- Read aloud to practice fluency.
- Read "Why the Larks Flew Away."
- Summarize a story by retelling important details.
- Order a story's events in sequence.
- Compare and contrast details from a fable and another story.
- Practice vocabulary words.
- Develop letter formation fluency.

GET READY

Introduction to "Why the Larks Flew Away"

Students will get a glimpse of what they will learn about in the lesson. They will also read the lesson goals and keywords. Have students select each keyword and preview its definition.

Spelling List 4 Review Game

Students will practice all spelling words from the workshop.

Read and Record

Good readers read quickly, smoothly, and with expression. This is called *fluency*. Students will record themselves reading aloud. They will listen to their recording and think about how quick, smooth, and expressive they sound.

TIP Encourage students to rerecord as needed.

Reading Foundations: Decoding and Multisyllabic Words

Reading Foundations activities serve to remind students of basic reading skills and reading behaviors mastered in earlier grades. The activities cover topics such as advanced decoding skills and various strategies for improving comprehension.

Before You Read "Why the Larks Flew Away"

Students will be introduced to some key vocabulary words that they will encounter in the upcoming reading and answer questions to help them activate their background knowledge for their reading.

READ

"Why the Larks Flew Away"

Students will read "Why the Larks Flew Away" in *Expeditions in Reading*.

Check-In: "Why the Larks Flew Away"

Students will answer several questions to demonstrate their comprehension of "Why the Larks Flew Away."

LEARN AND TRY IT

LEARN Summarizing and Sequencing

Students will learn that they can check their understanding of a story by giving a summary, or a short retelling, of the story. They will also learn that a summary should include a story's most important details in sequence.

TRY IT Summarize and Sequence

Students will practice determining details that should be included in a summary and creating summaries by placing details in sequence.

TRY IT Apply: Characters and Their Actions

Students will apply to a new work what they've learned about how characters' actions affect plot events.

TRY IT Compare Two Stories

Students will complete Compare Two Stories in *Summit English Language Arts 3 Activity Book*. Students will record information in a chart to compare and contrast details in "Why the Larks Flew Away" and "Cinderella."

LEARNING COACH CHECK-IN Student will refer to this activity page for a later writing activity, so it's important that you review students' responses. Give students feedback, using the sample answers provided to guide you.

TRY IT

"Why the Larks Flew Away"

Compare Two Stories

Read the beginning of "Cinderella."

Once upon a time, there was a lovely young woman named Cinderella. She lived in a small kingdom with her wicked stepmother and two stepsisters. They treated her like a servant. Even though they made her do all the work, she was always kind. One day, they were all invited to a ball in honor of the prince. But Cinderella's stepmother would not let her go. Instead, she was forced to help her stepsisters prepare for the ball. When they left for the palace, Cinderella stayed behind.

As the door closed, Cinderella began to cry. Suddenly, a fairy godmother appeared. She said, "Do not weep. I will help you go to the ball." This made her cry harder, saying, "I have nothing to wear but rags." At that, the fairy godmother waved her magic wand. Cinderella's rags turned into a beautiful gown. Then the fairy godmother touched Cinderella's feet with her wand. In a blink, tiny glass slippers appeared on her feet.

Complete the chart to compare "Cinderella" with "Why the Larks Flew Away." You do not need to use complete sentences.

Story Element	"Cinderella"	"Why the Larks Flew Away"
Characters	Cinderella Stepmother Stepsisters Fairy Godmother	Mother Lark Baby Larks Farmer Son
Setting	A small kingdom	A wheat field
Problem	Cinderella is not allowed to go to the ball.	The larks do not know when the farmer will cut the wheat, so they don't know when they must leave their nest.

Story Element	"Cinderella"	"Why the Larks Flew Away"
Solution	A fairy godmother helps Cinderella go to the ball.	The baby larks listen to the farmer to find out when the wheat will be cut.
Is the story a fable or fairy tale? How do you know?	fairy tale Possible answers: The story starts with "once upon a time"; the fairy godmother uses magic.	fable Possible answers: The animals act like people; the story has a moral.

TRY IT Practice Words from "Why the Larks Flew Away"

Students will answer questions to demonstrate their understanding of the vocabulary words from the reading.

WRAP-UP

Question About "Why the Larks Flew Away"

Students will answer a question to show that they understand the sequence of the story's events.

Handwriting

Students should gather their handwriting materials and begin where they left off. Remind students to form letters carefully and correctly.

TIP Set a timer to help students stay focused during handwriting practice.

"Why the Larks Flew Away" Wrap-Up

Lesson Overview

ACTIVITY	ACTIVITY TITLE	TIME	ONLINE/OFFLINE
GET READY	Introduction to "Why the Larks Flew Away" Wrap-Up	1 minute	online
	Read and Record	8 minutes	online
TRY IT	Write About Two Stories LEARNING COACH CHECK-IN	28 minutes	offline
	Review "Why the Larks Flew Away"	20 minutes	online
QUIZ	"Why the Larks Flew Away"	30 minutes	online
	Spelling List 4	10 minutes	online
WRAP-UP	More Language Arts Practice	15 minutes	online
	Handwriting	8 minutes	offline

Advance Preparation

Gather students' completed Compare Two Stories activity page from "Why the Larks Flew Away." Students will refer to this page during Try It: Write About Two Stories.

MATERIALS

Supplied

- *Summit English Language Arts 3 Activity Book*
  - Write About Two Stories
- handwriting workbook

Also Needed

- completed Compare Two Stories activity page from "Why the Larks Flew Away"

Lesson Goals

- Read aloud to practice fluency.
- Describe what's alike and what's different about a fable and another story.
- Review what you learned.
- Take a spelling quiz.
- Take a reading quiz.
- Develop letter formation fluency.

GET READY

Introduction to "Why the Larks Flew Away" Wrap-Up

Students will read the lesson goals.

Read and Record

Good readers read quickly, smoothly, and with expression. This is called *fluency*. Students will record themselves reading aloud. They will listen to their recording and think about how quick, smooth, and expressive they sound.

TIP Encourage students to rerecord as needed.

TRY IT

Write About Two Stories

Students will complete Write About Two Stories in *Summit English Language Arts 3 Activity Book*. Make sure students have their completed Compare Two Stories activity page from "Why the Larks Flew Away" to refer to during this activity.

LEARNING COACH CHECK-IN This activity page involves using information gathered in a chart and writing it in paragraph form, so it's important that you review students' responses. Give students feedback, using the sample answers provided to guide you.

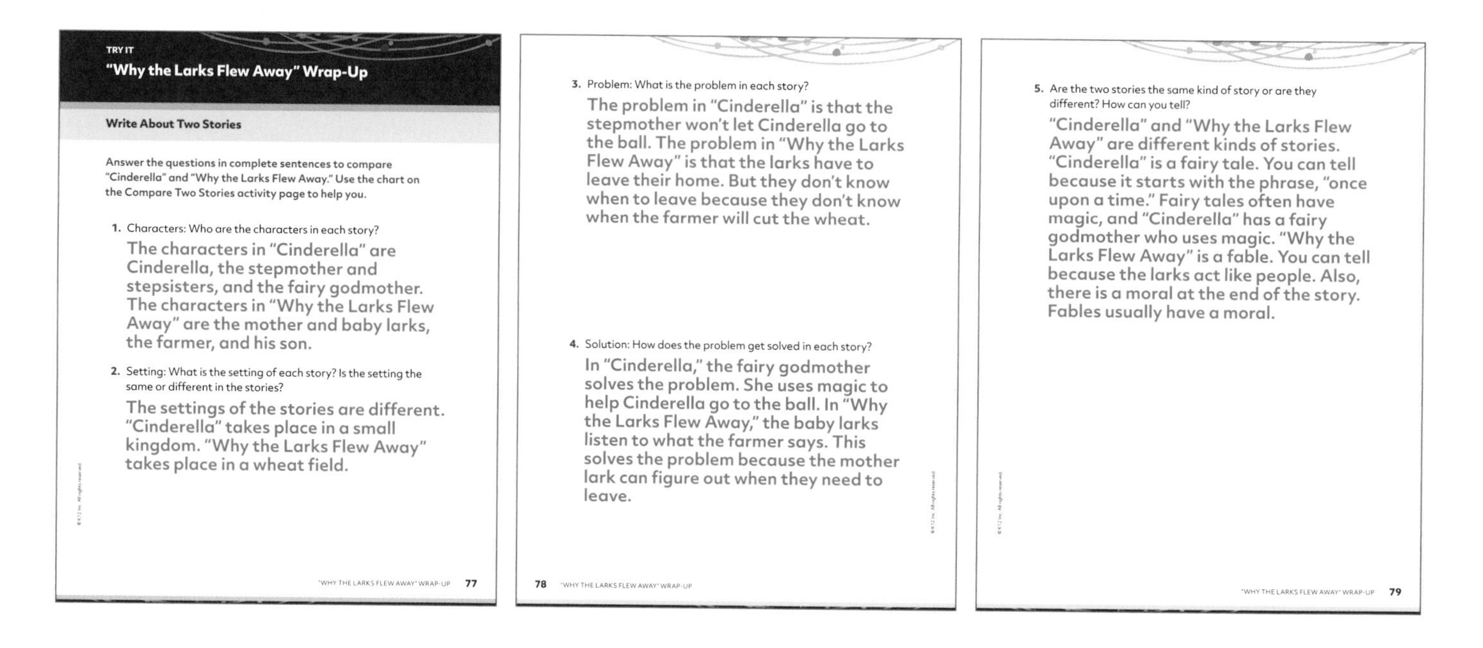

TRY IT

"Why the Larks Flew Away" Wrap-Up

Write About Two Stories

Answer the questions in complete sentences to compare "Cinderella" and "Why the Larks Flew Away." Use the chart on the Compare Two Stories activity page to help you.

1. Characters: Who are the characters in each story?
   The characters in "Cinderella" are Cinderella, the stepmother and stepsisters, and the fairy godmother. The characters in "Why the Larks Flew Away" are the mother and baby larks, the farmer, and his son.
2. Setting: What is the setting of each story? Is the setting the same or different in the stories?
   The settings of the stories are different. "Cinderella" takes place in a small kingdom. "Why the Larks Flew Away" takes place in a wheat field.

"WHY THE LARKS FLEW AWAY" WRAP-UP 77

3. Problem: What is the problem in each story?
   The problem in "Cinderella" is that the stepmother won't let Cinderella go to the ball. The problem in "Why the Larks Flew Away" is that the larks have to leave their home. But they don't know when to leave because they don't know when the farmer will cut the wheat.
4. Solution: How does the problem get solved in each story?
   In "Cinderella," the fairy godmother solves the problem. She uses magic to help Cinderella go to the ball. In "Why the Larks Flew Away," the baby larks listen to what the farmer says. This solves the problem because the mother lark can figure out when they need to leave.

78 "WHY THE LARKS FLEW AWAY" WRAP-UP

5. Are the two stories the same kind of story or are they different? How can you tell?
   "Cinderella" and "Why the Larks Flew Away" are different kinds of stories. "Cinderella" is a fairy tale. You can tell because it starts with the phrase, "once upon a time." Fairy tales often have magic, and "Cinderella" has a fairy godmother who uses magic. "Why the Larks Flew Away" is a fable. You can tell because the larks act like people. Also, there is a moral at the end of the story. Fables usually have a moral.

"WHY THE LARKS FLEW AWAY" WRAP-UP 79

Review "Why the Larks Flew Away"

Students will answer questions to review what they have learned about determining important details and summarizing a story in sequence.

QUIZ

"Why the Larks Flew Away"

Students will complete the "Why the Larks Flew Away" quiz.

Spelling List 4

Students will complete the Spelling List 4 quiz.

WRAP-UP

More Language Arts Practice

Students will practice skills according to their individual needs.

Handwriting

Students should gather their handwriting materials and begin where they left off. Remind students to form letters carefully and correctly.

TIP Set a timer to help students stay focused during handwriting practice.

Narrative Writing: Prewriting (A)

Lesson Overview

ACTIVITY	ACTIVITY TITLE	TIME	ONLINE/OFFLINE
GET READY	Introduction to Narrative Writing: Prewriting (A)	**1** minute	online
	Spelling List 5 Pretest LEARNING COACH CHECK-IN	**10** minutes	online and offline
	Look Back at Simple and Compound Sentences	**5** minutes	online
LEARN AND TRY IT	Complex Sentences	**10** minutes	online
	Write Complex Sentences	**10** minutes	online
	Explore a Model Short Story	**10** minutes	online
	Respond to a Short Story	**10** minutes	online
	Brainstorm for a Short Story	**10** minutes	online
	Brainstorm for Your Short Story LEARNING COACH CHECK-IN	**20** minutes	offline
WRAP-UP	Questions About Complex Sentences and Brainstorming	**4** minutes	online
	Handwriting	**8** minutes	offline
	Go Read!	**22** minutes	online or offline

Content Background

Students will begin working on a **short story**, which is a short, fictional narrative. They will complete this assignment over the course of several lessons by following the writing process. Students will begin by prewriting.

Writing Process

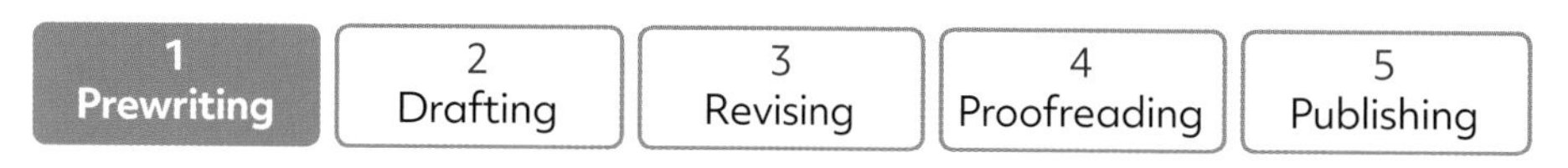

During **prewriting**, writers choose a topic and create a plan for their writing assignment. In this lesson, students will complete the first part of prewriting, choosing a topic. To do that, they'll **brainstorm** by listing and evaluating several different topics.

MATERIALS

Supplied

- *Summit English Language Arts 3 Activity Book*
  - Spelling List 5 Pretest
  - Model Short Story
  - Brainstorm for Your Short Story
- handwriting workbook

Also Needed

- folder for organizing short story assignment pages
- reading material for Go Read!

Grammar, Usage, and Mechanics A **complex sentence** is made up of an independent part and a dependent part. The independent part of a complex sentence expresses a complete idea and can stand alone.

Complex sentence: After the storm ended, the streets were flooded.

Independent part: the streets were flooded

Dependent part: After the storm ended

Advance Preparation

Gather a folder that students can use to keep all notes and activity pages related to their short story.

During the Go Read! activity, students will have the option of using the digital library. Allow extra time for students to make their reading selection, or have students make a selection before beginning the lesson.

KEYWORDS

brainstorming – before writing, a way for the writer to come up with ideas

complex sentence – a sentence that has one independent part and at least one dependent part

narrative – a kind of writing that tells a story

prewriting – the stage or step of writing in which a writer chooses a topic, gathers ideas, and plans what to write

Lesson Goals

- Take a spelling pretest.
- Write complex sentences.
- Read a model short story, and start planning your own.
- Develop letter formation fluency.
- Read independently to develop fluency.

GET READY

Introduction to Narrative Writing: Prewriting (A)

Students will get a glimpse of what they will learn about in the lesson. They will also read the lesson goals and keywords. Have students select each keyword and preview its definition.

Spelling List 5 Pretest

Students will take a spelling pretest and learn a new spelling pattern.

LEARNING COACH CHECK-IN Have students turn to Spelling List 5 Pretest in *Summit English Language Arts 3 Activity Book* and open the online Spelling Pretest activity. Online, students will listen to the spelling word, type the word in the space indicated, and then check their answer. In the activity book, students will write the correct spelling of the word in the tables provided and indicate with a ✓ or an ✗ if they spelled the word correctly or incorrectly online. Students will repeat this process with the remaining words.

As needed, help students with the interaction between the online activity and the activity book page until they become comfortable with what they need to do. As students practice their spelling words throughout the workshop, they should pay special attention to words they spelled incorrectly on the pretest.

This is the complete list of words students will be tested on.

Words with Long *i* Sound		
assign	island	shy
blind	July	sigh
child	lie	supply
entire	lightning	tie
Friday	might	while
inside	quite	

NOTE Have students keep their completed activity page in a safe place so they can refer to it later.

GET READY

Narrative Writing: Prewriting (A)

Spelling List 5 Pretest

1. Open the Spelling Pretest activity online. Listen to the first spelling word. Type the word. Check your answer.
2. Write the correct spelling of the word in the Word column of the Spelling Pretest table.

	Word	✓	✗
1	blindfold		

3. Put a check mark in the ✓ column if you spelled the word correctly online.

	Word	✓	✗
1	blindfold	✓	

Put an X in the ✗ column if you spelled the word incorrectly online.

	Word	✓	✗
1	blindfold		X

4. Repeat Steps 1–3 for the remaining words in the Spelling Pretest.

NARRATIVE WRITING: PREWRITING (A) 81

Narrative Writing: Prewriting (A)

Spelling List 5 Pretest

Write each spelling word in the Word column, making sure to spell it correctly.

	Word	✓	✗
1	assign		
2	blind		
3	child		
4	entire		
5	Friday		
6	inside		
7	island		
8	July		
9	lie		

	Word	✓	✗
10	lightning		
11	might		
12	quite		
13	shy		
14	sigh		
15	supply		
16	tie		
17	while		

Students should write the correct spelling of each word from the pretest and use the ✓ and X columns to indicate whether they spelled each word correctly or incorrectly online.

82 NARRATIVE WRITING: PREWRITING (A)

Look Back at Simple and Compound Sentences

Students will practice the prerequisite skill of writing simple and compound sentences.

LEARN AND TRY IT

LEARN Complex Sentences

Students will learn that a complex sentence is made up of an independent part and a dependent part. They will learn how to identify a complex sentence.

SUPPORT To understand what a complex sentence is, students must understand the words *independent* and *dependent*. Discuss examples of ways students themselves are independent and dependent.

TRY IT Write Complex Sentences

Students will practice identifying and completing complex sentences. They will also write complex sentences of their own by responding to prompts and using mentor sentences.

LEARN Explore a Model Short Story

By reading and exploring a model short story, students will learn what a short story is and how it is organized.

TIP The model short story that students read in the online activity is the same story on the Model Short Story activity page. Students may wish to reference and make notes on this page as they complete the online activity.

TRY IT Respond to a Short Story

Students will answer questions about the characters, setting, and plot of a short story.

LEARN Brainstorm for a Short Story

Students will learn about the writing process. Then they will learn how to choose a topic as they prepare to write their own short story.

TRY IT Brainstorm for Your Short Story

Students will complete Brainstorm for Your Short Story in *Summit English Language Arts 3 Activity Book*. They should have the Model Short Story activity page to refer to as they work.

LEARNING COACH CHECK-IN This activity page contains open-ended questions, so it's important that you review students' responses. Give students feedback about the characters, setting, and important events they have brainstormed for their short story.

NOTE Have students add the Model Short Story and their completed Brainstorm for Your Short Story activity page to the folder they are using to store their short story assignment pages.

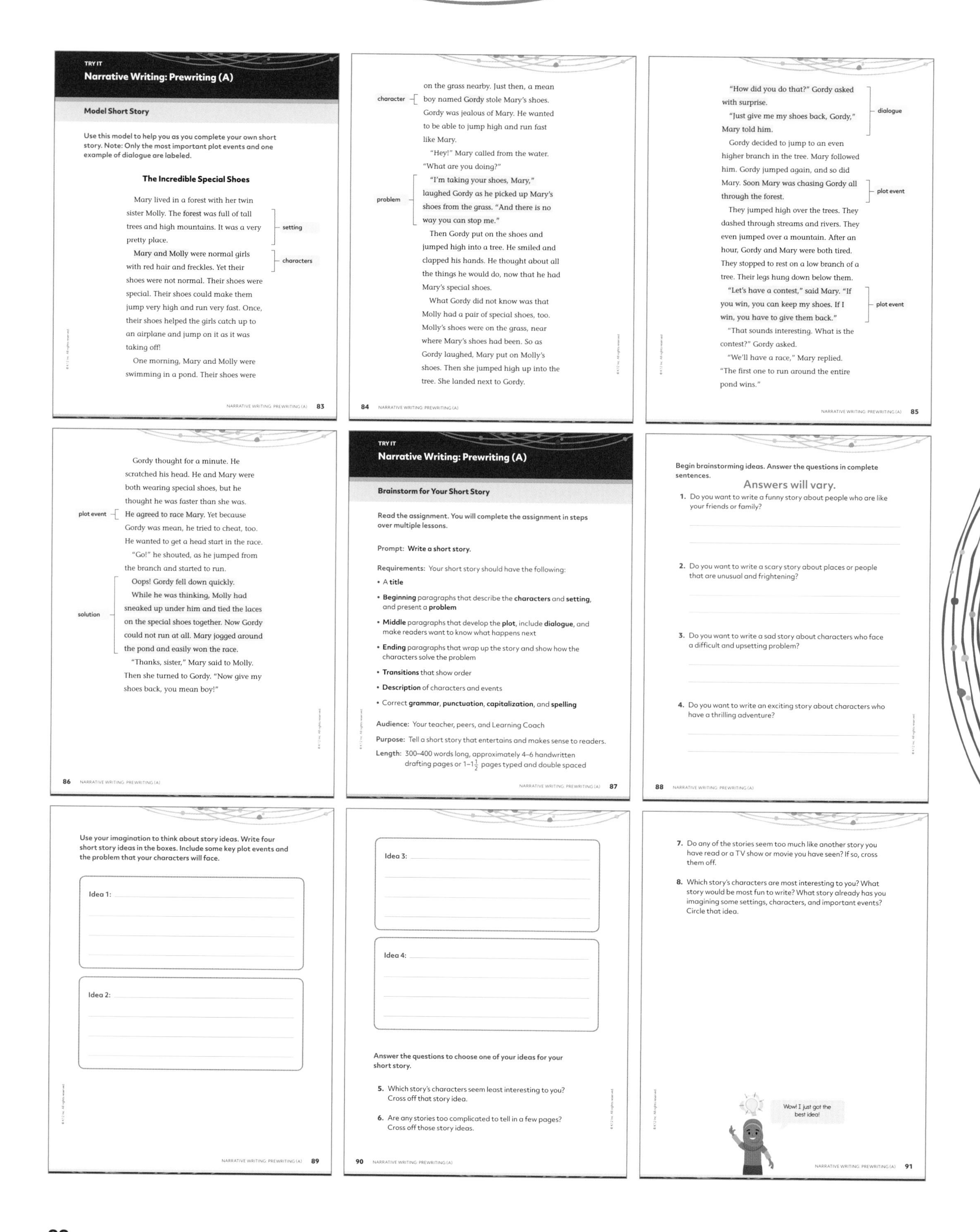

TRY IT

Narrative Writing: Prewriting (A)

Model Short Story

Use this model to help you as you complete your own short story. Note: Only the most important plot events and one example of dialogue are labeled.

The Incredible Special Shoes

Mary lived in a forest with her twin sister Molly. The forest was full of tall trees and high mountains. It was a very pretty place. *(setting)*

Mary and Molly were normal girls with red hair and freckles. *(characters)* Yet their shoes were not normal. Their shoes were special. Their shoes could make them jump very high and run very fast. Once, their shoes helped the girls catch up to an airplane and jump on it as it was taking off!

One morning, Mary and Molly were swimming in a pond. Their shoes were

NARRATIVE WRITING: PREWRITING (A) 83

on the grass nearby. Just then, a mean boy named Gordy stole Mary's shoes. *(character)* Gordy was jealous of Mary. He wanted to be able to jump high and run fast like Mary.

"Hey!" Mary called from the water. "What are you doing?"

"I'm taking your shoes, Mary," laughed Gordy as he picked up Mary's shoes from the grass. "And there is no way you can stop me." *(problem)*

Then Gordy put on the shoes and jumped high into a tree. He smiled and clapped his hands. He thought about all the things he would do, now that he had Mary's special shoes.

What Gordy did not know was that Molly had a pair of special shoes, too. Molly's shoes were on the grass, near where Mary's shoes had been. So as Gordy laughed, Mary put on Molly's shoes. Then she jumped high up into the tree. She landed next to Gordy.

84 NARRATIVE WRITING: PREWRITING (A)

"How did you do that?" Gordy asked with surprise.

"Just give me my shoes back, Gordy," Mary told him. *(dialogue)*

Gordy decided to jump to an even higher branch in the tree. Mary followed him. Gordy jumped again, and so did Mary. Soon Mary was chasing Gordy all through the forest. *(plot event)*

They jumped high over the trees. They dashed through streams and rivers. They even jumped over a mountain. After an hour, Gordy and Mary were both tired. They stopped to rest on a low branch of a tree. Their legs hung down below them.

"Let's have a contest," said Mary. "If you win, you can keep my shoes. If I win, you have to give them back." *(plot event)*

"That sounds interesting. What is the contest?" Gordy asked.

"We'll have a race," Mary replied. "The first one to run around the entire pond wins."

NARRATIVE WRITING: PREWRITING (A) 85

Gordy thought for a minute. He scratched his head. He and Mary were both wearing special shoes, but he thought he was faster than she was. He agreed to race Mary. *(plot event)* Yet because Gordy was mean, he tried to cheat, too. He wanted to get a head start in the race.

"Go!" he shouted, as he jumped from the branch and started to run.

Oops! Gordy fell down quickly. While he was thinking, Molly had sneaked up under him and tied the laces on the special shoes together. Now Gordy could not run at all. Mary jogged around the pond and easily won the race. *(solution)*

"Thanks, sister," Mary said to Molly. Then she turned to Gordy. "Now give my shoes back, you mean boy!"

86 NARRATIVE WRITING: PREWRITING (A)

TRY IT

Narrative Writing: Prewriting (A)

Brainstorm for Your Short Story

Read the assignment. You will complete the assignment in steps over multiple lessons.

Prompt: **Write a short story.**

Requirements: Your short story should have the following:

- A **title**
- **Beginning** paragraphs that describe the **characters** and **setting**, and present a **problem**
- **Middle** paragraphs that develop the **plot**, include **dialogue**, and make readers want to know what happens next
- **Ending** paragraphs that wrap up the story and show how the characters solve the problem
- **Transitions** that show order
- **Description** of characters and events
- Correct **grammar**, **punctuation**, **capitalization**, and **spelling**

Audience: Your teacher, peers, and Learning Coach

Purpose: Tell a short story that entertains and makes sense to readers.

Length: 300–400 words long, approximately 4–6 handwritten drafting pages or 1–1½ pages typed and double spaced

NARRATIVE WRITING: PREWRITING (A) 87

Begin brainstorming ideas. Answer the questions in complete sentences.

Answers will vary.

1. Do you want to write a funny story about people who are like your friends or family?
2. Do you want to write a scary story about places or people that are unusual and frightening?
3. Do you want to write a sad story about characters who face a difficult and upsetting problem?
4. Do you want to write an exciting story about characters who have a thrilling adventure?

88 NARRATIVE WRITING: PREWRITING (A)

Use your imagination to think about story ideas. Write four short story ideas in the boxes. Include some key plot events and the problem that your characters will face.

Idea 1:

Idea 2:

NARRATIVE WRITING: PREWRITING (A) 89

Idea 3:

Idea 4:

Answer the questions to choose one of your ideas for your short story.

5. Which story's characters seem least interesting to you? Cross off that story idea.
6. Are any stories too complicated to tell in a few pages? Cross off those story ideas.

90 NARRATIVE WRITING: PREWRITING (A)

7. Do any of the stories seem too much like another story you have read or a TV show or movie you have seen? If so, cross them off.
8. Which story's characters are most interesting to you? What story would be most fun to write? What story already has you imagining some settings, characters, and important events? Circle that idea.

NARRATIVE WRITING: PREWRITING (A) 91

WRAP-UP

Questions About Complex Sentences and Brainstorming

Students will answer questions to show that they understand how to form complex sentences and brainstorm for a short story.

Handwriting

Students should gather their handwriting materials and begin where they left off. Remind students to form letters carefully and correctly.

TIP Set a timer to help students stay focused during handwriting practice.

Go Read!

Students will read for pleasure. They should choose a book or a magazine that interests them, or they may choose a selection from the digital library, linked in the online lesson.

- Have students read aloud a few paragraphs of their selection.
- Then have students read silently for the rest of the time.

SUPPORT Students should make no more than five errors in decoding when they read aloud a few paragraphs of their Go Read! selection. If students struggle or make more than five errors, they need to select a different (and easier) text for the Go Read! activity.

TIP Have students select something to read ahead of time to help them stay focused.

Narrative Writing: Prewriting (B)

Lesson Overview

ACTIVITY	ACTIVITY TITLE	TIME	ONLINE/OFFLINE
GET READY	Introduction to Narrative Writing: Prewriting (B)	**1** minute	
	Spelling List 5 Activity Bank	**10** minutes	
LEARN AND **TRY IT**	Subordinating Conjunctions	**10** minutes	
	Use Subordinating Conjunctions	**10** minutes	
	Plan a Short Story	**15** minutes	
	Plan Your Short Story **LEARNING COACH CHECK-IN**	**40** minutes	
WRAP-UP	Questions About Subordinating Conjunctions and Organization	**4** minutes	
	Handwriting	**8** minutes	
	Go Read!	**22** minutes	or

Content Background

Students will continue working on their **short story**. They will complete this assignment over the course of several lessons by following the writing process. In this lesson, students will complete the prewriting step.

Writing Process

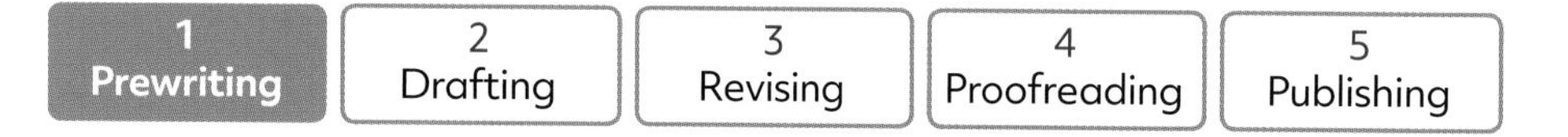

In this part of **prewriting**, students will plan key elements of their short story. They will determine what details readers need to know about the setting, characters, and plot. Then they will use a graphic organizer to organize the beginning, middle, and end of their story.

Grammar, Usage, and Mechanics A complex sentence is made up of an independent part and a dependent part. The dependent part of a complex sentence begins with a **subordinating conjunction**. Examples of subordinating conjunctions include *after*, *because*, *if*, *since*, *though*, *unless*, and *when*.

MATERIALS

Supplied

- *Summit English Language Arts 3 Activity Book*
  - Spelling List 5 Activity Bank
  - Plan Your Short Story
- Short Story Instructions (printout)
- handwriting workbook

Also Needed

- completed Spelling List 5 Pretest activity page from Narrative Writing: Prewriting (A)
- folder in which students are storing short story assignment pages
- reading material for Go Read!

In the following example, the subordinating conjunction *because* begins the dependent part of the complex sentence.

Complex sentence: I covered my nose **because** I didn't want to smell the trash.

Advance Preparation

Gather students' completed Spelling List 5 Pretest activity page from Narrative Writing: Prewriting (A). Students will refer to this page during Get Ready: Spelling List 5 Activity Bank.

Gather the folder that students are using to store the activity pages related to their short story. The folder should contain the following:

- Model Short Story activity page from Narrative Writing: Prewriting (A)
- Students' completed Brainstorm for Your Short Story activity page from Narrative Writing: Prewriting (A)

During the Go Read! activity, students will have the option of using the digital library. Allow extra time for students to make their reading selection, or have students make a selection before beginning the lesson.

KEYWORDS

character – a person or animal in a story

complex sentence – a sentence that has one independent part and at least one dependent part

graphic organizer – a visual tool used to show how ideas connect with each other; types of graphic organizers include webs, diagrams, and charts

narrative – a kind of writing that tells a story

plot – what happens in a story; the sequence of events

prewriting – the stage or step of writing in which a writer chooses a topic, gathers ideas, and plans what to write

setting – when and where a story takes place

subordinating conjunction – a word that is used to introduce a dependent clause

Lesson Goals

- Practice all spelling words offline.
- Identify and use subordinating conjunctions.
- Plan your short story.
- Develop letter formation fluency.
- Read independently to develop fluency.

GET READY

Introduction to Narrative Writing: Prewriting (B)

Students will get a glimpse of what they will learn about in the lesson. They will also read the lesson goals and keywords. Have students select each keyword and preview its definition.

Spelling List 5 Activity Bank

Students will practice all spelling words from the workshop by completing Spelling List 5 Activity Bank from *Summit English Language Arts 3 Activity Book*. Make sure students have their completed Spelling List 5 Pretest activity page from Narrative Writing: Prewriting (A) to refer to during this activity.

Remind students to pay special attention to words they spelled incorrectly on the Spelling Pretest.

GET READY

Narrative Writing: Prewriting (B)

Spelling List 5 Activity Bank

Circle any words in the box that you did not spell correctly on your pretest. Choose one activity to do with your circled words. Do as much of the activity as you can in the time given.

Did you spell all the words on the pretest correctly? Do the one activity with as many spelling words as you can.

assign	Friday	lie	quite	supply
blind	inside	lightning	shy	tie
child	island	might	sigh	while
entire	July			

Spelling Activity Choices

Alphabetizing

1. In the left column, write your spelling words in alphabetical order.
2. Correct any spelling errors.

NARRATIVE WRITING: PREWRITING (B) 93

Vowel-Free Words

1. In the left column, write only the consonants in each of your spelling words. Put a dot where each vowel should be.
2. Spell each word aloud, stating which vowels should be in the places with dots.
3. In the right column, rewrite the entire spelling word.
4. Correct any spelling errors.

Rhymes

1. In the left column, write your spelling words.
2. In the right column, write a word that rhymes with each spelling word.
3. Correct any spelling errors.

Uppercase and Lowercase

1. In the left column, write each of your spelling words in all uppercase letters.
2. In the right column, write each of your spelling words in all lowercase letters.
3. Correct any spelling errors.

94 NARRATIVE WRITING: PREWRITING (B)

Complete the activity that you chose.

My chosen activity: ______

1.
2.
3.
4.
5.
6.
7.
8.
9.
10.
11.
12.
13.
14.
15.
16.
17.

Students should use this page to complete all steps in their chosen activity.

NARRATIVE WRITING: PREWRITING (B) 95

LEARN AND TRY IT

LEARN Subordinating Conjunctions

Students will learn that a subordinating conjunction introduces the dependent part of a complex sentence. They will learn the meaning of some common subordinating conjunctions.

NOTE The dependent part of a sentence is sometimes called a *subordinate clause*.

TRY IT Use Subordinating Conjunctions

Students will practice identifying and using subordinating conjunctions in complex sentences. They will also write complex sentences of their own by responding to prompts and using mentor sentences.

LEARN Plan a Short Story

Students will learn how to plan the characters, setting, plot, and organization of a short story.

TRY IT Plan Your Short Story

Students will complete Plan Your Short Story in *Summit English Language Arts 3 Activity Book*. They should have their completed Brainstorm for Your Short Story activity page and Model Short Story to refer to as they work.

LEARNING COACH CHECK-IN Tell students that they do not have to complete the questions that come before the graphic organizers in order. For example, students may wish to plan their characters before they plan their setting. Or, planning their plot may give them a great idea for a character. Be sure to review all students' responses and give them feedback.

NOTE Have students add their completed Plan Your Short Story activity page to the folder they are using to store their short story assignment pages.

TRY IT

Narrative Writing: Prewriting (B)

Plan Your Short Story

Plan the setting for your short story by answering the questions.

Answers will vary.

1. When will your story take place? Check one box.
   - ☐ long ago
   - ☐ the present time
   - ☐ the future
2. What time of day will your story take place? Check one box.
   - ☐ morning
   - ☐ afternoon
   - ☐ evening
   - ☐ night

3. Where will each part of your story take place?
   a. Beginning:
   b. Middle:
   c. End:

Plan the characters. Write their names, describe them, and describe how they feel about the other characters.

4. Character 1
   a. Name:
   b. Description:

c. How this character feels about other characters:

5. Character 2
   a. Name:
   b. Description:
   c. How this character feels about other characters:
6. Character 3
   a. Name:
   b. Description:

c. How this character feels about other characters:

Develop the plot. Answer the questions in complete sentences.

7. What problem does the main character face?
8. What causes the problem?
9. How does the main character solve the problem?

Organize the story. Use your answers from Questions 1–9 to describe the setting, characters, and plot events for each part of the story.

Beginning

Setting

Characters

Plot Events (Include the problem.)

NARRATIVE WRITING: PREWRITING (B) 101

Middle

Setting

Characters

Plot Events

102 NARRATIVE WRITING: PREWRITING (B)

End

Setting

Characters

Plot Events (Include the solution.)

NARRATIVE WRITING: PREWRITING (B) 103

WRAP-UP

Questions About Subordinating Conjunctions and Organization

Students will answer questions to show that they understand how to use subordinating conjunctions and how to organize a short story.

Handwriting

Students should gather their handwriting materials and begin where they left off. Remind students to form letters carefully and correctly.

TIP Set a timer to help students stay focused during handwriting practice.

Go Read!

Students will read for pleasure. They should choose a book or a magazine that interests them, or they may choose a selection from the digital library, linked in the online lesson.

- Have students read aloud a few paragraphs of their selection.
- Then have students read silently for the rest of the time.

SUPPORT Students should make no more than five errors in decoding when they read aloud a few paragraphs of their Go Read! selection. If students struggle or make more than five errors, they need to select a different (and easier) text for the Go Read! activity.

TIP Have students select something to read ahead of time to help them stay focused.

Narrative Writing: Drafting (A)

Lesson Overview

ACTIVITY	ACTIVITY TITLE	TIME	ONLINE/OFFLINE
GET READY	Introduction to Narrative Writing: Drafting (A)	**1** minute	
	Spelling List 5 Review Game	**10** minutes	
LEARN AND **TRY IT**	Quotations	**10** minutes	
	Write Quotations	**10** minutes	
	Dialogue	**10** minutes	
	Think About Dialogue	**5** minutes	
	Draft a Short Story	**10** minutes	
	Draft Your Short Story **LEARNING COACH CHECK-IN**	**40** minutes	
WRAP-UP	Questions About Punctuating and Using Dialogue	**4** minutes	
	Go Read!	**20** minutes	or

Content Background

Students will continue working on their **short story**. They will complete this assignment over the course of several lessons by following the writing process. In this lesson, students will learn about dialogue and then begin drafting their short story.

Writing Process

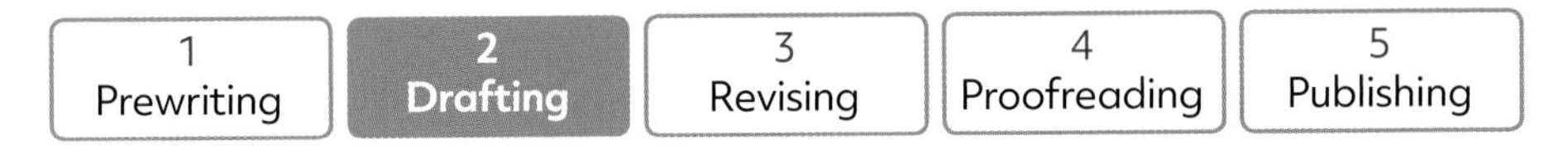

During **drafting**, students will use their prewriting as a guide as they write a rough draft of their short story. A rough draft (or *draft*) is a complete first version of a piece of writing. Writers create drafts to get all their ideas fleshed out and in order, from beginning to end.

Students are expected to write about **half** of their draft in this lesson (although they may write more if they wish). They will have time to finish and submit their draft in Narrative Writing: Drafting (B).

MATERIALS

Supplied

- *Summit English Language Arts 3 Activity Book*
  - Draft Your Short Story
- Short Story Instructions (printout)
- Drafting Paper (printout)

Also Needed

- folder in which students are storing short story assignment pages
- reading material for Go Read!

Grammar, Usage, and Mechanics Students will learn how to correctly write a quotation. A **quotation** is a person's or character's exact words. A quotation is enclosed in **quotation marks**, and it is usually separated from the **speaker tag** with a comma.

Example: Molly said**, "**That coat won't be warm enough.**"**

"I agree**,"** stated Mitch.

If a quotation ends with a question mark or exclamation point, that punctuation mark takes the place of a comma.

Example: **"**Are you sure**?"** asked Nya.

The first word of a quotation begins with a capital letter even if the quotation does not begin the sentence. Note how the word *That* is capitalized in the first example.

KEYWORDS

dialogue – the words that characters say in a written work

drafting – of writing, the stage or step in which the writer first writes the piece

narrative – a kind of writing that tells a story

quotation marks – punctuation that encloses a quotation, or the exact words of a speaker or writer

speaker tag – the part of a dialogue that identifies who is speaking

Advance Preparation

Gather the folder that students are using to store the activity pages related to their short story. The folder should contain the following:

- Model Short Story activity page from Narrative Writing: Prewriting (A)
- Students' completed Brainstorm for Your Short Story activity page from Narrative Writing: Prewriting (A)
- Students' completed Plan Your Short Story activity page from Narrative Writing: Prewriting (B)

During the Go Read! activity, students will have the option of using the digital library. Allow extra time for students to make their reading selection, or have students make a selection before beginning the lesson.

Lesson Goals

- Practice all spelling words online.
- Write dialogue with correct punctuation.
- Begin writing the draft of your short story.
- Read independently to develop fluency.

GET READY

Introduction to Narrative Writing: Drafting (A)

Students will get a glimpse of what they will learn about in the lesson. They will also read the lesson goals and keywords. Have students select each keyword and preview its definition.

Spelling List 5 Review Game

Students will practice all spelling words from the workshop.

LEARN AND TRY IT

LEARN Quotations

Students will learn how to correctly punctuate and capitalize quotations. They will learn the basic rules of enclosing a quotation in quotation marks, using a comma to separate the quotation from the tag, and capitalizing the first letter of a quotation.

NOTE There are exceptions to the rules for punctuating and capitalizing direct quotations. This lesson will focus on mastery of the rules, not on the exceptions.

TRY IT Write Quotations

Students will answer questions about punctuating and capitalizing direct quotations. They will receive feedback on their answers.

LEARN Dialogue

Dialogue is a conversation among characters in story. Students will learn about writing effective dialogue, including how to format dialogue within a passage, how to make dialogue realistic, and how dialogue can enhance a narrative.

TRY IT Think About Dialogue

Students will answer questions about how a writer uses dialogue in a short story.

LEARN Draft a Short Story

Students will explore how to use work completed during prewriting to draft a short story.

TIP Emphasize that drafts are not perfect. Even expert writers make many revisions to drafts.

TRY IT Draft Your Short Story

Students will complete half of their rough draft using Draft Your Short Story in *Summit English Language Arts 3 Activity Book*. Make sure students have their completed Plan Your Short Story activity page and Model Short Story to refer to as they work.

LEARNING COACH CHECK-IN Review students' in-progress draft. Ensure that students' draft is in line with the assignment criteria outlined on the Brainstorm for Your Short Story activity page. Students should store their draft in the folder they are using to organize their writing assignment pages.

NOTE If you or students wish, you can download and print another copy of the Short Story Instructions online. Additional sheets of Drafting Paper are also available online.

TRY IT
Narrative Writing: Drafting (A)

Draft Your Short Story

Write the first draft of your short story. Write only on the white rows. You will use the purple rows for revisions later.

Answers will vary.

Title:

start here ►

keep writing ►

Draft Page 1

NARRATIVE WRITING: DRAFTING (A) 105

keep writing ►

Draft Page 2

106 NARRATIVE WRITING: DRAFTING (A)

keep writing ►

Draft Page 3

NARRATIVE WRITING: DRAFTING (A) 107

keep writing ►

Draft Page 4

108 NARRATIVE WRITING: DRAFTING (A)

keep writing ►

Draft Page 5

NARRATIVE WRITING: DRAFTING (A) 109

Draft Page 6

110 NARRATIVE WRITING: DRAFTING (A)

WRAP-UP

Questions About Punctuating and Using Dialogue

Students will answer questions to show that they understand how to correctly punctuate dialogue and what purpose dialogue serves in a text.

Go Read!

Students will read for pleasure. They should choose a book or a magazine that interests them, or they may choose a selection from the digital library, linked in the online lesson.

- Have students read aloud a few paragraphs of their selection.
- Then have students read silently for the rest of the time.

SUPPORT Students should make no more than five errors in decoding when they read aloud a few paragraphs of their Go Read! selection. If students struggle or make more than five errors, they need to select a different (and easier) text for the Go Read! activity.

TIP Have students select something to read ahead of time to help them stay focused.

Narrative Writing: Drafting (B)

Lesson Overview

ACTIVITY	ACTIVITY TITLE	TIME	ONLINE/OFFLINE
GET READY	Introduction to Narrative Writing: Drafting (B)	**1** minute	
TRY IT	Review Complex Sentences, Conjunctions, and Quotations	**10** minutes	
QUIZ	Complex Sentences, Conjunctions, and Quotations	**20** minutes	
	Spelling List 5	**10** minutes	
TRY IT	Finish Drafting Your Short Story LEARNING COACH CHECK-IN	**45** minutes	
WRAP-UP	Turn In Your Short Story Draft	**1** minute	
	More Language Arts Practice	**15** minutes	
	Go Read!	**18** minutes	or

Content Background

Students will continue working on their **short story**. In this lesson, students will finish and submit their draft. In later lessons, students will revise, proofread, and publish their short story.

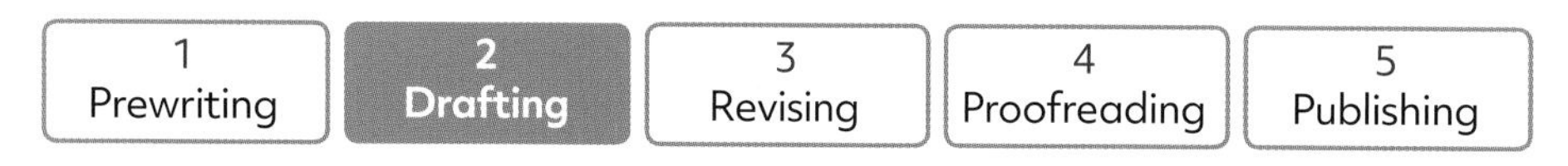

Advance Preparation

Gather the folder that students are using to store the activity pages related to their short story. The folder should contain the following:

- Model Short Story activity page from Narrative Writing: Prewriting (A)
- Students' completed Brainstorm for Your Short Story activity page from Narrative Writing: Prewriting (A)
- Students' completed Plan Your Short Story activity page from Narrative Writing: Prewriting (B)
- Students' in-progress Draft Your Short Story activity page from Narrative Writing: Drafting (A)

MATERIALS

Supplied

- *Summit English Language Arts 3 Activity Book*
  - Draft Your Short Story
- Short Story Instructions (printout)
- Drafting Paper (printout)

Also Needed

- folder in which students are storing short story assignment pages
- reading material for Go Read

During the Go Read! activity, students will have the option of using the digital library. Allow extra time for students to make their reading selection, or have students make a selection before beginning the lesson.

Lesson Goals

- Review complex sentences, subordinating conjunctions, and quotations.
- Take a quiz on complex sentences, subordinating conjunctions, and quotations.
- Take a spelling quiz.
- Finish and submit the draft of your short story.
- Read independently to develop fluency.

GET READY

Introduction to Narrative Writing: Drafting (B)

Students will get a glimpse of what they will learn about in the lesson. They will also read the lesson goals.

TRY IT

Review Complex Sentences, Conjunctions, and Quotations

Students will answer questions to review what they have learned about complex sentences, subordinating conjunctions, and quotations.

QUIZ

Complex Sentences, Conjunctions, and Quotations

Students will complete the Complex Sentences, Conjunctions, and Quotations quiz.

Spelling List 5

Students will complete the Spelling List 5 quiz.

TRY IT

Finish Drafting Your Short Story

Students will complete the draft of their short story using the Draft Your Short Story activity page in *Summit English Language Arts 3 Activity Book*. Make sure students have their completed Plan Your Short Story activity page and Model Short Story to refer to as they work.

LEARNING COACH CHECK-IN Review students' completed draft. Ensure that students' draft is in line with the assignment criteria outlined on the Brainstorm for Your Short Story activity page. Students should store their draft in the folder they are using to organize their writing assignment pages.

NOTE If you or students wish, you can download and print another copy of the Short Story Instructions online. Additional sheets of Drafting Paper are also available online.

TRY IT

Narrative Writing: Drafting (A)

Draft Your Short Story

Write the first draft of your short story. Write only on the white rows. You will use the purple rows for revisions later.

Answers will vary.

Title:

start here ►

keep writing ►

Draft Page 1

NARRATIVE WRITING: DRAFTING (A) 105

keep writing ►

Draft Page 2

106 NARRATIVE WRITING: DRAFTING (A)

keep writing ►

Draft Page 3

NARRATIVE WRITING: DRAFTING (A) 107

keep writing ►

Draft Page 4

108 NARRATIVE WRITING: DRAFTING (A)

keep writing ►

Draft Page 5

NARRATIVE WRITING: DRAFTING (A) 109

Draft Page 6

110 NARRATIVE WRITING: DRAFTING (A)

WRAP-UP

Turn In Your Short Story Draft

Students will submit their completed draft to their teacher.

More Language Arts Practice

Students will practice skills according to their individual needs.

Go Read!

Students will read for pleasure. They should choose a book or a magazine that interests them, or they may choose a selection from the digital library, linked in the online lesson.

- Have students read aloud a few paragraphs of their selection.
- Then have students read silently for the rest of the time.

SUPPORT Students should make no more than five errors in decoding when they read aloud a few paragraphs of their Go Read! selection. If students struggle or make more than five errors, they need to select a different (and easier) text for the Go Read! activity.

TIP Have students select something to read ahead of time to help them stay focused.

Nuance and Shades of Meaning

Lesson Overview

ACTIVITY	ACTIVITY TITLE	TIME	ONLINE/OFFLINE
GET READY	Introduction to Nuance and Shades of Meaning	**1** minute	online
	Look Back at Synonyms	**4** minutes	online
LEARN AND TRY IT	Nuance and Shades of Meaning	**10** minutes	online
	Practice Using Nuance and Shades of Meaning	**10** minutes	online
	Apply: Nuance and Shades of Meaning LEARNING COACH CHECK-IN	**15** minutes	offline
	Review Nuance and Shades of Meaning	**15** minutes	online
QUIZ	Nuance and Shades of Meaning	**15** minutes	online
WRAP-UP	More Language Arts Practice	**15** minutes	online
	Go Write! Look Out the Window	**15** minutes	offline
	Go Read!	**20** minutes	online or offline

Content Background

In this lesson, students will learn several words whose meanings are similar but subtly different. These subtle differences in meaning are called *nuances*, or shades of meaning. Students will use context clues to help them figure out which word among those with similar meanings is the best word in a situation.

For example, the words *annoyed* and *exasperated* have similar meanings. Because of the nuance between the two words, you would use *annoyed* to describe something slightly bothersome, like your dog running off with the newspaper. But, your neighbor might become *exasperated*, reaching the point of losing their patience, if your dog barked all night long.

Advance Preparation

During the Go Read! activity, students will have the option of using the digital library. Allow extra time for students to make their reading selection, or have students make a selection before beginning the lesson.

MATERIALS

Supplied

- *Summit English Language Arts 3 Activity Book*
  - Apply: Nuance and Shades of Meaning
  - Go Write! Look Out the Window

Also Needed

- reading material for Go Read!

KEYWORDS

nuance – a very small difference in meaning

Lesson Goals

- Practice vocabulary words.
- Use context clues to recognize small differences in the meanings of words.
- Take the Nuance and Shades of Meaning quiz.
- Freewrite about a topic to develop writing fluency and practice letter formation.
- Read independently to develop fluency.

GET READY

Introduction to Nuance and Shades of Meaning

Students will get a glimpse of what they will learn about in the lesson. They will also read the lesson goals and keywords. Have students select each keyword and preview its definition.

Look Back at Synonyms

Students will practice the prerequisite skill of identifying synonyms.

LEARN AND TRY IT

LEARN Nuance and Shades of Meaning

Students will be introduced to the vocabulary words for the lesson. Then they will learn the subtle differences in meaning of the new vocabulary words.

TRY IT Practice Using Nuance and Shades of Meaning

Students will practice recognizing nuance and choosing between words with subtly different meanings.

TRY IT Apply: Nuance and Shades of Meaning

Students will complete Apply: Nuance and Shades of Meaning in *Summit English Language Arts 3 Activity Book*. First students will complete sentences by choosing between words with subtly different meanings. Then they will write sentences with blanks and ask someone which word of those with different shades of meaning best completes their sentences.

OPTIONAL Have students write sentences with blanks for the remainder of the vocabulary words, and then have someone try to correctly complete their sentences.

LEARNING COACH CHECK-IN This activity requires students to share their sentences with someone. Either discuss students' sentences yourself, or help students make this connection.

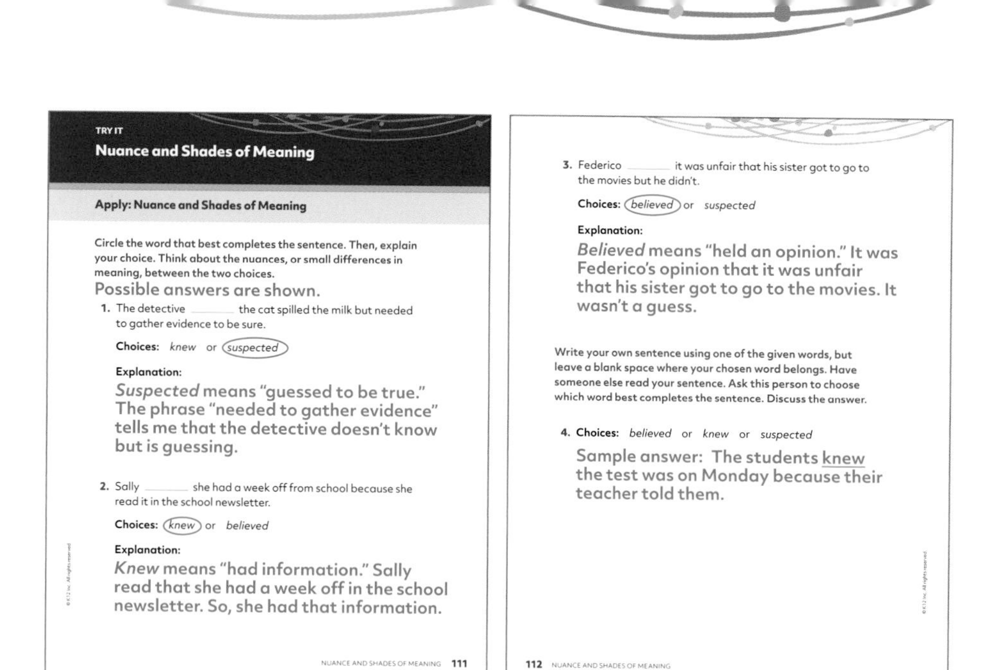
TRY IT
Nuance and Shades of Meaning

Apply: Nuance and Shades of Meaning

Circle the word that best completes the sentence. Then, explain your choice. Think about the nuances, or small differences in meaning, between the two choices.

Possible answers are shown.

1. The detective ______ the cat spilled the milk but needed to gather evidence to be sure.

   Choices: *knew* or *suspected* (circled: *suspected*)

   Explanation:

   Suspected means "guessed to be true." The phrase "needed to gather evidence" tells me that the detective doesn't know but is guessing.

2. Sally ______ she had a week off from school because she read it in the school newsletter.

   Choices: *knew* or *believed* (circled: *knew*)

   Explanation:

   Knew means "had information." Sally read that she had a week off in the school newsletter. So, she had that information.

NUANCE AND SHADES OF MEANING 111

3. Federico ______ it was unfair that his sister got to go to the movies but he didn't.

   Choices: *believed* or *suspected* (circled: *believed*)

   Explanation:

   Believed means "held an opinion." It was Federico's opinion that it was unfair that his sister got to go to the movies. It wasn't a guess.

Write your own sentence using one of the given words, but leave a blank space where your chosen word belongs. Have someone else read your sentence. Ask this person to choose which word best completes the sentence. Discuss the answer.

4. **Choices:** *believed* or *knew* or *suspected*

   Sample answer: The students knew the test was on Monday because their teacher told them.

112 NUANCE AND SHADES OF MEANING

TRY IT Review Nuance and Shades of Meaning

Students will answer questions to review what they have learned about nuance and shades of meaning.

QUIZ

Nuance and Shades of Meaning

Students will complete the Nuance and Shades of Meaning quiz.

WRAP-UP

More Language Arts Practice

Students will practice skills according to their individual needs.

Go Write! Look Out the Window

Students will complete Go Write! Look Out the Window in *Summit English Language Arts 3 Activity Book*. They will have the option to either respond to a prompt or write about a topic of their choice.

NOTE This activity is intended to build writing fluency. Students should write for the entire allotted time.

SUPPORT If students have trouble writing for the allotted time, prompt them with questions. For example, *Can you tell me more about this? How did you feel when this happened?*

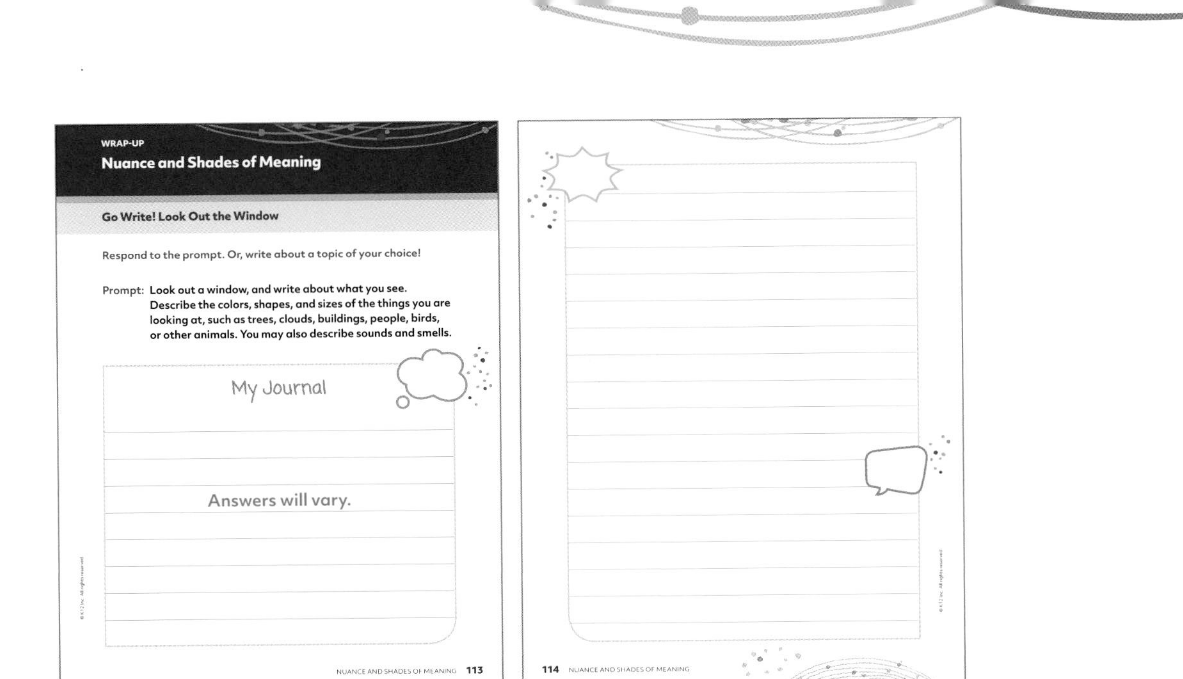
WRAP-UP

Nuance and Shades of Meaning

Go Write! Look Out the Window

Respond to the prompt. Or, write about a topic of your choice!

Prompt: Look out a window, and write about what you see. Describe the colors, shapes, and sizes of the things you are looking at, such as trees, clouds, buildings, people, birds, or other animals. You may also describe sounds and smells.

My Journal

Answers will vary.

NUANCE AND SHADES OF MEANING 113

114 NUANCE AND SHADES OF MEANING

Go Read!

Students will read for pleasure. They should choose a book or a magazine that interests them, or they may choose a selection from the digital library, linked in the online lesson.

- Have students read aloud a few paragraphs of their selection.
- Then have students read silently for the rest of the time.

SUPPORT Students should make no more than five errors in decoding when they read aloud a few paragraphs of their Go Read! selection. If students struggle or make more than five errors, they need to select a different (and easier) text for the Go Read! activity.

TIP Have students select something to read ahead of time to help them stay focused.

Big Ideas: Mini-Project

Lesson Overview

Big Ideas lessons provide students the opportunity to further apply the knowledge acquired and skills learned throughout the unit workshops. Each Big Ideas lesson consists of these parts:

1. **Cumulative Review:** Students keep their skills fresh by reviewing prior content.
2. **Preview:** Students practice answering the types of questions they will commonly find on standardized tests.
3. **Synthesis:** Students complete an assignment that allows them to connect and apply what they have learned. Synthesis assignments vary throughout the course.

   In the Synthesis portion of this Big Ideas lesson, students will complete a small creative project that ties together concepts and skills they have encountered across workshops. These small projects are designed to deepen students' understanding of those concepts and skills.

   LEARNING COACH CHECK-IN Make sure students complete, review, and submit the assignment to their teacher.

All materials needed for this lesson are linked online and not provided in the activity book.

MATERIALS

Supplied

- Mini-Project Instructions (printout)

Folktales and Legends

Words to Show Time and Space

Lesson Overview

ACTIVITY	ACTIVITY TITLE	TIME	ONLINE/OFFLINE
GET READY	Introduction to Words to Show Time and Space	**2** minutes	online
	Look Back at Content Vocabulary	**4** minutes	online
LEARN AND TRY IT	Words to Show Time and Space	**10** minutes	online
	Practice Using Words to Show Time and Space	**10** minutes	online
	Apply: Words to Show Time and Space **LEARNING COACH CHECK-IN**	**15** minutes	offline
	Review Words to Show Time and Space	**15** minutes	online
QUIZ	Words to Show Time and Space	**15** minutes	online
WRAP-UP	More Language Arts Practice	**19** minutes	online
	Go Write! Who Gives Good Advice?	**15** minutes	offline
	Go Read!	**15** minutes	online or offline

Content Background

In this lesson, students will learn words to show time and space, frequently used to describe our experience of the world around us. They will use context clues to help determine the meaning of these unknown words. Further, students will write a paragraph using the vocabulary words to describe their day.

Advance Preparation

During the Go Read! activity, students will have the option of using the digital library. Allow extra time for students to make their reading selection, or have students make a selection before beginning the lesson.

MATERIALS

Supplied

- *Summit English Language Arts 3 Activity Book*
  - Apply: Words to Show Time and Space
  - Go Write! Who Gives Good Advice?

Also Needed

- reading material for Go Read!

Lesson Goals

- Practice vocabulary words.
- Use context clues to determine the meaning of unknown words.
- Correctly use words to show time and space to describe your day.
- Take the Words to Show Time and Space quiz.
- Freewrite about a topic to develop writing fluency and practice letter formation.
- Read independently to develop fluency.

GET READY

Introduction to Words to Show Time and Space

After a quick introductory activity, students will read the lesson goals.

Look Back at Content Vocabulary

Students will practice the prerequisite skill of understanding content vocabulary.

LEARN AND TRY IT

LEARN Words to Show Time and Space

Students will be introduced to the vocabulary words for the lesson. Then they will learn how to use the vocabulary words to show time and space by seeing them in context.

TRY IT Practice Using Words to Show Time and Space

Students will practice recognizing the correct word to accurately show time and space.

TRY IT Apply: Words to Show Time and Space

Students will complete Apply: Words to Show Time and Space in *Summit English Language Arts 3 Activity Book*. They will practice using words to show time and space by writing a short paragraph describing their day using the vocabulary words.

OPTIONAL Have students look up, or provide them with, more words to show time and space—for example, *before* and *above*. Have them add to their paragraph using these additional words to further describe their day.

OPTIONAL Have students read their paragraph aloud to you, using hand gestures that demonstrate understanding of how the vocabulary words show time or space.

LEARNING COACH CHECK-IN This activity contains an open-ended response, so it's important that you review students' response. Give students feedback, using the sample answer provided to guide you.

TRY IT
Words to Show Time and Space

Apply: Words to Show Time and Space

The words *meanwhile, during,* and *afterward* show time. Use these words to write a short paragraph that describes your day. Use the sample response as a model.

Sample response: During the morning, I did my schoolwork. Afterward, I had lunch. Now, I'm waiting for my brother to get home. In the meanwhile, I am playing cards with my friend Maria.

Students should use the words ***meanwhile***, ***during***, and ***afterward*** in a short paragraph that describes their day.

WORDS TO SHOW TIME AND SPACE 115

Meanwhile,
I will have lunch!

116 WORDS TO SHOW TIME AND SPACE

TRY IT **Review Words to Show Time and Space**

Students will answer questions to review what they have learned about words to show time and space.

QUIZ

Words to Show Time and Space

Students will complete the Words to Show Time and Space quiz.

WRAP-UP

More Language Arts Practice

Students will practice skills according to their individual needs.

Go Write! Who Gives Good Advice?

Students will complete Go Write! Who Gives Good Advice? in *Summit English Language Arts 3 Activity Book*. They will have the option to either respond to a prompt or write about a topic of their choice.

NOTE This activity is intended to build writing fluency. Students should write for the entire allotted time.

SUPPORT If students have trouble writing for the allotted time, prompt them with questions. For example, *Can you tell me more about this? How did you feel when this happened?*

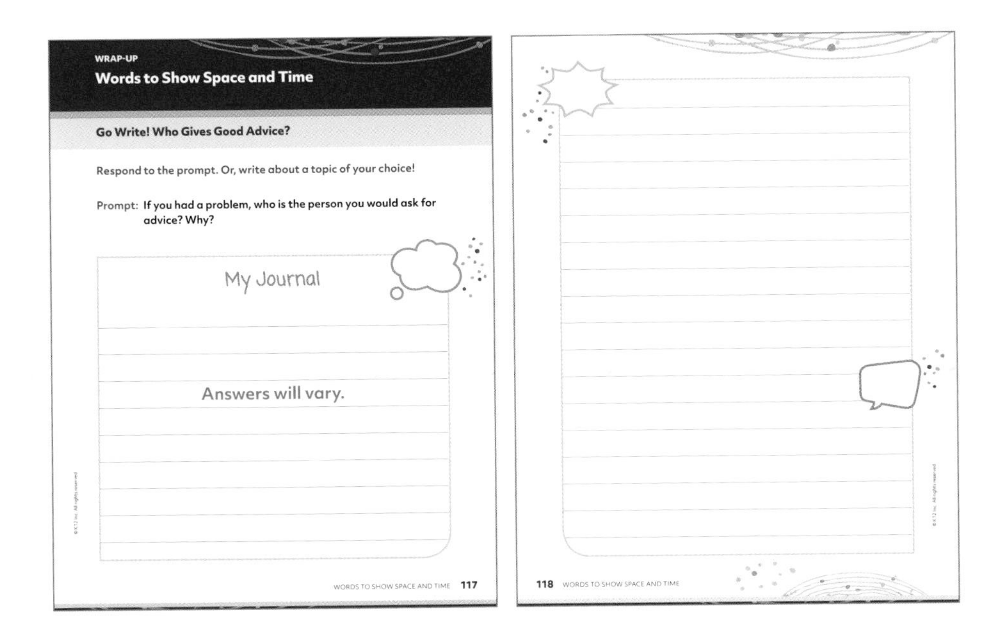
WRAP-UP

Words to Show Space and Time

Go Write! Who Gives Good Advice?

Respond to the prompt. Or, write about a topic of your choice!

Prompt: If you had a problem, who is the person you would ask for advice? Why?

My Journal

Answers will vary.

WORDS TO SHOW SPACE AND TIME 117

118 WORDS TO SHOW SPACE AND TIME

Go Read!

Students will read for pleasure. They should choose a book or a magazine that interests them, or they may choose a selection from the digital library, linked in the online lesson.

- Have students read aloud a few paragraphs of their selection.
- Then have students read silently for the rest of the time.

SUPPORT Students should make no more than five errors in decoding when they read aloud a few paragraphs of their Go Read! selection. If students struggle or make more than five errors, they need to select a different (and easier) text for the Go Read! activity.

TIP Have students select something to read ahead of time to help them stay focused.

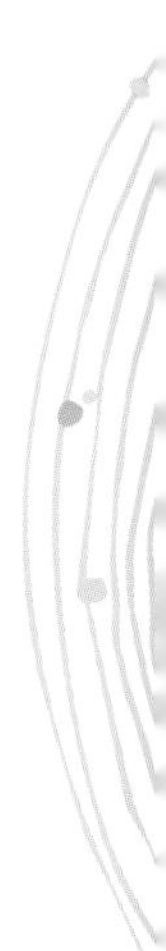

"The Stone in the Road" (A)

Lesson Overview

ACTIVITY	ACTIVITY TITLE	TIME	ONLINE/OFFLINE
GET READY	Introduction to "The Stone in the Road" (A)	**1** minute	online
	Spelling List 6 Pretest **LEARNING COACH CHECK-IN**	**10** minutes	online and offline
	Read and Record	**8** minutes	online
	Reading Foundations: Visualize	**5** minutes	online
	Before You Read "The Stone in the Road: A Story"	**10** minutes	online
READ	"The Stone in the Road: A Story"	**20** minutes	offline
	Check-In: "The Stone in the Road: A Story"	**5** minutes	online
LEARN AND **TRY IT**	Retelling and Identifying Problem and Solution	**10** minutes	online
	Retell and Identify Problem and Solution	**10** minutes	online
	Apply: Sequence of Events	**13** minutes	online
	Describe a Sequence of Events **LEARNING COACH CHECK-IN**	**10** minutes	offline
	Practice Words from "The Stone in the Road: A Story"	**8** minutes	online
WRAP-UP	Question About Sequence of Events	**2** minutes	online
	Handwriting	**8** minutes	offline

Content Background

Students will read a folktale called "The Stone in the Road." A *folktale* usually teaches a lesson that is important to the culture that it comes from. The folktale is often passed down from generation to generation as a way of passing on the lesson. Students will also spend some time talking about the sequence of events in the story and practice determining which details are important enough to include in a summary of a story.

MATERIALS

Supplied

- *Summit English Language Arts 3 Expeditions in Reading*
  - "The Stone in the Road: A Story"
- *Summit English Language Arts 3 Activity Book*
  - Describe a Sequence of Events
- handwriting workbook

"The Stone in the Road: A Story" Synopsis

In this folktale, a farmer, a soldier, and a group of merchants all come across a large stone in the middle of the road. All of them complain about having to go around the stone, yet none of them move it. A milkmaid sees the stone and decides to move it. She doesn't want anyone to get hurt by stumbling across the stone in the dark. The next day, the king gathers his subjects at the place where the stone was in the road. He explains that he placed the stone there as a test and that only the milkmaid passed. She was the only person to take responsibility for moving the stone. He rewards her with gold coins from a small box that was hidden under the stone.

KEYWORDS

folktale – a story, which usually teaches a lesson important to a culture, that is passed down through many generations

problem-solution structure – organizational pattern in which a problem is described, followed by descriptions of its solution or possible solutions

sequence of events – the order in which things happen in a story

Lesson Goals

- Take a spelling pretest.
- Read aloud to practice fluency.
- Read "The Stone in the Road: A Story."
- Retell a story.
- Identify a problem and solution in a story.
- Practice vocabulary words.
- Develop letter formation fluency.

GET READY

Introduction to "The Stone in the Road" (A)

Students will get a glimpse of what they will learn about in the lesson. They will also read the lesson goals and keywords. Have students select each keyword and preview its definition.

Spelling List 6 Pretest

Students will take a spelling pretest and learn a new spelling pattern.

LEARNING COACH CHECK-IN Have students turn to Spelling List 6 Pretest in *Summit English Language Arts 3 Activity Book* and open the online Spelling Pretest activity. Online, students will listen to the spelling word, type the word in the space indicated, and then check their answer. In the activity book, students will write the correct spelling of the word in the tables provided and indicate with a ✓ or an ✗ if they spelled the word correctly or incorrectly online. Students will repeat this process with the remaining words.

As needed, help students with the interaction between the online activity and the activity book page until they become comfortable with what they need to do. As students practice their spelling words throughout the workshop, they should pay special attention to words they spelled incorrectly on the pretest.

This is the complete list of words students will be tested on.

Words with Long *o* Sound		
almost	focus	phone
alone	follow	rowboat
although	hole	sailboat
crossroad	known	tiptoe
doe	locate	window
dough	open	

NOTE Have students keep their completed activity page in a safe place so they can refer to it later.

GET READY

"The Stone in the Road" (A)

Spelling List 6 Pretest

1. Open the Spelling Pretest activity online. Listen to the first spelling word. Type the word. Check your answer.

2. Write the correct spelling of the word in the Word column of the Spelling Pretest table.

	Word	✓	✗
1	blindfold		

3. Put a check mark in the ✓ column if you spelled the word correctly online.

	Word	✓	✗
1	blindfold	✓	

Put an X in the ✗ column if you spelled the word incorrectly online.

	Word	✓	✗
1	blindfold		X

4. Repeat Steps 1–3 for the remaining words in the Spelling Pretest.

"THE STONE IN THE ROAD" (A) 119

"The Stone in the Road" (A)

Spelling List 6 Pretest

Write each spelling word in the Word column, making sure to spell it correctly.

	Word	✓	✗
1	almost		
2	alone		
3	although		
4	crossroad		
5	doe		
6	dough		
7	focus		
8	follow		
9	hole		

	Word	✓	✗
10	known		
11	locate		
12	open		
13	phone		
14	rowboat		
15	sailboat		
16	tiptoe		
17	window		

Students should write the correct spelling of each word from the pretest and use the ✓ and X columns to indicate whether they spelled each word correctly or incorrectly online.

120 "THE STONE IN THE ROAD" (A)

Read and Record

Good readers read quickly, smoothly, and with expression. This is called *fluency*. Students will record themselves reading aloud. They will listen to their recording and think about how quick, smooth, and expressive they sound.

TIP Encourage students to rerecord as needed.

Reading Foundations: Visualize

Reading Foundations activities serve to remind students of basic reading skills and reading behaviors mastered in earlier grades. The activities cover topics such as advanced decoding skills and various strategies for improving comprehension.

Before You Read "The Stone in the Road: A Story"

Students will be introduced to some key vocabulary words that they will encounter in the upcoming reading and learn some important background related to the reading.

READ

"The Stone in the Road: A Story"

Students will read "The Stone in the Road: A Story" in *Expeditions in Reading*.

Check-In: "The Stone in the Road: A Story"

Students will answer several questions to demonstrate their comprehension of "The Stone in the Road: A Story."

LEARN AND TRY IT

LEARN Retelling and Identifying Problem and Solution

Students will learn how to retell a story and how to identify the problem and solution in a story.

TRY IT Retell and Identify Problem and Solution

Students will determine the key details they should include when retelling a story, including the problem and solution the characters face.

TRY IT Apply: Sequence of Events

Students will apply to a new work what they've learned about sequence of events when retelling a story.

TRY IT Describe a Sequence of Events

Students will complete Describe a Sequence of Events in *Summit English Language Arts 3 Activity Book*.

SUPPORT If students need help understanding sequence of events, ask them to copy you as you model three simple movements (patting your head, clapping your hands, stomping your feet). Then, ask them which movement came first, which came next, and which came last.

LEARNING COACH CHECK-IN This activity page contains open-ended questions, so it's important that you review students' responses. Give students feedback, using the sample answers provided to guide you.

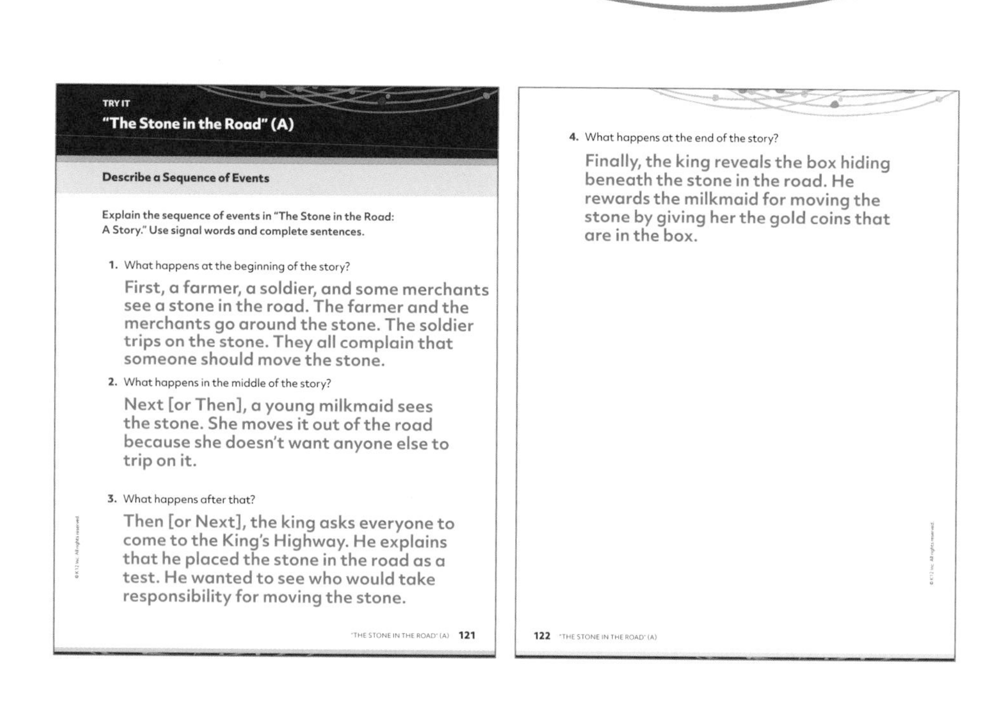
TRY IT
"The Stone in the Road" (A)

Describe a Sequence of Events

Explain the sequence of events in "The Stone in the Road: A Story." Use signal words and complete sentences.

1. What happens at the beginning of the story?
   First, a farmer, a soldier, and some merchants see a stone in the road. The farmer and the merchants go around the stone. The soldier trips on the stone. They all complain that someone should move the stone.
2. What happens in the middle of the story?
   Next [or Then], a young milkmaid sees the stone. She moves it out of the road because she doesn't want anyone else to trip on it.
3. What happens after that?
   Then [or Next], the king asks everyone to come to the King's Highway. He explains that he placed the stone in the road as a test. He wanted to see who would take responsibility for moving the stone.

"THE STONE IN THE ROAD" (A) 121

4. What happens at the end of the story?
   Finally, the king reveals the box hiding beneath the stone in the road. He rewards the milkmaid for moving the stone by giving her the gold coins that are in the box.

122 "THE STONE IN THE ROAD" (A)

TRY IT **Practice Words from "The Stone in the Road: A Story"**

Students will answer questions to demonstrate their understanding of the vocabulary words from the reading.

WRAP-UP

Question About Sequence of Events

Students will answer a question to show that they understand the sequence of events in "The Stone in the Road: A Story."

Handwriting

Students should gather their handwriting materials and begin where they left off. Remind students to form letters carefully and correctly.

TIP Set a timer to help students stay focused during handwriting practice.

"The Stone in the Road" (B)

Lesson Overview

ACTIVITY	ACTIVITY TITLE	TIME	ONLINE/OFFLINE
GET READY	Introduction to "The Stone in the Road" (B)	**1** minute	
	Spelling List 6 Activity Bank	**8** minutes	
	Read and Record	**10** minutes	
	Reading Foundations: Does It Make Sense?	**5** minutes	
	Recall "The Stone in the Road: A Story"	**5** minutes	
	Before You Read "The Stone in the Road: A Play"	**5** minutes	
READ	"The Stone in the Road: A Play"	**23** minutes	
	Check-In: "The Stone in the Road: A Play"	**5** minutes	
LEARN AND **TRY IT**	Identifying Scenes and Theme in Drama	**10** minutes	
	Identify Theme in Drama	**10** minutes	
	Apply: Identifying Theme	**10** minutes	
	Support a Theme **LEARNING COACH CHECK-IN**	**10** minutes	
	Practice Words from "The Stone in the Road: A Play"	**8** minutes	
WRAP-UP	Question About "The Stone in the Road: A Play"	**2** minutes	
	Handwriting	**8** minutes	

Content Background

Students will read a second version of "The Stone in the Road." This version is a *drama*, or a play. The characters in the drama version are slightly different than the characters in the story version. Students will also learn about different elements of drama, work to identify theme in the play, and determine a few details that support the theme they identify.

Advance Preparation

Gather students' completed Spelling List 6 Pretest activity page from "The Stone in the Road" (A). Students will refer to this page during Get Ready: Spelling List 6 Activity Bank.

"The Stone in the Road: A Play" Synopsis

In this dramatic version of the folktale, King Alvis instructs his knight, Sir Gavin, to place a stone in the middle of a road.Then, he and Sir Gavin hide behind a tree to watch what happens. A farmer and two soldiers all come across the stone in the middle of the road. All of them complain about having to go around the stone, yet none of them move it. After each visitor, King Alvis asks Sir Gavin if he knows why the king put the stone in the road. Sir Gavin is unable to come up with an answer. A milkmaid sees the stone and decides to move it. She doesn't want anyone to get hurt by stumbling across the stone in the dark. King Alvis instructs Sir Gavin to gather his subjects on the road the next morning. He explains that he placed the stone there as a test and that only the milkmaid passed. She was the only person to solve the problem of the stone in the road. He rewards her with gold coins from a small box that was hidden under the stone.

Lesson Goals

- Practice all spelling words offline.
- Read aloud to practice fluency.
- Read "The Stone in the Road: A Play."
- Identify parts of a play and theme.
- Practice vocabulary words.
- Develop letter formation fluency.

MATERIALS

Supplied

- *Summit English Language Arts 3 Expeditions in Reading*
  - "The Stone in the Road: A Play"
- *Summit English Language Arts 3 Activity Book*
  - Spelling List 6 Activity Bank
  - Support a Theme
- handwriting workbook

Also Needed

- completed Spelling List 6 Pretest activity page from "The Stone in the Road" (A)

KEYWORDS

character – a person or animal in a story

dialogue – the words that characters say in a written work

drama – another word for *play*

scene – a part of an act of a play that happens at a fixed time and place

setting – when and where a story takes place

stage directions – instructions in a play that tell the actors what to do

theme – the author's message or big idea

GET READY

Introduction to "The Stone in the Road" (B)

Students will get a glimpse of what they will learn about in the lesson. They will also read the lesson goals and keywords. Have students select each keyword and preview its definition.

Spelling List 6 Activity Bank

Students will practice all spelling words from the workshop by completing Spelling List 6 Activity Bank from *Summit English Language Arts 3 Activity Book*. Make sure students have their completed Spelling List 6 Pretest activity page from "The Stone in the Road" (A) to refer to during this activity.

Remind students to pay special attention to words they spelled incorrectly on the Spelling Pretest.

GET READY

"The Stone in the Road" (B)

Spelling List 6 Activity Bank

Circle any words in the box that you did not spell correctly on the pretest. Choose one activity to do with your circled words. Do as much of the activity as you can in the time given.

Did you spell all the words on the pretest correctly? Do the one activity with as many spelling words as you can.

almost	doe	hole	open	sailboat
alone	dough	known	phone	tiptoe
although	focus	locate	rowboat	window
crossroad	follow			

Spelling Activity Choices

Silly Sentences

1. Write a silly sentence for each of your spelling words.
2. Underline the spelling word in each sentence.
   Example: The dog was driving a car.
3. Correct any spelling errors.

"THE STONE IN THE ROAD" (B) 123

Spelling Story

1. Write a very short story using each of your spelling words.
2. Underline the spelling words in the story.
3. Correct any spelling errors.

Riddle Me This

1. Write a riddle for each of your spelling words.
   Example: "I have a trunk, but it's not on my car."
2. Write the answer, which is your word, for each riddle.
   Example: Answer: elephant
3. Correct any spelling errors.

RunOnWord

1. Gather some crayons, colored pencils, or markers. Use a different color to write each of your spelling words. Write the words end to end as one long word.
   Example: dogcatbirdfishturtle
2. Rewrite the words correctly and with proper spacing.
3. Correct any spelling errors.

124 "THE STONE IN THE ROAD" (B)

Complete the activity that you chose.

My chosen activity:

Students should use this page to complete all steps in their chosen activity.

"THE STONE IN THE ROAD" (B) 125

Read and Record

Good readers read quickly, smoothly, and with expression. This is called *fluency*. Students will record themselves reading aloud. They will listen to their recording and think about how quick, smooth, and expressive they sound.

TIP Encourage students to rerecord as needed.

Reading Foundations: Does It Make Sense?

Reading Foundations activities serve to remind students of basic reading skills and reading behaviors mastered in earlier grades. The activities cover topics such as advanced decoding skills and various strategies for improving comprehension.

Recall "The Stone in the Road: A Story"

Students will answer some questions to review the reading that they have already completed.

Before You Read "The Stone in the Road: A Play"

Students will be introduced to some key vocabulary words that they will encounter in the upcoming reading and learn some important background related to the reading.

READ

"The Stone in the Road: A Play"

Students will read "The Stone in the Road: A Play" in *Expeditions in Reading*.

Check-In: "The Stone in the Road: A Play"

Students will answer several questions to demonstrate their comprehension of "The Stone in the Road: A Play."

LEARN AND TRY IT

LEARN Identifying Scenes and Theme in Drama

Students will learn about different elements found in a play, how scenes build on one another in a play, and how the theme is revealed in a play.

TRY IT Identify Theme in Drama

Students will identify the theme of "The Stone in the Road: A Play" and details in the play that support the theme.

TRY IT Apply: Identifying Theme

Students will apply to a new work what they've learned about identifying theme.

TRY IT Support a Theme

Students will complete Support a Theme in *Summit English Language Arts 3 Activity Book*.

LEARNING COACH CHECK-IN This activity page contains open-ended questions about supporting the theme in the text, so it's important that you review students' responses. Give students feedback, using the sample answers provided to guide you.

TIP Ask students, *What did King Alvis see the character do or say? Does that action or dialogue have anything to do with the author's message?*

TRY IT

"The Stone in the Road" (B)

Support a Theme

Answer the questions in complete sentences.

1. Identify a theme in "The Stone in the Road: A Play."
   We need to work hard to solve our own problems instead of relying on someone else to solve them for us.

Choose two scenes in the play. Record a detail from each scene that supports the theme you identified in Question 1. The detail can be an action or a line of dialogue. Explain how the detail supports the theme.

2. First Scene: Scene 3
   a. Detail
   The milkmaid says, "And now it is getting dark, and anyone else who comes down the road might also stumble or hurt themselves. I must do something about that."

"THE STONE IN THE ROAD" (B) 127

   b. Explanation
   The milkmaid solves the problem of the stone in the road. She moves it herself. She doesn't complain or wait for someone else to move it. Her dialogue supports the theme that we should work hard to solve our own problems.

3. Second Scene: Scene 4
   a. Detail
   King Alvis rewards the milkmaid for moving the stone. He gives her gold coins.

   b. Explanation
   King Alvis rewards the milkmaid because she solved the problem herself. He says others should follow her example. It supports the theme that we should work hard to solve our own problems.

128 "THE STONE IN THE ROAD" (B)

TRY IT Practice Words from "The Stone in the Road: A Play"

Students will answer questions to demonstrate their understanding of the vocabulary words from the reading.

WRAP-UP

Question About "The Stone in the Road: A Play"

Students will answer a question to show that they understand different elements of "The Stone in the Road: A Play."

Handwriting

Students should gather their handwriting materials and begin where they left off. Remind students to form letters carefully and correctly.

TIP Set a timer to help students stay focused during handwriting practice.

"The Stone in the Road" (C)

Lesson Overview

ACTIVITY	ACTIVITY TITLE	TIME	ONLINE/OFFLINE
GET READY	Introduction to "The Stone in the Road" (C)	**1** minute	online
	Spelling List 6 Review Game	**10** minutes	online
	Read and Record	**8** minutes	online
	Recall "The Stone in the Road: A Play"	**5** minutes	online
READ	Review "The Stone in the Road"	**11** minutes	offline
LEARN AND **TRY IT**	Comparing & Contrasting Two Versions: "The Stone in the Road"	**15** minutes	online
	Contrast Two Versions of "The Stone in the Road"	**15** minutes	online
	Apply: Compare and Contrast	**15** minutes	online
	Compare a Story and a Play LEARNING COACH CHECK-IN	**30** minutes	offline
WRAP-UP	Question About "The Stone in the Road"	**2** minutes	online
	Handwriting	**8** minutes	offline

Content Background

Students will spend much of the lesson comparing and contrasting the two versions of "The Stone in the Road." Instead of reading new content, they should skim and scan the two texts to review the characters, settings, plot events, and themes in both works.

Lesson Goals

- Practice all spelling words online.
- Read aloud to practice fluency.
- Review "The Stone in the Road: A Story" and "The Stone in the Road: A Play."
- Compare and contrast the two versions of "The Stone in the Road."
- Develop letter formation fluency.

MATERIALS

Supplied

- *Summit English Language Arts 3 Expeditions in Reading*
- *Summit English Language Arts 3 Activity Book*
  - Compare a Story and a Play
- handwriting workbook

KEYWORDS

drama – another word for *play*

GET READY

Introduction to "The Stone in the Road" (C)

Students will get a glimpse of what they will learn about in the lesson. They will also read the lesson goals and keywords. Have students select each keyword and preview its definition.

Spelling List 6 Review Game

Students will practice all spelling words from the workshop.

Read and Record

Good readers read quickly, smoothly, and with expression. This is called *fluency*. Students will record themselves reading aloud. They will listen to their recording and think about how quick, smooth, and expressive they sound.

Encourage students to rerecord as needed.

Recall "The Stone in the Road: A Play"

Students will answer some questions to review the reading that they have already completed.

READ

Review "The Stone in the Road"

Students will review "The Stone in the Road: A Story" and "The Stone in the Road: A Play" in *Expeditions in Reading*.

LEARN AND TRY IT

LEARN Comparing & Contrasting Two Versions: "The Stone in the Road"

Students will learn about the similarities and differences between the two versions of the same story.

TIP Remind students that *compare* means "to determine how two things are alike or similar." *Contrast* means "to determine how two things are different."

TRY IT Contrast Two Versions of "The Stone in the Road"

Students will identify differences between the two versions of the story they read.

TRY IT Apply: Compare and Contrast

Students will apply to a new work what they've learned about comparing and contrasting text elements.

TRY IT Compare a Story and a Play

Students will complete Compare a Story and a Play in *Summit English Language Arts 3 Activity Book*.

LEARNING COACH CHECK-IN This activity page contains an open-ended question, so it's important that you review students' responses. Give students feedback, using the sample answers provided to guide you.

TRY IT

"The Stone in the Road" (C)

Compare a Story and a Play

Fill in the chart to compare "The Stone in the Road: A Story" with "The Stone in the Road: A Play." The first entry in the chart has been completed for you.

Question	"The Stone in the Road: A Story"	"The Stone in the Road: A Play"
Who are the main characters?	king milkmaid	King Alvis Sir Gavin Milkmaid
What is the setting?	a road	a road in a kingdom
What happens first?	A farmer, a soldier, and merchants go around or trip over a stone in road.	King Alvis and Sir Gavin place a stone in road.

"THE STONE IN THE ROAD" (C) 129

Question	"The Stone in the Road: A Story"	"The Stone in the Road: A Play"
What happens second?	A milkmaid moves the stone so no one trips on it.	Farmer and two Soldiers go around or trip over the stone in road.
What happens next?	The king explains he put stone in road.	Milkmaid moves the stone.
What happens at the end?	The king rewards the milkmaid for moving the stone.	King Alvis rewards Milkmaid for moving the stone.

130 "THE STONE IN THE ROAD" (C)

Question	"The Stone in the Road: A Story"	"The Stone in the Road: A Play"
What is the theme?	Do not expect someone else to solve your problems for you.	Do not expect someone else to solve your problems for you.

Answer the question in complete sentences. Use three details to support your answer.

Which version of "The Stone in the Road" do you like better? Why?

Students should indicate which version they prefer and include three details to support their response. Possible answer: I like "The Stone in the Road: A Play" better. First, I like how easy it is to just read the dialogue. I also like the character of Sir Gavin. He is funny. He isn't in the story version. Finally, I like the stage directions because they make it easy to picture what is happening in the story.

"THE STONE IN THE ROAD" (C) 131

Personally, I think a musical version would be neat.

132 "THE STONE IN THE ROAD" (C)

WRAP-UP

Question About "The Stone in the Road"

Students will answer a question to show that they understand the similarities between the two versions of "The Stone in the Road" they read.

Handwriting

Students should gather their handwriting materials and begin where they left off. Remind students to form letters carefully and correctly.

TIP Set a timer to help students stay focused during handwriting practice.

"The Stone in the Road" Wrap-Up

Lesson Overview

ACTIVITY	ACTIVITY TITLE	TIME	ONLINE/OFFLINE
GET READY	Introduction to "The Stone in the Road" Wrap-Up	**1** minute	online
	Read and Record	**8** minutes	online
TRY IT	Plan a Folktale LEARNING COACH CHECK-IN	**30** minutes	offline
	Review "The Stone in the Road"	**20** minutes	online
QUIZ	"The Stone in the Road"	**30** minutes	online
	Spelling List 6	**10** minutes	online
WRAP-UP	More Language Arts Practice	**14** minutes	online
	Handwriting	**8** minutes	offline

Lesson Goals

- Read aloud to practice fluency.
- Plan your own folktale.
- Review what you learned.
- Take a reading quiz.
- Take a spelling quiz.
- Develop letter formation fluency.

MATERIALS

Supplied

- *Summit English Language Arts 3 Activity Book*
  - Plan a Folktale

GET READY

Introduction to "The Stone in the Road" Wrap-Up

Students will read the lesson goals.

Read and Record

Good readers read quickly, smoothly, and with expression. This is called *fluency*. Students will record themselves reading aloud. They will listen to their recording and think about how quick, smooth, and expressive they sound.

TIP Encourage students to rerecord as needed.

TRY IT

Plan a Folktale

Students will complete Plan a Folktale in *Summit English Language Arts 3 Activity Book*. They are not expected to write out their folktale. They should complete the graphic organizer to plan the elements of a folktale as if they are writing it. They should illustrate one event from their folktale in the space provided.

LEARNING COACH CHECK-IN This activity page contains open-ended questions, so it's important that you review students' responses. If students have difficulty coming up with ideas, suggest that they start with the lesson they want to teach others in the folktale.

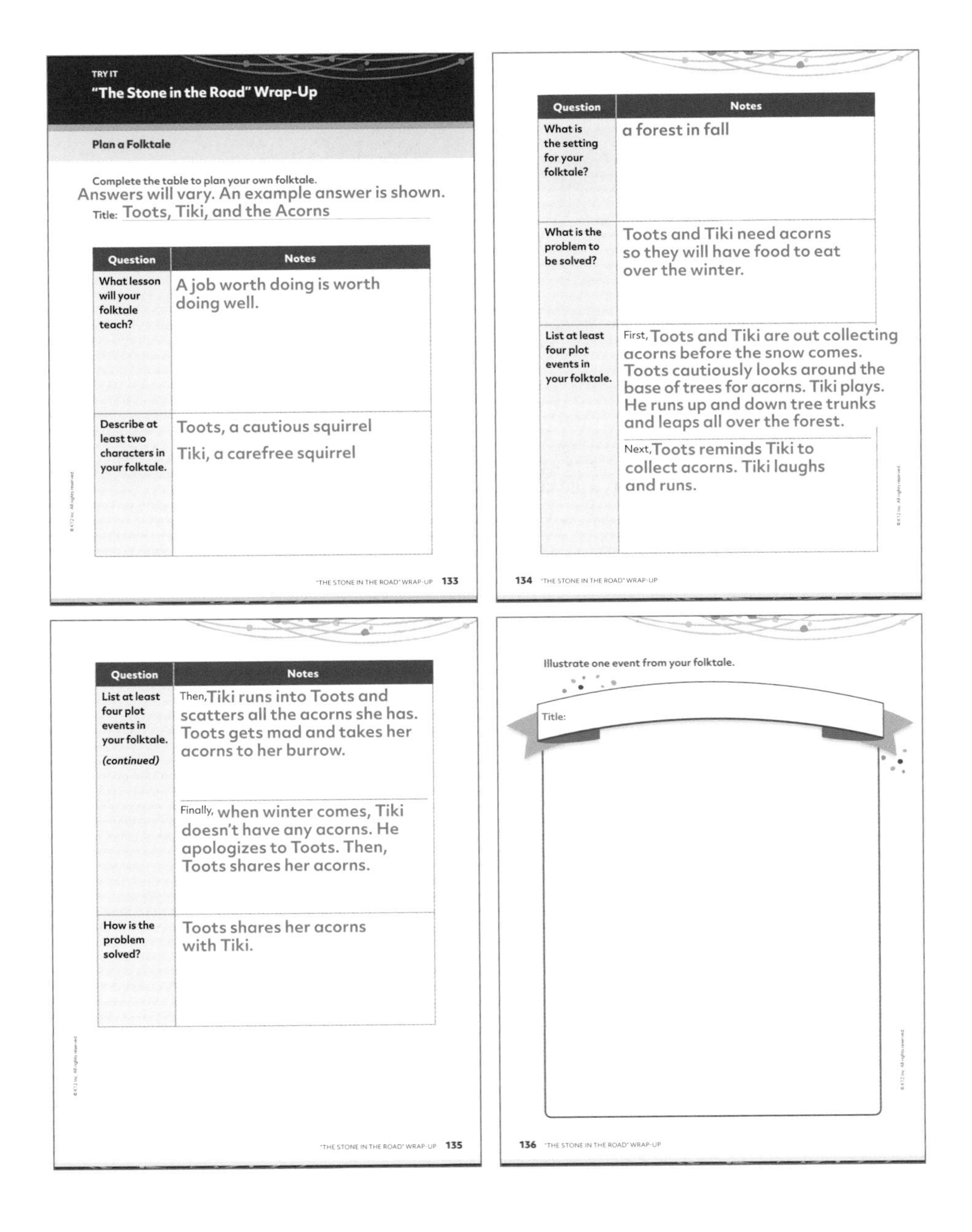

TRY IT

"The Stone in the Road" Wrap-Up

Plan a Folktale

Complete the table to plan your own folktale.

Answers will vary. An example answer is shown.

Title: Toots, Tiki, and the Acorns

Question	Notes
What lesson will your folktale teach?	A job worth doing is worth doing well.
Describe at least two characters in your folktale.	Toots, a cautious squirrel Tiki, a carefree squirrel

"THE STONE IN THE ROAD" WRAP-UP 133

Question	Notes
What is the setting for your folktale?	a forest in fall
What is the problem to be solved?	Toots and Tiki need acorns so they will have food to eat over the winter.
List at least four plot events in your folktale.	First, Toots and Tiki are out collecting acorns before the snow comes. Toots cautiously looks around the base of trees for acorns. Tiki plays. He runs up and down tree trunks and leaps all over the forest. Next, Toots reminds Tiki to collect acorns. Tiki laughs and runs.

134 "THE STONE IN THE ROAD" WRAP-UP

Question	Notes
List at least four plot events in your folktale. *(continued)*	Then, Tiki runs into Toots and scatters all the acorns she has. Toots gets mad and takes her acorns to her burrow. Finally, when winter comes, Tiki doesn't have any acorns. He apologizes to Toots. Then, Toots shares her acorns.
How is the problem solved?	Toots shares her acorns with Tiki.

"THE STONE IN THE ROAD" WRAP-UP 135

Illustrate one event from your folktale.

Title:

136 "THE STONE IN THE ROAD" WRAP-UP

Review "The Stone in the Road"

Students will answer questions to review what they have learned about the parts of a play, identifying and sequencing plot events, explaining how scenes in a play build on one another, and determining theme.

QUIZ

"The Stone in the Road"

Students will complete the "The Stone in the Road" quiz.

Spelling List 6

Students will complete the Spelling List 6 quiz.

WRAP-UP

More Language Arts Practice

Students will practice skills according to their individual needs.

Handwriting

Students should gather their handwriting materials and begin where they left off. Remind students to form letters carefully and correctly.

TIP Set a timer to help students stay focused during handwriting practice.

Narrative Writing: Revising

Lesson Overview

ACTIVITY	ACTIVITY TITLE	TIME	ONLINE/OFFLINE
GET READY	Introduction to Narrative Writing: Revising	**1** minute	online
LEARN AND **TRY IT**	Look Back at a Model Short Story	**10** minutes	online
	Revising a Short Story	**20** minutes	online
	Revise Your Short Story **LEARNING COACH CHECK-IN**	**55** minutes	offline
WRAP-UP	Question About Revising a Short Story	**2** minutes	online
	Handwriting	**8** minutes	offline
	Go Read!	**24** minutes	online or offline

Content Background

Students will continue working on their **short story**. In this lesson, students will **revise** their draft.

In the revising step of the writing process, writers look back at their work and find ways to improve it. They focus on their ideas and organization, not on punctuation, grammar, and so on.

Students will use a checklist to revise their short story. The checklist focuses on ideas (*Do I use dialogue to develop characters and events?*) and organization (*Are my ideas in chronological order?*).

Students may not understand the difference between revising and proofreading. When revising, writers focus on large issues, such as the order of ideas or the amount of dialogue. When proofreading, writers fix errors in grammar, usage, and mechanics, such as spelling or punctuation mistakes. Encourage students to focus on revising during this lesson. In the Narrative Writing: Proofreading lesson, students will proofread their short story.

MATERIALS

Supplied

- *Summit English Language Arts 3 Activity Book*
  - Revise Your Short Story
- Short Story: Revision Feedback Sheet (printout)
- Short Story Instructions (printout)
- handwriting workbook

Also Needed

- folder in which students are storing short story writing assignment pages
- reading material for Go Read!

Advance Preparation

Gather the folder that students are using to store the activity pages related to their short story. The folder should contain the following:

- Model Short Story activity page from Narrative Writing: Prewriting (A)
- Students' completed Brainstorm for Your Short Story activity page from Narrative Writing: Prewriting (A)
- Students' completed Plan Your Short Story activity page from Narrative Writing: Prewriting (B)
- Students' completed draft from Narrative Writing: Drafting (B)

Prior to the Revise Your Short Story activity in this lesson, read students' draft and complete the Short Story: Revision Feedback Sheet.

During the Go Read! activity, students will have the option of using the digital library. Allow extra time for students to make their reading selection, or have students make a selection before beginning the lesson.

KEYWORDS

narrative – a kind of writing that tells a story

revising – the step of the writing process for reviewing and fixing ideas and organization

Lesson Goals

- Use a checklist to revise your short story.
- Develop letter formation fluency.
- Read independently to develop fluency.

GET READY

Introduction to Narrative Writing: Revising

Students will get a glimpse of what they will learn about in the lesson. They will also read the lesson goals and keywords. Have students select each keyword and preview its definition.

Look Back at a Model Short Story

Students will review the key elements of an effective short story.

LEARN AND TRY IT

LEARN Revising a Short Story

Through a guided activity, students will explore how a student revises a short story.

TRY IT Revise Your Short Story

Students will revise their short story using Revise Your Short Story in *Summit English Language Arts 3 Activity Book*, which is a revising checklist. They will need their completed short story draft from Narrative Writing: Drafting (B).

LEARNING COACH CHECK-IN Guide students through the revision process.

1. Gather and use the Short Story: Revision Feedback Sheet that you filled out to guide a discussion with students.
   - Tell students the strengths of their story. Provide positive comments about the message, ideas, description, organization, or other elements that you enjoyed.
   - Walk through your feedback with students. As you discuss the feedback, encourage students to actively revise their draft in response. Reassure students that it's okay to remove or move around ideas and sentences. Students should revise their draft directly on the drafting pages, using the lines they left blank.
2. Have students review their draft once independently, using the revising checklist from the activity book.
   - For students having difficulty recognizing areas they should revise, suggest a revision, and think aloud to model your revising. For example: *This sentence tells about something that happened before the events in that sentence. We could switch the order of those sentences to make sure readers don't get confused. Is there a transition word we can add to make the order of events even clearer?*
3. Make sure students store their revised draft in the folder they are using to organize their writing assignment pages.

TIP Remind students to focus on the checklist questions. Emphasize that they should not worry about spelling, punctuation, grammar, and so on.

NOTE If you or students wish, you can download and print another copy of the Short Story Instructions online.

TRY IT

Narrative Writing: Revising

Revise Your Short Story

Read your short story draft. Then, use the checklist to improve your organization and ideas. Make changes to your short story draft.

Ideas

- ☑ Do I begin by describing the characters and setting, and presenting the problem?
- ☑ Do I develop the plot in the middle paragraphs?
- ☑ Do I end by showing how the characters solve the problem?
- ☑ Do I use dialogue to develop characters and events?
- ☑ Do I *show* instead of *tell*, when possible?

Organization

- ☑ Are my ideas in chronological order?
- ☑ Do I use transitions to show order?

Students should check off each item after they make any necessary changes to their short story draft.

NARRATIVE WRITING: REVISING 137

WRAP-UP

Question About Revising a Short Story

Students will answer a question to show that they understand a key revision skill.

Handwriting

Students should gather their handwriting materials and begin where they left off. Remind students to form letters carefully and correctly.

TIP Set a timer to help students stay focused during handwriting practice.

Go Read!

Students will read for pleasure. They should choose a book or a magazine that interests them, or they may choose a selection from the digital library, linked in the online lesson.

- Have students read aloud a few paragraphs of their selection.
- Then have students read silently for the rest of the time.

SUPPORT Students should make no more than five errors in decoding when they read aloud a few paragraphs of their Go Read! selection. If students struggle or make more than five errors, they need to select a different (and easier) text for the Go Read! activity.

TIP Have students select something to read ahead of time to help them stay focused.

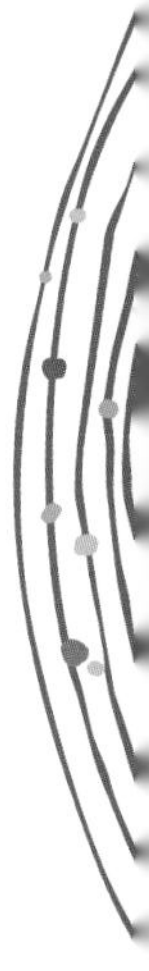

Narrative Writing: Proofreading

Lesson Overview

ACTIVITY	ACTIVITY TITLE	TIME	ONLINE/OFFLINE
GET READY	Introduction to Narrative Writing: Proofreading	**1** minute	online
	Look Back at Writing Sentences	**10** minutes	online
LEARN AND TRY IT	Reference Materials for Spelling	**10** minutes	online
	Practice Using Reference Materials for Spelling	**5** minutes	online
	Proofreading a Short Story	**15** minutes	online
	Proofread Your Short Story LEARNING COACH CHECK-IN	**45** minutes	offline
WRAP-UP	Question About Proofreading a Short Story	**2** minutes	online
	Handwriting	**8** minutes	offline
	Go Read!	**24** minutes	online or offline

Content Background

Students will continue working on their **short story**. In this lesson, students will **proofread** their revised draft.

Writing Process

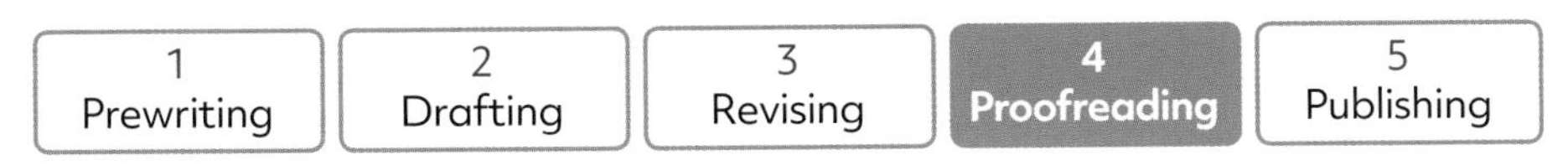

Students will use a checklist to proofread their short story. The checklist focuses on grammar and usage (*Are all sentences complete and correct?*) and mechanics (*Is every word spelled correctly?*).

Proofreading is often thought of as a hunt for errors, but that's not completely accurate. During proofreading, writers evaluate whether the way they use words, capitalization, punctuation, and sentence structure makes their writing as clear as possible. Sometimes, that means fixing an error, like misspelled word. Other times, that means changing something that wasn't necessarily "wrong," such as combining two sentences or using a more appropriate conjunction in a sentence.

Proofreading is sometimes called *editing*.

MATERIALS

Supplied

- *Summit English Language Arts 3 Activity Book*
  - Proofread Your Short Story
- Short Story: Proofreading Feedback Sheet (printout)
- Short Story Instructions (printout)
- handwriting workbook

Also Needed

- folder in which students are storing short story writing assignment pages
- reading material for Go Read!

Advance Preparation

Gather the folder that students are using to store the activity pages related to their short story. The folder should contain the following:

- Model Short Story activity page from Narrative Writing: Prewriting (A)
- Students' completed Brainstorm for Your Short Story activity page from Narrative Writing: Prewriting (A)
- Students' completed Plan Your Short Story activity page from Narrative Writing: Prewriting (B)
- Students' revised draft from Narrative Writing: Revising

Prior to the Proofread Your Short Story activity in this lesson, read students' revised draft and complete the Short Story: Proofreading Feedback Sheet.

During the Go Read! activity, students will have the option of using the digital library. Allow extra time for students to make their reading selection, or have students make a selection before beginning the lesson.

KEYWORDS

narrative – a kind of writing that tells a story

proofreading – the step of the writing process for checking and fixing errors in grammar, punctuation, capitalization, and spelling

Lesson Goals

- Use reference materials to check spelling.
- Use a checklist to proofread your short story.
- Develop letter formation fluency.
- Read independently to develop fluency.

GET READY

Introduction to Narrative Writing: Proofreading

Students will get a glimpse of what they will learn about in the lesson. They will also read the lesson goals and keywords. Have students select each keyword and preview its definition.

Look Back at Writing Sentences

Students will practice writing and identifying correctly written simple, compound, and complex sentences. This skill is a key one that students will use as they proofread their short story.

LEARN AND TRY IT

LEARN Reference Materials for Spelling

Students will learn how to use dictionaries and other reference materials to check spelling. They will also learn how to create personalized spelling references for words they commonly misspell.

TIP Help students create a space to display words that they commonly misspell. A whiteboard would be great for this purpose. An easily accessible digital space, such as a bookmarked digital document, would also be effective.

TRY IT Practice Using Reference Materials for Spelling

Students will practice using reference materials to check spelling.

LEARN Proofreading a Short Story

Through a guided activity, students will explore how a student proofreads a short story.

TRY IT Proofread Your Short Story

Students will proofread their short story using Proofread Your Short Story in *Summit English Language Arts 3 Activity Book*, which is a proofreading checklist. They will need their revised short story from Narrative Writing: Revising.

LEARNING COACH CHECK-IN Guide students through the proofreading process.

1. Have students read their draft aloud, listening for blatant errors such as missing words and incomplete sentences. As students catch errors, have them fix the errors on their draft, using the lines they left blank.
2. Have students review their draft again, using the proofreading checklist from the activity book.
3. Review with students your comments on the Short Story: Proofreading Feedback Sheet. Praise students for the improvements they made, and guide students to recognize any other critical improvements. **It is important that you don't edit students' story for them, but it's appropriate to ask questions such as, *How will readers know whether a character is speaking? What punctuation makes this clear?***
4. Make sure students store their edited draft in the folder they are using to organize their writing assignment pages.

OPTIONAL Have students exchange revised short stories with a peer and use the proofreading checklist from the activity book to proofread each other's short stories.

NOTE If you or students wish, you can download and print another copy of the Short Story Instructions online.

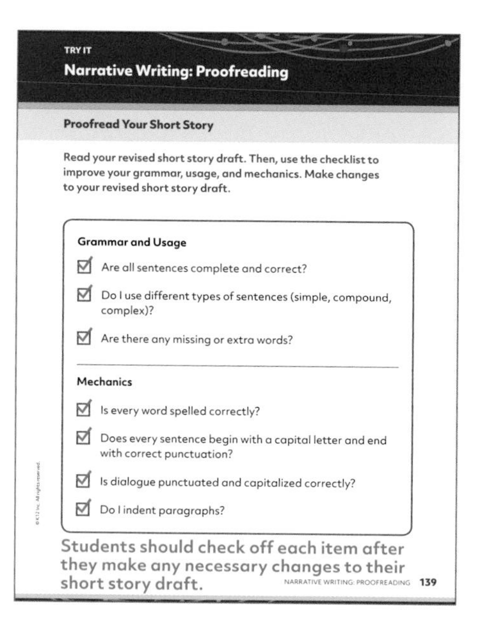
TRY IT

Narrative Writing: Proofreading

Proofread Your Short Story

Read your revised short story draft. Then, use the checklist to improve your grammar, usage, and mechanics. Make changes to your revised short story draft.

Grammar and Usage

- [x] Are all sentences complete and correct?
- [x] Do I use different types of sentences (simple, compound, complex)?
- [x] Are there any missing or extra words?

Mechanics

- [x] Is every word spelled correctly?
- [x] Does every sentence begin with a capital letter and end with correct punctuation?
- [x] Is dialogue punctuated and capitalized correctly?
- [x] Do I indent paragraphs?

Students should check off each item after they make any necessary changes to their short story draft.

NARRATIVE WRITING: PROOFREADING 139

WRAP-UP

Question About Proofreading a Short Story

Students will answer a question to show that they understand a key proofreading skill.

Handwriting

Students should gather their handwriting materials and begin where they left off. Remind students to form letters carefully and correctly.

TIP Set a timer to help students stay focused during handwriting practice.

Go Read!

Students will read for pleasure. They should choose a book or a magazine that interests them, or they may choose a selection from the digital library, linked in the online lesson.

- Have students read aloud a few paragraphs of their selection.
- Then have students read silently for the rest of the time.

SUPPORT Students should make no more than five errors in decoding when they read aloud a few paragraphs of their Go Read! selection. If students struggle or make more than five errors, they need to select a different (and easier) text for the Go Read! activity.

TIP Have students select something to read ahead of time to help them stay focused.

Narrative Writing: Publishing

Lesson Overview

ACTIVITY	ACTIVITY TITLE	TIME	ONLINE/OFFLINE
GET READY	Introduction to Narrative Writing: Publishing	1 minute	online
LEARN AND TRY IT	Publishing a Short Story	15 minutes	online
	Publish Your Short Story	60 minutes	online or offline
WRAP-UP	Turn In Your Short Story	1 minute	online
	More Language Arts Practice	15 minutes	online
	Handwriting	8 minutes	offline
	Go Read!	20 minutes	online or offline

Content Background

Students will continue working on their **short story**. In this lesson, students will **publish** their short story. Then they will submit their completed short story to their teacher.

Writing Process

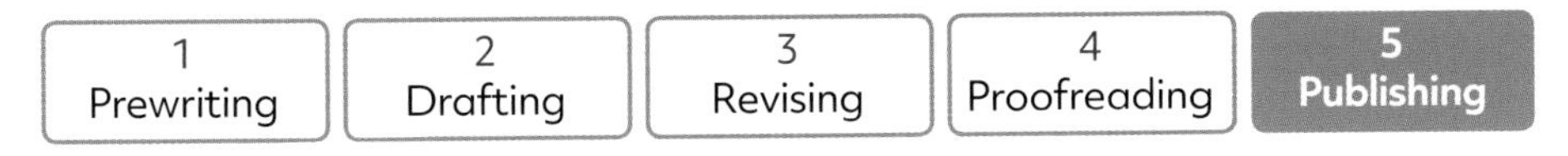

Students may create their final copy using print or cursive handwriting or by typing in a word-processing program. They will complete an activity to review basic word-processing skills.

Advance Preparation

Gather the folder that students are using to store the activity pages related to their short story. The folder should contain the following:

- Model Short Story activity page from Narrative Writing: Prewriting (A)
- Students' completed Brainstorm for Your Short Story activity page from Narrative Writing: Prewriting (A)
- Students' completed Plan Your Short Story activity page from Narrative Writing: Prewriting (B)
- Students' revised and edited draft from Narrative Writing: Proofreading

MATERIALS

Supplied

- Short Story Instructions (printout)
- handwriting workbook

Also Needed

- folder in which students are storing short story writing assignment pages
- reading material for Go Read!

KEYWORDS

narrative – a kind of writing that tells a story

publishing – the step of the writing process for making a clean copy of the piece and sharing it

During the Go Read! activity, students will have the option of using the digital library. Allow extra time for students to make their reading selection, or have students make a selection before beginning the lesson.

Lesson Goals

- Make a clean copy of your short story.
- Submit your short story to your teacher.
- Develop letter formation fluency.
- Read independently to develop fluency.

GET READY

Introduction to Narrative Writing: Publishing

Students will get a glimpse of what they will learn about in the lesson. They will also read the lesson goals and keywords. Have students select each keyword and preview its definition.

LEARN AND TRY IT

LEARN Publishing a Short Story

Students will learn about the publishing step of the writing process. They will also learn some basic keyboarding skills, such as how to center text in a document.

TRY IT Publish Your Short Story

Students will create a final copy of their short story. They should gather their revised and edited draft, and they should create a clean copy that incorporates all the changes they made in the workshop. They may either write their clean copy in print or cursive, or they may type it.

NOTE If you or students wish, you can download and print another copy of the Short Story Instructions online.

WRAP-UP

Turn In Your Short Story

Students will submit their writing assignment to their teacher.

More Language Arts Practice

Students will practice skills according to their individual needs.

Handwriting

Students should gather their handwriting materials and begin where they left off. Remind students to form letters carefully and correctly.

TIP Set a timer to help students stay focused during handwriting practice.

Go Read!

Students will read for pleasure. They should choose a book or a magazine that interests them, or they may choose a selection from the digital library, linked in the online lesson.

- Have students read aloud a few paragraphs of their selection.
- Then have students read silently for the rest of the time.

SUPPORT Students should make no more than five errors in decoding when they read aloud a few paragraphs of their Go Read! selection. If students struggle or make more than five errors, they need to select a different (and easier) text for the Go Read! activity.

TIP Have students select something to read ahead of time to help them stay focused.

"The Tiger, the Brahman, and the Jackal"

Lesson Overview

ACTIVITY	ACTIVITY TITLE	TIME	ONLINE/OFFLINE
GET READY	Introduction to "The Tiger, the Brahman, and the Jackal"	1 minute	online
	Spelling List 7 Pretest LEARNING COACH CHECK-IN	10 minutes	online and offline
	Read and Record	8 minutes	online
	Reading Foundations: Restate What You've Read	5 minutes	online
	Before You Read "The Tiger, the Brahman, and the Jackal"	10 minutes	online
READ	"The Tiger, the Brahman, and the Jackal"	20 minutes	offline
	Check-In: "The Tiger, the Brahman, and the Jackal"	5 minutes	online
LEARN AND TRY IT	Determining Character Traits	12 minutes	online
	Determine How Characters Affect Plot	11 minutes	online
	Apply: Character Traits	10 minutes	online
	Retell the Story LEARNING COACH CHECK-IN	10 minutes	offline
	Practice Words from "The Tiger, the Brahman, and the Jackal"	8 minutes	online
WRAP-UP	Question About "The Tiger, the Brahman, and the Jackal"	2 minutes	online
	Handwriting	8 minutes	offline

Content Background

Students will read a folktale from India. They will learn about character traits and how characters' actions and traits affect plot in the story. They will also retell the story in their own words.

Character traits are qualities that characters have. Steer students away from generalizations like "good" and "bad." Instead, encourage them to think of words that describe the characters' thoughts and actions in the story. For example, a character who takes time to understand something is patient. A character who asks a lot of questions may be curious—or in the case of this story, clever!

MATERIALS

Supplied

- *Summit English Language Arts 3 Expeditions in Reading*
  - "The Tiger, the Brahman, and the Jackal"
- *Summit English Language Arts 3 Activity Book*
  - Spelling List 7 Pretest
  - Retell the Story
- handwriting workbook

"The Tiger, the Brahman, and the Jackal" Synopsis

This folktale is from India. In it, a Brahman (or holy man) comes across a tiger trapped in a cage in the forest. The tiger pleads with the Brahman to release him from the cage. The Brahman refuses, as he is afraid the tiger will eat him when released. The tiger promises not to eat the Brahman, the Brahman sets him free, and the tiger then threatens to eat the Brahman. The Brahman asks for mercy and asks if he can find three things to agree that he should not be eaten, the tiger will not eat him. The tiger agrees, and the Brahman asks the tree, the buffalo, and the road what they think. None of them agree with the Brahman, and as he is preparing for his fate, a jackal walks up. The jackal tricks the tiger back into the cage and slams and locks the door.

KEYWORDS

character trait – a quality that a person has

folktale – a story, which usually teaches a lesson important to a culture, that is passed down through many generations

Lesson Goals

- Take a spelling pretest.
- Read aloud to practice fluency.
- Read "The Tiger, the Brahman, and the Jackal."
- Describe characters' traits.
- Explain how characters' actions contribute to the plot of a story.
- Retell a story.
- Practice vocabulary words.
- Develop letter formation fluency.

GET READY

Introduction to "The Tiger, the Brahman, and the Jackal"

Students will get a glimpse of what they will learn about in the lesson. They will also read the lesson goals and keywords. Have students select each keyword and preview its definition.

Spelling List 7 Pretest

Students will take a spelling pretest and learn a new spelling pattern.

LEARNING COACH CHECK-IN Have students turn to Spelling List 7 Pretest in *Summit English Language Arts 3 Activity Book* and open the online Spelling Pretest activity. Online, students will listen to the spelling word, type the word

in the space indicated, and then check their answer. In the activity book, students will write the correct spelling of the word in the tables provided and indicate with a ✓ or an ✗ if they spelled the word correctly or incorrectly online. Students will repeat this process with the remaining words.

As needed, help students with the interaction between the online activity and the activity book page until they become comfortable with what they need to do. As students practice their spelling words throughout the workshop, they should pay special attention to words they spelled incorrectly on the pretest.

This is the complete list of words students will be tested on.

Words with Long *e* Sound		
agreed	eclipse	probably
athlete	even	real
between	field	safety
body	least	steel
chief	leave	teaching
complete	melody	

NOTE Have students keep their completed activity page in a safe place so they can refer to it later.

GET READY

"The Tiger, the Brahman, and the Jackal"

Spelling List 7 Pretest

1. Open the Spelling Pretest activity online. Listen to the first spelling word. Type the word. Check your answer.
2. Write the correct spelling of the word in the Word column of the Spelling Pretest table.

	Word	✓	✗
1	blindfold		

3. Put a check mark in the ✓ column if you spelled the word correctly online.

	Word	✓	✗
1	blindfold	✓	

Put an X in the ✗ column if you spelled the word incorrectly online.

	Word	✓	✗
1	blindfold		X

4. Repeat Steps 1–3 for the remaining words in the Spelling Pretest.

"THE TIGER, THE BRAHMAN, AND THE JACKAL" 141

"The Tiger, the Brahman, and the Jackal"

Spelling List 7 Pretest

Write each spelling word in the Word column, making sure to spell it correctly.

	Word	✓	✗		Word	✓	✗
1	agreed			10	least		
2	athlete			11	leave		
3	between			12	melody		
4	body			13	probably		
5	chief			14	real		
6	complete			15	safety		
7	eclipse			16	steel		
8	even			17	teaching		
9	field						

Students should write the correct spelling of each word from the pretest and use the ✓ and X columns to indicate whether they spelled each word correctly or incorrectly online.

142 "THE TIGER, THE BRAHMAN, AND THE JACKAL"

Read and Record

Good readers read quickly, smoothly, and with expression. This is called *fluency*. Students will record themselves reading aloud. They will listen to their recording and think about how quick, smooth, and expressive they sound.

TIP Encourage students to rerecord as needed.

Reading Foundations: Restate What You've Read

Reading Foundations activities serve to remind students of basic reading skills and reading behaviors mastered in earlier grades. The activities cover topics such as advanced decoding skills and various strategies for improving comprehension.

Before You Read "The Tiger, the Brahman, and the Jackal"

Students will be introduced to some key vocabulary words that they will encounter in the upcoming reading, learn some important background related to the reading, and answer a question to help them set a purpose for their reading.

NOTE Students will make a prediction before reading the folktale.

READ

"The Tiger, the Brahman, and the Jackal"

Students will read "The Tiger, the Brahman, and the Jackal" in *Expeditions in Reading*.

Check-In: "The Tiger, the Brahman, and the Jackal"

Students will answer several questions to demonstrate their comprehension of "The Tiger, the Brahman, and the Jackal."

LEARN AND TRY IT

LEARN Determining Character Traits

Students will learn how to determine character traits for each main character in the story.

TRY IT Determine How Characters Affect Plot

Students will determine how characters' traits and actions affect the plot in the story.

TRY IT Apply: Character Traits

Students will apply to a new work what they've learned about determining character traits.

TRY IT Retell the Story

Students will complete Retell the Story in *Summit English Language Arts 3 Activity Book*.

LEARNING COACH CHECK-IN This activity page contains open-ended questions, so it's important that you review students' responses. Give students feedback, using the sample answers provided to guide you.

TIP Remind students that when they retell a story, they should use their own words. They should also retell the events in the story in the order in which they happened. If students need help, ask them, *What happened first in the story?* and *Then what happened?* to help them remember the sequence of events.

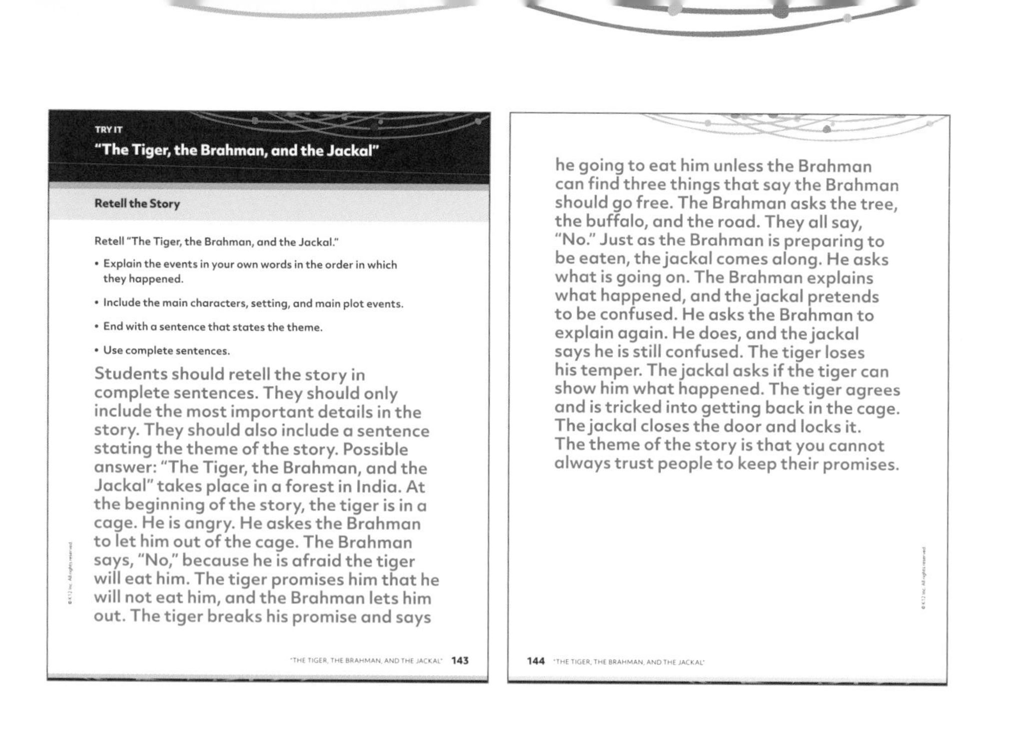
TRY IT
"The Tiger, the Brahman, and the Jackal"

Retell the Story

Retell "The Tiger, the Brahman, and the Jackal."

- Explain the events in your own words in the order in which they happened.
- Include the main characters, setting, and main plot events.
- End with a sentence that states the theme.
- Use complete sentences.

Students should retell the story in complete sentences. They should only include the most important details in the story. They should also include a sentence stating the theme of the story. Possible answer: "The Tiger, the Brahman, and the Jackal" takes place in a forest in India. At the beginning of the story, the tiger is in a cage. He is angry. He askes the Brahman to let him out of the cage. The Brahman says, "No," because he is afraid the tiger will eat him. The tiger promises him that he will not eat him, and the Brahman lets him out. The tiger breaks his promise and says he going to eat him unless the Brahman can find three things that say the Brahman should go free. The Brahman asks the tree, the buffalo, and the road. They all say, "No." Just as the Brahman is preparing to be eaten, the jackal comes along. He asks what is going on. The Brahman explains what happened, and the jackal pretends to be confused. He asks the Brahman to explain again. He does, and the jackal says he is still confused. The tiger loses his temper. The jackal asks if the tiger can show him what happened. The tiger agrees and is tricked into getting back in the cage. The jackal closes the door and locks it. The theme of the story is that you cannot always trust people to keep their promises.

"THE TIGER, THE BRAHMAN, AND THE JACKAL" 143

144 "THE TIGER, THE BRAHMAN, AND THE JACKAL"

TRY IT **Practice Words from "The Tiger, the Brahman, and the Jackal"**

Students will answer questions to demonstrate their understanding of the vocabulary words from the reading.

WRAP-UP

Question About "The Tiger, the Brahman, and the Jackal"

Students will answer a question to show that they understand the traits characters have in the story.

Handwriting

Students should gather their handwriting materials and begin where they left off. Remind students to form letters carefully and correctly.

TIP Set a timer to help students stay focused during handwriting practice.

"The Tiger, the Brahman, and the Jackal" Wrap-Up

Lesson Overview

ACTIVITY	ACTIVITY TITLE	TIME	ONLINE/OFFLINE
GET READY	Introduction: "The Tiger, the Brahman, and the Jackal" Wrap-Up	**1** minute	online
	Spelling List 7 Activity Bank	**10** minutes	offline
	Read and Record	**8** minutes	online
TRY IT	What Would Change? LEARNING COACH CHECK-IN	**25** minutes	offline
	Review "The Tiger, the Brahman, and the Jackal"	**20** minutes	online
QUIZ	"The Tiger, the Brahman, and the Jackal"	**30** minutes	online
WRAP-UP	More Language Arts Practice	**18** minutes	online
	Handwriting	**8** minutes	offline

Advance Preparation

Gather students' completed Spelling List 7 Pretest activity page from "The Tiger, the Brahman, and the Jackal." Students will refer to this page during Get Ready: Spelling List 7 Activity Bank.

Lesson Goals

- Practice all spelling words offline.
- Read aloud to practice fluency.
- Write about how a change in a character's traits would change the outcome of a story.
- Review what you learned.
- Take a reading quiz.
- Develop letter formation fluency.

MATERIALS

Supplied

- *Summit English Language Arts 3 Activity Book*
  - Spelling List 7 Activity Bank
  - What Would Change?
- handwriting workbook

Also Needed

- completed Spelling List 7 Pretest activity page from "The Tiger, the Brahman, and the Jackal"

GET READY

Introduction: "The Tiger, the Brahman, and the Jackal" Wrap-Up

Students will read the lesson goals.

Spelling List 7 Activity Bank

Students will practice all spelling words from the workshop by completing Spelling List 7 Activity Bank from *Summit English Language Arts 3 Activity Book*. Make sure students have their completed Spelling List 7 Pretest activity page from "The Tiger, the Brahman, and the Jackal" to refer to during this activity.

Remind students to pay special attention to words they spelled incorrectly on the Spelling Pretest.

GET READY

"The Tiger, the Brahman, and the Jackal" Wrap-Up

Spelling List 7 Activity Bank

Circle any words in the box that you did not spell correctly on your pretest. Choose one activity to do with your circled words. Do as much of the activity as you can in the time given.

Did you spell all the words on the pretest correctly? Do the one activity with as many spelling words as you can.

agreed	chief	field	melody	safety
athlete	complete	least	probably	steel
between	eclipse	leave	real	teaching
body	even			

Spelling Activity Choices

Hidden Words

1. Draw a picture. "Hide" as many of your spelling words as you can inside the picture.
2. See if others can find the words you hid in the picture.

"THE TIGER, THE BRAHMAN, AND THE JACKAL" WRAP-UP 145

Triangle Spelling

Write each of your spelling words in a triangle.

d
do
dog

Ghost Words

1. Use a white crayon to write each of your spelling words.
2. Write over the words in white crayon with a colored marker.

146 "THE TIGER, THE BRAHMAN, AND THE JACKAL" WRAP-UP

Complete the activity that you chose.

My chosen activity: ____________

Students should use this page to complete all steps in their chosen activity.

"THE TIGER, THE BRAHMAN, AND THE JACKAL" WRAP-UP 147

Read and Record

Good readers read quickly, smoothly, and with expression. This is called *fluency*. Students will record themselves reading aloud. They will listen to their recording and think about how quick, smooth, and expressive they sound.

TIP Encourage students to rerecord as needed.

TRY IT

What Would Change?

Students will complete What Would Change? in *Summit English Language Arts 3 Activity Book*.

LEARNING COACH CHECK-IN This activity page contains open-ended questions, so it's important that you review students' responses. Give students feedback, using the sample answers provided to guide you.

SUPPORT If students need help coming up with alternate character traits, consider asking them to identify what the opposite trait might be. For example, students might imagine a character who is optimistic, or has a positive outlook on life, changing to a pessimist, who has a negative outlook on life.

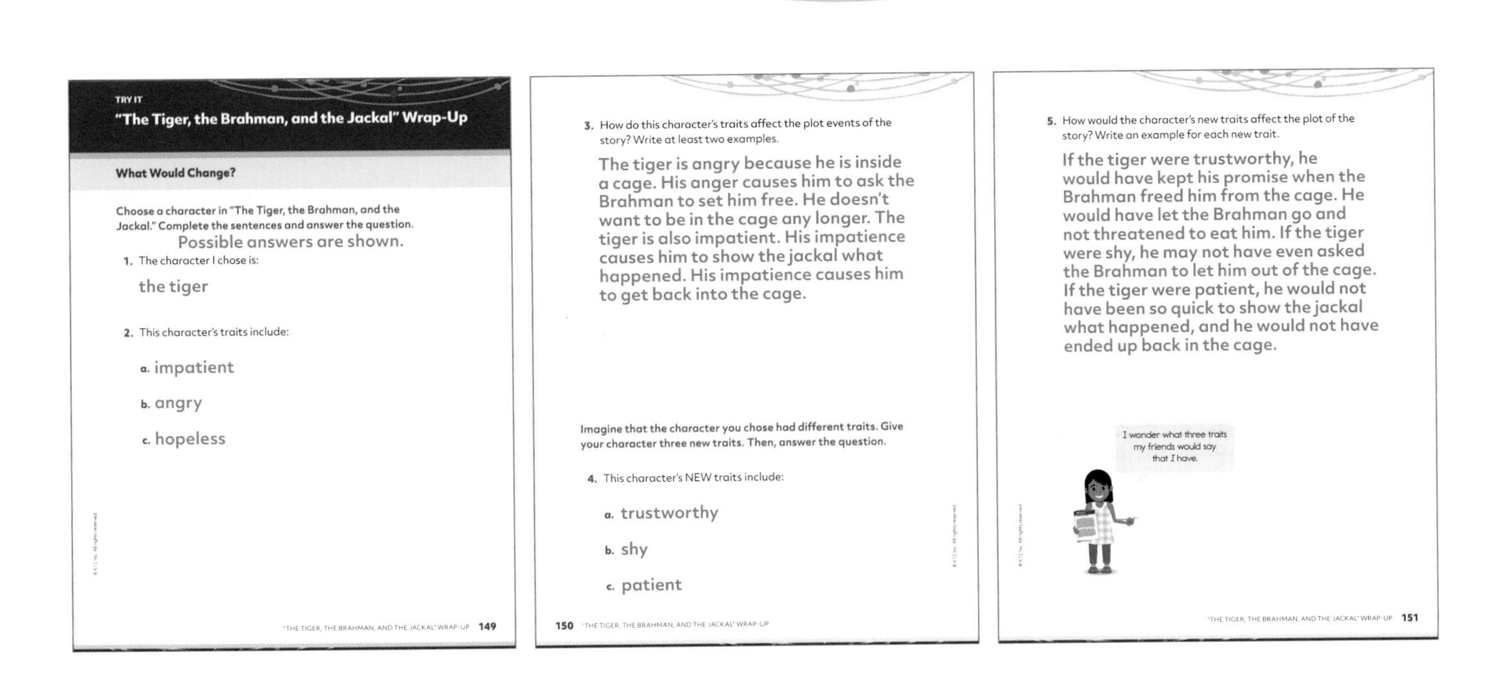
TRY IT
"The Tiger, the Brahman, and the Jackal" Wrap-Up

What Would Change?

Choose a character in "The Tiger, the Brahman, and the Jackal." Complete the sentences and answer the question.
Possible answers are shown.

1. The character I chose is:
the tiger

2. This character's traits include:
a. impatient
b. angry
c. hopeless

"THE TIGER, THE BRAHMAN, AND THE JACKAL" WRAP-UP 149

3. How do this character's traits affect the plot events of the story? Write at least two examples.
The tiger is angry because he is inside a cage. His anger causes him to ask the Brahman to set him free. He doesn't want to be in the cage any longer. The tiger is also impatient. His impatience causes him to show the jackal what happened. His impatience causes him to get back into the cage.

Imagine that the character you chose had different traits. Give your character three new traits. Then, answer the question.

4. This character's NEW traits include:
a. trustworthy
b. shy
c. patient

150 "THE TIGER, THE BRAHMAN, AND THE JACKAL" WRAP-UP

5. How would the character's new traits affect the plot of the story? Write an example for each new trait.
If the tiger were trustworthy, he would have kept his promise when the Brahman freed him from the cage. He would have let the Brahman go and not threatened to eat him. If the tiger were shy, he may not have even asked the Brahman to let him out of the cage. If the tiger were patient, he would not have been so quick to show the jackal what happened, and he would not have ended up back in the cage.

"THE TIGER, THE BRAHMAN, AND THE JACKAL" WRAP-UP 151

Review "The Tiger, the Brahman, and the Jackal"

Students will answer questions to review what they have learned about themes or lessons in the story, character traits and actions, and how traits and actions affect what happens in a story's plot.

QUIZ

"The Tiger, the Brahman, and the Jackal"

Students will complete the "The Tiger, the Brahman, and the Jackal" quiz.

WRAP-UP

More Language Arts Practice

Students will practice skills according to their individual needs.

Handwriting

Students should gather their handwriting materials and begin where they left off. Remind students to form letters carefully and correctly.

TIP Set a timer to help students stay focused during handwriting practice.

"Bruce and the Spider"

Lesson Overview

ACTIVITY	ACTIVITY TITLE	TIME	ONLINE/OFFLINE
GET READY	Introduction to "Bruce and the Spider"	**1** minute	🖥
	Spelling List 7 Review Game	**10** minutes	🖥
	Read and Record	**8** minutes	🖥
	Reading Foundations: Connect	**5** minutes	🖥
	Before You Read "Bruce and the Spider"	**5** minutes	🖥
READ	"Bruce and the Spider"	**23** minutes	📄
	Check-In: "Bruce and the Spider"	**5** minutes	🖥
LEARN AND TRY IT	Problem, Solution, and Character Traits	**10** minutes	🖥
	Determine Character Traits and Actions	**10** minutes	🖥
	Apply: Character's Actions	**15** minutes	🖥
	Describe Robert Bruce **LEARNING COACH CHECK-IN**	**10** minutes	📄
	Practice Words from "Bruce and the Spider"	**8** minutes	🖥
WRAP-UP	Question About "Bruce and the Spider"	**2** minutes	🖥
	Handwriting	**8** minutes	📄

Content Background

Students will read a *legend*, which is a story that is passed down through generations. A legend teaches the values of a culture; it may be about historical events or people. This legend is about Robert Bruce, a medieval king of Scotland who led his army in a fight against England to free Scotland from English rule. After many battles in which the Scottish army was outnumbered, he eventually triumphed and was made king of Scotland. As king, he was called Robert I of Scotland.

MATERIALS

Supplied

- *Summit English Language Arts 3 Expeditions in Reading*
  - "Bruce and the Spider"
- *Summit English Language Arts 3 Activity Book*
  - Describe Robert Bruce
- handwriting workbook

"Bruce and the Spider" Synopsis

In this legend, Robert Bruce, a king of Scotland from long ago, is ready to give up the fight against his enemies. In his hideout, Bruce sees a spider repeatedly try to build a web. Bruce is inspired by the spider's persistence and decides to fight on.

Lesson Goals

- Practice all spelling words online.
- Read aloud to practice fluency.
- Read "Bruce and the Spider."
- Identify the problem and solution in a legend.
- Determine and describe Robert Bruce's character traits and actions.
- Practice vocabulary words.
- Develop letter formation fluency.

KEYWORDS

legend – a story that is passed down for many years to teach the values of a culture; a legend may or may not contain some true events or people

main character – an important person, animal, or other being who is central to the plot

problem – an issue a character must solve in a story

solution – how a character solves a problem in a story

GET READY

Introduction to "Bruce and the Spider"

Students will get a glimpse of what they will learn about in the lesson. They will also read the lesson goals and keywords. Have students select each keyword and preview its definition.

Spelling List 7 Review Game

Students will practice all spelling words from the workshop.

Read and Record

Good readers read quickly, smoothly, and with expression. This is called *fluency*. Students will record themselves reading aloud. They will listen to their recording and think about how quick, smooth, and expressive they sound.

TIP Encourage students to rerecord as needed.

Reading Foundations: Connect

Reading Foundations activities serve to remind students of basic reading skills and reading behaviors mastered in earlier grades. The activities cover topics such as advanced decoding skills and various strategies for improving comprehension.

Before You Read "Bruce and the Spider"

Students will be introduced to some key vocabulary words that they will encounter in the upcoming reading.

READ

"Bruce and the Spider"

Students will read "Bruce and the Spider" in *Expeditions in Reading*.

Check-In: "Bruce and the Spider"

Students will answer several questions to demonstrate their comprehension of "Bruce and the Spider."

LEARN AND TRY IT

LEARN Problem, Solution, and Character Traits

Students will learn about the problem posed in the legend and how Robert Bruce solves the problem.

TIP Students may ask about the difference between folktales and legends. Folktales feature talking animals and often have a "trickster" component to them. Legends, on the other hand, are often based on people and events from history. Both folktales and legends tend to have histories of being passed down from person to person. Most importantly, both types of stories teach a valuable life lesson that students will be able to carry with them.

TRY IT Determine Character Traits and Actions

Students will determine Robert Bruce's character traits at the beginning and end of the legend.

TRY IT Apply: Character's Actions

Students will apply to a new work what they've learned about how a character's actions influence the plot in a story.

TRY IT Describe Robert Bruce

Students will complete Describe Robert Bruce in *Summit English Language Arts 3 Activity Book*.

LEARNING COACH CHECK-IN This activity page contains open-ended questions, so it's important that you review students' responses. Give students feedback, using the sample answers provided to guide you.

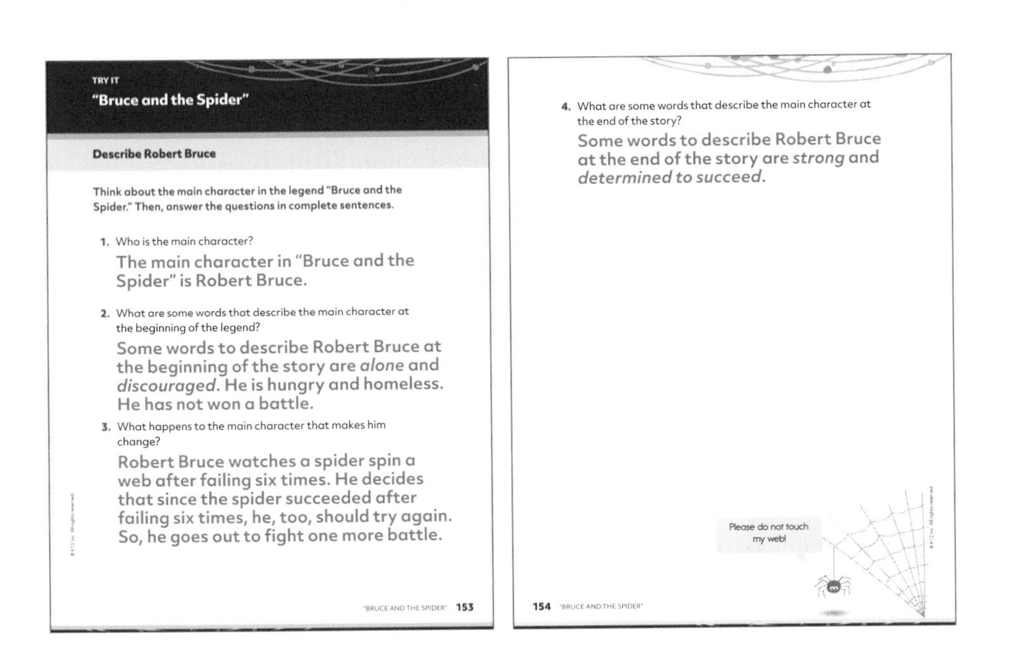
TRY IT
"Bruce and the Spider"

Describe Robert Bruce

Think about the main character in the legend "Bruce and the Spider." Then, answer the questions in complete sentences.

1. Who is the main character?
   The main character in "Bruce and the Spider" is Robert Bruce.
2. What are some words that describe the main character at the beginning of the legend?
   Some words to describe Robert Bruce at the beginning of the story are *alone* and *discouraged*. He is hungry and homeless. He has not won a battle.
3. What happens to the main character that makes him change?
   Robert Bruce watches a spider spin a web after failing six times. He decides that since the spider succeeded after failing six times, he, too, should try again. So, he goes out to fight one more battle.

"BRUCE AND THE SPIDER" 153

4. What are some words that describe the main character at the end of the story?
   Some words to describe Robert Bruce at the end of the story are *strong* and *determined to succeed.*

154 "BRUCE AND THE SPIDER"

TRY IT **Practice Words from "Bruce and the Spider"**

Students will answer questions to demonstrate their understanding of the vocabulary words from the reading.

WRAP-UP

Question About "Bruce and the Spider"

Students will answer a question to show that they understand what a legend is.

Handwriting

Students should gather their handwriting materials and begin where they left off. Remind students to form letters carefully and correctly.

TIP Set a timer to help students stay focused during handwriting practice.

"Bruce and the Spider" Wrap-Up

Lesson Overview

ACTIVITY	ACTIVITY TITLE	TIME	ONLINE/OFFLINE
GET READY	Introduction to "Bruce and the Spider" Wrap-Up	**1** minute	online
	Read and Record	**8** minutes	online
TRY IT	Write About a Lesson Learned LEARNING COACH CHECK-IN	**33** minutes	offline
	Review "Bruce and the Spider"	**20** minutes	online
QUIZ	"Bruce and the Spider"	**30** minutes	online
	Spelling List 7	**10** minutes	online
WRAP-UP	More Language Arts Practice	**10** minutes	online
	Handwriting	**8** minutes	offline

Lesson Goals

- Read aloud to practice fluency.
- Write about character traits and a lesson learned.
- Review what you learned.
- Take a reading quiz.
- Take a spelling quiz.
- Develop letter formation fluency.

MATERIALS

Supplied

- *Summit English Language Arts 3 Activity Book*
  - Write About a Lesson Learned

GET READY

Introduction to "Bruce and the Spider" Wrap-Up

Students will read the lesson goals.

Read and Record

Good readers read quickly, smoothly, and with expression. This is called *fluency*. Students will record themselves reading aloud. They will listen to their recording and think about how quick, smooth, and expressive they sound.

TIP Encourage students to rerecord as needed.

TRY IT

Write About a Lesson Learned

Students will complete Write About a Lesson Learned in *Summit English Language Arts 3 Activity Book*.

TIP Students should use the graphic organizer in the first part of the activity page to complete the second part. Remind students to look back at the text to find supporting details to complete the page.

LEARNING COACH CHECK-IN This activity page contains open-ended questions, so it's important that you review students' responses. Give students feedback, using the sample answers provided to guide you.

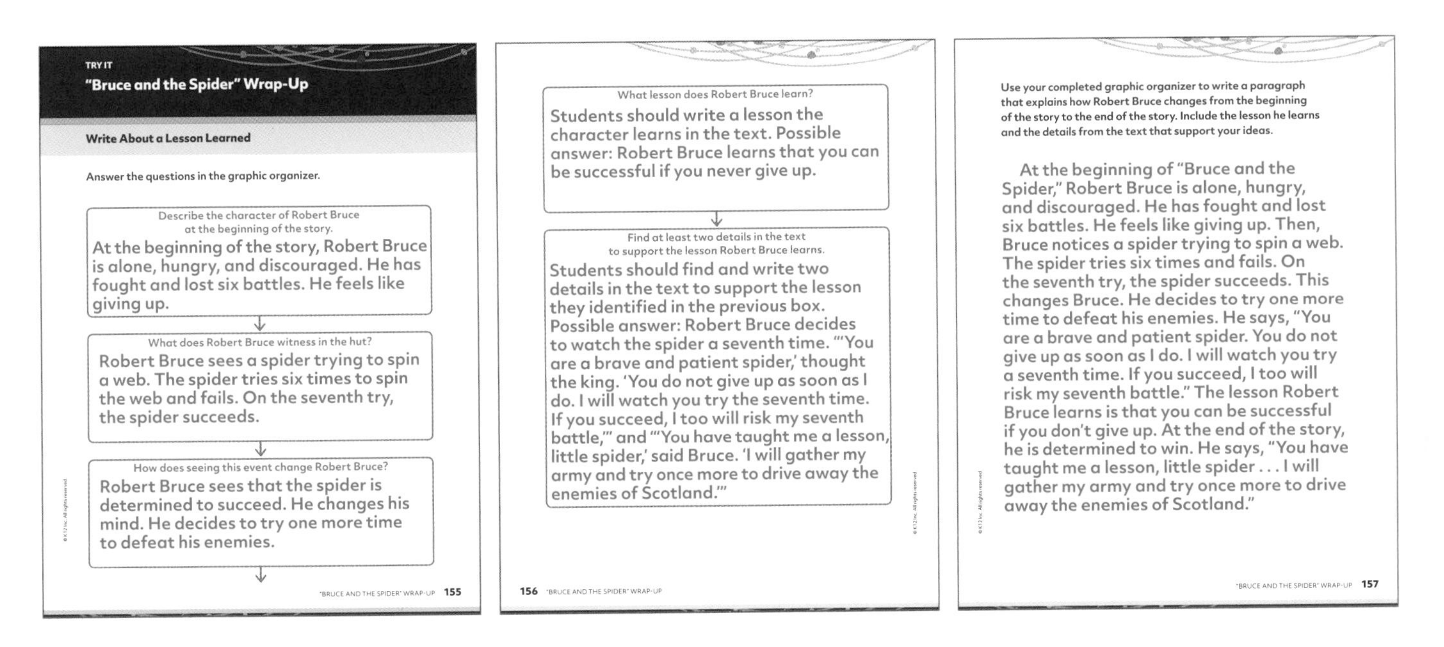
TRY IT

"Bruce and the Spider" Wrap-Up

Write About a Lesson Learned

Answer the questions in the graphic organizer.

Describe the character of Robert Bruce at the beginning of the story.

At the beginning of the story, Robert Bruce is alone, hungry, and discouraged. He has fought and lost six battles. He feels like giving up.

What does Robert Bruce witness in the hut?

Robert Bruce sees a spider trying to spin a web. The spider tries six times to spin the web and fails. On the seventh try, the spider succeeds.

How does seeing this event change Robert Bruce?

Robert Bruce sees that the spider is determined to succeed. He changes his mind. He decides to try one more time to defeat his enemies.

"BRUCE AND THE SPIDER" WRAP-UP 155

What lesson does Robert Bruce learn?

Students should write a lesson the character learns in the text. Possible answer: Robert Bruce learns that you can be successful if you never give up.

Find at least two details in the text to support the lesson Robert Bruce learns.

Students should find and write two details in the text to support the lesson they identified in the previous box. Possible answer: Robert Bruce decides to watch the spider a seventh time. "'You are a brave and patient spider,' thought the king. 'You do not give up as soon as I do. I will watch you try the seventh time. If you succeed, I too will risk my seventh battle,'" and "'You have taught me a lesson, little spider,' said Bruce. 'I will gather my army and try once more to drive away the enemies of Scotland.'"

156 "BRUCE AND THE SPIDER" WRAP-UP

Use your completed graphic organizer to write a paragraph that explains how Robert Bruce changes from the beginning of the story to the end of the story. Include the lesson he learns and the details from the text that support your ideas.

At the beginning of "Bruce and the Spider," Robert Bruce is alone, hungry, and discouraged. He has fought and lost six battles. He feels like giving up. Then, Bruce notices a spider trying to spin a web. The spider tries six times and fails. On the seventh try, the spider succeeds. This changes Bruce. He decides to try one more time to defeat his enemies. He says, "You are a brave and patient spider. You do not give up as soon as I do. I will watch you try a seventh time. If you succeed, I too will risk my seventh battle." The lesson Robert Bruce learns is that you can be successful if you don't give up. At the end of the story, he is determined to win. He says, "You have taught me a lesson, little spider . . . I will gather my army and try once more to drive away the enemies of Scotland."

"BRUCE AND THE SPIDER" WRAP-UP 157

TRY IT Review "Bruce and the Spider"

Students will answer questions to review what they have learned about determining lessons and theme in a text, describing character traits, and explaining how characters' actions and traits influence what happens in a text.

QUIZ

"Bruce and the Spider"

Students will complete the "Bruce and the Spider" quiz.

Spelling List 7

Students will complete the Spelling List 7 quiz.

WRAP-UP

More Language Arts Practice

Students will practice skills according to their individual needs.

Handwriting

Students should gather their handwriting materials and begin where they left off. Remind students to form letters carefully and correctly.

TIP Set a timer to help students stay focused during handwriting practice.

Big Ideas: Respond to a Prompt

Lesson Overview

Big Ideas lessons provide students the opportunity to further apply the knowledge acquired and skills learned throughout the unit workshops. Each Big Ideas lesson consists of these parts:

1. **Cumulative Review:** Students keep their skills fresh by reviewing prior content.
2. **Preview:** Students practice answering the types of questions they will commonly find on standardized tests.
3. **Synthesis:** Students complete an assignment that allows them to connect and apply what they have learned. Synthesis assignments vary throughout the course.

   In the Synthesis portion of this Big Ideas lesson, students will respond to an essay prompt based on reading selections. To respond meaningfully, students will need to use their own ideas as well as examples from the readings. Students' writing will be assessed in four categories: purpose and content; structure and organization; language and word choice; and grammar, usage, and mechanics.

   LEARNING COACH CHECK-IN This is a graded assessment. Make sure students complete, review, and submit the assignment to their teacher.

All materials needed for this lesson are linked online and not provided in the activity book.

MATERIALS

Supplied

- Respond to a Prompt (printout)

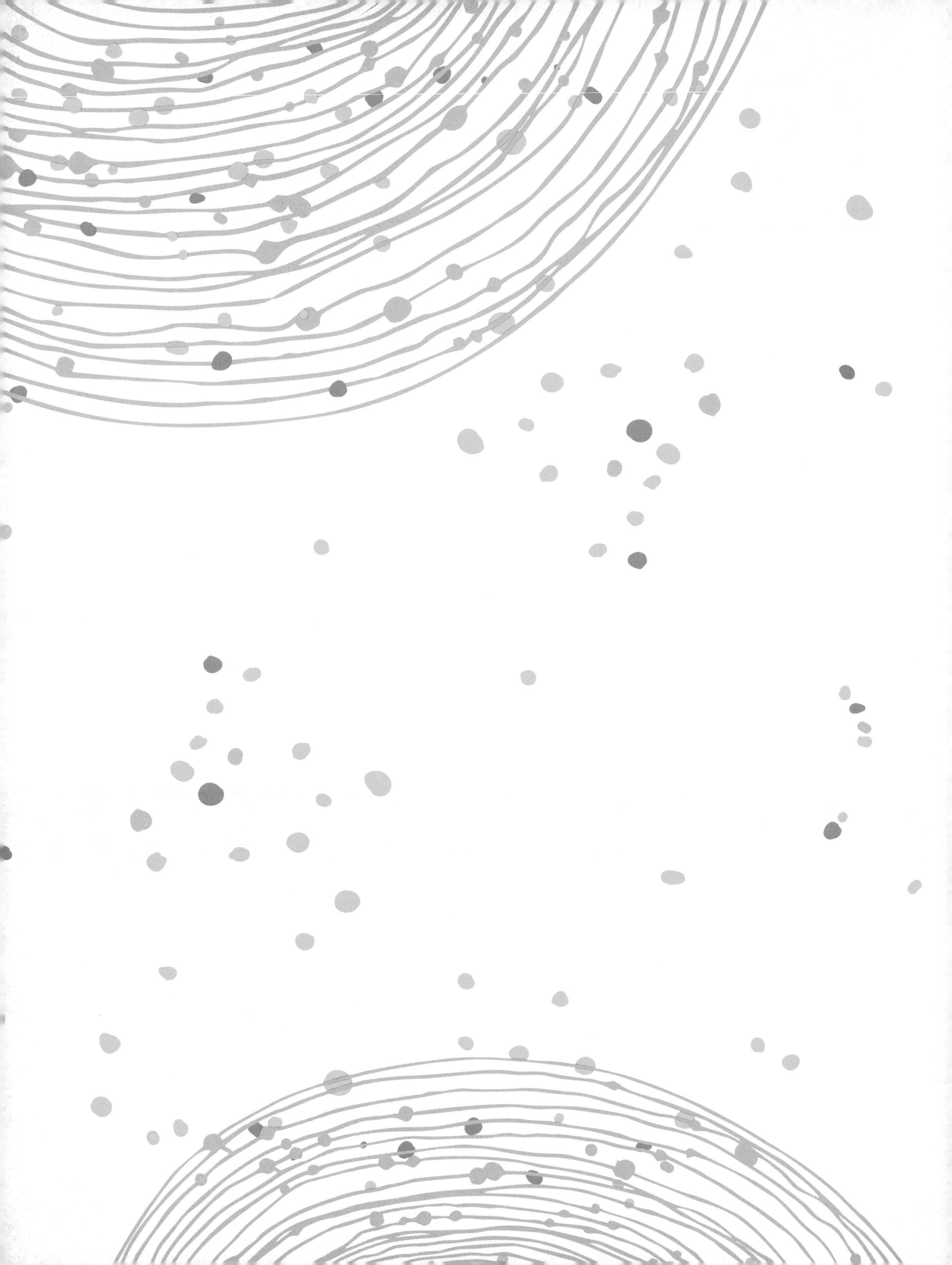

Snowy Days

Dictionary Skills

Lesson Overview

ACTIVITY	ACTIVITY TITLE	TIME	ONLINE/OFFLINE
GET READY	Introduction to Dictionary Skills	2 minutes	online
	Look Back at Beginning Dictionaries	4 minutes	online
LEARN AND TRY IT	Dictionary Skills	10 minutes	online
	Practice Using Dictionary Skills	10 minutes	online
	Apply: Dictionary Skills LEARNING COACH CHECK-IN	15 minutes	offline
	Review Dictionary Skills	15 minutes	online
QUIZ	Dictionary Skills	15 minutes	online
WRAP-UP	More Language Arts Practice	19 minutes	online
	Go Write! What Do You Do Well?	15 minutes	offline
	Go Read!	15 minutes	online or offline

Content Background

A dictionary is a helpful resource for learning the meaning of unknown words. Students will learn about putting words in *alphabetical order*, or alphabetizing, and how to use this skill to find words in a dictionary. When alphabetizing words that begin with the same letter, look at the second letter to put the words in order. Likewise, if words begin with the same first two letters, look at the third letter to alphabetize them.

Words in Alphabetical Order:

rebel
recall
reduce
regular
responsible
retreat

MATERIALS

Supplied

- *Summit English Language Arts 3 Activity Book*
  - Apply: Dictionary Skills
  - Go Write! What Do You Do Well?

Also Needed

- dictionary
- reading material for Go Read!

KEYWORDS

alphabetical order – a way to put things in order according to the alphabet; Example: in alphabetical order, *at* comes before *bat*, which comes before *cat*

Advance Preparation

During the Go Read! activity, students will have the option of using the digital library. Allow extra time for students to make their reading selection, or have students make a selection before beginning the lesson.

Lesson Goals

- Practice vocabulary words.
- Learn to alphabetize to the third letter, and practice putting words in alphabetical order.
- Look up words in a dictionary and write their definitions.
- Take the Dictionary Skills quiz.
- Freewrite about a topic to develop writing fluency and practice letter formation.
- Read independently to develop fluency.

GET READY

Introduction to Dictionary Skills

After a quick introductory activity, students will read the lesson goals and keywords. Have students select each keyword and preview its definition.

Look Back at Beginning Dictionaries

Students will practice the prerequisite skill of understanding beginning dictionaries.

LEARN AND TRY IT

LEARN Dictionary Skills

Students will be introduced to the vocabulary words for the lesson. They will learn how to use the vocabulary words by seeing them in context. Then they will learn about dictionaries and how to use them.

TRY IT Practice Using Dictionary Skills

Students will practice alphabetizing words.

TRY IT Apply: Dictionary Skills

Students will complete Apply: Dictionary Skills in *Summit English Language Arts 3 Activity Book*. They will practice using dictionary skills by alphabetizing words and finding and writing definitions.

OPTIONAL Provide students with several more words to add to their alphabetized list. Make sure to include words that require students to alphabetize up to the third letter.

Examples: afford, annoyed, arrive, desk, develop, dust

LEARNING COACH CHECK-IN Make sure students use a dictionary, either a print or online reference, to complete this activity. If necessary, help students find the appropriate resource. Review students' responses. Give students feedback, using the sample answers provided to guide you.

TRY IT

Dictionary Skills

Apply: Dictionary Skills

Alphabetize the words in the Word Bank.

Word Bank

believed	explore	afterward
explain	around	during

1. afterward
2. around
3. believed
4. during
5. explain
6. explore

DICTIONARY SKILLS 159

Look up the word in a dictionary. Then, write the part of speech and the definition next to each word.

7. **celebrate**
   part of speech: verb
   definition: Possible answer: to honor a holiday or event in a special way

8. **gradual**
   part of speech: adjective
   definition: Possible answer: slowly, over time

9. **odor**
   part of speech: noun
   definition: Possible answer: a smell

160 DICTIONARY SKILLS

Read the sentences. Then, look up the word *chair* in the dictionary. Write the part of speech and the definition that best match how the word *chair* is used in the sentence.

10. Our recycling club had a big meeting last weekend. We held a vote to decide who would be our club **chair** for the next year. Our previous leader is moving away, so we needed to choose a new one.

    chair
    part of speech: noun
    definition: Possible answer: the head of a group or one who conducts a meeting

DICTIONARY SKILLS 161

TRY IT Review Dictionary Skills

Students will answer questions to review vocabulary word definitions and practice using the words in sentences.

QUIZ

Dictionary Skills

Students will complete the Dictionary Skills quiz.

WRAP-UP

More Language Arts Practice

Students will practice skills according to their individual needs.

Go Write! What Do You Do Well?

Students will complete Go Write! What Do You Do Well? in *Summit English Language Arts 3 Activity Book*. They will have the option to either respond to a prompt or write about a topic of their choice.

NOTE This activity is intended to build writing fluency. Students should write for the entire allotted time.

SUPPORT If students have trouble writing for the allotted time, prompt them with questions. For example, *Can you tell me more about this? How did you feel when you do this?*

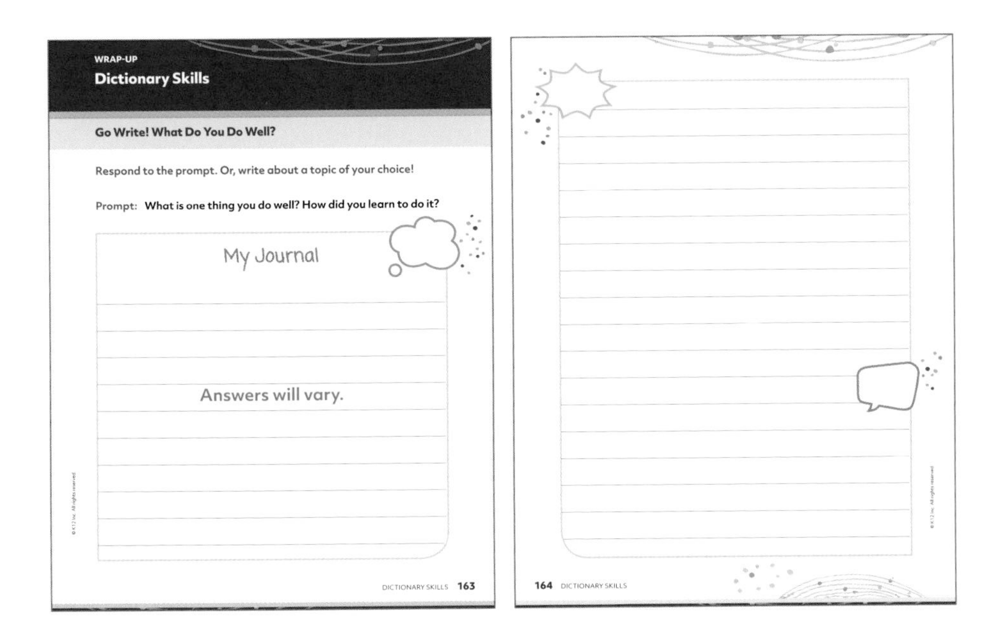

Go Read!

Students will read for pleasure. They should choose a book or a magazine that interests them, or they may choose a selection from the digital library, linked in the online lesson.

- Have students read aloud a few paragraphs of their selection.
- Then have students read silently for the rest of the time.

SUPPORT Students should make no more than five errors in decoding when they read aloud a few paragraphs of their Go Read! selection. If students struggle or make more than five errors, they need to select a different (and easier) text for the Go Read! activity.

TIP Have students select something to read ahead of time to help them stay focused.

Snowy Days (A)

Lesson Overview

ACTIVITY	ACTIVITY TITLE	TIME	ONLINE/OFFLINE
GET READY	Introduction to Snowy Days (A)	**1** minute	online
	Spelling List 8 Pretest LEARNING COACH CHECK-IN	**10** minutes	online and offline
	Read and Record	**8** minutes	online
	Reading Foundations: Open and Closed Syllables	**5** minutes	online
	Before You Read *Our Wonderful Weather: Snow*	**15** minutes	online and offline
READ	*Our Wonderful Weather: Snow*	**13** minutes	online
	Check-In: *Our Wonderful Weather: Snow*	**5** minutes	online
LEARN AND TRY IT	Showing What You Know	**10** minutes	online
	Show What You Know	**10** minutes	online
	Apply: Text Features	**15** minutes	online
	What Do You Know About Snow? LEARNING COACH CHECK-IN	**10** minutes	offline
	Practice Words from *Our Wonderful Weather: Snow*	**8** minutes	online
WRAP-UP	Question About *Our Wonderful Weather: Snow*	**2** minutes	online
	Handwriting	**8** minutes	offline

Content Background

In this lesson, students will learn about the *glossary*, a text feature found at the back of many informational texts. The glossary defines words in the text that appear in heavy type or a different color of type. Students will also learn that information that demonstrates their understanding of a text can be found not only in the main text, called the *body*, in a piece of writing. It can also be found in text features such as photographs and captions.

MATERIALS

Supplied

- *Our Wonderful Weather: Snow* by Valerie Bodden
- *Summit English Language Arts 3 Activity Book*
  - Spelling List 8 Pretest
  - What Do You Know About Snow?
- handwriting workbook

Our Wonderful Weather: Snow Synopsis

This informational text explains the process through which snowflakes form and the various structures of snowflakes. It explains that meteorologists forecast the weather by using radar and satellites. It also describes historical blizzards and the potential dangers of blizzards.

KEYWORDS

body – the main text of a piece of writing

glossary – a list of important terms and their meanings that is usually found in the back of a book

Lesson Goals

- Take a spelling pretest.
- Read aloud to practice fluency.
- Practice using a glossary.
- Think about what you know about a topic.
- Read *Our Wonderful Weather: Snow*.
- Use information found in body text, photographs, and captions to demonstrate understanding.
- Record what you learn about snow and what more you want to learn about snow.
- Practice vocabulary words.
- Develop letter formation fluency.

GET READY

Introduction to Snowy Days (A)

Students will get a glimpse of what they will learn about in the lesson. They will also read the lesson goals and keywords. Have students select each keyword and preview its definition.

Spelling List 8 Pretest

Students will take a spelling pretest and learn a new spelling pattern.

LEARNING COACH CHECK-IN Have students turn to Spelling List 8 Pretest in *Summit English Language Arts 3 Activity Book* and open the online Spelling Pretest activity. Online, students will listen to the spelling word, type the word in the space indicated, and then check their answer. In the activity book, students will write the correct spelling of the word in the tables provided and indicate with a ✓ or an ✗ if they spelled the word correctly or incorrectly online. Students will repeat this process with the remaining words.

As needed, help students with the interaction between the online activity and the activity book page until they become comfortable with what they need

to do. As students practice their spelling words throughout the workshop, they should pay special attention to words they spelled incorrectly on the pretest.

This is the complete list of words students will be tested on.

Words with Long *u* Sound		
argue	human	rescue
continue	menu	unit
curfew	molecule	use
cute	music	value
fuel	nephew	view
fumes	pew	

NOTE Have students keep their completed activity page in a safe place so they can refer to it later.

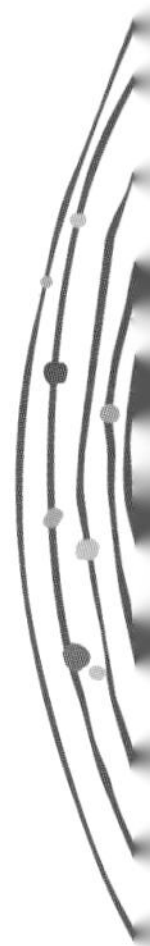

GET READY

Snowy Days (A)

Spelling List 8 Pretest

1. Open the Spelling Pretest activity online. Listen to the first spelling word. Type the word. Check your answer.
2. Write the correct spelling of the word in the Word column of the Spelling Pretest table.

	Word	✓	✗
1	blindfold		

3. Put a check mark in the ✓ column if you spelled the word correctly online.

	Word	✓	✗
1	blindfold	✓	

Put an X in the ✗ column if you spelled the word incorrectly online.

	Word	✓	✗
1	blindfold		X

4. Repeat Steps 1–3 for the remaining words in the Spelling Pretest.

SNOWY DAYS (A) 165

Snowy Days (A)

Spelling List 8 Pretest

Write each spelling word in the Word column, making sure to spell it correctly.

	Word	✓	✗
1	argue		
2	continue		
3	curfew		
4	cute		
5	fuel		
6	fumes		
7	human		
8	menu		
9	molecule		

	Word	✓	✗
10	music		
11	nephew		
12	pew		
13	rescue		
14	unit		
15	use		
16	value		
17	view		

Students should write the correct spelling of each word from the pretest and use the ✓and X columns to indicate whether they spelled each word correctly or incorrectly online.

166 SNOWY DAYS (A)

Read and Record

Good readers read quickly, smoothly, and with expression. This is called *fluency*. Students will record themselves reading aloud. They will listen to their recording and think about how quick, smooth, and expressive they sound.

TIP Encourage students to rerecord as needed.

Reading Foundations: Open and Closed Syllables

Reading Foundations activities serve to remind students of basic reading skills and reading behaviors mastered in earlier grades. The activities cover topics such as advanced decoding skills and various strategies for improving comprehension.

Before You Read *Our Wonderful Weather: Snow*

Students will be introduced to a glossary, make a prediction about the content of the book *Our Wonderful Weather: Snow*, and record background knowledge that they already have about the book's topic, snow.

NOTE Students will answer Questions 1 and 2 on the What Do You Know About Snow? activity page during this activity. Activity pages are not typically done at this point in a lesson, so make sure that students know when to access the activity page.

READ

Our Wonderful Weather: Snow

Students will read *Our Wonderful Weather: Snow* by Valerie Bodden. This book is accessed through the digital library, linked in the online lesson.

Check-In: *Our Wonderful Weather: Snow*

Students will answer several questions to demonstrate their comprehension of *Our Wonderful Weather: Snow*.

LEARN AND TRY IT

LEARN Showing What You Know

Students will learn that information to answer questions and show understanding is found in more than just the body. It can also be found in text features such as photographs and captions.

TRY IT Show What You Know

Students will practice determining which source of information in a text best answers a particular question: body, photograph, or caption.

TRY IT Apply: Text Features

Students will apply to a new work what they've learned about using information in the body and text features to demonstrate their understanding.

TRY IT What Do You Know About Snow?

Students will answer Questions 3 and 4 on the What Do You Know About Snow? activity page in *Summit English Language Arts 3 Activity Book*.

LEARNING COACH CHECK-IN This activity page contains open-ended questions, so it's important that you review students' responses.

NOTE Have students keep their activity page in a safe place so they can refer to it later.

TRY IT

Snowy Days (A)

What Do You Know About Snow?

Before you read *Our Wonderful Weather: Snow*, preview the cover, table of contents, and photos in the book. Answer the questions in complete sentences.

Answers will vary.

1. What do you predict *Our Wonderful Weather: Snow* will be about?

2. What do you know about snow?

SNOWY DAYS (A) 167

After you read *Our Wonderful Weather: Snow*, answer the questions. Use complete sentences.

3. What did you learn from *Our Wonderful Weather: Snow*? List at least three things you learned.

168 SNOWY DAYS (A)

4. What else do you want to learn about snow? List at least three questions that you hope to find answers for as you read more about snow.

SNOWY DAYS (A) 169

TRY IT Practice Words from *Our Wonderful Weather: Snow*

Students will answer questions to demonstrate their understanding of the words that appear in the glossary of *Our Wonderful Weather: Snow*.

WRAP-UP

Question About *Our Wonderful Weather: Snow*

Students will answer a question to show that they know how to use text features to demonstrate that they understand a text.

Handwriting

Students should gather their handwriting materials and begin where they left off. Remind students to form letters carefully and correctly.

TIP Set a timer to help students stay focused during handwriting practice.

Snowy Days (B)

Lesson Overview

ACTIVITY	ACTIVITY TITLE	TIME	ONLINE/OFFLINE
GET READY	Introduction to Snowy Days (B)	**1** minute	
	Spelling List 8 Activity Bank	**8** minutes	
	Read and Record	**5** minutes	
	Reading Foundations: *r*-Controlled Vowel Syllables	**5** minutes	
	Recall *Our Wonderful Weather: Snow*	**5** minutes	
	Before You Read *Curious About Snow*	**5** minutes	
READ	*Curious About Snow*	**25** minutes	
	Check-In: *Curious About Snow*	**5** minutes	
LEARN AND **TRY IT**	Using Text-Based Evidence	**10** minutes	
	Use Text-Based Evidence	**10** minutes	
	Apply: Text Evidence	**15** minutes	
	What Did You Learn from *Curious About Snow?* **LEARNING COACH CHECK-IN**	**10** minutes	
	Practice Words from *Curious About Snow*	**8** minutes	
WRAP-UP	Question About *Curious About Snow*	**2** minutes	
	Handwriting	**6** minutes	

Content Background

Students will be introduced to the term *text-based evidence*. Text-based evidence is proof that comes from facts and information in a text. Text-based evidence can be used to answer questions. It also can be used to indicate how concepts are related, such as cause-and-effect relationships. For example, this lesson's reading, *Curious About Snow*, includes the sentence: "To snow, the temperature must be below 32°F (Fahrenheit) or 0°C (Celsius), the freezing point of water." This sentence is text-based evidence of the cause-and-effect relationship of snow and temperature. Students will also learn that text features such as photographs can provide evidence. For example, photographs of snowflakes provide evidence of their structure.

Advance Preparation

Gather students' completed Spelling List 8 Pretest activity page from Snowy Days (A). Students will refer to this page during Get Ready: Spelling List 8 Activity Bank.

Gather students' completed What Do You Know About Snow? activity page from Snowy Days (A). Students will refer to this page during Try It: What Did You Learn from *Curious About Snow*?

Curious About Snow Synopsis

This informational text explains the process through which snowflakes form and the conditions necessary for snow to fall. It includes biographical information about Wilson Bentley, a man who spent his life studying snow and was the first to photograph snowflakes. Through Bentley's work and his photographs, some of which are included in the book, we know the possible shapes of snowflakes and the conditions under which each shape forms. The text describes different types of snowstorms and the dangers of these storms. It also includes records set by snowflakes and snowstorms and how people have fun in snow.

Lesson Goals

- Practice all spelling words offline.
- Read aloud to practice fluency.
- Read *Curious About Snow*.
- Use evidence in text to answer questions and show how ideas are related.
- Record information learned from the reading.
- Practice vocabulary words.
- Develop letter formation fluency.

MATERIALS

Supplied

- *Curious About Snow* by Gina Shaw
- *Summit English Language Arts 3 Activity Book*
  - What Did You Learn from *Curious About Snow?*
- handwriting workbook

Also Needed

- completed Spelling List 8 Pretest activity page from Snowy Days (A)
- completed What Do You Know About Snow? activity page from Snowy Days (A)

KEYWORDS

text-based evidence – proof found in a text that supports an idea or answers a question

GET READY

Introduction to Snowy Days (B)

Students will get a glimpse of what they will learn about in the lesson. They will also read the lesson goals and keywords. Have students select each keyword and preview its definition.

Spelling List 8 Activity Bank

Students will practice spelling words by completing Spelling List 8 Activity Bank from *Summit English Language Arts 3 Activity Book*. Make sure students have their completed Spelling List 8 Pretest activity page from Snowy Days (A) to refer to during this activity.

Remind students to pay special attention to words they spelled incorrectly on the Spelling Pretest.

GET READY

Snowy Days (B)

Spelling List 8 Activity Bank

Circle any words in the box that you did not spell correctly on your pretest. Choose one activity to do with your circled words. Do as much of the activity as you can in the time given.

Did you spell all the words on the pretest correctly? Do the one activity with as many spelling words as you can.

argue	fuel	molecule	pew	use
continue	fumes	music	rescue	value
curfew	human	nephew	unit	view
cute	menu			

Spelling Activity Choices

Create a Crossword

1. Write one of your spelling words going down in the center of the grid.

2. Write another spelling word going across that shares a letter with the first word. See how many words you can connect.

Example:

Word Search Puzzle

1. Draw a box on the grid. The box should be large enough to hold your spelling words.
2. Fill in the grid with your spelling words. Write them across, up and down, and diagonally. You can write them forward and backward.
3. Fill in the rest of the box with random letters.
4. Ask someone to find and circle your words in the puzzle.

Complete the activity that you chose.

My chosen activity: ______

Students should use this page to complete all steps in their chosen activity.

Read and Record

Good readers read quickly, smoothly, and with expression. This is called *fluency*. Students will record themselves reading aloud. They will listen to their recording and think about how quick, smooth, and expressive they sound.

TIP Encourage students to rerecord as needed.

Reading Foundations: *r*-Controlled Vowel Syllables

Reading Foundations activities serve to remind students of basic reading skills and reading behaviors mastered in earlier grades. The activities cover topics such as advanced decoding skills and various strategies for improving comprehension.

Recall *Our Wonderful Weather: Snow*

Students will answer some questions to review the reading that they have already completed.

Before You Read *Curious About Snow*

Students will be introduced to some key vocabulary words that they will encounter in the upcoming reading.

READ

Curious About Snow

Students will read *Curious About Snow* by Gina Shaw.

Check-In: *Curious About Snow*

Students will answer several questions to demonstrate their comprehension of *Curious About Snow*.

LEARN AND TRY IT

LEARN Using Text-Based Evidence

Student will learn the definition of the term *text-based evidence*. They will learn that text-based evidence can be used to answer questions and explain how ideas are related. They will learn that text-based evidence can be found in the body and text features such as photographs.

TRY IT Use Text-Based Evidence

Students will practice locating text-based evidence to support answers to questions and explain relationships of ideas in text.

TRY IT Apply: Text Evidence

Students will apply to a new work what they've learned about how they can use text-based evidence to answer questions and support their ideas.

TRY IT What Did You Learn from *Curious About Snow*?

Students will complete What Did You Learn from *Curious About Snow*? in *Summit English Language Arts 3 Activity Book*. Students should refer to their response to Question 4 on the What Do You Know About Snow? activity page from Snowy Days (A) to complete this activity page.

LEARNING COACH CHECK-IN This activity page includes an open-ended question, so it's important that you review students' responses.

TRY IT

Snowy Days (B)

What Did You Learn from *Curious About Snow*?

Answer the questions in complete sentences.

Answers will vary.

1. What did you learn from *Curious About Snow*? List at least three things you learned.

SNOWY DAYS (B) 175

Refer to what you wrote for Question 4 on the What Do You Know About Snow? activity page.

2. Did you find the answer to any of your questions about snow in *Curious About Snow*? If so, how would you answer your question(s)?

176 SNOWY DAYS (B)

TRY IT Practice Words from *Curious About Snow*

Students will answer questions to demonstrate their understanding of the vocabulary words from the reading.

WRAP-UP

Question About *Curious About Snow*

Students will answer a question to show that they understand how ideas are related in an informational text.

Handwriting

Students should gather their handwriting materials and begin where they left off. Remind students to form letters carefully and correctly.

TIP Set a timer to help students stay focused during handwriting practice.

Snowy Days (C)

Lesson Overview

ACTIVITY	ACTIVITY TITLE	TIME	ONLINE/OFFLINE
GET READY	Introduction to Snowy Days (C)	**1** minute	
	Spelling List 8 Review Game	**10** minutes	
	Read and Record	**8** minutes	
	Reading Foundations: Vowel Team Syllables	**5** minutes	
	Recall *Curious About Snow*	**5** minutes	
	Before You Read *Snowflake Bentley*, Part 1	**10** minutes	
READ	*Snowflake Bentley*, Part 1	**20** minutes	
	Check-In: *Snowflake Bentley*, Part 1	**5** minutes	
LEARN AND **TRY IT**	Finding the Main Idea	**10** minutes	
	Find the Main Idea	**10** minutes	
	Apply: Main Idea	**10** minutes	
	What Did You Learn from *Snowflake Bentley*, Part 1? LEARNING COACH CHECK-IN	**10** minutes	
	Practice Words from *Snowflake Bentley*, Part 1	**8** minutes	
WRAP-UP	Question About *Snowflake Bentley*, Part 1	**2** minutes	
	Handwriting	**6** minutes	

Content Background

In this lesson, students will learn about main ideas and supporting details in nonfiction text. The *main idea* is what the text is mostly about, an important point that the author makes. A text can have an overall main idea and main ideas within passages of the text. *Supporting details*, which can also be called key details, are details that tell more about the main idea. Sometimes the main idea is directly stated in a text. When the main idea is not stated, readers must use the supporting details to figure out the main idea. Readers can do this by asking themselves questions such as, "What are these details mostly about?" and "What important point is the author making?"

Advance Preparation

Gather students' completed What Do You Know About Snow? activity page from Snowy Days (A). Students will refer to this page during Try It: What Did You Learn from *Snowflake Bentley*, Part 1?

Snowflake Bentley, Part 1 Synopsis

In 1865, Wilson Bentley is born in Vermont where the annual snowfall is about 120 inches. He loves snow and spends the snowy days of his childhood catching and studying snowflakes. During his teens, he begins using a microscope to view the intricate patterns of snowflakes. He discovers that most snowflakes have six sides, but no two snowflakes are alike. Bentley is determined to share the wonders of snowflakes with others. At first, he attempts to draw ice crystals he views through a microscope. But eventually, through winters of experimentation, he discovers how to photograph snowflakes.

Lesson Goals

- Practice all spelling words online.
- Read aloud to practice fluency.
- Read *Snowflake Bentley*.
- Find the main idea and supporting details of text passages.
- Record information learned from the reading.
- Practice vocabulary words.
- Develop letter formation fluency.

MATERIALS

Supplied

- *Snowflake Bentley* by Jacqueline Briggs Martin
- *Summit English Language Arts 3 Activity Book*
  - What Did You Learn from *Snowflake Bentley*, Part 1?
- handwriting workbook

Also Needed

- completed What Do You Know About Snow? activity page from Snowy Days (A)

KEYWORDS

main idea – the most important point the author makes; it may be stated or unstated

nonfiction – writing that presents facts and information in order to explain, describe, or persuade; Example: newspaper articles and biographies are nonfiction

supporting detail – a detail that gives more information about a main idea

GET READY

Introduction to Snowy Days (C)

Students will get a glimpse of what they will learn about in the lesson. They will also read the lesson goals and keywords. Have students select each keyword and preview its definition.

Spelling List 8 Review Game

Students will practice all spelling words from the workshop.

Read and Record

Good readers read quickly, smoothly, and with expression. This is called *fluency*. Students will record themselves reading aloud. They will listen to their recording and think about how quick, smooth, and expressive they sound.

TIP Encourage students to rerecord as needed.

Reading Foundations: Vowel Team Syllables

Reading Foundations activities serve to remind students of basic reading skills and reading behaviors mastered in earlier grades. The activities cover topics such as advanced decoding skills and various strategies for improving comprehension.

Recall *Curious About Snow*

Students will answer some questions to review the reading that they have already completed.

Before You Read *Snowflake Bentley*, Part 1

Students will be introduced to some key vocabulary words that they will encounter in the upcoming reading.

READ

Snowflake Bentley, Part 1

Students will read Part 1 of *Snowflake Bentley* by Jacqueline Briggs Martin. Students will read the first 15 pages. They should stop after reading the page that ends with the sentence, "This etching meant extra hours of work for each photograph, but Willie didn't mind."

NOTE Be sure students understand that they are to read the body and the sidebar text, which is the text on the sides of the pages.

Check-In: *Snowflake Bentley*, Part 1

Students will answer several questions to demonstrate their comprehension of *Snowflake Bentley*, Part 1.

LEARN AND TRY IT

LEARN Finding the Main Idea

Students will learn about main ideas and how supporting details can help them determine a main idea.

TRY IT Find the Main Idea

Students will analyze passages and answer questions about the main ideas and supporting details.

SUPPORT For students having difficulty determining the main idea of a passage, explain that they can test their thinking by following these steps:

1. State what they believe is the main idea.
2. Read each sentence in the passage.
   - If **most** of the sentences are related to their stated main idea, then they are probably correct.
   - If most of the sentences are **not** related to their stated main idea, then they are not correct.
3. If they are not correct, repeat these steps with a new statement of the main idea.

TRY IT Apply: Main Idea

Students will apply to a new work what they've learned about how to find the main idea of a piece of writing.

TRY IT What Did You Learn from *Snowflake Bentley*, Part 1?

Students will complete What Did You Learn from *Snowflake Bentley*, Part 1? in *Summit English Language Arts 3 Activity Book*. Make sure students have their completed What Do You Know About Snow? activity page from Snowy Days (A) to refer to during this activity.

LEARNING COACH CHECK-IN This activity page contains open-ended questions, so it's important that you review students' responses.

TRY IT

Snowy Days (C)

What Did You Learn from *Snowflake Bentley*, Part 1?

Answer the questions in complete sentences.

Answers will vary.

1. What did you learn from Part 1 of the book *Snowflake Bentley*? List at least three things you learned.

SNOWY DAYS (C) 177

Refer to what you wrote for Question 4 on the What Do You Know About Snow? activity page.

2. Did you find the answer to any of your questions about snow in Part 1 of *Snowflake Bentley*? If so, how would you answer your question(s)?

Don't tell my brother, but I hid a snowball in the freezer!

178 SNOWY DAYS (C)

TRY IT Practice Words from *Snowflake Bentley*, Part 1

Students will answer questions to demonstrate their understanding of the vocabulary words from the reading.

WRAP-UP

Question About *Snowflake Bentley*, Part 1

Students will answer a question to show that they understand how a key detail supports a main idea.

Handwriting

Students should gather their handwriting materials and begin where they left off. Remind students to form letters carefully and correctly.

TIP Set a timer to help students stay focused during handwriting practice.

Snowy Days (D)

Lesson Overview

ACTIVITY	ACTIVITY TITLE	TIME	ONLINE/OFFLINE
GET READY	Introduction to Snowy Days (D)	**1** minute	
	Read and Record	**8** minutes	
	Reading Foundations: Vowel-Consonant-e Syllables	**5** minutes	
	Recall *Snowflake Bentley*, Part 1	**5** minutes	
	Before You Read *Snowflake Bentley*, Part 2	**10** minutes	
READ	*Snowflake Bentley*, Part 2	**20** minutes	
	Check-In: *Snowflake Bentley*, Part 2	**5** minutes	
LEARN AND **TRY IT**	Finding Key Details to Summarize	**10** minutes	
	Find Key Details to Summarize	**10** minutes	
	Apply: Key Details	**10** minutes	
	What Did You Learn from *Snowflake Bentley*, Part 2? **LEARNING COACH CHECK-IN**	**10** minutes	
	Practice Words from *Snowflake Bentley*, Part 2	**8** minutes	
QUIZ	Spelling List 8	**10** minutes	
WRAP-UP	Question About *Snowflake Bentley*, Part 2	**2** minutes	
	Handwriting	**6** minutes	

Content Background

In this lesson, students will be introduced to sidebars, a nonfiction text feature. A *sidebar* is a short text within a longer text that provides related information to the main text. Sidebars often appear in a box on the side of a page. Students will also learn about key details, which are the most important details in a text. *Key details* are the details that support an important idea in a passage. They are also the most important details within a text. Students will learn that key details are used to summarize a passage or text, while less important details are not.

Advance Preparation

Gather students' completed What Do You Know About Snow? activity page from Snowy Days (A). Students will refer to this page during Try It: What Did You Learn from *Snowflake Bentley*, Part 2?

Snowflake Bentley, Part 2 Synopsis

Even with his special camera, Wilson Bentley faces challenges in his attempts to photograph snow. He often waits hours for just the right crystal. But through his photographs, Bentley unlocks the secrets of snowflakes. He learns the process through which snowflakes form and how weather conditions affect a snowflake's structure. He shares his photos of snowflakes with friends and family. And, he shares his knowledge with scholars through magazines and speeches. Many colleges and universities buy lantern slide copies of his photos. After 50 years of studying and photographing snow, Bentley publishes his book *Snow Crystals*, which is still used as a reference today. Forty years after his death, children in his village of Jericho work to set up a museum in Wilson Bentley's honor.

Lesson Goals

- Read aloud to practice fluency.
- Read *Snowflake Bentley*.
- Identify key details that support an important idea and belong in a summary of text.
- Record information learned from the reading.
- Practice vocabulary words.
- Take a spelling quiz.
- Develop letter formation fluency.

MATERIALS

Supplied

- *Snowflake Bentley* by Jacqueline Briggs Martin
- *Summit English Language Arts 3 Activity Book*
  - What Did You Learn from *Snowflake Bentley*, Part 2?
  - handwriting workbook

Also Needed

- completed What Do You Know About Snow? activity page from Snowy Days (A)

KEYWORDS

detail – a fact or description that tells more about a topic

sidebar – a short text within a larger text that tells about something related to the main text

summary – a short retelling that includes only the most important ideas or events of a text

text feature – part of a text that helps a reader locate information and determine what is most important; Examples: title, table of contents, headings, pictures, and glossary

GET READY

Introduction to Snowy Days (D)

Students will get a glimpse of what they will learn about in the lesson. They will also read the lesson goals and keywords. Have students select each keyword and preview its definition.

Read and Record

Good readers read quickly, smoothly, and with expression. This is called *fluency*. Students will record themselves reading aloud. They will listen to their recording and think about how quick, smooth, and expressive they sound.

TIP Encourage students to rerecord as needed.

Reading Foundations: Vowel-Consonant-e Syllables

Reading Foundations activities serve to remind students of basic reading skills and reading behaviors mastered in earlier grades. The activities cover topics such as advanced decoding skills and various strategies for improving comprehension.

Recall *Snowflake Bentley*, Part 1

Students will answer some questions to review the reading that they have already completed.

Before You Read *Snowflake Bentley*, Part 2

Students will be introduced to some key vocabulary words and nonfiction text features that they will encounter in the upcoming reading.

READ

Snowflake Bentley, Part 2

Students will read Part 2 of *Snowflake Bentley* by Jacqueline Briggs Martin. They will finish reading the book.

NOTE Be sure students understand that they are to read the body and the sidebar text, which is the text on the sides of the pages.

Check-In: *Snowflake Bentley*, Part 2

Students will answer several questions to demonstrate their comprehension of *Snowflake Bentley*, Part 2.

LEARN AND TRY IT

LEARN Finding Key Details to Summarize

Students will learn about key details in a text and how key details are used to summarize a passage or text.

TRY IT Find Key Details to Summarize

Students will practice identifying key details that support an important idea. They will also identify key details that belong in a summary.

TRY IT Apply: Key Details

Students will apply to a new work what they've learned about how to identify key details.

TRY IT What Did You Learn from *Snowflake Bentley*, Part 2?

Students will complete What Did You Learn from *Snowflake Bentley*, Part 2? in *Summit English Language Arts 3 Activity Book*. Make sure students have their completed What Do You Know About Snow? activity page from Snowy Days (A) to refer to during this activity.

LEARNING COACH CHECK-IN This activity page contains open-ended questions, so it's important that you review students' responses.

TRY IT

Snowy Days (D)

What Did You Learn from *Snowflake Bentley*, Part 2?

Answer the questions in complete sentences.

Answers will vary.

1. What did you learn from Part 2 of the book *Snowflake Bentley*? List at least three things you learned.

SNOWY DAYS (D) 179

Refer to what you wrote for Question 4 on the What Do You Know About Snow? activity page.

2. Did you find the answer to any of your questions about snow in Part 2 of *Snowflake Bentley*? If so, how would you answer your question(s)?

180 SNOWY DAYS (D)

TRY IT Practice Words from *Snowflake Bentley*, Part 2

Students will answer questions to demonstrate their understanding of the vocabulary words from the reading.

QUIZ

Spelling List 8

Students will complete the Spelling List 8 quiz.

WRAP-UP

Question About *Snowflake Bentley*, Part 2

Students will answer a question to show that they understand how to identify key details.

Handwriting

Students should gather their handwriting materials and begin where they left off. Remind students to form letters carefully and correctly.

TIP Set a timer to help students stay focused during handwriting practice.

Snowy Days (E)

Lesson Overview

ACTIVITY	ACTIVITY TITLE	TIME	ONLINE/OFFLINE
GET READY	Introduction to Snowy Days (E)	**1** minute	
	Spelling List 9 Pretest LEARNING COACH CHECK-IN	**10** minutes	and
	Read and Record	**8** minutes	
	Reading Foundations: Consonant-*le* Syllables	**5** minutes	
	Recall *Snowflake Bentley*, Part 2	**5** minutes	
	Before You Read *Bear and Wolf*	**5** minutes	
READ	*Bear and Wolf*	**15** minutes	
	Check-In: *Bear and Wolf*	**5** minutes	
LEARN AND **TRY IT**	Describing the Narrator	**8** minutes	
	Describe the Narrator	**6** minutes	
	Thinking About Setting and Mood	**8** minutes	
	Think About Setting and Mood	**6** minutes	
	Apply: Setting	**10** minutes	
	Illustrations and Setting LEARNING COACH CHECK-IN	**14** minutes	
	Practice Words from *Bear and Wolf*	**6** minutes	
WRAP-UP	Question About *Bear and Wolf*	**2** minutes	
	Handwriting	**6** minutes	

Content Background

In this lesson, students will learn about two types of narrators. Students will not yet be introduced to the terms *first-person point of view* or *third-person point of view*. Instead, they will learn that a *narrator* can be inside of a story or outside of a story. A narrator inside of a story is a character in the story. When a narrator is outside of a story, it's as if somebody is describing what is happening in the story but is not taking part in it.

Students will learn about how *illustrations* show more about a story's setting than is shared in the words of a text. They will also learn that Illustrations work with the words of a story to convey a *mood*, or feeling. For example, an illustration with soft, muted colors might work with the words of the story to convey a calm, peaceful mood. Or, an illustration with vivid colors might help convey a joyous mood.

Bear and Wolf Synopsis

Bear and Wolf come across each other as they are out separately on a winter night, enjoying the snowy woods. They take a friendly walk together exploring the sights, sounds, and smells of the woods and the frozen lake. When they say goodbye, Bear returns to her family to hibernate for the winter, while Wolf returns to his pack to follow the caribou. When spring arrives, the friends find each other again and enjoy the awakening woods together.

Lesson Goals

- Take a spelling pretest.
- Read aloud to practice fluency.
- Read *Bear and Wolf*.
- Identify the narrator of a story.
- Determine how illustrations contribute information about the setting and mood of a story.
- Practice vocabulary words.
- Develop letter formation fluency.

MATERIALS

Supplied

- *Bear and Wolf* by Daniel Salmieri
- *Summit English Language Arts 3 Activity Book*
  - Spelling 9 Pretest
  - Illustrations and Setting
- handwriting workbook

KEYWORDS

illustration – a drawing

mood – the feeling that an author shows with words and pictures

narrator – the teller of a story

setting – where and when a literary work takes place

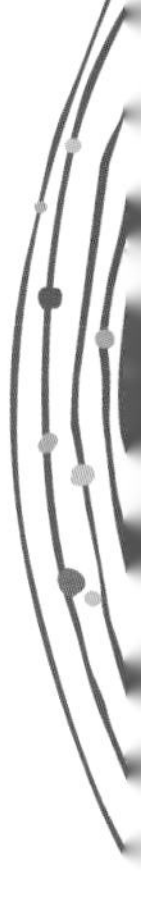

GET READY

Introduction to Snowy Days (E)

Students will get a glimpse of what they will learn about in the lesson. They will also read the lesson goals and keywords. Have students select each keyword and preview its definition.

Spelling List 9 Pretest

Students will take a spelling pretest and learn a new spelling pattern.

LEARNING COACH CHECK-IN Have students turn to Spelling List 9 Pretest in *Summit English Language Arts 3 Activity Book* and open the online Spelling Pretest activity. Online, students will listen to the spelling word, type the word in the space indicated, and then check their answer. In the activity book, students will write the correct spelling of the word in the tables provided and indicate with a ✓ or an ✗ if they spelled the word correctly or incorrectly online. Students will repeat this process with the remaining words.

As needed, help students with the interaction between the online activity and the activity book page until they become comfortable with what they need to do. As students practice their spelling words throughout the workshop, they should pay special attention to words they spelled incorrectly on the pretest.

This is the complete list of words students will be tested on.

Words with Long Double *o* Sound		
bamboo	group	soup
bruise	include	student
flew	poof	suit
fruit	ruby	true
glue	rule	youth
grew	smooth	

NOTE Have students keep their completed activity page in a safe place so they can refer to it later.

GET READY

Snowy Days (E)

Spelling List 9 Pretest

1. Open the Spelling Pretest activity online. Listen to the first spelling word. Type the word. Check your answer.
2. Write the correct spelling of the word in the Word column of the Spelling Pretest table.

	Word	✓	✗
1	blindfold		

3. Put a check mark in the ✓ column if you spelled the word correctly online.

	Word	✓	✗
1	blindfold	✓	

Put an X in the ✗ column if you spelled the word incorrectly online.

	Word	✓	✗
1	blindfold		X

4. Repeat Steps 1–3 for the remaining words in the Spelling Pretest.

SNOWY DAYS (E) 181

Snowy Days (E)

Spelling List 9 Pretest

Write each spelling word in the Word column, making sure to spell it correctly.

	Word	✓	✗
1	bamboo		
2	bruise		
3	flew		
4	fruit		
5	glue		
6	grew		
7	group		
8	include		
9	poof		

	Word	✓	✗
10	ruby		
11	rule		
12	smooth		
13	soup		
14	student		
15	suit		
16	true		
17	youth		

Students should write the correct spelling of each word from the pretest and use the ✓ and X columns to indicate whether they spelled each word correctly or incorrectly online.

182 SNOWY DAYS (E)

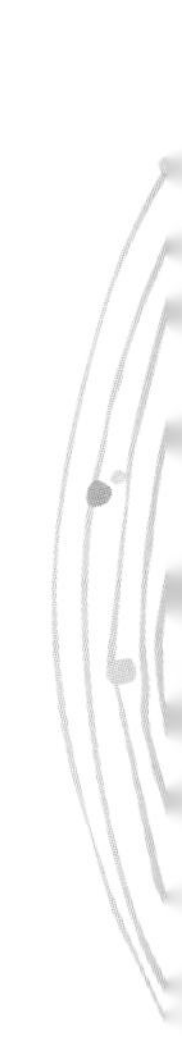

Read and Record

Good readers read quickly, smoothly, and with expression. This is called *fluency*. Students will record themselves reading aloud. They will listen to their recording and think about how quick, smooth, and expressive they sound.

TIP Encourage students to rerecord as needed.

Reading Foundations: Consonant-*le* Syllables

Reading Foundations activities serve to remind students of basic reading skills and reading behaviors mastered in earlier grades. The activities cover topics such as advanced decoding skills and various strategies for improving comprehension.

Recall *Snowflake Bentley*, Part 2

Students will answer some questions to review the reading that they have already completed.

Before You Read *Bear and Wolf*

Students will be introduced to some key vocabulary words that they will encounter in the upcoming reading.

READ

Bear and Wolf

Students will read *Bear and Wolf* by Daniel Salmieri.

Check-In: *Bear and Wolf*

Students will answer several questions to demonstrate their comprehension of *Bear and Wolf*.

LEARN AND TRY IT

LEARN Describing the Narrator

Students will learn how to identify if a story's narrator is a character inside the story or somebody outside of the story.

TRY IT Describe the Narrator

Students will practice identifying the narrator of a story.

LEARN Thinking About Setting and Mood

Students will learn that illustrations can show details about a story's setting that are not included in the story's words. They will also learn that pictures help convey the mood, or feeling, of a story.

TRY IT Think About Setting and Mood

Students will practice identifying what the story's illustrations convey about the setting and mood.

TRY IT Apply: Setting

Students will apply to a new work what they've learned about the setting of a story.

TRY IT Illustrations and Setting

Students will complete Illustrations and Setting in *Summit English Language Arts 3 Activity Book*.

LEARNING COACH CHECK-IN This activity page contains open-ended questions, so it's important that you review students' responses.

TRY IT

Snowy Days (E)

Illustrations and Setting

Follow the instructions to draw a picture and write about it.

Answers will vary.

1. Draw a picture of a place you know well.

SNOWY DAYS (E) 183

2. Write one or two sentences that explain why you chose to draw this place.

3. What does your picture show about this place that is not in the sentences you wrote about it?

184 SNOWY DAYS (E)

TRY IT Practice Words from *Bear and Wolf*

Students will answer questions to demonstrate their understanding of the vocabulary words from the reading.

WRAP-UP

Question About *Bear and Wolf*

Students will answer a question to show that they understand how to identify the narrator of a story.

Handwriting

Students should gather their handwriting materials and begin where they left off. Remind students to form letters carefully and correctly.

TIP Set a timer to help students stay focused during handwriting practice.

Snowy Days (F)

Lesson Overview

ACTIVITY	ACTIVITY TITLE	TIME	ONLINE/OFFLINE
GET READY	Introduction to Snowy Days (F)	**1** minute	
	Spelling List 9 Activity Bank	**10** minutes	
	Read and Record	**8** minutes	
	Recall *Bear and Wolf*	**5** minutes	
READ	Review Snowy Days Texts	**16** minutes	and
LEARN AND **TRY IT**	Comparing and Contrasting Fiction and Nonfiction	**10** minutes	
	Compare and Contrast Fiction and Nonfiction	**10** minutes	
	Comparing and Contrasting Nonfiction Texts	**10** minutes	
	Compare and Contrast Nonfiction Texts	**10** minutes	
	Apply: Compare Texts	**15** minutes	
	Prepare to Write a Compare-and-Contrast Essay **LEARNING COACH CHECK-IN**	**15** minutes	
WRAP-UP	Question About Comparing Texts	**2** minutes	
	Handwriting	**8** minutes	

Content Background

In this lesson, students will compare and contrast works of fiction and nonfiction that share a similar topic. Students will first compare and contrast a fictional story, *Bear and Wolf*, with a nonfiction text, *Our Wonderful Weather: Snow*. Then they will compare and contrast two nonfiction books, *Curious About Snow* and *Snowflake Bentley*.

To *compare* text means "to determine what is the same." To *contrast* text means "to determine what is different." Comparing and contrasting text is an important skill that builds readers' critical thinking. It helps readers remember important content. The focus on important details when comparing and contrasting improves reading comprehension.

Elements in text that students will learn to compare and contrast include topics, important ideas, author's purpose, nonfiction text features, and visual features such as photographs and illustrations.

Advance Preparation

Gather students' completed Spelling List 9 Pretest activity page from Snowy Days (E). Students will refer to this page during Get Ready: Spelling List 9 Activity Bank.

Lesson Goals

- Practice all spelling words offline.
- Read aloud to practice fluency.
- Review books read in the Snowy Days workshop.
- Compare and contrast texts.
- Answer questions about nonfiction texts to prepare for writing an essay.
- Develop letter formation fluency.

MATERIALS

Supplied

- *Our Wonderful Weather: Snow* by Valerie Bodden
- *Curious About Snow* by Gina Shaw
- *Snowflake Bentley* by Jacqueline Briggs Martin
- *Bear and Wolf* by Daniel Salmieri
- *Summit English Language Arts 3 Activity Book*
  - Spelling List 9 Activity Bank
  - Prepare to Write a Compare-and-Contrast Essay
- handwriting workbook

Also Needed

- completed Spelling List 9 Pretest activity page from Snowy Days (E)

GET READY

Introduction to Snowy Days (F)

Students will get a glimpse of what they will learn about in the lesson. They will also read the lesson goals and keywords. Have students select each keyword and preview its definition.

Spelling List 9 Activity Bank

Students will practice spelling words by completing Spelling List 9 Activity Bank from *Summit English Language Arts 3 Activity Book*. Make sure students have their completed Spelling List 9 Pretest activity page from Snowy Days (E) to refer to during this activity.

Remind students to pay special attention to words they spelled incorrectly on the Spelling Pretest.

KEYWORDS

compare – to explain how two or more things are alike

contrast – to explain how two or more things are different

fiction – make-believe stories

nonfiction – writing that presents facts and information in order to explain, describe, or persuade; Example: newspaper articles and biographies are nonfiction

topic – the subject of a text

GET READY

Snowy Days (F)

Spelling List 9 Activity Bank

Circle any words in the box that you did not spell correctly on your pretest. Choose one activity to do with your circled words. Do as much of the activity as you can in the time given.

Did you spell all the words on the pretest correctly? Do the one activity with as many spelling words as you can.

bamboo	glue	poof	smooth	suit
bruise	grew	ruby	soup	true
flew	group	rule	student	youth
fruit	include			

Spelling Activity Choices

Alphabetizing

1. In the left column, write your spelling words in alphabetical order.
2. Correct any spelling errors.

SNOWY DAYS (F) 185

Vowel-Free Words

1. In the left column, write only the consonants in each of your spelling words. Put a dot where each vowel should be.
2. Spell each word aloud, stating which vowels should be in the places with dots.
3. In the right column, rewrite the entire spelling word.
4. Correct any spelling errors.

Rhymes

1. In the left column, write your spelling words.
2. In the right column, write a word that rhymes with each spelling word.
3. Correct any spelling errors.

Uppercase and Lowercase

1. In the left column, write each of your spelling words in all uppercase letters.
2. In the right column, write each of your spelling words in all lowercase letters.
3. Correct any spelling errors.

186 SNOWY DAYS (F)

Complete the activity that you chose.

My chosen activity: ______

1.
2.
3.
4.
5.
6.
7.
8.
9.
10.
11.
12.
13.
14.
15.
16.
17.

Students should use this page to complete all steps in their chosen activity.

SNOWY DAYS (F) 187

Read and Record

Good readers read quickly, smoothly, and with expression. This is called *fluency*. Students will record themselves reading aloud. They will listen to their recording and think about how quick, smooth, and expressive they sound.

TIP Encourage students to rerecord as needed.

Recall *Bear and Wolf*

Students will answer some questions to review the reading that they have already completed.

READ

Review Snowy Days Texts

Students will review the books they have read in the Snowy Days workshop.

NOTE Students will access *Our Wonderful Weather: Snow* by Valerie Bodden through the digital library, linked in the online lesson.

LEARN AND TRY IT

LEARN Comparing and Contrasting Fiction and Nonfiction

Students will learn about features typically found in fiction and nonfiction texts. They will learn that comparing and contrasting details can help readers determine whether a text is fiction or nonfiction.

TRY IT **Compare and Contrast Fiction and Nonfiction**

Students will practice comparing and contrasting passages from fiction and nonfiction texts. They will use what they have learned to determine whether a passage is fiction or nonfiction.

LEARN **Comparing and Contrasting Nonfiction Texts**

Students will learn about comparing and contrasting two works of nonfiction on a similar topic.

TRY IT **Compare and Contrast Nonfiction Texts**

Students will analyze passages to identify what is alike and different about two works of nonfiction.

TRY IT **Apply: Compare Texts**

Students will apply to a new work what they've learned about comparing texts.

TRY IT **Prepare to Write a Compare-and-Contrast Essay**

Students will complete Prepare to Write a Compare-and-Contrast Essay in *Summit English Language Arts 3 Activity Book*. Students will answer questions about *Curious About Snow* and *Snowflake Bentley*. They will refer to this information in a later lesson write an essay that compares and contrasts the two books.

SUPPORT For students having difficulty identifying topics of each book, remind them that a topic is stated as a word or phrase. Ask them, "What is something the book talks about?" Provide an example answer such as: *Curious About Snow* talks about the different shapes of snowflakes. "The different shape of snowflakes" is a topic.

LEARNING COACH CHECK-IN Students will refer to the information they write on the activity page when they write their essay, so it's important that you review students' responses. Give students feedback, using the sample answers provided to guide you.

NOTE Have students keep their activity page in a safe place so they can refer to it later.

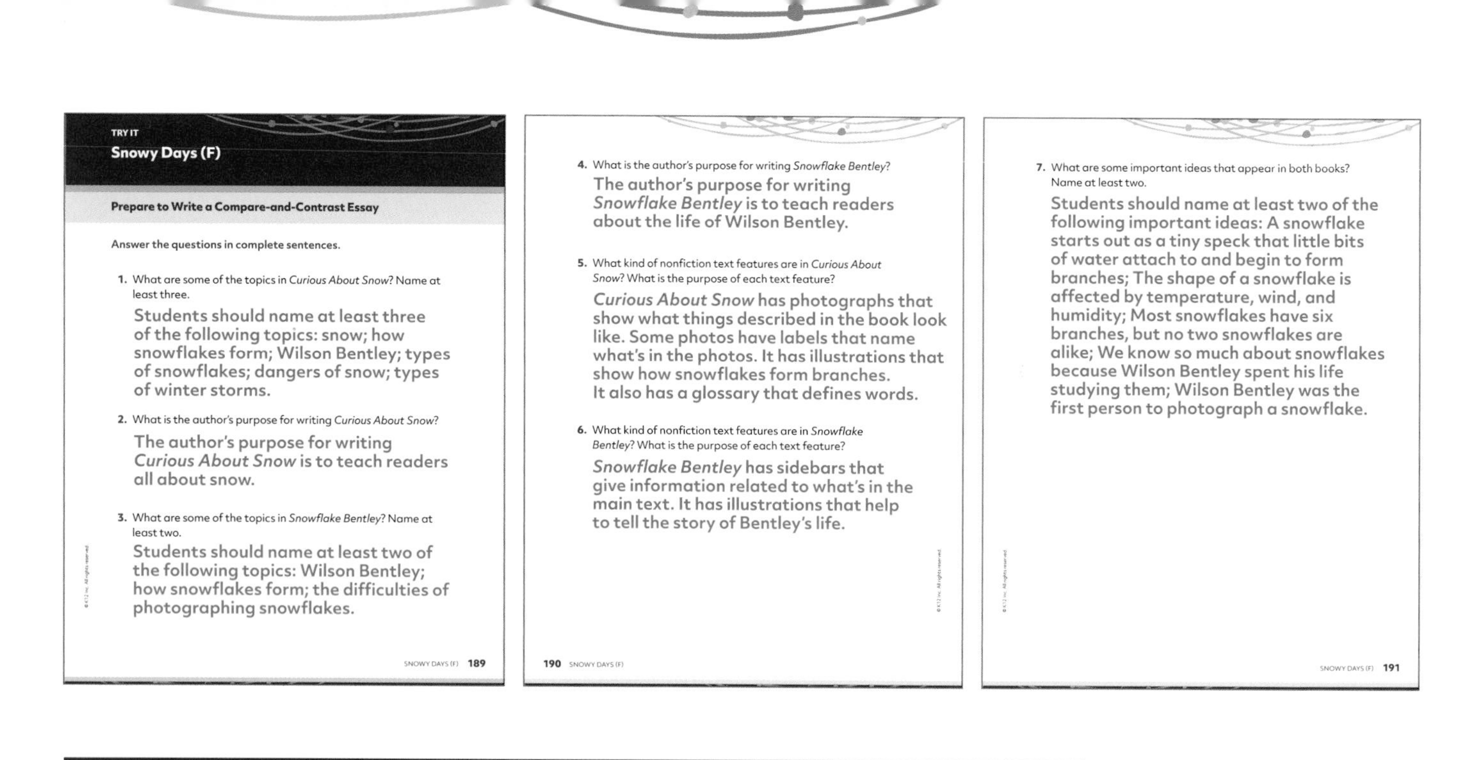
TRY IT
Snowy Days (F)

Prepare to Write a Compare-and-Contrast Essay

Answer the questions in complete sentences.

1. What are some of the topics in *Curious About Snow*? Name at least three.
Students should name at least three of the following topics: snow; how snowflakes form; Wilson Bentley; types of snowflakes; dangers of snow; types of winter storms.

2. What is the author's purpose for writing *Curious About Snow*?
The author's purpose for writing *Curious About Snow* is to teach readers all about snow.

3. What are some of the topics in *Snowflake Bentley*? Name at least two.
Students should name at least two of the following topics: Wilson Bentley; how snowflakes form; the difficulties of photographing snowflakes.

SNOWY DAYS (F) 189

4. What is the author's purpose for writing *Snowflake Bentley*?
The author's purpose for writing *Snowflake Bentley* is to teach readers about the life of Wilson Bentley.

5. What kind of nonfiction text features are in *Curious About Snow*? What is the purpose of each text feature?
Curious About Snow has photographs that show what things described in the book look like. Some photos have labels that name what's in the photos. It has illustrations that show how snowflakes form branches. It also has a glossary that defines words.

6. What kind of nonfiction text features are in *Snowflake Bentley*? What is the purpose of each text feature?
Snowflake Bentley has sidebars that give information related to what's in the main text. It has illustrations that help to tell the story of Bentley's life.

190 SNOWY DAYS (F)

7. What are some important ideas that appear in both books? Name at least two.
Students should name at least two of the following important ideas: A snowflake starts out as a tiny speck that little bits of water attach to and begin to form branches; The shape of a snowflake is affected by temperature, wind, and humidity; Most snowflakes have six branches, but no two snowflakes are alike; We know so much about snowflakes because Wilson Bentley spent his life studying them; Wilson Bentley was the first person to photograph a snowflake.

SNOWY DAYS (F) 191

WRAP-UP

Question About Comparing Texts

Students will answer a question to show that they understand how to compare key details in nonfiction texts.

Handwriting

Students should gather their handwriting materials and begin where they left off. Remind students to form letters carefully and correctly.

TIP Set a timer to help students stay focused during handwriting practice.

Snowy Days (G)

Lesson Overview

ACTIVITY	ACTIVITY TITLE	TIME	ONLINE/OFFLINE
GET READY	Introduction to Snowy Days (G)	**1** minute	online
	Spelling List 9 Review Game	**10** minutes	online
	Read and Record	**10** minutes	online
LEARN AND TRY IT	Explore a Model Compare-and-Contrast Essay	**10** minutes	online
	Respond to a Model Compare-and-Contrast Essay	**5** minutes	online
	Write a Compare-and-Contrast Essay LEARNING COACH CHECK-IN	**50** minutes	offline
WRAP-UP	Question About Writing a Compare-and-Contrast Essay	**2** minutes	online
	Handwriting	**8** minutes	offline
	Go Read!	**24** minutes	online or offline

Content Background

In this lesson, students will learn about and then write a compare-and-contrast essay about two of the books from the Snowy Days workshop. A *compare-and-contrast essay* is a type of informative writing. It can also be called analytic, explanatory, or informational writing. Students will learn about the structure and elements of a compare-and-contrast essay by exploring a model essay.

There are many ways to structure informative writing. A compare-and-contrast essay uses a compare-and-contrast structure. This structure begins with a paragraph that introduces the main idea of the essay. It has a body that has two parts, one that explains what is alike about the two books and one that explains what is different. (For this essay, students will only be expected to write one compare paragraph and one contrast paragraph.) It finishes with a concluding paragraph that restates the main idea of the essay and offers some final thoughts.

Advance Preparation

Gather students' completed Prepare to Write a Compare-and-Contrast Essay activity page from Snowy Days (F). Students will refer to this page during Try It: Write a Compare-and-Contrast Essay.

MATERIALS

Supplied
- *Curious About Snow* by Gina Shaw
- *Snowflake Bentley* by Jacqueline Briggs Martin
- *Summit English Language Arts 3 Activity Book*
  - Model Compare-and-Contrast Essay
  - Write a Compare-and-Contrast Essay
- handwriting workbook

Also Needed
- completed Prepare to Write a Compare-and-Contrast Essay activity page from Snowy Days (F)
- reading material for Go Read!

During the Go Read! activity, students will have the option of using the digital library. Allow extra time for students to make their reading selection, or have students make a selection before beginning the lesson.

Lesson Goals

- Practice all spelling words online.
- Read aloud to practice fluency.
- Explore features of a compare-and-contrast essay.
- Write a compare-and-contrast essay.
- Develop letter formation fluency.
- Read independently to develop fluency.

KEYWORDS

compare-and-contrast organization – a structure for text that shows how two or more things are similar and different

main idea – the most important point the author makes; it may be stated or unstated

topic – the subject of a text

topic sentence – the sentence that expresses the main idea of the paragraph

transition – a word, phrase, or clause that connects ideas

GET READY

Introduction to Snow Days (G)

Students will get a glimpse of what they will learn about in the lesson. They will also read the lesson goals and keywords. Have students select each keyword and preview its definition.

Spelling List 9 Review Game

Students will practice all spelling words from the workshop.

Read and Record

Good readers read quickly, smoothly, and with expression. This is called *fluency*. Students will record themselves reading aloud. They will listen to their recording and think about how quick, smooth, and expressive they sound.

TIP Encourage students to rerecord as needed.

LEARN AND TRY IT

LEARN Explore a Model Compare-and-Contrast Essay

By reading and exploring a model compare-and-contrast essay, students will learn what a compare-and-contrast essay is and how it is organized.

TIP The model compare-and-contrast essay that students read in the online activity is the same essay on the Model Compare-and-Contrast Essay activity page. Students may wish to reference and make notes on this page as they complete the activity.

TRY IT Respond to a Model Compare-and-Contrast Essay

Students will answer questions to check their understanding of the elements of a compare-and-contrast essay.

TRY IT Write a Compare-and-Contrast Essay

Students will complete Write a Compare-and-Contrast Essay in *Summit English Language Arts 3 Activity Book*. Make sure students have their completed Prepare to Write a Compare-and-Contrast Essay activity page from Snowy Days (F) to refer to during this activity. They should use the information they recorded on this activity page for writing their essay.

LEARNING COACH CHECK-IN If necessary, work closely with students, referring to the Model Compare-and-Contrast Essay to help them with ideas and organization for their essay.

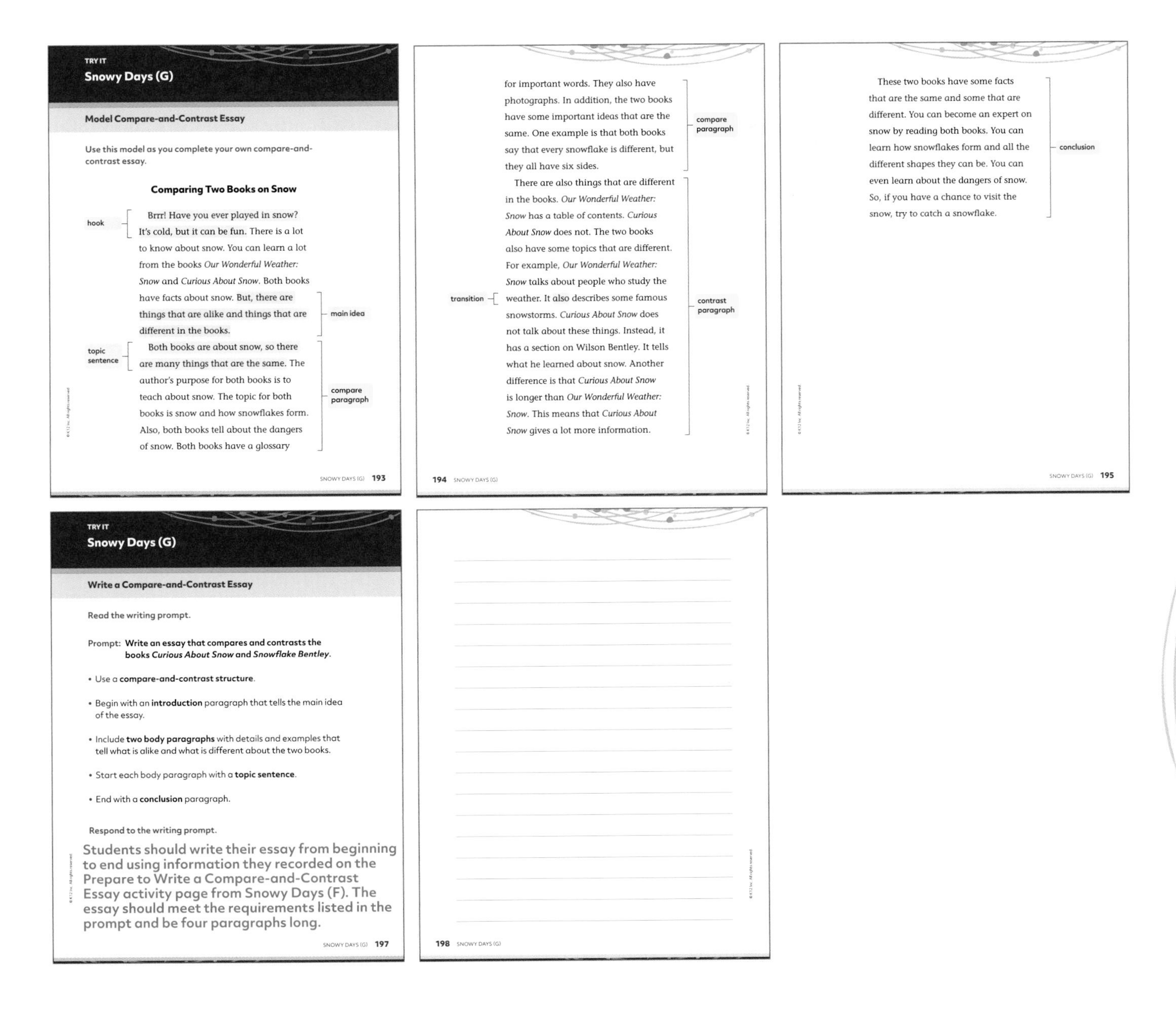

TRY IT

Snowy Days (G)

Model Compare-and-Contrast Essay

Use this model as you complete your own compare-and-contrast essay.

Comparing Two Books on Snow

[hook] Brrr! Have you ever played in snow? It's cold, but it can be fun. There is a lot to know about snow. You can learn a lot from the books *Our Wonderful Weather: Snow* and *Curious About Snow*. [main idea] Both books have facts about snow. But, there are things that are alike and things that are different in the books.

[compare paragraph] [topic sentence] Both books are about snow, so there are many things that are the same. The author's purpose for both books is to teach about snow. The topic for both books is snow and how snowflakes form. Also, both books tell about the dangers of snow. Both books have a glossary for important words. They also have photographs. In addition, the two books have some important ideas that are the same. One example is that both books say that every snowflake is different, but they all have six sides.

[contrast paragraph] There are also things that are different in the books. *Our Wonderful Weather: Snow* has a table of contents. *Curious About Snow* does not. The two books also have some topics that are different. For example, *Our Wonderful Weather: Snow* talks about people who study the weather. It also describes some famous snowstorms. *Curious About Snow* does not talk about these things. [transition] Instead, it has a section on Wilson Bentley. It tells what he learned about snow. Another difference is that *Curious About Snow* is longer than *Our Wonderful Weather: Snow*. This means that *Curious About Snow* gives a lot more information.

[conclusion] These two books have some facts that are the same and some that are different. You can become an expert on snow by reading both books. You can learn how snowflakes form and all the different shapes they can be. You can even learn about the dangers of snow. So, if you have a chance to visit the snow, try to catch a snowflake.

TRY IT

Snowy Days (G)

Write a Compare-and-Contrast Essay

Read the writing prompt.

Prompt: **Write an essay that compares and contrasts the books *Curious About Snow* and *Snowflake Bentley*.**

- Use a **compare-and-contrast structure**.
- Begin with an **introduction** paragraph that tells the main idea of the essay.
- Include **two body paragraphs** with details and examples that tell what is alike and what is different about the two books.
- Start each body paragraph with a **topic sentence**.
- End with a **conclusion** paragraph.

Respond to the writing prompt.

Students should write their essay from beginning to end using information they recorded on the Prepare to Write a Compare-and-Contrast Essay activity page from Snowy Days (F). The essay should meet the requirements listed in the prompt and be four paragraphs long.

WRAP-UP

Question About Writing a Compare-and-Contrast Essay

Students will answer a question to show that they understand the purpose of elements in a compare-and-contrast essay.

Handwriting

Students should gather their handwriting materials and begin where they left off. Remind students to form letters carefully and correctly.

TIP Set a timer to help students stay focused during handwriting practice.

Go Read!

Students will read for pleasure. They should choose a book or a magazine that interests them, or they may choose a selection from the digital library, linked in the online lesson.

- Have students read aloud a few paragraphs of their selection.
- Then have students read silently for the rest of the time.

SUPPORT Students should make no more than five errors in decoding when they read aloud a few paragraphs of their Go Read! selection. If students struggle or make more than five errors, they need to select a different (and easier) text for the Go Read! activity.

TIP Have students select something to read ahead of time to help them stay focused.

Snowy Days Wrap-Up

Lesson Overview

ACTIVITY	ACTIVITY TITLE	TIME	ONLINE/OFFLINE
GET READY	Introduction to Snowy Days Wrap-Up	**1** minute	online
	Read and Record	**10** minutes	online
TRY IT	Can You Answer Your Questions? LEARNING COACH CHECK-IN	**25** minutes	offline
	Review Snowy Days	**20** minutes	online
QUIZ	Snowy Days	**30** minutes	online
	Spelling List 9	**10** minutes	online
WRAP-UP	More Language Arts Practice	**16** minutes	online
	Handwriting	**8** minutes	offline

Advance Preparation

Gather students' completed What Do You Know About Snow? activity page from Snowy Days (A). Students will refer to this page during Try It: Can You Answer Your Questions?

Lesson Goals

- Read aloud to practice fluency.
- Record information learned in this workshop.
- Review what you learned.
- Take a reading quiz.
- Take a spelling quiz.
- Develop letter formation fluency.

MATERIALS

Supplied

- *Summit English Language Arts 3 Activity Book*
  - Can You Answer Your Questions?
- handwriting workbook

Also Needed

- completed What Do You Know About Snow? activity page from Snowy Days (A)

GET READY

Introduction to Snowy Days Wrap-Up

Students will read the lesson goals.

Read and Record

Good readers read quickly, smoothly, and with expression. This is called *fluency*. Students will record themselves reading aloud. They will listen to their recording and think about how quick, smooth, and expressive they sound.

TIP Encourage students to rerecord as needed.

TRY IT

Can You Answer Your Questions?

Students will complete Can You Answer Your Questions? in *Summit English Language Arts 3 Activity Book*. Make sure students have their completed What Do You Know About Snow? activity page from Snowy Days (A) to refer to during this activity.

LEARNING COACH CHECK-IN This activity page contains open-ended question that refer back to questions students asked in Snowy Days (A). So, it's important that you review students' responses. Give students feedback, and guide them to the texts read in the workshop that may hold answers to their questions.

TRY IT

Snowy Days Wrap-Up

Can You Answer Your Questions?

Refer to what you wrote for Question 4 on the What Do You Know About Snow? activity page. Then, answer the questions in complete sentences.

Answers will vary.

1. What is the first question you listed that you wanted to find an answer to as you read more about snow?

2. Did you find the answer to your question? If so, write the answer here.

3. What is the second question you listed that you wanted to find an answer to?

4. Did you find the answer to your question? If so, write the answer here.

5. What is the third question you listed that you wanted to find an answer to?

6. Did you find the answer to your question? If so, write the answer here.

Review Snowy Days

Students will answer questions to review what they have learned in the Snowy Days workshop.

QUIZ

Snowy Days

Students will complete the Snowy Days quiz.

Spelling List 9

Students will complete the Spelling List 9 quiz.

WRAP-UP

More Language Arts Practice

Students will practice skills according to their individual needs.

Handwriting

Students should gather their handwriting materials and begin where they left off. Remind students to form letters carefully and correctly.

TIP Set a timer to help students stay focused during handwriting practice.

Informative Writing Skills (A)

Lesson Overview

ACTIVITY	ACTIVITY TITLE	TIME	ONLINE/OFFLINE
GET READY	Introduction to Informative Writing Skills (A)	**1** minute	online
	Spelling List 10 Pretest **LEARNING COACH CHECK-IN**	**10** minutes	online and offline
	Look Back at Nouns	**4** minutes	online
LEARN AND **TRY IT**	Common and Proper Nouns	**10** minutes	online
	Explain the Function of Common and Proper Nouns	**10** minutes	online
	Explore a Model Informative Essay	**10** minutes	online
	Respond to a Model Informative Essay	**5** minutes	online
	Plan an Informative Essay	**10** minutes	online
	Plan Your Informative Essay **LEARNING COACH CHECK-IN**	**25** minutes	offline
WRAP-UP	Questions About Nouns and Organizing an Informative Essay	**4** minutes	online
	Handwriting	**8** minutes	offline
	Go Read!	**23** minutes	online or offline

Content Background

Informative text (also called *informational text*) is factual text written to share information. Throughout this workshop, students will build informative writing skills by analyzing a model informative essay and writing their own informative essay. In this lesson, students will focus on how writers organize, or structure, an informative essay.

There are many types of informative writing, including compare-and-contrast essays, how-to essays, and biographies. The type of writing influences the structure of the writing. For example, a compare-and-contrast essay typically has part of the body devoted to comparing and part to contrasting; a biography typically has a chronological structure. The informative essay that students will explore and use as a model has the following simple structure:

MATERIALS

Supplied

- *Summit English Language Arts 3 Activity Book*
  - Spelling List 10 Pretest
  - Model Informative Essay
  - Plan Your Informative Essay
- handwriting workbook

Also Needed

- folder for organizing informative essay assignment pages
- reading material for Go Read!

- An introduction that introduces the topic and tells readers what they will learn
- A body that provides facts and details about a topic (The model essay has only one body paragraph.)
- A conclusion that summarizes the essay and provides final thoughts

The informative essay is a short writing assignment, so students will follow an abbreviated version of the writing process. In this lesson, they will *prewrite* by choosing a topic and organizing their ideas.

Grammar, Usage, and Mechanics A **noun** is a word that names a person, place, thing, or idea. A **common noun** refers to any person, place, or thing—it's generic. A **proper noun** refers to a particular person, place, or thing. (Nouns that name ideas are called *abstract nouns* and are covered in a different lesson.)

A proper noun always begins with a capital letter. If the proper noun is made up of more than one word, each word begins with a capital letter. Note that students will learn the rules for capitalizing titles of works in a different lesson.

A common noun does not begin with a capital letter (unless it is the first word of a sentence).

Examples of Common Nouns	Examples of Proper Nouns
song	"Oh Susannah"
lake	Lake Erie
friend	Mr. Lee

All nouns can function as subjects, objects, and predicate nominatives.

The **subject** performs the action in a sentence.

Example: **Micah** lost his keys.

An **object** receives the action in a sentence. There are three kinds of objects: direct objects, indirect objects, and objects of prepositions. Students will focus on direct and indirect objects in this lesson.

A **direct object** answers the question *whom* or *what* after an action verb.

Example: Micah lost his **keys**. (*What did Micah lose?*)

An **indirect object** answers the question *for whom* or *for what*.

Example: Micah gave **Mom** a sad look. (*For whom was the sad look?*)

An **object of a preposition** is part of a prepositional phrase.

Example: Micah noticed his keys on the **table**. (*The prepositional phrase is "on the table."*)

KEYWORDS

body – the main text of a piece of writing

common noun – a noun that names any person, place, thing, or idea; Examples: *girl*, *mountain*, *book*, and *joy*

conclusion – the final paragraph of a written work

informative essay – a kind of writing that explains or informs

introduction – the first paragraph of an essay, identifying the topic and stating the main idea

noun – a word that names a person, place, thing, or idea

proper noun – noun that names a particular person, place, thing, or idea

A **predicate nominative** follows a linking verb and renames the subject.

> **Example:** The table was the **location** of the keys. (*The noun "location" follows the linking verb "was" and renames the subject, "table."*)

Advance Preparation

Gather a folder that students can use to keep all notes and activity pages related to their informative essay.

During the Go Read! activity, students will have the option of using the digital library. Allow extra time for students to make their reading selection, or have students make a selection before beginning the lesson.

Lesson Goals

- Take a spelling pretest.
- Explain the function of common and proper nouns.
- Read a model informative essay, and start planning your own.
- Develop letter formation fluency.
- Read independently to develop fluency.

GET READY

Introduction to Informative Writing Skills (A)

Students will get a glimpse of what they will learn about in the lesson. They will also read the lesson goals and keywords. Have students select each keyword and preview its definition.

Spelling List 10 Pretest

Students will take a spelling pretest and learn a new spelling pattern.

LEARNING COACH CHECK-IN Have students turn to Spelling List 10 Pretest in *Summit English Language Arts 3 Activity Book* and open the online Spelling Pretest activity. Online, students will listen to the spelling word, type the word in the space indicated, and then check their answer. In the activity book, students will write the correct spelling of the word in the tables provided and indicate with a ✓ or an ✗ if they spelled the word correctly or incorrectly online. Students will repeat this process with the remaining words.

As needed, help students with the interaction between the online activity and the activity book page until they become comfortable with what they need to do. As students practice their spelling words throughout the workshop, they should pay special attention to words they spelled incorrectly on the pretest.

This is the complete list of words students will be tested on.

Words with /ow/ and /oi/ Sounds		
about	pounce	enjoy
crown	thousands	joint
downtown	vowel	loyal
flowers	avoid	ploy
mountain	choice	soil
outline	destroy	

NOTE Have students keep their completed activity page in a safe place so they can refer to it later.

GET READY
Informative Writing Skills (A)

Spelling List 10 Pretest

1. Open the Spelling Pretest activity online. Listen to the first spelling word. Type the word. Check your answer.
2. Write the correct spelling of the word in the Word column of the Spelling Pretest table.

	Word	✓	⊗
1	blindfold		

3. Put a check mark in the ✓ column if you spelled the word correctly online.

	Word	✓	⊗
1	blindfold	✓	

Put an X in the ⊗ column if you spelled the word incorrectly online.

	Word	✓	⊗
1	blindfold		X

4. Repeat Steps 1–3 for the remaining words in the Spelling Pretest.

INFORMATIVE WRITING SKILLS (A) 203

Informative Writing Skills (A)

Spelling List 10 Pretest

Write each spelling word in the Word column, making sure to spell it correctly.

	Word	✓	⊗
1	about		
2	crown		
3	downtown		
4	flowers		
5	mountain		
6	outline		
7	pounce		
8	thousands		
9	vowel		

	Word	✓	⊗
10	avoid		
11	choice		
12	destroy		
13	enjoy		
14	joint		
15	loyal		
16	ploy		
17	soil		

Students should write the correct spelling of each word from the pretest and use the ✓and X columns to indicate whether they spelled each word correctly or incorrectly online.

204 INFORMATIVE WRITING SKILLS (A)

Look Back at Nouns

Students will practice the prerequisite skill of identifying a noun in a sentence.

LEARN AND TRY IT

LEARN Common and Proper Nouns

Students will learn the difference between a common and proper noun. They will learn that both common and proper nouns can function as subjects, direct and indirect objects, and predicate nominatives.

TRY IT **Explain the Function of Common and Proper Nouns**

Students will practice explaining how common and proper nouns function in sentences. They will also write sentences that use nouns in different ways, using mentor sentences as models.

LEARN **Explore a Model Informative Essay**

By reading and exploring a model informative essay, students will learn what an informative essay is and how it is organized.

TIP The model informative essay that students read in the online activity is the same essay on the Model Informative Essay activity page. Students may wish to reference and make notes on the activity page as they complete the online activity.

TRY IT **Respond to a Model Informative Essay**

Students will answer questions to check and expand their understanding of the organization of an informative essay.

LEARN **Plan an Informative Essay**

Students will learn how to choose a topic and organize their ideas in preparation to begin writing their own informative essay.

TRY IT **Plan Your Informative Essay**

Students will complete Plan Your Informative Essay in *Summit English Language Arts 3 Activity Book*. They should have the Model Informative Essay activity page to refer to as they work.

SUPPORT Work through the brainstorming process together. Remind students that topics for an informative essay don't need to be "academic" in nature. For example, students can write about a sport or a hobby that they know a lot about.

LEARNING COACH CHECK-IN This activity page contains open-ended questions, so it's important that you review students' responses.

NOTE Have students add the Model Informative Essay and their completed Plan Your Informative Essay activity page to the folder they are using to store their informative essay assignment pages.

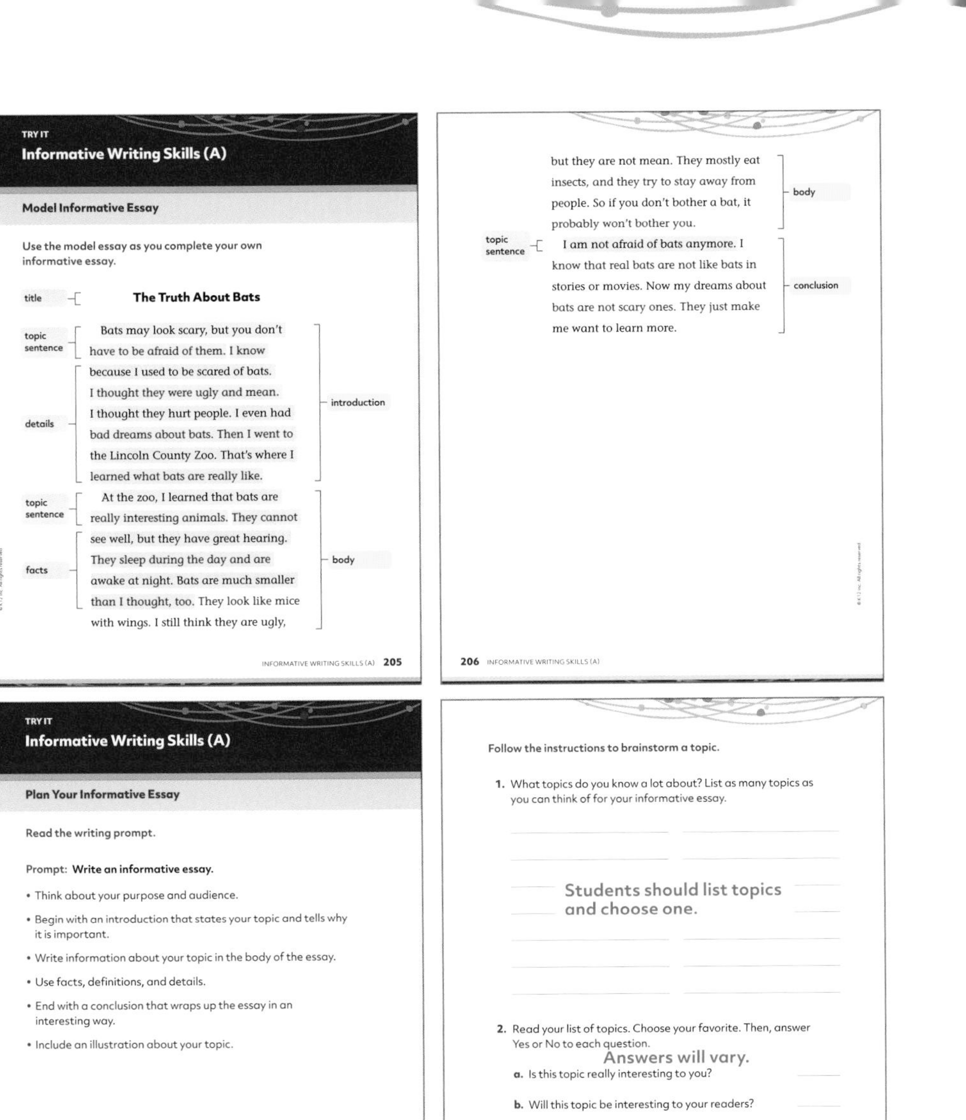

TRY IT

Informative Writing Skills (A)

Model Informative Essay

Use the model essay as you complete your own informative essay.

title — **The Truth About Bats**

topic sentence — Bats may look scary, but you don't have to be afraid of them. I know

details — because I used to be scared of bats. I thought they were ugly and mean. I thought they hurt people. I even had bad dreams about bats. Then I went to the Lincoln County Zoo. That's where I learned what bats are really like.

(introduction)

topic sentence — At the zoo, I learned that bats are really interesting animals. They cannot

facts — see well, but they have great hearing. They sleep during the day and are awake at night. Bats are much smaller than I thought, too. They look like mice with wings. I still think they are ugly,

(body)

INFORMATIVE WRITING SKILLS (A) 205

but they are not mean. They mostly eat insects, and they try to stay away from people. So if you don't bother a bat, it probably won't bother you.

(body)

topic sentence — I am not afraid of bats anymore. I know that real bats are not like bats in stories or movies. Now my dreams about bats are not scary ones. They just make me want to learn more.

(conclusion)

206 INFORMATIVE WRITING SKILLS (A)

TRY IT

Informative Writing Skills (A)

Plan Your Informative Essay

Read the writing prompt.

Prompt: **Write an informative essay.**

- Think about your purpose and audience.
- Begin with an introduction that states your topic and tells why it is important.
- Write information about your topic in the body of the essay.
- Use facts, definitions, and details.
- End with a conclusion that wraps up the essay in an interesting way.
- Include an illustration about your topic.

INFORMATIVE WRITING SKILLS (A) 207

Follow the instructions to brainstorm a topic.

1. What topics do you know a lot about? List as many topics as you can think of for your informative essay.

   Students should list topics and choose one.

2. Read your list of topics. Choose your favorite. Then, answer Yes or No to each question.

   Answers will vary.

   a. Is this topic really interesting to you?

   b. Will this topic be interesting to your readers?

   c. Do you know enough about the topic?

   d. Is this topic something you can write about in three paragraphs (something that is not too simple and not too complicated)?

208 INFORMATIVE WRITING SKILLS (A)

3. Did you answer Yes to Parts a–d of Question 2? If not, answer the question for another topic in your list. Repeat until you find a topic that works.

   Informative essay topic:
   Students should list their chosen topic.

Follow the instructions to plan your essay.

4. State your audience and purpose.

   a. Audience: Answers will vary.

   b. Purpose: Answers will vary.

I am deciding between two topics: dimetrodons or pteranodons.

INFORMATIVE WRITING SKILLS (A) 209

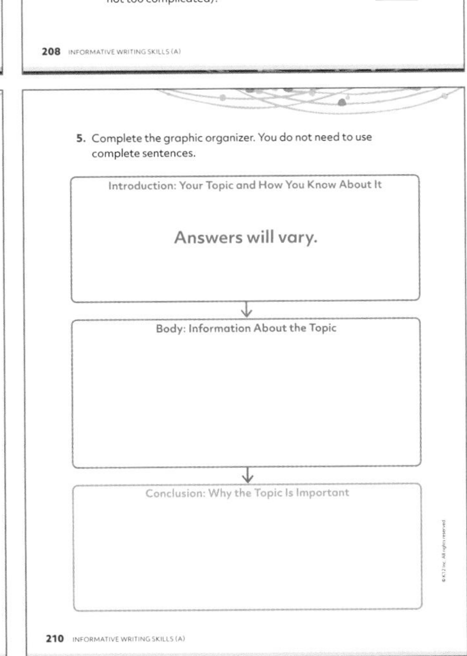

5. Complete the graphic organizer. You do not need to use complete sentences.

Introduction: Your Topic and How You Know About It

Answers will vary.

Body: Information About the Topic

Conclusion: Why the Topic Is Important

210 INFORMATIVE WRITING SKILLS (A)

WRAP-UP

Questions About Nouns and Organizing an Informative Essay

Students will answer questions to show that they understand how a noun functions and how to organize an informative essay.

Handwriting

Students should gather their handwriting materials and begin where they left off. Remind students to form letters carefully and correctly.

TIP Set a timer to help students stay focused during handwriting practice.

Go Read!

Students will read for pleasure. They should choose a book or a magazine that interests them, or they may choose a selection from the digital library, linked in the online lesson.

- Have students read aloud a few paragraphs of their selection.
- Then have students read silently for the rest of the time.

SUPPORT Students should make no more than five errors in decoding when they read aloud a few paragraphs of their Go Read! selection. If students struggle or make more than five errors, they need to select a different (and easier) text for the Go Read! activity.

TIP Have students select something to read ahead of time to help them stay focused.

Informative Writing Skills (B)

Lesson Overview

ACTIVITY	ACTIVITY TITLE	TIME	ONLINE/OFFLINE
GET READY	Introduction to Informative Writing Skills (B)	**1** minute	
	Spelling List 10 Activity Bank	**10** minutes	
LEARN AND TRY IT	Abstract Nouns	**10** minutes	
	Use Abstract Nouns	**10** minutes	
	Begin Writing an Informative Essay	**15** minutes	
	Respond to an Introduction, Body, and Transitions	**5** minutes	
	Begin Writing Your Informative Essay LEARNING COACH CHECK-IN	**35** minutes	
WRAP-UP	Questions About Abstract Nouns and Supporting Details	**4** minutes	
	Handwriting	**8** minutes	
	Go Read!	**22** minutes	or

Content Background

Students will learn about the introduction and body of an informative essay. Strong informative writing begins with an *introduction*, which clearly states the topic and conveys why that topic is important enough to read about. The introduction should also engage readers.

The *body*, or main text, of informative writing is divided into paragraphs that begin with topic sentences. Facts and details support the topic sentence and ultimately support the writer's purpose. Good informative writing also includes transitions to connect ideas. Examples of transitions include *also*, *another*, *but*, and *and*.

Students will continue working on their own informative essay. In this lesson, they will draft about half their essay (the introduction and half of the body). Note that students will not be revising or proofreading the informative essay in this course.

Grammar, Usage, and Mechanics An **abstract noun** is a word that names an idea, such as *happiness*. Abstract nouns can function as subjects, objects, and predicate nominatives.

MATERIALS

Supplied

- *Summit English Language Arts 3 Activity Book*
  - Spelling List 10 Activity Bank
  - Write Your Informative Essay
- handwriting workbook

Also Needed

- completed Spelling List 10 Pretest activity page from Informative Writing Skills (A)
- folder in which students are storing informative essay assignment pages
- reading material for Go Read!

Subject: Fear affected my choice.

Direct object: We wanted **peace** more than anything else.

Predicate nominative: That statement is the **truth**.

While it is possible for an abstract noun to function as an indirect object, it is not common. Additionally, an abstract noun may function as the object of a preposition, but that is not covered in this lesson.

Advance Preparation

Gather students' completed Spelling List 10 Pretest activity page from Informative Writing Skills (A). Students will refer to this page during Get Ready: Spelling List 10 Activity Bank.

Gather the folder that students are using to store the activity pages related to their informative essay. The folder should contain the following:

- Model Informative Essay activity page from Informative Writing Skills (A)
- Students' completed Plan Your Informative Essay activity page from Informative Writing Skills (A)

During the Go Read! activity, students will have the option of using the digital library. Allow extra time for students to make their reading selection, or have students make a selection before beginning the lesson.

KEYWORDS

abstract noun – a word that names an idea

body – the main text of a piece of writing

detail – a fact or description that tells more about a topic

fact – something that can be proven true

informative essay – a kind of writing that explains or informs

introduction – the first paragraph of an essay, identifying the topic and stating the main idea

noun – a word that names a person, place, thing, or idea

transition – a word, phrase, or clause that connects ideas

Lesson Goals

- Practice all spelling words offline.
- Use abstract nouns.
- Explore the introduction, body, and transitions in a model informative essay.
- Begin writing your informative essay.
- Develop letter formation fluency.
- Read independently to develop fluency.

GET READY

Introduction to Informative Writing Skills (B)

Students will get a glimpse of what they will learn about in the lesson. They will also read the lesson goals and keywords. Have students select each keyword and preview its definition.

Spelling List 10 Activity Bank

Students will practice all spelling words from the workshop by completing Spelling List 10 Activity Bank from *Summit English Language Arts 3 Activity Book*. Make sure students have their completed Spelling List 10 Pretest activity page from Informative Writing Skills (A) to refer to during this activity.

Remind students to pay special attention to words they spelled incorrectly on the Spelling Pretest.

GET READY
Informative Writing Skills (B)

Spelling List 10 Activity Bank

Circle any words in the box that you did not spell correctly on the pretest. Choose one activity to do with your circled words. Do as much of the activity as you can in the time given.

Did you spell all the words on the pretest correctly? Do the one activity with as many spelling words as you can.

about	mountain	vowel	destroy	loyal
crown	outline	avoid	enjoy	ploy
downtown	pounce	choice	joint	soil
flowers	thousands			

Spelling Activity Choices

Silly Sentences

1. Write a silly sentence for each of your spelling words.
2. Underline the spelling word in each sentence.
   Example: The dog was driving a car.
3. Correct any spelling errors.

Spelling Story

1. Write a very short story using each of your spelling words.
2. Underline the spelling words in the story.
3. Correct any spelling errors.

Riddle Me This

1. Write a riddle for each of your spelling words.
   Example: "I have a trunk, but it's not on my car."
2. Write the answer, which is your word, for each riddle.
   Example: Answer: elephant
3. Correct any spelling errors.

RunOnWord

1. Gather some crayons, colored pencils, or markers. Use a different color to write each of your spelling words. Write the words end to end as one long word.
   Example: dogcatbirdfishturtle
2. Rewrite the words correctly and with proper spacing.
3. Correct any spelling errors.

Complete the activity that you chose.

My chosen activity: ____________

Students should use this page to complete all steps in their chosen activity.

LEARN AND TRY IT

LEARN Abstract Nouns

Students will learn how to identify abstract nouns and use them in sentences.

SUPPORT Search the term *abstract nouns* online, as you will find lists of commonly used abstract nouns. Take turns with students picking an abstract noun from such a list and using that noun in a sentence. Discuss how the abstract nouns function in your sentences (as subjects, objects, or predicate nominatives).

TIP The opposite of an abstract noun is a concrete noun.

TRY IT Use Abstract Nouns

Students will practice using abstract nouns in sentences. They will write their own sentences that use abstract nouns by modeling mentor sentences.

LEARN Begin Writing an Informative Essay

Students will explore the introduction and body of a model informative essay. They will explore how the writer effectively uses a topic sentence, supporting facts and details, and transitions to develop the body.

TIP The words *facts* and *details* are often used interchangeably. A *fact* is something that can be proven true. A *detail* may be a fact, but it could also be an example, description, or elaboration. For students, the distinction isn't that important—it's most important that the information is true and supports the main idea of their essay.

TRY IT Respond to an Introduction, Body, and Transitions

Students will answer questions about introductions, bodies, and transitions in informative writing.

TRY IT Begin Writing Your Informative Essay

Students will begin writing their informative essay using Write Your Informative Essay in *Summit English Language Arts 3 Activity Book*. They will write the introduction and at least half of the body. They should have their completed Plan Your Informative Essay activity page and Model Informative Essay from Informative Writing Skills (A) to refer to as they work.

LEARNING COACH CHECK-IN Students should write about half of their informative essay in this activity (they may write more if they wish). They should use the prewriting work they have done to guide them as they write. Give students feedback on their introduction and body, paying particular attention to their use of facts, details, and transitions. Most importantly of all, encourage students to keep writing!

NOTE Have students add their in-progress Write Your Informative Essay activity page to the folder they are using to store their informative essay assignment pages.

TRY IT

Informative Writing Skills (B)

Write Your Informative Essay

Read the writing prompt.

Prompt: **Write an informative essay.**

- Think about your purpose and audience.
- Begin with an introduction that states your topic and tells why it is important.
- Write information about your topic in the body of the essay.
- Use facts, definitions, and details.
- End with a conclusion that wraps up the essay in an interesting way.
- Include an illustration about your topic.

Respond to the writing prompt.

Students should begin writing their informative essay (introduction and at least half the body) in Informative Writing Skills (B) and finish (remainder of essay and illustration) in Informative Writing Skills (C).

INFORMATIVE WRITING SKILLS (B) 215

216 INFORMATIVE WRITING SKILLS (B)

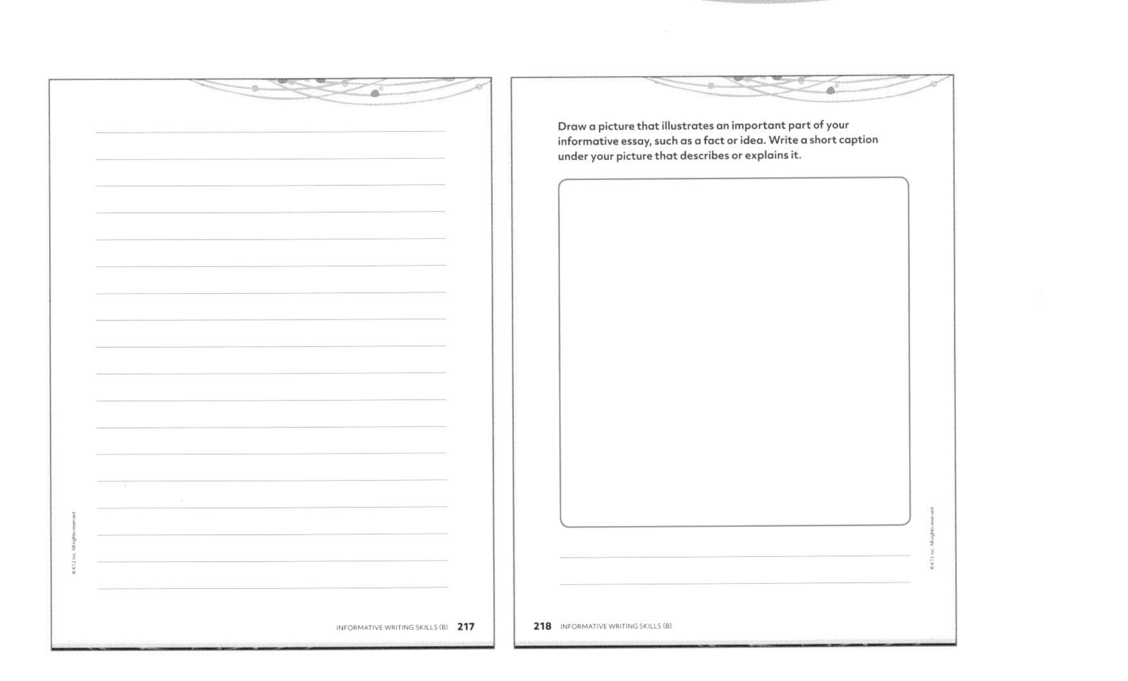

WRAP-UP

Questions About Abstract Nouns and Supporting Details

Students will answer questions to show that they understand how to use abstract nouns and supporting details.

Handwriting

Students should gather their handwriting materials and begin where they left off. Remind students to form letters carefully and correctly.

TIP Set a timer to help students stay focused during handwriting practice.

Go Read!

Students will read for pleasure. They should choose a book or a magazine that interests them, or they may choose a selection from the digital library, linked in the online lesson.

- Have students read aloud a few paragraphs of their selection.
- Then have students read silently for the rest of the time.

SUPPORT Students should make no more than five errors in decoding when they read aloud a few paragraphs of their Go Read! selection. If students struggle or make more than five errors, they need to select a different (and easier) text for the Go Read! activity.

TIP Have students select something to read ahead of time to help them stay focused.

Informative Writing Skills (C)

Lesson Overview

ACTIVITY	ACTIVITY TITLE	TIME	ONLINE/OFFLINE
GET READY	Introduction to Informative Writing Skills (C)	**1** minute	online
	Spelling List 10 Review Game	**10** minutes	online
LEARN AND TRY IT	Plural Nouns	**10** minutes	online
	Use Plural Nouns	**10** minutes	online
	Finish Writing an Informative Essay	**15** minutes	online
	Respond to a Conclusion and a Picture	**5** minutes	online
	Finish Writing Your Informative Essay LEARNING COACH CHECK-IN	**35** minutes	offline
WRAP-UP	Questions About Nouns and Conclusions	**4** minutes	online
	Handwriting	**8** minutes	offline
	Go Read!	**22** minutes	online or offline

Content Background

Students will learn about the conclusion of an informative essay. The *conclusion*, or end, of an informative essay restates the main idea in a new way and conveys why the topic is important to the writer (and thus should be important to readers). Most importantly, the conclusion should wrap up the essay and make sense.

Students will also learn that writers use *illustrations* to support their ideas. Effective illustrations relate to the writer's audience and purpose. They may include a *caption*, or short written description of the illustration.

In this lesson, students will finish drafting their informative essay. As part of the draft, they will create an illustration that supports their essay. Note that students will not be revising or proofreading the informative essay in this course.

Grammar, Usage, and Mechanics A **plural noun** names more than one person, place, thing, or idea. Most plural nouns are formed by adding –*s*:

Example: The **bears** hid among the **trees**.

MATERIALS

Supplied

- *Summit English Language Arts 3 Activity Book*
  - Write Your Informative Essay
- handwriting workbook

Also Needed

- folder in which students are storing informative essay assignment pages
- reading material for Go Read!

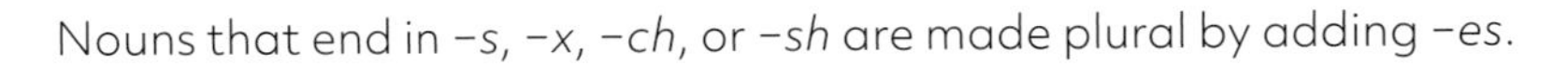

Nouns that end in *–s*, *–x*, *–ch*, or *–sh* are made plural by adding *–es*.

Example: Are those **foxes** wearing **watches**?

Nouns that end in a consonant and a *–y* are made plural by changing the *y* to *i* and adding *–es*.

Example: The **puppies** love their new toys.

Note that in the previous example, *toy* is made plural by adding *–s* only. That's because the word *toy* ends in a *vowel* and the letter *y*.

Many nouns that end in *–f* or *–fe* are made plural by change the *f* or *fe* to *v* and adding *–es*.

Example: Those **knives** don't belong on the **shelves**!

Irregular plural nouns do not end in *–s* or *–es*. Common irregular plural nouns are *men*, *feet*, *oxen*, *mice*, and *cacti*. Some irregular plural nouns are the same as their singular form, such as *deer*, *fish*, and *sheep*.

KEYWORDS

caption – text that tells more about an illustration, a photograph, or other graphic

conclusion – the final paragraph of a written work

illustration – a drawing

informative essay – a kind of writing that informs or explains

noun – a word that names a person, place, thing, or idea

plural noun – a word that names more than one person, place, thing, or idea

Advance Preparation

Gather the folder that students are using to store the activity pages related to their informative essay. The folder should contain the following:

- Model Informative Essay activity page from Informative Writing Skills (A)
- Students' completed Plan Your Informative Essay activity page from Informative Writing Skills (A)
- Students' in-progress Write Your Informative Essay activity page from Informative Writing Skills (B)

During the Go Read! activity, students will have the option of using the digital library. Allow extra time for students to make their reading selection, or have students make a selection before beginning the lesson.

Lesson Goals

- Practice all spelling words online.
- Form and use plural nouns.
- Explore conclusions and illustrations in a model informative essay.
- Finish writing your informative essay, and add an illustration.
- Develop letter formation fluency.
- Read independently to develop fluency.

GET READY

Introduction to Informative Writing Skills (C)

Students will get a glimpse of what they will learn about in the lesson. They will also read the lesson goals and keywords. Have students select each keyword and preview its definition.

Spelling List 10 Review Game

Students will practice all spelling words from the workshop.

LEARN AND TRY IT

LEARN Plural Nouns

Students will learn what a plural noun is and the rules for forming plural nouns. They will also learn that some plural nouns are irregular and do not follow rules. Irregular plural forms must be memorized.

TIP If students are unsure of the spelling of a plural noun, they can look up the singular form of the noun in a dictionary. The dictionary entry will have the correct plural spelling.

TRY IT Use Plural Nouns

Students will practice forming regular and irregular plural nouns and using them in sentences. They will write their own sentences that use plural nouns by modeling mentor sentences.

LEARN Finish Writing an Informative Essay

Students will explore the conclusion of a model informative essay. They will also explore how writers use illustrations and captions to enhance an informative essay.

TRY IT Respond to a Conclusion and a Picture

Students will answer questions about conclusions and illustrations in informative writing.

TRY IT Finish Writing Your Informative Essay

Students will complete their informative essay using Write Your Informative Essay in *Summit English Language Arts 3 Activity Book*. Make sure they have their completed Plan Your Informative Essay activity page and Model Informative Essay from Informative Writing Skills (A) to refer to as they work.

LEARNING COACH CHECK-IN Students should write about the remainder of their essay and create an illustration that supports their main idea. They should use the prewriting work they have done to guide them as they write. Give students feedback and encouragement as they write.

OPTIONAL Provide students with colored pencils, crayons, or other art supplies to create their illustrations.

NOTE Have students add their completed Write Your Informative Essay activity page to the folder they are using to store their informative essay assignment pages.

TRY IT

Informative Writing Skills (B)

Write Your Informative Essay

Read the writing prompt.

Prompt: **Write an informative essay.**

- Think about your purpose and audience.
- Begin with an introduction that states your topic and tells why it is important.
- Write information about your topic in the body of the essay.
- Use facts, definitions, and details.
- End with a conclusion that wraps up the essay in an interesting way.
- Include an illustration about your topic.

Respond to the writing prompt.

Students should begin writing their informative essay (introduction and at least half the body) in Informative Writing Skills (B) and finish (remainder of essay and illustration) in Informative Writing Skills (C).

INFORMATIVE WRITING SKILLS (B) 215

216 INFORMATIVE WRITING SKILLS (B)

INFORMATIVE WRITING SKILLS (B) 217

Draw a picture that illustrates an important part of your informative essay, such as a fact or idea. Write a short caption under your picture that describes or explains it.

218 INFORMATIVE WRITING SKILLS (B)

WRAP-UP

Questions About Plural Nouns and Conclusions

Students will answer questions to show that they understand how to form plural nouns and conclude an informative essay.

Handwriting

Students should gather their handwriting materials and begin where they left off. Remind students to form letters carefully and correctly.

TIP Set a timer to help students stay focused during handwriting practice.

Go Read!

Students will read for pleasure. They should choose a book or a magazine that interests them, or they may choose a selection from the digital library, linked in the online lesson.

- Have students read aloud a few paragraphs of their selection.
- Then have students read silently for the rest of the time.

SUPPORT Students should make no more than five errors in decoding when they read aloud a few paragraphs of their Go Read! selection. If students struggle or make more than five errors, they need to select a different (and easier) text for the Go Read! activity.

TIP Have students select something to read ahead of time to help them stay focused.

Informative Writing Skills Wrap-Up

Lesson Overview

ACTIVITY	ACTIVITY TITLE	TIME	ONLINE/OFFLINE
GET READY	Introduction to Informative Writing Skills Wrap-Up	**1** minute	online
TRY IT	Reflect on Your Informative Essay LEARNING COACH CHECK-IN	**30** minutes	offline
	Review Nouns	**15** minutes	online
QUIZ	Nouns and Informative Writing Skills	**20** minutes	online
	Spelling List 10	**10** minutes	online
WRAP-UP	More Language Arts Practice	**20** minutes	online
	Handwriting	**8** minutes	offline
	Go Read!	**16** minutes	online or offline

Advance Preparation

Gather the folder that students are using to store the activity pages related to their informative essay. The folder should contain the following:

- Model Informative Essay activity page from Informative Writing Skills (A)
- Students' completed Plan Your Informative Essay activity page from Informative Writing Skills (A)
- Students' completed Write Your Informative Essay activity page from Informative Writing Skills (C)

During the Go Read! activity, students will have the option of using the digital library. Allow extra time for students to make their reading selection, or have students make a selection before beginning the lesson.

MATERIALS

Supplied

- *Summit English Language Arts 3 Activity Book*
  - Reflect on Your Informative Essay
- handwriting workbook

Also Needed

- folder in which students are storing informative essay assignment pages
- reading material for Go Read!

Lesson Goals

- Reflect on your informative essay.
- Review common nouns, proper nouns, abstract nouns, plural nouns, and functions of nouns.
- Take a quiz on nouns and informative writing skills.
- Take a spelling quiz.
- Develop letter formation fluency.
- Read independently to develop fluency.

GET READY

Introduction to Informative Writing Skills Wrap-Up

Students will read the lesson goals.

TRY IT

Reflect on Your Informative Essay

Students will complete Reflect on Your Informative Essay in *Summit English Language Arts 3 Activity Book*. They should have their completed Write Your Informative Essay activity page from Informative Writing Skills (C) to refer to as they work.

LEARNING COACH CHECK-IN This activity page contains open-ended questions, so it's important that you review students' responses and give them feedback. Help students reflect by pointing out things that they did well in their essay as well as offering a few suggestions for improvement.

TRY IT

Informative Writing Skills Wrap-Up

Reflect on Your Informative Essay

Read your informative essay. Then, answer the questions in complete sentences.

1. A strong informative essay begins with a clear introduction.
   a. Does your introduction clearly tell what your essay is about? Explain your answer.
      Answers will vary but may include reflection on language that clearly states the topic of the essay.
   b. What do you think you could improve?
      Answers will vary.

INFORMATIVE WRITING SKILLS WRAP-UP 219

2. The body of an informative essay includes facts and details that develop the topic.
   a. List two facts or details from your essay.
      Answers will vary.
   b. Explain why each fact or detail is important to your audience and purpose.
      Answers will vary.
3. Good writers use transitions to connect ideas.
   a. List one sentence that includes a transition.
      Answers will vary.

220 INFORMATIVE WRITING SKILLS WRAP-UP

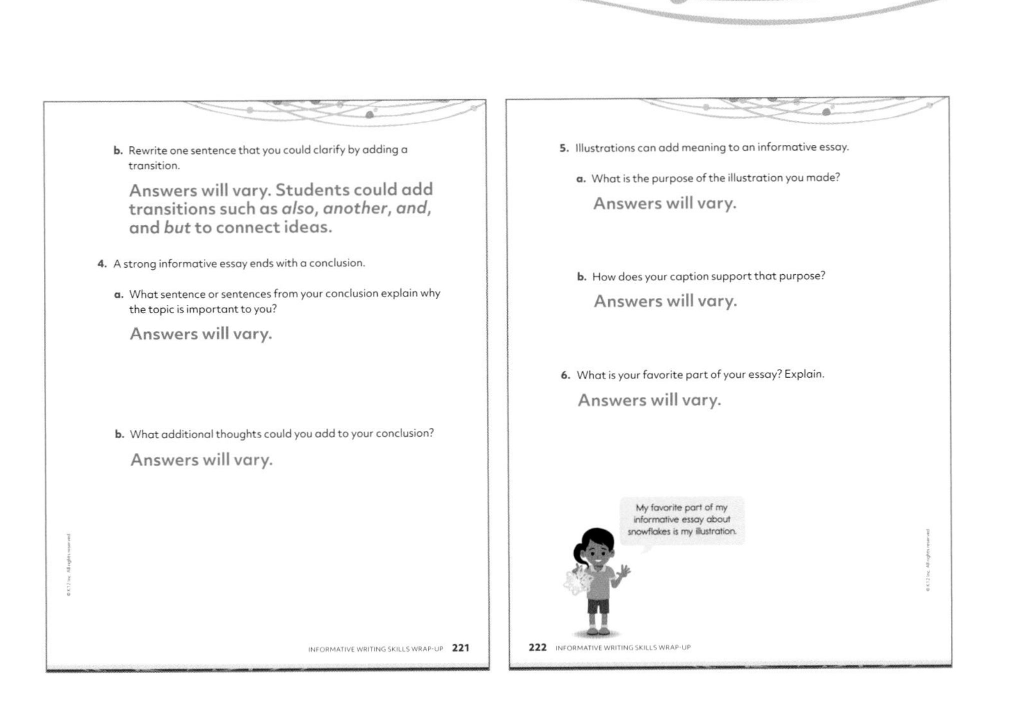

b. Rewrite one sentence that you could clarify by adding a transition.

Answers will vary. Students could add transitions such as *also*, *another*, *and*, and *but* to connect ideas.

4. A strong informative essay ends with a conclusion.

a. What sentence or sentences from your conclusion explain why the topic is important to you?

Answers will vary.

b. What additional thoughts could you add to your conclusion?

Answers will vary.

INFORMATIVE WRITING SKILLS WRAP-UP 221

5. Illustrations can add meaning to an informative essay.

a. What is the purpose of the illustration you made?

Answers will vary.

b. How does your caption support that purpose?

Answers will vary.

6. What is your favorite part of your essay? Explain.

Answers will vary.

My favorite part of my informative essay about snowflakes is my illustration.

222 INFORMATIVE WRITING SKILLS WRAP-UP

Review Nouns

Students will answer questions to review what they have learned about common nouns, proper nouns, abstract nouns, plural nouns, and functions of nouns.

QUIZ

Nouns and Informative Writing Skills

Students will complete the Nouns and Informative Writing Skills quiz.

Spelling List 10

Students will complete the Spelling List 10 quiz.

WRAP-UP

More Language Arts Practice

Students will practice skills according to their individual needs.

Handwriting

Students should gather their handwriting materials and begin where they left off. Remind students to form letters carefully and correctly.

TIP Set a timer to help students stay focused during handwriting practice.

Go Read!

Students will read for pleasure. They should choose a book or a magazine that interests them, or they may choose a selection from the digital library, linked in the online lesson.

- Have students read aloud a few paragraphs of their selection.
- Then have students read silently for the rest of the time.

SUPPORT Students should make no more than five errors in decoding when they read aloud a few paragraphs of their Go Read! selection. If students struggle or make more than five errors, they need to select a different (and easier) text for the Go Read! activity.

TIP Have students select something to read ahead of time to help them stay focused.

Big Ideas: Critical Skills Assignment

Lesson Overview

Big Ideas lessons provide students the opportunity to further apply the knowledge acquired and skills learned throughout the unit workshops. Each Big Ideas lesson consists of these parts:

1. **Cumulative Review:** Students keep their skills fresh by reviewing prior content.
2. **Preview:** Students practice answering the types of questions they will commonly find on standardized tests.
3. **Synthesis:** Students complete an assignment that allows them to connect and apply what they have learned. Synthesis assignments vary throughout the course.

   In the Synthesis portion of this Big Ideas lesson, students will read new selections. They will answer literal and inferential comprehension questions and complete writing questions that ask for short responses about the reading selections. Students should refer to the selections while answering the questions, because the questions emphasize using textual evidence. The questions call for students to demonstrate critical thinking, reading, and writing skills.

   LEARNING COACH CHECK-IN This is a graded assessment. Make sure students complete, review, and submit the assignment to their teacher.

All materials needed for this lesson are linked online and not provided in the activity book.

MATERIALS

Supplied

- Critical Skills Assignment (printout)

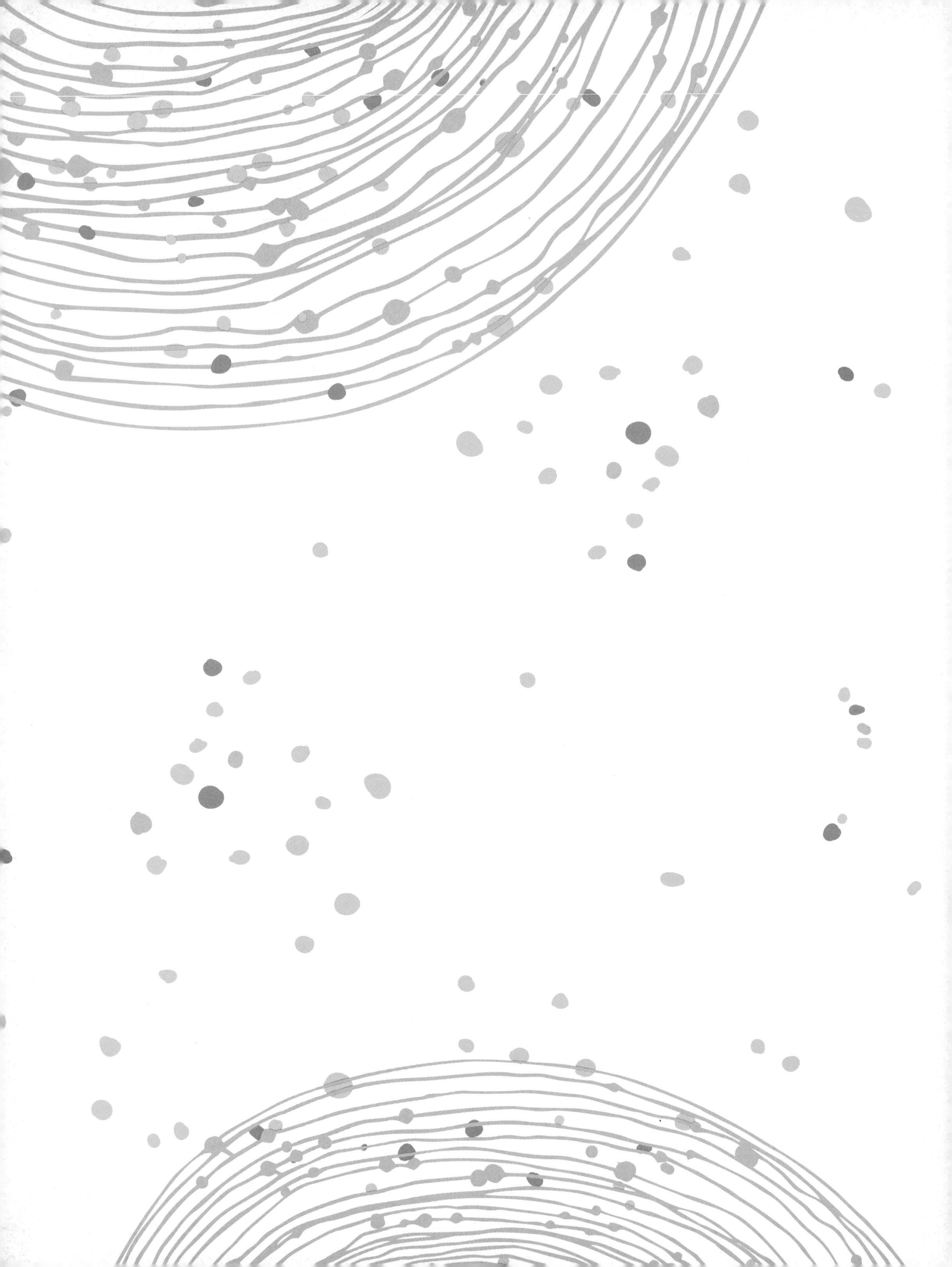

Ancient Greece

Roots and Affixes

Lesson Overview

ACTIVITY	ACTIVITY TITLE	TIME	ONLINE/OFFLINE
GET READY	Introduction to Roots and Affixes	**2** minutes	
	Look Back at Roots and Affixes	**4** minutes	
LEARN AND TRY IT	Roots and Affixes	**10** minutes	
	Practice Roots and Affixes	**10** minutes	
	Apply: Roots and Affixes LEARNING COACH CHECK-IN	**14** minutes	
	Review Roots and Affixes	**15** minutes	
QUIZ	Roots and Affixes	**15** minutes	
WRAP-UP	More Language Arts Practice	**15** minutes	
	Go Write! Your Favorite Place	**15** minutes	
	Go Read!	**20** minutes	or

Content Background

A **root** is a word part that helps give a word its meaning. Most roots are not words on their own. Words are formed when other letters or word parts, called *affixes*, are added to a root. A **prefix** is an affix that appears at the beginning of a root. A **suffix** is an affix that appears at the end of a root. Prefixes and suffixes have meanings, too. Knowing the meanings of roots, prefixes, and suffixes helps determine the meanings of new words.

Root **aud**	Prefix **com–**	Suffixes **–able** and **–ible**
audience	companion	enjoyable
audition	company	sensible

MATERIALS

Supplied

- *Summit English Language Arts 3 Activity Book*
  - Apply: Roots and Affixes
  - Go Write! Your Favorite Place

Also Needed

- reading material for Go Read!

Advance Preparation

During the Go Read! activity, students will have the option of using the digital library. Allow extra time for students to make their reading selection, or have students make a selection before beginning the lesson.

Lesson Goals

- Practice vocabulary words.
- Learn and use roots, prefixes, and suffixes.
- Take the Roots and Affixes quiz.
- Freewrite about a topic to develop writing fluency and practice letter formation.
- Read independently to develop fluency.

KEYWORDS

affix – a word part attached to a root or base word to create a new word

prefix – a word part with its own meaning that can be added to the beginning of a base word or root to make a new word

root – a word part with a special meaning to which prefixes and suffixes can be added; Example: *spec* is a root that means "see"

suffix – a word part added to the end of a base word or root that changes the meaning or part of speech of a word

GET READY

Introduction to Roots and Affixes

After a quick introductory activity, students will read the lesson goals and keywords. Have students select each keyword and preview its definition.

Look Back at Roots and Affixes

Students will practice the prerequisite skill of understanding the meaning of and how to use roots and affixes.

LEARN AND TRY IT

LEARN Roots and Affixes

Students will be introduced to the vocabulary words for the lesson. Then they will learn the roots *act* and *aud* and how adding suffixes to the roots creates words with different meanings.

TRY IT Practice Roots and Affixes

Students will learn and answer questions about the prefix *com–* and the suffixes *–able* and *–ible*.

TRY IT Apply: Roots and Affixes

Students will complete Apply: Roots and Affixes in *Summit English Language Arts 3 Activity Book*. They will create new words by adding the suffix *–able* or the suffix *–ible* to different words. Then they will determine and write the meaning of the new words.

OPTIONAL Have students write sentences using the words they formed and defined.

LEARNING COACH CHECK-IN This activity page contains open-ended questions, so it's important that you review students' responses. Give students feedback, using the sample answers provided to guide you.

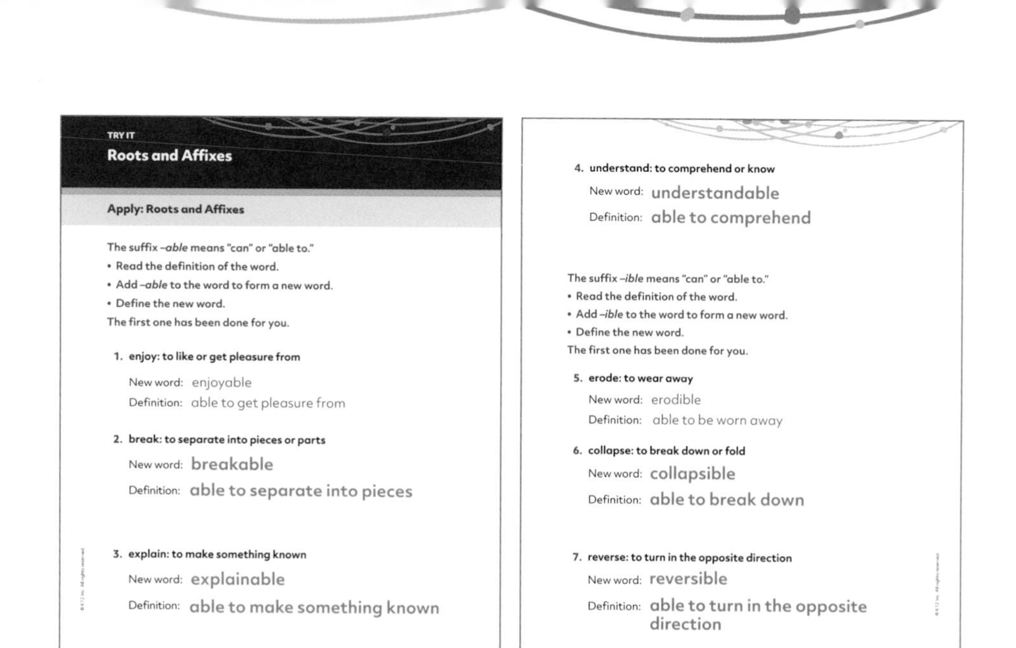
TRY IT
Roots and Affixes

Apply: Roots and Affixes

The suffix *–able* means "can" or "able to."
- Read the definition of the word.
- Add *–able* to the word to form a new word.
- Define the new word.

The first one has been done for you.

1. enjoy: to like or get pleasure from
   New word: enjoyable
   Definition: able to get pleasure from
2. break: to separate into pieces or parts
   New word: breakable
   Definition: able to separate into pieces
3. explain: to make something known
   New word: explainable
   Definition: able to make something known

ROOTS AND AFFIXES 223

4. understand: to comprehend or know
   New word: understandable
   Definition: able to comprehend

The suffix *–ible* means "can" or "able to."
- Read the definition of the word.
- Add *–ible* to the word to form a new word.
- Define the new word.

The first one has been done for you.

5. erode: to wear away
   New word: erodible
   Definition: able to be worn away
6. collapse: to break down or fold
   New word: collapsible
   Definition: able to break down
7. reverse: to turn in the opposite direction
   New word: reversible
   Definition: able to turn in the opposite direction

224 ROOTS AND AFFIXES

TRY IT Review Roots and Affixes

Students will answer questions to review vocabulary word definitions and practice using the words in sentences.

QUIZ

Roots and Affixes

Students will complete the Roots and Affixes quiz.

WRAP-UP

More Language Arts Practice

Students will practice skills according to their individual needs.

Go Write! Your Favorite Place

Students will complete Go Write! Your Favorite Place in *Summit English Language Arts 3 Activity Book*. They will have the option to either respond to a prompt or write about a topic of their choice.

NOTE This activity is intended to build writing fluency. Students should write for the entire allotted time.

SUPPORT If students have trouble writing for the allotted time, prompt them with questions. For example, *Can you provide more details about your favorite place? Why is this your favorite place?*

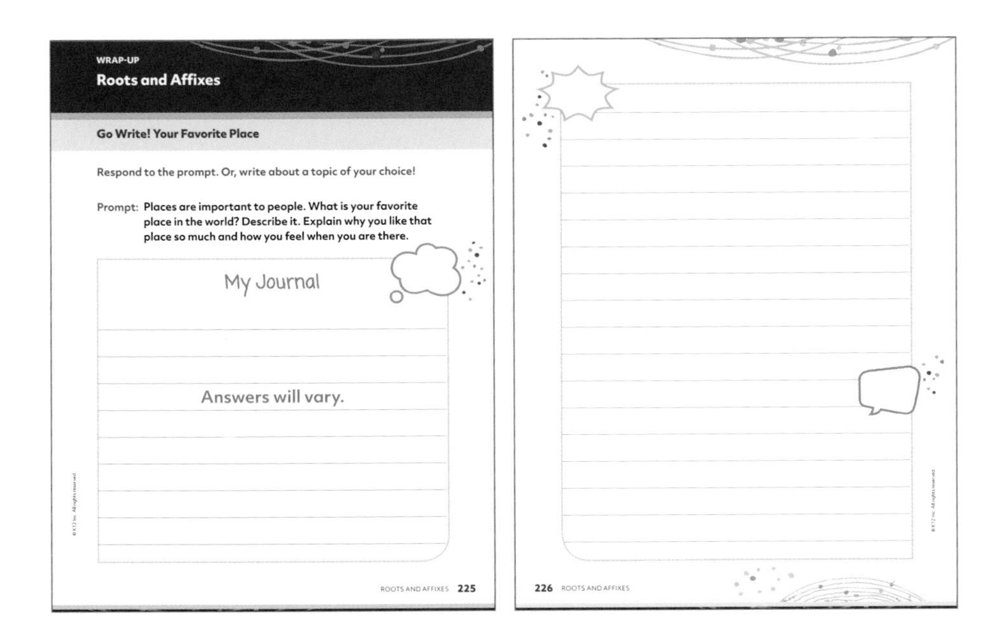

WRAP-UP
Roots and Affixes

Go Write! Your Favorite Place

Respond to the prompt. Or, write about a topic of your choice!

Prompt: Places are important to people. What is your favorite place in the world? Describe it. Explain why you like that place so much and how you feel when you are there.

My Journal

Answers will vary.

ROOTS AND AFFIXES 225

226 ROOTS AND AFFIXES

Go Read!

Students will read for pleasure. They should choose a book or a magazine that interests them, or they may choose a selection from the digital library, linked in the online lesson.

- Have students read aloud a few paragraphs of their selection.
- Then have students read silently for the rest of the time.

SUPPORT Students should make no more than five errors in decoding when they read aloud a few paragraphs of their Go Read! selection. If students struggle or make more than five errors, they need to select a different (and easier) text for the Go Read! activity.

TIP Have students select something to read ahead of time to help them stay focused.

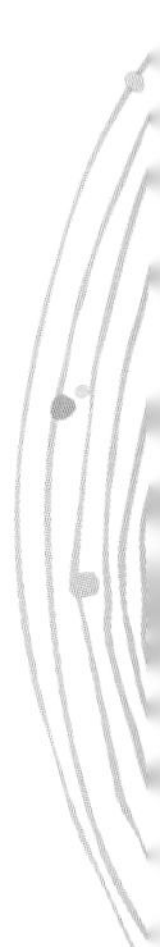

The Glory of Greece (A)

Lesson Overview

ACTIVITY	ACTIVITY TITLE	TIME	ONLINE/OFFLINE
GET READY	Introduction to *The Glory of Greece* (A)	**1** minute	
	Spelling List 11 Pretest **LEARNING COACH CHECK-IN**	**10** minutes	and
	Read and Record	**8** minutes	
	Reading Foundations: Text Features	**5** minutes	
	Before You Read *The Glory of Greece*, Chapters 1 and 2	**13** minutes	
READ	*The Glory of Greece*, Chapters 1 and 2	**15** minutes	
	Check-In: *The Glory of Greece*, Chapters 1 and 2	**5** minutes	
LEARN AND **TRY IT**	Using Text Features	**10** minutes	
	Use Text Features	**10** minutes	
	Apply: Text Features	**15** minutes	
	Practice Using Text Features **LEARNING COACH CHECK-IN**	**10** minutes	
	Practice Words from *The Glory of Greece*, Chapters 1 and 2	**8** minutes	
WRAP-UP	Question About *The Glory of Greece*, Chapters 1 and 2	**2** minutes	
	Handwriting	**8** minutes	

Content Background

The Glory of Greece is a nonfiction chapter book that introduces students to the geography, religion, political system, and culture of ancient Greece. Students will use this text to learn about the country and time period.

Students will also spend some time learning about text features. They will be introduced to text features they will encounter in nonfiction reading material. This lesson will primarily focus on headings, key words, pictures, captions, and maps.

The Glory of Greece, Chapters 1 and 2 Synopsis

Ancient Greek civilization came into being in the eighth century B.C. The civilization lasted for four centuries. Despite existing so long ago, ancient Greece remains an influence on life today.

Land in ancient Greece was rocky and hilly, which made it difficult to farm. Ancient Greeks adapted to the land by growing grains, grapes, and olives. They also gathered along the sea. Greece is a peninsula, and people took advantage of being close to the water to fish, sail, and trade.

Ancient Greeks were polytheists and looked to religion to explain things that happened in their world. They told stories, called myths, about their gods. The judgment of Paris is one myth. It explains how the Trojan War began. Zeus did not want to choose who was fairest among three goddesses: Hera, Aphrodite, and Athena. So Zeus asked Paris to choose. In the end, Paris chose Aphrodite, who promised him a wife. Aphrodite cast a spell over Helen, the most beautiful woman in the land, who also happened to be married to a Greek king. Paris convinced Helen to come with him to Troy. When the Greek king found out, he was angry and declared war on Troy.

MATERIALS

Supplied

- *The Glory of Greece* by Beth Zemble and John Holdren
- *Summit English Language Arts 3 Activity Book*
  - Spelling List 11 Pretest
  - Practice Using Text Features

KEYWORDS

text feature – part of a text that helps a reader locate information and determine what is most important; Examples: title, table of contents, headings, pictures, and glossary

Lesson Goals

- Take a spelling pretest.
- Read Chapters 1 and 2 of *The Glory of Greece*.
- Identify and use text features.
- Explain information found in maps.
- Practice vocabulary words.
- Develop letter formation fluency.

GET READY

Introduction to *The Glory of Greece* (A)

Students will get a glimpse of what they will learn about in the lesson. They will also read the lesson goals and keywords. Have students select each keyword and preview its definition.

Spelling List 11 Pretest

Students will take a spelling pretest and learn a new spelling pattern.

LEARNING COACH CHECK-IN Have students turn to Spelling List 11 Pretest in *Summit English Language Arts 3 Activity Book* and open the online Spelling Pretest activity. Online, students will listen to the spelling word, type the word in the space indicated, and then check their answer. In the activity book, students will write the correct spelling of the word in the tables provided and indicate with a ✓ or an **x** if they spelled the word correctly or incorrectly online. Students will repeat this process with the remaining words.

As needed, help students with the interaction between the online activity and the activity book page until they become comfortable with what they need to do. As students practice their spelling words throughout the workshop, they should pay special attention to words they spelled incorrectly on the pretest.

This is the complete list of words students will be tested on.

Words with /ur/ Sound				
chirp	doctor	earth	pattern	together
circle	dollar	forward	return	turkey
collar	early	learn	Saturday	western
color	earn	numeral	third	worth
curtain				

NOTE Have students keep their completed activity page in a safe place so they can refer to it later.

GET READY

***The Glory of Greece* (A)**

Spelling List 11 Pretest

1. Open the Spelling Pretest activity online. Listen to the first spelling word. Type the word. Check your answer.

2. Write the correct spelling of the word in the Word column of the Spelling Pretest table.

	Word	✓	✗
1	blindfold		

3. Put a check mark in the ✓ column if you spelled the word correctly online.

	Word	✓	✗
1	blindfold	✓	

Put an X in the ✗ column if you spelled the word incorrectly online.

	Word	✓	✗
1	blindfold		X

4. Repeat Steps 1–3 for the remaining words in the Spelling Pretest.

THE GLORY OF GREECE (A) 227

***The Glory of Greece* (A)**

Spelling List 11 Pretest

Write each spelling word in the Word column, making sure to spell it correctly.

	Word	✓	✗
1	chirp		
2	circle		
3	collar		
4	color		
5	curtain		
6	doctor		
7	dollar		
8	early		
9	earn		
10	earth		
11	forward		

	Word	✓	✗
12	learn		
13	numeral		
14	pattern		
15	return		
16	Saturday		
17	third		
18	together		
19	turkey		
20	western		
21	worth		

Students should write the correct spelling of each word from the pretest and use the ✓and X columns to indicate whether they spelled each word correctly or incorrectly online.

228 THE GLORY OF GREECE (A)

Read and Record

Good readers read quickly, smoothly, and with expression. This is called *fluency*. Students will record themselves reading aloud. They will listen to their recording and think about how quick, smooth, and expressive they sound.

TIP Encourage students to rerecord as needed.

Reading Foundations: Text Features

Reading Foundations activities serve to remind students of basic reading skills and reading behaviors mastered in earlier grades. The activities cover topics such as advanced decoding skills and various strategies for improving comprehension.

Before You Read *The Glory of Greece*, Chapters 1 and 2

Students will be introduced to some key vocabulary words that they will encounter in the upcoming reading, review text features, and answer questions to help them set a purpose for their reading.

READ

The Glory of Greece, Chapters 1 and 2

Students will read Chapters 1 and 2 of *The Glory of Greece* by Beth Zemble and John Holdren.

TIP Ensure that students take time to look at all text features they encounter. These features communicate information that might not be explained in the body of the text.

Check-In: *The Glory of Greece*, Chapters 1 and 2

Students will answer several questions to demonstrate their comprehension of Chapters 1 and 2 of *The Glory of Greece*.

LEARN AND TRY IT

LEARN Using Text Features

Students will learn about different features of nonfiction text, including headings, glossaries, illustrations, photographs, captions, and maps.

TRY IT Use Text Features

Students will practice using maps, headings, and captions.

TRY IT Apply: Text Features

Students will apply to a new work what they've learned about using text features.

TRY IT Practice Using Text Features

Students will complete Practice Using Text Features from *Summit English Language Arts 3 Activity Book*.

LEARNING COACH CHECK-IN This activity page contains open-ended questions, so it's important that you review students' responses. Give students feedback, using the sample answers provided to guide you.

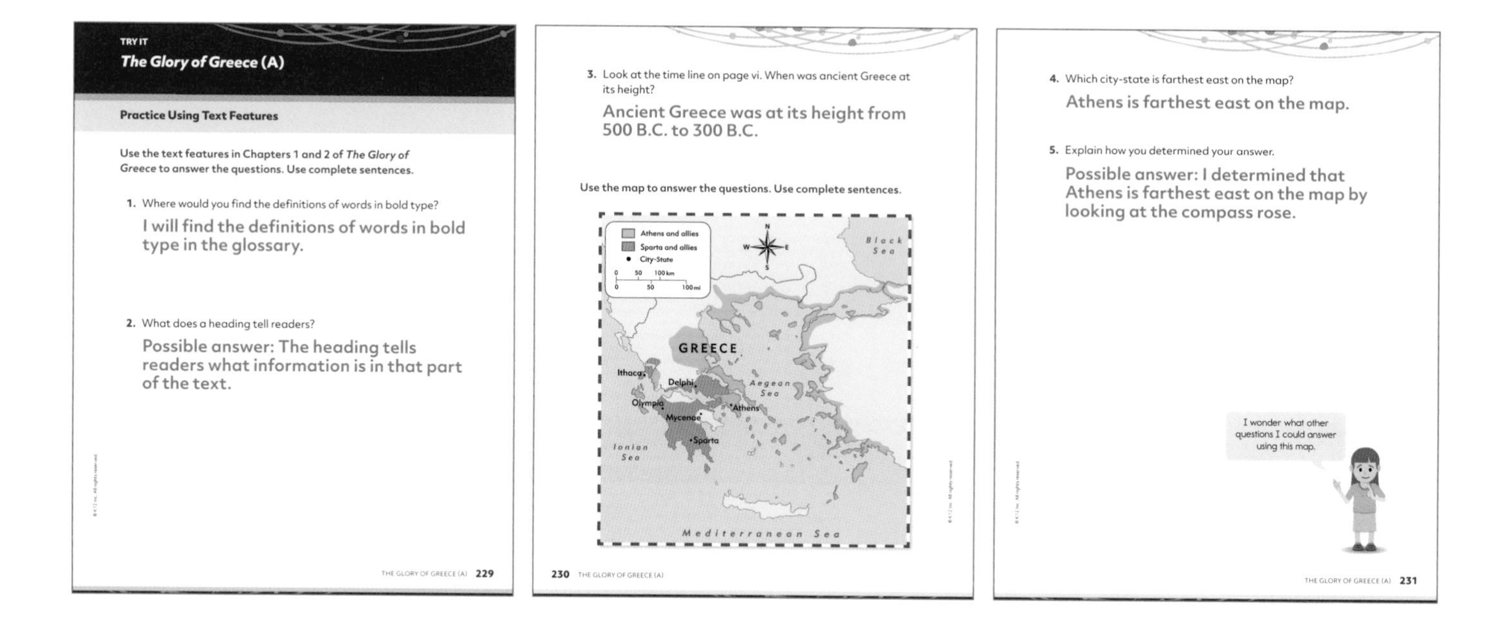

TRY IT

***The Glory of Greece* (A)**

Practice Using Text Features

Use the text features in Chapters 1 and 2 of *The Glory of Greece* to answer the questions. Use complete sentences.

1. Where would you find the definitions of words in bold type?

   I will find the definitions of words in bold type in the glossary.

2. What does a heading tell readers?

   Possible answer: The heading tells readers what information is in that part of the text.

THE GLORY OF GREECE (A) 229

3. Look at the time line on page vi. When was ancient Greece at its height?

   Ancient Greece was at its height from 500 B.C. to 300 B.C.

Use the map to answer the questions. Use complete sentences.

230 THE GLORY OF GREECE (A)

4. Which city-state is farthest east on the map?

   Athens is farthest east on the map.

5. Explain how you determined your answer.

   Possible answer: I determined that Athens is farthest east on the map by looking at the compass rose.

THE GLORY OF GREECE (A) 231

TRY IT Practice Words from *The Glory of Greece*, Chapters 1 and 2

Students will answer questions to demonstrate their understanding of the vocabulary words from the reading.

WRAP-UP

Question About *The Glory of Greece*, Chapters 1 and 2

Students will answer a question to show that they understand how to use a map to find information.

Handwriting

Students should gather their handwriting materials and begin where they left off. Remind students to form letters carefully and correctly.

TIP Set a timer to help students stay focused during handwriting practice.

The Glory of Greece (B)

Lesson Overview

ACTIVITY	ACTIVITY TITLE	TIME	ONLINE/OFFLINE
GET READY	Introduction to *The Glory of Greece* (B)	**1** minute	
	Spelling List 11 Activity Bank	**10** minutes	
	Read and Record	**8** minutes	
	Reading Foundations: Inferences	**5** minutes	
	Recall *The Glory of Greece*, Chapters 1 and 2	**5** minutes	
	Before You Read *The Glory of Greece*, Chapters 3 and 4	**8** minutes	
READ	*The Glory of Greece*, Chapters 3 and 4	**12** minutes	
	Check-In: *The Glory of Greece*, Chapters 3 and 4	**5** minutes	
LEARN AND TRY IT	How to Paraphrase	**8** minutes	
	Try Paraphrasing	**8** minutes	
	Comparing and Contrasting Sparta and Athens	**5** minutes	
	Compare and Contrast Sparta and Athens	**5** minutes	
	Apply: Compare and Contrast	**10** minutes	
	Paraphrase, Compare, and Contrast **LEARNING COACH CHECK-IN**	**12** minutes	
	Practice Words from *The Glory of Greece*, Chapters 3 and 4	**8** minutes	
WRAP-UP	Question About *The Glory of Greece*, Chapters 3 and 4	**2** minutes	
	Handwriting	**8** minutes	

Content Background

Students will read Chapters 3 and 4 of *The Glory of Greece* and review how to paraphrase a text. They will also compare and contrast two city-states in ancient Greece, Sparta and Athens.

Another word for *paraphrasing* is *retelling*. When students paraphrase, they retell what they learn in their own words. Ensure that students include only key details when

they paraphrase. They should also retell information in the same order the information occurs in the text.

Students will also learn about compare-and-contrast text structure, which authors use to organize information. Authors often include signal words, such as *but* and *same*, to indicate that they are using this text structure. When students encounter these and other signal words, they should look for information to compare and contrast.

Advance Preparation

Gather students' completed Spelling List 11 Pretest activity page from *The Glory of Greece* (A). Students will refer to this page during Get Ready: Spelling List 11 Activity Bank.

The Glory of Greece, Chapters 3 and 4 Synopsis

Chapter 3 of *The Glory of Greece* describes two city-states in ancient Greece, Sparta and Athens. Spartans valued war, honor, and glory, while Athenians valued discussion, wisdom, and beauty. Spartans believed in following orders from their leaders, while Athenians worked to form a democracy—a new style of government in which citizens elect their leaders. All people were not equal in Athens. Only free men were considered citizens and could vote. Women and enslaved people did not have this right. U.S. democracy descends from Athenian democracy. Athenian democracy also included a public meeting called the Assembly, in which citizens discussed laws, leadership, and whether to go to war. When people were accused of crimes, a jury of citizens determined whether they were guilty and if so, what punishment they would receive.

Chapter 4 follows the daily routine of a Nestor, an 11-year-old boy who lives in Athens. Nestor wears a tunic, goes to an altar in his house to offer a prayer to Athena, and then washes. He eats breakfast before he heads to school, where he studies poetry, public speaking, math, and philosophy. Nestor walks through the agora, or marketplace, on his way to school and meets up with his friend Darius, with whom he wrestles.

MATERIALS

Supplied

- *The Glory of Greece* by Beth Zemble and John Holdren
- *Summit English Language Arts 3 Activity Book*
  - Spelling List 11 Activity Bank
  - Paraphrase, Compare, and Contrast
- handwriting workbook

Also Needed

- completed Spelling List 11 Pretest activity page from *The Glory of Greece* (A)

KEYWORDS

compare – to explain how two or more things are alike

compare-and-contrast organization – a structure for text that shows how two or more things are similar and different

contrast – to explain how two or more things are different

paraphrase – to restate information in one's own words

Lesson Goals

- Practice spelling words offline.
- Read Chapters 3 and 4 of *The Glory of Greece*.
- Use text features, including maps, illustrations, and headings.
- Paraphrase information in a nonfiction text.
- Compare and contrast information in a nonfiction text.
- Practice vocabulary words.
- Develop letter formation fluency.

GET READY

Introduction to *The Glory of Greece* (B)

Students will get a glimpse of what they will learn about in the lesson. They will also read the lesson goals and keywords. Have students select each keyword and preview its definition.

Spelling List 11 Activity Bank

Students will practice all spelling words from the workshop by completing Spelling List 11 Activity Bank from *Summit English Language Arts 3 Activity Book*. Make sure students have their completed Spelling List 11 Pretest activity page from *The Glory of Greece* (A) to refer to during this activity.

Remind students to pay special attention to words they spelled incorrectly on the Spelling Pretest.

GET READY

***The Glory of Greece* (B)**

Spelling List 11 Activity Bank

Circle any words in the box that you did not spell correctly on your pretest. Choose one activity to do with your circled words. Do as much of the activity as you can in the time given.

Did you spell all the words on the pretest correctly? Do the one activity with as many spelling words as you can.

chirp	doctor	earth	pattern	together
circle	dollar	forward	return	turkey
collar	early	learn	Saturday	western
color	earn	numeral	third	worth
curtain				

Spelling Activity Choices

Hidden Words

1. Draw a picture. "Hide" as many of your spelling words as you can inside the picture.
2. See if others can find the words you hid in the picture.

THE GLORY OF GREECE (B) 233

Triangle Spelling

Write each of your spelling words in a triangle.

d
do
dog

Ghost Words

1. Use a white crayon to write each of your spelling words.
2. Write over the words in white crayon with a colored marker.

234 THE GLORY OF GREECE (B)

Complete the activity that you chose.

My chosen activity: ______

Students should use this page to complete all steps in their chosen activity.

THE GLORY OF GREECE (B) 235

Read and Record

Good readers read quickly, smoothly, and with expression. This is called *fluency*. Students will record themselves reading aloud. They will listen to their recording and think about how quick, smooth, and expressive they sound.

TIP Encourage students to rerecord as needed.

Reading Foundations: Inferences

Reading Foundations activities serve to remind students of basic reading skills and reading behaviors mastered in earlier grades. The activities cover topics such as advanced decoding skills and various strategies for improving comprehension.

Recall *The Glory of Greece*, Chapters 1 and 2

Students will answer some questions to review the reading that they have already completed.

Before You Read *The Glory of Greece*, Chapters 3 and 4

Students will be introduced to some key vocabulary words that they will encounter in the upcoming reading, review text features, and answer questions to help them set a purpose for their reading.

READ

The Glory of Greece, Chapters 3 and 4

Students will read Chapters 3 and 4 of *The Glory of Greece* by Beth Zemble and John Holdren.

Check-In: *The Glory of Greece*, Chapters 3 and 4

Students will answer several questions to demonstrate their comprehension of Chapters 3 and 4 of *The Glory of Greece*.

LEARN AND TRY IT

LEARN How to Paraphrase

Students will learn how to paraphrase a text, including which key details to include and how to organize their paraphrase.

TRY IT Try Paraphrasing

Students will determine what to include and what not to include when paraphrasing text.

LEARN Comparing and Contrasting Sparta and Athens

Students will learn about compare-and-contrast text structure and signal words. They will also learn that the ancient Greek city-states of Sparta and Athens were alike and different.

TRY IT Compare and Contrast Sparta and Athens

Students will use compare-and-contrast text structure to determine how Sparta and Athens were alike and different.

TIP Remind students to look for signal words as they compare and contrast Sparta and Athens.

TRY IT Apply: Compare and Contrast

Students will apply to a new work what they've learned about paraphrasing, comparing, and contrasting effectively.

TRY IT Paraphrase, Compare, and Contrast

Students will complete Paraphrase, Compare, and Contrast in *Summit English Language Arts 3 Activity Book*.

LEARNING COACH CHECK-IN This activity page contains open-ended questions, so it's important that you review students' responses. You may need to help students understand what a Venn diagram is and how to fill it out.

TRY IT

***The Glory of Greece* (B)**

Paraphrase, Compare, and Contrast

Read the excerpt from *The Glory of Greece* by Beth Zemble and John Holdren.

> Democracy in Athens was not perfect. It did not include all the people. In Athens, the citizens voted to choose their leaders. But only free adult men were citizens. Women and slaves were not citizens.
>
> Even though democracy in Athens was not perfect, it was still a bold new idea. In most ancient lands, the people were ruled by kings or by the strongest soldiers or by a few rich men. But in Athens, the citizens could finally rule themselves.

Answer the question in complete sentences.

1. Paraphrase the information about democracy and voting from the passage.

   Democracy in Athens did not include everyone. Citizens voted to choose a leader. Free adult men were citizens, but women and slaves were not. Democracy was a new idea. Usually, kings, strong soldiers, or rich men were in charge. In Athens, the people ruled.

Read pages 17 and 19 of *The Glory of Greece*.

2. Fill in the Venn diagram to show how Sparta and Athens were alike and different.

TRY IT Practice Words from *The Glory of Greece*, Chapters 3 and 4

Students will answer questions to demonstrate their understanding of the vocabulary words from the reading.

WRAP-UP

Question About *The Glory of Greece*, Chapters 3 and 4

Students will answer a question to show that they understand how to compare and contrast information in a text.

Handwriting

Students should gather their handwriting materials and begin where they left off. Remind students to form letters carefully and correctly.

TIP Set a timer to help students stay focused during handwriting practice.

The Glory of Greece (C)

Lesson Overview

ACTIVITY	ACTIVITY TITLE	TIME	ONLINE/OFFLINE
GET READY	Introduction to *The Glory of Greece* (C)	**1** minute	online
	Spelling List 11 Practice	**10** minutes	online
	Read and Record	**5** minutes	online
	Reading Foundations: Asking Questions for Nonfiction Text	**5** minutes	online
	Recall *The Glory of Greece*, Chapters 3 and 4	**5** minutes	online
	Before You Read *The Glory of Greece*, Chapters 5–7	**8** minutes	online
READ	*The Glory of Greece*, Chapters 5–7	**17** minutes	offline
	Check-In: *The Glory of Greece*, Chapters 5–7	**5** minutes	online
LEARN AND **TRY IT**	Using Other Text Features	**5** minutes	online
	Use Other Text Features	**5** minutes	online
	Relating Text Events	**8** minutes	online
	Relate Text Events	**8** minutes	online
	Apply: Relationships Between Events	**8** minutes	online
	They Came from Ancient Greece **LEARNING COACH CHECK-IN**	**12** minutes	offline
	Practice Words from *The Glory of Greece*, Chapters 5–7	**8** minutes	online
WRAP-UP	Question About *The Glory of Greece*, Chapters 5–7	**2** minutes	online
	Handwriting	**8** minutes	offline

Content Background

Students will read Chapters 5–7 of *The Glory of Greece*. They will review text features often found in informational text, such as time lines, appendices, and charts. Students will also explore three ways events in a text may be related: sequence text structure (chronological or time order), cause-and-effect text structure, and compare-and-contrast text structure. Finding signal words in the text, such as *first*, *next*, *then*, and *finally*, will help students determine which events come first in a text that is organized chronologically.

The Glory of Greece, Chapters 5–7 Synopsis

Chapter 5 of *The Glory of Greece* describes ancient Greek art and architecture. It introduces the Parthenon, a Greek temple built 2,500 years ago to honor Athena. The ruins of the Parthenon are still standing on the Acropolis in Athens, Greece. Ancient Greek architecture used three different types of columns: Doric, Ionic, and Corinthian. Ancient Greek artworks included sculptures, friezes, and pottery.

Chapter 6 presents an important part of cultural life in ancient Greece: going to the theater. Most large cities had theaters, and ancient Greeks spent days at the theater watching comedies and tragedies. All actors in ancient Greece were men, and they used masks to project emotions. Most Greek plays contained a chorus that commented on the play's action.

Chapter 7 focuses on the Olympic Games, past and present. The games originally started as a running race at the foot of Mount Olympus. Eventually, other events were added to the games, including the *pankration*, an event that combined boxing and wrestling. The Olympics were so important that fighting ceased for three months during the games.

MATERIALS

Supplied

- *The Glory of Greece* by Beth Zemble and John Holdren
- *Summit English Language Arts 3 Activity Book*
  - They Came from Ancient Greece
- handwriting workbook

KEYWORDS

cause and effect – when one thing—the cause—makes another thing—the effect—happen

compare-and-contrast organization – a structure for text that shows how two or more things are similar and different

text feature – part of a text that helps a reader locate information and determine what is most important; Examples: title, table of contents, headings, pictures, and glossary

time order – arrangement of ideas according to when they happen

Lesson Goals

- Practice spelling words online.
- Read Chapters 5–7 of *The Glory of Greece*.
- Use text features, including time lines, appendices, and charts.
- Identify relationships among events in a text.
- Practice vocabulary words.
- Develop letter formation fluency.

GET READY

Introduction to *The Glory of Greece* (C)

Students will get a glimpse of what they will learn about in the lesson. They will also read the lesson goals and keywords. Have students select each keyword and preview its definition.

Spelling List 11 Practice

Students will practice all spelling words from the workshop.

OPTIONAL Students may do an activity from Spelling List 11 Activity Bank instead of the online practice activity.

Read and Record

Good readers read quickly, smoothly, and with expression. This is called *fluency*. Students will record themselves reading aloud. They will listen to their recording and think about how quick, smooth, and expressive they sound.

TIP Encourage students to rerecord as needed.

Reading Foundations: Asking Questions for Nonfiction Text

Reading Foundations activities serve to remind students of basic reading skills and reading behaviors mastered in earlier grades. The activities cover topics such as advanced decoding skills and various strategies for improving comprehension.

Recall *The Glory of Greece*, Chapters 3 and 4

Students will answer some questions to review the reading that they have already completed.

Before You Read *The Glory of Greece*, Chapters 5–7

Students will be introduced to some key vocabulary words that they will encounter in the upcoming reading, learn more about using text features, and answer questions to make predictions and help them set a purpose for their reading.

READ

The Glory of Greece, Chapters 5–7

Students will read Chapters 5–7 of *The Glory of Greece* by Beth Zemble and John Holdren.

Check-In: *The Glory of Greece*, Chapters 5–7

Students will answer several questions to demonstrate their comprehension of Chapters 5–7 of *The Glory of Greece*.

LEARN AND TRY IT

LEARN Using Other Text Features

Students will explore text features that frequently appear in nonfiction text: a time line, an appendix, and a chart.

NOTE If students struggle with the idea of a time line, help them create a time line of their own life, beginning with their birth and including other important events. This exercise may help them understand how time and events are related and can be visualized.

TRY IT Use Other Text Features

Students will practice using text features to find information.

LEARN Relating Text Events

Students will explore three different ways events in texts can be related: sequence structure, cause-and-effect structure, and compare-and-contrast structure.

TRY IT Relate Text Events

Student will practice determining which text structure an author uses to indicate how events in a text are related.

TRY IT Apply: Relationships Between Events

Students will apply to a new work what they've learned about other text features and how events in a text are related.

TRY IT They Came from Ancient Greece

Students will complete They Came from Ancient Greece in *Summit English Language Arts 3 Activity Book*.

LEARNING COACH CHECK-IN This activity page contains open-ended questions, so it's important that you review students' responses. Assist students in identifying three ideas or events that originated in ancient Greece and how those ideas or events affect life today.

NOTE Have students keep their completed activity page in a safe place so they can refer to it later.

TRY IT

The Glory of Greece (C)

They Came from Ancient Greece

Many ideas and events that were born in ancient Greece still exist and happen today. Choose three ideas or events from the list. Brainstorm how those ideas or events affect our lives today.

Olympic Games   art and architecture   trial by jury
going to plays   democracy

Event/Idea 1: ______

Students should choose three events or ideas from the box. For each event or idea, they should explain how it affects life today.

Possible answer for "Olympic Games": The Olympic Games from ancient Greece affect our lives today because we still take time to watch the best athletes in the world and celebrate the winners.

THE GLORY OF GREECE (C) 241

Event/Idea 2: ______

Event/Idea 3: ______

242 THE GLORY OF GREECE (C)

TRY IT **Practice Words from *The Glory of Greece*, Chapters 5–7**

Students will answer questions to demonstrate their understanding of the vocabulary words from the reading.

WRAP-UP

Question About *The Glory of Greece*, Chapters 5–7

Students will answer a question to show that they understand how events are related in the text.

Handwriting

Students should gather their handwriting materials and begin where they left off. Remind students to form letters carefully and correctly.

TIP Set a timer to help students stay focused during handwriting practice.

The Glory of Greece (D)

Lesson Overview

ACTIVITY	ACTIVITY TITLE	TIME	ONLINE/OFFLINE
GET READY	Introduction to *The Glory of Greece* (D)	**1** minute	
	Spelling List 11 Review Game	**10** minutes	
	Read and Record	**5** minutes	
	Reading Foundations: Context	**5** minutes	
	Recall *The Glory of Greece*, Chapters 5–7	**5** minutes	
	Before You Read *The Glory of Greece*, Chapter 8 and Conclusion	**5** minutes	
READ	*The Glory of Greece*, Chapter 8 and Conclusion	**23** minutes	
	Check-In: *The Glory of Greece*, Chapter 8 and Conclusion	**5** minutes	
LEARN AND **TRY IT**	Making Inferences and Drawing Conclusions	**8** minutes	
	Make Inferences and Draw Conclusions	**10** minutes	
	Apply: Make Inferences	**10** minutes	
	Draw a Conclusion **LEARNING COACH CHECK-IN**	**15** minutes	
	Practice Words from *The Glory of Greece*, Chapter 8, Conclusion	**8** minutes	
WRAP-UP	Question About *The Glory of Greece*, Chapter 8	**2** minutes	
	Handwriting	**8** minutes	

Content Background

Students will read Chapter 8 and the conclusion of *The Glory of Greece*. They will review using text features to make a prediction. Students will also review how to make an inference based on information in the text and learn how to draw a conclusion from what they already know. Good readers use these important skills, so it is key that students understand how to infer and conclude.

If students struggle with the difference between inferring and concluding, it can be helpful to point out that an inference is a guess that they make when looking at evidence in the text. An inference sometimes answers the question, "What might come next?" A conclusion, on the other hand, is a decision they make or opinion they form after they have finished reading.

Advance Preparation

Gather students' completed They Came from Ancient Greece activity page from *The Glory of Greece* (C). Students will refer to this page during Try It: Draw a Conclusion.

MATERIALS

Supplied

- *The Glory of Greece* by Beth Zemble and John Holdren
- *Summit English Language Arts 3 Activity Book*
  - Draw a Conclusion
- handwriting workbook

Also Needed

- completed They Came from Ancient Greece activity page from *The Glory of Greece* (C)

The Glory of Greece, Chapter 8 and Conclusion Synopsis

Chapter 8 of *The Glory of Greece* presents four philosophers who lived, wrote, and asked questions in ancient Greece. Socrates led his students to wisdom by asking questions and encouraging people to think about the best ways to live their lives. Socrates's student, Plato, wrote books and recorded some of the questions Socrates asked. Plato also founded the Academy, a school where people discussed big questions and studied math and science. Plato's student, Aristotle, asked lots of "why" questions and built a school. Aristotle also wrote the first encyclopedia. Hippocrates is often called the father of modern medicine. He determined that bodily illness was not a punishment from the gods but rather a problem in body.

The conclusion to *The Glory of Greece* briefly explains the legacy of ancient Greece, including how archaeologists study ruins and artifacts and how Homer's stories were passed orally through the centuries. The book concludes with a quick wrap-up of the things from ancient Greece still in existence in modern life, including democracy.

Lesson Goals

- Practice all spelling words online.
- Read Chapter 8 and the conclusion of *The Glory of Greece*.
- Make inferences and draw conclusions.
- Convey ideas in writing.
- Practice vocabulary words.
- Develop letter formation fluency.

GET READY

Introduction to *The Glory of Greece* (D)

Students will get a glimpse of what they will learn about in the lesson. They will also read the lesson goals and keywords. Have students select each keyword and preview its definition.

Spelling List 11 Review Game

Students will practice all spelling words from the workshop.

Read and Record

Good readers read quickly, smoothly, and with expression. This is called *fluency*. Students will record themselves reading aloud. They will listen to their recording and think about how quick, smooth, and expressive they sound.

TIP Encourage students to rerecord as needed.

Reading Foundations: Context

Reading Foundations activities serve to remind students of basic reading skills and reading behaviors mastered in earlier grades. The activities cover topics such as advanced decoding skills and various strategies for improving comprehension.

Recall *The Glory of Greece*, Chapter 5–7

Students will answer some questions to review the reading that they have already completed.

Before You Read *The Glory of Greece*, Chapter 8 and Conclusion

Students will be introduced to some key vocabulary words that they will encounter in the upcoming reading and answer questions to help them set a purpose for their reading.

READ

The Glory of Greece, Chapter 8 and Conclusion

Students will read Chapter 8 and the conclusion of *The Glory of Greece* by Beth Zemble and John Holdren.

Check-In: *The Glory of Greece*, Chapter 8 and Conclusion

Students will answer several questions to demonstrate their comprehension of Chapter 8 and the conclusion of *The Glory of Greece*.

LEARN AND TRY IT

LEARN Making Inferences and Drawing Conclusions

Students will review how to make inferences based on information in a text and learn how to draw conclusions.

NOTE It may be helpful to explain to students that there are two types of conclusions used in English Language Arts:

conclusion: a decision made, or opinion formed, about something not stated, using information provided and what is already known

conclusion: the final paragraph (or chapter) of a written work

Though both will be mentioned in this lesson, students will primarily explore the first type.

TRY IT Make Inferences and Draw Conclusions

Students will practice making inferences and drawing conclusions.

TRY IT Apply: Make Inferences

Students will apply to a new work what they've learned about making inferences and drawing conclusions.

TRY IT Draw a Conclusion

Students will complete Draw a Conclusion in *Summit English Language Arts 3 Activity Book*. Make sure students have their completed They Came from Ancient Greece activity page from *The Glory of Greece* (C) to refer to during this activity.

LEARNING COACH CHECK-IN This activity page contains open-ended responses, so it's important that you review students' responses. Guide students to a conclusion about what from ancient Greece remains with us today and why.

NOTE Have students keep their completed activity page in a safe place so they can refer to it later.

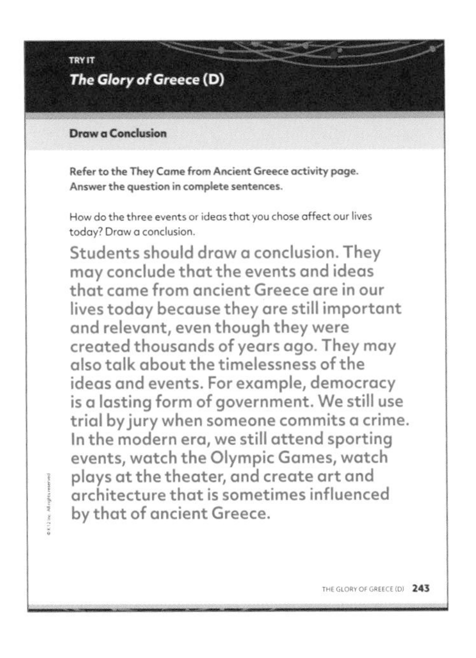
TRY IT
The Glory of Greece (D)

Draw a Conclusion

Refer to the They Came from Ancient Greece activity page. Answer the question in complete sentences.

How do the three events or ideas that you chose affect our lives today? Draw a conclusion.

Students should draw a conclusion. They may conclude that the events and ideas that came from ancient Greece are in our lives today because they are still important and relevant, even though they were created thousands of years ago. They may also talk about the timelessness of the ideas and events. For example, democracy is a lasting form of government. We still use trial by jury when someone commits a crime. In the modern era, we still attend sporting events, watch the Olympic Games, watch plays at the theater, and create art and architecture that is sometimes influenced by that of ancient Greece.

THE GLORY OF GREECE (D) 243

TRY IT **Practice Words from *The Glory of Greece*, Chapter 8, Conclusion**

Students will answer questions to demonstrate their understanding of the vocabulary words from the reading.

WRAP-UP

Question About *The Glory of Greece*, Chapter 8

Students will answer a question to show that they understand the information presented in Chapter 8.

Handwriting

Students should gather their handwriting materials and begin where they left off. Remind students to form letters carefully and correctly.

TIP Set a timer to help students stay focused during handwriting practice.

The Glory of Greece Wrap-Up

Lesson Overview

ACTIVITY	ACTIVITY TITLE	TIME	ONLINE/OFFLINE
GET READY	Introduction to *The Glory of Greece* Wrap-Up	**1** minute	online
	Read and Record	**8** minutes	online
TRY IT	Ancient Greece and Modern Life LEARNING COACH CHECK-IN	**30** minutes	offline
	Review *The Glory of Greece*	**20** minutes	online
QUIZ	*The Glory of Greece*	**30** minutes	online
	Spelling List 11	**10** minutes	online
WRAP-UP	More Language Arts Practice	**13** minutes	online
	Handwriting	**8** minutes	offline

Advance Preparation

Gather students' completed They Came from Ancient Greece activity page from *The Glory of Greece* (C) and Draw a Conclusion activity page from *The Glory of Greece* (D). Students will refer to these pages during Try It: Ancient Greece and Modern Life.

MATERIALS

Supplied

- *The Glory of Greece* by Beth Zemble and John Holdren
- *Summit English Language Arts 3 Activity Book*
  - Ancient Greece and Modern Life
- handwriting workbook

Also Needed

- completed They Came from Ancient Greece activity page from *The Glory of Greece* (C)
- completed Draw a Conclusion activity page from *The Glory of Greece* (D)

Lesson Goals

- Make inferences and draw conclusions.
- Use text features such as maps and images.
- Explain how events and parts of a text are related.
- Take a reading quiz.
- Take a spelling quiz.
- Develop letter formation fluency.

GET READY

Introduction to *The Glory of Greece* Wrap-Up

Students will read the lesson goals.

Read and Record

Good readers read quickly, smoothly, and with expression. This is called *fluency*. Students will record themselves reading aloud. They will listen to their recording and think about how quick, smooth, and expressive they sound.

TIP Encourage students to rerecord as needed.

TRY IT

Ancient Greece and Modern Life

Students will complete Ancient Greece and Modern Life in *Summit English Language Arts 3 Activity Book*. Make sure students have their completed They Came from Ancient Greece activity page from *The Glory of Greece* (C) and Draw a Conclusion activity page from *The Glory of Greece* (D) to refer to during this activity.

LEARNING COACH CHECK-IN This activity page contains an open-ended prompt, so it's important that you review students' responses. Give students feedback, using the sample answers provided to guide you.

TRY IT

***The Glory of Greece* Wrap-Up**

Ancient Greece and Modern Life

Read the writing prompt.

Prompt: **Write an essay about ancient Greece and modern life. Include the following:**

- An introduction
- A body that describes your three ideas or events from the They Came from Ancient Greece activity page
- Your conclusion from the Draw a Conclusion activity page
- Transitions such as *for example* and *also*

Respond to the writing prompt.

Students should write about three events or ideas that originated in ancient Greece and are still relevant today. They should draw a conclusion at the end of their writing. A possible conclusion they might draw is that the ideas and events from ancient Greece are still part of modern-day life because they are important or timeless.

THE GLORY OF GREECE WRAP-UP 245

246 THE GLORY OF GREECE WRAP-UP

Review *The Glory of Greece*

Students will answer questions to review what they have learned about using text features, determining how events are related in a text, making inferences, and drawing conclusions.

QUIZ

The Glory of Greece

Students will complete *The Glory of Greece* quiz.

Spelling List 11

Students will complete the Spelling List 11 quiz.

WRAP-UP

More Language Arts Practice

Students will practice skills according to their individual needs.

Handwriting

Students should gather their handwriting materials and begin where they left off. Remind students to form letters carefully and correctly.

TIP Set a timer to help students stay focused during handwriting practice.

Informative Writing: Prewriting (A)

Lesson Overview

ACTIVITY	ACTIVITY TITLE	TIME	ONLINE/OFFLINE
GET READY	Introduction to Informative Writing: Prewriting (A)	**1** minute	(online)
	Spelling List 12 Pretest **LEARNING COACH CHECK-IN**	**10** minutes	(online) and (offline)
	Look Back at Contractions	**4** minutes	(online)
LEARN AND **TRY IT**	Singular Possessive Nouns	**10** minutes	(online)
	Form and Use Singular Possessive Nouns	**10** minutes	(online)
	Explore a Model Research Report	**10** minutes	(online)
	Respond to a Research Report	**10** minutes	(online)
	Brainstorming for a Research Report	**10** minutes	(online)
	Brainstorm for Your Research Report **LEARNING COACH CHECK-IN**	**20** minutes	(offline)
WRAP-UP	Questions About Possessive Nouns and Brainstorming	**4** minutes	(online)
	Handwriting	**8** minutes	(offline)
	Go Read!	**23** minutes	(online) or (offline)

Content Background

Students will begin working on a **research report** about a U.S. state. They will complete this assignment over the course of several lessons by following the writing process. Students will begin by prewriting.

Writing Process

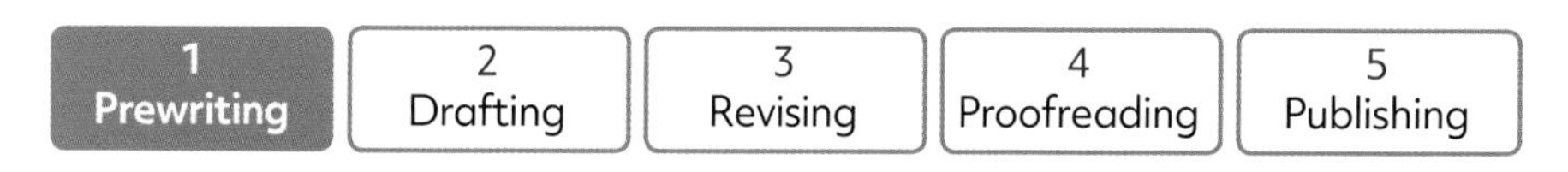

During **prewriting**, writers choose a topic and create a plan for their writing assignment. In this lesson, students will complete the first part of prewriting, choosing a topic. To do that, they'll **brainstorm** by answering questions intended to activate their prior knowledge and interest about U.S. states (e.g., *Which states would you visit if you could?*).

MATERIALS

Supplied

- *Summit English Language Arts 3 Activity Book*
  - Spelling List 12 Pretest
  - Model Research Report
  - Brainstorm for Your Research Report
- handwriting workbook

Also Needed

- folder for organizing research report assignment pages
- reading material for Go Read!

Grammar, Usage, and Mechanics A **possessive noun** shows ownership. To make a singular noun possessive, add an apostrophe and an –*s* to the end of the word.

In the following example, the name belongs to Eli, and the cover belongs to the book.

> **Example:** Is that **Eli's** name on the **book's** cover?

Even if a singular noun ends with an –*s*, add an apostrophe and an –*s* to make it possessive.

> **Example:** **James's** goal is to finish the race.

KEYWORDS

brainstorming – before writing, a way for the writer to come up with ideas

possessive noun – the form of a noun that shows ownership

prewriting – the stage or step of writing in which a writer chooses a topic, gathers ideas, and plans what to write

research report – a type of essay based mainly on the author's research

Advance Preparation

Gather a folder that students can use to keep all notes and activity pages related to their research report.

During the Go Read! activity, students will have the option of using the digital library. Allow extra time for students to make their reading selection, or have students make a selection before beginning the lesson.

Lesson Goals

- Take a spelling pretest.
- Form and use singular possessive nouns.
- Read a model research report, and start planning your own.
- Develop letter formation fluency.
- Read independently to develop fluency.

GET READY

Introduction to Informative Writing: Prewriting (A)

Students will get a glimpse of what they will learn about in the lesson. They will also read the lesson goals and keywords. Have students select each keyword and preview its definition.

Spelling List 12 Pretest

Students will take a spelling pretest and learn a new spelling pattern.

LEARNING COACH CHECK-IN Have students turn to Spelling List 12 Pretest in *Summit English Language Arts 3 Activity Book* and open the online Spelling Pretest activity. Online, students will listen to the spelling word, type the word in the space indicated, and then check their answer. In the activity book,

students will write the correct spelling of the word in the tables provided and indicate with a ✓ or an ✗ if they spelled the word correctly or incorrectly online. Students will repeat this process with the remaining words.

As needed, help students with the interaction between the online activity and the activity book page until they become comfortable with what they need to do. As students practice their spelling words throughout the workshop, they should pay special attention to words they spelled incorrectly on the pretest.

This is the complete list of words students will be tested on.

Words with Long *e* or Long *i* Spelled *y*		
copy	many	crybaby
country	penny	deny
empty	story	myself
fluffy	study	notify
fuzzy	sturdy	pry
hungry	windy	reply
hurry	apply	spy

NOTE Have students keep their completed activity page in a safe place so they can refer to it later.

GET READY

Informative Writing: Prewriting (A)

Spelling List 12 Pretest

1. Open the Spelling Pretest activity online. Listen to the first spelling word. Type the word. Check your answer.
2. Write the correct spelling of the word in the Word column of the Spelling Pretest table.

	Word	✓	✗
1	blindfold		

3. Put a check mark in the ✓ column if you spelled the word correctly online.

	Word	✓	✗
1	blindfold	✓	

Put an X in the ✗ column if you spelled the word incorrectly online.

	Word	✓	✗
1	blindfold		X

4. Repeat Steps 1–3 for the remaining words in the Spelling Pretest.

INFORMATIVE WRITING: PREWRITING (A) 249

Informative Writing: Prewriting (A)

Spelling List 12 Pretest

Write each spelling word in the Word column, making sure to spell it correctly.

	Word	✓	✗		Word	✓	✗
1	copy			12	sturdy		
2	country			13	windy		
3	empty			14	apply		
4	fluffy			15	crybaby		
5	fuzzy			16	deny		
6	hungry			17	myself		
7	hurry			18	notify		
8	many			19	pry		
9	penny			20	reply		
10	story			21	spy		
11	study						

Students should write the correct spelling of each word from the pretest and use the ✓ and X columns to indicate whether they spelled each word correctly or incorrectly online.

250 INFORMATIVE WRITING: PREWRITING (A)

Look Back at Contractions

Students will practice the prerequisite skill of using apostrophes to form contractions.

LEARN AND TRY IT

LEARN Singular Possessive Nouns

Students will learn how to form and use singular possessive nouns.

TIP After learning about the apostrophe, students may overuse it. Watch for students who use the apostrophe to form plural nouns that are not possessive.

TRY IT Form and Use Singular Possessive Nouns

Students will practice forming singular possessive nouns and using them correctly in sentences.

LEARN Explore a Model Research Report

By reading and exploring a model research report, students will learn what a research report is and how it is organized.

TIP The model research report that students read in the online activity is the same piece of writing on the Model Research Report activity page. Students may wish to reference and make notes on this page as they complete the online activity.

TRY IT Respond to a Research Report

Students will answer questions about the ideas and organization of the model research report to ensure that they understand the genre and their writing assignment.

LEARN Brainstorming for a Research Report

Students will explore how a writer uses a questionnaire to narrow down a topic for a research report.

TRY IT Brainstorm for Your Research Report

Students will complete Brainstorm for Your Research Report in *Summit English Language Arts 3 Activity Book*. They should have the Model Research Report activity page to refer to as they work.

LEARNING COACH CHECK-IN This activity page contains open-ended questions, so it's important that you review students' responses. Work with students to ensure that they choose a state that they are excited to learn more about.

NOTE Have students add the Model Research Report and their completed Brainstorm for Your Research Report activity page to the folder they are using to store their research report assignment pages.

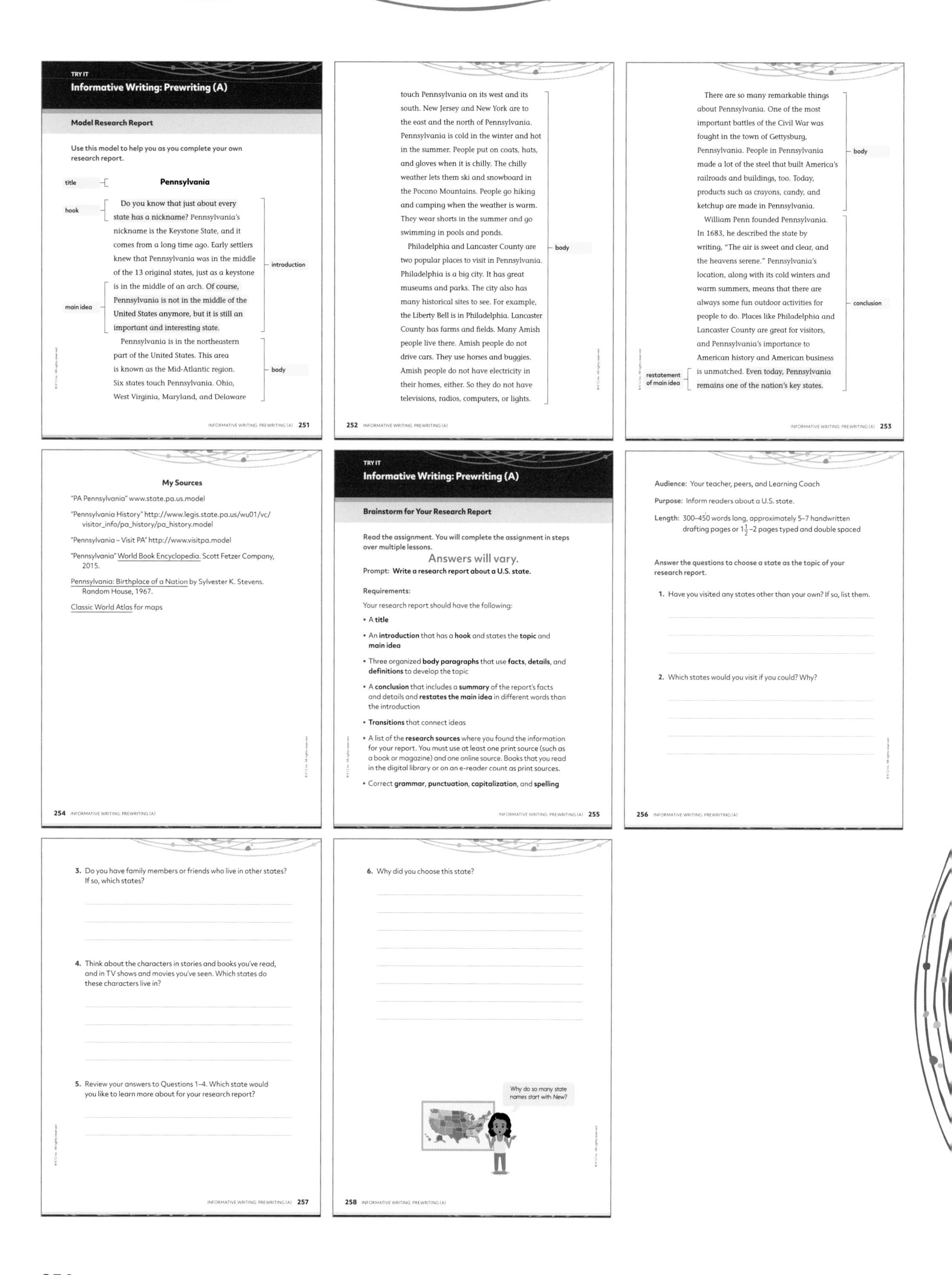

TRY IT

Informative Writing: Prewriting (A)

Model Research Report

Use this model to help you as you complete your own research report.

title — **Pennsylvania**

hook — Do you know that just about every state has a nickname? Pennsylvania's nickname is the Keystone State, and it comes from a long time ago. Early settlers knew that Pennsylvania was in the middle of the 13 original states, just as a keystone is in the middle of an arch. Of course, Pennsylvania is not in the middle of the United States anymore, but it is still an important and interesting state. — introduction (main idea)

Pennsylvania is in the northeastern part of the United States. This area is known as the Mid-Atlantic region. Six states touch Pennsylvania. Ohio, West Virginia, Maryland, and Delaware touch Pennsylvania on its west and its south. New Jersey and New York are to the east and the north of Pennsylvania. Pennsylvania is cold in the winter and hot in the summer. People put on coats, hats, and gloves when it is chilly. The chilly weather lets them ski and snowboard in the Pocono Mountains. People go hiking and camping when the weather is warm. They wear shorts in the summer and go swimming in pools and ponds. — body

Philadelphia and Lancaster County are two popular places to visit in Pennsylvania. Philadelphia is a big city. It has great museums and parks. The city also has many historical sites to see. For example, the Liberty Bell is in Philadelphia. Lancaster County has farms and fields. Many Amish people live there. Amish people do not drive cars. They use horses and buggies. Amish people do not have electricity in their homes, either. So they do not have televisions, radios, computers, or lights. — body

There are so many remarkable things about Pennsylvania. One of the most important battles of the Civil War was fought in the town of Gettysburg, Pennsylvania. People in Pennsylvania made a lot of the steel that built America's railroads and buildings, too. Today, products such as crayons, candy, and ketchup are made in Pennsylvania. — body

William Penn founded Pennsylvania. In 1683, he described the state by writing, "The air is sweet and clear, and the heavens serene." Pennsylvania's location, along with its cold winters and warm summers, means that there are always some fun outdoor activities for people to do. Places like Philadelphia and Lancaster County are great for visitors, and Pennsylvania's importance to American history and American business is unmatched. Even today, Pennsylvania remains one of the nation's key states. — conclusion (restatement of main idea)

My Sources

"PA Pennsylvania" www.state.pa.us.model

"Pennsylvania History" http://www.legis.state.pa.us/wu01/vc/visitor_info/pa_history/pa_history.model

"Pennsylvania – Visit PA" http://www.visitpa.model

"Pennsylvania" World Book Encyclopedia. Scott Fetzer Company, 2015.

Pennsylvania: Birthplace of a Nation by Sylvester K. Stevens. Random House, 1967.

Classic World Atlas for maps

TRY IT

Informative Writing: Prewriting (A)

Brainstorm for Your Research Report

Read the assignment. You will complete the assignment in steps over multiple lessons.

Answers will vary.

Prompt: **Write a research report about a U.S. state.**

Requirements:

Your research report should have the following:

- A **title**
- An **introduction** that has a **hook** and states the **topic** and **main idea**
- Three organized **body paragraphs** that use **facts**, **details**, and **definitions** to develop the topic
- A **conclusion** that includes a **summary** of the report's facts and details and **restates the main idea** in different words than the introduction
- **Transitions** that connect ideas
- A list of the **research sources** where you found the information for your report. You must use at least one print source (such as a book or magazine) and one online source. Books that you read in the digital library or on an e-reader count as print sources.
- Correct **grammar**, **punctuation**, **capitalization**, and **spelling**

Audience: Your teacher, peers, and Learning Coach

Purpose: Inform readers about a U.S. state.

Length: 300–450 words long, approximately 5–7 handwritten drafting pages or $1\frac{1}{2}$–2 pages typed and double spaced

Answer the questions to choose a state as the topic of your research report.

1. Have you visited any states other than your own? If so, list them.
2. Which states would you visit if you could? Why?
3. Do you have family members or friends who live in other states? If so, which states?
4. Think about the characters in stories and books you've read, and in TV shows and movies you've seen. Which states do these characters live in?
5. Review your answers to Questions 1–4. Which state would you like to learn more about for your research report?
6. Why did you choose this state?

INFORMATIVE WRITING: PREWRITING (A) 251 · 252 · 253 · 254 · 255 · 256 · 257 · 258

WRAP-UP

Questions About Possessive Nouns and Brainstorming

Students will answer questions to show that they understand how to form singular possessive nouns and brainstorm for a research report.

Handwriting

Students should gather their handwriting materials and begin where they left off. Remind students to form letters carefully and correctly.

TIP Set a timer to help students stay focused during handwriting practice.

Go Read!

Students will read for pleasure. They should choose a book or a magazine that interests them, or they may choose a selection from the digital library, linked in the online lesson.

- Have students read aloud a few paragraphs of their selection.
- Then have students read silently for the rest of the time.

SUPPORT Students should make no more than five errors in decoding when they read aloud a few paragraphs of their Go Read! selection. If students struggle or make more than five errors, they need to select a different (and easier) text for the Go Read! activity.

TIP Have students select something to read ahead of time to help them stay focused.

Informative Writing: Prewriting (B)

Lesson Overview

ACTIVITY	ACTIVITY TITLE	TIME	ONLINE/OFFLINE
GET READY	Introduction to Informative Writing: Prewriting (B)	**1** minute	online
	Spelling List 12 Activity Bank	**10** minutes	offline
LEARN AND TRY IT	Plural Possessive Nouns	**10** minutes	online
	Form and Use Plural Possessive Nouns	**10** minutes	online
	Conducting Research	**15** minutes	online
	Conduct Your Research LEARNING COACH CHECK-IN	**62** minutes	online and offline
WRAP-UP	Questions About Possessive Nouns and Research	**4** minutes	online
	Handwriting	**8** minutes	offline

Content Background

Students will continue to work on their **research report** about a U.S. state, an assignment that they will complete over the course of several lessons by following the writing process. In this lesson, students will continue prewriting by conducting research.

Writing Process

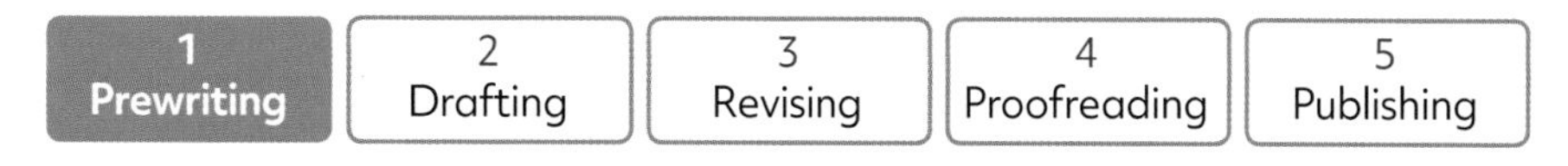

Students will conduct **research** by using trustworthy print and online sources.

- Print sources include books, magazines, atlases, and encyclopedias. Digital versions of print sources are acceptable to use and can be found in the digital library, which is linked in the online lesson.
- Online sources include websites and video clips.

After identifying appropriate sources, students will read the sources and write notes about important information that they learn. They will gather information that relates to five prescribed subtopics about their chosen state: general information, location and climate, outdoor activities, popular places to visit, and interesting facts.

MATERIALS

Supplied

- *Summit English Language Arts 3 Activity Book*
  - Spelling List 12 Activity Bank
  - Conduct Your Research
- Research Report Instructions (printout)
- handwriting workbook

Also Needed

- completed Spelling List 12 Pretest activity page from Informative Writing: Prewriting (A)
- folder in which students are storing research report assignment pages
- index cards (20)

Grammar, Usage, and Mechanics A **possessive noun** shows ownership. To make a plural noun possessive, follow these guidelines:

If a plural noun ends with an *-s*, add an apostrophe to the end of the word to make it possessive. In the following example, the room belongs to more than one brother.

Example: My **brothers'** room has a set of bunk beds.

If a plural noun doesn't end with an *-s*, add an apostrophe and an *-s* to make it possessive.

Example: Did you see the **children's** faces?

Advance Preparation

Gather students' completed Spelling List 12 Pretest activity page from Informative Writing: Prewriting (A). Students will refer to this page during Get Ready: Spelling List 12 Activity Bank.

Gather the folder that students are using to store the activity pages related to their research report. The folder should contain the following:

- Model Research Report activity page from Informative Writing: Prewriting (A)
- Students' completed Brainstorm for Your Research Report activity page from Informative Writing: Prewriting (A)

Students will need to complete research during Try It: Conduct Your Research, and they will need to use both *print* (e.g., books, magazines, encyclopedias) and *online* (e.g., websites, video clips) research sources. Print sources can be found at a library. If access to a library isn't possible, students can find print sources in the digital library, which is linked in the online lesson. (Note that students may also use sources from the digital library *in addition* to sources from a physical library.)

Lesson Goals

- Practice all spelling words offline.
- Form and use plural possessive nouns.
- Find research sources, and take notes.
- Develop letter formation fluency.

KEYWORDS

possessive noun – the form of a noun that shows ownership

prewriting – the stage or step of writing in which a writer chooses a topic, gathers ideas, and plans what to write

research – to find information through study rather than through personal experience

research report – a type of essay based mainly on the author's research

source – a provider of information; a book, a historical document, online materials, and an interviewee are all sources

GET READY

Introduction to Informative Writing: Prewriting (B)

Students will get a glimpse of what they will learn about in the lesson. They will also read the lesson goals and keywords. Have students select each keyword and preview its definition.

Spelling List 12 Activity Bank

Students will practice all spelling words from the workshop by completing Spelling List 12 Activity Bank from *Summit English Language Arts 3 Activity Book*. Make sure students have their completed Spelling List 12 Pretest activity page from Informative Writing: Prewriting (A) to refer to during this activity.

Remind students to pay special attention to words they spelled incorrectly on the Spelling Pretest.

GET READY
Informative Writing: Prewriting (B)

Spelling List 12 Activity Bank

Circle any words in the box that you did not spell correctly on your pretest. Choose one activity to do with your circled words. Do as much of the activity as you can in the time given.

Did you spell all the words on the pretest correctly? Do the one activity with as many spelling words as you can.

copy	hungry	story	apply	notify
country	hurry	study	crybaby	pry
empty	many	sturdy	deny	reply
fluffy	penny	windy	myself	spy
fuzzy				

Spelling Activity Choices

Create a Crossword

1. Write one of your spelling words going down in the center of the grid.

INFORMATIVE WRITING: PREWRITING (B) 259

2. Write another spelling word going across that shares a letter with the first word. See how many words you can connect.

Example:

Word Search Puzzle

1. Draw a box on the grid. The box should be large enough to hold your spelling words.
2. Fill in the grid with your spelling words. Write them across, up and down, and diagonally. You can write them forward and backward.
3. Fill in the rest of the box with random letters.
4. Ask someone to find and circle your words in the puzzle.

260 INFORMATIVE WRITING: PREWRITING (B)

Complete the activity that you chose.

My chosen activity:

Students should use this page to complete all steps in their chosen activity.

INFORMATIVE WRITING: PREWRITING (B) 261

LEARN AND TRY IT

LEARN Plural Possessive Nouns

Students will learn how to form and use plural possessive nouns.

TIP Discuss how the meanings of these two sentences are different. Emphasize that whether a sentence is *correct* depends on what a writer is trying to say.

The girl's toys are in the bin.

The girls' toys are in the bin.

TRY IT Form and Use Plural Possessive Nouns

Students will practice forming plural possessive nouns and using them correctly in sentences.

LEARN Conducting Research

Students will learn how to identify research sources and take notes from these sources.

TIP The online activity models how to take notes using index cards. Students may take notes in an online document instead if they prefer.

TRY IT Conduct Your Research

Students will complete Conduct Your Research in *Summit English Language Arts 3 Activity Book*. They will need approximately 20 index cards on which to take notes, and they will need access to reliable print and online research sources. They should have their completed Brainstorm for Your Research Report activity page to refer to as they work.

LEARNING COACH CHECK-IN Work with students to find reliable print and online research sources. The activity page has space to list six sources, but two or three sources are plenty. (Note that at least one source should be a print source, and one should be an online source.) Print sources may be obtained from your local library or from the digital library, which is linked in the online lesson.

TIP Many online websites, such as state government websites, are reliable sources but may be difficult for students to read. Search "state websites for kids" to find sources. Some suggested websites are linked in the online lesson.

OPTIONAL Students may complete their research using an online document instead of using index cards. It's critical, however, that the document is organized. Help students create a table to organize their notes. Students should only put information from one source in each row, adding rows as needed. An example table is shown.

Topic	Notes	Source
Outdoor Activities	• skiing and snowboarding in the Pocono Mountains • hiking and camping • swimming in pools and ponds • polka dancing • boating and fishing	#1
Location and Climate	• Mid-Atlantic region • PA bordered by NY, NJ, DE, MD, WV, and OH • looks like a rectangle • has lots of rivers	#6, pages 60 and 71

NOTE If you or students wish, you can download and print another copy of the Research Report Instructions online. Have students add their Conduct Your Research activity page and index cards to the folder they are using to store their research report assignment pages.

TRY IT

Informative Writing: Prewriting (B)

Conduct Your Research

Search for sources of information about the state you chose for your research report.

Use the Internet and go to a library. For each source you find, fill out one section on the form as follows:

- For print sources (a book, an entry in an encyclopedia, an atlas, a magazine, or newspaper article), write the title, author, publisher, year of publication, and notes about each source.
- For online sources (websites), write the name, URL, and notes about each source.

Example

Online or Print: online

Name or Title: PA Pennsylvania

URL or Author: www.state.pa.us.model

Publisher/Year of Publication: —

Notes: lots of info about state history and things to do for fun

INFORMATIVE WRITING: PREWRITING (B) 263

Answers will vary.

Source 1

Online or Print:

Name or Title:

URL or Author:

Publisher/Year of Publication:

Notes:

Source 2

Online or Print:

Name or Title:

URL or Author:

Publisher/Year of Publication:

Notes:

264 INFORMATIVE WRITING: PREWRITING (B)

Source 3

Online or Print:

Name or Title:

URL or Author:

Publisher/Year of Publication:

Notes:

Source 4

Online or Print:

Name or Title:

URL or Author:

Publisher/Year of Publication:

Notes:

INFORMATIVE WRITING: PREWRITING (B) 265

Source 5

Online or Print:

Name or Title:

URL or Author:

Publisher/Year of Publication:

Notes:

Source 6

Online or Print:

Name or Title:

URL or Author:

Publisher/Year of Publication:

Notes:

266 INFORMATIVE WRITING: PREWRITING (B)

Follow the instructions to take notes about your research topic.

1. Gather index cards. Write each of the following labels at the top of three index cards. Label three cards "General Information," three cards "Location and Climate," and so on.
   - General Information
   - Location and Climate
   - Outdoor Activities
   - Popular Places to Visit
   - Interesting Facts
2. Pick a source from your list and read about your state. As you read, look for information that relates to the labels on your cards.
3. When you read something important, find the correct note card and write down the key information. Write information from just one source per card.
4. For each card that you complete, write down the number of the source you used to find the information. If it is a print source, write down chapter or page numbers, too.
5. Continue to read and take notes from all of your sources. Make more cards when you need to. Keep your cards together in a safe place.

INFORMATIVE WRITING: PREWRITING (B) 267

Sample card for an online source

Outdoor Activities

- skiing and snowboarding in the Pocono Mountains
- hiking and camping
- swimming in pools and ponds
- polka dancing
- boating and fishing

Source #1

Sample card for a print source

Location and Climate

- Mid-Atlantic region
- PA bordered by NY, NJ, DE, MD, WV, and OH
- looks like a rectangle
- has lots of rivers

Source #6, pages 60 and 71

268 INFORMATIVE WRITING: PREWRITING (B)

WRAP-UP

Questions About Possessive Nouns and Research

Students will answer questions to show that they understand how to form plural possessive nouns and conduct research.

Handwriting

Students should gather their handwriting materials and begin where they left off. Remind students to form letters carefully and correctly.

TIP Set a timer to help students stay focused during handwriting practice.

Informative Writing: Prewriting (C)

Lesson Overview

ACTIVITY	ACTIVITY TITLE	TIME	ONLINE/OFFLINE
GET READY	Introduction to Informative Writing: Prewriting (C)	1 minute	online
	Spelling List 12 Practice	10 minutes	online
LEARN AND TRY IT	Titles of Works	10 minutes	online
	Write Titles of Works	10 minutes	online
	Organizing a Research Report	10 minutes	online
	Organize Your Research Report LEARNING COACH CHECK-IN	50 minutes	offline
WRAP-UP	Questions About Titles and Organization	4 minutes	online
	Handwriting	8 minutes	offline
	Go Read!	17 minutes	online or offline

Content Background

Students will continue to work on their **research report** about a U.S. state, an assignment that they will complete over the course of several lessons by following the writing process. In this lesson, students will complete prewriting by creating an outline.

Writing Process

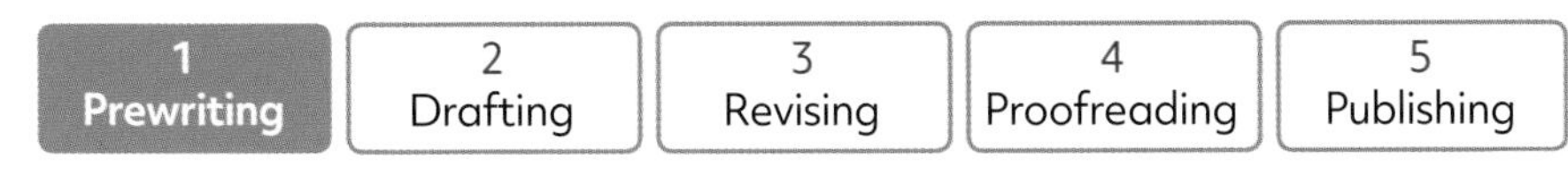

An **outline** is an organized list of information. The outline is designed to help students group related information and put the information in the order in which they will write it in their report.

Grammar, Usage, and Mechanics The important words in titles of works, such as books, magazines, poems, songs, and paintings, are capitalized according to these rules:

MATERIALS

Supplied

- *Summit English Language Arts 3 Activity Book*
  - Organize Your Research Report
- Research Report Instructions (printout)
- handwriting workbook

Also Needed

- folder in which students are storing research report assignment pages
- reading material for Go Read!

1. Capitalize the first and last words.
2. Lowercase the following, unless they are the first or last words:
   - *the*, *a*, or *an*
   - coordinating conjunctions, such as *and* and *or*
   - prepositions that have four or fewer letters
3. Capitalize all other words.

   Examples:

   "Goldilocks and the Three Bears"

   The Tale of Peter Rabbit

   "The Farmer in the Dell"

In this course, proper formatting of titles (quotation marks, italicizing, and underlining) is not addressed.

KEYWORDS

outline – an organized list of topics in an essay

prewriting – the stage or step of writing in which a writer chooses a topic, gathers ideas, and plans what to write

research report – a type of essay based mainly on the author's research

Advance Preparation

Gather the folder that students are using to store the activity pages related to their research report. The folder should contain the following:

- Model Research Report activity page from Informative Writing: Prewriting (A)
- Students' completed Brainstorm for Your Research Report activity page from Informative Writing: Prewriting (A)
- Students' completed Conduct Your Research activity page from Informative Writing: Prewriting (B)
- Students' completed index cards from Informative Writing: Prewriting (B)

During the Go Read! activity, students will have the option of using the digital library. Allow extra time for students to make their reading selection, or have students make a selection before beginning the lesson.

Lesson Goals

- Practice all spelling words online.
- Capitalize the correct words in titles.
- Make an outline for your research report.
- Develop letter formation fluency.
- Read independently to develop fluency.

GET READY

Introduction to Informative Writing: Prewriting (C)

Students will get a glimpse of what they will learn about in the lesson. They will also read the lesson goals and keywords. Have students select each keyword and preview its definition.

Spelling List 12 Practice

Students will practice all spelling words from the workshop.

OPTIONAL Students may do an activity from Spelling List 12 Activity Bank instead of the online practice activity.

LEARN AND TRY IT

LEARN Titles of Works

Students will learn the rules of capitalizing titles of works.

TIP Before completing the online activity, compare titles of books at home or in the digital library. Discuss what students notice about capitalization.

TRY IT Write Titles of Works

Students will practice correctly capitalizing titles of works.

LEARN Organizing a Research Report

Students will learn how to organize their research notes in an outline.

TRY IT Organize Your Research Report

Students will complete Organize Your Research Report in *Summit English Language Arts 3 Activity Book*. They should have their completed research notes from Informative Writing (B) and the Model Research Report to refer to as they work.

LEARNING COACH CHECK-IN Review students' outline, providing guidance as needed. Remind students that they do not need to include all the information that they found during research in their outline. Explain that professional writers often spend years researching and only wind up using a small portion of that research in their final product.

NOTE If you or students wish, you can download and print another copy of the Research Report Instructions online. Have students add their Organize Your Research Report activity page to the folder they are using to store their research report assignment pages.

TRY IT

Informative Writing: Prewriting (C)

Organize Your Research Report

Use your notes to create an outline for your research report.

Answers will vary.

Paragraph 1: Introduction

A. Main idea of research report

B. General information

INFORMATIVE WRITING: PREWRITING (C) 269

Paragraph 2: Location and climate

A. Region of the United States and bordering states

B. Winter weather

1. Clothing
2. Outdoor activities

C. Summer weather

1. Clothing
2. Outdoor activities

270 INFORMATIVE WRITING: PREWRITING (C)

Paragraph 3: Popular places to visit

A. Name of first place to visit

1. Description
2. Reason for being popular

B. Name of second place to visit

1. Description
2. Reason for being popular

INFORMATIVE WRITING: PREWRITING (C) 271

Paragraph 4: Other interesting facts

A. Historical facts about the state

B. Current facts about the state

Did you know that Tennessee's nickname is "The Volunteer State"?

272 INFORMATIVE WRITING: PREWRITING (C)

Paragraph 5: Conclusion

A. Short summary

B. Restatement of main idea

INFORMATIVE WRITING: PREWRITING (C) 273

WRAP-UP

Questions About Titles and Organization

Students will answer questions to show that they understand how to capitalize titles of works and organize information for a research report.

Handwriting

Students should gather their handwriting materials and begin where they left off. Remind students to form letters carefully and correctly.

TIP Set a timer to help students stay focused during handwriting practice.

Go Read!

Students will read for pleasure. They should choose a book or a magazine that interests them, or they may choose a selection from the digital library, linked in the online lesson.

- Have students read aloud a few paragraphs of their selection.
- Then have students read silently for the rest of the time.

SUPPORT Students should make no more than five errors in decoding when they read aloud a few paragraphs of their Go Read! selection. If students struggle or make more than five errors, they need to select a different (and easier) text for the Go Read! activity.

TIP Have students select something to read ahead of time to help them stay focused.

Informative Writing: Drafting (A)

Lesson Overview

ACTIVITY	ACTIVITY TITLE	TIME	ONLINE/OFFLINE
GET READY	Introduction to Informative Writing: Drafting (A)	**1** minute	online
	Spelling List 12 Review Game	**10** minutes	online
LEARN AND TRY IT	Strong Details	**10** minutes	online
	Use Strong Details	**10** minutes	online
	Drafting a Research Report	**10** minutes	online
	Draft Your Research Report LEARNING COACH CHECK-IN	**55** minutes	offline
WRAP-UP	Questions About Details and Drafting	**4** minutes	online
	Go Read!	**20** minutes	online or offline

Content Background

Students will continue to work on their **research report** about a U.S. state, an assignment that they will complete over the course of several lessons by following the writing process. In this lesson, students will begin drafting their report.

Writing Process

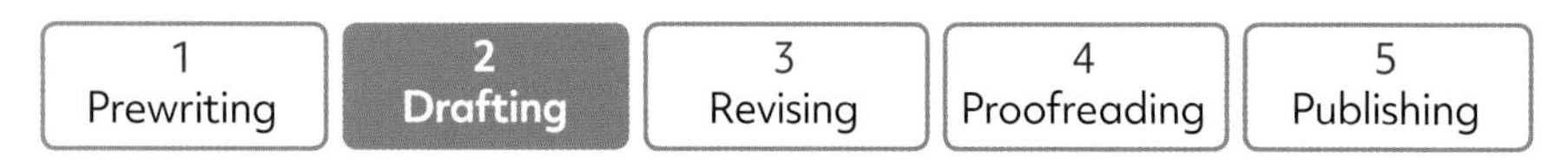

During **drafting**, students will follow their completed outline to write a draft of their research report. Students are expected to write about half of their draft in this lesson (although they may write more if they wish). They will have time to finish and submit their draft in Informative Writing: Drafting (B).

Grammar, Usage, and Mechanics By adding details, writers can clarify the meaning of their writing. Details are important in all types of writing.

Sentence with few details: The bird sang.

Revised sentence: The yellow bird sang noisily in the tree.

Sentence with few details: An important battle was fought in Pennsylvania.

Revised sentence: One of the most important battles of the Civil War was fought in the town of Gettysburg, Pennsylvania.

MATERIALS

Supplied

- *Summit English Language Arts 3 Activity Book*
  - Draft Your Research Report
- Research Report Instructions (printout)
- Drafting Paper (printout)

Also Needed

- folder in which students are storing research report assignment pages
- reading material for Go Read!

KEYWORDS

drafting – of writing, the stage or step in which the writer first writes the piece

research report – a type of essay based mainly on the author's research

Advance Preparation

Gather the folder that students are using to store the activity pages related to their research report. The folder should contain the following:

- Model Research Report activity page from Informative Writing: Prewriting (A)
- Students' completed Brainstorm for Your Research Report activity page from Informative Writing: Prewriting (A)
- Students' completed Conduct Your Research activity page from Informative Writing: Prewriting (B)
- Students' completed index cards from Informative Writing: Prewriting (B)
- Students' completed Organize Your Research Report activity page from Informative Writing: Prewriting (C)

During the Go Read! activity, students will have the option of using the digital library. Allow extra time for students to make their reading selection, or have students make a selection before beginning the lesson.

Lesson Goals

- Practice all spelling words online.
- Use strong details in writing.
- Begin drafting your research report.
- Read independently to develop fluency.

GET READY

Introduction to Informative Writing: Drafting (A)

Students will get a glimpse of what they will learn about in the lesson. They will also read the lesson goals and keywords. Have students select each keyword and preview its definition.

Spelling List 12 Review Game

Students will practice all spelling words from the workshop.

LEARN AND TRY IT

LEARN Strong Details

Students will learn that using strong details can improve writing.

TIP Adding detail can improve writing. Changing details can, too. Ask students to replace the words *so cool* in this sentence with one or more words to make the meaning of the sentence clearer: *My teacher is so cool.*

TRY IT Use Strong Details

Students will practice using strong details to improve writing.

LEARN Drafting a Research Report

Students will explore how to use an outline to complete a draft.

TIP The outline is like the frame of a building. As students write, they will add walls, paint, furniture—all the details that will complete the building.

TRY IT Draft Your Research Report

Students will complete half of their draft using Draft Your Research Report in *Summit English Language Arts 3 Activity Book*. Make sure students have their completed Organize Your Research Report activity page, research notes, and other prewriting work to refer to as they work.

LEARNING COACH CHECK-IN Review students' in-progress draft. Ensure that students' draft is in line with the assignment criteria outlined on the Brainstorm for Your Research Report activity page. Students should store their draft in the folder they are using to organize their writing assignment pages.

TIP Encourage students to reread the Model Research Report before beginning their own draft. Discuss the strengths of the model.

SUPPORT Have students use their outline to talk through each paragraph, speaking in complete sentences and adding to what they've written in their outline. Point out to students when they add a detail (and prompt them to add details at appropriate points). Repeat this process for each paragraph, as needed.

NOTE If you or students wish, you can download and print another copy of the Research Report Instructions online. Additional sheets of Drafting Paper are also available online. Have students add their in-progress Draft Your Research Report activity page to the folder they are using to store their research report assignment pages.

TRY IT

Informative Writing: Drafting (A)

Draft Your Research Report

Write the first draft of your research report. Write only on the white rows. You will use the purple rows for revisions later.

Title:

start here ►

Answers will vary.

keep writing ►

Draft Page 1

keep writing ►

Draft Page 2

keep writing ►

Draft Page 3

keep writing ►

Draft Page 4

keep writing ►

Draft Page 5

keep writing ►

Draft Page 6

keep writing ►

Draft Page 7

Draft Page 8

WRAP-UP

Questions About Details and Drafting

Students will answer questions to show that they understand how to add appropriate details to writing and how to draft a research report.

Go Read!

Students will read for pleasure. They should choose a book or a magazine that interests them, or they may choose a selection from the digital library, linked in the online lesson.

- Have students read aloud a few paragraphs of their selection.
- Then have students read silently for the rest of the time.

SUPPORT Students should make no more than five errors in decoding when they read aloud a few paragraphs of their Go Read! selection. If students struggle or make more than five errors, they need to select a different (and easier) text for the Go Read! activity.

TIP Have students select something to read ahead of time to help them stay focused.

Informative Writing: Drafting (B)

Lesson Overview

ACTIVITY	ACTIVITY TITLE	TIME	ONLINE/OFFLINE
GET READY	Introduction to Informative Writing: Drafting (B)	**1** minute	online
TRY IT	Review Possessives, Titles, and Details	**10** minutes	online
QUIZ	Possessives, Titles, and Details	**20** minutes	online
	Spelling List 12	**10** minutes	online
TRY IT	Finish Drafting Your Research Report LEARNING COACH CHECK-IN	**45** minutes	offline
WRAP-UP	Turn In Your Research Report Draft	**1** minute	online
	More Language Arts Practice	**15** minutes	online
	Go Read!	**18** minutes	online or offline

Content Background

Students will continue working on their **research report** about a U.S. state. In this lesson, students will finish and submit their draft. In later lessons, students will revise, proofread, and publish their research report.

Writing Process

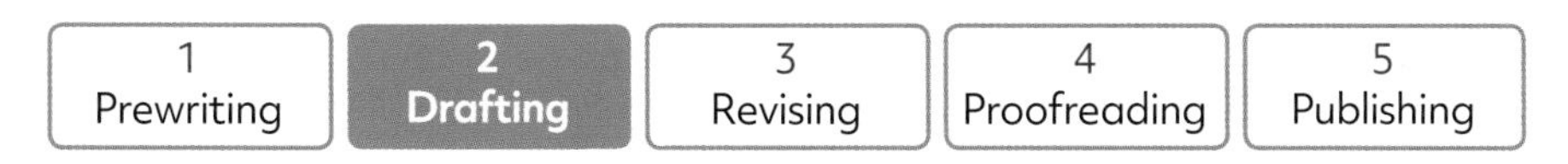

Advance Preparation

Gather the folder that students are using to store the activity pages related to their research report. The folder should contain the following:

- Model Research Report activity page from Informative Writing: Prewriting (A)
- Students' completed Brainstorm for Your Research Report activity page from Informative Writing: Prewriting (A)
- Students' completed Conduct Your Research activity page from Informative Writing: Prewriting (B)
- Students' completed index cards from Informative Writing: Prewriting (B)

MATERIALS

Supplied

- *Summit English Language Arts 3 Activity Book*
  - Draft Your Research Report
- Research Report Instructions (printout)
- Drafting Paper (printout)

Also Needed

- folder in which students are storing research report assignment pages
- reading material for Go Read!

- Students' completed Organize Your Research Report activity page from Informative Writing: Prewriting (C)
- Students' in-progress Draft Your Research Report activity page from Informative Writing: Drafting (A)

During the Go Read! activity, students will have the option of using the digital library. Allow extra time for students to make their reading selection, or have students make a selection before beginning the lesson.

Lesson Goals

- Review possessive nouns, titles of works, and strong details.
- Take a quiz on possessive nouns, titles of works, and strong details.
- Take a spelling quiz.
- Finish and submit the draft of your research report.
- Read independently to develop fluency.

GET READY

Introduction to Informative Writing: Drafting (B)

Students will get a glimpse of what they will learn about in the lesson. They will also read the lesson goals.

TRY IT

Review Possessives, Titles, and Details

Students will answer questions to review what they have learned about forming possessive nouns, capitalizing titles of works, and using strong details.

QUIZ

Possessive, Titles, and Details

Students will complete the Possessives, Titles, and Details quiz.

Spelling List 12

Students will complete the Spelling List 12 quiz.

TRY IT

Finish Drafting Your Research Report

Students will complete the draft of their research report using the Draft Your Research Report activity page in *Summit English Language Arts 3 Activity Book*. Make sure students have their prewriting work to refer to as they work. Most important is their Organize Your Research Report activity page—they should follow this outline closely as they write.

LEARNING COACH CHECK-IN Review students' completed draft. Ensure that students' draft is in line with the assignment criteria outlined on the Brainstorm for Your Research Report activity page. Students should store their draft in the folder they are using to organize their writing assignment pages.

NOTE If you or students wish, you can download and print another copy of the Research Report Instructions online. Additional sheets of Drafting Paper are also available online.

TRY IT
Informative Writing: Drafting (A)

Draft Your Research Report

Write the first draft of your research report. Write only on the white rows. You will use the purple rows for revisions later.

Title:

start here ►

Answers will vary.

keep writing ►

Draft Page 1

INFORMATIVE WRITING: DRAFTING (A) 275

keep writing ►

Draft Page 2

276 INFORMATIVE WRITING: DRAFTING (A)

keep writing ►

Draft Page 3

INFORMATIVE WRITING: DRAFTING (A) 277

keep writing ►

Draft Page 4

278 INFORMATIVE WRITING: DRAFTING (A)

keep writing ►

Draft Page 5

INFORMATIVE WRITING: DRAFTING (A) 279

keep writing ►

Draft Page 6

280 INFORMATIVE WRITING: DRAFTING (A)

keep writing ►

Draft Page 7

INFORMATIVE WRITING: DRAFTING (A) 281

Draft Page 8

282 INFORMATIVE WRITING: DRAFTING (A)

WRAP-UP

Turn In Your Research Report Draft

Students will submit their completed draft to their teacher.

More Language Arts Practice

Students will practice skills according to their individual needs.

Go Read!

Students will read for pleasure. They should choose a book or a magazine that interests them, or they may choose a selection from the digital library, linked in the online lesson.

- Have students read aloud a few paragraphs of their selection.
- Then have students read silently for the rest of the time.

SUPPORT Students should make no more than five errors in decoding when they read aloud a few paragraphs of their Go Read! selection. If students struggle or make more than five errors, they need to select a different (and easier) text for the Go Read! activity.

TIP Have students select something to read ahead of time to help them stay focused.

Big Ideas: Mini-Project

Lesson Overview

Big Ideas lessons provide students the opportunity to further apply the knowledge acquired and skills learned throughout the unit workshops. Each Big Ideas lesson consists of these parts:

1. **Cumulative Review:** Students keep their skills fresh by reviewing prior content.
2. **Preview:** Students practice answering the types of questions they will commonly find on standardized tests.
3. **Synthesis:** Students complete an assignment that allows them to connect and apply what they have learned. Synthesis assignments vary throughout the course.

   In the Synthesis portion of this Big Ideas lesson, students will complete a small creative project that ties together concepts and skills they have encountered across workshops. These small projects are designed to deepen students' understanding of those concepts and skills.

   LEARNING COACH CHECK-IN Make sure students complete, review, and submit the assignment to their teacher.

All materials needed for this lesson are linked online and not provided in the activity book.

MATERIALS

Supplied

- Mini-Project Instructions (printout)

Myths

Multiple-Meaning Words

Lesson Overview

ACTIVITY	ACTIVITY TITLE	TIME	ONLINE/OFFLINE
GET READY	Introduction to Multiple-Meaning Words	**2** minutes	online
	Look Back at Using Context Clues	**4** minutes	online
LEARN AND TRY IT	Multiple-Meaning Words	**10** minutes	online
	Practice Using Multiple-Meaning Words	**10** minutes	online
	Apply: Multiple-Meaning Words LEARNING COACH CHECK-IN	**15** minutes	offline
	Review Multiple-Meaning Words	**14** minutes	online
QUIZ	Multiple-Meaning Words	**15** minutes	online
WRAP-UP	More Language Arts Practice	**15** minutes	online
	Go Write! Under Water or in the Air	**15** minutes	offline
	Go Read!	**20** minutes	online or offline

Content Background

Words that are spelled and said the same but have different meanings are called multiple-meaning words. Sometimes, multiple-meaning words have different parts of speech. Knowing the part of speech and using context clues can help students figure out which meaning is correct in a sentence.

Advance Preparation

During the Go Read! activity, students will have the option of using the digital library. Allow extra time for students to make their reading selection, or have students make a selection before beginning the lesson.

MATERIALS

Supplied

- *Summit English Language Arts 3 Activity Book*
  - Apply: Multiple-Meaning Words
  - Go Write! Under Water or in the Air

Also Needed

- reading material for Go Read!

Lesson Goals

- Practice vocabulary words.
- Use context clues to determine the meaning of multiple-meaning words.
- Take the Multiple-Meaning Words quiz.
- Freewrite about a topic to develop writing fluency and practice letter formation.
- Read independently to develop fluency.

KEYWORDS

context clue – a word or phrase in a text that helps you figure out the meaning of an unknown word

GET READY

Introduction to Multiple-Meaning Words

After a quick introductory activity, students will read the lesson goals and keywords. Have students select each keyword and preview its definition.

Look Back at Using Context Clues

Students will practice the prerequisite skill of using words and phrases in a sentence or paragraph to figure out the meaning of unknown words.

LEARN AND TRY IT

LEARN Multiple-Meaning Words

Students will be introduced to the vocabulary words for the lesson. Then they will learn how to determine which meaning of a multiple-meaning word is being used in a passage.

TRY IT Practice Using Multiple-Meaning Words

Students will practice using multiple-meaning words.

TRY IT Apply: Multiple-Meaning Words

Students will complete Apply: Multiple-Meaning Words in *Summit English Language Arts 3 Activity Book*. They will practice using context clues and knowledge of parts of speech to determine the correct multiple-meaning word to complete a sentence.

LEARNING COACH CHECK-IN Have students explain the context clues that helped them determine the correct word to complete each sentence.

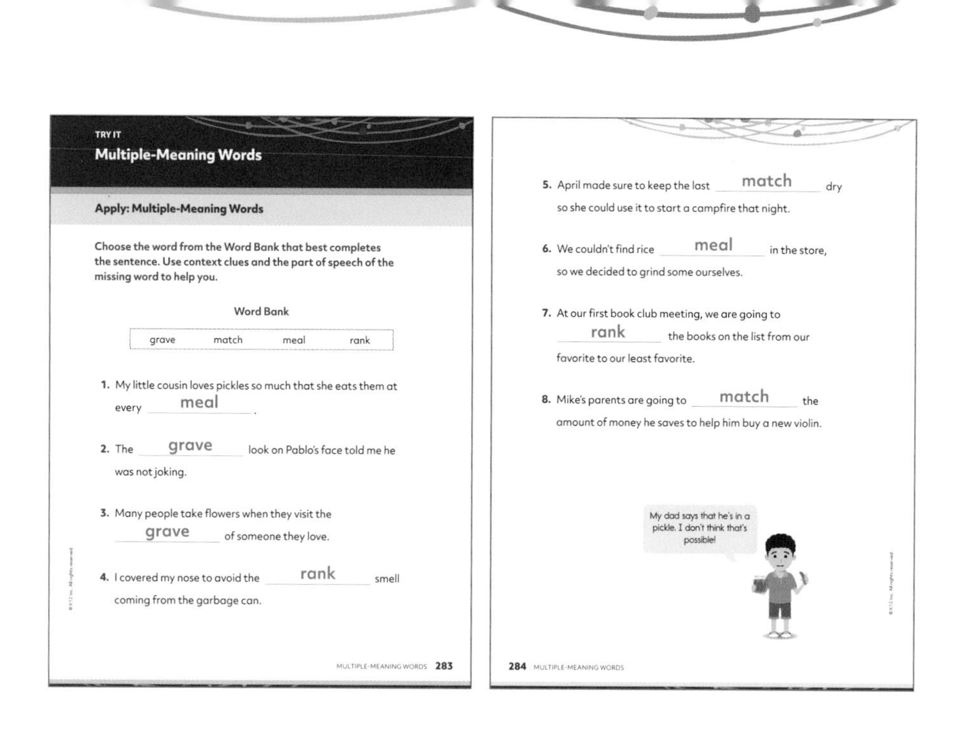
TRY IT
Multiple-Meaning Words

Apply: Multiple-Meaning Words

Choose the word from the Word Bank that best completes the sentence. Use context clues and the part of speech of the missing word to help you.

Word Bank

grave	match	meal	rank

1. My little cousin loves pickles so much that she eats them at every meal.
2. The grave look on Pablo's face told me he was not joking.
3. Many people take flowers when they visit the grave of someone they love.
4. I covered my nose to avoid the rank smell coming from the garbage can.

MULTIPLE-MEANING WORDS 283

5. April made sure to keep the last match dry so she could use it to start a campfire that night.
6. We couldn't find rice meal in the store, so we decided to grind some ourselves.
7. At our first book club meeting, we are going to rank the books on the list from our favorite to our least favorite.
8. Mike's parents are going to match the amount of money he saves to help him buy a new violin.

284 MULTIPLE-MEANING WORDS

TRY IT Review Multiple-Meaning Words

Students will answer questions to review what they have learned about multiple-meaning words.

QUIZ

Multiple-Meaning Words

Students will complete the Multiple-Meaning Words quiz.

WRAP-UP

More Language Arts Practice

Students will practice skills according to their individual needs.

Go Write! Under Water or in the Air

Students will complete Go Write! Under Water or in the Air in *Summit English Language Arts 3 Activity Book*. They will have the option to either respond to a prompt or write about a topic of their choice.

NOTE This activity is intended to build writing fluency. Students should write for the entire allotted time.

SUPPORT If students have trouble writing for the allotted time, prompt them with questions. For example, *Can you tell me more about this? Why did you choose to write about this?*

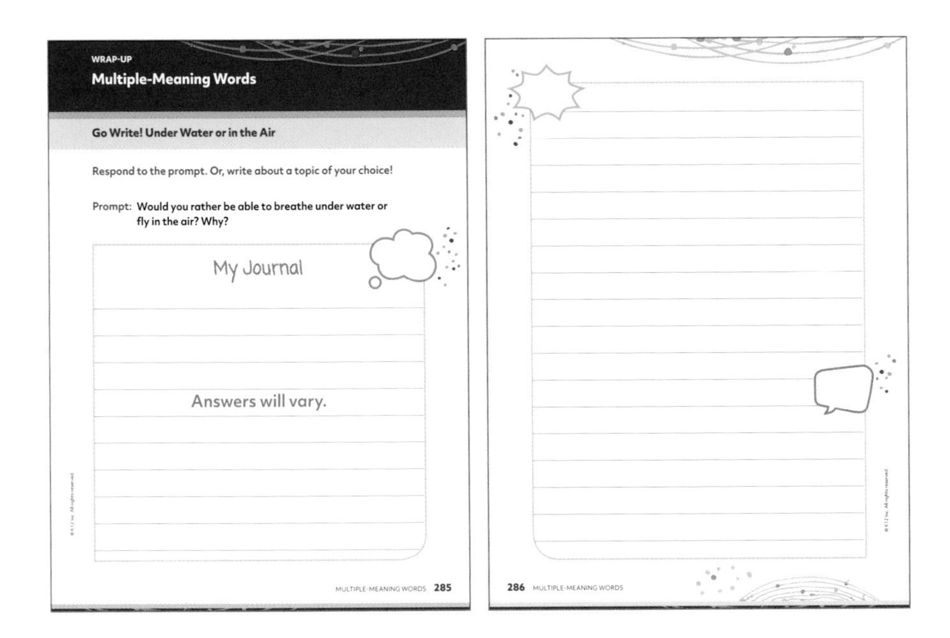
WRAP-UP

Multiple-Meaning Words

Go Write! Under Water or in the Air

Respond to the prompt. Or, write about a topic of your choice!

Prompt: Would you rather be able to breathe under water or fly in the air? Why?

My Journal

Answers will vary.

MULTIPLE-MEANING WORDS 285

286 MULTIPLE-MEANING WORDS

Go Read!

Students will read for pleasure. They should choose a book or a magazine that interests them, or they may choose a selection from the digital library, linked in the online lesson.

- Have students read aloud a few paragraphs of their selection.
- Then have students read silently for the rest of the time.

SUPPORT Students should make no more than five errors in decoding when they read aloud a few paragraphs of their Go Read! selection. If students struggle or make more than five errors, they need to select a different (and easier) text for the Go Read! activity.

TIP Have students select something to read ahead of time to help them stay focused.

Myths (A)

Lesson Overview

ACTIVITY	ACTIVITY TITLE	TIME	ONLINE/OFFLINE
GET READY	Introduction to Myths (A)	**1** minute	
	Spelling List 13 Pretest **LEARNING COACH CHECK-IN**	**10** minutes	and
	Read and Record	**8** minutes	
	Reading Foundations: Prefixes	**5** minutes	
	Before You Read "Tangled Webs"	**9** minutes	
READ	"Tangled Webs"	**20** minutes	
	Check-In: "Tangled Webs"	**5** minutes	
LEARN AND **TRY IT**	Finding Themes in Myths	**10** minutes	
	Find Themes in Myths	**10** minutes	
	Apply: Theme	**14** minutes	
	Retell a Myth **LEARNING COACH CHECK-IN**	**10** minutes	
	Practice Words from "Tangled Webs"	**8** minutes	
WRAP-UP	Question About "Tangled Webs"	**2** minutes	
	Handwriting	**8** minutes	

Content Background

In this lesson, students will explore characteristics of myths. They will learn that myths were created by ancient people to explain things in their world, including things such as why we have lightning and where spiders came from. Another feature that helps readers recognize a myth is characters that are supernatural beings. In myths from ancient Greece, these supernatural beings are the gods and goddesses that the Greeks worshipped. Student will also learn that myths teach lessons. The lessons of a myth are its themes. They will learn to identify themes by analyzing characters' actions and the consequences of those actions.

MATERIALS

Supplied

- *Summit English Language Arts 3 Expeditions in Reading*
  - "Tangled Webs"
- *Summit English Language Arts 3 Activity Book*
  - Spelling List 13 Pretest
  - Retell a Myth
- handwriting workbook

"Tangled Webs" Synopsis

In this myth, a young woman named Arachne boasts that she is the best weaver in the world—even better than the goddess Athena. Athena challenges Arachne to a weaving contest. The one who loses may never weave again. Not surprisingly, Athena wins. The powerful goddess takes pity on Arachne and turns her into a spider, so she and her kind may continue to weave forever.

KEYWORDS

myth – a story that explains how something came to be and that usually contains magical figures as characters

theme – the author's message or big idea

Lesson Goals

- Take a spelling pretest.
- Read aloud to practice fluency.
- Read "Tangled Webs."
- Determine themes of a myth.
- Retell a myth in writing.
- Practice vocabulary words.
- Develop letter formation fluency.

GET READY

Introduction to Myths (A)

Students will get a glimpse of what they will learn about in the lesson. They will also read the lesson goals and keywords. Have students select each keyword and preview its definition.

Spelling List 13 Pretest

Students will take a spelling pretest and learn a new spelling pattern.

LEARNING COACH CHECK-IN Have students turn to Spelling List 13 Pretest in *Summit English Language Arts 3 Activity Book* and open the online Spelling Pretest activity. Online, students will listen to the spelling word, type the word in the space indicated, and then check their answer. In the activity book, students will write the correct spelling of the word in the tables provided and indicate with a ✓ or an **x** if they spelled the word correctly or incorrectly online. Students will repeat this process with the remaining words.

As needed, help students with the interaction between the online activity and the activity book page until they become comfortable with what they need to do. As students practice their spelling words throughout the workshop, they should pay special attention to words they spelled incorrectly on the pretest.

This is the complete list of words students will be tested on.

Words with *y* + Vowel Suffixes				
annoying	crazier	grouchier	marries	spies
berries	cried	happier	ponies	stickier
bunnies	easier	hurried	prettier	studying
burying	flies	ladies	replies	trying
carrying				

NOTE Have students keep their completed activity page in a safe place so they can refer to it later.

GET READY

Myths (A)

Spelling List 13 Pretest

1. Open the Spelling Pretest activity online. Listen to the first spelling word. Type the word. Check your answer.
2. Write the correct spelling of the word in the Word column of the Spelling Pretest table.

	Word	✓	✗
1	blindfold		

3. Put a check mark in the ✓ column if you spelled the word correctly online.

	Word	✓	✗
1	blindfold	✓	

Put an X in the ✗ column if you spelled the word incorrectly online.

	Word	✓	✗
1	blindfold		X

4. Repeat Steps 1–3 for the remaining words in the Spelling Pretest.

MYTHS (A) 287

Myths (A)

Spelling List 13 Pretest

Write each spelling word in the Word column, making sure to spell it correctly.

	Word	✓	✗
1	annoying		
2	berries		
3	bunnies		
4	burying		
5	carrying		
6	crazier		
7	cried		
8	easier		
9	flies		
10	grouchier		
11	happier		

	Word	✓	✗
12	hurried		
13	ladies		
14	marries		
15	ponies		
16	prettier		
17	replies		
18	spies		
19	stickier		
20	studying		
21	trying		

Students should write the correct spelling of each word from the pretest and use the ✓and X columns to indicate whether they spelled each word correctly or incorrectly online.

288 MYTHS (A)

Read and Record

Good readers read quickly, smoothly, and with expression. This is called *fluency*. Students will record themselves reading aloud. They will listen to their recording and think about how quick, smooth, and expressive they sound.

TIP Encourage students to rerecord as needed.

Reading Foundations: Prefixes

Reading Foundations activities serve to remind students of basic reading skills and reading behaviors mastered in earlier grades. The activities cover topics such as advanced decoding skills and various strategies for improving comprehension.

Before You Read "Tangled Webs"

Students will be introduced to some key vocabulary words that they will encounter in the upcoming reading, learn some important historical background related to the reading, and answer questions to help them set a purpose for their reading.

READ

"Tangled Webs"

Students will read "Tangled Webs" in *Expeditions in Reading*.

Check-In: "Tangled Webs"

Students will answer several questions to demonstrate their comprehension of "Tangled Webs."

LEARN AND TRY IT

LEARN Finding Themes in Myths

Students will learn about characteristics of myths and how to determine themes of a myth.

TRY IT Find Themes in Myths

Students will analyze passages to determine themes of a myth that are developed by characters' actions.

TRY IT Apply: Theme

Students will apply to a new work what they've learned about determining themes of a story.

TRY IT Retell a Myth

Students will complete Retell a Myth in *Summit English Language Arts 3 Activity Book*.

LEARNING COACH CHECK-IN It's important that you review students' responses. Give students feedback, using the sample answers provided to guide you.

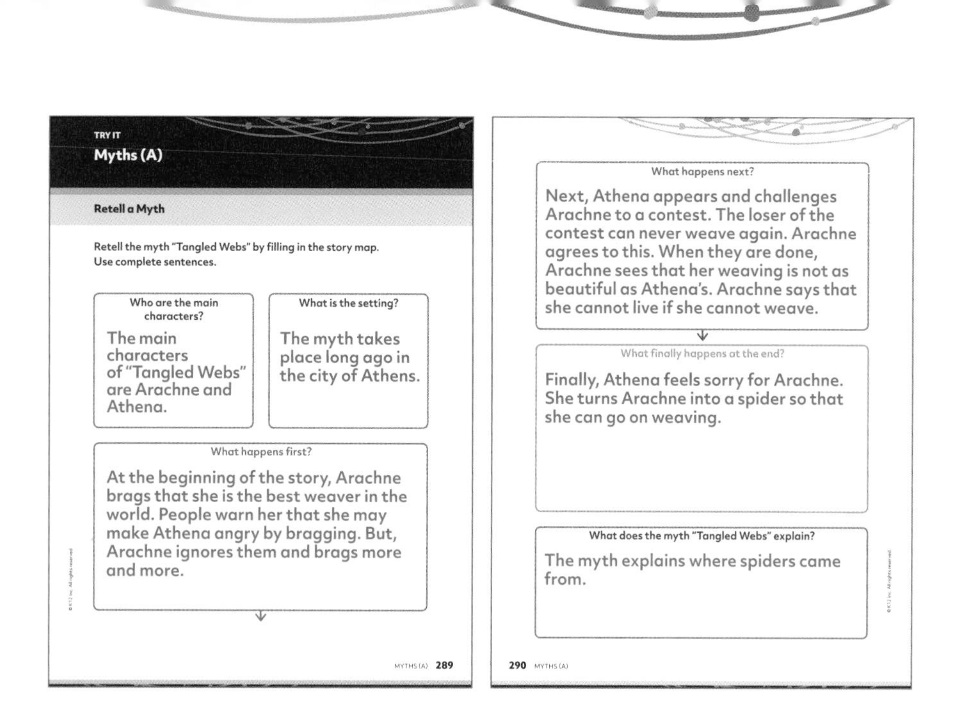
TRY IT

Myths (A)

Retell a Myth

Retell the myth "Tangled Webs" by filling in the story map. Use complete sentences.

Who are the main characters?

The main characters of "Tangled Webs" are Arachne and Athena.

What is the setting?

The myth takes place long ago in the city of Athens.

What happens first?

At the beginning of the story, Arachne brags that she is the best weaver in the world. People warn her that she may make Athena angry by bragging. But, Arachne ignores them and brags more and more.

MYTHS (A) 289

What happens next?

Next, Athena appears and challenges Arachne to a contest. The loser of the contest can never weave again. Arachne agrees to this. When they are done, Arachne sees that her weaving is not as beautiful as Athena's. Arachne says that she cannot live if she cannot weave.

What finally happens at the end?

Finally, Athena feels sorry for Arachne. She turns Arachne into a spider so that she can go on weaving.

What does the myth "Tangled Webs" explain?

The myth explains where spiders came from.

290 MYTHS (A)

TRY IT Practice Words from "Tangled Webs"

Students will answer questions to demonstrate their understanding of the vocabulary words from the reading.

WRAP-UP

Question About "Tangled Webs"

Students will answer a question to show that they understand the characteristics of myths.

Handwriting

Students should gather their handwriting materials and begin where they left off. Remind students to form letters carefully and correctly.

TIP Set a timer to help students stay focused during handwriting practice.

Myths (B)

Lesson Overview

ACTIVITY	ACTIVITY TITLE	TIME	ONLINE/OFFLINE
GET READY	Introduction to Myths (B)	1 minute	
	Spelling List 13 Activity Bank	10 minutes	
	Read and Record	8 minutes	
	Reading Foundations: Homophones	5 minutes	
	Recall "Tangled Webs"	5 minutes	
	Before You Read "Repeat After Me, Me, Me..."	5 minutes	
READ	"Repeat After Me, Me, Me..."	15 minutes	
	Check-In: "Repeat After Me, Me, Me..."	5 minutes	
LEARN AND TRY IT	Comparing Myths	10 minutes	
	Compare Myths	10 minutes	
	Apply: Compare or Contrast Plots	13 minutes	
	Compare Two Goddesses LEARNING COACH CHECK-IN	15 minutes	
	Practice Words from "Repeat After Me, Me, Me..."	8 minutes	
WRAP-UP	Question About "Repeat After Me, Me, Me..."	2 minutes	
	Handwriting	8 minutes	

Content Background

In this lesson, students will compare and contrast two Greek myths with similar characters and a similar pattern of events. *Compare* means "to determine how things are alike." *Contrast* means "to determine how things are different." While students will learn about some differences, the main emphasis will be on similarities. This emphasis is meant to help students recognize the features that make a story a myth. It is also meant to show how ideas commonly found in myths indicate the beliefs of the ancient Greeks who created the myths.

An example of what students will explore is how characters in the myths "Tangled Webs" and "Repeat After Me, Me, Me..." act in similar ways, which leads to a similar result. The main characters in the myths both offend a goddess, leading to the characters being

punished. The characters' actions and the ensuing punishment emphasize certain beliefs of the ancient Greeks. These beliefs include that no human is better than a god and that the gods must be respected.

Advance Preparation

Gather students' completed Spelling List 13 Pretest activity page from Myths (A). Students will refer to this page during Get Ready: Spelling List 13 Activity Bank.

"Repeat After Me, Me, Me..." Synopsis

Echo is a nymph who is never at a loss for words. She is so well-known for her conversational skills that her fame eventually attracts the attention of Zeus, the king of the gods. Zeus seeks out Echo and spends a day walking and talking with her. When he asks Echo to return to Mount Olympus with him, a jealous Hera appears. She is extremely angry that Zeus has gone behind her back to visit Echo. When Echo makes a casual remark that offends Hera, Hera curses Echo. Echo will no longer be able speak her own words. She will only be able to repeat the words that another has just spoken.

Lesson Goals

- Practice all spelling words offline.
- Read aloud to practice fluency.
- Read "Repeat After Me, Me, Me...."
- Compare details from two myths.
- Practice vocabulary words.
- Develop letter formation fluency.

MATERIALS

Supplied
- *Summit English Language Arts 3 Expeditions in Reading*
  - "Repeat After Me, Me, Me..."
- *Summit English Language Arts 3 Activity Book*
  - Spelling List 13 Activity Bank
  - Compare Two Goddesses
- handwriting workbook

Also Needed
- completed Spelling List 13 Pretest activity page from Myths (A)

KEYWORDS

compare – to explain how two or more things are alike

contrast – to explain how two or more things are different

myth – a story that explains how something came to be and that usually contains magical figures as characters

plot – what happens in a story; the sequence of events

GET READY

Introduction to Myths (B)

Students will get a glimpse of what they will learn about in the lesson. They will also read the lesson goals and keywords. Have students select each keyword and preview its definition.

Spelling List 13 Activity Bank

Students will practice all spelling words from the workshop by completing Spelling List 13 Activity Bank from *Summit English Language Arts 3 Activity Book*. Make sure students have their completed Spelling List 13 Pretest activity page from Myths (A) to refer to during this activity.

Remind students to pay special attention to words they spelled incorrectly on the Spelling Pretest.

GET READY

Myths (B)

Spelling List 13 Activity Bank

Circle any words in the box that you did not spell correctly on your pretest. Choose one activity to do with your circled words. Do as much of the activity as you can in the time given.

Did you spell all the words on the pretest correctly? Do the one activity with as many spelling words as you can.

annoying	crazier	grouchier	marries	spies
berries	cried	happier	ponies	stickier
bunnies	easier	hurried	prettier	studying
burying	flies	ladies	replies	trying
carrying				

Spelling Activity Choices

Alphabetizing

1. In the left column, write your spelling words in alphabetical order.
2. Correct any spelling errors.

MYTHS (B) 291

Vowel-Free Words

1. In the left column, write only the consonants in each of your spelling words. Put a dot where each vowel should be.
2. Spell each word aloud, stating which vowels should be in the places with dots.
3. In the right column, rewrite the entire spelling word.
4. Correct any spelling errors.

Rhymes

1. In the left column, write your spelling words.
2. In the right column, write a word that rhymes with each spelling word.
3. Correct any spelling errors.

Uppercase and Lowercase

1. In the left column, write each of your spelling words in all uppercase letters.
2. In the right column, write each of your spelling words in all lowercase letters.
3. Correct any spelling errors.

292 MYTHS (B)

Complete the activity that you chose.

My chosen activity: __________

1.
2.
3.
4.
5.
6.
7.
8.
9.
10.
11.
12.
13.
14.
15.
16.

Students should use these pages to complete all steps in their chosen activity.

MYTHS (B) 293

17.
18.
19.
20.
21.

294 MYTHS (B)

Read and Record

Good readers read quickly, smoothly, and with expression. This is called *fluency*. Students will record themselves reading aloud. They will listen to their recording and think about how quick, smooth, and expressive they sound.

TIP Encourage students to rerecord as needed.

Reading Foundations: Homophones

Reading Foundations activities serve to remind students of basic reading skills and reading behaviors mastered in earlier grades. The activities cover topics such as advanced decoding skills and various strategies for improving comprehension.

Recall "Tangled Webs"

Students will answer some questions to review the reading that they have already completed.

Before You Read "Repeat After Me, Me, Me..."

Students will be introduced to some key vocabulary words that they will encounter in the upcoming reading.

READ

"Repeat After Me, Me, Me..."

Students will read "Repeat After Me, Me, Me..." in *Expeditions in Reading*.

Check-In: "Repeat After Me, Me, Me..."

Students will answer several questions to demonstrate their comprehension of "Repeat After Me, Me, Me...."

LEARN AND TRY IT

LEARN Comparing Myths

Students will learn about comparing two myths with similar characters and plot events.

TIP Students will be comparing today's reading to the myth "Tangled Webs," so encourage them to refer to the complete version of the story in *Expeditions in Reading* if necessary.

TRY IT Compare Myths

Students will practice identifying similarities between two myths with similar characters and plot events.

TRY IT Apply: Compare or Contrast Plots

Students will apply to a new work what they've learned about comparing or contrasting plots of two stories.

TRY IT Compare Two Goddesses

Students will complete Compare Two Goddesses in *Summit English Language Arts 3 Activity Book*.

LEARNING COACH CHECK-IN This activity page contains a Venn diagram that must be completed first. The information in the diagram will be used to write a paragraph, so it's important that you review students' responses. Give students feedback, using the sample answers provided to guide you.

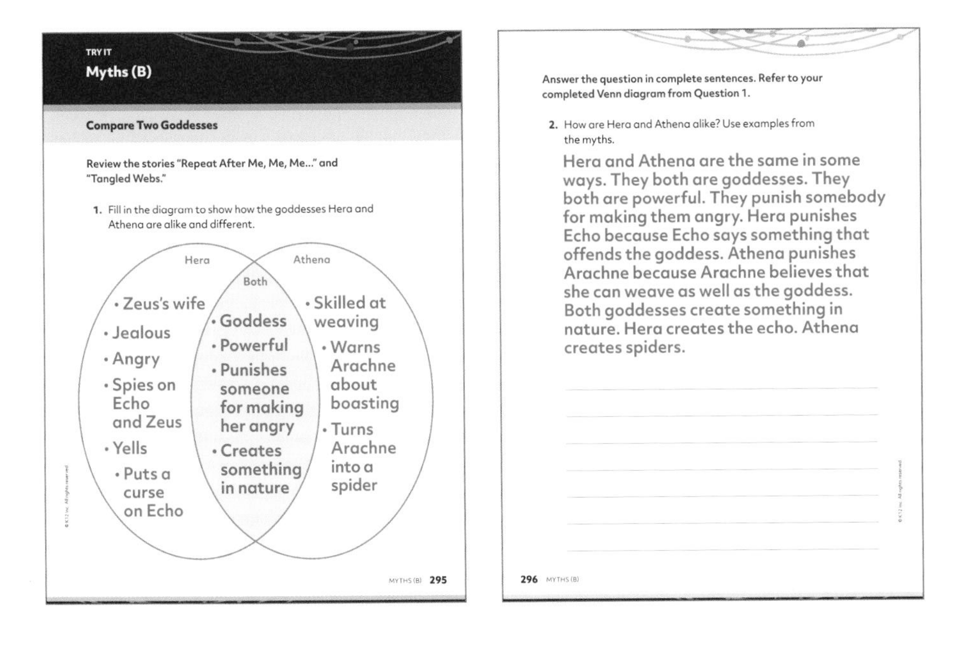

TRY IT

Myths (B)

Compare Two Goddesses

Review the stories "Repeat After Me, Me, Me..." and "Tangled Webs."

1. Fill in the diagram to show how the goddesses Hera and Athena are alike and different.

MYTHS (B) 295

Answer the question in complete sentences. Refer to your completed Venn diagram from Question 1.

2. How are Hera and Athena alike? Use examples from the myths.

Hera and Athena are the same in some ways. They both are goddesses. They both are powerful. They punish somebody for making them angry. Hera punishes Echo because Echo says something that offends the goddess. Athena punishes Arachne because Arachne believes that she can weave as well as the goddess. Both goddesses create something in nature. Hera creates the echo. Athena creates spiders.

296 MYTHS (B)

TRY IT Practice Words from "Repeat After Me, Me, Me..."

Students will answer questions to demonstrate their understanding of the vocabulary words from the reading.

WRAP-UP

Question About "Repeat After Me, Me, Me..."

Students will answer a question to show that they understand how to find similarities in passages from myths.

Handwriting

Students should gather their handwriting materials and begin where they left off. Remind students to form letters carefully and correctly.

TIP Set a timer to help students stay focused during handwriting practice.

Myths (C)

Lesson Overview

ACTIVITY	ACTIVITY TITLE	TIME	ONLINE/OFFLINE
GET READY	Introduction to Myths (C)	1 minute	online
	Spelling List 13 Practice	10 minutes	online
	Read and Record	8 minutes	online
	Reading Foundations: Contractions	5 minutes	online
	Recall "Repeat After Me, Me, Me..."	5 minutes	online
	Before You Read "A Flight Through the Sky"	5 minutes	online
READ	"A Flight Through the Sky"	23 minutes	offline
	Check-In: "A Flight Through the Sky"	5 minutes	online
LEARN AND TRY IT	Describing Characters and How They Make Things Happen	10 minutes	online
	Describe Characters and How They Make Things Happen	10 minutes	online
	Apply: Character's Actions	10 minutes	online
	What's That Character Like? LEARNING COACH CHECK-IN	10 minutes	offline
	Practice Words from "A Flight Through the Sky"	8 minutes	online
WRAP-UP	Question About "A Flight Through the Sky"	2 minutes	online
	Handwriting	8 minutes	offline

Content Background

In this lesson, students will learn about determining a character's traits from details in the text.

At times, traits may be stated directly in the text. For example, in the myth "A Flight Through the Sky," the text states, "Daedalus was famed throughout the land for his skill with his hands." This detail tells readers that the character of Daedalus is skillful.

Other times, readers will use text details to make an inference about a character. For example, the myth states, "The cruel king of the island knew

MATERIALS

Supplied

- *Summit English Language Arts 3 Expeditions in Reading*
  - "A Flight Through the Sky"
- *Summit English Language Arts 3 Activity Book*
  - What's That Character Like?
- handwriting workbook

how skillful he was and would not let him go away." From this detail, readers can infer that the king is a selfish person.

Students will also learn about how characters affect the plot of a story. The plot is the events that happen in a story.

A character's actions often cause other things to happen. Thus, the character affects the plot. For example, in "A Flight Through the Sky," the king places ships around the island to prevent Daedalus from escaping by sea. As a result, Daedalus decides that he will escape by flying away. The characters' actions shape the story. If the king had not placed ships around the island, Daedalus may not have tried to escape by flying. The events of the story would have been different.

KEYWORDS

character trait – a quality of a person or character; part of a personality

myth – a story that explains how something came to be and that usually contains magical figures as characters

plot – what happens in a story; the sequence of events

"A Flight Through the Sky" Synopsis

In this Greek myth, Daedalus, a skilled builder, is being held captive on an island by a king. Daedalus plans to escape. He builds wings for himself and his son Icarus using wood and feathers held together with wax. As they prepare to escape, Daedalus warns Icarus not to fly too close to the sun. With the excitement of flying, Icarus forgets his father's warning and flies too close to the sun. The wax holding the feathers to the wings melts, and Icarus falls into the sea. The story can be read as a warning to children to be mindful of their parents, or as a warning to those who would choose to defy the gods or become godlike.

Lesson Goals

- Practice all spelling words online.
- Read aloud to practice fluency.
- Read "A Flight Through the Sky."
- Identify traits of a story's characters.
- Explain how a character's actions affect the events of a story.
- Practice vocabulary words.
- Develop letter formation fluency.

GET READY

Introduction to Myths (C)

Students will get a glimpse of what they will learn about in the lesson. They will also read the lesson goals and keywords. Have students select each keyword and preview its definition.

Spelling List 13 Practice

Students will practice all spelling words from the workshop.

OPTIONAL Students may do an activity from Spelling List 13 Activity Bank instead of the online practice activity.

Read and Record

Good readers read quickly, smoothly, and with expression. This is called *fluency*. Students will record themselves reading aloud. They will listen to their recording and think about how quick, smooth, and expressive they sound.

TIP Encourage students to rerecord as needed.

Reading Foundations: Contractions

Reading Foundations activities serve to remind students of basic reading skills and reading behaviors mastered in earlier grades. The activities cover topics such as advanced decoding skills and various strategies for improving comprehension.

Recall "Repeat After Me, Me, Me..."

Students will answer some questions to review the reading that they have already completed.

Before You Read "A Flight Through the Sky"

Students will be introduced to some key vocabulary words that they will encounter in the upcoming reading.

READ

"A Flight Through the Sky"

Students will read "A Flight Through the Sky" in *Expeditions in Reading*.

Check-In: "A Flight Through the Sky"

Students will answer several questions to demonstrate their comprehension of "A Flight Through the Sky."

LEARN AND TRY IT

LEARN Describing Characters and How They Make Things Happen

Students will learn that characters' traits may be directly stated in text or can be inferred from what the characters think, say, and do. Students will also learn that a character's actions cause other events to happen.

TRY IT Describe Characters and How They Make Things Happen

Students will practice identifying characters' traits and determining how a character's actions affect the plot of a story.

TRY IT Apply: Character's Actions

Students will apply to a new work what they've learned about how a character's actions affect the plot of a story.

TRY IT What's That Character Like?

Students will complete What's That Character Like? in *Summit English Language Arts 3 Activity Book*.

LEARNING COACH CHECK-IN This activity page contains a choice of characters to describe. The sample answer provided to guide you may not match choices made by students. So, it's important that you review students' responses and use your knowledge of the story's characters to provide feedback.

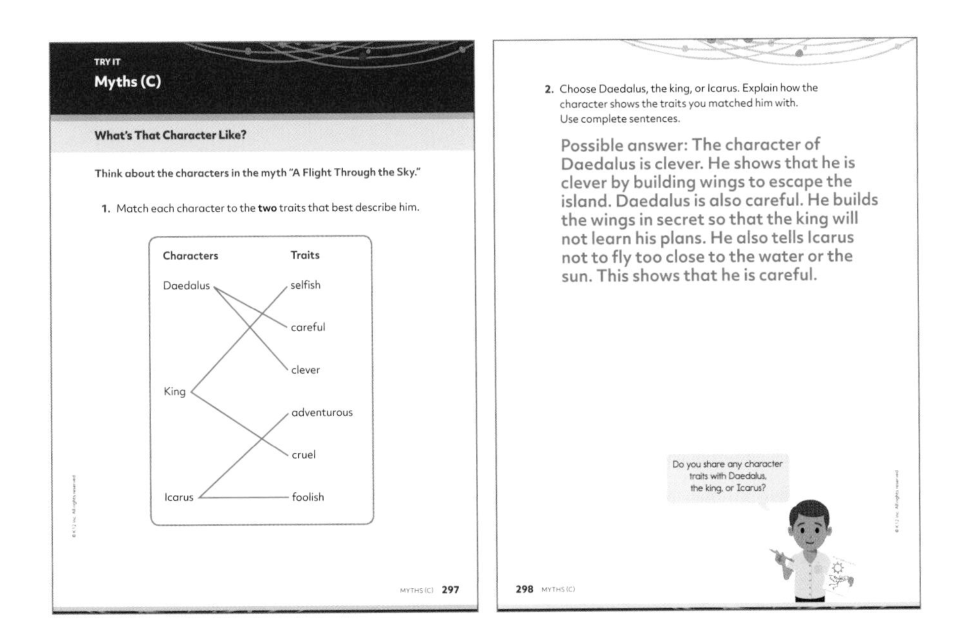

TRY IT

Myths (C)

What's That Character Like?

Think about the characters in the myth "A Flight Through the Sky."

1. Match each character to the **two** traits that best describe him.

Characters	Traits
Daedalus	selfish
	careful
	clever
King	adventurous
	cruel
Icarus	foolish

MYTHS (C) 297

2. Choose Daedalus, the king, or Icarus. Explain how the character shows the traits you matched him with. Use complete sentences.

Possible answer: The character of Daedalus is clever. He shows that he is clever by building wings to escape the island. Daedalus is also careful. He builds the wings in secret so that the king will not learn his plans. He also tells Icarus not to fly too close to the water or the sun. This shows that he is careful.

298 MYTHS (C)

TRY IT Practice Words from "A Flight Through the Sky"

Students will answer questions to demonstrate their understanding of the vocabulary words from the reading.

WRAP-UP

Question About "A Flight Through the Sky"

Students will answer a question to show that they understand how to identify character traits.

Handwriting

Students should gather their handwriting materials and begin where they left off. Remind students to form letters carefully and correctly.

TIP Set a timer to help students stay focused during handwriting practice.

Myths (D)

Lesson Overview

ACTIVITY	ACTIVITY TITLE	TIME	ONLINE/OFFLINE
GET READY	Introduction to Myths (D)	1 minute	online
	Spelling List 13 Review Game	10 minutes	online
	Read and Record	8 minutes	online
	Reading Foundations: Irregular Vowel Patterns	5 minutes	online
	Recall "A Flight Through the Sky"	5 minutes	online
	Before You Read "Roll, Roll, Roll That Rock"	5 minutes	online
READ	"Roll, Roll, Roll That Rock"	23 minutes	offline
	Check-In: "Roll, Roll, Roll That Rock"	5 minutes	online
LEARN AND TRY IT	Using Evidence to Support Answers	10 minutes	online
	Use Evidence to Support Answers	10 minutes	online
	Apply: Text-Based Evidence	10 minutes	online
	Prepare to Compare Two Myths LEARNING COACH CHECK-IN	10 minutes	offline
	Practice Words from "Roll, Roll, Roll That Rock"	8 minutes	online
WRAP-UP	Question About "Roll, Roll, Roll That Rock"	2 minutes	online
	Handwriting	8 minutes	offline

Content Background

In this lesson, students will learn how to support answers to comprehension questions with text-based evidence. Text-based evidence is a quotation directly from a story that supports, or proves, an answer to a comprehension question. For example, if a student were asked to describe the character of Sisyphus in the myth "Roll, Roll, Roll That Rock," one possible answer would be that Sisyphus is selfish. Sisyphus shows that he is selfish when he agrees to help someone, but only if that person first helps him. The evidence from the text is when Sisyphus says, "But first, you must do something for me."

MATERIALS

Supplied

- *Summit English Language Arts 3 Expeditions in Reading*
  - "Roll, Roll, Roll That Rock"
- *Summit English Language Arts 3 Activity Book*
  - Prepare to Compare Two Myths
- handwriting workbook

Students will also learn about comparing and contrasting myths with similar characters and events. They will learn that text-based evidence from two stories can prove how things in the stories are alike and different.

"Roll, Roll, Roll That Rock" Synopsis

In this Greek myth, Sisyphus, a cruel and selfish king, claims that he is more powerful than the gods. He belief is reinforced when Asopus, a river god, asks for his help. Zeus has carried off Asopus's daughter, Aegina, and Asopus thinks that Sisyphus may know where Zeus has taken her. Sisyphus tells Asopus what he knows, but only after Asopus makes a freshwater spring appear in Sisyphus's palace.

When Asopus tries to rescue his daughter, Zeus refuses to return her. Zeus then demands to know how Asopus found him. Asopus reveals that Sisyphus told him. This makes Zeus so angry that he puts a curse on Sisyphus. Sisyphus is doomed to push a boulder up a hill in the underworld for all time.

KEYWORDS

compare – to explain how two or more things are alike

contrast – to explain how two or more things are different

myth – a story that explains how something came to be and that usually contains magical figures as characters

plot – what happens in a story; the sequence of events

text-based evidence – proof in a text that supports an idea or answers a question

Lesson Goals

- Practice all spelling words online.
- Read aloud to practice fluency.
- Read "Roll, Roll, Roll That Rock."
- Describe what's alike and what's different in two myths.
- Support answers to questions with text-based evidence.
- Practice vocabulary words.
- Develop letter formation fluency.

GET READY

Introduction to Myths (D)

Students will get a glimpse of what they will learn about in the lesson. They will also read the lesson goals and keywords. Have students select each keyword and preview its definition.

Spelling List 13 Review Game

Students will practice all spelling words from the workshop.

Read and Record

Good readers read quickly, smoothly, and with expression. This is called *fluency*. Students will record themselves reading aloud. They will listen to their recording and think about how quick, smooth, and expressive they sound.

TIP Encourage students to rerecord as needed.

Reading Foundations: Irregular Vowel Patterns

Reading Foundations activities serve to remind students of basic reading skills and reading behaviors mastered in earlier grades. The activities cover topics such as advanced decoding skills and various strategies for improving comprehension.

Recall "A Flight Through the Sky"

Students will answer some questions to review the reading that they have already completed.

Before You Read "Roll, Roll, Roll That Rock"

Students will be introduced to some key vocabulary words that they will encounter in the upcoming reading.

READ

"Roll, Roll, Roll That Rock"

Students will read "Roll, Roll, Roll That Rock" in *Expeditions in Reading*.

Check-In: "Roll, Roll, Roll That Rock"

Students will answer several questions to demonstrate their comprehension of "Roll, Roll, Roll That Rock."

LEARN AND TRY IT

LEARN Using Evidence to Support Answers

Students will use text-based evidence to compare characters and plot events in myths.

TRY IT Use Evidence to Support Answers

Students will practice supporting answers to comprehension questions with text-based evidence.

TRY IT Apply: Text-Based Evidence

Students will apply to a new work what they've learned about using text-based evidence to support answers.

TRY IT **Prepare to Compare Two Myths**

Students will complete Prepare to Compare Two Myths in *English Language Arts 3 Activity Book*.

LEARNING COACH CHECK-IN Students will use answers on this activity page to help them complete an activity in Myths Wrap-Up, so it's important that you review students' responses. Give students feedback, using the sample answers provided to guide you.

NOTE Have students keep their completed activity page in a safe place so they can refer to it later.

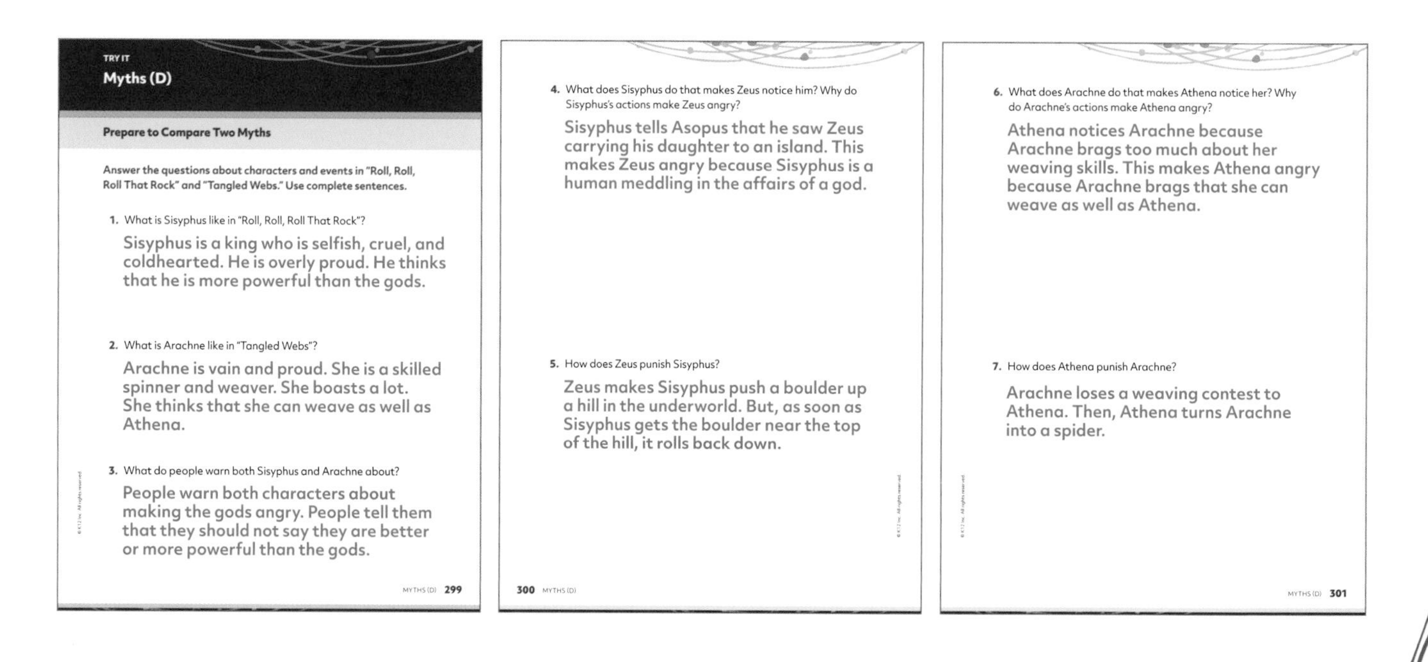

TRY IT

Myths (D)

Prepare to Compare Two Myths

Answer the questions about characters and events in "Roll, Roll, Roll That Rock" and "Tangled Webs." Use complete sentences.

1. What is Sisyphus like in "Roll, Roll, Roll That Rock"?

   Sisyphus is a king who is selfish, cruel, and coldhearted. He is overly proud. He thinks that he is more powerful than the gods.

2. What is Arachne like in "Tangled Webs"?

   Arachne is vain and proud. She is a skilled spinner and weaver. She boasts a lot. She thinks that she can weave as well as Athena.

3. What do people warn both Sisyphus and Arachne about?

   People warn both characters about making the gods angry. People tell them that they should not say they are better or more powerful than the gods.

MYTHS (D) 299

4. What does Sisyphus do that makes Zeus notice him? Why do Sisyphus's actions make Zeus angry?

   Sisyphus tells Asopus that he saw Zeus carrying his daughter to an island. This makes Zeus angry because Sisyphus is a human meddling in the affairs of a god.

5. How does Zeus punish Sisyphus?

   Zeus makes Sisyphus push a boulder up a hill in the underworld. But, as soon as Sisyphus gets the boulder near the top of the hill, it rolls back down.

300 MYTHS (D)

6. What does Arachne do that makes Athena notice her? Why do Arachne's actions make Athena angry?

   Athena notices Arachne because Arachne brags too much about her weaving skills. This makes Athena angry because Arachne brags that she can weave as well as Athena.

7. How does Athena punish Arachne?

   Arachne loses a weaving contest to Athena. Then, Athena turns Arachne into a spider.

MYTHS (D) 301

TRY IT **Practice Words from "Roll, Roll, Roll That Rock"**

Students will answer questions to demonstrate their understanding of the vocabulary words from the reading.

WRAP-UP

Question About "Roll, Roll, Roll That Rock"

Students will answer a question to show that they understand how to identify text-based evidence that supports an idea found in a story.

Handwriting

Students should gather their handwriting materials and begin where they left off. Remind students to form letters carefully and correctly.

TIP Set a timer to help students stay focused during handwriting practice.

Myths Wrap-Up

Lesson Overview

ACTIVITY	ACTIVITY TITLE	TIME	ONLINE/OFFLINE
GET READY	Introduction to Myths Wrap-Up	**1** minute	online
	Read and Record	**8** minutes	online
TRY IT	Compare Two Myths LEARNING COACH CHECK-IN	**30** minutes	offline
	Review Myths	**20** minutes	online
QUIZ	Myths	**30** minutes	online
	Spelling List 13	**10** minutes	online
WRAP-UP	More Language Arts Practice	**13** minutes	online
	Handwriting	**8** minutes	offline

Advance Preparation

Gather students' completed Prepare to Compare Two Myths activity page from Myths (D). Students will refer to this page during Try It: Compare Two Myths.

Lesson Goals

- Read aloud to practice fluency.
- Compare and contrast two myths.
- Review what you learned.
- Take a reading quiz.
- Take a spelling quiz.
- Develop letter formation fluency.

MATERIALS

Supplied

- *Summit English Language Arts 3 Activity Book*
  - Compare Two Myths
- handwriting workbook

Also Needed

- completed Prepare to Compare Two Myths activity page from Myths (D)

GET READY

Introduction to Myths Wrap-Up

Students will read the lesson goals.

Read and Record

Good readers read quickly, smoothly, and with expression. This is called *fluency*. Students will record themselves reading aloud. They will listen to their recording and think about how quick, smooth, and expressive they sound.

TIP Encourage students to rerecord as needed.

TRY IT

Compare Two Myths

Students will complete Compare Two Myths in *Summit English Language Arts 3 Activity Book*. Make sure students have their completed Prepare to Compare Two Myths activity page from Myths (D) to refer to during this activity.

LEARNING COACH CHECK-IN It's important that you review students' responses. Give students feedback, using the sample answers provided to guide you.

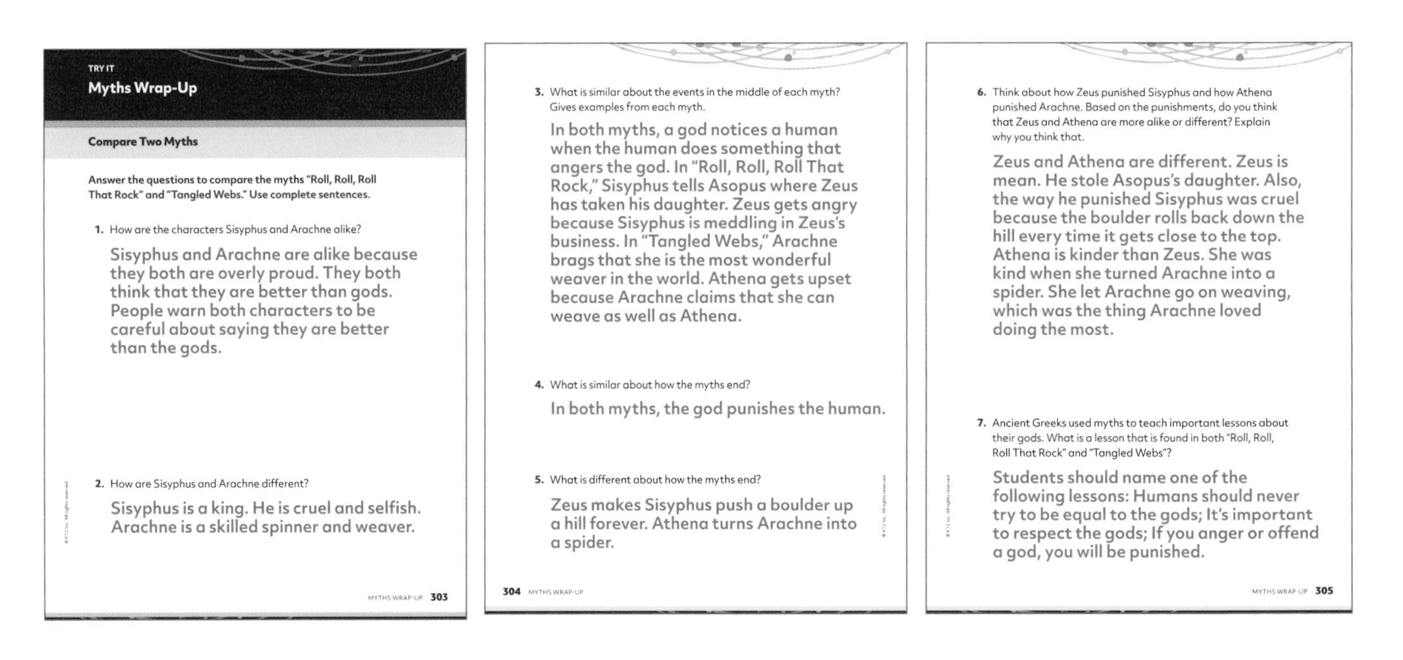
TRY IT

Myths Wrap-Up

Compare Two Myths

Answer the questions to compare the myths "Roll, Roll, Roll That Rock" and "Tangled Webs." Use complete sentences.

1. How are the characters Sisyphus and Arachne alike?

   Sisyphus and Arachne are alike because they both are overly proud. They both think that they are better than gods. People warn both characters to be careful about saying they are better than the gods.

2. How are Sisyphus and Arachne different?

   Sisyphus is a king. He is cruel and selfish. Arachne is a skilled spinner and weaver.

MYTHS WRAP-UP 303

3. What is similar about the events in the middle of each myth? Gives examples from each myth.

   In both myths, a god notices a human when the human does something that angers the god. In "Roll, Roll, Roll That Rock," Sisyphus tells Asopus where Zeus has taken his daughter. Zeus gets angry because Sisyphus is meddling in Zeus's business. In "Tangled Webs," Arachne brags that she is the most wonderful weaver in the world. Athena gets upset because Arachne claims that she can weave as well as Athena.

4. What is similar about how the myths end?

   In both myths, the god punishes the human.

5. What is different about how the myths end?

   Zeus makes Sisyphus push a boulder up a hill forever. Athena turns Arachne into a spider.

304 MYTHS WRAP-UP

6. Think about how Zeus punished Sisyphus and how Athena punished Arachne. Based on the punishments, do you think that Zeus and Athena are more alike or different? Explain why you think that.

   Zeus and Athena are different. Zeus is mean. He stole Asopus's daughter. Also, the way he punished Sisyphus was cruel because the boulder rolls back down the hill every time it gets close to the top. Athena is kinder than Zeus. She was kind when she turned Arachne into a spider. She let Arachne go on weaving, which was the thing Arachne loved doing the most.

7. Ancient Greeks used myths to teach important lessons about their gods. What is a lesson that is found in both "Roll, Roll, Roll That Rock" and "Tangled Webs"?

   Students should name one of the following lessons: Humans should never try to be equal to the gods; It's important to respect the gods; If you anger or offend a god, you will be punished.

MYTHS WRAP-UP 305

Review Myths

Students will answer questions to review what they have learned in this Reading workshop.

QUIZ

Myths

Students will complete the Myths quiz.

Spelling List 13

Students will complete the Spelling List 13 quiz.

WRAP-UP

More Language Arts Practice

Students will practice skills according to their individual needs.

Handwriting

Students should gather their handwriting materials and begin where they left off. Remind students to form letters carefully and correctly.

TIP Set a timer to help students stay focused during handwriting practice.

Informative Writing: Revising

Lesson Overview

ACTIVITY	ACTIVITY TITLE	TIME	ONLINE/OFFLINE
GET READY	Introduction to Informative Writing: Revising	**1** minute	online
	Look Back at a Model Research Report	**10** minutes	online
LEARN AND TRY IT	Revising a Research Report	**20** minutes	online
	Revising Your Research Report LEARNING COACH CHECK-IN	**55** minutes	offline
WRAP-UP	Question About Revising a Research Report	**2** minutes	online
	Handwriting	**8** minutes	offline
	Go Read!	**24** minutes	online or offline

Content Background

Students will continue working on their **research report** about a U.S. state. In this lesson, students will **revise** their draft.

Writing Process

In the revising step of the writing process, writers look back at their work and find ways to improve it. They focus on their ideas and organization, not on punctuation, grammar, and so on.

Students will use a checklist to revise their research report. The checklist focuses on ideas (*Does my introduction clearly state the topic and main idea?*) and organization (*Do I use transitions to connect ideas?*).

Students may not understand the difference between revising and proofreading. When revising, writers focus on large issues, such as the development and grouping of ideas. When proofreading, writers fix errors in grammar, usage, and mechanics, such as spelling or punctuation mistakes. Encourage students to focus on revising during this lesson. In the Informative Writing: Proofreading lesson, students will proofread their research report.

MATERIALS

Supplied

- *Summit English Language Arts 3 Activity Book*
  - Revise Your Research Report
- Research Report: Revision Feedback Sheet (printout)
- Research Report Instructions (printout)
- handwriting workbook

Also Needed

- folder in which students are storing research report writing assignment pages
- reading material for Go Read!

Advance Preparation

Gather the folder that students are using to store the activity pages related to their research report. The folder should contain the following:

- Model Research Report activity page from Informative Writing: Prewriting (A)
- Students' completed Brainstorm for Your Research Report activity page from Informative Writing: Prewriting (A)
- Students' completed Conduct Your Research activity page from Informative Writing: Prewriting (B)
- Students' completed index cards or online document from Informative Writing: Prewriting (B)
- Students' completed Organize Your Research Report activity page from Informative Writing: Prewriting (C)
- Students' completed draft from Informative Writing: Drafting (B)

Prior to the Revise Your Research Report activity in this lesson, read students' draft and complete the Research Report: Revision Feedback Sheet.

During the Go Read! activity, students will have the option of using the digital library. Allow extra time for students to make their reading selection, or have students make a selection before beginning the lesson.

KEYWORDS

research report – a type of essay based mainly on the author's research

revising – the step of the writing process for reviewing and fixing ideas and organization

Lesson Goals

- Use a checklist to revise your research report.
- Develop letter formation fluency.
- Read independently to develop fluency.

GET READY

Introduction to Informative Writing: Revising

Students will get a glimpse of what they will learn about in the lesson. They will also read the lesson goals and keywords. Have students select each keyword and preview its definition.

Look Back at a Model Research Report

Students will review the key elements of an effective research report.

LEARN AND TRY IT

LEARN Revising a Research Report

Through a guided activity, students will explore how a student revises a research report.

TRY IT Revise Your Research Report

Students will revise their research report using Revise Your Research Report in *Summit English Language Arts 3 Activity Book*, which is a revising checklist. They will need their completed research report draft from Informative Writing: Drafting (B).

LEARNING COACH CHECK-IN Guide students through the revision process.

1. Gather and use the Research Report: Revision Feedback Sheet that you filled out to guide a discussion with students.
   - Tell students the strengths of their report. Provide positive comments about the hook, supporting details and facts, organization, or other elements that you enjoyed.
   - Walk through your feedback with students. As you discuss the feedback, encourage students to actively revise their draft in response. Reassure students that it's okay to remove or move around ideas and sentences. Students should revise their draft directly on the drafting pages, using the lines they left blank.
2. Have students review their draft once independently, using the revising checklist from the activity book.
   - For students having difficulty recognizing areas they should revise, suggest a revision, and think aloud to model your revising. For example: *Your conclusion introduces a new idea. Is there a different paragraph where this idea would fit better?*
3. Make sure students store their revised draft in the folder they are using to organize their writing assignment pages.

TIP Remind students to focus on the checklist questions. Emphasize that they should not worry about spelling, punctuation, grammar, and so on.

NOTE If you or students wish, you can download and print another copy of the Research Report Instructions online.

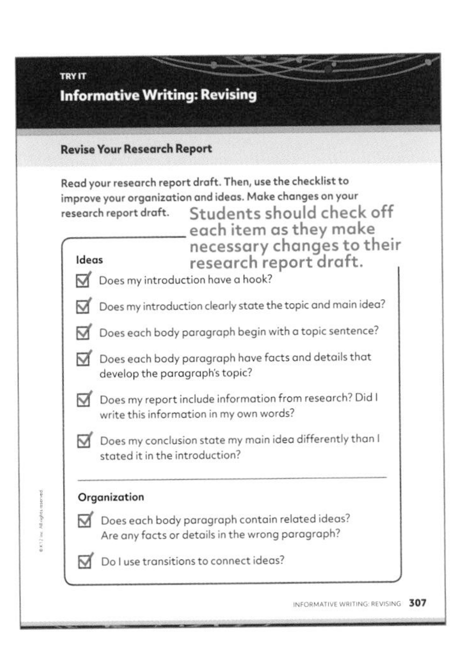
TRY IT

Informative Writing: Revising

Revise Your Research Report

Read your research report draft. Then, use the checklist to improve your organization and ideas. Make changes on your research report draft. Students should check off each item as they make necessary changes to their research report draft.

Ideas

- ☑ Does my introduction have a hook?
- ☑ Does my introduction clearly state the topic and main idea?
- ☑ Does each body paragraph begin with a topic sentence?
- ☑ Does each body paragraph have facts and details that develop the paragraph's topic?
- ☑ Does my report include information from research? Did I write this information in my own words?
- ☑ Does my conclusion state my main idea differently than I stated it in the introduction?

Organization

- ☑ Does each body paragraph contain related ideas? Are any facts or details in the wrong paragraph?
- ☑ Do I use transitions to connect ideas?

INFORMATIVE WRITING: REVISING 307

WRAP-UP

Question About Revising a Research Report

Students will answer a question to show that they understand a key revision skill.

Handwriting

Students should gather their handwriting materials and begin where they left off. Remind students to form letters carefully and correctly.

TIP Set a timer to help students stay focused during handwriting practice.

Go Read!

Students will read for pleasure. They should choose a book or a magazine that interests them, or they may choose a selection from the digital library, linked in the online lesson.

- Have students read aloud a few paragraphs of their selection.
- Then have students read silently for the rest of the time.

SUPPORT Students should make no more than five errors in decoding when they read aloud a few paragraphs of their Go Read! selection. If students struggle or make more than five errors, they need to select a different (and easier) text for the Go Read! activity.

TIP Have students select something to read ahead of time to help them stay focused.

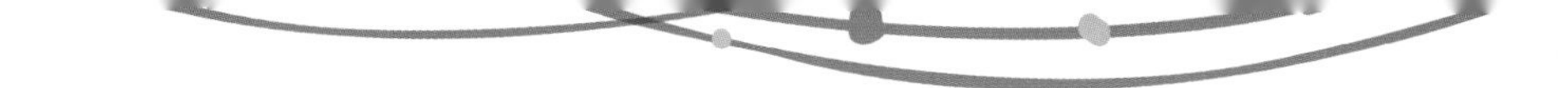

Informative Writing: Proofreading

Lesson Overview

ACTIVITY	ACTIVITY TITLE	TIME	ONLINE/OFFLINE
GET READY	Introduction to Informative Writing: Proofreading	**1** minute	
	Look Back at Nouns, Titles, and Quotations	**10** minutes	
LEARN AND **TRY IT**	Proofreading a Research Report	**20** minutes	
	Proofread Your Research Report **LEARNING COACH CHECK-IN**	**55** minutes	
WRAP-UP	Question About Proofreading a Research Report	**2** minutes	
	Handwriting	**8** minutes	
	Go Read!	**24** minutes	or

Content Background

Students will continue working on their **research report** about a U.S. state. In this lesson, students will **proofread** their draft.

Writing Process

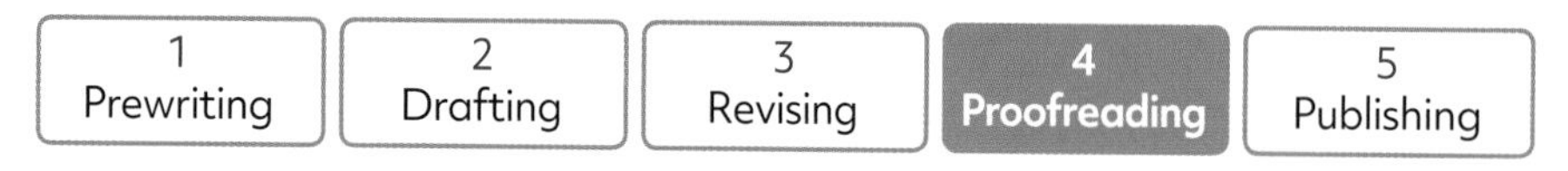

Students will use a checklist to proofread their research report. The checklist focuses on grammar and usage (*Are all sentences complete and correct?*) and mechanics (*Are plural and possessive nouns formed correctly?*).

Proofreading is often thought of as a hunt for errors, but that's not completely accurate. During proofreading, writers evaluate whether the way they use words, capitalization, punctuation, and sentence structure makes their writing as clear as possible. Sometimes, that means fixing an error, like a misspelled word. Other times, that means changing something that wasn't necessarily "wrong," such as combining two sentences or using a more appropriate noun in a sentence.

Proofreading is sometimes called *editing*.

MATERIALS

Supplied

- *Summit English Language Arts 3 Activity Book*
  - Proofread Your Research Report
- Research Report: Proofreading Feedback Sheet (printout)
- Research Report Instructions (printout)
- handwriting workbook

Also Needed

- folder in which students are storing research report writing assignment pages
- reading material for Go Read!

Advance Preparation

Gather the folder that students are using to store the activity pages related to their research report. The folder should contain the following:

- Model Research Report activity page from Informative Writing: Prewriting (A)
- Students' completed Brainstorm for Your Research Report activity page from Informative Writing: Prewriting (A)
- Students' completed Conduct Your Research activity page from Informative Writing: Prewriting (B)
- Students' completed index cards or online document from Informative Writing: Prewriting (B)
- Students' completed Organize Your Research Report activity page from Informative Writing: Prewriting (C)
- Students' revised draft from Informative Writing: Revising

Prior to the Proofread Your Research Report activity in this lesson, read students' draft and complete the Research Report: Proofreading Feedback Sheet.

During the Go Read! activity, students will have the option of using the digital library. Allow extra time for students to make their reading selection, or have students make a selection before beginning the lesson.

KEYWORDS

proofreading – the step of the writing process for checking and fixing errors in grammar, punctuation, capitalization, and spelling

research report – a type of essay based mainly on the author's research

Lesson Goals

- Use a checklist to proofread your research report.
- Develop letter formation fluency.
- Read independently to develop fluency.

GET READY

Introduction to Informative Writing: Proofreading

Students will get a glimpse of what they will learn about in the lesson. They will also read the lesson goals and keywords. Have students select each keyword and preview its definition.

Look Back at Nouns, Titles, and Quotations

Students will practice using various types of nouns, forming plural and possessive nouns, capitalizing the correct words in titles, and punctuating direct quotations. These are skills that students will use as they proofread their research report.

LEARN AND TRY IT

LEARN Proofreading a Research Report

Through a guided activity, students will explore how a student proofreads a research report.

TRY IT Proofread Your Research Report

Students will proofread their research report using Proofread Your Research Report in *Summit English Language Arts 3 Activity Book*, which is a proofreading checklist. They will need their revised research report from Informative Writing: Revising.

LEARNING COACH CHECK-IN Guide students through the proofreading process.

1. Have students read their draft aloud, listening for blatant errors such as missing words and incomplete sentences. As students catch errors, have them fix the errors on their draft, using the lines they left blank.
2. Have students review their draft again, using the proofreading checklist from the activity book.
3. Review with students your comments on the Research Report: Proofreading Feedback Sheet. Praise students for the improvements they made, and guide students to recognize any other critical improvements.
   - It is important that you don't edit students' report for them, but it's appropriate to guide students with observations and questions such as, *In this sentence, the word tourists is written as plural. Do you mean more than one tourist? Or do you mean that something belongs to the tourist?*
4. Have students store their edited draft in the folder they are using to organize their writing assignment pages.

OPTIONAL Have students exchange revised research reports with a peer and use the proofreading checklist from the activity book to proofread each other's reports.

NOTE If you or students wish, you can download and print another copy of the Research Report Instructions online.

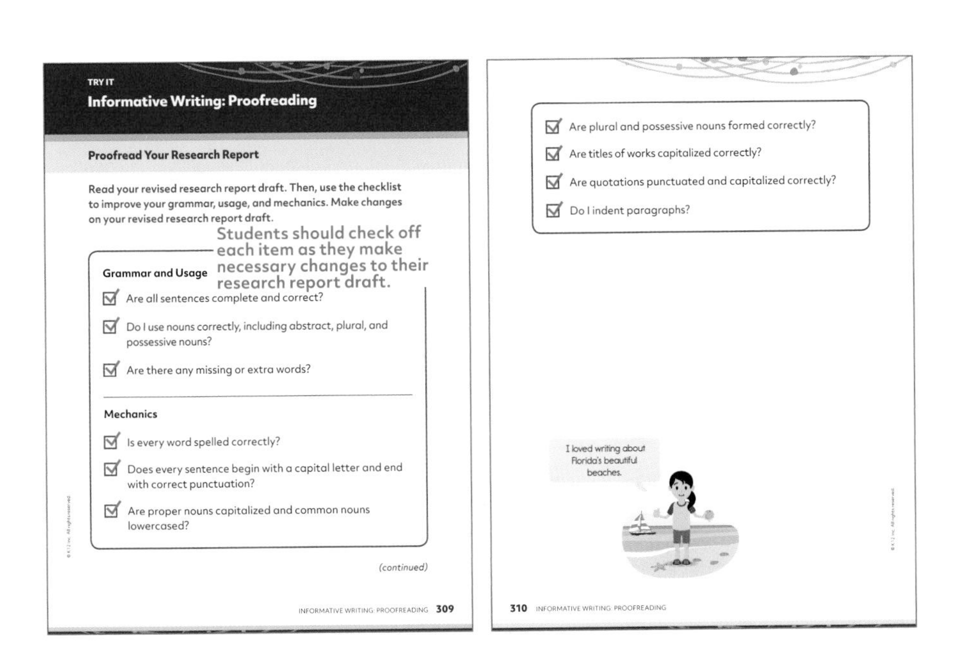
TRY IT
Informative Writing: Proofreading

Proofread Your Research Report

Read your revised research report draft. Then, use the checklist to improve your grammar, usage, and mechanics. Make changes on your revised research report draft.

Students should check off each item as they make necessary changes to their research report draft.

Grammar and Usage

- ☑ Are all sentences complete and correct?
- ☑ Do I use nouns correctly, including abstract, plural, and possessive nouns?
- ☑ Are there any missing or extra words?

Mechanics

- ☑ Is every word spelled correctly?
- ☑ Does every sentence begin with a capital letter and end with correct punctuation?
- ☑ Are proper nouns capitalized and common nouns lowercased?

(continued)

INFORMATIVE WRITING: PROOFREADING 309

- ☑ Are plural and possessive nouns formed correctly?
- ☑ Are titles of works capitalized correctly?
- ☑ Are quotations punctuated and capitalized correctly?
- ☑ Do I indent paragraphs?

310 INFORMATIVE WRITING: PROOFREADING

WRAP-UP

Question About Proofreading a Research Report

Students will answer a question to show that they understand a key proofreading skill.

Handwriting

Students should gather their handwriting materials and begin where they left off. Remind students to form letters carefully and correctly.

TIP Set a timer to help students stay focused during handwriting practice.

Go Read!

Students will read for pleasure. They should choose a book or a magazine that interests them, or they may choose a selection from the digital library, linked in the online lesson.

- Have students read aloud a few paragraphs of their selection.
- Then have students read silently for the rest of the time.

SUPPORT Students should make no more than five errors in decoding when they read aloud a few paragraphs of their Go Read! selection. If students struggle or make more than five errors, they need to select a different (and easier) text for the Go Read! activity.

TIP Have students select something to read ahead of time to help them stay focused.

Informative Writing: Publishing

Lesson Overview

ACTIVITY	ACTIVITY TITLE	TIME	ONLINE/OFFLINE
GET READY	Introduction to Informative Writing: Publishing	**1** minute	Online
	Look Back at Publishing Skills	**5** minutes	Online
LEARN AND TRY IT	Formatting a Source List	**10** minutes	Online
	Publish Your Research Report LEARNING COACH CHECK-IN	**60** minutes	Online or Offline
WRAP-UP	Turn In Your Research Report	**1** minute	Online
	More Language Arts Practice	**15** minutes	Online
	Handwriting	**8** minutes	Offline
	Go Read!	**20** minutes	Online or Offline

Content Background

Students will continue working on their **research report** about a U.S. state. In this lesson, students will format their source list and **publish** their research report. Then they will submit their completed research report to their teacher.

Writing Process

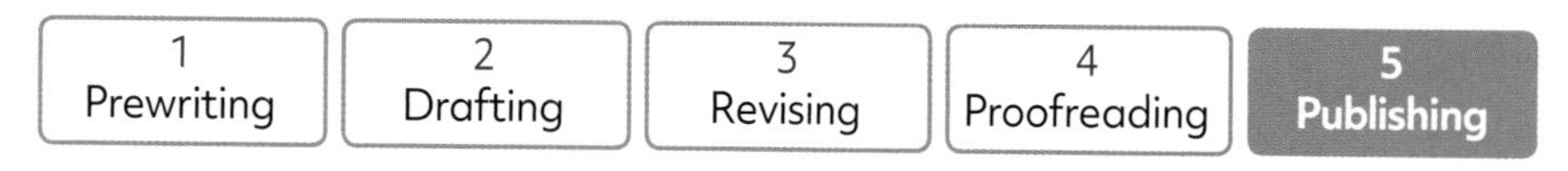

A *source list* is a list of students' research sources. Different style manuals have different rules for formatting a source list. In this course, students will learn the following basic rules:

- Website: "title of website" full URL
- Book: title of book by author. Publisher, year of publication.
- Article from reference book, such as encyclopedia: "title of article" title of book by author. Publisher, year of publication.

Not all sources will include all of the elements listed, and that's okay. Students should include the information available. What is most critical is that students understand the importance of crediting their research sources.

MATERIALS

Supplied

- Research Report Instructions (printout)
- handwriting workbook

Also Needed

- folder in which students are storing research report writing assignment pages
- reading material for Go Read!

Students may create their final copy using cursive handwriting or by typing in a word-processing program. They will complete an activity to review basic word-processing skills.

Advance Preparation

Gather the folder that students are using to store the activity pages related to their research report. The folder should contain the following:

- Model Research Report activity page from Informative Writing: Prewriting (A)
- Students' completed Brainstorm for Your Research Report activity page from Informative Writing: Prewriting (A)
- Students' completed Conduct Your Research activity page from Informative Writing: Prewriting (B)
- Students' completed index cards from Informative Writing: Prewriting (B)
- Students' completed Organize Your Research Report activity page from Informative Writing: Prewriting (C)
- Students' revised and edited draft from Informative Writing: Proofreading

During the Go Read! activity, students will have the option of using the digital library. Allow extra time for students to make their reading selection, or have students make a selection before beginning the lesson.

KEYWORDS

publishing – the step of the writing process for making a clean copy of the piece and sharing it

research report – a type of essay based mainly on the author's research

source – a provider of information; a book, a historical document, online materials, and an interviewee are all sources

Lesson Goals

- Format the source list for your research report.
- Make a clean copy of your research report.
- Submit your research report to your teacher.
- Develop letter formation fluency.
- Read independently to develop fluency.

GET READY

Introduction to Informative Writing: Publishing

Students will get a glimpse of what they will learn about in the lesson. They will also read the lesson goals and keywords. Have students select each keyword and preview its definition.

Look Back at Publishing Skills

Students will review what writers do during the publishing step of the writing process. They will also review basic keyboarding skills.

LEARN AND TRY IT

LEARN Formatting a Source List

Students will learn how to format their list of research sources for their research report.

TIP A source list is sometimes called a *bibliography*.

TRY IT Publish Your Research Report

Students will create a final copy of their research report. Students should gather their revised and edited draft, and they should create a clean copy that incorporates all of the changes they made in the workshop. They may either write their clean copy in cursive or type it.

NOTE If you or students wish, you can download and print another copy of the Research Report Instructions online.

WRAP-UP

Turn In Your Research Report

Students will submit their writing assignment to their teacher.

More Language Arts Practice

Students will practice skills according to their individual needs.

Handwriting

Students should gather their handwriting materials and begin where they left off. Remind students to form letters carefully and correctly.

TIP Set a timer to help students stay focused during handwriting practice.

Go Read!

Students will read for pleasure. They should choose a book or a magazine that interests them, or they may choose a selection from the digital library, linked in the online lesson.

- Have students read aloud a few paragraphs of their selection.
- Then have students read silently for the rest of the time.

SUPPORT Students should make no more than five errors in decoding when they read aloud a few paragraphs of their Go Read! selection. If students struggle or make more than five errors, they need to select a different (and easier) text for the Go Read! activity.

TIP Have students select something to read ahead of time to help them stay focused.

Big Ideas: Respond to a Prompt

Lesson Overview

Big Ideas lessons provide students the opportunity to further apply the knowledge acquired and skills learned throughout the unit workshops. Each Big Ideas lesson consists of these parts:

1. **Cumulative Review:** Students keep their skills fresh by reviewing prior content.
2. **Preview:** Students practice answering the types of questions they will commonly find on standardized tests.
3. **Synthesis:** Students complete an assignment that allows them to connect and apply what they have learned. Synthesis assignments vary throughout the course.

   In the Synthesis portion of this Big Ideas lesson, students will respond to an essay prompt based on reading selections. To respond meaningfully, students will need to use their own ideas as well as examples from the readings. Students' writing will be assessed in four categories: purpose and content; structure and organization; language and word choice; and grammar, usage, and mechanics.

   LEARNING COACH CHECK-IN This is a graded assessment. Make sure students complete, review, and submit the assignment to their teacher.

All materials needed for this lesson are linked online and not provided in the activity book.

MATERIALS

Supplied

- Respond to a Prompt (printout)

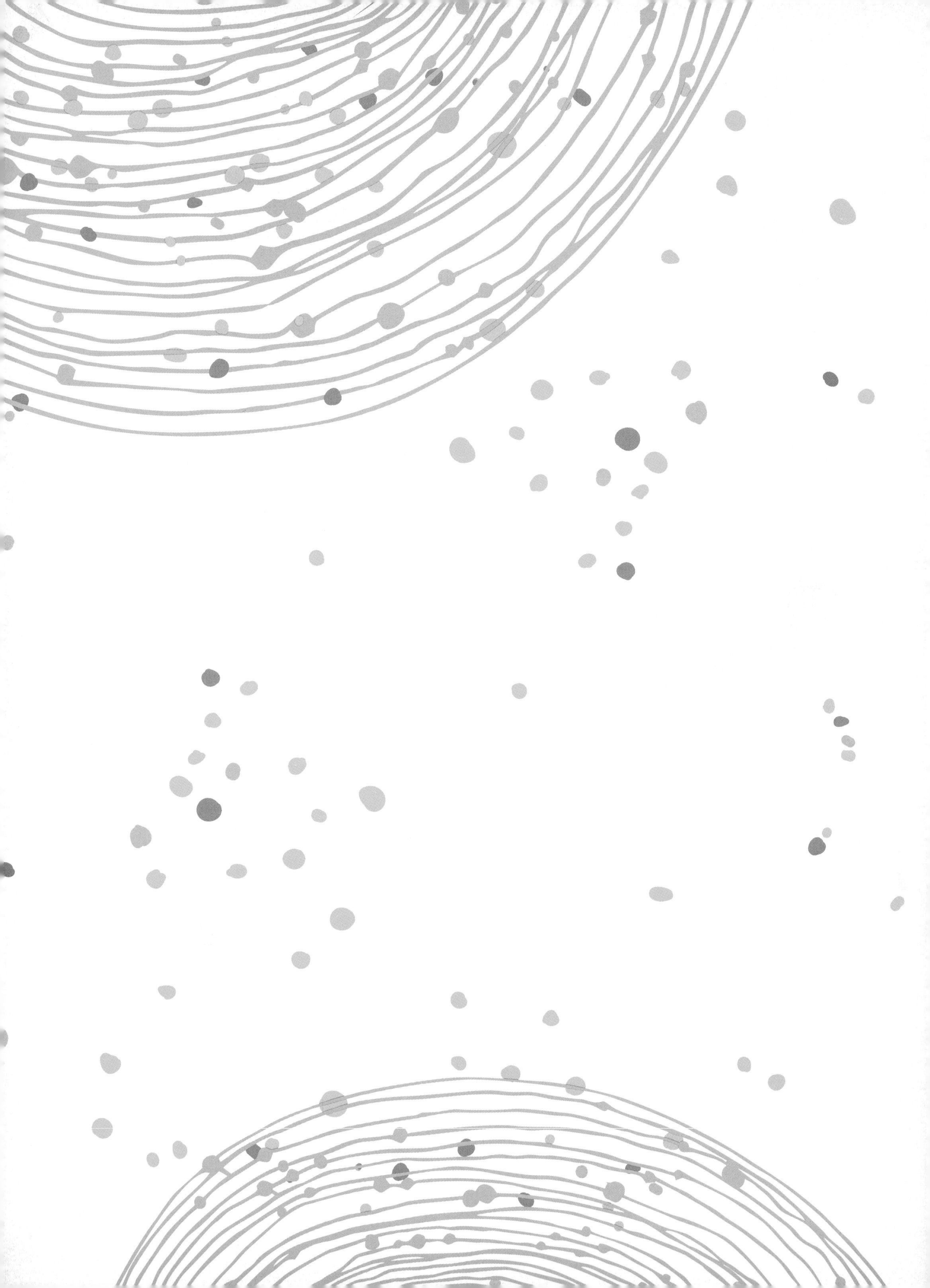

What Do You Think?

Utility Wires (A)

Lesson Overview

ACTIVITY	ACTIVITY TITLE	TIME	ONLINE/OFFLINE
GET READY	Introduction to Utility Wires (A)	**2** minutes	online
	Spelling List 14 Pretest LEARNING COACH CHECK-IN	**10** minutes	online and offline
	Before You Read "Bury All Utility Wires"	**12** minutes	online
READ	"Bury All Utility Wires"	**20** minutes	offline
	Check-In: "Bury All Utility Wires"	**6** minutes	online
LEARN AND **TRY IT**	Determining Main Idea and Author's Purpose	**10** minutes	online
	Determine Supporting Details	**5** minutes	online
	Determining Author's Point of View	**10** minutes	online
	Determine Author's Point of View	**5** minutes	online
	Apply: Main Idea	**12** minutes	online
	Write About Main Idea and Supporting Details LEARNING COACH CHECK-IN	**10** minutes	offline
	Practice Words from "Bury All Utility Wires"	**8** minutes	online
WRAP-UP	Question About "Bury All Utility Wires"	**2** minutes	online
	Handwriting	**8** minutes	offline

Content Background

Students will read a nonfiction article about utility wires. The author of the article believes that all utility wires should be buried. Students will learn how to determine the main idea, supporting details, and purpose of the article. In addition, students will spend some time learning what *point of view* is and how to determine an author's point of view.

MATERIALS

Supplied

- *Summit English Language Arts 3 Expeditions in Reading*
  - "Bury All Utility Wires"
- *Summit English Language Arts 3 Activity Book*
  - Spelling List 14 Pretest
  - Write About Main Idea and Supporting Details
- handwriting workbook

"Bury All Utility Wires" Synopsis

This nonfiction article is about utility poles and wires. The author believes that all utility poles should be taken down and that all utility wires should be buried underground. Burying wires will protect them from the weather and will protect people and animals from potential injuries. Additionally, burying wires and removing utility poles will make the landscape prettier. The author acknowledges that some people will not agree and that they will worry about the cost and the length of time it will take to bury the wires. Burying the wires will save money in the long run. The author also states that it won't take as long to bury the wires as people might think.

KEYWORDS

author's purpose – the reason the author wrote a text: to entertain, to inform, to express an opinion, or to persuade

main idea – the most important point the author makes; it may be stated or unstated

point of view – who is telling the story

supporting detail – a detail that gives more information about a main idea

Lesson Goals

- Take a spelling pretest.
- Read "Bury All Utility Wires."
- Determine the main idea, supporting details, and purpose of a nonfiction article.
- Determine an author's point of view.
- Practice vocabulary words.
- Develop letter formation fluency.

GET READY

Introduction to Utility Wires (A)

After a quick introductory activity, students will read the lesson goals and keywords. Have students select each keyword and preview its definition.

Spelling List 14 Pretest

Students will take a spelling pretest and learn a new spelling pattern.

LEARNING COACH CHECK-IN Have students turn to Spelling List 14 Pretest in *Summit English Language Arts 3 Activity Book* and open the online Spelling Pretest activity. Online, students will listen to the spelling word, type the word in the space indicated, and then check their answer. In the activity book, students will write the correct spelling of the word in the tables provided and indicate with a ✓ or an ✗ if they spelled the word correctly or incorrectly online. Students will repeat this process with the remaining words.

As needed, help students with the interaction between the online activity and the activity book page until they become comfortable with what they need to do. As students practice their spelling words throughout the workshop, they should pay special attention to words they spelled incorrectly on the pretest.

This is the complete list of words students will be tested on.

Words with soft c Sound				
braces	center	excite	police	space
celebrate	cereal	fancy	recess	spruce
celery	decide	lettuce	sentence	surface
cell	decimal	office	since	trace
cent	except	piece	sincere	voice

NOTE Have students keep their completed activity page in a safe place so they can refer to it later.

GET READY

Utility Wires (A)

Spelling List 14 Pretest

1. Open the Spelling Pretest activity online. Listen to the first spelling word. Type the word. Check your answer.
2. Write the correct spelling of the word in the Word column of the Spelling Pretest table.

	Word	✓	✗
1	blindfold		

3. Put a check mark in the ✓ column if you spelled the word correctly online.

	Word	✓	✗
1	blindfold	✓	

Put an X in the ✗ column if you spelled the word incorrectly online.

	Word	✓	✗
1	blindfold		X

4. Repeat Steps 1–3 for the remaining words in the Spelling Pretest.

UTILITY WIRES (A) 311

Utility Wires (A)

Spelling List 14 Pretest

Write each spelling word in the Word column, making sure to spell it correctly.

	Word	✓	✗
1	braces		
2	celebrate		
3	celery		
4	cell		
5	cent		
6	center		
7	cereal		
8	decide		
9	decimal		
10	except		
11	excite		
12	fancy		
13	lettuce		

	Word	✓	✗
14	office		
15	piece		
16	police		
17	recess		
18	sentence		
19	since		
20	sincere		
21	space		
22	spruce		
23	surface		
24	trace		
25	voice		

Students should write the correct spelling of each word from the pretest and use the ✓ and X columns to indicate whether they spelled each word correctly or incorrectly online.

312

Before You Read "Bury All Utility Wires"

Students will be introduced to some key vocabulary words that they will encounter in the upcoming reading and learn some important background related to the reading.

READ

"Bury All Utility Wires"

Students will read "Bury All Utility Wires" in *Expeditions in Reading*.

Check-In: "Bury All Utility Wires"

Students will answer several questions to demonstrate their comprehension of "Bury All Utility Wires."

LEARN AND TRY IT

LEARN Determining Main Idea and Author's Purpose

Students will learn how to determine the main idea, supporting details, and author's purpose for writing a nonfiction text.

TRY IT Determine Supporting Details

Students will determine supporting details in a nonfiction text.

LEARN Determining Author's Point of View

Students will learn how to determine an author's point of view in a nonfiction text.

Point of view is the perspective a story or an article is told from. All writers have a point of view from which they write; some authors' points of view are more obvious than others. The author's point of view in "Bury All Utility Wires" should be fairly obvious to students. The author believes all power lines should be buried and gives a variety of reasons for this opinion.

TIP If students struggle with the idea of point of view, consider rereading one of their favorite picture books or fairy tale, such as "Cinderella" or "Little Red Riding Hood." Then ask them to think about how they would retell the story from a different character's point of view (such as the stepmother in "Cinderella" or the Big Bad Wolf in "Little Red Riding Hood"). This exercise can help them with the concept of perspective.

TRY IT Determine Author's Point of View

Students will determine details that support an author's point of view in a nonfiction text.

TRY IT Apply: Main Idea

Students will apply to a new work what they've learned about determining the main idea in a text.

TRY IT Write About Main Idea and Supporting Details

Students will complete Write About Main Idea and Supporting Details in *Summit English Language Arts 3 Activity Book*.

LEARNING COACH CHECK-IN This activity page contains open-ended questions, so it's important that you review students' responses. Give students feedback, using the sample answers provided to guide you.

NOTE Have students keep their completed activity page in a safe place so they can refer to it later.

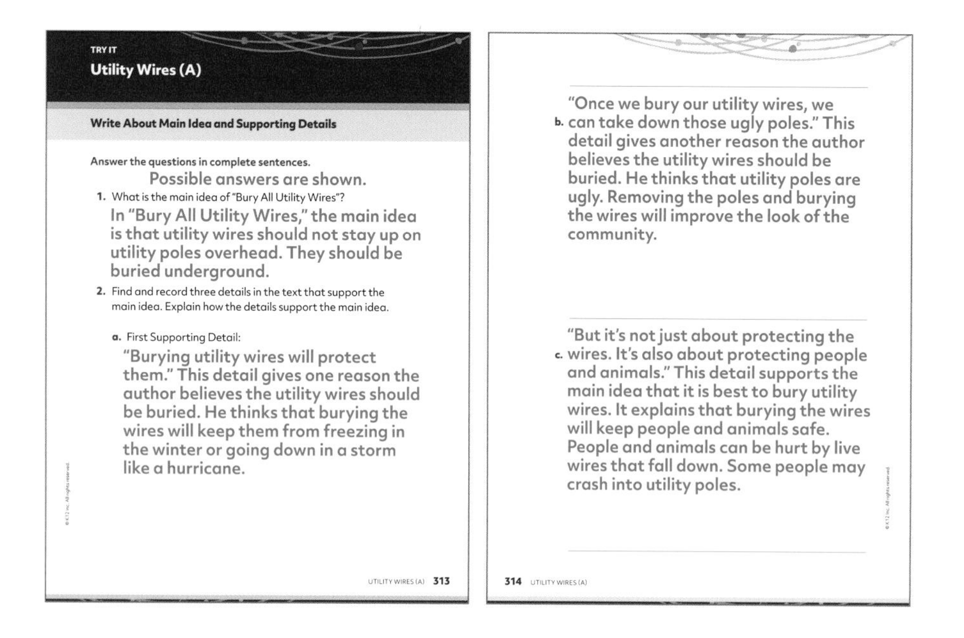

TRY IT

Utility Wires (A)

Write About Main Idea and Supporting Details

Answer the questions in complete sentences.

Possible answers are shown.

1. What is the main idea of "Bury All Utility Wires"?

   In "Bury All Utility Wires," the main idea is that utility wires should not stay up on utility poles overhead. They should be buried underground.

2. Find and record three details in the text that support the main idea. Explain how the details support the main idea.

   a. First Supporting Detail:

   "Burying utility wires will protect them." This detail gives one reason the author believes the utility wires should be buried. He thinks that burying the wires will keep them from freezing in the winter or going down in a storm like a hurricane.

UTILITY WIRES (A) 313

b. "Once we bury our utility wires, we can take down those ugly poles." This detail gives another reason the author believes the utility wires should be buried. He thinks that utility poles are ugly. Removing the poles and burying the wires will improve the look of the community.

c. "But it's not just about protecting the wires. It's also about protecting people and animals." This detail supports the main idea that it is best to bury utility wires. It explains that burying the wires will keep people and animals safe. People and animals can be hurt by live wires that fall down. Some people may crash into utility poles.

314 UTILITY WIRES (A)

TRY IT Practice Words from "Bury All Utility Wires"

Students will answer questions to demonstrate their understanding of the vocabulary words from the reading.

WRAP-UP

Question About "Bury all Utility Wires"

Students will answer a question to show that they understand the main idea of a paragraph.

Handwriting

Students should gather their handwriting materials and begin where they left off. Remind students to form letters carefully and correctly.

TIP Set a timer to help students stay focused during handwriting practice.

Utility Wires (B)

Lesson Overview

ACTIVITY	ACTIVITY TITLE	TIME	ONLINE/OFFLINE
GET READY	Introduction to Utility Wires (B)	**1** minute	online
	Spelling List 14 Activity Bank	**10** minutes	offline
	Recall "Bury All Utility Wires"	**5** minutes	online
	Before You Read "Keep Our Wires High in the Sky"	**5** minutes	online
READ	"Keep Our Wires High in the Sky"	**21** minutes	offline
	Check-In: "Keep Our Wires High in the Sky"	**5** minutes	online
LEARN AND TRY IT	Determining Purpose and Point of View	**15** minutes	online
	Determine Purpose and Point of View	**10** minutes	online
	Apply: Supporting Details	**15** minutes	online
	Write About Main Idea, Supporting Details, and Your Opinion LEARNING COACH CHECK-IN	**15** minutes	offline
	Practice Words from "Keep Our Wires High in the Sky"	**8** minutes	online
WRAP-UP	Question About "Keep Our Wires High in the Sky"	**2** minutes	online
	Handwriting	**8** minutes	offline

Content Background

Students will read "Keep Our Wires High in the Sky," an article that expresses the author's opinion that utility wires and poles should stay above the ground. Students will explore the article's main idea and supporting details. They will also explore the author's opinion and point of view. Finally, they will be asked to share their own point of view on where utility wires should be located.

Advance Preparation

Gather students' completed Spelling List 14 Pretest activity page from Utility Wires (A). Students will refer to this page during Get Ready: Spelling List 14 Activity Bank.

"Keep Our Wires High in the Sky" Synopsis

This nonfiction article is about utility poles and wires. The author believes that all utility poles and wires should remain above the ground. Burying wires is a waste of money and time and that power outages and accidents will happen no matter where wires are located. The author believes that burying wires will make them more difficult to repair. Whether the poles and wires make an area less attractive is a matter of opinion and that burying wires will put people who repair them out of work.

Lesson Goals

- Practice all spelling words offline.
- Read "Keep Our Wires High in the Sky."
- Determine an article's main idea and supporting details.
- Determine an author's purpose for writing an article and an author's point of view.
- Write about one's own point of view.
- Practice vocabulary words.
- Develop letter formation fluency.

MATERIALS

Supplied

- *Summit English Language Arts 3 Expeditions in Reading*
  - "Keep Our Wires High in the Sky"
- *Summit English Language Arts 3 Activity Book*
  - Spelling List 14 Activity Bank
  - Write About Main Idea, Supporting Details, and Your Opinion
- handwriting workbook

Also Needed

- completed Spelling List 14 Pretest activity page from Utility Wires (A)

KEYWORDS

author's purpose – the reason the author wrote a text: to entertain, to inform, to express an opinion, or to persuade

main idea – the most important point the author makes; it may be stated or unstated

point of view – who is telling the story

supporting detail – a detail that gives more information about a main idea

GET READY

Introduction to Utility Wires (B)

Students will get a glimpse of what they will learn about in the lesson. They will also read the lesson goals and keywords. Have students select each keyword and preview its definition.

Spelling List 14 Activity Bank

Students will practice all spelling words from the workshop by completing Spelling List 14 Activity Bank from *Summit English Language Arts 3 Activity Book*. Make sure students have their completed Spelling List 14 Pretest activity page from Utility Wires (A) to refer to during this activity.

Remind students to pay special attention to words they spelled incorrectly on the Spelling Pretest.

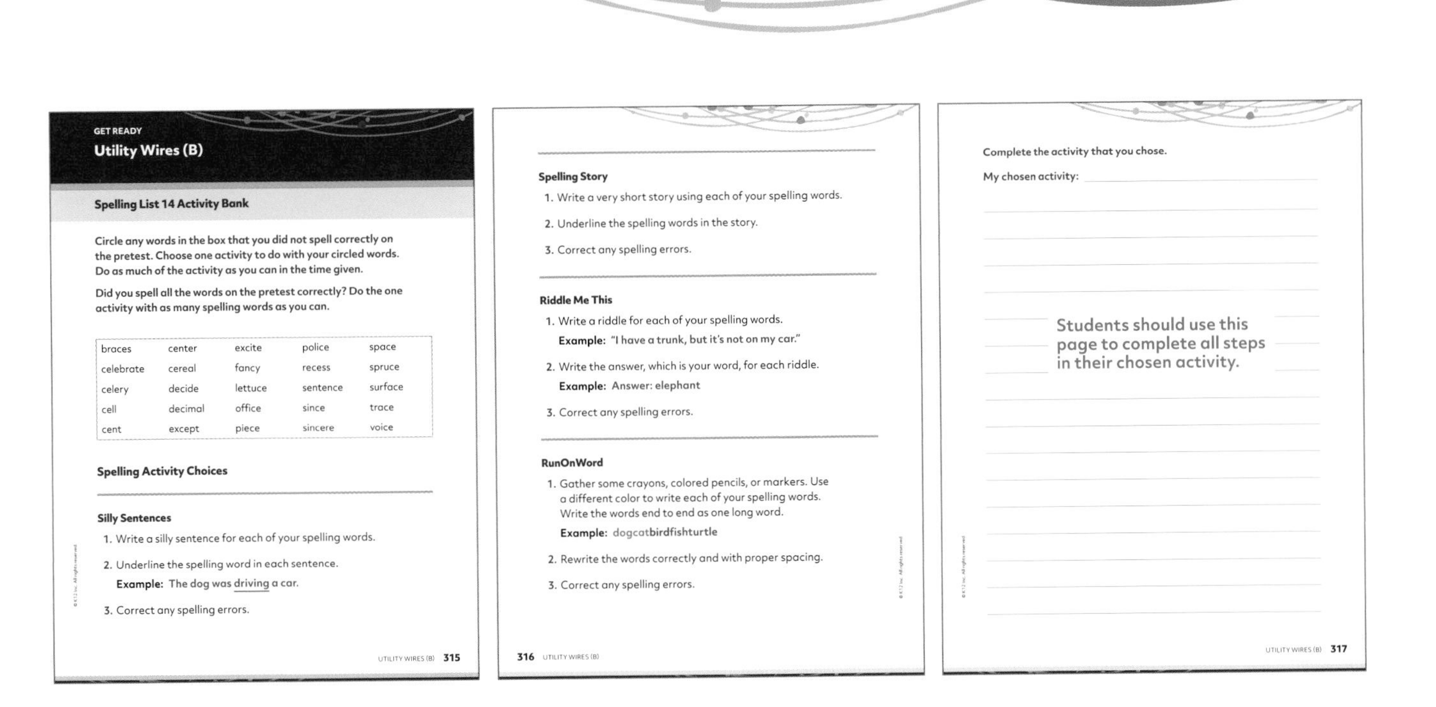
GET READY

Utility Wires (B)

Spelling List 14 Activity Bank

Circle any words in the box that you did not spell correctly on the pretest. Choose one activity to do with your circled words. Do as much of the activity as you can in the time given.

Did you spell all the words on the pretest correctly? Do the one activity with as many spelling words as you can.

braces	center	excite	police	space
celebrate	cereal	fancy	recess	spruce
celery	decide	lettuce	sentence	surface
cell	decimal	office	since	trace
cent	except	piece	sincere	voice

Spelling Activity Choices

Silly Sentences

1. Write a silly sentence for each of your spelling words.
2. Underline the spelling word in each sentence.
   Example: The dog was driving a car.
3. Correct any spelling errors.

UTILITY WIRES (B) 315

Spelling Story

1. Write a very short story using each of your spelling words.
2. Underline the spelling words in the story.
3. Correct any spelling errors.

Riddle Me This

1. Write a riddle for each of your spelling words.
   Example: "I have a trunk, but it's not on my car."
2. Write the answer, which is your word, for each riddle.
   Example: Answer: elephant
3. Correct any spelling errors.

RunOnWord

1. Gather some crayons, colored pencils, or markers. Use a different color to write each of your spelling words. Write the words end to end as one long word.
   Example: dogcatbirdfishturtle
2. Rewrite the words correctly and with proper spacing.
3. Correct any spelling errors.

316 UTILITY WIRES (B)

Complete the activity that you chose.

My chosen activity:

Students should use this page to complete all steps in their chosen activity.

UTILITY WIRES (B) 317

Recall "Bury All Utility Wires"

Students will answer some questions to review the reading that they have already completed.

Before You Read "Keep Our Wires High in the Sky"

Students will be introduced to some key vocabulary words that they will encounter in the upcoming reading.

READ

"Keep Our Wires High in the Sky"

Students will read "Keep Our Wires High in the Sky" in *Expeditions in Reading*.

Check-In: "Keep Our Wires High in the Sky"

Students will answer several questions to demonstrate their comprehension of "Keep Our Wires High in the Sky."

LEARN AND TRY IT

LEARN Determining Purpose and Point of View

Students will review main idea, supporting details, author's purpose, and author's point of view. They will then learn how to determine their own point of view.

TRY IT **Determine Purpose and Point of View**

Students will determine the main idea, supporting details, author's purpose, and author's point of view in the article they read.

TRY IT **Apply: Supporting Details**

Students will apply to a new work what they've learned about determining supporting details in a text.

TRY IT **Write About Main Idea, Supporting Details, and Your Opinion**

Students will complete Write About Main Idea, Supporting Details, and Your Opinion in *Summit English Language Arts 3 Activity Book*.

LEARNING COACH CHECK-IN This activity page contains open-ended questions, so it's important that you review students' responses. Give students feedback, using the sample answers provided to guide you.

TIP To guide students on developing their own point of view, it may be helpful to explore how utilities are handled in students' own communities.

NOTE Have students keep their completed activity page in a safe place so they can refer to it later.

TRY IT

Utility Wires (B)

Write About Main Idea, Supporting Details, and Your Opinion

Answer the questions in complete sentences.

Possible answers are shown.

1. What is the main idea of "Keep Our Wires High in the Sky"?

   In "Keep Our Wires High in the Sky," the main idea is that utility wires should stay up on utility poles overhead. They should not be buried underground.

2. Find and record three details in the text that support the main idea. Explain how the details support the main idea.

   a. First Supporting Detail:

   "Outages are a fact of life. Disruptions will happen. This is true no matter where the wires are placed." This detail gives one reason why the author believes the utility wires should stay above the ground. He believes that it doesn't matter if the wires are above or below ground. Outages will happen either way.

UTILITY WIRES (B) 319

   b. Second Supporting Detail:

   "Burying wires will only make them harder to repair." This detail gives another reason why the author believes that utility wires should stay above the ground. He thinks that it will take more effort to fix wires if they are underground.

   c. Third Supporting Detail:

   "Do you know what's worse than hitting a pole? When a kid digging a hole strikes one of the buried wires. Or when that car slides past where a utility pole would have been and smashes into a storefront." This detail gives a third reason why the author doesn't believe that burying the wires is a good idea. He thinks that accidents will still happen when wires are buried.

320 UTILITY WIRES (B)

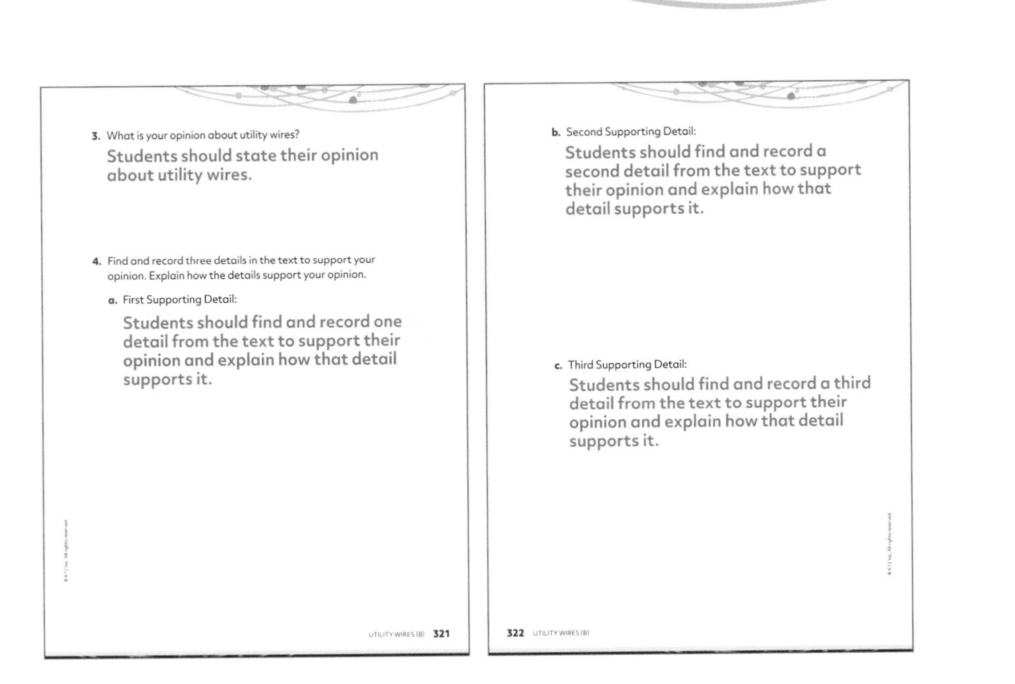
3. What is your opinion about utility wires?

Students should state their opinion about utility wires.

4. Find and record three details in the text to support your opinion. Explain how the details support your opinion.

a. First Supporting Detail:

Students should find and record one detail from the text to support their opinion and explain how that detail supports it.

UTILITY WIRES (B) 321

b. Second Supporting Detail:

Students should find and record a second detail from the text to support their opinion and explain how that detail supports it.

c. Third Supporting Detail:

Students should find and record a third detail from the text to support their opinion and explain how that detail supports it.

322 UTILITY WIRES (B)

TRY IT Practice Words from "Keep Our Wires High in the Sky"

Students will answer questions to demonstrate their understanding of the vocabulary words from the reading.

WRAP-UP

Question About "Keep Our Wires High in the Sky"

Students will answer a question to show that they understand an author's opinion.

Handwriting

Students should gather their handwriting materials and begin where they left off. Remind students to form letters carefully and correctly.

TIP Set a timer to help students stay focused during handwriting practice.

Utility Wires Wrap-Up

Lesson Overview

ACTIVITY	ACTIVITY TITLE	TIME	ONLINE/OFFLINE
GET READY	Introduction to Utility Wires Wrap-Up	**1** minute	online
	Read and Record	**8** minutes	online
	Spelling List 14 Practice	**10** minutes	online
TRY IT	Compare and Contrast Points of View LEARNING COACH CHECK-IN	**30** minutes	offline
	Review Utility Wires	**20** minutes	online
QUIZ	Utility Wires	**30** minutes	online
WRAP-UP	More Language Arts Practice	**15** minutes	online
	Handwriting	**6** minutes	offline

Advance Preparation

Gather students' completed Write About Main Idea and Supporting Details activity page from Utility Wires (A) and Write About Main Idea, Supporting Details, and Your Opinion activity page from Utility Wires (B). Students will refer to these pages during Try It: Compare and Contrast Points of View.

MATERIALS

Supplied

- *Summit English Language Arts 3 Expeditions in Reading*
- *Summit English Language Arts 3 Activity Book*
  - Compare and Contrast Points of View
- handwriting notebook

Also Needed

- completed Write About Main Idea and Supporting Details activity page from Utility Wires (A)
- completed Write About Main Idea, Supporting Details, and Your Opinion activity page from Utility Wires (B)

Lesson Goals

- Read aloud to practice fluency.
- Practice all spelling words online.
- Compare and contrast different points of view on the same topic.
- Review what you learned.
- Take a reading quiz.
- Develop letter formation fluency.

GET READY

Introduction to Utility Wires Wrap-Up

Students will read the lesson goals.

Read and Record

Good readers read quickly, smoothly, and with expression. This is called *fluency*. Students will record themselves reading aloud. They will listen to their recording and think about how quick, smooth, and expressive they sound.

TIP Encourage students to rerecord as needed.

Spelling List 14 Practice

Students will practice all spelling words from the workshop.

OPTIONAL Students may do an activity from Spelling List 14 Activity Bank instead of the online practice activity.

TRY IT

Compare and Contrast Points of View

Students will complete Compare and Contrast Points of View in *Summit English Language Arts 3 Activity Book*. Make sure students have their completed Write About Main Idea and Supporting Details activity page from Utility Wires (A) and Write About Main Idea, Supporting Details, and Your Opinion activity page from Utility Wires (B) to refer to during this activity.

LEARNING COACH CHECK-IN This activity page contains the framework for building a dialogue, so it's important that you review students' responses. Give students feedback, using the sample answers provided to guide you.

SUPPORT For students having difficulty with the idea of writing a dialogue, it may be helpful to revisit "The Stone in the Road: A Play" in *Expeditions in Reading*. The play provides an example of dialogue exchanges that students can use when they are writing the dialogue for the activity page.

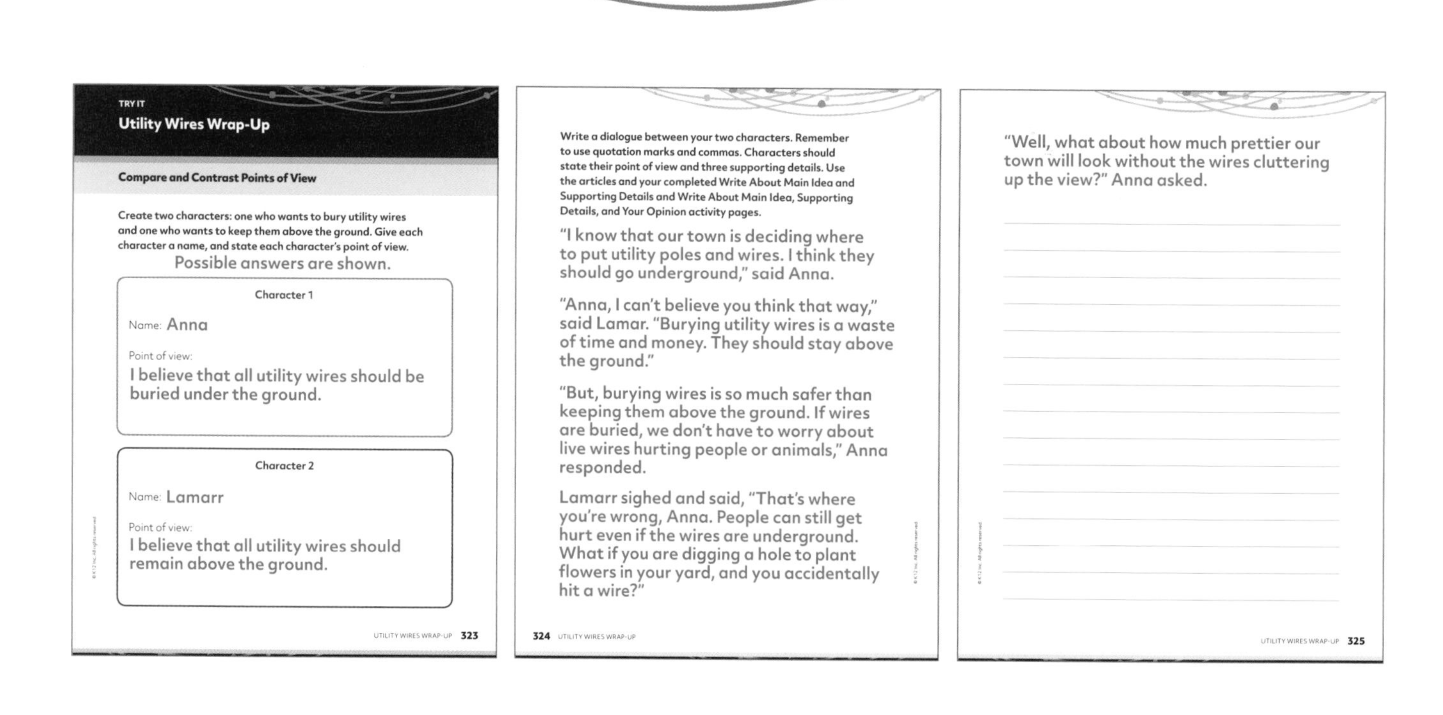
TRY IT
Utility Wires Wrap-Up

Compare and Contrast Points of View

Create two characters: one who wants to bury utility wires and one who wants to keep them above the ground. Give each character a name, and state each character's point of view.
Possible answers are shown.

Character 1
Name: Anna
Point of view:
I believe that all utility wires should be buried under the ground.

Character 2
Name: Lamarr
Point of view:
I believe that all utility wires should remain above the ground.

UTILITY WIRES WRAP-UP 323

Write a dialogue between your two characters. Remember to use quotation marks and commas. Characters should state their point of view and three supporting details. Use the articles and your completed Write About Main Idea and Supporting Details and Write About Main Idea, Supporting Details, and Your Opinion activity pages.

"I know that our town is deciding where to put utility poles and wires. I think they should go underground," said Anna.

"Anna, I can't believe you think that way," said Lamar. "Burying utility wires is a waste of time and money. They should stay above the ground."

"But, burying wires is so much safer than keeping them above the ground. If wires are buried, we don't have to worry about live wires hurting people or animals," Anna responded.

Lamarr sighed and said, "That's where you're wrong, Anna. People can still get hurt even if the wires are underground. What if you are digging a hole to plant flowers in your yard, and you accidentally hit a wire?"

324 UTILITY WIRES WRAP-UP

"Well, what about how much prettier our town will look without the wires cluttering up the view?" Anna asked.

UTILITY WIRES WRAP-UP 325

Review Utility Wires

Students will answer questions to review what they have learned about determining main idea, supporting details, author's purpose, and author's point of view.

QUIZ

Utility Wires

Students will complete the Utility Wires quiz.

WRAP-UP

More Language Arts Practice

Students will practice skills according to their individual needs.

Handwriting

Students should gather their handwriting materials and begin where they left off. Remind students to form letters carefully and correctly.

TIP Set a timer to help students stay focused during handwriting practice.

Fast Food (A)

Lesson Overview

ACTIVITY	ACTIVITY TITLE	TIME	ONLINE/OFFLINE
GET READY	Introduction to Fast Food (A)	**1** minute	
	Spelling List 14 More Practice	**10** minutes	
	Before You Read "Down with Fast Food"	**6** minutes	
READ	"Down with Fast Food"	**25** minutes	
	Check-In: "Down with Fast Food"	**5** minutes	
LEARN AND **TRY IT**	Distinguishing Facts from Opinions	**15** minutes	
	Distinguish Facts from Opinions	**10** minutes	
	Apply: Author's Purpose	**15** minutes	
	Write About Points of View LEARNING COACH CHECK-IN	**15** minutes	
	Practice Words from "Down with Fast Food"	**8** minutes	
WRAP-UP	Question About Fact and Opinion	**2** minutes	
	Handwriting	**8** minutes	

Content Background

Students will read the first of two persuasive articles about fast food. They will learn about the difference between facts and opinions. A *fact* is information that can be proven to be true, whereas an *opinion* is something that a writer feels or believes. An opinion cannot be proven to be true. Students can verify facts by looking for the same information in another source, such as a nonfiction book, a reputable website, or an expert interview.

MATERIALS

Supplied

- *Summit English Language Arts 3 Expeditions in Reading*
  - "Down with Fast Food"
- *Summit English Language Arts 3 Activity Book*
  - Write About Points of View
- handwriting workbook

"Down with Fast Food" Synopsis

"Down with Fast Food" is an informational article. The purpose of the article is to persuade readers to agree with the author's point of view—namely, fast food is very unhealthy and should never be eaten. The author believes that eating fast food leads to health problems such as a heart disease and diabetes. The author thinks that fast food is addictive and that the ingredients used in fast food are of poor quality. Finally, the author takes issue with people who say that it is cheaper to feed a family of four at a fast food restaurant, as the author was able to cook a meal for six for $18.

KEYWORDS

fact – something that can be proven true

opinion – something that a person thinks or believes but that cannot be proven to be true

point of view – who is telling the story

Lesson Goals

- Practice all spelling words online.
- Read "Down with Fast Food."
- Distinguish facts from opinions.
- Determine an author's point of view.
- Practice vocabulary words.
- Develop letter formation fluency.

GET READY

Introduction to Fast Food (A)

Students will get a glimpse of what they will learn about in the lesson. They will also read the lesson goals and keywords. Have students select each keyword and preview its definition.

Spelling List 14 More Practice

Students will practice all spelling words from the workshop.

OPTIONAL Students may do an activity from Spelling List 14 Activity Bank instead of the online practice activity.

Before You Read "Down with Fast Food"

Students will be introduced to some key vocabulary words that they will encounter in the upcoming reading.

READ

"Down with Fast Food"

Students will read "Down with Fast Food" in *Expeditions in Reading*.

NOTE K12 does not take a stance on the consumption of fast food. The writers are using this issue as a way of presenting two different points of view on the same topic. It is up to each family to make choices that are right for them.

Check-In: "Down with Fast Food"

Students will answer several questions to demonstrate their comprehension of "Down with Fast Food."

LEARN AND TRY IT

LEARN Distinguishing Facts from Opinions

Students will learn the difference between facts and opinions, as well as why authors use facts in persuasive texts.

TRY IT Distinguish Fact from Opinion

Students will identify facts and opinions and explain how authors support their opinions with facts.

TRY IT Apply: Author's Purpose

Students will apply to a new work what they've learned about the reasons authors write specific texts.

TRY IT Write About Points of View

Students will complete Write About Points of View in *Summit English Language Arts 3 Activity Book*.

LEARNING COACH CHECK-IN This activity page contains open-ended questions, so it's important that you review students' responses. Give students feedback, using the sample answers provided to guide you.

TIP The second half of this activity asks students for their point of view about eating fast food. If students struggle to come up with a point of view, encourage them to begin thinking about their own experience with fast food.

NOTE Have students keep their completed activity page in a safe place so they can refer to it later.

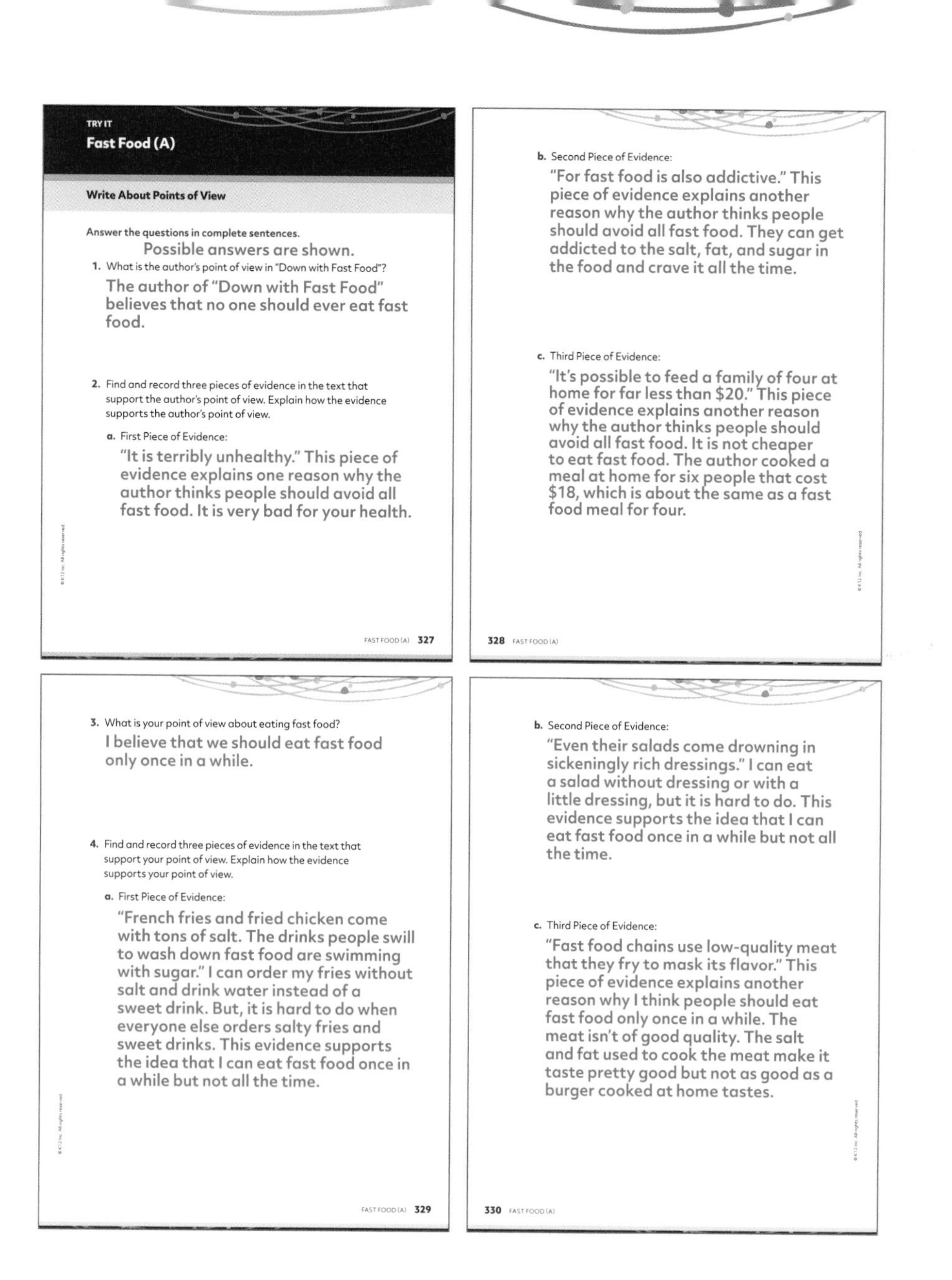
TRY IT

Fast Food (A)

Write About Points of View

Answer the questions in complete sentences.

Possible answers are shown.

1. What is the author's point of view in "Down with Fast Food"?

The author of "Down with Fast Food" believes that no one should ever eat fast food.

2. Find and record three pieces of evidence in the text that support the author's point of view. Explain how the evidence supports the author's point of view.

a. First Piece of Evidence:

"It is terribly unhealthy." This piece of evidence explains one reason why the author thinks people should avoid all fast food. It is very bad for your health.

FAST FOOD (A) 327

b. Second Piece of Evidence:

"For fast food is also addictive." This piece of evidence explains another reason why the author thinks people should avoid all fast food. They can get addicted to the salt, fat, and sugar in the food and crave it all the time.

c. Third Piece of Evidence:

"It's possible to feed a family of four at home for far less than $20." This piece of evidence explains another reason why the author thinks people should avoid all fast food. It is not cheaper to eat fast food. The author cooked a meal at home for six people that cost $18, which is about the same as a fast food meal for four.

328 FAST FOOD (A)

3. What is your point of view about eating fast food?

I believe that we should eat fast food only once in a while.

4. Find and record three pieces of evidence in the text that support your point of view. Explain how the evidence supports your point of view.

a. First Piece of Evidence:

"French fries and fried chicken come with tons of salt. The drinks people swill to wash down fast food are swimming with sugar." I can order my fries without salt and drink water instead of a sweet drink. But, it is hard to do when everyone else orders salty fries and sweet drinks. This evidence supports the idea that I can eat fast food once in a while but not all the time.

FAST FOOD (A) 329

b. Second Piece of Evidence:

"Even their salads come drowning in sickeningly rich dressings." I can eat a salad without dressing or with a little dressing, but it is hard to do. This evidence supports the idea that I can eat fast food once in a while but not all the time.

c. Third Piece of Evidence:

"Fast food chains use low-quality meat that they fry to mask its flavor." This piece of evidence explains another reason why I think people should eat fast food only once in a while. The meat isn't of good quality. The salt and fat used to cook the meat make it taste pretty good but not as good as a burger cooked at home tastes.

330 FAST FOOD (A)

TRY IT Practice Words from "Down with Fast Food"

Students will answer questions to demonstrate their understanding of the vocabulary words from the reading.

WRAP-UP

Question About Fact and Opinion

Students will answer a question to show that they understand the difference between a fact and an opinion.

Handwriting

Students should gather their handwriting materials and begin where they left off. Remind students to form letters carefully and correctly.

TIP Set a timer to help students stay focused during handwriting practice.

Fast Food (B)

Lesson Overview

ACTIVITY	ACTIVITY TITLE	TIME	ONLINE/OFFLINE
GET READY	Introduction to Fast Food (B)	1 minute	online
	Spelling List 14 Review Game	10 minutes	online
	Recall "Down with Fast Food"	5 minutes	online
	Before You Read "In Favor of Fast Food"	5 minutes	online
READ	"In Favor of Fast Food"	30 minutes	offline
	Check-In: "In Favor of Fast Food"	5 minutes	online
LEARN AND TRY IT	Determining Points of View	15 minutes	online
	Explain Your Point of View	5 minutes	online
	Apply: Author's Point of View	11 minutes	online
	Compare Points of View LEARNING COACH CHECK-IN	15 minutes	offline
	Practice Words from "In Favor of Fast Food"	8 minutes	online
WRAP-UP	Question About "In Favor of Fast Food"	2 minutes	online
	Handwriting	8 minutes	offline

Content Background

Students will read the second of two persuasive articles about fast food. They will identify the author's point of view and their own point of view. They will focus on how their point of view may be similar to or differ from the points of view presented in the articles they read.

MATERIALS

Supplied

- *Summit English Language Arts 3 Expeditions in Reading*
  - "In Favor of Fast Food"
- *Summit English Language Arts 3 Activity Book*
  - Compare Points of View
- handwriting workbook

"In Favor of Fast Food" Synopsis

"In Favor of Fast Food" is an informational article. The purpose of the article is to persuade readers to agree with the author's point of view, which is that it is okay to eat fast food. The author believes that fast food has a place at the table, particularly when one orders salad or other healthy options. The author urges readers to be logical in their assessment of fast food and not dismiss it because of the unhealthy options available. The author also believes that people eat fast food because they like the taste of what they order and that eating fast food saves busy families time.

KEYWORDS

opinion – something that a person thinks or believes but that cannot be proven to be true

point of view – who is telling the story

Lesson Goals

- Practice all spelling words online.
- Read "In Favor of Fast Food."
- Determine an author's point of view.
- Explain your own point of view.
- Compare points of view.
- Practice vocabulary words.
- Develop letter formation fluency.

GET READY

Introduction to Fast Food (B)

Students will get a glimpse of what they will learn about in the lesson. They will also read the lesson goals and keywords. Have students select each keyword and preview its definition.

Spelling List 14 Review Game

Students will practice all spelling words from the workshop.

Recall "Down with Fast Food"

Students will answer some questions to review the reading that they have already completed.

Before You Read "In Favor of Fast Food"

Students will be introduced to some key vocabulary words that they will encounter in the upcoming reading.

READ

"In Favor of Fast Food"

Students will read "In Favor of Fast Food" in *Expeditions in Reading*.

NOTE K12 does not take a stance on the consumption of fast food. The writers are using this issue as a way of presenting two different points of view on the same topic. It is up to each family to make choices that are right for them.

Check-In: "In Favor of Fast Food"

Students will answer several questions to demonstrate their comprehension of "In Favor of Fast Food."

LEARN AND TRY IT

LEARN Determining Points of View

Students will review the two articles they read and figure out each author's point of view.

TRY IT Explain Your Point of View

Students will record their point of view about eating fast food.

NOTE Encourage students to respond fully to the question in this activity. They should list reasons they hold their point of view. They should also identify details in the text(s) that support their point of view. Students will use their response as a jumping-off point for their work on the activity page.

TRY IT Apply: Author's Point of View

Students will apply to a new work what they've learned about determining an author's point of view in a text.

TRY IT Compare Points of View

Students will complete Compare Points of View in *Summit English Language Arts 3 Activity Book*.

LEARNING COACH CHECK-IN This activity page contains open-ended questions, so it's important that you review students' responses. Give students feedback, using the sample answers provided to guide you. Remind students that there is no single "correct" point of view. They just need to be able to support their point of view with examples and details from the text(s).

NOTE Have students keep their completed activity page in a safe place so they can refer to it later.

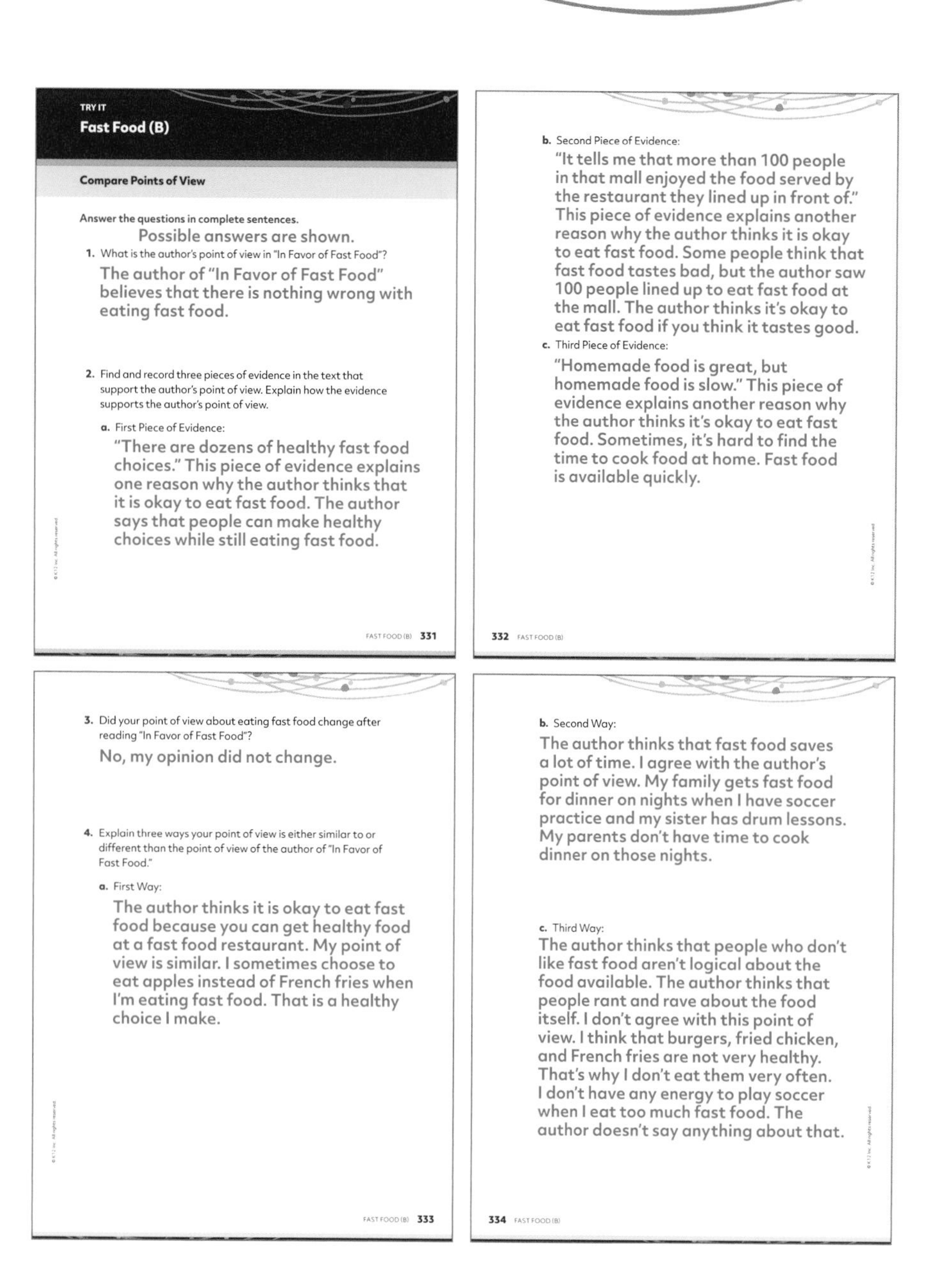
TRY IT

Fast Food (B)

Compare Points of View

Answer the questions in complete sentences.

Possible answers are shown.

1. What is the author's point of view in "In Favor of Fast Food"?

The author of "In Favor of Fast Food" believes that there is nothing wrong with eating fast food.

2. Find and record three pieces of evidence in the text that support the author's point of view. Explain how the evidence supports the author's point of view.

a. First Piece of Evidence:

"There are dozens of healthy fast food choices." This piece of evidence explains one reason why the author thinks that it is okay to eat fast food. The author says that people can make healthy choices while still eating fast food.

FAST FOOD (B) 331

b. Second Piece of Evidence:

"It tells me that more than 100 people in that mall enjoyed the food served by the restaurant they lined up in front of." This piece of evidence explains another reason why the author thinks it is okay to eat fast food. Some people think that fast food tastes bad, but the author saw 100 people lined up to eat fast food at the mall. The author thinks it's okay to eat fast food if you think it tastes good.

c. Third Piece of Evidence:

"Homemade food is great, but homemade food is slow." This piece of evidence explains another reason why the author thinks it's okay to eat fast food. Sometimes, it's hard to find the time to cook food at home. Fast food is available quickly.

332 FAST FOOD (B)

3. Did your point of view about eating fast food change after reading "In Favor of Fast Food"?

No, my opinion did not change.

4. Explain three ways your point of view is either similar to or different than the point of view of the author of "In Favor of Fast Food."

a. First Way:

The author thinks it is okay to eat fast food because you can get healthy food at a fast food restaurant. My point of view is similar. I sometimes choose to eat apples instead of French fries when I'm eating fast food. That is a healthy choice I make.

FAST FOOD (B) 333

b. Second Way:

The author thinks that fast food saves a lot of time. I agree with the author's point of view. My family gets fast food for dinner on nights when I have soccer practice and my sister has drum lessons. My parents don't have time to cook dinner on those nights.

c. Third Way:

The author thinks that people who don't like fast food aren't logical about the food available. The author thinks that people rant and rave about the food itself. I don't agree with this point of view. I think that burgers, fried chicken, and French fries are not very healthy. That's why I don't eat them very often. I don't have any energy to play soccer when I eat too much fast food. The author doesn't say anything about that.

334 FAST FOOD (B)

TRY IT Practice Words from "In Favor of Fast Food"

Students will answer questions to demonstrate their understanding of the vocabulary words from the reading.

WRAP-UP

Question About "In Favor of Fast Food"

Students will answer a question to show that they understand supporting details in "In Favor of Fast Food."

Handwriting

Students should gather their handwriting materials and begin where they left off. Remind students to form letters carefully and correctly.

TIP Set a timer to help students stay focused during handwriting practice.

Fast Food Wrap-Up

Lesson Overview

ACTIVITY	ACTIVITY TITLE	TIME	ONLINE/OFFLINE
GET READY	Introduction to Fast Food Wrap-Up	**1** minute	online
	Read and Record	**8** minutes	online
TRY IT	Create a Mini-Book LEARNING COACH CHECK-IN	**30** minutes	offline
	Review Fast Food	**20** minutes	online
QUIZ	Fast Food	**30** minutes	online
	Spelling List 14	**10** minutes	online
WRAP-UP	More Language Arts Practice	**15** minutes	online
	Handwriting	**6** minutes	offline

Advance Preparation

Gather students' completed Write About Points of View activity page from Fast Food (A) and Compare Points of View activity page from Fast Food (B). Students will refer to these pages during Try It: Create a Mini-Book.

Lesson Goals

- Read aloud to practice fluency.
- Compare and contrast opinions.
- Compare main idea, key details, author's purpose, and author's point of view.
- Review what you learned.
- Take a reading quiz.
- Take a spelling quiz.
- Develop letter formation fluency.

MATERIALS

Supplied

- *Summit English Language Arts 3 Expeditions in Reading*
- *Summit English Language Arts 3 Activity Book*
  - Create a Mini-Book
- handwriting workbook

Also Needed

- completed Write About Points of View activity page from Fast Food (A)
- completed Compare Points of View activity page from Fast Food (B)

GET READY

Introduction to Fast Food Wrap-Up

Students will read the lesson goals.

Read and Record

Good readers read quickly, smoothly, and with expression. This is called *fluency*. Students will record themselves reading aloud. They will listen to their recording and think about how quick, smooth, and expressive they sound.

TIP Encourage students to rerecord as needed.

TRY IT

Create a Mini-Book

Students will complete Create a Mini-Book in *Summit English Language Arts 3 Activity Book*. They should use their best cursive handwriting when completing this activity page. Make sure students have their completed Write About Points of View activity page from Fast Food (A) and Compare Points of View activity page from Fast Food (B) to refer to during this activity.

LEARNING COACH CHECK-IN This activity page contains open-ended questions, so it's important that you review students' responses. Give students feedback, using the sample answers provided to guide you.

TRY IT

Fast Food Wrap-Up

Create a Mini-Book

Write a mini-book about fast food. Use the articles and your completed Write About Points of View and Compare Points of View activity pages.

To create your mini-book, tear out page 337. Fold the page in half. Use your best cursive handwriting to add your title and name to your mini-book.

Use the lines inside your mini-book to write two paragraphs.

- The first paragraph should explain your opinion about fast food. Include examples to support your opinion.
- The second paragraph should compare the author's opinion in one of the articles you read to your own opinion.

Use the boxes inside your mini-book to illustrate your opinion.

What's a frog's favorite fast food? French flies!

FAST FOOD WRAP-UP 335

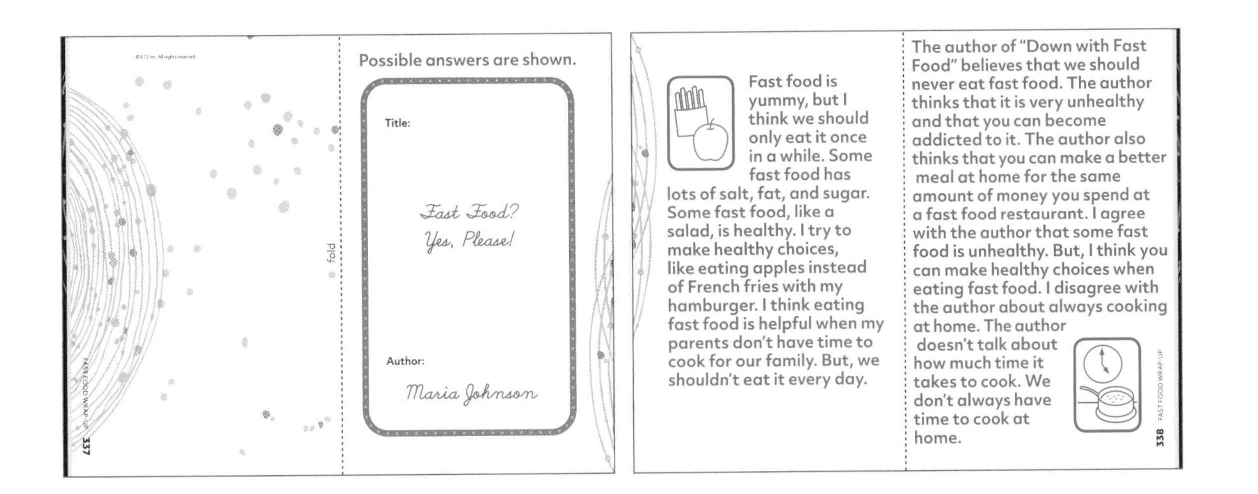
Possible answers are shown.

Title:

Fast Food? Yes, Please!

Author:

Maria Johnson

Fast food is yummy, but I think we should only eat it once in a while. Some fast food has lots of salt, fat, and sugar. Some fast food, like a salad, is healthy. I try to make healthy choices, like eating apples instead of French fries with my hamburger. I think eating fast food is helpful when my parents don't have time to cook for our family. But, we shouldn't eat it every day.

The author of "Down with Fast Food" believes that we should never eat fast food. The author thinks that it is very unhealthy and that you can become addicted to it. The author also thinks that you can make a better meal at home for the same amount of money you spend at a fast food restaurant. I agree with the author that some fast food is unhealthy. But, I think you can make healthy choices when eating fast food. I disagree with the author about always cooking at home. The author doesn't talk about how much time it takes to cook. We don't always have time to cook at home.

337 FAST FOOD WRAP-UP

338 FAST FOOD WRAP-UP

Review Fast Food

Students will answer questions to review what they have learned about determining, comparing, and contrasting main idea, supporting details, author's purpose, and author's point of view.

QUIZ

Fast Food

Students will complete the Fast Food quiz.

Spelling List 14

Students will complete the Spelling List 14 quiz.

WRAP-UP

More Language Arts Practice

Students will practice skills according to their individual needs.

Handwriting

Students should gather their handwriting materials and begin where they left off. Remind students to form letters carefully and correctly.

TIP Set a timer to help students stay focused during handwriting practice.

Opinion Writing Skills (A)

Lesson Overview

ACTIVITY	ACTIVITY TITLE	TIME	ONLINE/OFFLINE
GET READY	Introduction to Opinion Writing Skills (A)	**1** minute	online
	Spelling List 15 Pretest LEARNING COACH CHECK-IN	**10** minutes	online and offline
	Look Back at Verbs	**4** minutes	online
LEARN AND TRY IT	Present Tense Verbs	**10** minutes	online
	Use Present Tense Verbs	**10** minutes	online
	Explore a Model Opinion Essay	**10** minutes	online
	Respond to a Model Opinion Essay	**5** minutes	online
	Choose a Topic and State an Opinion	**10** minutes	online
	Choose Your Topic and State Your Opinion LEARNING COACH CHECK-IN	**25** minutes	offline
WRAP-UP	Questions About Present Tense Verbs and Opinion Statements	**4** minutes	online
	Handwriting	**8** minutes	offline
	Go Read!	**23** minutes	online or offline

Content Background

Your opinion is what you think or feel about something. People often share opinions by writing about them. This type of writing is called *opinion writing*. Throughout this workshop, students will build opinion writing skills by analyzing a model opinion essay and writing their own opinion essay.

The opinion essay is a short writing assignment, so students will follow an abbreviated version of the writing process. In this lesson, they will **prewrite** by choosing a topic and writing a clear opinion statement.

Grammar, Usage, and Mechanics A **verb** shows action or a state of being. A verb has four principal parts, or forms: the present, the present participle, the past, and the past participle. Regular verbs form the past and past participle by adding *–ed* or *–d* to the present form.

MATERIALS

Supplied

- *Summit English Language Arts 3 Activity Book*
  - Spelling List 15 Pretest
  - Model Opinion Essay
  - Choose Your Topic and State Your Opinion
- handwriting workbook

Also Needed

- folder for storing opinion essay assignment pages
- reading material for Go Read!

Present: play

Present participle: (is) playing

Past: played

Past participle: (has) played

The principal parts of a verb are not the same as a verb's **tense**, which is the time the verb expresses. The principal parts are used to form a verb's tense. Note that while students should be aware of all the principal verb parts, only the present and past parts are used to form the simple verb tenses (which are the only tenses covered in this course).

A verb in the **present tense** shows being or action that is happening now. It also shows action that happens regularly.

Action happening now: She **brushes** her teeth.

Action happening regularly: Every Sunday night, they **watch** a movie.

To form the present tense, use the present form of the verb. If the subject is singular, add -*s* or -*es*.

Example: The dog **runs** and **fetches**.

If the subject is plural, the pronoun *I*, or the pronoun *you*, do not add -*s* or -*es* to the present form.

Example: Two dogs **run** and **fetch**.

Example: I **throw** the ball over and over again.

KEYWORDS

opinion – something that a person thinks or believes but that cannot be proven to be true

present tense – the verb form that tells what is happening now

tense – the time that verbs show, such as present, future, or past

verb – a word that shows action or a state of being

Advance Preparation

Gather a folder that students can use to keep all notes and activity pages related to their opinion essay.

During the Go Read! activity, students will have the option of using the digital library. Allow extra time for students to make their reading selection, or have students make a selection before beginning the lesson.

Lesson Goals

- Take a spelling pretest.
- Form and use present tense verbs.
- Read a model opinion essay, and choose a topic for your own.
- Develop letter formation fluency.
- Read independently to develop fluency.

GET READY

Introduction to Opinion Writing Skills (A)

Students will get a glimpse of what they will learn about in the lesson. They will also read the lesson goals and keywords. Have students select each keyword and preview its definition.

Spelling List 15 Pretest

Students will take a spelling pretest and learn a new spelling pattern.

LEARNING COACH CHECK-IN Have students turn to Spelling List 15 Pretest in *Summit English Language Arts 3 Activity Book* and open the online Spelling Pretest activity. Online, students will listen to the spelling word, type the word in the space indicated, and then check their answer. In the activity book, students will write the correct spelling of the word in the tables provided and indicate with a ✓ or an ✕ if they spelled the word correctly or incorrectly online. Students will repeat this process with the remaining words.

As needed, help students with the interaction between the online activity and the activity book page until they become comfortable with what they need to do. As students practice their spelling words throughout the workshop, they should pay special attention to words they spelled incorrectly on the pretest.

This is the complete list of words students will be tested on.

Adding a Vowel Suffix to Words with a Silent e		
danced dancer dancing graded grading hoped	hoping liked liking smiled smiling used	using wasted wasting write writing

NOTE Have students keep their completed activity page in a safe place so they can refer to it later.

GET READY

Opinion Writing Skills (A)

Spelling List 15 Pretest

1. Open the Spelling Pretest activity online. Listen to the first spelling word. Type the word. Check your answer.

2. Write the correct spelling of the word in the Word column of the Spelling Pretest table.

	Word	✓	⊗
1	blindfold		

3. Put a check mark in the ✓ column if you spelled the word correctly online.

	Word	✓	⊗
1	blindfold	✓	

Put an X in the ⊗ column if you spelled the word incorrectly online.

	Word	✓	⊗
1	blindfold		X

4. Repeat Steps 1–3 for the remaining words in the Spelling Pretest.

OPINION WRITING SKILLS (A) 339

Opinion Writing Skills (A)

Spelling List 15 Pretest

Write each spelling word in the Word column, making sure to spell it correctly.

	Word	✓	⊗
1	danced		
2	dancer		
3	dancing		
4	graded		
5	grading		
6	hoped		
7	hoping		
8	liked		
9	liking		

	Word	✓	⊗
10	smiled		
11	smiling		
12	used		
13	using		
14	wasted		
15	wasting		
16	write		
17	writing		

Students should write the correct spelling of each word from the pretest and use the ✓and X columns to indicate whether they spelled each word correctly or incorrectly online.

340 OPINION WRITING SKILLS (A)

Look Back at Verbs

Students will practice the prerequisite skill of identifying a verb in a sentence.

LEARN AND TRY IT

LEARN Present Tense Verbs

Students will briefly learn about the four principal parts of verbs. Then they will learn how to form and use the present verb tense.

TIP The present tense is also called the "simple present tense."

TRY IT Use Present Tense Verbs

Students will practice forming present tense verbs and using present tense verbs in sentences. They will write their own sentences that use present tense verbs by modeling mentor sentences.

SUPPORT Have students identify present tense verbs in a book, magazine, email, or other text. Choose a couple of the verbs and discuss how each verb's tense affects the meaning of the text.

LEARN Explore a Model Opinion Essay

By reading and exploring a model opinion essay, students will learn what an opinion essay is and how it is organized.

TIP The model opinion essay that students read in the online activity is the same essay on the Model Opinion Essay activity page. Students may wish to reference and make notes on the activity page as they complete the online activity.

TRY IT Respond to a Model Opinion Essay

Students will answer questions to check and expand their understanding of the organization of an opinion essay.

LEARN Choose a Topic and State an Opinion

Students will learn one way to choose a topic for an opinion essay. They will also learn how to clearly state an opinion.

TRY IT Choose Your Topic and State Your Opinion

Students will complete Choose Your Topic and State Your Opinion in *Summit English Language Arts 3 Activity Book*. They should have the Model Opinion Essay activity page to refer to as they work.

SUPPORT Have students complete the sentence "I believe that ____" or "I feel that ____" to help them articulate an opinion. (When students actually write their opinion, have them omit those words.)

LEARNING COACH CHECK-IN This activity page contains open-ended questions, so it's important that you review students' responses.

NOTE Have students add the Model Opinion Essay and their completed Choose Your Topic and State Your Opinion activity page to the folder they are using to store their opinion essay assignment pages.

TRY IT
Opinion Writing Skills (A)

Model Opinion Essay

Use this model as you complete your own opinion essay.

Kickball

Imagine you are playing baseball. You hit the ball and sprint around first base. What a thrill! Now, imagine you are playing soccer. You kick the ball from midfield with a loud smack. There is a game that combines the best parts of baseball and soccer. The game is played on a baseball field, but there are no gloves, bat, or baseball. Instead, a pitcher tosses a large rubber ball from the pitcher's mound, and the player who is "at bat" kicks the ball. This game is kickball. Kickball is a fun sport that everyone should try. — introduction; opinion statement

OPINION WRITING SKILLS (A) 341

There are many reasons that kickball is a fun sport. First, it is fun because many people can play at the same time. There are so many roles in kickball. For example, there are people in the field and at each base. There is a pitcher and a catcher. And, there are the people kicking the ball and running the bases. Almost everyone is active the whole game, so kickball is never dull. Next, players get to do different things while they play. Players switch between the field and kicking often. During a game, players get to throw, catch, run, tag, and kick. — topic sentence; supporting reasons

Kickball is a game that everyone should try. Kickball is easy to play because you only need a ball, a field, and some friends. Players don't need helmets or mouth guards either. Kickball is also a great way to get exercise since it involves a lot of running. Everyone needs exercise! Therefore, everyone should give kickball a try. — topic sentence; supporting reasons; body

342 OPINION WRITING SKILLS (A)

Kickball is an entertaining sport. It does not use a lot of special equipment, and it is a great way to get exercise. There are a lot of ways to spend a sunny day, but kickball is the best way. — conclusion; restatement of opinion

OPINION WRITING SKILLS (A) 343

TRY IT

Opinion Writing Skills (A)

Choose Your Topic and State Your Opinion

Read the writing prompt.

Prompt: **Write an essay that expresses your opinion on a topic.**

- Write an **introduction** that gives information about your topic and clearly states your opinion.
- Write **one or two body paragraphs** that give reasons that support your opinion. Use transitions such as *because* and *for example* to connect your reasons and opinion.
- Write a **conclusion** that restates your opinion in a new way.

In my opinion, polka dots match everything!

In my opinion...

OPINION WRITING SKILLS (A) 345

Follow the instructions to choose a topic and state your opinion.

1. List as many possible topics for your opinion essay as you can think of. You should have an opinion about the topics.

   Students should list topics and choose one.

2. Read your list of topics. State an opinion about each topic. If you don't have an opinion about a topic, cross it off! Cross off any topics you are not excited to write about. Keep crossing off topics until you have one left. Circle that topic.

3. Write the opinion that you will support in your essay.

   Sample answers:
   Watermelon is the perfect summer dessert.
   All kids should learn about ancient Egypt.
   The voting age should be changed to 10 years old.

   Students should state an opinion about the topic they chose in Question 1.

346 OPINION WRITING SKILLS (A)

WRAP-UP

Questions About Present Tense Verbs and Opinion Statements

Students will answer questions to show that they understand how to form present tense verbs and write an opinion statement.

Handwriting

Students should gather their handwriting materials and begin where they left off. Remind students to form letters carefully and correctly.

TIP Set a timer to help students stay focused during handwriting practice.

Go Read!

Students will read for pleasure. They should choose a book or a magazine that interests them, or they may choose a selection from the digital library, linked in the online lesson.

- Have students read aloud a few paragraphs of their selection.
- Then have students read silently for the rest of the time.

SUPPORT Students should make no more than five errors in decoding when they read aloud a few paragraphs of their Go Read! selection. If students struggle or make more than five errors, they need to select a different (and easier) text for the Go Read! activity.

TIP Have students select something to read ahead of time to help them stay focused.

Opinion Writing Skills (B)

Lesson Overview

ACTIVITY	ACTIVITY TITLE	TIME	ONLINE/OFFLINE
GET READY	Introduction to Opinion Writing Skills (B)	**1** minute	online
	Spelling List 15 Activity Bank	**10** minutes	offline
LEARN AND TRY IT	Future Tense and Regular Past Tense Verbs	**10** minutes	online
	Use Future Tense and Regular Past Tense Verbs	**15** minutes	online
	Support an Opinion with Reasons	**10** minutes	online
	Respond to Support in an Opinion Essay	**5** minutes	online
	Support Your Opinion with Reasons LEARNING COACH CHECK-IN	**35** minutes	offline
WRAP-UP	Questions About Verb Tense and Supporting an Opinion	**4** minutes	online
	Handwriting	**8** minutes	offline
	Go Read!	**22** minutes	online or offline

Content Background

Students will learn that writers support their opinion with reasons in an opinion essay. Effective reasons are directly related to the opinion, written clearly, and based in fact. Consider these reasons for the opinion "Kickball is a fun sport that everyone should try":

Fact-based reason: Many people can play at the same time.

Opinion-based reason: Kickball is truly the most amazing sport.

Students will also learn that details and examples strengthen reasons.

Fact-based reason with details: Many people can play at the same time. There are so many roles in kickball. For example, there are people in the field and at each base. There is a pitcher and a catcher.

Students will continue working on their own opinion essay. In this lesson, they will complete a graphic organizer, focusing on adding and developing reasons to support their opinion.

MATERIALS

Supplied

- *Summit English Language Arts 3 Activity Book*
  - Spelling List 15 Activity Bank
  - Support Your Opinion with Reasons
- handwriting workbook

Also Needed

- completed Spelling List 15 Pretest activity page from Opinion Writing Skills (A)
- folder in which students are storing opinion essay assignment pages
- reading material for Go Read!

Grammar, Usage, and Mechanics A **verb** in the **future tense** shows being or action that will happen later. To form the future tense, use the word *will* or *shall* plus the present form of the verb. Note that *will* is more common than *shall* in everyday language.

Example: Tomorrow, I **will hike** up a mountain.

A verb in the **past tense** shows being or action that has already happened. To form the past tense of verb, use the past form of the verb. For regular verbs, the past is formed by adding *-ed* or *-d* to the present form. In this lesson, students will work with the past tense of regular verbs only.

Example: Yesterday, I **hiked** up a mountain.

Example: After the long hike, I **rested**.

KEYWORDS

future tense – a form of a verb that names an action that will happen later

opinion – something that a person thinks or believes but that cannot be proven to be true

past tense – form of the verb that tells what has already happened

reason – a statement that explains why something is or why it should bes

tense – the time that verbs show, such as present, future, or past

verb – a word that shows action or a state of being

Advance Preparation

Gather students' completed Spelling List 15 Pretest activity page from Opinion Writing Skills (A). Students will refer to this page during Get Ready: Spelling List 15 Activity Bank.

Gather the folder that students are using to store the activity pages related to their opinion essay. The folder should contain the following:

- Model Opinion Essay activity page from Opinion Writing Skills (A)
- Students' completed Choose Your Topic and State Your Opinion activity page from Opinion Writing Skills (A)

During the Go Read! activity, students will have the option of using the digital library. Allow extra time for students to make their reading selection, or have students make a selection before beginning the lesson.

Lesson Goals

- Practice all spelling words offline.
- Form and use future and regular past tense verbs.
- Explore how to support an opinion with reasons.
- Write reasons to support your opinion statement.
- Develop letter formation fluency.
- Read independently to develop fluency.

GET READY

Introduction to Opinion Writing Skills (B)

Students will get a glimpse of what they will learn about in the lesson. They will also read the lesson goals and keywords. Have students select each keyword and preview its definition.

Spelling List 15 Activity Bank

Students will practice all spelling words from the workshop by completing Spelling List 15 Activity Bank from *Summit English Language Arts 3 Activity Book*. Make sure students have their completed Spelling List 15 Pretest activity page from Opinion Writing Skills (A) to refer to during this activity.

Remind students to pay special attention to words they spelled incorrectly on the Spelling Pretest.

GET READY

Opinion Writing Skills (B)

Spelling List 15 Activity Bank

Circle any words in the box that you did not spell correctly on your pretest. Choose one activity to do with your circled words. Do as much of the activity as you can in the time given.

Did you spell all the words on the pretest correctly? Do the one activity with as many spelling words as you can.

danced	grading	liking	used	wasting
dancer	hoped	smiled	using	write
dancing	hoping	smiling	wasted	writing
graded	liked			

Spelling Activity Choices

Hidden Words

1. Draw a picture. "Hide" as many of your spelling words as you can inside the picture.
2. See if others can find the words you hid in the picture.

OPINION WRITING SKILLS (B) 347

Triangle Spelling

Write each of your spelling words in a triangle.

d
do
dog

Ghost Words

1. Use a white crayon to write each of your spelling words.
2. Write over the words in white crayon with a colored marker.

348 OPINION WRITING SKILLS (B)

Complete the activity that you chose.

My chosen activity: ______

Students should use this page to complete all steps in their chosen activity.

OPINION WRITING SKILLS (B) 349

LEARN AND TRY IT

LEARN Future Tense and Regular Past Tense Verbs

Students will learn how to form and use future tense verbs and regular past tense verbs.

TIP The future tense is also called the "simple future tense," and the past tense is also called the "simple past tense."

TRY IT Use Future Tense and Regular Past Tense Verbs

Students will practice forming and using future tense verbs and regular past tense verbs. They will write their own sentences that use future tense verbs and regular past tense verbs by modeling mentor sentences.

SUPPORT Have students identify future tense verbs and regular past tense verbs in a book, magazine, email, or other text. Choose a couple of the verbs and discuss how their tense affects the meaning of the text.

TIP To form the past tense of some regular verbs, you must double the last consonant before adding *–ed*. For example, the past tense of *stop* is *stopped*. Encourage students to check the dictionary if they are unsure of the spelling of a past tense verb.

LEARN Support an Opinion with Reasons

Students will learn how to effectively support an opinion with reasons.

TRY IT Respond to Support in an Opinion Essay

Students will answer questions about how a writer supports an opinion with reasons.

TRY IT Support Your Opinion with Reasons

Students will complete Support Your Opinion with Reasons in *Summit English Language Arts 3 Activity Book*. Make sure they have their completed Choose Your Topic and State Your Opinion activity page and Model Opinion Essay to refer to as they work.

SUPPORT If students' reasons are vague or opinion based, guide them to revise or elaborate on their reasons. For example, if students write, "Summer is the best season because it is awesome," ask, "What makes summer awesome? What activities can you do in the summer that you cannot do in other seasons?"

LEARNING COACH CHECK-IN This activity page contains open-ended questions, so it's important that you review students' responses.

NOTE Have students add their completed Support Your Opinion with Reasons activity page to the folder they are using to store their opinion essay assignment pages.

TRY IT

Opinion Writing Skills (B)

Support Your Opinion with Reasons

Read the writing prompt.

Prompt: **Write an essay that expresses your opinion on a topic.**

- Write an **introduction** that gives information about your topic and clearly states your opinion.
- Write **one or two body paragraphs** that give reasons that support your opinion. Use transitions such as *because* and *for example* to connect your reasons and opinion.
- Write a **conclusion** that restates your opinion in a new way.

Complete the chart to plan your opinion essay. Make sure your reasons are clear. Add details to support your reasons.

Introduce Topic

Opinion

Students should complete the chart to plan their opinion essay. They should include details to support the reasons they listed in their chart.

OPINION WRITING SKILLS (B) 351

Reason

Reason

Reason

Reason

Restate Opinion

352 OPINION WRITING SKILLS (B)

WRAP-UP

Questions About Verb Tense and Supporting an Opinion

Students will answer questions to show that they understand how to form a future tense or regular past tense verb and how to write a reason that effectively supports an opinion.

Handwriting

Students should gather their handwriting materials and begin where they left off. Remind students to form letters carefully and correctly.

TIP Set a timer to help students stay focused during handwriting practice.

Go Read!

Students will read for pleasure. They should choose a book or a magazine that interests them, or they may choose a selection from the digital library, linked in the online lesson.

- Have students read aloud a few paragraphs of their selection.
- Then have students read silently for the rest of the time.

SUPPORT Students should make no more than five errors in decoding when they read aloud a few paragraphs of their Go Read! selection. If students struggle or make more than five errors, they need to select a different (and easier) text for the Go Read! activity.

TIP Have students select something to read ahead of time to help them stay focused.

Opinion Writing Skills (C)

Lesson Overview

ACTIVITY	ACTIVITY TITLE	TIME	ONLINE/OFFLINE
GET READY	Introduction to Opinion Writing Skills (C)	**1** minute	online
	Spelling List 15 Review Game	**10** minutes	online
LEARN AND TRY IT	Irregular Past Tense Verbs	**10** minutes	online
	Use Irregular Past Tense Verbs	**10** minutes	online
	Write an Opinion Essay	**10** minutes	online
	Respond to the Introduction, Conclusion, and Transitions	**7** minutes	online
	Write Your Opinion Essay LEARNING COACH CHECK-IN	**40** minutes	offline
WRAP-UP	Questions About Irregular Past Tense Verbs and Transitions	**4** minutes	online
	Handwriting	**8** minutes	offline
	Go Read!	**20** minutes	online or offline

Content Background

Students will learn about introductions, conclusions, and transitions in opinion writing. Introductions and conclusions in opinion writing are similar in many ways to introductions and conclusions in informative writing. An *introduction* captures readers' attention, clarifies the topic of the essay, and states the main idea. In opinion writing, the main idea is an opinion statement. The *conclusion* restates the main idea (opinion statement) and logically wraps up the essay.

Transitions show how ideas relate. Students will learn specifically about transitions that connect reasons to an opinion. These transitions include *because*, *since*, *therefore*, and *for example*. Note that students may use other transitions in their essay, such as transitions that show order (e.g., *first* and *next*).

Students will continue working on their opinion essay. In this lesson, they will **draft** their essay, writing it from beginning to end. Note that students will not revise or proofread their opinion essay in this course.

MATERIALS

Supplied

- *Summit English Language Arts 3 Activity Book*
  - Write Your Opinion Essay
- handwriting workbook

Also Needed

- folder in which students are storing opinion essay assignment pages
- reading material for Go Read!

Grammar, Usage, and Mechanics A verb in the **past tense** shows being or action that has already happened. To form the past tense of verb, use the past form of the verb. For irregular verbs, the past is not formed by adding *-ed* or *-d*. Still, there are some patterns to forming the past of irregular verbs.

The vowel in the present form may change to an *a* in the past form.

Example: Just as we **began** the movie, the phone **rang**.

The *ee* in the present form may change to *e_t* in the past form.

Example: I **felt** angry, but I **kept** that feeling to myself.

The vowel before a *w* in the present form may change to an *e* in the past form.

Example: Alex **grew** restless because he **knew** the answer.

For some irregular verbs, there is no pattern to forming the past form.

Example: I **brought** a water bottle with me when I **went** to camp.

Advance Preparation

Gather the folder that students are using to store the activity pages related to their opinion essay. The folder should contain the following:

- Model Opinion Essay activity page from Opinion Writing Skills (A)
- Students' completed Choose Your Topic and State Your Opinion activity page from Opinion Writing Skills (A)
- Students' completed Support Your Opinion with Reasons activity page from Opinion Writing Skills (B)

During the Go Read! activity, students will have the option of using the digital library. Allow extra time for students to make their reading selection, or have students make a selection before beginning the lesson.

KEYWORDS

conclusion – the final paragraph of a written work

introduction – the first paragraph of an essay, identifying the topic and stating the main idea

opinion – something that a person thinks or believes but that cannot be proven to be true

past tense – form of the verb that tells what has already happened

reason – a statement that explains why something is or why it should be

tense – the time that verbs show, such as present, future, or past

transition – a word, phrase, or clause that connects ideas

verb – a word that shows action or a state of being

Lesson Goals

- Practice all spelling words online.
- Form and use irregular past tense verbs.
- Explore the introduction, conclusion, and transitions in a model opinion essay.
- Write your opinion essay.
- Develop letter formation fluency.
- Read independently to develop fluency.

GET READY

Introduction to Opinion Writing Skills (C)

Students will get a glimpse of what they will learn about in the lesson. They will also read the lesson goals and keywords. Have students select each keyword and preview its definition.

Spelling List 15 Review Game

Students will practice all spelling words from the workshop.

LEARN AND TRY IT

LEARN Irregular Past Tense Verbs

Students will learn to form and use the past tense of irregular verbs.

TRY IT Use Irregular Past Tense Verbs

Students will practice forming and using irregular past tense verbs. They will write their own sentences that use irregular past tense verbs by modeling mentor sentences.

NOTE There are regional differences to how people form the past tense of some verbs. For example, the past tense *learnt* is commonly used in British English and some American dialects but considered nonstandard in American English. This course teaches what is considered standard American English.

LEARN Write an Opinion Essay

Students will learn how to write the introduction and conclusion to an opinion essay. They will also learn how to use transitions to connect reasons to an opinion.

TRY IT Respond to the Introduction, Conclusion, and Transitions

Students will answer questions about the introduction, conclusion, and transitions in an opinion essay.

TRY IT Write Your Opinion Essay

Students will complete Write Your Opinion Essay in *Summit English Language Arts 3 Activity Book*. They should have their completed prewriting work to refer to as they write.

LEARNING COACH CHECK-IN Students will write their entire opinion essay in this activity. They should use the prewriting work they have done to guide them as they write. Give students feedback on their introduction, reasons and details, transitions, and conclusion. Most importantly of all, encourage students to keep writing!

NOTE Have students add their completed Write Your Opinion Essay activity page to the folder they are using to store their opinion essay assignment pages.

TRY IT
Opinion Writing Skills (C)

Write Your Opinion Essay

Read the writing prompt.

Prompt: **Write an essay that expresses your opinion on a topic.**

- Write an **introduction** that gives information about your topic and clearly states your opinion.
- Write **one or two body paragraphs** that give reasons that support your opinion. Use transitions such as *because* and *for example* to connect your reasons and opinion.
- Write a **conclusion** that restates your opinion in a new way.

Respond to the writing prompt. Use your prewriting work to help you.

Students should write their opinion essay from beginning to end. Their essay should meet the requirements listed in the prompt.

OPINION WRITING SKILLS (C) 353

354 OPINION WRITING SKILLS (C)

OPINION WRITING SKILLS (C) 355

356 OPINION WRITING SKILLS (C)

WRAP-UP

Questions About Irregular Past Tense Verbs and Transitions

Students will answer questions to show that they understand how to form an irregular past tense verb and how to use transitions effectively in opinion writing.

Handwriting

Students should gather their handwriting materials and begin where they left off. Remind students to form letters carefully and correctly.

TIP Set a timer to help students stay focused during handwriting practice.

Go Read!

Students will read for pleasure. They should choose a book or a magazine that interests them, or they may choose a selection from the digital library, linked in the online lesson.

- Have students read aloud a few paragraphs of their selection.
- Then have students read silently for the rest of the time.

SUPPORT Students should make no more than five errors in decoding when they read aloud a few paragraphs of their Go Read! selection. If students struggle or make more than five errors, they need to select a different (and easier) text for the Go Read! activity.

TIP Have students select something to read ahead of time to help them stay focused.

Opinion Writing Skills Wrap-Up

Lesson Overview

ACTIVITY	ACTIVITY TITLE	TIME	ONLINE/OFFLINE
GET READY	Introduction to Opinion Writing Skills Wrap-Up	**1** minute	online
TRY IT	Reflect on Your Opinion Essay LEARNING COACH CHECK-IN	**20** minutes	offline
	Review Verbs	**15** minutes	online
QUIZ	Verb Tense and Opinion Writing Skills	**30** minutes	online
	Spelling List 15	**10** minutes	online
WRAP-UP	More Language Arts Practice	**20** minutes	online
	Handwriting	**8** minutes	offline
	Go Read!	**16** minutes	online or offline

Advance Preparation

Gather the folder that students are using to store the activity pages related to their opinion essay. The folder should contain the following:

- Model Opinion Essay activity page from Opinion Writing Skills (A)
- Students' completed Choose Your Topic and State Your Opinion activity page from Opinion Writing Skills (A)
- Students' completed Support Your Opinion with Reasons activity page from Opinion Writing Skills (B)
- Students' completed Write Your Opinion Essay activity page from Opinion Writing Skills (C)

During the Go Read! activity, students will have the option of using the digital library. Allow extra time for students to make their reading selection, or have students make a selection before beginning the lesson.

MATERIALS

Supplied

- *Summit English Language Arts 3 Activity Book*
  - Reflect on Your Opinion Essay
- handwriting workbook

Also Needed

- folder in which students are storing opinion essay assignment pages
- reading material for Go Read!

Lesson Goals

- Reflect on your opinion essay.
- Review the past, present, and future verb tenses.
- Take a quiz on verb tense and opinion writing skills.
- Take a spelling quiz.
- Develop letter formation fluency.
- Read independently to develop fluency.

GET READY

Introduction to Opinion Writing Skills Wrap-Up

Students will read the lesson goals.

TRY IT

Reflect on Your Opinion Essay

Students will complete Reflect on Your Opinion Essay in *Summit English Language Arts 3 Activity Book*. They should have their completed Write Your Opinion Essay activity page to refer to as they work.

LEARNING COACH CHECK-IN This activity page contains open-ended questions, so it's important that you review students' responses and give them feedback. Be sure to point out things students did well in their essay, as well as offer a few suggestions for improvement.

TRY IT

Opinion Writing Skills Wrap-Up

Reflect on Your Opinion Essay

Read your opinion essay. Then, answer the questions in complete sentences.

Answers will vary.

1. A strong opinion essay begins with information about the topic and a clear opinion statement.
   a. What did you tell readers about your topic? How will that information help readers understand your opinion?
   b. Is there anything else about your topic you should tell readers?

   c. Write one way you could make your opinion statement stronger. For example, you might change a vague word or add a detail.

2. The body of an opinion essay includes reasons that support the writer's opinion.
   a. Which of your reasons is the strongest? Why?
   b. Rewrite one sentence from your body to improve it. Explain how your revision makes that sentence stronger.

   Revised sentence:

   Explanation:

3. Transitions like *because*, *since*, and *for example* can connect an opinion and reason.
   a. Write one sentence from your essay that has a transition.
   b. Rewrite one sentence from your essay so that it has a transition.

4. A strong opinion essay ends with a conclusion.
   a. Which sentence or sentences from your conclusion restate your opinion?
   b. If you did not restate your opinion in a new way, revise the sentences you wrote in Part a.

Review Verbs

Students will answer questions to review what they have learned about past, present, and future tense verbs.

QUIZ

Verb Tense and Opinion Writing Skills

Students will complete the Verb Tense and Opinion Writing Skills quiz.

Spelling List 15

Students will complete the Spelling List 15 quiz.

WRAP-UP

More Language Arts Practice

Students will practice skills according to their individual needs.

Handwriting

Students should gather their handwriting materials and begin where they left off. Remind students to form letters carefully and correctly.

TIP Set a timer to help students stay focused during handwriting practice.

Go Read!

Students will read for pleasure. They should choose a book or a magazine that interests them, or they may choose a selection from the digital library, linked in the online lesson.

- Have students read aloud a few paragraphs of their selection.
- Then have students read silently for the rest of the time.

SUPPORT Students should make no more than five errors in decoding when they read aloud a few paragraphs of their Go Read! selection. If students struggle or make more than five errors, they need to select a different (and easier) text for the Go Read! activity.

TIP Have students select something to read ahead of time to help them stay focused.

Figurative Language

Lesson Overview

ACTIVITY	ACTIVITY TITLE	TIME	ONLINE/OFFLINE
GET READY	Introduction to Figurative Language	**1** minute	
	Look Back at Context Clues	**4** minutes	
LEARN AND **TRY IT**	Figurative Language	**10** minutes	
	Practice Using Figurative Language	**10** minutes	
	Apply: Figurative Language **LEARNING COACH CHECK-IN**	**15** minutes	
	Review Figurative Language	**15** minutes	
QUIZ	Figurative Language	**15** minutes	
WRAP-UP	More Language Arts Practice	**15** minutes	
	Go Write! The Best Book or Movie	**15** minutes	
	Go Read!	**20** minutes	or

Content Backgrounds

In this lesson, students will learn about *figurative language*, also called nonliteral language. The form of figurative language students will learn is idioms, although the term idiom will not yet be introduced. They will learn that these phrases mean something different than the words suggest. For example, the phrase "in the same boat" can be used to explain that some people are literally sitting in the same boat. However, the nonliteral meaning of "in the same boat" is more commonly used. It is a way of expressing that people are in the same situation.

Advance Preparation

During the Go Read! activity, students will have the option of using the digital library. Allow extra time for students to make their reading selection, or have students make a selection before beginning the lesson.

MATERIALS

Supplied

- *Summit English Language Arts 3 Activity Book*
  - Apply: Figurative Language
  - Go Write! The Best Book or Movie

Also Needed

- reading material for Go Read!

Lesson Goals

- Practice vocabulary words.
- Identify figurative language in text.
- Use context clues to determine the meaning of figurative language.
- Determine the difference between the literal and nonliteral meanings of phrases.
- Take the Figurative Language quiz.
- Freewrite about a topic to develop writing fluency and practice letter formation.
- Read independently to develop fluency.

KEYWORDS

figurative language – words that describe something by comparing it to something completely different; figure of speech; Example: Rain fell in buckets and the streets looked like rivers.

literal language – language that uses words according to their exact, or factual, meanings

nonliteral language – figures of speech or words and phrases that change their usual meaning based on how they are used in a sentence

GET READY

Introduction to Figurative Language

After a quick introductory activity, students will read the lesson goals and keywords. Have students select each keyword and preview its definition.

Look Back at Context Clues

Students will practice the prerequisite skill of using context clues, the words and phrases in a sentence or paragraph, to figure out the meaning of unknown words.

LEARN AND TRY IT

LEARN Figurative Language

Students will be introduced to the vocabulary for the lesson. Then they will learn how to determine the meaning of figurative language being used in a passage.

TRY IT Practice Using Figurative Language

Students will practice using context clues to determine the meaning of figurative language. They will also practice identifying the difference between the literal and nonliteral meanings of phrases.

TRY IT Apply: Figurative Language

Students will complete Apply: Figurative Language in *Summit English Language Arts 3 Activity Book*. They will practice using figurative language

by using context clues to determine the phrase that best fits a passage. Then they will write a short passage with a blank and ask someone which phrase best completes their passage.

LEARNING COACH CHECK-IN Have students explain the context clues that helped them determine the correct phrase to complete each passage.

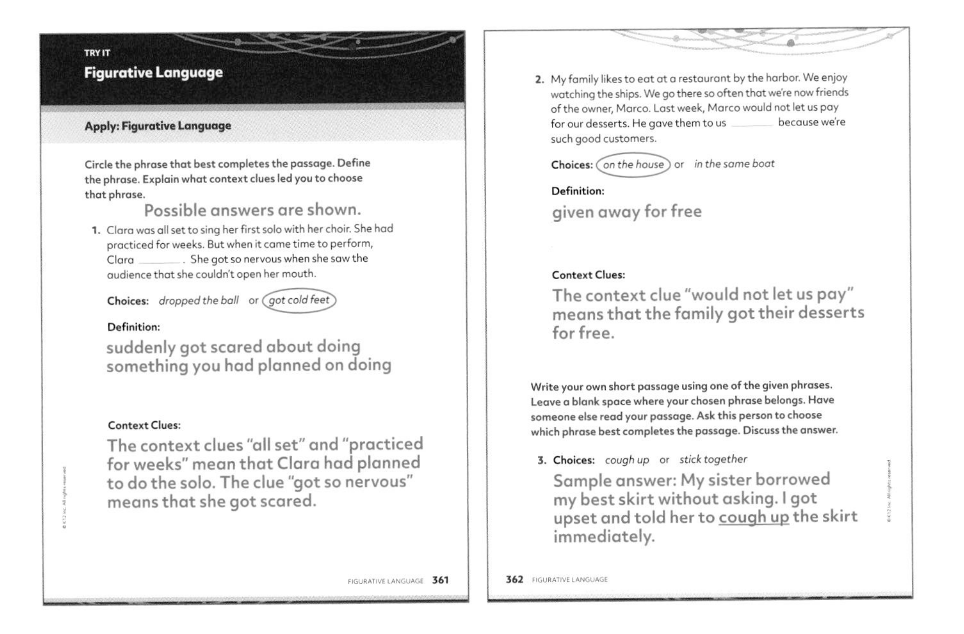

TRY IT

Figurative Language

Apply: Figurative Language

Circle the phrase that best completes the passage. Define the phrase. Explain what context clues led you to choose that phrase.

Possible answers are shown.

1. Clara was all set to sing her first solo with her choir. She had practiced for weeks. But when it came time to perform, Clara ______. She got so nervous when she saw the audience that she couldn't open her mouth.

Choices: *dropped the ball* or *got cold feet* (circled)

Definition:

suddenly got scared about doing something you had planned on doing

Context Clues:

The context clues "all set" and "practiced for weeks" mean that Clara had planned to do the solo. The clue "got so nervous" means that she got scared.

FIGURATIVE LANGUAGE 361

2. My family likes to eat at a restaurant by the harbor. We enjoy watching the ships. We go there so often that we're now friends of the owner, Marco. Last week, Marco would not let us pay for our desserts. He gave them to us ______ because we're such good customers.

Choices: *on the house* (circled) or *in the same boat*

Definition:

given away for free

Context Clues:

The context clue "would not let us pay" means that the family got their desserts for free.

Write your own short passage using one of the given phrases. Leave a blank space where your chosen phrase belongs. Have someone else read your passage. Ask this person to choose which phrase best completes the passage. Discuss the answer.

3. **Choices:** *cough up* or *stick together*

Sample answer: My sister borrowed my best skirt without asking. I got upset and told her to cough up the skirt immediately.

362 FIGURATIVE LANGUAGE

TRY IT Review Figurative Language

Students will answer questions to review what they have learned about figurative language.

QUIZ

Figurative Language

Students will complete the Figurative Language quiz.

WRAP-UP

More Language Arts Practice

Students will practice skills according to their individual needs.

Go Write! The Best Book or Movie

Students will complete Go Write! The Best Book or Movie in *Summit English Language Arts 3 Activity Book*. They will have the option to either respond to a prompt or write about a topic of their choice.

NOTE This activity is intended to build writing fluency. Students should write for the entire allotted time.

SUPPORT If students have trouble writing for the allotted time, prompt them with questions. For example, *Can you tell me more about this? How did the book/movie make you feel?*

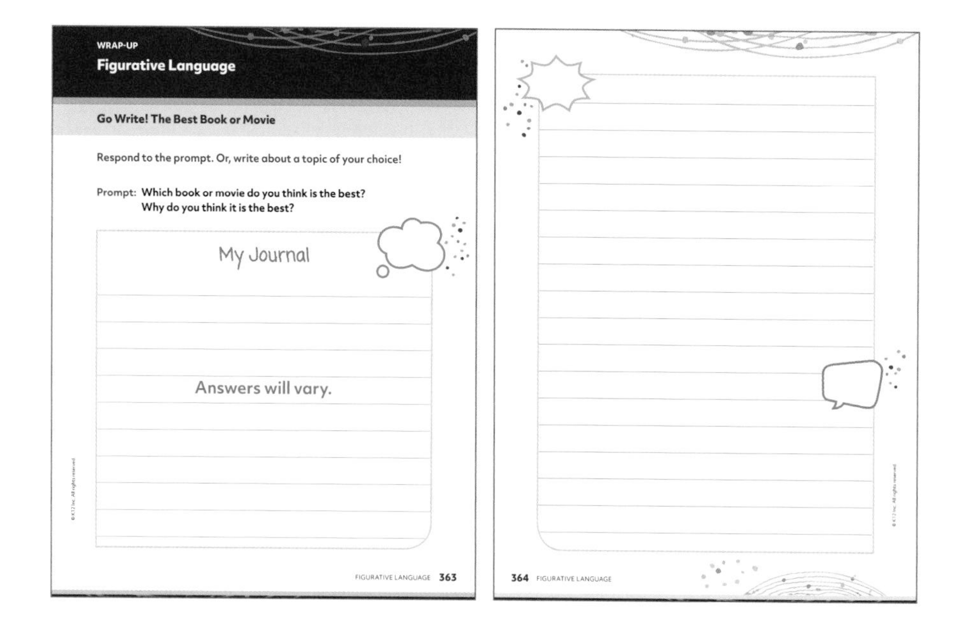
WRAP-UP
Figurative Language
Go Write! The Best Book or Movie
Respond to the prompt. Or, write about a topic of your choice!
Prompt: Which book or movie do you think is the best?
Why do you think it is the best?
My Journal
Answers will vary.
FIGURATIVE LANGUAGE 363
364 FIGURATIVE LANGUAGE

Go Read!

Students will read for pleasure. They should choose a book or a magazine that interests them, or they may choose a selection from the digital library, linked in the online lesson.

- Have students read aloud a few paragraphs of their selection.
- Then have students read silently for the rest of the time.

SUPPORT Students should make no more than five errors in decoding when they read aloud a few paragraphs of their Go Read! selection. If students struggle or make more than five errors, they need to select a different (and easier) text for the Go Read! activity.

TIP Have students select something to read ahead of time to help them stay focused.

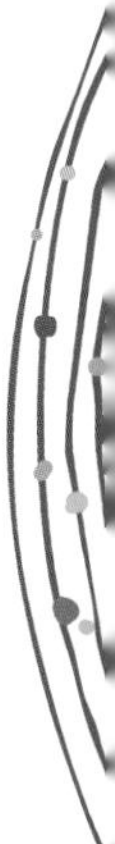

Big Ideas: Critical Skills Assignment

Lesson Overview

Big Ideas lessons provide students the opportunity to further apply the knowledge acquired and skills learned throughout the unit workshops. Each Big Ideas lesson consists of these parts:

1. **Cumulative Review:** Students keep their skills fresh by reviewing prior content.
2. **Preview:** Students practice answering the types of questions they will commonly find on standardized tests.
3. **Synthesis:** Students complete an assignment that allows them to connect and apply what they have learned. Synthesis assignments vary throughout the course.

   In the Synthesis portion of this Big Ideas lesson, students will read new selections. They will answer literal and inferential comprehension questions and complete writing questions that ask for short responses about the reading selections. Students should refer to the selections while answering the questions, because the questions emphasize using textual evidence. The questions call for students to demonstrate critical thinking, reading, and writing skills.

   LEARNING COACH CHECK-IN This is a graded assessment. Make sure students complete, review, and submit the assignment to their teacher.

All materials needed for this lesson are linked online and not provided in the activity book.

MATERIALS

Supplied

- Critical Skills Assignment (printout)

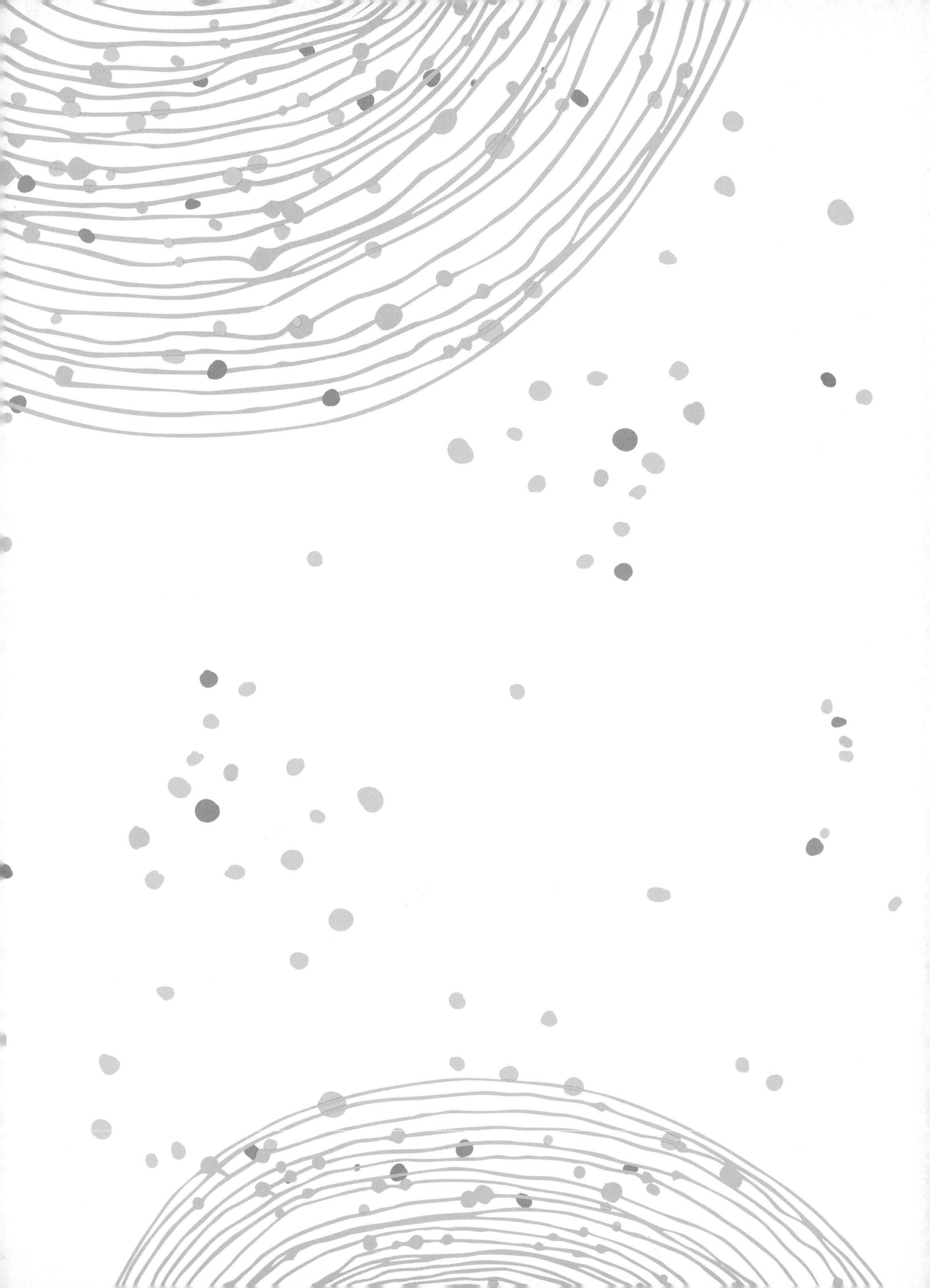

The Tale of Despereaux

The Tale of Despereaux (A)

Lesson Overview

ACTIVITY	ACTIVITY TITLE	TIME	ONLINE/OFFLINE
GET READY	Introduction to *The Tale of Despereaux* (A)	**2** minutes	online
	Spelling List 16 Pretest LEARNING COACH CHECK-IN	**10** minutes	online and offline
	Before You Read *The Tale of Despereaux*, Chapters 1–8	**10** minutes	online
READ	*The Tale of Despereaux*, Chapters 1–8	**35** minutes	offline
	Check-In: *The Tale of Despereaux*, Chapters 1–8	**5** minutes	online
LEARN AND TRY IT	Figuring Out Character Traits	**10** minutes	online
	Figure Out Character Traits	**10** minutes	online
	Apply: Character Traits	**10** minutes	online
	Describe Despereaux LEARNING COACH CHECK-IN	**10** minutes	offline
	Practice Words from *The Tale of Despereaux*, Chapters 1–8	**8** minutes	online
WRAP-UP	Question About *The Tale of Despereaux*, Chapters 1–8	**2** minutes	online
	Handwriting	**8** minutes	offline

Content Background

In this lesson, students will begin reading the fictional novel, *The Tale of Despereaux*. They will learn about using evidence from text to describe characters and explain their actions.

At times, authors will directly state details that describe a character. For example, in *The Tale of Despereaux*, the text states, "'His ears are too big,' said his sister Merlot." This detail tells readers that the character of Despereaux has big ears.

Other times, readers will make an inference about a character based on evidence in the text. For example, the text states the following about the character of Despereaux's mother: "The mouse mother, whose name was Antoinette, looked at her reflection and gasped aloud. 'Toulèse,' she said to one of her sons, 'get for me my makeup bag. My eyes are a fright.'" From this, readers can infer that Despereaux's mother is vain.

MATERIALS

Supplied

- *The Tale of Despereaux* by Kate DiCamillo
- *Summit English Language Arts 3 Activity Book*
  - Spelling List 16 Pretest
  - Describe Despereaux
- handwriting workbook

The Tale of Despereaux, Chapters 1–8 Synopsis

Despereaux Tilling is a very small mouse with very large ears. He does not act like a normal mouse, which causes his family and the mouse community much concern. He prefers staring dreamily at stained-glass windows to learning how to scurry out of danger. And, he won't nibble the pages of a book because it would ruin the story of the fair maiden and the knight who rescued her. When Despereaux follows the sound of the king's music, he ignores his instincts and reveals himself to humans. One of those humans is Princess Pea. When she smiles at Despereaux, he falls in love. Despereaux's behavior with humans is seen as a threat to the mouse community. The Mouse Council, which includes Despereaux's father, decides that Despereaux cannot be trusted and must go to the rats in the dungeon.

KEYWORDS

character – a person or animal in a story

character trait – a quality of a person or character; part of a personality

text-based evidence – proof in a text that supports an idea or answers a question

Lesson Goals

- Take a spelling pretest.
- Read Chapters 1–8 of *The Tale of Despereaux*.
- Describe actions and traits of story characters.
- Provide text evidence to support the description of a character.
- Practice vocabulary words.
- Develop letter formation fluency.

GET READY

Introduction to *The Tale of Despereaux* (A)

After a quick introductory activity, students will read the lesson goals and keywords. Have students select each keyword and preview its definition.

Spelling List 16 Pretest

Students will take a spelling pretest and learn a new spelling pattern.

LEARNING COACH CHECK-IN Have students turn to Spelling List 16 Pretest in *Summit English Language Arts 3 Activity Book* and open the online Spelling Pretest activity. Online, students will listen to the spelling word, type the word in the space indicated, and then check their answer. In the activity book, students will write the correct spelling of the word in the tables provided and indicate with a ✓ or an ✗ if they spelled the word correctly or incorrectly online. Students will repeat this process with the remaining words.

As needed, help students with the interaction between the online activity and the activity book page until they become comfortable with what they need to do. As students practice their spelling words throughout the workshop, they should pay special attention to words they spelled incorrectly on the pretest.

This is the complete list of words students will be tested on.

Words with a Consonant Ending and Vowel Suffix				
asked	founded	melting	quitting	speaker
beginning	heaped	mixed	runner	stopped
boating	hunter	mopping	shouted	trapped
crashed	looking	pinching	sleeping	warming
dotted				

NOTE Have students keep their completed activity page in a safe place so they can refer to it later.

GET READY

***The Tale of Despereaux* (A)**

Spelling List 16 Pretest

1. Open the Spelling Pretest activity online. Listen to the first spelling word. Type the word. Check your answer.
2. Write the correct spelling of the word in the Word column of the Spelling Pretest table.

	Word	✓	⊗
1	blindfold		

3. Put a check mark in the ✓ column if you spelled the word correctly online.

	Word	✓	⊗
1	blindfold	✓	

Put an X in the ⊗ column if you spelled the word incorrectly online.

	Word	✓	⊗
1	blindfold		X

4. Repeat Steps 1–3 for the remaining words in the Spelling Pretest.

THE TALE OF DESPEREAUX (A) 365

***The Tale of Despereaux* (A)**

Spelling List 16 Pretest

Write each spelling word in the Word column, making sure to spell it correctly.

	Word	✓	⊗		Word	✓	⊗
1	asked			12	mopping		
2	beginning			13	pinching		
3	boating			14	quitting		
4	crashed			15	runner		
5	dotted			16	shouted		
6	founded			17	sleeping		
7	heaped			18	speaker		
8	hunter			19	stopped		
9	looking			20	trapped		
10	melting			21	warming		
11	mixed						

Students should write the correct spelling of each word from the pretest and use the ✓ and X columns to indicate whether they spelled each word correctly or incorrectly online.

366 THE TALE OF DESPEREAUX (A)

Before You Read *The Tale of Despereaux*, Chapters 1–8

Students will be introduced to some key vocabulary words that they will encounter in the upcoming reading, learn some important background related to the reading, and answer a question to help them set a purpose for their reading.

READ

The Tale of Despereaux, Chapters 1–8

Students will read Chapters 1–8 of *The Tale of Despereaux* by Kate DiCamillo.

Check-In: *Tale of Despereaux*, Chapters 1–8

Students will answer several questions to demonstrate their comprehension of Chapters 1–8 of *The Tale of Despereaux*.

LEARN AND TRY IT

LEARN Figuring Out Character Traits

Students will learn about making inferences about characters' personalities based on what the characters think, say, and do.

TRY IT Figure Out Character Traits

Students will analyze passages to determine characters' traits and describe characters' actions.

TRY IT Apply: Character Traits

Students will apply to a new work what they've learned about determining the traits of a character.

TRY IT Describe Despereaux

Students will complete Describe Despereaux in *Summit English Language Arts 3 Activity Book*.

LEARNING COACH CHECK-IN Students may describe Despereaux in many different ways, so it's important to review students' responses. Give students feedback, using the sample answers provided to guide you.

TRY IT

***The Tale of Despereaux* (A)**

Describe Despereaux

Describe Despereaux using evidence from the text.

It can be inferred that Despereaux is not like other mice. Write a paragraph that describes at least two ways that Despereaux is different from other mice. Use quotations from the text as evidence to support your description.

Students' paragraph should include at least two of the following descriptions. Quotations from the story may vary.

- Despereaux has very big ears, so he has better hearing than other mice. "He was listening with his big ears, to the sweet sound that no other mouse seemed to hear."
- He doesn't think about food all the time. "He was not intent on tracking down every crumb."
- He is very curious. "'Furlough,' he said, 'what is this thing? What are all these colors? Are we in heaven?'"

THE TALE OF DESPEREAUX (A) 367

- He can read. "...he read the story of a beautiful princess and the brave knight who serves and honors her."
- He loves music. "The sound of the king's music made Despereaux's soul grow large and light inside of him."
- He doesn't follow the rules that other mice follow. He lets humans see him, and he talks to the princess. "...he revealed himself; and in no time at all, he was spied by the sharp-eyed Princess Pea."

I found evidence to support my idea!

368 THE TALE OF DESPEREAUX (A)

TRY IT Practice Words from *The Tale of Despereaux*, Chapters 1–8

Students will answer questions to demonstrate their understanding of the vocabulary words from the reading.

WRAP-UP

Question About *The Tale of Despereaux*, Chapters 1–8

Students will answer a question to show that they understand how to describe a character's actions.

Handwriting

Students should gather their handwriting materials and begin where they left off. Remind students to form letters carefully and correctly.

TIP Set a timer to help students stay focused during handwriting practice.

The Tale of Despereaux (B)

Lesson Overview

ACTIVITY	ACTIVITY TITLE	TIME	ONLINE/OFFLINE
GET READY	Introduction to *The Tale of Despereaux* (B)	**1** minute	online
	Spelling List 16 Activity Bank	**10** minutes	offline
	Recall *The Tale of Despereaux*, Chapters 1–8	**5** minutes	online
	Before You Read *The Tale of Despereaux*, Chapters 9–15	**5** minutes	online
READ	*The Tale of Despereaux*, Chapters 9–15	**36** minutes	offline
	Check-In: *The Tale of Despereaux*, Chapters 9–15	**5** minutes	online
LEARN AND TRY IT	Describing the Setting	**10** minutes	online
	Describe the Setting	**10** minutes	online
	Apply: Setting	**10** minutes	online
	Describe the Castle LEARNING COACH CHECK-IN	**10** minutes	offline
	Practice Words from *The Tale of Despereaux*, Chapters 9–15	**8** minutes	online
WRAP-UP	Question About *The Tale of Despereaux*, Chapters 9–15	**2** minutes	online
	Handwriting	**8** minutes	offline

Content Background

In this lesson, students will continue to read *The Tale of Despereaux* by Kate DiCamillo. They will learn about using text details to describe the setting.

The *setting* is where and when the story takes place. The author may provide explicit details that tell readers about the setting. For example, in the first sentence of the novel, the author explicitly states that the story takes place in a castle.

At times though, readers must use text details to make inferences about the setting. For example, the author of *The Tale of Despereaux* never states the time period of the novel. But, we can make an inference based on details. Events happen in a castle in which a king and princess live. The castle has a dungeon that holds prisoners. From these details, we can infer that the story happens long ago.

MATERIALS

Supplied

- *The Tale of Despereaux* by Kate DiCamillo
- *Summit English Language Arts 3 Activity Book*
    - Spelling List 16 Activity Bank
    - Describe the Castle
- handwriting workbook

Also Needed

- completed Spelling List 16 Pretest activity page from *The Tale of Despereaux* (A)

Advance Preparation

Gather students' completed Spelling List 16 Pretest activity page from *The Tale of Despereaux* (A). Students will refer to this page during Get Ready: Spelling List 16 Activity Bank.

KEYWORDS

infer – to use clues and what you already know to make a guess

inference – a guess that readers make using the clues that an author gives them in a piece of writing

setting – where and when a story takes place

The Tale of Despereaux, Chapters 9–15 Synopsis

Despereaux is called before the Mouse Council and the entire mouse community to account for his behavior with the king and princess. Despereaux does not deny his actions and is condemned to go to the rats in the dungeon. A red thread is tied around his neck to mark him as condemned. He is then led through the castle and down to the dungeon by two hooded mice. On the way, Despereaux discovers that his own brother, Furlough, is one of the mice delivering him to the dungeon. Despereaux is pushed down the stairs into the dark dungeon. There he encounters Gregory the jailer, who tells Despereaux about the ways of the dungeon and the foolishness of love. Gregory says that he has never saved any of the other mice sent to the dungeon. But, he will save Despereaux because Despereaux can bring some light to his life by telling him a story.

Lesson Goals

- Practice all spelling words offline.
- Read Chapters 9–15 of *The Tale of Despereaux.*
- Use text details to describe and make inferences about the setting.
- Practice vocabulary words.
- Develop letter formation fluency.

GET READY

Introduction to *The Tale of Despereaux* (B)

Students will get a glimpse of what they will learn about in the lesson. They will also read the lesson goals and keywords. Have students select each keyword and preview its definition.

Spelling List 16 Activity Bank

Students will practice spelling words by completing Spelling List 16 Activity Bank from *Summit English Language Arts 3 Activity Book*. Make sure students have their completed Spelling List 16 Pretest activity page from *The Tale of Despereaux* (A) to refer to during this activity.

Remind students to pay special attention to words they spelled incorrectly on the Spelling Pretest.

GET READY

***The Tale of Despereaux* (B)**

Spelling List 16 Activity Bank

Circle any words in the box that you did not spell correctly on your pretest. Choose one activity to do with your circled words. Do as much of the activity as you can in the time given.

Did you spell all the words on the pretest correctly? Do the one activity with as many spelling words as you can.

asked	founded	melting	quitting	speaker
beginning	heaped	mixed	runner	stopped
boating	hunter	mopping	shouted	trapped
crashed	looking	pinching	sleeping	warming
dotted				

Spelling Activity Choices

Create a Crossword

1. Write one of your spelling words going down in the center of the grid.

THE TALE OF DESPEREAUX (B) 369

2. Write another spelling word going across that shares a letter with the first word. See how many words you can connect.

Example:

Word Search Puzzle

1. Draw a box on the grid. The box should be large enough to hold your spelling words.
2. Fill in the grid with your spelling words. Write them across, up and down, and diagonally. You can write them forward and backward.
3. Fill in the rest of the box with random letters.
4. Ask someone to find and circle your words in the puzzle.

370 THE TALE OF DESPEREAUX (B)

Complete the activity that you chose.

My chosen activity:

Students should use this page to complete all steps in their chosen activity.

THE TALE OF DESPEREAUX (B) 371

Recall *The Tale of Despereaux*, Chapters 1–8

Students will answer some questions to review the reading that they have already completed.

Before You Read *The Tale of Despereaux*, Chapters 9–15

Students will be introduced to some key vocabulary words that they will encounter in the upcoming reading.

READ

The Tale of Despereaux, Chapters 9–15

Students will read Chapters 9–15 of *The Tale of Despereaux* by Kate DiCamillo.

Check-In: *The Tale of Despereaux*, Chapters 9–15

Students will answer several questions to demonstrate their comprehension of Chapters 9–15 of *The Tale of Despereaux*.

LEARN AND TRY IT

LEARN Describing the Setting

Students will learn that details from text provide information about a story's setting.

TRY IT Describe the Setting

Students will analyze passages to describe and make inferences about a story's setting.

TRY IT Apply: Setting

Students will apply to a new work what they've learned about describing the setting of a story.

TRY IT Describe the Castle

Students will complete Describe the Castle in *Summit English Language Arts 3 Activity Book*.

LEARNING COACH CHECK-IN This activity page contains a writing task for which students may choose which descriptions to include, so it's important that you review students' responses. Give students feedback, using the sample answers provided to guide you.

TRY IT
The Tale of Despereaux (B)

Describe the Castle

Describe what you imagine the inside of the castle is like.

Write a paragraph that describes what the inside of the castle is like. Base your description on details directly stated in the story and inferences you make from the details. Use at least three examples from the text to support your description.

Students' paragraph may include any of the following details:

- The castle is large based on the description of Despereaux being led to the dungeon.
- The inside is made with beautiful items based on the description of the golden staircase, marble floors, and velvet curtains.
- The castle has many stained-glass windows based on the description of Despereaux looking at the windows.
- The castle has many levels based on the description of Despereaux being led far down into the dungeon.

THE TALE OF DESPEREAUX (B) 373

- There are many holes in the walls based on the description of the mice disappearing into holes.
- There are spaces inside the walls where the mice live based on the description of the meeting of the Mouse Council.

374 THE TALE OF DESPEREAUX (B)

TRY IT Practice Words from *The Tale of Despereaux*, Chapters 9–15

Students will answer questions to demonstrate their understanding of the vocabulary words from the reading.

WRAP-UP

Question About *The Tale of Despereaux*, Chapters 9–15

Students will answer a question to show that they understand how to make an inference about a story's setting.

Handwriting

Students should gather their handwriting materials and begin where they left off. Remind students to form letters carefully and correctly.

TIP Set a timer to help students stay focused during handwriting practice.

The Tale of Despereaux (C)

Lesson Overview

ACTIVITY	ACTIVITY TITLE	TIME	ONLINE/OFFLINE
GET READY	Introduction to *The Tale of Despereaux* (C)	**1** minute	online
	Spelling List 16 Practice	**10** minutes	online
	Recall *The Tale of Despereaux*, Chapters 9–15	**5** minutes	online
	Before You Read *The Tale of Despereaux*, Chapters 16–19	**8** minutes	online
READ	*The Tale of Despereaux*, Chapters 16–19	**23** minutes	offline
	Check-In: *The Tale of Despereaux*, Chapters 16–19	**5** minutes	online
LEARN AND TRY IT	Identifying the Narrator	**10** minutes	online
	Identify the Narrator	**5** minutes	online
	Illustrations Reveal Things About Characters	**10** minutes	online
	What Do Illustrations Reveal About Characters?	**5** minutes	online
	Apply: Narrator	**10** minutes	online
	Create a Scene LEARNING COACH CHECK-IN	**10** minutes	offline
	Practice Words from *The Tale of Despereaux*, Chapters 16–19	**8** minutes	online
WRAP-UP	Question About *The Tale of Despereaux*, Chapters 16–19	**2** minutes	online
	Handwriting	**8** minutes	offline

Content Background

In this lesson, students will learn about a story's narrator. They will learn that a *narrator* can be inside of a story or outside of a story. A narrator inside of a story is a character in the story. When a narrator is outside of a story, it's as if somebody is describing what is happening in the story but is not taking part in it. Students will learn that the narrator of *The Tale of Despereaux* is outside of the story but is a bit unusual. This narrator speaks directly to readers.

Students will also learn that *illustrations* show more about a story's characters than is shared in the words of a text. For example, the illustration of Despereaux's birth shows much about Despereaux's mother. She is

MATERIALS

Supplied

- *The Tale of Despereaux* by Kate DiCamillo
- *Summit English Language Arts 3 Activity Book*
  - Create a Scene
- handwriting workbook

staring into a mirror with a concerned look on her face. She is not paying any attention to her newborn child. This illustration shows that she is vain and selfish.

KEYWORDS

illustration – a drawing

narrator – the teller of a story

The Tale of Despereaux, Chapters 16–19 Synopsis

The story now goes back in time and introduces the reader to Roscuro, a rat born in the dark dungeon. As a young rat, Roscuro nibbles on Gregory the jailer's rope. Gregory teaches Roscuro a lesson by lighting a matching and burning Roscuro's whiskers. This action does not have the desired effect, though. Instead, it is the beginning of Roscuro's belief that the meaning of life is light. Botticelli, an older rat, tries to teach Roscuro that making prisoners suffer is the meaning of life. Botticelli instructs Roscuro to torture a new prisoner by taking away the man's only means of comfort, a red tablecloth. Roscuro tricks the prisoner and takes the cloth. But, he is disappointed. He realizes that what he needs is not the cloth, but the light from the world above. Roscuro goes upstairs and happily wanders the rooms of the castle until he comes upon a light-filled gathering in the banquet hall.

Lesson Goals

- Practice all spelling words online.
- Read Chapters 16–19 of *The Tale of Despereaux*.
- Identify the narrator of a story.
- Explain how pictures show things about a story's characters.
- Illustrate a scene from a story, and explain what it shows about the setting.
- Practice vocabulary words.
- Develop letter formation fluency.

GET READY

Introduction to *The Tale of Despereaux* (C)

Students will get a glimpse of what they will learn about in the lesson. They will also read the lesson goals and keywords. Have students select each keyword and preview its definition.

Spelling List 16 Practice

Students will practice all spelling words from the workshop.

OPTIONAL Students may do an activity from Spelling List 16 Activity Bank instead of the online practice activity.

Recall *The Tale of Despereaux*, Chapters 9–15

Students will answer some questions to review the reading that they have already completed.

Before You Read *The Tale of Despereaux*, Chapters 16–19

Students will be introduced to some key vocabulary words that they will encounter in the upcoming reading.

READ

The Tale of Despereaux, Chapters 16–19

Students will read Chapters 16–19 of *The Tale of Despereaux* by Kate DiCamillo.

Check-In: *The Tale of Despereaux*, Chapters 16–19

Students will answer several questions to demonstrate their comprehension of Chapters 16–19 of *The Tale of Despereaux*.

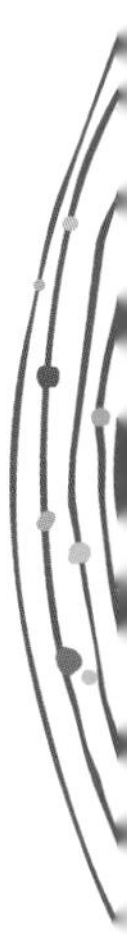

LEARN AND TRY IT

LEARN Identifying the Narrator

Students will learn how to determine whether a story's narrator is a character in the story or somebody outside of the story.

TRY IT Identify the Narrator

Students will analyze passages to determine who is narrating the story.

LEARN Illustrations Reveal Things About Characters

Students will learn that illustrations can show more about characters than the words of the text say.

TRY IT What Do Illustrations Reveal About Characters?

Student will analyze illustrations from *The Tale of Despereaux* to explain what they convey about the story's characters.

TRY IT Apply: Narrator

Students will apply to a new work what they've learned about identifying the narrator of a story.

TRY IT **Create a Scene**

Students will complete Create a Scene in *Summit English Language Arts 3 Activity Book*.

LEARNING COACH CHECK-IN This activity page requires students to draw a picture that shows a scene from the story, and then explain what it conveys about the setting. Encourage students to include details in their picture that are not included in the text. Give students feedback on their picture before they begin writing about it.

TRY IT

The Tale of Despereaux (C)

Create a Scene

Read the excerpt from *The Tale of Despereaux* by Kate DiCamillo.

Answers will vary.

The rat waltzed happily from room to room until he found himself at the door to the banquet hall. He looked inside and saw gathered there King Phillip, Queen Rosemary, the Princess Pea, twenty noble people, a juggler, four minstrels, and all the king's men. This party, reader, was a sight for a rat's eyes. Roscuro had never seen happy people. He had known only the miserable ones. Gregory the jailer and those who were consigned to his domain did not laugh or smile or clink glasses with the person sitting next to them.

THE TALE OF DESPEREAUX (C) 375

Follow the instructions to draw a picture and write about it.

1. Draw a picture that shows the setting of the banquet hall. Add details from your imagination that may not be described in the passsage.

376 THE TALE OF DESPEREAUX (C)

2. What does your picture help the passage show about the setting of the banquet hall?

THE TALE OF DESPEREAUX (C) 377

TRY IT **Practice Words from *The Tale of Despereaux*, Chapters 16–19**

Students will answer questions to demonstrate their understanding of the vocabulary words from the reading.

WRAP-UP

Question About *The Tale of Despereaux*, Chapters 16–19

Students will answer a question to show that they understand how to identify the narrator of a story.

Handwriting

Students should gather their handwriting materials and begin where they left off. Remind students to form letters carefully and correctly.

TIP Set a timer to help students stay focused during handwriting practice.

The Tale of Despereaux (D)

Lesson Overview

ACTIVITY	ACTIVITY TITLE	TIME	ONLINE/OFFLINE
GET READY	Introduction to *The Tale of Despereaux* (D)	**1** minute	online
	Spelling List 16 Review Game	**10** minutes	online
	Recall *The Tale of Despereaux*, Chapters 16–19	**5** minutes	online
	Before You Read *The Tale of Despereaux*, Chapters 20–23	**5** minutes	online
READ	*The Tale of Despereaux*, Chapters 20–23	**22** minutes	offline
	Check-In: *The Tale of Despereaux*, Chapters 20–23	**5** minutes	online
LEARN AND TRY IT	Describing Conflicts	**10** minutes	online
	Describe Conflicts	**7** minutes	online
	Learn About Chapters	**10** minutes	online
	Describe Chapters	**7** minutes	online
	Apply: Plot	**10** minutes	online
	Describe a Chapter's Events LEARNING COACH CHECK-IN	**10** minutes	offline
	Practice Words from *The Tale of Despereaux*, Chapters 20–23	**8** minutes	online
WRAP-UP	Question About *The Tale of Despereaux*, Chapters 20–23	**2** minutes	online
	Handwriting	**8** minutes	offline

Content Background

In this lesson, students will learn that part of a story's plot is conflict. A *conflict* is a problem that a character faces in a story. Students may have previously learned the term *problem*. Conflict is the same thing as problem. A story usually has one main conflict, but it can have other smaller conflicts. For example, a conflict Despereaux has is that he is sent to the dungeon for breaking the rules of the mouse community. A conflict can be with other characters, or it can be within a character. Students will learn that this type of conflict is usually related to a character's feelings. For example, one of Roscuro's conflicts is that he does not want to be a rat.

MATERIALS

Supplied

- *The Tale of Despereaux* by Kate DiCamillo
- *Summit English Language Arts 3 Activity Book*
  - Describe a Chapter's Events
- handwriting workbook

Students will also learn that a novel is divided into chapters. *Chapters* provide readers a chance to pause and think about how the plot is developing. They usually tell a story's events in order. Chapters build on each other by connecting events to other chapters. They work together to tell a complete story.

KEYWORDS

chapter – a main part of a written work, usually numbered or titled

conflict – a problem or issue that a character faces in a story

plot – what happens in a story; the sequence of events

The Tale of Despereaux, Chapters 20–23 Synopsis

Once Roscuro discovers the lively banquet, he climbs up to a chandelier to view the scene from above. Princess Pea spots him and yells out that a rat is hanging from the chandelier. Hearing the word *rat* used like a curse, Roscuro falls from the chandelier, right into the queen's soup. The shock to the queen is so great that she dies. As Roscuro runs away, he looks back at the princess to see her looking at him with disgust. Roscuro returns to the darkness of the dungeon with a broken heart and a desire to make the princess suffer for how she looked at him. Because the queen dies while eating soup, the heartbroken king outlaws soup and all the utensils needed to make and eat it. These items are collected from the people of the kingdom and stored in the dungeon. The king also orders that all rats be killed. However, this order only results in many of the king's men becoming lost in the maze of the dungeon and never returning. As Roscuro plans his revenge, Despereaux is upstairs hearing music for the first time, and a girl named Miggery Sow arrives at the castle.

Lesson Goals

- Practice all spelling words online.
- Read Chapters 20–23 of *The Tale of Despereaux*.
- Identify and describe conflicts in the plot of a story.
- Define what a chapter is.
- Describe a chapter's events and how those events connect to events in other chapters.
- Practice vocabulary words.
- Develop letter formation fluency.

GET READY

Introduction to *The Tale of Despereaux* (D)

Students will get a glimpse of what they will learn about in the lesson. They will also read the lesson goals and keywords. Have students select each keyword and preview its definition.

Spelling List 16 Review Game

Students will practice all spelling words from the workshop.

Recall *The Tale of Despereaux*, Chapters 16–19

Students will answer some questions to review the reading that they have already completed.

Before You Read *The Tale of Despereaux*, Chapters 20–23

Students will be introduced to some key vocabulary words that they will encounter in the upcoming reading.

READ

The Tale of Despereaux, Chapters 20–23

Students will read Chapters 20–23 of *The Tale of Despereaux* by Kate DiCamillo.

Check-In: *The Tale of Despereaux*, Chapters 20–23

Students will answer several questions to demonstrate their comprehension of Chapters 20–23 of *The Tale of Despereaux*.

LEARN AND TRY IT

LEARN Describing Conflicts

Students will learn that a part of the story's plot is conflict. There can be more than one conflict in a story. Many plot events involve characters trying to resolve a conflict.

TRY IT Describe Conflicts

Students will identify and describe conflicts in the story.

LEARN Learn About Chapters

Students will learn the purpose for a book's chapters and how chapters build on each other and work together to tell a story.

TRY IT Describe Chapters

Students will describe how the events of a chapter build on events of previous chapters.

TRY IT Apply: Plot

Students will apply to a new work what they've learned about describing elements of a story's plot.

TRY IT Describe a Chapter's Events

Students will complete Describe a Chapter's Events in *Summit English Language Arts 3 Activity Book*.

LEARNING COACH CHECK-IN It's important that you review students' responses. Give students feedback, using the sample answers provided to guide you.

TRY IT

***The Tale of Despereaux* (D)**

Describe a Chapter's Events

Answer the questions in complete sentences.

1. What is the definition of a chapter?
   A chapter is a main section of a book.

2. Describe the events of Chapter Twenty "a view from a chandelier" from *The Tale of Despereaux*. Tell the events in order.
   Roscuro hangs from the chandelier to watch the banquet. But then, Princess Pea sees him. She shouts that a rat is hanging from the chandelier. No one hears her except Roscuro. He thinks that *rat* is an ugly word. It feels like a curse to him. He realizes that he doesn't want to be a rat. Then, he loses his grip on the chandelier and falls into the queen's soup.

THE TALE OF DESPEREAUX (D) 379

380 THE TALE OF DESPEREAUX (D)

TRY IT Practice Words from *The Tale of Despereaux*, Chapters 20–23

Students will answer questions to demonstrate their understanding of the vocabulary words from the reading.

WRAP-UP

Question About *The Tale of Despereaux*, Chapters 20–23

Students will answer a question to show that they understand how events from one chapter build on events from previous chapters.

Handwriting

Students should gather their handwriting materials and begin where they left off. Remind students to form letters carefully and correctly.

TIP Set a timer to help students stay focused during handwriting practice.

The Tale of Despereaux (E)

Lesson Overview

ACTIVITY	ACTIVITY TITLE	TIME	ONLINE/OFFLINE
GET READY	Introduction to *The Tale of Despereaux* (E)	**1** minute	online
	Recall *The Tale of Despereaux*, Chapters 20–23	**5** minutes	online
	Before You Read *The Tale of Despereaux*, Chapters 24–29	**5** minutes	online
READ	*The Tale of Despereaux*, Chapters 24–29	**35** minutes	offline
	Check-In: *The Tale of Despereaux*, Chapters 24–29	**5** minutes	online
LEARN AND TRY IT	Understanding Sensory and Nonliteral Language	**11** minutes	online
	Sensory and Nonliteral Language	**7** minutes	online
	Apply: Nonliteral Language	**10** minutes	online
	Literal Versus Nonliteral LEARNING COACH CHECK-IN	**15** minutes	offline
	Practice Words from *The Tale of Despereaux*, Chapters 24–29	**8** minutes	online
WRAP-UP	Question About *The Tale of Despereaux*, Chapters 24–29	**2** minutes	online
QUIZ	Spelling List 16	**10** minutes	online
WRAP-UP	Handwriting	**6** minutes	offline

Content Background

In this lesson, students will learn about expressive forms of language that authors use to make their writing more vivid and imaginative. Students will learn about sensory language. *Sensory language* helps readers connect to the five senses: sight, hearing, touch, smell, and taste. For example, in the sentence "I heard the screeching tires," the word *screeching* is sensory language that helps readers hear the sound of the tires.

Students will also learn about nonliteral language, which is also called *figurative language*. *Nonliteral language* is language that means something different than how the words are defined in the dictionary. For example, the idiom "It's raining cats and dogs" is an example of figurative language. It does not mean that cats and dogs are falling out of the sky. It means that it is raining very hard.

MATERIALS

Supplied

- *The Tale of Despereaux* by Kate DiCamillo
- *Summit English Language Arts 3 Activity Book*
  - Literal Versus Nonliteral
- handwriting workbook

The Tale of Despereaux, Chapters 24–29 Synopsis

The story goes back in time, and we meet Miggery Sow who, at the age of six, loses her mother and is sold into service by her father. Mig calls the man who buys her *Uncle*, and spends her days cooking, cleaning, and tending sheep. The uncle often gives Mig a good clout to the ears, which causes her to lose most of her hearing. She is caught in a cycle of hearing less, understanding less, making more mistakes, and receiving more clouts to the ears. On the day that Mig turns seven, she sees the royal family ride by in all their glowing splendor. The sight leads Mig to hope that she will be a princess someday. Years later, when the king outlaws soup, the king's men come to the uncle's home to collect all spoons, kettles, and bowls. They discover that the uncle owns Mig, which is against the law. The soldiers take Mig from the uncle and bring her to the castle to be a servant. On her first day as a servant in the castle, Mig meets the princess while delivering a spool of red thread to her.

KEYWORDS

nonliteral language – figures of speech or words and phrases that change their usual meaning based on how they are used in a sentence

sensory language – language that appeals to the five senses

Lesson Goals

- Read Chapters 24–29 of *The Tale of Despereaux*.
- Identify and define examples of sensory language and figurative language.
- Illustrate the literal and nonliteral meanings of figurative language.
- Practice vocabulary words.
- Take a spelling quiz.
- Develop letter formation fluency.

GET READY

Introduction to *The Tale of Despereaux* (E)

Students will get a glimpse of what they will learn about in the lesson. They will also read the lesson goals and keywords. Have students select each keyword and preview its definition.

Recall *The Tale of Despereaux*, Chapters 20–23

Students will answer some questions to review the reading that they have already completed.

Before You Read *The Tale of Despereaux*, Chapters 24–29

Students will be introduced to some key vocabulary words that they will encounter in the upcoming reading.

READ

The Tale of Despereaux, Chapters 24–29

Students will read Chapters 24–29 of *The Tale of Despereaux* by Kate DiCamillo.

Check-In: *The Tale of Despereaux*, Chapters 24–29

Students will answer several questions to demonstrate their comprehension of Chapters 24–29 of *The Tale of Despereaux*.

LEARN AND TRY IT

LEARN Understanding Sensory and Nonliteral Language

Students will learn about sensory language, or words and phrases an author uses that appeal to the five senses. They will also learn about nonliteral language, also called *figurative language*, or words used to mean something different than how the words are defined in the dictionary.

TRY IT Sensory and Nonliteral Language

Students will identify sensory language and nonliteral language in passages. They will also define figurative language as it is used in passages from the story.

TRY IT Apply: Nonliteral Language

Students will apply to a new work what they've learned about identifying nonliteral, or figurative, language.

TRY IT Literal Versus Nonliteral

Students will complete Literal Versus Nonliteral in *Summit English Language Arts 3 Activity Book*. Students will draw two pictures to illustrate the literal and nonliteral meanings of an example of figurative language.

LEARNING COACH CHECK-IN This activity page requires students to understand the difference between the literal and nonliteral meanings of phrases. It's important that you make sure students are clear about the difference before they begin drawing their pictures. Give students feedback, using the sample answers provided to guide you.

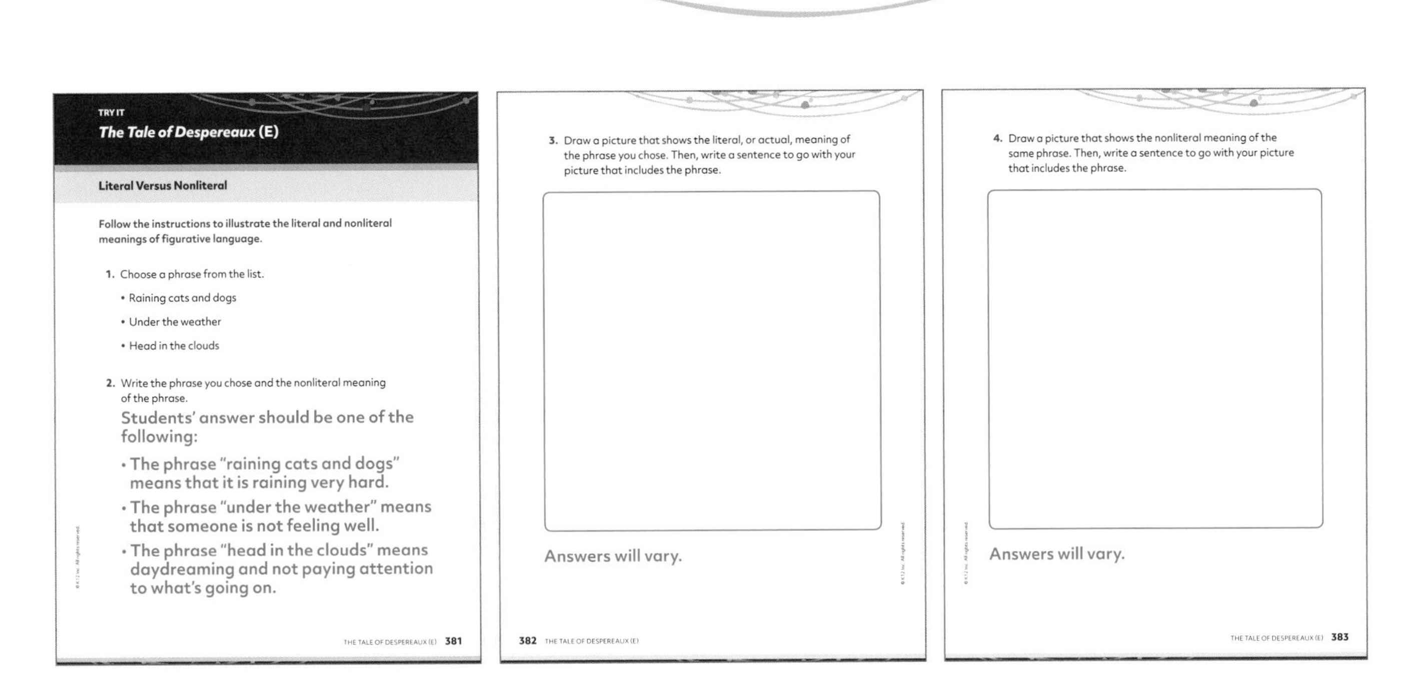
TRY IT
The Tale of Despereaux (E)
Literal Versus Nonliteral
Follow the instructions to illustrate the literal and nonliteral meanings of figurative language.
1. Choose a phrase from the list.
• Raining cats and dogs
• Under the weather
• Head in the clouds
2. Write the phrase you chose and the nonliteral meaning of the phrase.
Students' answer should be one of the following:
• The phrase "raining cats and dogs" means that it is raining very hard.
• The phrase "under the weather" means that someone is not feeling well.
• The phrase "head in the clouds" means daydreaming and not paying attention to what's going on.
THE TALE OF DESPEREAUX (E) 381
3. Draw a picture that shows the literal, or actual, meaning of the phrase you chose. Then, write a sentence to go with your picture that includes the phrase.
Answers will vary.
382 THE TALE OF DESPEREAUX (E)
4. Draw a picture that shows the nonliteral meaning of the same phrase. Then, write a sentence to go with your picture that includes the phrase.
Answers will vary.
THE TALE OF DESPEREAUX (E) 383

TRY IT Practice Words from *The Tale of Despereaux*, Chapters 24–29

Students will answer questions to demonstrate their understanding of the vocabulary words from the reading.

WRAP-UP

Question About *The Tale of Despereaux*, Chapters 24–29

Students will answer a question to show that they understand the meaning of nonliteral, or figurative, language.

QUIZ

Spelling List 16

Students will complete the Spelling List 16 quiz.

WRAP-UP

Handwriting

Students should gather their handwriting materials and begin where they left off. Remind students to form letters carefully and correctly.

TIP Set a timer to help students stay focused during handwriting practice.

The Tale of Despereaux (F)

Lesson Overview

ACTIVITY	ACTIVITY TITLE	TIME	ONLINE/OFFLINE
GET READY	Introduction to *The Tale of Despereaux* (F)	**1** minute	online
	Spelling List 17 Pretest **LEARNING COACH CHECK-IN**	**10** minutes	online and offline
	Recall *The Tale of Despereaux*, Chapters 24–29	**5** minutes	online
	Before You Read *The Tale of Despereaux*, Chapters 30–35	**5** minutes	online
READ	*The Tale of Despereaux*, Chapters 30–35	**31** minutes	offline
	Check-In: *The Tale of Despereaux*, Chapters 30–35	**5** minutes	online
LEARN AND TRY IT	Describing Characters' Actions, Feelings, Motivation	**13** minutes	online
	Describe Characters' Feelings and Motivation	**12** minutes	online
	Apply: Characters and Their Feelings	**10** minutes	online
	What Are the Results? **LEARNING COACH CHECK-IN**	**10** minutes	offline
	Practice Words from *The Tale of Despereaux*, Chapters 30–35	**8** minutes	online
WRAP-UP	Question About *The Tale of Despereaux*, Chapters 30–35	**2** minutes	online
	Handwriting	**8** minutes	offline

Content Background

In this lesson, students will learn more about characters. They will learn that characters' actions affect the plot. This means that characters' actions cause other actions to happen. For example, Roscuro's action of falling into the queen's soup causes the queen to die.

Students will learn that they can infer characters' feelings from their actions. For example, after Mig has failed at many tasks, Cook shouts at her. From this action, we can infer that Cook feels very frustrated.

Finally, students will learn about characters' motivation, or the reason for their actions. It is why characters do what they do. Often characters' motivation is related to their feelings. For example, Roscuro wants to punish the princess. His motivation, or reason, for this is because he felt deeply wounded when the princess looked at him with anger and disgust.

MATERIALS

Supplied

- *The Tale of Despereaux* by Kate DiCamillo
- *Summit English Language Arts 3 Activity Book*
  - Spelling List 17 Pretest
  - What Are the Results?
- handwriting workbook

The Tale of Despereaux, Chapters 30–35 Synopsis

Mig settles into life in the castle, but her inability to accomplish the simplest task leads to her working in the kitchen. Finally, she is given the daily task of going to the dungeon to deliver Gregory his meal. Roscuro listens as Mig tells Gregory of her dream to be a princess. He decides to use Mig's wish to help him get his revenge on Princess Pea. Roscuro tells Mig his plan of making her a princess and bringing the real princess to the dungeon. In the meantime, Gregory has hidden Despereaux in a napkin, which he places on his meal tray. While hidden in the napkin, Despereaux hears Roscuro's plan. Without knowing it, Mig then brings Despereaux out of the dungeon and into the kitchen. When Despereaux is discovered, he must run for his life as Cook tells Mig to kill him. Despereaux escapes to the pantry, but not before Mig cuts off his tail. Despereaux weeps with pain but also with joy for escaping the dungeon in time to save the princess.

KEYWORDS

plot – what happens in a story; the sequence of events

Lesson Goals

- Take a spelling pretest.
- Read Chapters 30–35 of *The Tale of Despereaux*.
- Determine characters' feelings and motivation.
- Determine how characters' actions cause events to happen.
- Practice vocabulary words.
- Develop letter formation fluency.

GET READY

Introduction to *The Tale of Despereaux* (F)

Students will get a glimpse of what they will learn about in the lesson. They will also read the lesson goals and keywords. Have students select each keyword and preview its definition.

Spelling List 17 Pretest

Students will take a spelling pretest and learn a new spelling pattern.

LEARNING COACH CHECK-IN Have students turn to Spelling List 17 Pretest in *Summit English Language Arts 3 Activity Book* and open the online Spelling Pretest activity. Online, students will listen to the spelling word, type the word

in the space indicated, and then check their answer. In the activity book, students will write the correct spelling of the word in the tables provided and indicate with a ✓ or an ✗ if they spelled the word correctly or incorrectly online. Students will repeat this process with the remaining words.

As needed, help students with the interaction between the online activity and the activity book page until they become comfortable with what they need to do. As students practice their spelling words throughout the workshop, they should pay special attention to words they spelled incorrectly on the pretest.

This is the complete list of words students will be tested on.

Words with /z/ Sound				
breeze	easy	praise	rise	those
cheese	elbows	prison	rosebush	Thursday
chose	hose	raise	suppose	Tuesday
details	means	raisin	surprise	Wednesday
disease				

NOTE Have students keep their completed activity page in a safe place so they can refer to it later.

GET READY
***The Tale of Despereaux* (F)**

Spelling List 17 Pretest

1. Open the Spelling Pretest activity online. Listen to the first spelling word. Type the word. Check your answer.
2. Write the correct spelling of the word in the Word column of the Spelling Pretest table.

	Word	✓	✗
1	blindfold		

3. Put a check mark in the ✓ column if you spelled the word correctly online.

	Word	✓	✗
1	blindfold	✓	

Put an X in the ✗ column if you spelled the word incorrectly online.

	Word	✓	✗
1	blindfold		X

4. Repeat Steps 1–3 for the remaining words in the Spelling Pretest.

THE TALE OF DESPEREAUX (F) 385

***The Tale of Despereaux* (F)**

Spelling List 17 Pretest

Write each spelling word in the Word column, making sure to spell it correctly.

	Word	✓	✗
1	breeze		
2	cheese		
3	chose		
4	details		
5	disease		
6	easy		
7	elbows		
8	hose		
9	means		
10	praise		
11	prison		

	Word	✓	✗
12	raise		
13	raisin		
14	rise		
15	rosebush		
16	suppose		
17	surprise		
18	those		
19	Thursday		
20	Tuesday		
21	Wednesday		

Students should write the correct spelling of each word from the pretest and use the ✓ and X columns to indicate whether they spelled each word correctly or incorrectly online.

386 THE TALE OF DESPEREAUX (F)

Recall *The Tale of Despereaux*, Chapters 24–29

Students will answer some questions to review the reading that they have already completed.

Before You Read *The Tale of Despereaux*, Chapters 30–35

Students will be introduced to some key vocabulary words that they will encounter in the upcoming reading.

READ

The Tale of Despereaux, Chapters 30–35

Students will read Chapters 30–35 of *The Tale of Despereaux* by Kate DiCamillo.

Check-In: *The Tale of Despereaux*, Chapters 30–35

Students will answer several questions to demonstrate their comprehension of Chapters 30–35 of *The Tale of Despereaux*.

LEARN AND TRY IT

LEARN Describing Characters' Actions, Feelings, Motivation

Students will learn that characters' actions can cause events in the story to happen. They will learn that they can figure out characters' feelings from their actions. They will also learn that characters' motivation is the reason for their actions.

TRY IT Describe Characters' Feelings and Motivation

Students will analyze passages to determine characters' feelings and motivation.

TRY IT Apply: Characters and Their Feelings

Students will apply to a new work what they've learned about determining characters' feelings.

TRY IT What Are the Results?

Students will complete What Are the Results? in *Summit English Language Arts 3 Activity Book*.

LEARNING COACH CHECK-IN This activity page requires students to determine a chain of related events. Give students feedback, using the sample answers provided to guide you.

SUPPORT Some students may have difficulty recognizing the cause-and-effect chain that results from Mig going to the dungeon. For those students, ask them guiding questions to help them recognize that one event leads to another. For example, *What happens because Mig can't do anything right in the kitchen?* (Answer: *Cook sends her to the dungeon.*) *What happens because Mig goes to the dungeon?* (Answer: *She meets Roscuro.*) *What happens because Mig meets Roscuro?* (Answer: *He tells her his plan.*) Continue in this manner.

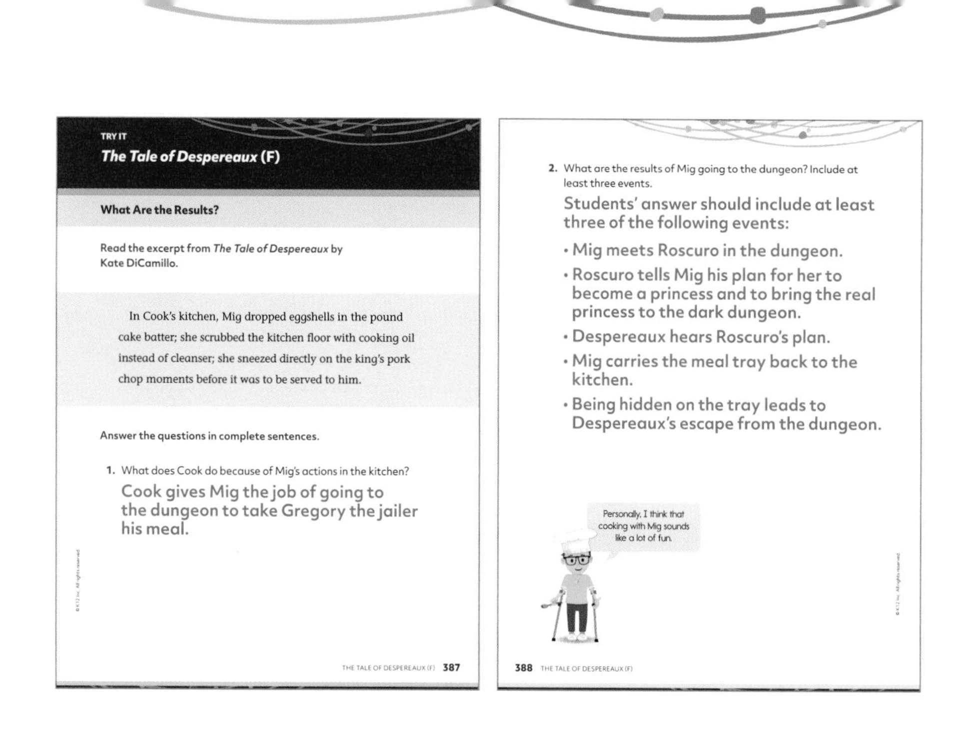

TRY IT
The Tale of Despereaux (F)

What Are the Results?

Read the excerpt from *The Tale of Despereaux* by Kate DiCamillo.

> In Cook's kitchen, Mig dropped eggshells in the pound cake batter; she scrubbed the kitchen floor with cooking oil instead of cleanser; she sneezed directly on the king's pork chop moments before it was to be served to him.

Answer the questions in complete sentences.

1. What does Cook do because of Mig's actions in the kitchen?
   Cook gives Mig the job of going to the dungeon to take Gregory the jailer his meal.

THE TALE OF DESPEREAUX (F) 387

2. What are the results of Mig going to the dungeon? Include at least three events.
   Students' answer should include at least three of the following events:
   - Mig meets Roscuro in the dungeon.
   - Roscuro tells Mig his plan for her to become a princess and to bring the real princess to the dark dungeon.
   - Despereaux hears Roscuro's plan.
   - Mig carries the meal tray back to the kitchen.
   - Being hidden on the tray leads to Despereaux's escape from the dungeon.

388 THE TALE OF DESPEREAUX (F)

TRY IT **Practice Words from *The Tale of Despereaux*, Chapters 30–35**

Students will answer questions to demonstrate their understanding of the vocabulary words from the reading.

WRAP-UP

Question About *The Tale of Despereaux*, Chapters 30–35

Students will answer a question to show that they understand how characters' actions cause events in the story to happen.

Handwriting

Students should gather their handwriting materials and begin where they left off. Remind students to form letters carefully and correctly.

TIP Set a timer to help students stay focused during handwriting practice.

The Tale of Despereaux (G)

Lesson Overview

ACTIVITY	ACTIVITY TITLE	TIME	ONLINE/OFFLINE
GET READY	Introduction to *The Tale of Despereaux* (G)	**1** minute	
	Spelling List 17 Activity Bank	**10** minutes	
	Recall *The Tale of Despereaux*, Chapters 30–35	**5** minutes	
	Before You Read *The Tale of Despereaux*, Chapters 36–40	**5** minutes	
READ	*The Tale of Despereaux*, Chapters 36–40	**30** minutes	
	Check-In: *The Tale of Despereaux*, Chapters 36–40	**5** minutes	
LEARN AND **TRY IT**	Focusing on Plot	**10** minutes	
	Focus on Plot	**5** minutes	
	Describing Nonliteral Language	**10** minutes	
	Identify Nonliteral Language	**5** minutes	
	Apply: Meaning of Nonliteral Words	**10** minutes	
	Events Affect Future Events **LEARNING COACH CHECK-IN**	**10** minutes	
	Practice Words from *The Tale of Despereaux*, Chapters 36–40	**6** minutes	
WRAP-UP	Question About *The Tale of Despereaux*, Chapters 36–40	**2** minutes	
	Handwriting	**6** minutes	

Content Background

In this lesson, students will learn about a story's *plot*. They will learn that events in a story happen in sequence, or the order in which events occur. They will also learn that events can cause other events to happen right away or in the future. For example, Mig sees the royal family. This event causes her to want to be a princess. Several years in the future, this even causes her to take part in Roscuro's plan so that she can become a princess.

Students will learn about a story's conflict and resolution. Conflict and resolution are the same as problem and solution. A *conflict* is a problem that a character faces. A *resolution* is defined as the outcome of a story. It is essentially how a conflict is resolved. A story usually has a main conflict, which is the biggest problem characters face. For

example, the main problem in *The Tale of Despereaux* is that Roscuro and Mig take the princess and hide her in the dungeon. But, a story can also have smaller conflicts. For example, Despereaux has a conflict when he is sent to the dungeon. The resolution to this conflict is that Despereaux escapes from the dungeon with Gregory's help.

Students will learn more about nonliteral language, also called *figurative language*. They will review that *nonliteral language* means something different than the words suggest. For example, the phrase "wash your hands" of something means that you no longer want anything to do with something. They will learn something new about figurative language. It can compare one thing to something different. For example, the sentence, "Stories are light," compares a story to something completely different, light. This figurative language emphasizes the wonder of a story.

Advance Preparation

Gather students' completed Spelling List 17 Pretest activity page from *The Tale of Despereaux* (F). Students will refer to this page during Get Ready: Spelling List 17 Activity Bank.

The Tale of Despereaux, Chapters 36–40 Synopsis

Roscuro puts his plan for revenge into action. Mig helps him because he has convinced her that the plan is for her to be a princess and the princess to be her maid. However, his real plan is to chain the princess in the dungeon. In the middle of the night, Mig threatens Pea with a knife, while Roscuro makes her dress in the gown she wore to the banquet. Then, while everyone in the castle sleeps, Roscuro and Mig take Pea to the dungeon. Despereaux awakes to discover that Pea is missing and Gregory is dead. Despereaux sets out to find the king and comes across the Mouse Council and his father. When they see Despereaux, they think he is a ghost. Despereaux's father seems to have aged many years, which has a strong impact on Despereaux. His father asks Despereaux to forgive him, which he does.

MATERIALS

Supplied

- *The Tale of Despereaux* by Kate DiCamillo
- *Summit English Language Arts 3 Activity Book*
  - Spelling List 17 Activity Bank
  - Events Affect Future Events
- handwriting workbook

Also Needed

- completed Spelling List 17 Pretest activity page from *The Tale of Despereaux* (F)

KEYWORDS

conflict – a problem or issue that a character faces in a story

nonliteral language – figures of speech or words and phrases that change their usual meaning based on how they are used in a sentence

plot – what happens in a story; the sequence of events

resolution – the outcome of a story

Lesson Goals

- Practice all spelling words offline.
- Read Chapters 36–40 of *The Tale of Despereaux*.
- Put plot events in sequence.
- Identify conflict and resolution in a story.
- Identify and define nonliteral language.
- Explain how plot events cause future events to happen.
- Practice vocabulary words.
- Develop letter formation fluency.

GET READY

Introduction to *The Tale of Despereaux* (G)

Students will get a glimpse of what they will learn about in the lesson. They will also read the lesson goals and keywords. Have students select each keyword and preview its definition.

Spelling List 17 Activity Bank

Students will practice all spelling words by completing Spelling List 17 Activity Bank from *Summit English Language Arts 3 Activity Book*. Make sure students have their completed Spelling List 17 Pretest activity page from *The Tale of Despereaux* (F) to refer to during this activity.

Remind students to pay special attention to words they spelled incorrectly on the Spelling Pretest.

GET READY

***The Tale of Despereaux* (G)**

Spelling List 17 Activity Bank

Circle any words in the box that you did not spell correctly on your pretest. Choose one activity to do with your circled words. Do as much of the activity as you can in the time given.

Did you spell all the words on the pretest correctly? Do the one activity with as many spelling words as you can.

breeze	easy	praise	rise	those
cheese	elbows	prison	rosebush	Thursday
chose	hose	raise	suppose	Tuesday
details	means	raisin	surprise	Wednesday
disease				

Spelling Activity Choices

Alphabetizing

1. In the left column, write your spelling words in alphabetical order.
2. Correct any spelling errors.

THE TALE OF DESPEREAUX (G) 389

Vowel-Free Words

1. In the left column, write only the consonants in each of your spelling words. Put a dot where each vowel should be.
2. Spell each word aloud, stating which vowels should be in the places with dots.
3. In the right column, rewrite the entire spelling word.
4. Correct any spelling errors.

Rhymes

1. In the left column, write your spelling words.
2. In the right column, write a word that rhymes with each spelling word.
3. Correct any spelling errors.

Uppercase and Lowercase

1. In the left column, write each of your spelling words in all uppercase letters.
2. In the right column, write each of your spelling words in all lowercase letters.
3. Correct any spelling errors.

390 THE TALE OF DESPEREAUX (G)

Complete the activity that you chose.

My chosen activity: ______

1. ______ ______
2. ______ ______
3. ______ ______
4. ______ ______
5. ______ ______
6. ______ ______
7. ______ ______
8. ______ ______
9. ______ ______
10. ______ ______
11. ______ ______
12. ______ ______
13. ______ ______
14. ______ ______
15. ______ ______
16. ______ ______

Students should use this page and the next to complete all steps in their chosen activity.

THE TALE OF DESPEREAUX (G) 391

17. ______ ______
18. ______ ______
19. ______ ______
20. ______ ______
21. ______ ______

392 THE TALE OF DESPEREAUX (G)

Recall *The Tale of Despereaux*, Chapters 30–35

Students will answer some questions to review the reading that they have already completed.

Before You Read *The Tale of Despereaux*, Chapters 36–40

Students will be introduced to some key vocabulary words that they will encounter in the upcoming reading.

READ

The Tale of Despereaux, Chapters 36–40

Students will read Chapters 36–40 of *The Tale of Despereaux* by Kate DiCamillo.

Check-In: *The Tale of Despereaux*, Chapters 36–40

Students will answer several questions to demonstrate their comprehension of Chapters 36–40 of *The Tale of Despereaux*.

LEARN AND TRY IT

LEARN Focusing on Plot

Students will learn about putting plot events in order and how events can influence other events in the future. They will also learn about conflict and resolution in a story's plot.

TRY IT Focus on Plot

Students will place plot events in sequence. They will also determine the main conflict of *The Tale of Despereaux* and a smaller conflict and its resolution.

LEARN Describing Nonliteral Language

Students will learn more about nonliteral, or figurative, language. They will learn that figurative language can mean something different than the words suggest. But, other forms of figurative language compare one thing to something completely different.

TRY IT Identify Nonliteral Language

Students will identify nonliteral, or figurative, language in passages and determine the meaning of the phrases.

TRY IT Apply: Meaning of Nonliteral Words

Students will apply to a new work what they've learned about determining the meaning of nonliteral, or figurative, language.

TRY IT Events Affect Future Events

Students will complete Events Affect Future Events in *Summit English Language Arts 3 Activity Book*.

LEARNING COACH CHECK-IN It's important that you review students' responses in case they do not fully understand the idea that an event can cause something to happen in the future. Give students feedback, using the sample answers provided to guide you.

TRY IT

***The Tale of Despereaux* (G)**

Events Affect Future Events

Read the excerpt from *The Tale of Despereaux* by Kate DiCamillo.

> He looked back.
>
> And he saw that the princess was glaring at him. Her eyes were filled with disgust and anger.
>
> "Go back to the dungeon" was what the look she gave him said. "Go back into the darkness where you belong."
>
> This look, reader, broke Roscuro's heart.

Answer the questions in complete sentences.

1. The passage describes events after Roscuro falls into the queen's soup and the queen dies. What does Roscuro do right after these events?

   Roscuro goes back to the dungeon. He says that he will have something beautiful. He says that he will have revenge.

THE TALE OF DESPEREAUX (G) 393

2. What does Roscuro do in the future because of the events in the passage?

   Roscuro comes up with a plan to get revenge on the princess. He talks Mig into helping him. He and Mig take the princess to the dungeon. Roscuro plans on keeping the princess in the dungeon forever.

394 THE TALE OF DESPEREAUX (G)

TRY IT Practice Words from *The Tale of Despereaux*, Chapters 36–40

Students will answer questions to demonstrate their understanding of the vocabulary words from the reading.

WRAP-UP

Question About *The Tale of Despereaux*, Chapters 36–40

Students will answer a question to show that they can distinguish nonliteral language from literal language.

Handwriting

Students should gather their handwriting materials and begin where they left off. Remind students to form letters carefully and correctly.

TIP Set a timer to help students stay focused during handwriting practice.

The Tale of Despereaux (H)

Lesson Overview

ACTIVITY	ACTIVITY TITLE	TIME	ONLINE/OFFLINE
GET READY	Introduction to *The Tale of Despereaux* (H)	**1** minute	online
	Spelling List 17 Practice	**10** minutes	online
	Recall *The Tale of Despereaux*, Chapters 36–40	**5** minutes	online
	Before You Read *The Tale of Despereaux*, Chapters 41–46	**5** minutes	online
READ	*The Tale of Despereaux*, Chapters 41–46	**30** minutes	offline
	Check-In: *The Tale of Despereaux*, Chapters 41–46	**5** minutes	online
LEARN AND **TRY IT**	Describing Characters' Interactions and Relationships	**9** minutes	online
	Describe Characters' Interactions and Relationships	**4** minutes	online
	Identifying Personification	**9** minutes	online
	Identify Personification	**4** minutes	online
	Apply: Interaction Among Characters	**10** minutes	online
	Describe Interactions Among Characters **LEARNING COACH CHECK-IN**	**10** minutes	offline
	Practice Words from *The Tale of Despereaux*, Chapters 41–46	**8** minutes	online
WRAP-UP	Question About *The Tale of Despereaux*, Chapters 41–46	**2** minutes	online
	Handwriting	**8** minutes	offline

Content Background

In this lesson, students will learn about interactions and relationships among characters. Characters' interactions affect characters and the plot of the story. For example, the princess and Roscuro interact just after the queen dies. The princess looks at Roscuro with disgust, which affects Roscuro and makes him feel bitter. It affects the story's plot because he sets out to get revenge on the princess.

Students will learn that relationships are formed when characters connect with one another. Relationships are closely tied to interactions because characters make connections through interactions. For example, Despereaux

MATERIALS

Supplied

- *The Tale of Despereaux* by Kate DiCamillo
- *Summit English Language Arts 3 Activity Book*
  - Describe Interactions Among Characters
- handwriting workbook

interacts with the princess when he listens to the king's song. Through this interaction, Despereaux and the princess form a relationship. Characters develop because of their interactions and relationships. They cause characters to grow and change.

Students will also learn about another form of figurative language, personification. *Personification* is giving human qualities to something that is not human. An example of personification is the phrase "sleepy garden walls." The phrase gives the human quality of feeling sleepy to something that is not human, garden walls.

KEYWORDS

personification – giving human qualities to something that is not human; Example: The thunder shouted from the clouds.

The Tale of Despereaux, Chapters 41–46 Synopsis

Despereaux seeks out the king to tell him that the princess is in the dungeon. But, the king refuses to believe him. This leads Despereaux to realize that he must rescue the princess himself. Despereaux finds the threadmaster, Hovis, to ask for thread. He needs it to help him find the way back out of the dungeon once he has located the princess. Hovis gives Despereaux a spool of thread and a needle to be his sword. As Despereaux pushes the spool of thread to the dungeon, he comes across Cook making soup in the kitchen. Despereaux realizes that he must make it across the kitchen without being seen by the mouse-hating Cook. Despereaux is afraid for his life. But, Cook is so relieved that he is not a soldier, she does not threaten him. Instead, she acts kindly and feeds Despereaux soup. Despereaux then enters the dungeon, rolling the thread in front of him. However, the thread leaps down the stairs ahead of him, landing at the feet of the rat Botticelli.

Lesson Goals

- Practice all spelling words online.
- Read Chapters 41–46 of *The Tale of Despereaux*.
- Describe interactions and relationships among characters in a story.
- Identify and explain the use of personification in a story.
- Practice vocabulary words.
- Develop letter formation fluency.

GET READY

Introduction to *The Tale of Despereaux* (H)

Students will get a glimpse of what they will learn about in the lesson. They will also read the lesson goals and keywords. Have students select each keyword and preview its definition.

Spelling List 17 Practice

Students will practice all spelling words from the workshop.

OPTIONAL Students may do an activity from Spelling List 17 Activity Bank instead of the online practice activity.

Recall *The Tale of Despereaux*, Chapters 36–40

Students will answer some questions to review the reading that they have already completed.

Before You Read *The Tale of Despereaux*, Chapters 41–46

Students will be introduced to some key vocabulary words that they will encounter in the upcoming reading.

READ

The Tale of Despereaux, Chapters 41–46

Students will read Chapters 41–46 of *The Tale of Despereaux* by Kate DiCamillo.

Check-In: *The Tale of Despereaux*, Chapters 41–46

Students will answer several questions to demonstrate their comprehension of Chapters 41–46 of *The Tale of Despereaux*.

LEARN AND TRY IT

LEARN Describing Characters' Interactions and Relationships

Students will learn about interactions and relationships among characters, which can be positive or negative, and affect characters and the story's plot.

TRY IT Describe Characters' Interactions and Relationships

Students will analyze passages to determine the effects of interactions and relationships among characters.

LEARN Identifying Personification

Students will learn that personification is a form of figurative language that gives human traits to nonhuman things.

TRY IT Identify Personification

Students will identify examples of personification and determine how personification affects meaning.

TRY IT **Apply: Interaction Among Characters**

Students will apply to a new work what they've learned about interactions among characters.

TRY IT **Describe Interactions Among Characters**

Students will complete Describe Interactions Among Characters in *Summit English Language Arts 3 Activity Book*.

LEARNING COACH CHECK-IN This activity page asks students to recall events from Chapter Thirty-Four "kill 'em, even if they're already dead," so you may need to refer them to that chapter. It's important that you review students' responses. Give students feedback, using the sample answers provided to guide you.

TRY IT

***The Tale of Despereaux* (H)**

Describe Interactions Among Characters

Read the excerpt from *The Tale of Despereaux* by Kate DiCamillo.

> "Mouse," said Cook, "would you like some soup?"...
> "Come closer," she said. "I don't aim to hurt you. I promise."
> Despereaux sniffed. The soup smelled wonderful, incredible. Keeping one eye on Cook, he stepped out from behind the spool of thread and crept closer.
> "Go on," said Cook, "taste it."
> Despereaux stepped onto the saucer....He sipped. Oh, it was lovely....
> "How is it?" asked Cook anxiously.
> "Wonderful," said Despereaux....
> Cook smiled. "See?" she said. "There ain't a body, be it mouse or man, that ain't made better by a little soup."

THE TALE OF DESPEREAUX (H) 395

Answer the questions in complete sentences.

1. Think back to when Despereaux escaped from the dungeon and Cook saw him in the kitchen. Describe the interaction between Cook, Mig, and Despereaux at that point in the story.

   Cook was upset that there was a mouse in her kitchen. She said that the only kind of mouse to have is a dead mouse. She yelled at Mig to kill Despereaux. Mig tried to kill him, but she ended up cutting off his tail instead. Despereaux escaped into the pantry. Then, Cook was angry with Mig.

2. Is the relationship between Cook, Mig, and Despereaux positive or negative?

   The relationship is negative.

396 THE TALE OF DESPEREAUX (H)

3. The events of the excerpt happen right before Despereaux enters the dungeon to rescue Princess Pea. How do Cook and Despereaux act toward each other in the excerpt?

   Cook is nice to Despereaux and offers him soup. But, Despereaux isn't sure he trusts Cook. Cook is anxious because she's not sure that her soup is good. Despereaux makes her feel better when he says that the soup is wonderful. Cook's soup makes Despereaux feel better.

4. How has the relationship between Cook and Despereaux changed?

   Their relationship is more positive. They make each other feel better.

THE TALE OF DESPEREAUX (H) 397

TRY IT **Practice Words from *The Tale of Despereaux*, Chapters 41–46**

Students will answer questions to demonstrate their understanding of the vocabulary words from the reading.

WRAP-UP

Question About *The Tale of Despereaux*, Chapters 41–46

Students will answer a question to show that they understand how to identify personification.

Handwriting

Students should gather their handwriting materials and begin where they left off. Remind students to form letters carefully and correctly.

TIP Set a timer to help students stay focused during handwriting practice.

The Tale of Despereaux (I)

Lesson Overview

ACTIVITY	ACTIVITY TITLE	TIME	ONLINE/OFFLINE
GET READY	Introduction to *The Tale of Despereaux* (I)	**1** minute	online
	Spelling List 17 Review Game	**10** minutes	online
	Recall *The Tale of Despereaux*, Chapters 41–46	**5** minutes	online
	Before You Read *The Tale of Despereaux*, Chapters 47–Coda	**5** minutes	online
READ	*The Tale of Despereaux*, Chapters 47–Coda	**30** minutes	offline
	Check-In: *The Tale of Despereaux*, Chapters 47–Coda	**5** minutes	online
LEARN AND TRY IT	A Theme Is a Lesson About Life	**10** minutes	online
	Determine Themes	**10** minutes	online
	Apply: Theme	**13** minutes	online
	Write About a Theme LEARNING COACH CHECK-IN	**15** minutes	offline
	Practice Words from *The Tale of Despereaux*, Chapters 47–Coda	**8** minutes	online
WRAP-UP	Question About *The Tale of Despereaux*, Chapters 47–Coda	**2** minutes	online
	Handwriting	**6** minutes	offline

Content Background

In this lesson, students will finish reading *The Tale of Despereaux*. They will explore the themes in the novel. They will learn that themes are usually not stated directly but can be determined from the characters' actions and experiences.

A *theme* is a message the author conveys in the story. A story may have more than one theme. For example, one theme of *The Tale of Despereaux* is that one's words can seriously affect others. This theme is supported by details that explain how hearing the princess use the word *rat* like an insult dramatically impacts Roscuro. He decides he does not want to be a rat, and he feels ashamed of being a rat.

Students will learn that a topic and a theme are not the same thing, but they are related. A *topic* is stated in one or two words, while a theme is stated in a complete sentence. A *theme* is a lesson the author conveys about a topic. For

MATERIALS

Supplied

- *The Tale of Despereaux* by Kate DiCamillo
- *Summit English Language Arts 3 Activity Book*
  - Write About a Theme
- handwriting workbook

KEYWORDS

theme – the author's message or big idea

topic – the subject of a text

example, "overcoming obstacles" is a topic found throughout *The Tale of Despereaux*. One of the novel's themes related to this topic is "having hope can help you overcome obstacles."

The Tale of Despereaux, Chapters 47–Coda Synopsis

After losing the spool of thread, Despereaux wants to turn back but continues on into the dungeon. There he comes across the rat Botticelli, who tricks Despereaux into thinking that he wants to help rescue the princess. Botticelli leads Despereaux through the maze of the dungeon heading toward the princess. The story then goes back in time to Roscuro leading Mig and Pea into the dungeon. Roscuro reveals his true intention to keep the princess in the dungeon, a different plan than he had told Mig. When Mig realizes this, she sobs that she wants her mother. Having recently lost her own mother, Pea empathizes with Mig and acts kindly toward her. Roscuro demands that Mig chain up the princess, but Mig refuses. She threatens Roscuro with the knife and tells him to lead them out of the dungeon. Roscuro refuses, so the three sit in the dark dungeon until Despereaux arrives. Roscuro threatens Despereaux, which prompts Mig to cut off Roscuro's tail. Despereaux holds Roscuro at bay with his needle, but he realizes he does not want to kill Roscuro. Roscuro smells soup on Despereaux, which makes him cry. He explains that he brought the princess to the dungeon only because he wanted some light of his own. The princess promises Roscuro that, if he leads them out of the dungeon, she will have Cook make him soup. They then all go upstairs and have soup.

Lesson Goals

- Practice all spelling words online.
- Read Chapters 47–Coda of *The Tale of Despereaux*.
- Determine themes of a story.
- Find details that support themes of a story.
- Practice vocabulary words.
- Develop letter formation fluency.

GET READY

Introduction to *The Tale of Despereaux* (I)

Students will get a glimpse of what they will learn about in the lesson. They will also read the lesson goals and keywords. Have students select each keyword and preview its definition.

Spelling List 17 Review Game

Students will practice all spelling words from the workshop.

Recall *The Tale of Despereaux*, Chapters 41–46

Students will answer some questions to review the reading that they have already completed.

Before You Read *The Tale of Despereaux*, Chapters 47–Coda

Students will be introduced to some key vocabulary words that they will encounter in the upcoming reading.

READ

The Tale of Despereaux, Chapters 47–Coda

Students will read Chapters 47–Coda of *The Tale of Despereaux* by Kate DiCamillo.

Check-In: *The Tale of Despereaux*, Chapters 47–Coda

Students will answer several questions to demonstrate their comprehension of Chapters 47–Coda of *The Tale of Despereaux*.

LEARN AND TRY IT

LEARN A Theme Is a Lesson About Life

Student will learn that themes are developed through characters' actions and experiences.

TRY IT Determine Themes

Students will analyze passages to determine themes of *The Tale of Despereaux* and find details that support those themes.

TRY IT Apply: Theme

Students will apply to a new work what they've learned about determining the theme of a story.

TRY IT Write About a Theme

Students will complete Write About a Theme in *Summit English Language Arts 3 Activity Book*.

LEARNING COACH CHECK-IN This activity page provides students a choice of characters to focus on. Their answers will vary depending on the character they choose, so it's important that you review students' responses. Give students feedback, using the sample answers provided to guide you.

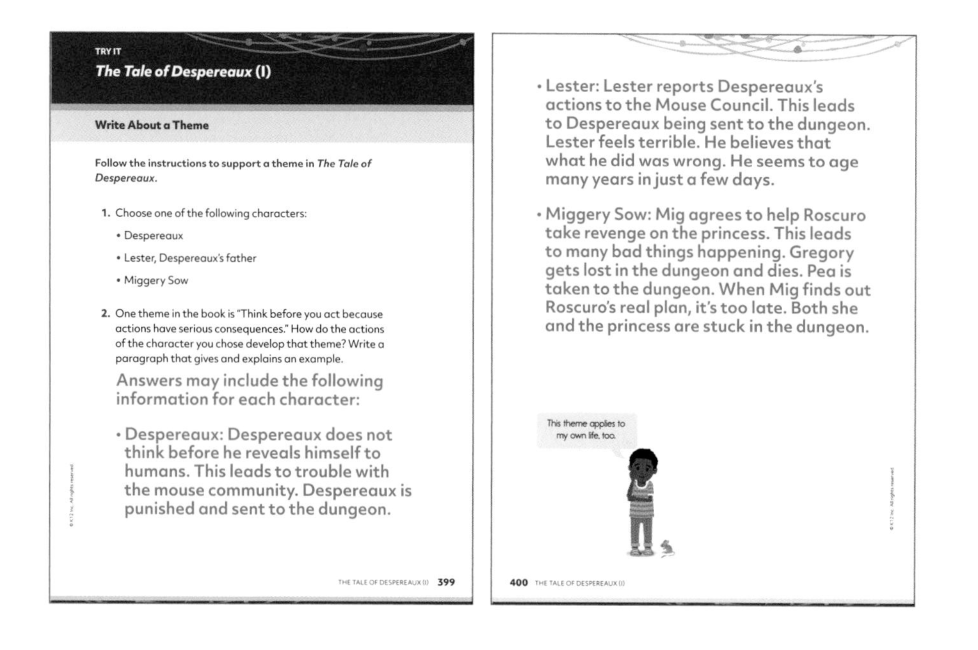

TRY IT

The Tale of Despereaux (I)

Write About a Theme

Follow the instructions to support a theme in *The Tale of Despereaux*.

1. Choose one of the following characters:
   - Despereaux
   - Lester, Despereaux's father
   - Miggery Sow
2. One theme in the book is "Think before you act because actions have serious consequences." How do the actions of the character you chose develop that theme? Write a paragraph that gives and explains an example.

   Answers may include the following information for each character:

   - Despereaux: Despereaux does not think before he reveals himself to humans. This leads to trouble with the mouse community. Despereaux is punished and sent to the dungeon.

THE TALE OF DESPEREAUX (I) 399

- Lester: Lester reports Despereaux's actions to the Mouse Council. This leads to Despereaux being sent to the dungeon. Lester feels terrible. He believes that what he did was wrong. He seems to age many years in just a few days.
- Miggery Sow: Mig agrees to help Roscuro take revenge on the princess. This leads to many bad things happening. Gregory gets lost in the dungeon and dies. Pea is taken to the dungeon. When Mig finds out Roscuro's real plan, it's too late. Both she and the princess are stuck in the dungeon.

400 THE TALE OF DESPEREAUX (I)

TRY IT Practice Words from *The Tale of Despereaux*, Chapters 47–Coda

Students will answer questions to demonstrate their understanding of the vocabulary words from the reading.

WRAP-UP

Question About *The Tale of Despereaux*, Chapters 47–Coda

Students will answer a question to show that they understand how to determine the theme of a story.

Handwriting

Students should gather their handwriting materials and begin where they left off. Remind students to form letters carefully and correctly.

TIP Set a timer to help students stay focused during handwriting practice.

The Tale of Despereaux Wrap-Up

Lesson Overview

ACTIVITY	ACTIVITY TITLE	TIME	ONLINE/OFFLINE
GET READY	Introduction to *The Tale of Despereaux* Wrap-Up	**1** minute	online
TRY IT	Read and Record	**8** minutes	online
	Reflect on Overcoming Obstacles LEARNING COACH CHECK-IN	**30** minutes	offline
	Review *The Tale of Despereaux*	**20** minutes	online
QUIZ	*The Tale of Despereaux*	**30** minutes	online
	Spelling List 17	**10** minutes	online
WRAP-UP	More Language Arts Practice	**15** minutes	online
	Handwriting	**6** minutes	offline

Lesson Goals

- Read aloud to practice fluency.
- Write about the idea of overcoming obstacles.
- Review what you learned.
- Take a reading quiz.
- Take a spelling quiz.
- Develop letter formation fluency.

MATERIALS

Supplied

- *The Tale of Despereaux* by Kate DiCamillo
- *Summit English Language Arts 3 Activity Book*
  - Reflect on Overcoming Obstacles
- handwriting workbook

GET READY

Introduction to *The Tale of Despereaux* Wrap-Up

Students will read the lesson goals.

TRY IT

Read and Record

Good readers read quickly, smoothly, and with expression. This is called *fluency*. Students will record themselves reading aloud. They will listen to their recording and think about how quick, smooth, and expressive they sound.

TIP Encourage students to rerecord as needed.

Reflect on Overcoming Obstacles

Students will complete Reflect on Overcoming Obstacles in *Summit English Language Arts 3 Activity Book*.

LEARNING COACH CHECK-IN This activity page contains open-ended questions, so it's important that you review students' responses.

TRY IT

***The Tale of Despereaux* Wrap-Up**

Reflect on Overcoming Obstacles

Answer the questions in complete sentences.

Answers will vary.

1. The idea of overcoming obstacles is throughout *The Tale of Despereaux*. Think of a time that you had to overcome an obstacle. What was the obstacle?

2. How did you overcome that obstacle?

THE TALE OF DESPEREAUX WRAP-UP **401**

3. What did you learn from your experience?

402 THE TALE OF DESPEREAUX WRAP-UP

Review *The Tale of Despereaux*

Students will answer questions to review what they have learned about *The Tale of Despereaux*.

QUIZ

The Tale of Despereaux

Students will complete the *The Tale of Despereaux* quiz.

Spelling List 17

Students will complete the Spelling List 17 quiz.

WRAP-UP

More Language Arts Practice

Students will practice skills according to their individual needs.

Handwriting

Students should gather their handwriting materials and begin where they left off. Remind students to form letters carefully and correctly.

TIP Set a timer to help students stay focused during handwriting practice.

Prefixes

Lesson Overview

ACTIVITY	ACTIVITY TITLE	TIME	ONLINE/OFFLINE
GET READY	Introduction to Prefixes	**1** minute	online
	Look Back at Prefixes	**4** minutes	online
LEARN AND TRY IT	Prefixes	**10** minutes	online
	Practice Using Prefixes	**10** minutes	online
	Apply: Prefixes LEARNING COACH CHECK-IN	**15** minutes	offline
	Review Prefixes	**15** minutes	online
QUIZ	Prefixes	**15** minutes	online
WRAP-UP	More Language Arts Practice	**15** minutes	online
	Go Write! Why Read a Book?	**15** minutes	offline
	Go Read!	**20** minutes	online or offline

Content Background

In this lesson, students will learn that a prefix can be attached to the beginning of a root, or base word, to create a new word. A *prefix* is a word part with its own meaning. For example, *re–* is a prefix that means "again." When it is attached to the beginning of the base word *tell*, it forms *retell*, which means "to tell again." Students will learn the meanings of some of the more common prefixes: *dis–*, *in–*, *pre–*, *un–*, *re–*, and *mis–*. Knowing the meaning of prefixes can help students figure out the meanings of new words and determine words that fit the context of a text.

MATERIALS

Supplied

- *Summit English Language Arts 3 Activity Book*
  - Apply: Prefixes
  - Go Write! Why Read a Book?

Also Needed

- reading material for Go Read!

Advance Preparation

During the Go Read! activity, students will have the option of using the digital library. Allow extra time for students to make their reading selection, or have students make a selection before beginning the lesson.

Lesson Goals

- Practice vocabulary words.
- Identify and determine the meanings of prefixes.
- Use prefixes to determine the meanings of words.
- Take the Prefixes quiz.
- Freewrite about a topic to develop writing fluency and practice letter formation.
- Read independently to develop fluency.

KEYWORDS

affix – a word part attached to a root or base word to create a new word

prefix – a word part with its own meaning that can be added to the beginning of a base word or root to make a new word

GET READ

Introduction to Prefixes

Students will get a glimpse of what they will learn about in the lesson. They will also read the lesson goals and keywords. Have students select each keyword and preview its definition.

Look Back at Prefixes

Students will practice the prerequisite skill of determining the meaning of a word when a prefix is added.

LEARN AND TRY IT

LEARN Prefixes

Students will be introduced to the vocabulary words for the lesson. Then they will learn how to use known words and context clues to determine the meanings of prefixes and words formed with prefixes.

TRY IT Practice Using Prefixes

Students will practice determining the meaning of prefixes and using context clues to determine the prefix needed to correctly form a new word.

TRY IT Apply: Prefixes

Students will complete Apply: Prefixes in *Summit English Language Arts 3 Activity Book*. They will practice forming words with prefixes and using those words in sentences.

LEARNING COACH CHECK-IN This activity page contains open-ended questions, so it's important that you review students' responses. Give students feedback, using the sample answers provided to guide you.

TRY IT

Prefixes

Apply: Prefixes

Write the definition for each prefix.

1. *dis–* not, the opposite of *pre–* before
   in– not *re–* again
   mis– wrong *un–* not

Form new words with prefixes, and then use one of the new words in a sentence.

2. Add prefixes from Question 1 to the word *placed* to form words that match the definitions.
   mis placed: put in the wrong place
   re placed: put something in its place again
   dis placed: moved people or things so they are not in their usual place

3. Choose a word from Question 2. Write 1–2 sentences that show the meaning of the word.
   Possible answer: After my brother left my books on the table, I replaced them on my bookshelf.

PREFIXES 403

4. Add prefixes from Question 1 to the word *cooked* to form words that match the definitions.
   un cooked: not cooked
   re cooked: cooked again
   pre cooked: cooked before or ahead of time

5. Choose a word from Question 4. Write 1–2 sentences that show the meaning of the word.
   Possible answer: To get ready for the party, my mom precooked some of the food the day before.

Answer the question.

6. Which word correctly completes the sentence? Circle the word.
   pretest (inequality) dislike
   Nico said it was a case of ________ when his brother got a bigger piece of cake than he did.

404 PREFIXES

TRY IT Review Prefixes

Students will answer questions to review what they have learned about prefixes.

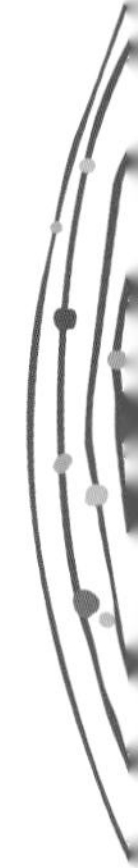

QUIZ

Prefixes

Students will complete the Prefixes quiz.

WRAP-UP

More Language Arts Practice

Students will practice skills according to their individual needs.

Go Write! Why Read a Book?

Students will complete Go Write! Why Read a Book? in *Summit English Language Arts 3 Activity Book*. They will have the option to either respond to a prompt or write about a topic of their choice.

NOTE This activity is intended to build writing fluency. Students should write for the entire allotted time.

SUPPORT If students have trouble writing for the allotted time, prompt them with questions. For example, *Can you tell me more about this?*

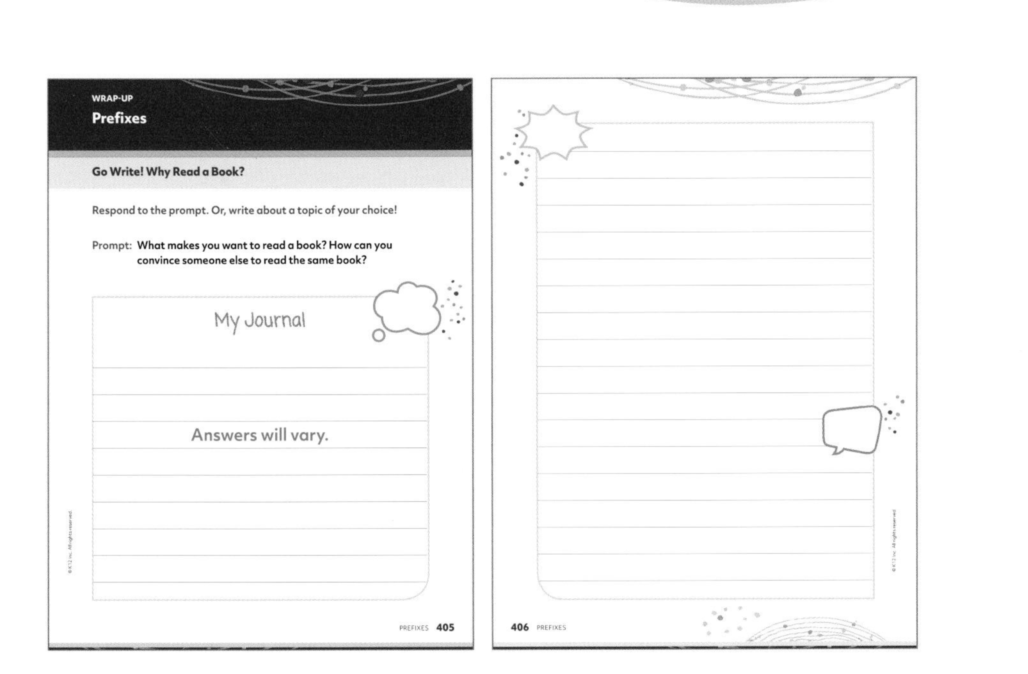

Go Read!

Students will read for pleasure. They should choose a book or a magazine that interests them, or they may choose a selection from the digital library, linked in the online lesson.

- Have students read aloud a few paragraphs of their selection.
- Then have students read silently for the rest of the time.

SUPPORT Students should make no more than five errors in decoding when they read aloud a few paragraphs of their Go Read! selection. If students struggle or make more than five errors, they need to select a different (and easier) text for the Go Read! activity.

TIP Have students select something to read ahead of time to help them stay focused.

Opinion Writing: Prewriting (A)

Lesson Overview

ACTIVITY	ACTIVITY TITLE	TIME	ONLINE/OFFLINE
GET READY	Introduction to Opinion Writing: Prewriting (A)	**1** minute	
	Spelling List 18 Pretest LEARNING COACH CHECK-IN	**10** minutes	and
	Look Back at Verb Tense	**4** minutes	
LEARN AND TRY IT	Subject-Verb Agreement	**10** minutes	
	Use Correct Subject-Verb Agreement	**15** minutes	
	Explore a Model Persuasive Essay	**10** minutes	
	Respond to a Persuasive Essay	**10** minutes	
	Brainstorming for a Persuasive Essay	**10** minutes	
	Brainstorm for Your Persuasive Essay LEARNING COACH CHECK-IN	**20** minutes	
WRAP-UP	Questions About Agreement and Brainstorming	**4** minutes	
	Handwriting	**8** minutes	
	Go Read!	**18** minutes	or

Content Background

Students will begin working on a **persuasive essay** about a way to improve their city, town, or neighborhood. They will complete this assignment over the course of several lessons by following the writing process. Students will begin by prewriting.

Writing Process

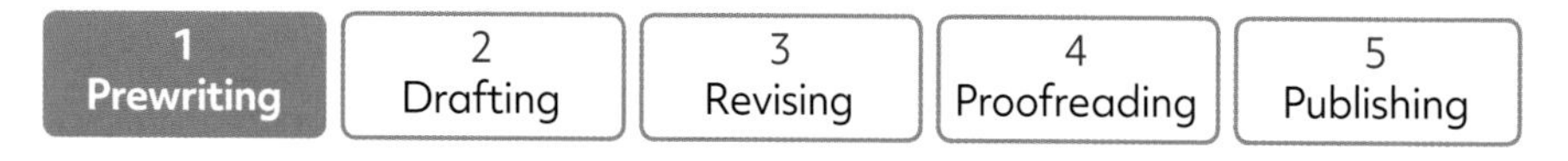

During **prewriting**, writers choose a topic and create a plan for their writing assignment. In this lesson, students will complete the first part of prewriting, choosing a topic. To do that, they'll **brainstorm** by listing and evaluating several different topics. They will also choose an audience for their essay.

MATERIALS

Supplied

- *Summit English Language Arts 3 Activity Book*
  - Spelling List 18 Pretest
  - Model Persuasive Essay
  - Brainstorm for Your Persuasive Essay
- handwriting workbook

Also Needed

- folder for organizing persuasive essay assignment pages
- reading material for Go Read!

Grammar, Usage, and Mechanics A **subject** and **verb** must agree. A singular subject agrees with a singular verb. A plural subject agrees with a plural verb.

Examples: A raindrop falls from the sky.

Raindrops fall from the sky.

The pronouns *I* and *you* agree with plural verbs.

Example: You say the most thoughtful things!

Other words in the sentence don't affect subject-verb agreement. In this example, the plural subject *days* agrees with the plural verb *make*.

Example: Cold and rainy days always make me sad.

A compound subject joined by *and* agrees with a plual verb.

Example: Pete and Mai swim on the same team.

In a compound or complex sentence, the subject and verb in each part agree.

Examples: My dad plays the drums, but I play the saxophone.

When we play together, the walls shake.

Note that there are many other rules related to subject-verb agreement. Those rules will be covered in later courses.

KEYWORDS

brainstorming – before writing, a way for the writer to come up with ideas

opinion – something that a person thinks or believes but that cannot be proven to be true

persuasive essay – an essay in which the writer tries to convince readers to agree with a stance on an issue

prewriting – the stage or step of writing in which a writer chooses a topic, gathers ideas, and plans what to write

subject – a word or words that tell whom or what the sentence is about

subject-verb agreement – the way a subject and verb match when both are singular or both are plural

verb – a word that shows action or a state of being

Advance Preparation

Gather a folder that students can use to keep all notes and activity pages related to their persuasive essay.

During the Go Read! activity, students will have the option of using the digital library. Allow extra time for students to make their reading selection, or have students make a selection before beginning the lesson.

Lesson Goals

- Take a spelling pretest.
- Use correct subject-verb agreement.
- Read a model persuasive essay, and start planning your own.
- Develop letter formation fluency.
- Read independently to develop fluency.

GET READY

Introduction to Opinion Writing: Prewriting (A)

Students will get a glimpse of what they will learn about in the lesson. They will also read the lesson goals and keywords. Have students select each keyword and preview its definition.

Spelling List 18 Pretest

Students will take a spelling pretest and learn a new spelling pattern.

LEARNING COACH CHECK-IN Have students turn to Spelling List 18 Pretest in *Summit English Language Arts 3 Activity Book* and open the online Spelling Pretest activity. Online, students will listen to the spelling word, type the word in the space indicated, and then check their answer. In the activity book, students will write the correct spelling of the word in the tables provided and indicate with a ✓ or an ✗ if they spelled the word correctly or incorrectly online. Students will repeat this process with the remaining words.

As needed, help students with the interaction between the online activity and the activity book page until they become comfortable with what they need to do. As students practice their spelling words throughout the workshop, they should pay special attention to words they spelled incorrectly on the pretest.

This is the complete list of words students will be tested on.

Word with Triple Consonant Blends				
scrap scrape scream splash splendid	splice split sprain spray	spring sprout squash squat	squeak squeeze squint stranger	strap straw strength stress

NOTE Have students keep their completed activity page in a safe place so they can refer to it later.

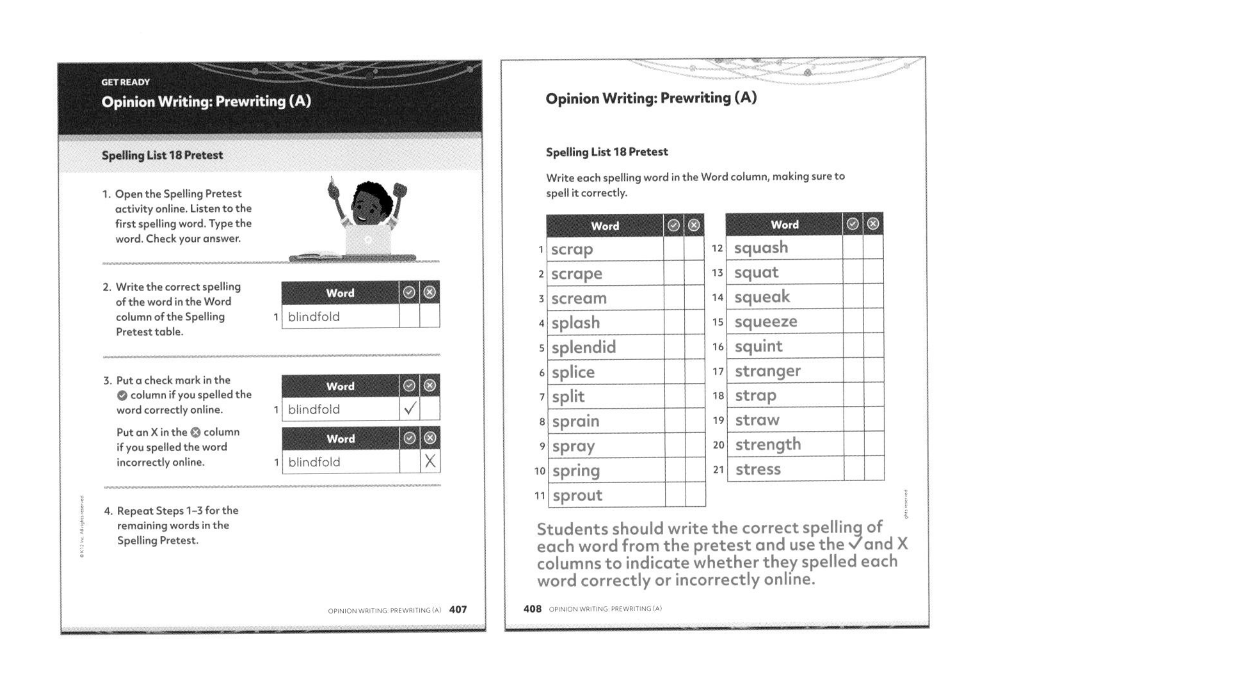

GET READY

Opinion Writing: Prewriting (A)

Spelling List 18 Pretest

1. Open the Spelling Pretest activity online. Listen to the first spelling word. Type the word. Check your answer.
2. Write the correct spelling of the word in the Word column of the Spelling Pretest table.

	Word	✓	⊗
1	blindfold		

3. Put a check mark in the ✓ column if you spelled the word correctly online.

	Word	✓	⊗
1	blindfold	✓	

Put an X in the ⊗ column if you spelled the word incorrectly online.

	Word	✓	⊗
1	blindfold		X

4. Repeat Steps 1–3 for the remaining words in the Spelling Pretest.

OPINION WRITING: PREWRITING (A) 407

Opinion Writing: Prewriting (A)

Spelling List 18 Pretest

Write each spelling word in the Word column, making sure to spell it correctly.

	Word	✓	⊗
1	scrap		
2	scrape		
3	scream		
4	splash		
5	splendid		
6	splice		
7	split		
8	sprain		
9	spray		
10	spring		
11	sprout		

	Word	✓	⊗
12	squash		
13	squat		
14	squeak		
15	squeeze		
16	squint		
17	stranger		
18	strap		
19	straw		
20	strength		
21	stress		

Students should write the correct spelling of each word from the pretest and use the ✓ and X columns to indicate whether they spelled each word correctly or incorrectly online.

408 OPINION WRITING: PREWRITING (A)

Look Back at Verb Tense

Students will practice the prerequisite skill of forming and using the simple past, present, and future verb tenses.

LEARN AND TRY IT

LEARN Subject-Verb Agreement

Students will learn that subjects must always agree with their verbs. They will learn some basic rules of subject-verb agreement.

NOTE This activity does not discuss agreement with *they* used as a singular pronoun. When *they* is used as a singular pronoun, it agrees with a plural verb (as do the pronouns *I* and *you*).

TRY IT Use Correct Subject-Verb Agreement

Students will practice using correct subject-verb agreement. They will answer questions as well as write sentences of their own.

LEARN Explore a Model Persuasive Essay

By reading and exploring a model persuasive essay, students will learn what a persuasive essay is and how it is organized.

TIP The model persuasive essay that students read in the online activity is the same piece of writing on the Model Persuasive Essay activity page. Students may wish to reference and make notes on this page as they complete the online activity.

TRY IT **Respond to a Persuasive Essay**

Students will answer questions about the ideas and organization of the model persuasive essay to ensure that they understand the genre and their writing assignment.

LEARN **Brainstorming for a Persuasive Essay**

Students will explore how a writer brainstorms and chooses a topic for a persuasive essay.

TRY IT **Brainstorm for Your Persuasive Essay**

Students will complete Brainstorm for Your Persuasive Essay in *Summit English Language Arts 3 Activity Book*. They should have the Model Persuasive Essay activity page to refer to as they work.

LEARNING COACH CHECK-IN This activity page contains open-ended questions, so it's important that you review students' responses. Work with students to ensure that they choose a topic that meets the requirements of the assignment. Students also may need help choosing an appropriate audience for the assignment. Note that the audience does not have to be someone who will actually read the essay; rather, it should be someone students have in mind as an audience as they write.

NOTE Have students add the Model Persuasive Essay and their completed Brainstorm for Your Persuasive Essay activity page to the folder they are using to store their persuasive essay assignment pages.

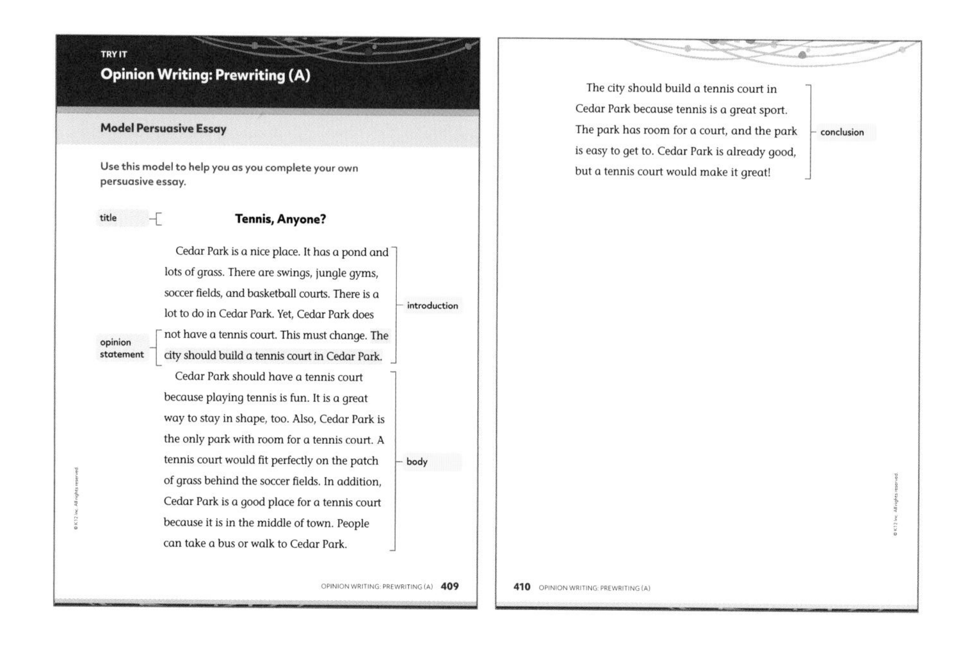

TRY IT

Opinion Writing: Prewriting (A)

Model Persuasive Essay

Use this model to help you as you complete your own persuasive essay.

title — **Tennis, Anyone?**

Cedar Park is a nice place. It has a pond and lots of grass. There are swings, jungle gyms, soccer fields, and basketball courts. There is a lot to do in Cedar Park. Yet, Cedar Park does not have a tennis court. This must change. The city should build a tennis court in Cedar Park. — introduction (opinion statement: "The city should build a tennis court in Cedar Park.")

Cedar Park should have a tennis court because playing tennis is fun. It is a great way to stay in shape, too. Also, Cedar Park is the only park with room for a tennis court. A tennis court would fit perfectly on the patch of grass behind the soccer fields. In addition, Cedar Park is a good place for a tennis court because it is in the middle of town. People can take a bus or walk to Cedar Park. — body

OPINION WRITING: PREWRITING (A) 409

The city should build a tennis court in Cedar Park because tennis is a great sport. The park has room for a court, and the park is easy to get to. Cedar Park is already good, but a tennis court would make it great! — conclusion

410 OPINION WRITING: PREWRITING (A)

TRY IT

Opinion Writing: Prewriting (A)

Brainstorm for Your Persuasive Essay

Read the assignment. You will complete the assignment in steps over multiple lessons.

Prompt: **Write a persuasive essay about a way to improve your city, town, or neighborhood.**

Requirements:

Your persuasive essay should have the following:

- A **title**
- An **introduction** that that gives information about your topic and clearly states your opinion
- At least two **body** paragraphs that have well-developed supporting reasons that are facts or reasonable opinions
- A **conclusion** that restates your opinion in a new way and summarizes your reasons
- **Transitions** such as *because* and *for example* that connect your opinion and reasons
- Words and phrases that are chosen for effect
- Correct **grammar**, **punctuation**, **capitalization**, and **spelling**

OPINION WRITING: PREWRITING (A) 411

Audience: You will choose an audience based on your topic and opinion.

Purpose: Persuade your audience to agree with your opinion.

Length: 350–450 words long, approximately 5–7 handwritten drafting pages or $1\frac{1}{2}$–2 pages typed and double spaced

Answer the questions to choose a topic for your persuasive essay.

1. Think about topics you care about. Examples are *pets*, *reading*, and *recycling*. List as many topics as you can.

   Students should list several topics.

2. Which topics on your list do you care most about?

   Answers to Questions 2 and 3 will vary.

412 OPINION WRITING: PREWRITING (A)

3. Which topics are good ones for a persuasive essay about improving your community? Choose two topics, and restate them as opinions.

   Sample opinion for the topic "pets": Our town should have a dog park.

4. Choose the opinion you most want to write about.

   Topic: Students' topic should be a clearly stated opinion about one way to improve their town, city, or neighborhood.

5. Based on your topic, choose the audience for your essay. Choose one person, business, or group of people.

   Audience: Students' audience should be tailored to their topic. For instance, students may write to a city or county official if they believe an intersection should have a stop sign. Or, students may write to the director of a local food pantry if they have an idea for a community fundraiser.

OPINION WRITING: PREWRITING (A) 413

WRAP-UP

Questions About Agreement and Brainstorming

Students will answer questions to show that they understand subject-verb agreement and how to brainstorm for a persuasive essay.

Handwriting

Students should gather their handwriting materials and begin where they left off. Remind students to form letters carefully and correctly.

TIP Set a timer to help students stay focused during handwriting practice.

Go Read!

Students will read for pleasure. They should choose a book or a magazine that interests them, or they may choose a selection from the digital library, linked in the online lesson.

- Have students read aloud a few paragraphs of their selection.
- Then have students read silently for the rest of the time.

SUPPORT Students should make no more than five errors in decoding when they read aloud a few paragraphs of their Go Read! selection. If students struggle or make more than five errors, they need to select a different (and easier) text for the Go Read! activity.

TIP Have students select something to read ahead of time to help them stay focused.

Opinion Writing: Prewriting (B)

Lesson Overview

ACTIVITY	ACTIVITY TITLE	TIME	ONLINE/OFFLINE
GET READY	Introduction to Opinion Writing: Prewriting (B)	**1** minute	online
	Spelling List 18 Activity Bank	**10** minutes	offline
LEARN AND TRY IT	Adjectives	**10** minutes	online
	Use Adjectives	**10** minutes	online
	Plan a Persuasive Essay	**15** minutes	online
	Plan Your Persuasive Essay LEARNING COACH CHECK-IN	**40** minutes	offline
WRAP-UP	Questions About Adjectives and Supporting an Opinion	**4** minutes	online
	Handwriting	**8** minutes	offline
	Go Read!	**22** minutes	online or offline

Content Background

Students will continue working on their **persuasive essay** about a way to improve their city, town, or neighborhood. They will complete this assignment over the course of several lessons by following the writing process. In this lesson, students will complete the prewriting step.

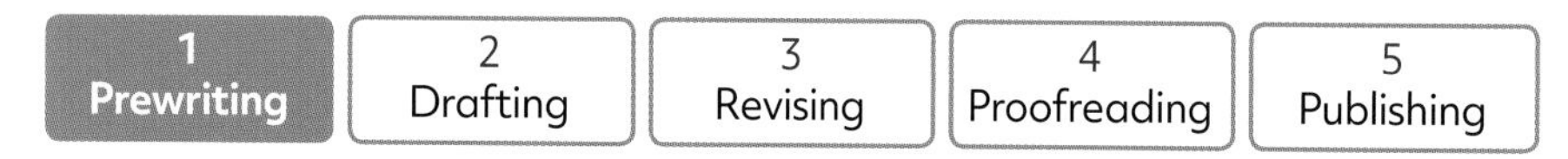

In this part of **prewriting**, students will brainstorm reasons that support their opinion and then complete a graphic organizer that includes what they determine are the most effective reasons to support their opinion.

In a persuasive essay, it's important that reasons are chosen with the essay's audience in mind. After all, the purpose of a persuasive essay is to persuade readers to agree with the opinion expressed in the essay.

MATERIALS

Supplied

- *Summit English Language Arts 3 Activity Book*
  - Spelling List 18 Activity Bank
  - Plan Your Persuasive Essay
- Persuasive Essay Instructions (printout)
- handwriting workbook

Also Needed

- completed Spelling List 18 Pretest activity page from Opinion Writing: Prewriting (A)
- folder in which students are storing persuasive essay assignment pages
- reading material for Go Read!

Grammar, Usage, and Mechanics An **adjective** is a word that describes a noun or pronoun. An adjective usually comes before a noun, but it does not have to. In both of the following examples, the adjective *red* describes the noun *bird*.

Examples: The **red** bird landed on the branch.
The bird was **red**.

An adjective can answer the question, *How many?* or *Which one?*.

Examples: I have **three** siblings.
This sibling is named Luke.

Advance Preparation

Gather students' completed Spelling List 18 Pretest activity page from Opinion Writing: Prewriting (A). Students will refer to this page during Get Ready: Spelling List 18 Activity Bank.

Gather the folder that students are using to store the activity pages related to their persuasive essay. The folder should contain the following:

- Model Persuasive Essay activity page from Opinion Writing: Prewriting (A)
- Students' completed Brainstorm for Your Persuasive Essay activity page from Opinion Writing: Prewriting (A)

During the Go Read! activity, students will have the option of using the digital library. Allow extra time for students to make their reading selection, or have students make a selection before beginning the lesson.

KEYWORDS

adjective – a word that describes a noun or pronoun

opinion – something that a person thinks or believes but that cannot be proven to be true

persuasive essay – an essay in which the writer tries to convince readers to agree with a stance on an issue

prewriting – the stage or step of writing in which a writer chooses a topic, gathers ideas, and plans what to write

reason – a statement that explains why something is or why it should be

Lesson Goals

- Practice all spelling words offline.
- Use an adjective in a sentence.
- Plan your persuasive essay.
- Develop letter formation fluency.
- Read independently to develop fluency.

GET READY

Introduction to Opinion Writing: Prewriting (B)

Students will get a glimpse of what they will learn about in the lesson. They will also read the lesson goals and keywords. Have students select each keyword and preview its definition.

Spelling List 18 Activity Bank

Students will practice all spelling words from the workshop by completing Spelling List 18 Activity Bank from *Summit English Language Arts 3 Activity Book*. Make sure students have their completed Spelling List 18 Pretest activity page from Opinion Writing: Prewriting (A) to refer to during this activity.

Remind students to pay special attention to words they spelled incorrectly on the Spelling Pretest.

GET READY

Opinion Writing: Prewriting (B)

Spelling List 18 Activity Bank

Circle any words in the box that you did not spell correctly on the pretest. Choose one activity to do with your circled words. Do as much of the activity as you can in the time given.

Did you spell all the words on the pretest correctly? Do the one activity with as many spelling words as you can.

scrap	splice	spring	squeak	strap
scrape	split	sprout	squeeze	straw
scream	sprain	squash	squint	strength
splash	spray	squat	stranger	stress
splendid				

Spelling Activity Choices

Silly Sentences

1. Write a silly sentence for each of your spelling words.
2. Underline the spelling word in each sentence.
   Example: The dog was driving a car.
3. Correct any spelling errors.

Spelling Story

1. Write a very short story using each of your spelling words.
2. Underline the spelling words in the story.
3. Correct any spelling errors.

Riddle Me This

1. Write a riddle for each of your spelling words.
   Example: "I have a trunk, but it's not on my car."
2. Write the answer, which is your word, for each riddle.
   Example: Answer: elephant
3. Correct any spelling errors.

RunOnWord

1. Gather some crayons, colored pencils, or markers. Use a different color to write each of your spelling words. Write the words end to end as one long word.
   Example: dogcat**birdfishturtle**
2. Rewrite the words correctly and with proper spacing.
3. Correct any spelling errors.

Complete the activity that you chose.

My chosen activity: ______________

Students should use this page to complete all steps in their chosen activity.

LEARN AND TRY IT

LEARN Adjectives

Students will learn that an adjective describes a noun or a pronoun. They will learn how to use an adjective in a sentence.

NOTE This activity is an introduction to adjectives. Students will continue to learn about adjectives (e.g., ordering adjectives, punctuating lists of adjectives) in future courses.

TRY IT Use Adjectives

Students will practice identifying, explaining the function of, and using adjectives in sentences. They will also write their own sentences that use adjectives.

LEARN Plan a Persuasive Essay

Students will learn how to brainstorm and choose reasons that support the opinion in their persuasive essay. They will also learn how to fill out a graphic organizer to plan their essay.

TRY IT Plan Your Persuasive Essay

Students will complete Plan Your Persuasive Essay in *Summit English Language Arts 3 Activity Book*. They should have their completed Brainstorm for Your Persuasive Essay activity page and Model Persuasive Essay to refer to as they work.

LEARNING COACH CHECK-IN This activity page contains open-ended questions, so it's important that you review students' responses. Give students feedback about their reasons and organization. Students should store their completed Plan Your Persuasive Essay activity page in the folder they are using to store their persuasive essay assignment pages.

NOTE If you or students wish, you can download and print another copy of the Persuasive Essay Instructions online.

TRY IT

Opinion Writing: Prewriting (B)

Plan Your Persuasive Essay

Write the topic for your persuasive essay. List reasons that support your opinion. Next to each reason, write an *F* if the reason is a fact or an *O* if the reason is an opinion.

My topic is Answers will vary.

Reasons	Fact or Opinion

Complete the graphic organizer to plan your persuasive essay.

Topic

My Opinion About the Topic

Reason 1

Reason 2

Reason 3

Why Readers Should Agree with Me

WRAP-UP

Questions About Adjectives and Supporting an Opinion

Students will answer questions to show that they understand the function of an adjective and how to effectively support an opinion.

Handwriting

Students should gather their handwriting materials and begin where they left off. Remind students to form letters carefully and correctly.

TIP Set a timer to help students stay focused during handwriting practice.

Go Read!

Students will read for pleasure. They should choose a book or a magazine that interests them, or they may choose a selection from the digital library, linked in the online lesson.

- Have students read aloud a few paragraphs of their selection.
- Then have students read silently for the rest of the time.

SUPPORT Students should make no more than five errors in decoding when they read aloud a few paragraphs of their Go Read! selection. If students struggle or make more than five errors, they need to select a different (and easier) text for the Go Read! activity.

TIP Have students select something to read ahead of time to help them stay focused.

Opinion Writing: Drafting (A)

Lesson Overview

ACTIVITY	ACTIVITY TITLE	TIME	ONLINE/OFFLINE
GET READY	Introduction to Opinion Writing: Drafting (A)	**1** minute	online
	Spelling List 18 Practice	**10** minutes	online
LEARN AND TRY IT	Adverbs	**10** minutes	online
	Use Adverbs	**10** minutes	online
	Draft a Persuasive Essay	**10** minutes	online
	Draft Your Persuasive Essay **LEARNING COACH CHECK-IN**	**55** minutes	offline
WRAP-UP	Questions About Adverbs and Introductions	**4** minutes	online
	Go Read!	**20** minutes	online or offline

Content Background

Students will continue working on their **persuasive essay** about a way to improve their city, town, or neighborhood. They will complete this assignment over the course of several lessons by following the writing process. In this lesson, students will begin drafting their essay.

Writing Process

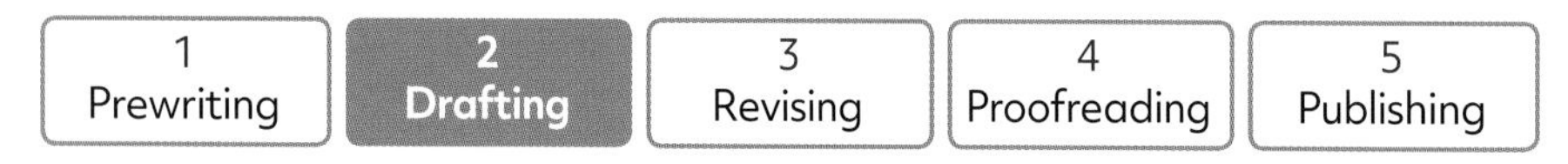

During **drafting**, students will follow their completed plan to write a draft of their persuasive essay. Students are expected to write about half of their draft in this lesson (although they may write more if they wish). They will have time to finish their draft in Opinion Writing: Drafting (B), and they will submit their draft in Opinion Writing: Drafting (C).

Grammar, Usage, and Mechanics An **adverb** is a word that describes a verb, an adjective, or another adverb. An adverb can describe how, when, or where an action takes place.

MATERIALS

Supplied

- *Summit English Language Arts 3 Activity Book*
  - Draft Your Persuasive Essay
- Persuasive Essay Instructions (printout)
- Drafting Paper (printout)

Also Needed

- folder in which students are storing persuasive essay assignment pages
- reading material for Go Read!

Describing How: Lisa walked **carefully** toward the door. (The adverb *carefully* tells how Lisa walked.)

Describing When: Rodney will jog **later**. (The adverb *later* tells when Rodney will jog.)

Describing Where: The children played a game **outside** for an hour. (The adverb *outside* tells where the children played.)

An adverb can tell more about an adjective or another adverb.

Describing an Adjective: The **incredibly** long race had a **very** close finish. (The adverb *incredibly* describes the adjective *long*, and the adverb *very* describes the adjective *close*.)

Describing Another Adverb: The second-place finisher ran *too* slowly at the end. (The adverb *too* describes the adverb *slowly*.)

Advance Preparation

Gather the folder that students are using to store the activity pages related to their persuasive essay. The folder should contain the following:

- Model Persuasive Essay activity page from Opinion Writing: Prewriting (A)
- Students' completed Brainstorm for Your Persuasive Essay activity page from Opinion Writing: Prewriting (A)
- Students' completed Plan Your Persuasive Essay activity page from Opinion Writing: Prewriting (B)

During the Go Read! activity, students will have the option of using the digital library. Allow extra time for students to make their reading selection, or have students make a selection before beginning the lesson.

Lesson Goals

- Practice all spelling words online.
- Use an adverb in a sentence.
- Begin drafting your persuasive essay.
- Read independently to develop fluency.

KEYWORDS

adverb – a word that describes a verb, an adjective, or another adverb

drafting – of writing, the stage or step in which the writer first writes the piece

opinion – something that a person thinks or believes but that cannot be proven to be true

persuasive essay – an essay in which the writer tries to convince readers to agree with a stance on an issue

reason – a statement that explains why something is or why it should be

GET READY

Introduction to Opinion Writing: Drafting (A)

Students will get a glimpse of what they will learn about in the lesson. They will also read the lesson goals and keywords. Have students select each keyword and preview its definition.

Spelling List 18 Practice

Students will practice all spelling words from the workshop.

OPTIONAL Students may do an activity from Spelling List 18 Activity Bank instead of the online practice activity.

LEARN AND TRY IT

LEARN Adverbs

Students will learn that an adverb describes a verb, an adjective, or another adverb. They will learn how to use an adverb in a sentence.

TIP Many adverbs end in the letters *–ly* (e.g., *quickly*, *nicely*), but some do not (e.g., *fast*, *soon*).

NOTE This activity is an introduction to adverbs. Students will continue to learn about adverbs (e.g., using relative adverbs, punctuation after an introductory adverb) in future courses.

TRY IT Use Adverbs

Students will practice identifying, explaining the function of, and using adverbs in sentences. They will also write their own sentences that use adverbs.

LEARN Draft a Persuasive Essay

Students will explore how to use their prewriting work to begin drafting their persuasive essay.

TRY IT Draft Your Persuasive Essay

Students will complete half of their draft using Draft Your Persuasive Essay in *Summit English Language Arts 3 Activity Book*. Make sure students have their completed Plan Your Persuasive Essay activity page to refer to as they work.

LEARNING COACH CHECK-IN Review students' in-progress draft. Ensure that students' draft is in line with the assignment criteria outlined on the Brainstorm for Your Persuasive Essay activity page. Students should store their draft in the folder they are using to organize their writing assignment pages.

TIP Encourage students to reread the Model Persuasive Essay before beginning their own draft. Discuss the strengths of the model.

SUPPORT Have students use their graphic organizer to talk through each paragraph, speaking in complete sentences, adding details to explain each of their reasons, and using transitions to connect ideas. Point out to students when they add a detail or transition (and prompt them to add details and transitions at appropriate points). Repeat this process for each paragraph, as needed.

NOTE If you or students wish, you can download and print another copy of the Persuasive Essay Instructions online. Additional sheets of Drafting Paper are also available online.

TRY IT

Opinion Writing: Drafting (A)

Draft Your Persuasive Essay

Write the first draft of your persuasive essay. Write only on the white rows. You will use the purple rows for revisions later.

Title:

start here ►

Answers will vary.

keep writing ►

Draft Page 1

OPINION WRITING: DRAFTING (A) 421

keep writing ►

Draft Page 2

422 OPINION WRITING: DRAFTING (A)

keep writing ►

Draft Page 3

OPINION WRITING: DRAFTING (A) 423

keep writing ►

Draft Page 4

424 OPINION WRITING: DRAFTING (A)

keep writing ►

Draft Page 5

OPINION WRITING: DRAFTING (A) 425

keep writing ►

Draft Page 6

426 OPINION WRITING: DRAFTING (A)

keep writing ►

Draft Page 7

OPINION WRITING: DRAFTING (A) 427

Draft Page 8

428 OPINION WRITING: DRAFTING (A)

WRAP-UP

Questions About Adverbs and Introductions

Students will answer questions to show that they understand the function of an adverb and how to draft the introduction to a persuasive essay.

Go Read!

Students will read for pleasure. They should choose a book or a magazine that interests them, or they may choose a selection from the digital library, linked in the online lesson.

- Have students read aloud a few paragraphs of their selection.
- Then have students read silently for the rest of the time.

SUPPORT Students should make no more than five errors in decoding when they read aloud a few paragraphs of their Go Read! selection. If students struggle or make more than five errors, they need to select a different (and easier) text for the Go Read! activity.

TIP Have students select something to read ahead of time to help them stay focused.

Opinion Writing: Drafting (B)

Lesson Overview

ACTIVITY	ACTIVITY TITLE	TIME	ONLINE/OFFLINE
GET READY	Introduction to Opinion Writing: Drafting (B)	1 minute	online
	Spelling List 18 Review Game	10 minutes	online
LEARN AND TRY IT	Comparative and Superlative Forms	10 minutes	online
	Use Comparative and Superlative Forms	15 minutes	online
	Finish Drafting a Persuasive Essay	10 minutes	online
	Finish Drafting Your Persuasive Essay LEARNING COACH CHECK-IN	50 minutes	offline
WRAP-UP	Questions About Comparisons and Conclusions	4 minutes	online
	Go Read!	20 minutes	online or offline

Content Background

Students will continue working on their **persuasive essay** about a way to improve their city, town, or neighborhood. They will complete this assignment over the course of several lessons by following the writing process. In this lesson, students will finish their draft. They will submit their draft in the next lesson. In later lessons, they will revise, proofread, and publish their draft as a business letter.

Writing Process

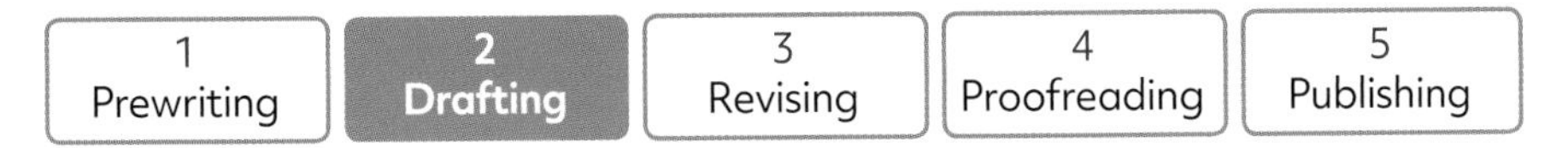

Grammar, Usage, and Mechanics Adjectives and adverbs can be used to compare things. A **comparative form** compares two things. A **superlative form** compares more than two things.

In general, form comparative adjectives by adding *–er*. Form most superlative adjectives by adding *–est*.

> **Examples:** Benji is loud, but his father is **louder**. (The comparative adjective *louder* compares two people: Benji and his father.)
>
> Benji is the **youngest** of the four children in his family. (The superlative adjective *youngest* compares four children.)

MATERIALS

Supplied

- *Summit English Language Arts 3 Activity Book*
  - Draft Your Persuasive Essay
- Persuasive Essay Instructions (printout)
- Drafting Paper (printout)

Also Needed

- folder in which students are storing persuasive essay assignment pages
- reading material for Go Read!

Many adjectives that have two syllables and all adjectives that have three or more syllables use *more* and *most* or *less* and *least* to form the comparative and superlative.

> **Example:** Chess is **more** difficult than checkers, but underwater chess is the **most** difficult game of all.

In general, use the words *more* or *less* to form comparative adverbs, and use *most* or *least* to form superlative adverbs.

> **Examples:** Esha runs quickly, but her brother runs **more quickly**. (The comparative adverb *more quickly* compares how Esha and her brother run.)
>
> Their dog Kippy runs the **most quickly** of the three of them. (The superlative adverb *most quickly* compares how Esha, her brother, and their dog run.)

Some short adverbs add *–er* and *–est* to make the comparative and superlative forms.

> **Example:** Esha runs **faster** than her brother, but their dog Kippy runs the **fastest** of all.

KEYWORDS

comparative form – the form of an adjective or adverb used to compare two things

drafting – of writing, the stage or step in which the writer first writes the piece

opinion – something that a person thinks or believes but that cannot be proven to be true

persuasive essay – an essay in which the writer tries to convince readers to agree with a stance on an issue

reason – a statement that explains why something is or why it should be

superlative form – the form of an adjective or adverb that compares more than two things

Advance Preparation

Gather the folder that students are using to store the activity pages related to their persuasive essay. The folder should contain the following:

- Model Persuasive Essay activity page from Opinion Writing: Prewriting (A)
- Students' completed Brainstorm for Your Persuasive Essay activity page from Opinion Writing: Prewriting (A)
- Students' completed Plan Your Persuasive Essay activity page from Opinion Writing: Prewriting (B)
- Students' in-progress Draft Your Persuasive Essay activity page from Opinion Writing: Drafting (A)

During the Go Read! activity, students will have the option of using the digital library. Allow extra time for students to make their reading selection, or have students make a selection before beginning the lesson.

Lesson Goals

- Practice all spelling words online.
- Form and use adjectives and adverbs that compare.
- Finish the draft of your persuasive essay.
- Read independently to develop fluency.

GET READY

Introduction to Opinion Writing: Drafting (B)

Students will get a glimpse of what they will learn about in the lesson. They will also read the lesson goals and keywords. Have students select each keyword and preview its definition.

Spelling List 18 Review Game

Students will practice all spelling words from the workshop.

LEARN AND TRY IT

LEARN Comparative and Superlative Forms

Students will learn how to form and use the comparative and superlative forms of adjectives and adverbs.

TIP Students' may accidentally use *more* or *most* in addition to *–er* and *–est*.

Incorrect: Today is *more warmer* than yesterday.

Correct: Today is *warmer* than yesterday.

TRY IT Use Comparative and Superlative Forms

Students will practice forming and using comparative and superlative forms of adjectives and adverbs. They will also write their own sentences that use these forms.

LEARN Finish Drafting a Persuasive Essay

Students will explore how to write the conclusion to a persuasive essay.

TRY IT Finish Drafting Your Persuasive Essay

Students will complete the draft of their persuasive essay using their Draft Your Persuasive Essay activity page in *Summit English Language Arts 3 Activity Book*. Make sure students have their prewriting work to refer to as they work.

LEARNING COACH CHECK-IN Review students' completed draft. Ensure that students' draft is in line with the assignment criteria outlined on the Brainstorm for Your Persuasive Essay activity page. Students should store their draft in the folder they are using to organize their writing assignment pages. They will turn in their draft in a later lesson.

NOTE If you or students wish, you can download and print another copy of the Persuasive Essay Instructions online. Additional sheets of Drafting Paper are also available online.

TRY IT

Opinion Writing: Drafting (A)

Draft Your Persuasive Essay

Write the first draft of your persuasive essay. Write only on the white rows. You will use the purple rows for revisions later.

Title: ____________________

start here ►

Answers will vary.

keep writing ►

Draft Page 1

OPINION WRITING: DRAFTING (A) 421

keep writing ►

Draft Page 2

422 OPINION WRITING: DRAFTING (A)

keep writing ►

Draft Page 3

OPINION WRITING: DRAFTING (A) 423

keep writing ►

Draft Page 4

424 OPINION WRITING: DRAFTING (A)

keep writing ►

Draft Page 5

OPINION WRITING: DRAFTING (A) 425

keep writing ►

Draft Page 6

426 OPINION WRITING: DRAFTING (A)

keep writing ►

Draft Page 7

OPINION WRITING: DRAFTING (A) 427

Draft Page 8

428 OPINION WRITING: DRAFTING (A)

WRAP-UP

Questions About Comparisons and Conclusions

Students will answer questions to show that they understand comparative and superlative forms and how to conclude a persuasive essay.

Go Read!

Students will read for pleasure. They should choose a book or a magazine that interests them, or they may choose a selection from the digital library, linked in the online lesson.

- Have students read aloud a few paragraphs of their selection.
- Then have students read silently for the rest of the time.

SUPPORT Students should make no more than five errors in decoding when they read aloud a few paragraphs of their Go Read! selection. If students struggle or make more than five errors, they need to select a different (and easier) text for the Go Read! activity.

TIP Have students select something to read ahead of time to help them stay focused.

Opinion Writing: Drafting (C)

Lesson Overview

ACTIVITY	ACTIVITY TITLE	TIME	ONLINE/OFFLINE
GET READY	Introduction to Opinion Writing: Drafting (C)	**1** minute	
TRY IT	Review Adjectives, Adverbs, and Agreement	**10** minutes	
QUIZ	Adjectives, Adverbs, and Agreement	**20** minutes	
	Spelling List 18	**10** minutes	
LEARN AND TRY IT	Parts of a Business Letter	**15** minutes	
	Turn Your Persuasive Essay into a Business Letter **LEARNING COACH CHECK-IN**	**20** minutes	
WRAP-UP	Turn In Your Persuasive Essay Draft and Business Letter Page	**1** minute	
	More Language Arts Practice	**15** minutes	
	Handwriting	**8** minutes	
	Go Read!	**20** minutes	or

Content Background

Students will continue working on their **persuasive essay** about a way to improve their city, town, or neighborhood. They will complete this assignment over the course of several lessons by following the writing process. In this lesson, students will draft the parts they need to turn their persuasive essay into a business letter. In later lessons, they will revise, proofread, and publish their draft as a business letter.

Writing Process

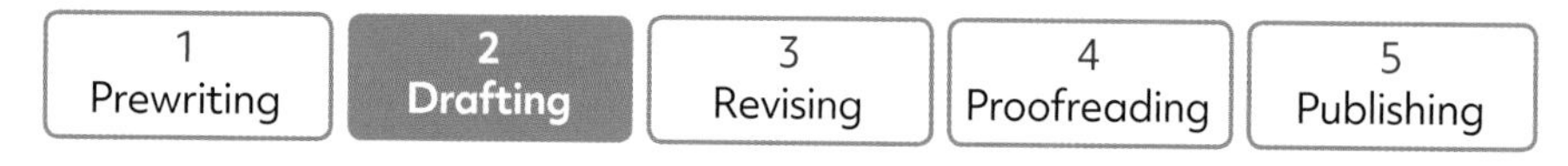

Students will learn that one way to use a persuasive essay in the real world is to turn it into a business letter. They will learn about the parts of a business letter, including the **heading**, **inside address**, **salutation**, **body**, **closing**, and **signature**. These parts are labeled on the Model Business Letter activity page.

MATERIALS

Supplied

- *Summit English Language Arts 3 Activity Book*
  - Model Business Letter
  - Turn Your Persuasive Essay into a Business Letter
- handwriting workbook

Also Needed

- folder in which students are storing persuasive essay assignment pages
- reading material for Go Read!

Grammar, Usage, and Mechanics When writing a letter, it is important to use proper punctuation. Use a comma to separate the day and the year in a date.

Example: August 11**,** 2020

Use a comma between the city and state in a U.S. address.

Example: 88 Lincoln Lane
Lexington**,** VA 24450

In a friendly letter, use a comma after the greeting. In a business letter, use a colon.

Examples: Dear Chloe**,**
Dear Ms. Hall**:**

Use a comma after the closing.

Example: Sincerely**,**

Advance Preparation

Gather the folder that students are using to store the activity pages related to their persuasive essay. The folder should contain the following:

- Model Persuasive Essay activity page from Opinion Writing: Prewriting (A)
- Students' completed Brainstorm for Your Persuasive Essay activity page from Opinion Writing: Prewriting (A)
- Students' completed Plan Your Persuasive Essay activity page from Opinion Writing: Prewriting (B)
- Students' completed draft from Opinion Writing: Drafting (B)

During the Go Read! activity, students will have the option of using the digital library. Allow extra time for students to make their reading selection, or have students make a selection before beginning the lesson.

Lesson Goals

- Review adjectives, adverbs, and subject-verb agreement.
- Take a quiz on adjectives, adverbs, and subject-verb agreement.
- Take a spelling quiz.
- Learn about the parts of a business letter.
- Write the parts that you need to turn your persuasive essay into a business letter.
- Submit your persuasive essay draft and business letter page.
- Develop letter formation fluency.
- Read independently to develop fluency.

KEYWORDS

body – the main text of a business letter

closing – the part of a business letter that follows the body text, containing a phrase such as "Sincerely" or "Yours truly"

heading – the first part of a letter that has the writer's address and the date

inside address – the part of a business or formal letter that comes after the heading and before the greeting, made up of the name and address of the person to whom the letter is written

salutation – the greeting of a business letter, which usually says, "Dear (name of recipient)"; it is followed by a colon

signature – the part of a business letter following the closing, consisting of the writer's signature above the writer's typed name

GET READY

Introduction to Opinion Writing: Drafting (C)

Students will get a glimpse of what they will learn about in the lesson. They will also read the lesson goals and keywords. Have students select each keyword and preview its definition.

TRY IT

Review Adjectives, Adverbs, and Agreement

Students will answer questions to review what they have learned about adjectives and adverbs (including comparative and superlative forms) and subject-verb agreement.

QUIZ

Adjectives, Adverbs, and Agreement

Students will complete the Adjectives, Adverbs, and Agreement quiz.

Spelling List 18

Students will complete the Spelling List 18 quiz.

LEARN AND TRY IT

LEARN Parts of a Business Letter

Students will learn about the parts of a business letter.

TIP The model business letter that students read in the online activity is the same piece of writing on the Model Business Letter activity page. Students may wish to reference and make notes on this page as they complete the online activity.

TRY IT Turn Your Persuasive Essay into a Business Letter

Students will complete Turn Your Persuasive Essay into a Business Letter in *Summit English Language Arts 3 Activity Book*. Make sure students have their completed persuasive essay draft, their prewriting work, and the Model Business Letter to refer to as they work.

LEARNING COACH CHECK-IN This activity page contains open-ended questions, so it's important that you review students' responses. Give students feedback, using the models provided on the activity page to guide you.

NOTE Have students add the Model Business Letter and their completed Turn Your Persuasive Essay into a Business Letter activity page to the folder they are using to store their persuasive essay assignment pages.

TRY IT

Opinion Writing: Drafting (C)

Model Business Letter

Use this model to help you as you complete your own business letter.

heading
88 Lincoln Lane
Lexington, VA 24450
August 11, 2020

inside address
Ms. Mary Hall
Town Council
15 Main Street
Lexington, VA 24450

salutation
Dear Ms. Hall:

body
Cedar Park is a nice place. It has a pond and lots of grass. There are swings, jungle gyms, soccer fields, and basketball courts. There is a lot to do in Cedar Park. Yet, Cedar Park does not have a tennis court. This must change. The city should build a tennis court in Cedar Park.

Cedar Park should have a tennis court because playing tennis is fun. It is a great way to stay in shape, too. Also, Cedar Park is the only park with room for a tennis court. A tennis court would fit perfectly on the patch of grass behind the soccer fields. In addition, Cedar Park is a good place for a tennis court because it is in the middle of town. People can take a bus or walk to Cedar Park.

OPINION WRITING: DRAFTING (C) 429

body
The city should build a tennis court in Cedar Park because tennis is a great sport. The park has room for a court, and the park is easy to get to. Cedar Park is already good, but a tennis court would make it great!

closing
Sincerely,

signature
Johnny
Johnny

430 OPINION WRITING: DRAFTING (C)

TRY IT

Opinion Writing: Drafting (C)

Turn Your Persuasive Essay into a Business Letter

Think about the audience for your persuasive essay.

Answers will vary.

1. If your audience is one person, write that person's name. If your audience is a group of people, narrow down that group to one person whose opinion you would like to change.

You will turn your persuasive essay into a business letter to your audience. Follow the instructions to write the parts you will need to add to your essay. You will add these parts in a later lesson.

2. Write the heading. This is your address and the date. Put a comma between the city and state and between the day and year.

Model heading:

88 Lincoln Lane
Lexington, VA 24450
August 11, 2020

Your heading:

OPINION WRITING: DRAFTING (C) 431

3. Write the inside address. This is the address of your audience. Put a comma between the city and state.

Model inside address:

Ms. Mary Hall
Town Council
15 Main Street
Lexington, VA 24450

Your inside address:

4. Write the salutation. Put a colon after the name.

Model salutation:

Dear Ms. Hall:

Your salutation:

432 OPINION WRITING: DRAFTING (C)

5. Write the closing. Put a comma after the closing.

Model closing:

Sincerely,

Your closing:

6. Write the signature. Sign your first and last names in cursive. Below that, clearly print your first and last names. (Johnny doesn't have a last name, but *you* do!)

Model signature:

Johnny
Johnny

Your signature:

It's a good thing I have been practicing cursive handwriting!

OPINION WRITING: DRAFTING (C) 433

WRAP-UP

Turn In Your Persuasive Essay Draft and Business Letter Page

Students will submit their completed persuasive essay draft and Turn Your Persuasive Essay into a Business Letter activity page to their teacher.

More Language Arts Practice

Students will practice skills according to their individual needs.

Handwriting

Students should gather their handwriting materials and begin where they left off. Remind students to form letters carefully and correctly.

TIP Set a timer to help students stay focused during handwriting practice.

Go Read!

Students will read for pleasure. They should choose a book or a magazine that interests them, or they may choose a selection from the digital library, linked in the online lesson.

- Have students read aloud a few paragraphs of their selection.
- Then have students read silently for the rest of the time.

SUPPORT Students should make no more than five errors in decoding when they read aloud a few paragraphs of their Go Read! selection. If students struggle or make more than five errors, they need to select a different (and easier) text for the Go Read! activity.

TIP Have students select something to read ahead of time to help them stay focused.

Big Ideas: Mini-Project

Lesson Overview

Big Ideas lessons provide students the opportunity to further apply the knowledge acquired and skills learned throughout the unit workshops. Each Big Ideas lesson consists of these parts:

1. **Cumulative Review:** Students keep their skills fresh by reviewing prior content.
2. **Preview:** Students practice answering the types of questions they will commonly find on standardized tests.
3. **Synthesis:** Students complete an assignment that allows them to connect and apply what they have learned. Synthesis assignments vary throughout the course.

   In the Synthesis portion of this Big Ideas lesson, students will complete a small creative project that ties together concepts and skills they have encountered across workshops. These small projects are designed to deepen students' understanding of those concepts and skills.

   LEARNING COACH CHECK-IN Make sure students complete, review, and submit the assignment to their teacher.

All materials needed for this lesson are linked online and not provided in the activity book.

MATERIALS

Supplied

- Mini-Project Instructions (printout)

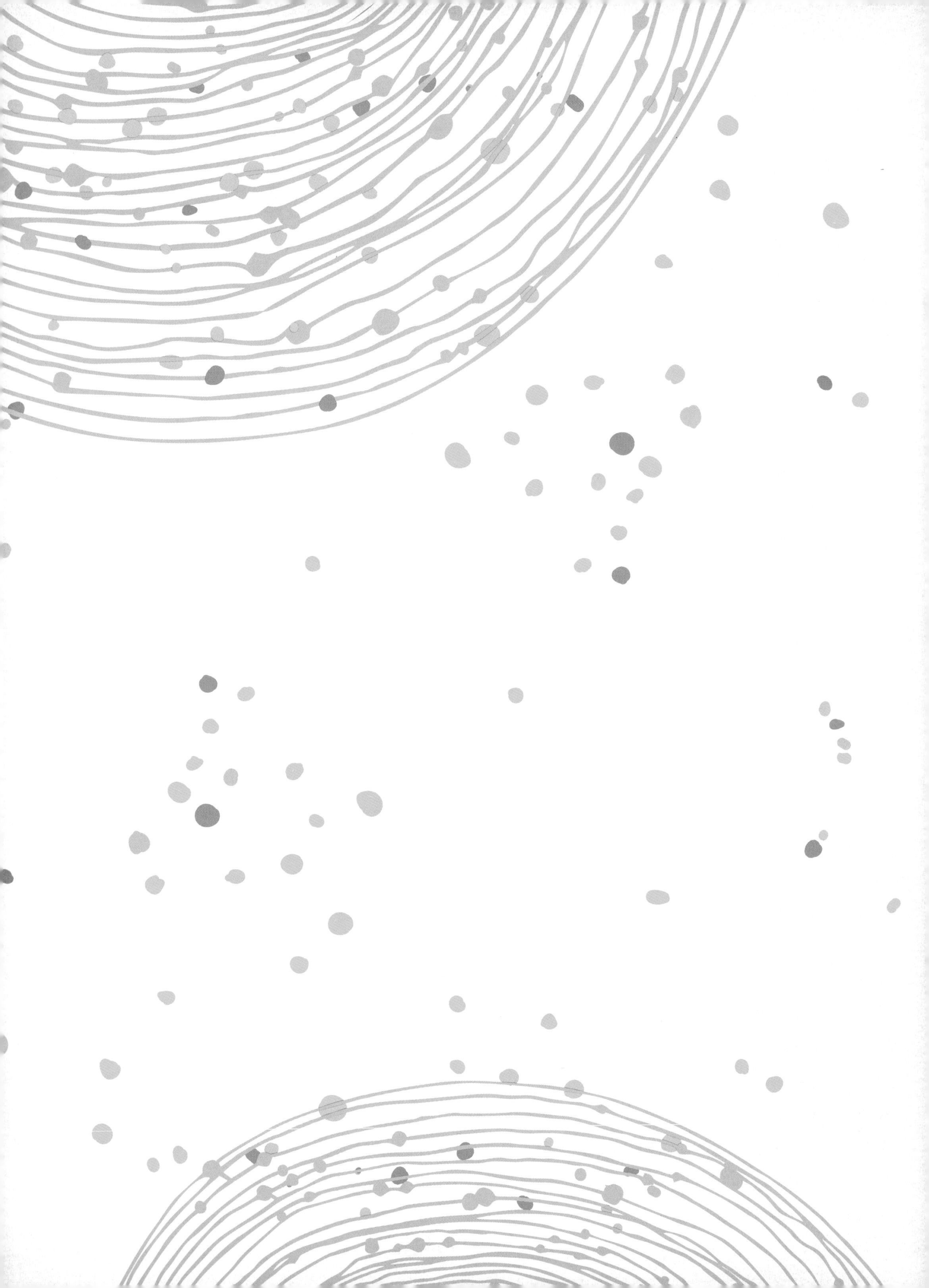

Weather, Weather Everywhere

"Forecasting the Weather"

Lesson Overview

ACTIVITY	ACTIVITY TITLE	TIME	ONLINE/OFFLINE
GET READY	Introduction to "Forecasting the Weather"	**2** minutes	
	Spelling List 19 Pretest LEARNING COACH CHECK-IN	**10** minutes	and
	Before You Read "Forecasting the Weather"	**10** minutes	
READ	"Forecasting the Weather"	**20** minutes	
	Check-In: "Forecasting the Weather"	**5** minutes	
LEARN AND TRY IT	Identifying Text Structures	**10** minutes	
	Identify Text Structures	**5** minutes	
	Using Text Features	**10** minutes	
	Use Text Features	**5** minutes	
	Apply: Text Features	**10** minutes	
	Write About Text Features LEARNING COACH CHECK-IN	**15** minutes	
	Practice Words from "Forecasting the Weather"	**8** minutes	
WRAP-UP	Question About "Forecasting the Weather"	**2** minutes	
	Handwriting	**8** minutes	

Content Background

Students will read an article in the nonfiction magazine *K12 World: Weather, Weather Everywhere*. They will explore the sequential organization of the article.

An article organized in *sequence* explains parts of a process in the order in which they occur. In this article, for example, meteorologists can't give a forecast before looking at data and computer models. These are two steps in the process of forecasting; one has to come before the other one or the process doesn't make sense.

Students will also explore text features in the article, including captions, sidebars, and a map.

MATERIALS

Supplied

- *K12 World: Weather, Weather Everywhere*
  - "Forecasting the Weather"
- *Summit English Language Arts 3 Activity Book*
  - Spelling List 19 Pretest
  - Write About Text Features
- handwriting workbook

"Forecasting the Weather" Synopsis

This nonfiction informational article discusses the process meteorologists go through when they create a weather forecast. First, they use tools and instruments such as satellites, radar, and Doppler radar to gather data about conditions in the atmosphere. Next, supercomputers organize and use the information from the instruments to create weather models. Then, meteorologists forecast the weather using maps to help people visualize weather conditions. Finally, meteorologists revisit and refine forecasts for accuracy.

Lesson Goals

- Take a spelling pretest.
- Read "Forecasting the Weather."
- Identify the way in which text is organized.
- Use text features.
- Practice vocabulary words.
- Develop letter formation fluency.

KEYWORDS

caption – text that tells more about an illustration, photograph, or other graphic

graphic – a picture, photograph, map, diagram, or other image

sequence – the order in which things happen

sidebar – a short text within a larger text that tells about something related to the main text

text feature – part of a text that helps a reader locate information and determine what is most important; Example: title, table of contents, headings, pictures, and glossary

GET READY

Introduction to "Forecasting the Weather"

After a quick introductory activity, students will read the lesson goals and keywords. Have students select each keyword and preview its definition.

Spelling List 19 Pretest

Students will take a spelling pretest and learn a new spelling pattern.

LEARNING COACH CHECK-IN Have students turn to Spelling List 19 Pretest in *Summit English Language Arts 3 Activity Book* and open the online Spelling Pretest activity. Online, students will listen to the spelling word, type the word in the space indicated, and then check their answer. In the activity book, students will write the correct spelling of the word in the tables provided and indicate with a ✓ or an ✗ if they spelled the word correctly or incorrectly online. Students will repeat this process with the remaining words.

As needed, help students with the interaction between the online activity and the activity book page until they become comfortable with what they need to do. As students practice their spelling words throughout the workshop, they should pay special attention to words they spelled incorrectly on the pretest.

This is the complete list of words students will be tested on.

Words with Digraphs and Trigraphs				
branch	lunch	shadow	thrill	kitchen
brothers	paragraph	shower	throne	match
bunch	phonics	shred	blotch	scratch
chatter	phrase	shrimp	catch	stretch
health	refresh	telephone	ketchup	watch

NOTE *Catsup* is a less common spelling of *ketchup*. For Spelling List 19, students are expected to learn and use the more common spelling, which has the trigraph *–tch*.

NOTE Have students keep their completed activity page in a safe place so they can refer to it later.

GET READY
"Forecasting the Weather"

Spelling List 19 Pretest

1. Open the Spelling Pretest activity online. Listen to the first spelling word. Type the word. Check your answer.
2. Write the correct spelling of the word in the Word column of the Spelling Pretest table.

	Word	✓	✗
1	blindfold		

3. Put a check mark in the ✓ column if you spelled the word correctly online.

	Word	✓	✗
1	blindfold	✓	

Put an X in the ✗ column if you spelled the word incorrectly online.

	Word	✓	✗
1	blindfold		X

4. Repeat Steps 1–3 for the remaining words in the Spelling Pretest.

"FORECASTING THE WEATHER" 435

"Forecasting the Weather"

Spelling List 19 Pretest

Write each spelling word in the Word column, making sure to spell it correctly.

	Word	✓	✗		Word	✓	✗
1	branch			14	shrimp		
2	brothers			15	telephone		
3	bunch			16	thrill		
4	chatter			17	throne		
5	health			18	blotch		
6	lunch			19	catch		
7	paragraph			20	ketchup		
8	phonics			21	kitchen		
9	phrase			22	match		
10	refresh			23	scratch		
11	shadow			24	stretch		
12	shower			25	watch		
13	shred						

Students should write the correct spelling of each word from the pretest and use the ✓ and X columns to indicate whether they spelled each word correctly or incorrectly online.

436

Before You Read "Forecasting the Weather"

Students will be introduced to some key vocabulary words that they will encounter in the upcoming reading and learn some important background related to the reading.

READ

"Forecasting the Weather"

Students will read "Forecasting the Weather" in *K12 World: Weather, Weather Everywhere*.

Check-In: "Forecasting the Weather"

Students will answer several questions to demonstrate their comprehension of "Forecasting the Weather."

LEARN AND TRY IT

LEARN Identifying Text Organization

Students will learn about one way of organizing text and the associated signal words.

TIP If students need help figuring out what *sequence* means, ask them to talk through how they get dressed to go outside when it is cold. If students say they put on their boots after they put on their socks or their pants, ask them why. The sequence of putting on clothes contains logical steps in a process. The same theory applies when organizing text sequentially—one step in the process has to happen before another.

TRY IT Identify Text Organization

Students will practice identifying how text is organized and signal words.

LEARN Using Text Features

Students will learn about different text features they will encounter in the magazine.

TRY IT Use Text Features

Students will use text features in the article to answer questions about it.

TRY IT Apply: Text Features

Students will apply to a new work what they've learned about using text features.

TRY IT Write About Text Features

Students will complete Write About Text Features in *Summit English Language Arts 3 Activity Book*.

LEARNING COACH CHECK-IN This activity page contains open-ended questions, so it's important that you review students' responses. Give students feedback, using the sample answers provided to guide you.

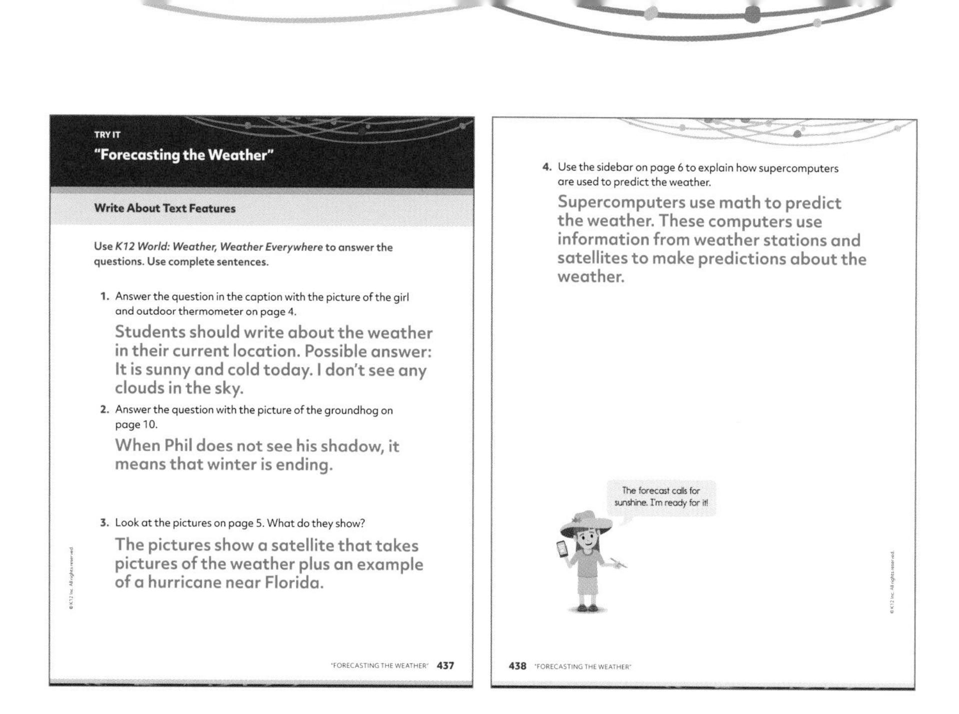
TRY IT
"Forecasting the Weather"

Write About Text Features

Use *K12 World: Weather, Weather Everywhere* to answer the questions. Use complete sentences.

1. Answer the question in the caption with the picture of the girl and outdoor thermometer on page 4.
   Students should write about the weather in their current location. Possible answer: It is sunny and cold today. I don't see any clouds in the sky.
2. Answer the question with the picture of the groundhog on page 10.
   When Phil does not see his shadow, it means that winter is ending.
3. Look at the pictures on page 5. What do they show?
   The pictures show a satellite that takes pictures of the weather plus an example of a hurricane near Florida.

"FORECASTING THE WEATHER" 437

4. Use the sidebar on page 6 to explain how supercomputers are used to predict the weather.
   Supercomputers use math to predict the weather. These computers use information from weather stations and satellites to make predictions about the weather.

438 "FORECASTING THE WEATHER"

TRY IT **Practice Words from "Forecasting the Weather"**

Students will answer questions to demonstrate their understanding of the vocabulary words from the reading.

WRAP-UP

Question About "Forecasting the Weather"

Students will answer a question to show that they understand information in "Forecasting the Weather."

Handwriting

Students should gather their handwriting materials and begin where they left off. Remind students to form letters carefully and correctly.

TIP Set a timer to help students stay focused during handwriting practice.

"Forecasting the Weather" Wrap-Up

Lesson Overview

ACTIVITY	ACTIVITY TITLE	TIME	ONLINE/OFFLINE
GET READY	Introduction to "Forecasting the Weather" Wrap-Up	**1** minute	
	Spelling List 19 Activity Bank	**10** minutes	
	Read and Record	**15** minutes	
TRY IT	Create a Comic Strip **LEARNING COACH CHECK-IN**	**40** minutes	
	Review "Forecasting the Weather"	**18** minutes	
QUIZ	"Forecasting the Weather"	**15** minutes	
WRAP-UP	More Language Arts Practice	**15** minutes	
	Handwriting	**6** minutes	

Advance Preparation

Gather students' completed Spelling List 19 Pretest activity page from "Forecasting the Weather." Students will refer to this page during Get Ready: Spelling List 19 Activity Bank.

Lesson Goals

- Practice all spelling words offline.
- Read aloud to practice fluency.
- Use and explain text organization by sequence.
- Review what you learned.
- Take a reading quiz.
- Develop letter formation fluency.

MATERIALS

Supplied

- *K12 World: Weather, Weather Everywhere*
- *Summit English Language Arts 3 Activity Book*
  - Spelling List 19 Activity Bank
  - Create a Comic Strip
- handwriting workbook

Also Needed

- completed Spelling List 19 Pretest activity page from "Forecasting the Weather"

GET READY

Introduction to "Forecasting the Weather" Wrap-Up

Students will read the lesson goals.

Spelling List 19 Activity Bank

Students will practice all spelling words from the workshop by completing Spelling List 19 Activity Bank from *Summit English Language Arts 3 Activity Book*. Make sure students have their completed Spelling List 19 Pretest activity page from "Forecasting the Weather" to refer to during this activity.

Remind students to pay special attention to words they spelled incorrectly on the Spelling Pretest.

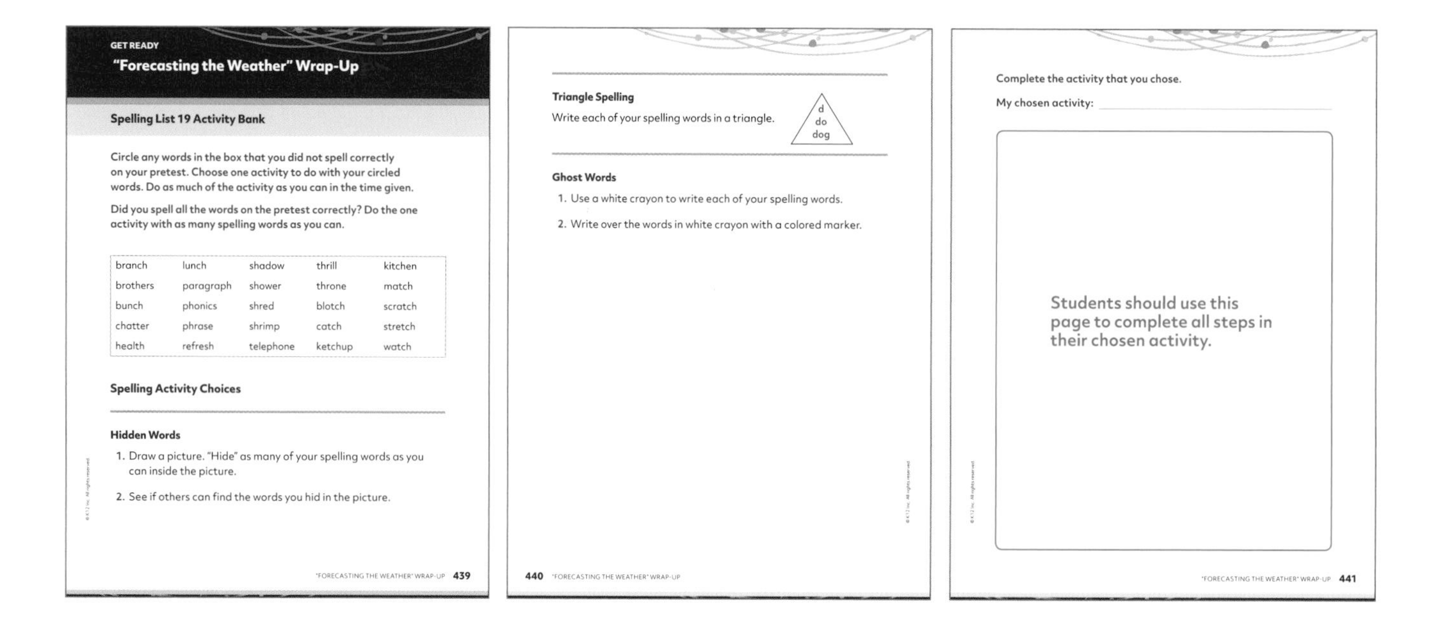
GET READY

"Forecasting the Weather" Wrap-Up

Spelling List 19 Activity Bank

Circle any words in the box that you did not spell correctly on your pretest. Choose one activity to do with your circled words. Do as much of the activity as you can in the time given.

Did you spell all the words on the pretest correctly? Do the one activity with as many spelling words as you can.

branch	lunch	shadow	thrill	kitchen
brothers	paragraph	shower	throne	match
bunch	phonics	shred	blotch	scratch
chatter	phrase	shrimp	catch	stretch
health	refresh	telephone	ketchup	watch

Spelling Activity Choices

Hidden Words

1. Draw a picture. "Hide" as many of your spelling words as you can inside the picture.
2. See if others can find the words you hid in the picture.

"FORECASTING THE WEATHER" WRAP-UP 439

Triangle Spelling

Write each of your spelling words in a triangle.

d
do
dog

Ghost Words

1. Use a white crayon to write each of your spelling words.
2. Write over the words in white crayon with a colored marker.

440 "FORECASTING THE WEATHER" WRAP-UP

Complete the activity that you chose.

My chosen activity:

Students should use this page to complete all steps in their chosen activity.

"FORECASTING THE WEATHER" WRAP-UP 441

Read and Record

Good readers read quickly, smoothly, and with expression. This is called *fluency*. Students will record themselves reading aloud. They will listen to their recording and think about how quick, smooth, and expressive they sound.

TIP Encourage students to rerecord as needed.

TRY IT

Create a Comic Strip

Students will complete Create a Comic Strip in *Summit English Language Arts 3 Activity Book*. They will use the information they've learned from "Forecasting the Weather" and signal words for organizing in sequence—*first*, *next*, *then*, and *finally*—to create and explain a comic strip about forecasting the weather.

LEARNING COACH CHECK-IN This activity page contains open-ended questions, so it's important that you review students' responses. Give students feedback, using the sample answers provided to guide you.

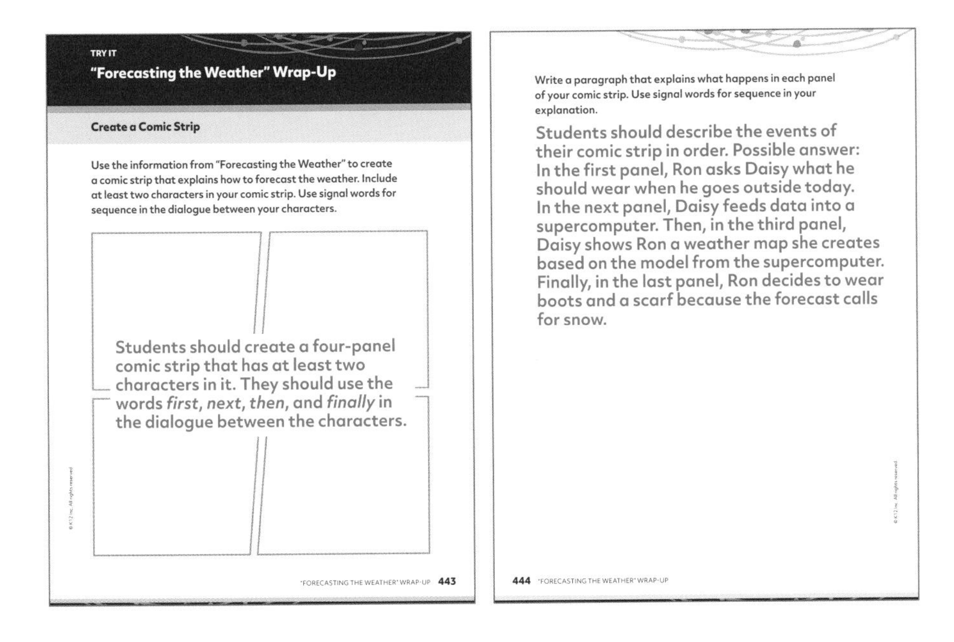

TRY IT

"Forecasting the Weather" Wrap-Up

Create a Comic Strip

Use the information from "Forecasting the Weather" to create a comic strip that explains how to forecast the weather. Include at least two characters in your comic strip. Use signal words for sequence in the dialogue between your characters.

Students should create a four-panel comic strip that has at least two characters in it. They should use the words *first*, *next*, *then*, and *finally* in the dialogue between the characters.

"FORECASTING THE WEATHER" WRAP-UP 443

Write a paragraph that explains what happens in each panel of your comic strip. Use signal words for sequence in your explanation.

Students should describe the events of their comic strip in order. Possible answer: In the first panel, Ron asks Daisy what he should wear when he goes outside today. In the next panel, Daisy feeds data into a supercomputer. Then, in the third panel, Daisy shows Ron a weather map she creates based on the model from the supercomputer. Finally, in the last panel, Ron decides to wear boots and a scarf because the forecast calls for snow.

444 "FORECASTING THE WEATHER" WRAP-UP

Review "Forecasting the Weather"

Students will answer questions to review what they have learned about text features and ordering text by sequence.

QUIZ

"Forecasting the Weather"

Students will complete the "Forecasting the Weather" quiz.

WRAP-UP

More Language Arts Practice

Students will practice skills according to their individual needs.

Handwriting

Students should gather their handwriting materials and begin where they left off. Remind students to form letters carefully and correctly.

TIP Set a timer to help students stay focused during handwriting practice.

"Let It Rain"

Lesson Overview

ACTIVITY	ACTIVITY TITLE	TIME	ONLINE/OFFLINE
GET READY	Introduction to "Let It Rain"	**1** minute	online
	Spelling List 19 Practice	**10** minutes	online
	Before You Read "Let It Rain"	**7** minutes	online
READ	"Let It Rain"	**20** minutes	offline
	Check-In: "Let It Rain"	**5** minutes	online
LEARN AND TRY IT	Using Descriptive Text Structure	**10** minutes	online
	Use Descriptive Text Structure	**7** minutes	online
	Determining Main Idea and Supporting Details	**5** minutes	online
	Determine Main Idea and Supporting Details	**12** minutes	online
	Apply: Main Idea	**15** minutes	online
	Write About Clouds LEARNING COACH CHECK-IN	**10** minutes	offline
	Practice Words from "Let It Rain"	**8** minutes	online
WRAP-UP	Question About Main Idea	**2** minutes	online
	Handwriting	**8** minutes	offline

Content Background

Students will read an informational article, "Let It Rain," in *K12 World: Weather, Weather Everywhere*. They will spend some time learning about descriptive text structure and will review main idea and key, or supporting, details.

Descriptive text structure is one way to organize ideas in a text. If a text is not organized in sequence or by compare and contrast, problem and solution, or cause and effect, it is most likely organized by description. A good example of this structure is on page 16 in the magazine. The author has organized the information by describing the different clouds we encounter.

Students will also review main idea and key, or supporting, details. Key details are sometimes called *supporting details* because they support the

MATERIALS

Supplied

- *K12 World: Weather, Weather Everywhere*
  - "Let It Rain"
- *Summit English Language Arts 3 Activity Book*
  - Write About Clouds
- handwriting workbook

main idea of a text. The *main idea* is the most important point an author makes in a text. We can determine main ideas of an entire article, a section of text, or even a paragraph. Students will spend time in this lesson working on main ideas of paragraphs

"Let It Rain" Synopsis

"Let It Rain" is a nonfiction article about water. It explains the five stages of the water cycle. It also details information about the different types of clouds in the sky and what we can expect when we see them. The article touches on why we need fresh water to live, as well as what happens when there is too much or not enough rain.

Lesson Goals

- Practice all spelling words online.
- Read "Let It Rain."
- Identify and use descriptive text structure.
- Determine main idea and key, or supporting, details in a text.
- Develop letter formation fluenc.

KEYWORDS

main idea – the most important point the author makes; it may be stated or unstated

supporting detail – a detail that gives more information about a main idea

GET READY

Introduction to "Let It Rain"

Students will get a glimpse of what they will learn about in the lesson. They will also read the lesson goals and keywords. Have students select each keyword and preview its definition.

Spelling List 19 Practice

Students will practice all spelling words from the workshop.

OPTIONAL Students may do an activity from Spelling List 19 Activity Bank instead of the online practice activity.

Before You Read "Let It Rain"

Students will be introduced to some key vocabulary words that they will encounter in the upcoming reading.

READ

"Let It Rain"

Students will read "Let It Rain" in *K12 World: Weather, Weather Everywhere*.

Check-In: "Let It Rain"

Students will answer several questions to demonstrate their comprehension of "Let It Rain."

LEARN AND TRY IT

LEARN Using Descriptive Text Structure

Students will learn that authors organize text using description.

TRY IT Use Descriptive Text Structure

Students will practice identifying when and how descriptive text structure is used in an article.

LEARN Determining Main Idea and Supporting Details

Students will review how to determine the main idea and supporting details of a text.

TRY IT Determine Main Idea and Supporting Details

Students will determine the main idea and supporting details of a selection from a text.

TRY IT Apply: Main Idea

Students will apply to a new work what they've learned about identifying a main idea.

TRY IT Write About Clouds

Students will complete Write About Clouds in *Summit English Language Arts 3 Activity Book*.

LEARNING COACH CHECK-IN This activity page contains open-ended questions, so it's important that you review students' responses. Remind students that they can and should restate the main idea in their own words.

NOTE Have students keep their completed activity page in a safe place so they can refer to it later.

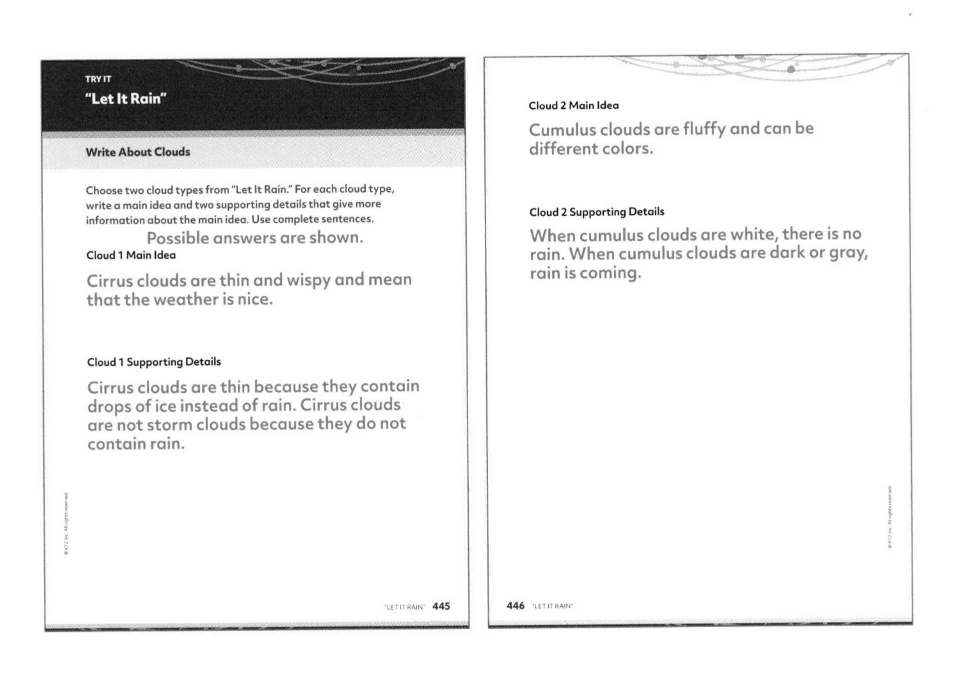
TRY IT
"Let It Rain"

Write About Clouds

Choose two cloud types from "Let It Rain." For each cloud type, write a main idea and two supporting details that give more information about the main idea. Use complete sentences.

Possible answers are shown.

Cloud 1 Main Idea

Cirrus clouds are thin and wispy and mean that the weather is nice.

Cloud 1 Supporting Details

Cirrus clouds are thin because they contain drops of ice instead of rain. Cirrus clouds are not storm clouds because they do not contain rain.

"LET IT RAIN" 445

Cloud 2 Main Idea

Cumulus clouds are fluffy and can be different colors.

Cloud 2 Supporting Details

When cumulus clouds are white, there is no rain. When cumulus clouds are dark or gray, rain is coming.

446 "LET IT RAIN"

TRY IT Practice Words from "Let It Rain"

Students will answer questions to demonstrate their understanding of the vocabulary words from the reading.

WRAP-UP

Question About Main Idea

Students will answer a question to show that they understand how to identify the main idea in a paragraph.

Handwriting

Students should gather their handwriting materials and begin where they left off. Remind students to form letters carefully and correctly.

TIP Set a timer to help students stay focused during handwriting practice.

"Let It Rain" Wrap-Up

Lesson Overview

ACTIVITY	ACTIVITY TITLE	TIME	ONLINE/OFFLINE
GET READY	Introduction to "Let It Rain" Wrap-Up	**1** minute	online
	Spelling List 19 More Practice	**10** minutes	online
	Read and Record	**15** minutes	online
TRY IT	Teach a Lesson About Clouds LEARNING COACH CHECK-IN	**38** minutes	offline
	Review "Let It Rain"	**20** minutes	online
QUIZ	"Let It Rain"	**15** minutes	online
WRAP-UP	More Language Arts Practice	**15** minutes	online
	Handwriting	**6** minutes	offline

Advance Preparation

Gather students' completed Write About Clouds activity page from "Let It Rain." Students will refer to this page during Try It: Teach a Lesson About Clouds.

MATERIALS

Supplied

- *K12 World: Weather, Weather Everywhere*
- *Summit English Language Arts 3 Activity Book*
  - Teach a Lesson About Clouds
- handwriting workbook

Also Needed

- completed Write About Clouds activity page from "Let It Rain"

Lesson Goals

- Practice all spelling words online.
- Read aloud to practice fluency.
- Review what you learned.
- Take a reading quiz.
- Develop letter formation fluency.

GET READY

Introduction to "Let It Rain" Wrap-Up

Students will read the lesson goals.

Spelling List 19 More Practice

Students will practice all spelling words from the workshop.

OPTIONAL Students may do an activity from Spelling List 19 Activity Bank instead of the online practice activity.

Read and Record

Good readers read quickly, smoothly, and with expression. This is called *fluency*. Students will record themselves reading aloud. They will listen to their recording and think about how quick, smooth, and expressive they sound.

TIP Encourage students to rerecord as needed.

TRY IT

Teach a Lesson About Clouds

Students will complete Teach a Lesson About Clouds in *Summit English Language Arts 3 Activity Book*. They should use what they wrote in their Write About Clouds activity page from "Let It Rain" to help them complete this page.

LEARNING COACH CHECK-IN This activity page contains open-ended questions, so it's important that you review students' responses. Give students feedback, using the sample answers provided to guide you.

TRY IT

"Let It Rain" Wrap-Up

Teach a Lesson About Clouds

It's time for you to be the teacher! Create a study guide.

- Identify two different cloud types.
- Explain as much as you can about each cloud using the article "Let It Rain" and the Write About Clouds activity page to help you. Use complete sentences.
- Illustrate the clouds.

Answers will vary.

Can't decide which clouds to write about? Look outside!

"LET IT RAIN" WRAP-UP 447

Cloud 1 Cirrus

Cirrus clouds are thin and wispy. They are found high in the sky, where the air is very cold. Since cirrus clouds are so high up, they contain ice instead of rain. When cirrus clouds are in the sky, there are no storms.

Students should illustrate Cloud 1.

448 "LET IT RAIN" WRAP-UP

Cloud 2 Cumulus

Cumulus clouds are fluffy clouds. These are the clouds people usually draw when someone asks them to draw a cloud. Cumulus clouds are different colors. If they are gray, cumulus clouds show that rain is coming. If they are white, cumulus clouds mean there is no rain coming.

Students should illustrate Cloud 2.

"LET IT RAIN" WRAP-UP 449

Review "Let It Rain"

Students will answer questions to review what they have learned about descriptive text structure, main idea, and key details.

QUIZ

"Let It Rain"

Students will complete the "Let It Rain" quiz.

WRAP-UP

More Language Arts Practice

Students will practice skills according to their individual needs.

Handwriting

Students should gather their handwriting materials and begin where they left off. Remind students to form letters carefully and correctly.

TIP Set a timer to help students stay focused during handwriting practice.

"Winter Storms"

Lesson Overview

ACTIVITY	ACTIVITY TITLE	TIME	ONLINE/OFFLINE
GET READY	Introduction to "Winter Storms"	1 minute	online
	Spelling List 19 Review Game	10 minutes	online
	Before You Read "Winter Storms"	5 minutes	online
READ	"Winter Storms"	22 minutes	offline
	Check-In: "Winter Storms"	5 minutes	online
LEARN AND TRY IT	Identifying Cause and Effect	12 minutes	online
	Identify Cause and Effect	5 minutes	online
	Identifying Steps in a Process	12 minutes	online
	Identify Steps in a Process	5 minutes	online
	Apply: Cause and Effect	15 minutes	online
	Prepare to Write About Cause and Effect LEARNING COACH CHECK-IN	10 minutes	offline
	Practice Words from "Winter Storms"	8 minutes	online
WRAP-UP	Question About Steps in a Process	2 minutes	online
	Handwriting	8 minutes	offline

Content Background

Students will read a nonfiction article about winter weather. They will also learn about two ways authors organize nonfiction text—by cause and effect and by sequence.

In *cause-and-effect text organization*, authors write about a situation (a cause) that results in something else happening (an effect). For example, if students put their sports equipment in the same place every day, then they will be able to find it when they need it. The cause is putting their equipment in the same place. The effect is being able to find it when they need it. When authors organize with cause and effect, they typically use signal words such as *if*, *then*, *because*, or *as a result*.

MATERIALS

Supplied

- *K12 World: Weather, Weather Everywhere*
  - "Winter Storms"
- *Summit English Language Arts 3 Activity Book*
  - Prepare to Write About Cause and Effect
- handwriting workbook

Authors use *sequential organization*, or steps in process, to organize information that occurs in a certain way. For example, when getting ready to go outside in the cold, students may first put on a coat and then gloves. These things have to be put on in order, since it is hard to zip or button a coat with gloves on.

KEYWORDS

cause – the reason something happens

cause and effect – when one thing—the cause—makes another thing—the effect—happen

effect – the result of a cause

sequence – the order in which things happen

"Winter Storms" Synopsis

The nonfiction article, "Winter Storms," introduces students to scientific concepts about winter weather, such as what has to happen to create snow and what conditions must be present to call a snowstorm a blizzard. Students also learn about different types of winter storm warnings and how sleet is formed.

Lesson Goals

- Practice all spelling words online.
- Read "Winter Storms."
- Identify and explain cause-and-effect text structure.
- Identify and explain sequential text structure.
- Write about cause and effect.
- Develop letter formation fluency.

GET READY

Introduction to "Winter Storms"

Students will get a glimpse of what they will learn about in the lesson. They will also read the lesson goals and keywords. Have students select each keyword and preview its definition.

Spelling List 19 Review Game

Students will practice all spelling words from the workshop.

Before You Read "Winter Storms"

Students will be introduced to some key vocabulary words that they will encounter in the upcoming reading.

READ

"Winter Storms"

Students will read "Winter Storms" in *K12 World: Weather, Weather Everywhere*.

Check-In: "Winter Storms"

Students will answer several questions to demonstrate their comprehension of "Winter Storms."

LEARN AND TRY IT

LEARN Identifying Cause and Effect

Students will learn about causes and effects and how to identify cause-and-effect organizational structure in a text.

TRY IT Identify Cause and Effect

Students will practice identifying causes and effects in a nonfiction text.

LEARN Identifying Steps in a Process

Students will learn about steps in a process and how to identify sequential organizational structure in a text.

TRY IT Identify Steps in a Process

Students will practice identifying steps in a process in a nonfiction text.

TRY IT Apply: Cause and Effect

Students will apply to a new work what they've learned about identifying cause-and-effect relationships.

TRY IT Prepare to Write About Cause and Effect

Students will complete Prepare to Write About Cause and Effect in *Summit English Language Arts 3 Activity Book*.

LEARNING COACH CHECK-IN This activity page contains open-ended questions, so it's important that you review students' responses. If students are having trouble, help them identify typical weather patterns where they live and what they do as a result of those patterns. For example, students who live in areas that are sunny most of the year may be in the habit of putting on sunscreen every day. Those who live in areas with lots of snow may own winter-weather clothing.

NOTE Have students keep their completed activity page in a safe place so they can refer to it later.

TRY IT
"Winter Storms"

Prepare to Write About Cause and Effect

Think about the weather where you live. What effect does it have on you? Brainstorm a cause and some effects.

Answers will vary.

Cause: the weather where I live

Where I live, it rains all the time. We do have sun, but we can count on rain many days during the fall, winter, and beginning of spring.

Effect: what I do or don't do because of the weather

- We keep raincoats and rain boots by the door all the time.
- I love jumping in puddles.
- It is very green where I live.

"WINTER STORMS" 451

TRY IT Practice Words from "Winter Storms"

Students will answer questions to demonstrate their understanding of the vocabulary words from the reading.

WRAP-UP

Question About Steps in a Process

Students will answer a question to show that they understand signal words used with steps in a process.

Handwriting

Students should gather their handwriting materials and begin where they left off. Remind students to form letters carefully and correctly.

TIP Set a timer to help students stay focused during handwriting practice.

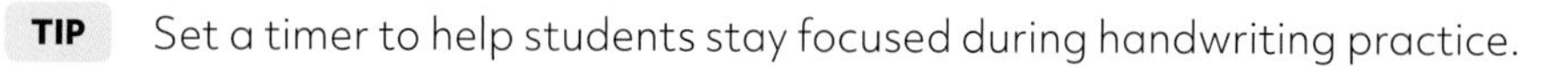

"Winter Storms" Wrap-Up

Lesson Overview

ACTIVITY	ACTIVITY TITLE	TIME	ONLINE/OFFLINE
GET READY	Introduction to "Winter Storms" Wrap-Up	1 minute	online
	Read and Record	8 minutes	online
TRY IT	Write About Cause and Effect LEARNING COACH CHECK-IN	35 minutes	offline
	Review "Winter Storms"	20 minutes	online
QUIZ	"Winter Storms"	25 minutes	online
	Spelling List 19	10 minutes	online
WRAP-UP	More Language Arts Practice	15 minutes	online
	Handwriting	6 minutes	offline

Advance Preparation

Gather students' completed Prepare to Write About Cause and Effect activity page from "Winter Storms." Students will refer to this page during Try it: Write About Cause and Effect.

MATERIALS

Supplied

- *K12 World: Weather, Weather Everywhere*
- *Summit English Language Arts 3 Activity Book*
  - Write About Cause and Effect
- handwriting workbook

Also Needed

- completed Prepare to Write About Cause and Effect activity page from "Winter Storms"

Lesson Goals

- Read aloud to practice fluency.
- Write about cause and effect.
- Review what you learned.
- Take a reading quiz.
- Take a spelling quiz.
- Develop letter formation fluency.

GET READY

Introduction to "Winter Storms" Wrap-Up

Students will read the lesson goals.

Read and Record

Good readers read quickly, smoothly, and with expression. This is called *fluency*. Students will record themselves reading aloud. They will listen to their recording and think about how quick, smooth, and expressive they sound.

TIP Encourage students to rerecord as needed.

TRY IT

Write About Cause and Effect

Students will complete Write About Cause and Effect in *Summit English Language Arts 3 Activity Book*. Students should write three paragraphs about the weather where they live and how it affects their lives. They should write an introduction, a body paragraph that explains the cause and effect, and a conclusion. Remind students to use words that signal cause and effect, such as *if*, *then*, *because*, or *as a result*. Make sure students have their completed Prepare to Write About Cause and Effect activity page from "Winter Storms" to refer to during this activity.

LEARNING COACH CHECK-IN This activity page contains an open-ended question, so it's important that you review students' responses. Give students feedback, using the sample answers provided to guide you.

TRY IT

"Winter Storms" Wrap-Up

Write About Cause and Effect

Answers will vary.

Read the writing prompt.

Prompt: **Write a three-paragraph essay about how the weather where you live affects you. Include the following:**

- A title
- Paragraph 1: An introduction to the topic
- Paragraph 2: A body paragraph that explains the effects of the weather
- Paragraph 3: A conclusion
- Signal words that connect your ideas and show cause and effect

Respond to the writing prompt. Use your completed Prepare to Write About Cause and Effect activity page to help you.

My Rainy Days

Where I live, it rains all the time. We have light rain in the fall and spring, and heavy rain in the winter. Because it rains all the time, we keep a lot of gear near the door to

"WINTER STORMS" WRAP-UP 453

help us stay dry. Umbrellas, raincoats, and rain boots pile up by the door as a result.

I love to play with my friends. When it rains, you can find us jumping in huge puddles. Since we have so much rain, it's hard to play outdoor sports with my friends. Because of this, I signed up for indoor soccer this year.

Rain is a part of my daily life. It has affected my life in many ways. I may not be able to play outdoor sports, but I barely ever need to use sun screen!

454 "WINTER STORMS" WRAP-UP

Review "Winter Storms"

Students will answer questions to review what they have learned about cause-and-effect text organization, sequential organization, main idea and key details, and using text features.

QUIZ

"Winter Storms"

Students will complete the "Winter Storms" quiz.

Spelling List 19

Students will complete the Spelling List 19 quiz.

WRAP-UP

More Language Arts Practice

Students will practice skills according to their individual needs.

Handwriting

Students should gather their handwriting materials and begin where they left off. Remind students to form letters carefully and correctly.

TIP Set a timer to help students stay focused during handwriting practice.

"Wind"

Lesson Overview

ACTIVITY	ACTIVITY TITLE	TIME	ONLINE/OFFLINE
GET READY	Introduction to "Wind"	1 minute	online
	Spelling List 20 Pretest LEARNING COACH CHECK-IN	10 minutes	online and offline
	Before You Read "Wind"	5 minutes	online
READ	"Wind"	24 minutes	offline
	Check-In: "Wind"	5 minutes	online
LEARN AND TRY IT	Identifying Question-and-Answer Text Structure	10 minutes	online
	Identify Question-and-Answer Text Structure	5 minutes	online
	Comparing and Contrasting Storms	10 minutes	online
	Compare and Contrast Storms	5 minutes	online
	Apply: Connections	15 minutes	online
	Compare and Contrast Types of Storms LEARNING COACH CHECK-IN	10 minutes	offline
	Practice Words from "Wind"	8 minutes	online
WRAP-UP	Question About Text Structures	2 minutes	online
	Handwriting	10 minutes	offline

Content Background

Students will learn about two ways authors organize text in informational articles: question-and-answer text organization and compare-and-contrast text organization.

With *question-and-answer organization*, authors pose a question and then answer it. Often, the question is the main idea, and the answers are the details that support or give more information about that main idea.

With *compare-and-contrast organization*, authors explain how two things are alike and how they are different. *Comparing* tells how things are alike; *contrasting* tells how things are different.

MATERIALS

Supplied

- *K12 World: Weather, Weather Everywhere*
  - "Wind"
- *Summit English Language Arts 3 Activity Book*
  - Spelling List 20 Pretest
  - Compare and Contrast Types of Storms
- handwriting workbook

"Wind" Synopsis

"Wind" is a nonfiction informational article that explains the different wind patterns that influence life on earth. Students learn about specific winds, how meteorologists measure wind, how storms are created when strong winds occur, and finally, how wind can be a force for good.

Lesson Goals

- Take a spelling pretest.
- Read "Wind."
- Identify question-and-answer text structure.
- Identify and use compare-and-contrast text structure.
- Practice vocabulary words.
- Develop letter formation fluency.

KEYWORDS

compare – to explain how two or more things are alike

compare-and-contrast organization – a structure for text that shows how two or more things are similar and different

contrast – to explain how two or more things are different

main idea – the most important point the author makes; it may be stated or unstated

supporting detail – a detail that gives more information about a main idea

GET READY

Introduction to "Wind"

Students will get a glimpse of what they will learn about in the lesson. They will also read the lesson goals and keywords. Have students select each keyword and preview its definition.

Spelling List 20 Pretest

Students will take a spelling pretest and learn a new spelling pattern.

LEARNING COACH CHECK-IN Have students turn to Spelling List 20 Pretest in *Summit English Language Arts 3 Activity Book* and open the online Spelling Pretest activity. Online, students will listen to the spelling word, type the word in the space indicated, and then check their answer. In the activity book, students will write the correct spelling of the word in the tables provided and indicate with a ✓ or an ✗ if they spelled the word correctly or incorrectly online. Students will repeat this process with the remaining words.

As needed, help students with the interaction between the online activity and the activity book page until they become comfortable with what they need to do. As students practice their spelling words throughout the workshop, they should pay special attention to words they spelled incorrectly on the pretest.

This is the complete list of words students will be tested on.

Words with Consonant Suffixes		
bravely	faithful	peaceful
careful	finally	quickly
dampness	hopeful	strangely
darkness	joyful	suddenly
delightful	kindness	totally
fairness	lonely	

NOTE Have students keep their completed activity page in a safe place so they can refer to it later.

GET READY
"Wind"

Spelling List 20 Pretest

1. Open the Spelling Pretest activity online. Listen to the first spelling word. Type the word. Check your answer.
2. Write the correct spelling of the word in the Word column of the Spelling Pretest table.

	Word	✓	✗
1	blindfold		

3. Put a check mark in the ✓ column if you spelled the word correctly online.

	Word	✓	✗
1	blindfold	✓	

Put an X in the ✗ column if you spelled the word incorrectly online.

	Word	✓	✗
1	blindfold		X

4. Repeat Steps 1–3 for the remaining words in the Spelling Pretest.

"WIND" 455

"Wind"

Spelling List 20 Pretest

Write each spelling word in the Word column, making sure to spell it correctly.

	Word	✓	✗		Word	✓	✗
1	bravely			10	joyful		
2	careful			11	kindness		
3	dampness			12	lonely		
4	darkness			13	peaceful		
5	delightful			14	quickly		
6	fairness			15	strangely		
7	faithful			16	suddenly		
8	finally			17	totally		
9	hopeful						

Students should write the correct spelling of each word from the pretest and use the ✓ and X columns to indicate whether they spelled each word correctly or incorrectly online.

456 "WIND"

Before You Read "Wind"

Students will be introduced to some key vocabulary words that they will encounter in the upcoming reading.

READ

"Wind"

Students will read "Wind" in *K12 World: Weather, Weather Everywhere*.

Check-In: "Wind"

Students will answer several questions to demonstrate their comprehension of "Wind."

LEARN AND TRY IT

LEARN Identifying Question-and-Answer Text Structure

Students will explore question-and-answer text structure as they identify a main idea and supporting details in a paragraph.

TRY IT Identify Question-and-Answer Text Structure

Students will answer questions to practice identifying question-and-answer text structure.

LEARN Comparing and Contrasting Storms

Students will learn that an author uses compare-and-contrast text structure to illustrate similarities and differences among storm types.

TRY IT Compare and Contrast Storms

Students will answer questions to practice identifying compare-and-contrast text structure.

TRY IT Apply: Connections

Students will apply to a new work what they've learned about how sentences are connected in a text.

TRY IT Compare and Contrast Types of Storms

Students will complete Compare and Contrast Types of Storms in *Summit English Language Arts 3 Activity Book*.

LEARNING COACH CHECK-IN This activity page contains an open-ended graphic organizer, so it's important that you review students' responses. Students need to read the information on storms carefully and look for signal words to help determine how hurricanes and tornadoes are alike and different.

TRY IT
"Wind"

Compare and Contrast Types of Storms

Complete the T chart to record the ways that hurricanes and tornadoes are alike and different.

One example for each column has been done for you. Write at least two more examples in each column.

Possible answers are shown.

Alike	Different
• Both are storms.	• Hurricanes form over warm water. Tornadoes form over land.
• Both contain strong winds.	• Hurricanes can be several miles wide. Tornadoes are less than a quarter mile wide.
• Both can knock down power lines and trees.	• Forecasters can predict hurricanes a few days before they occur. They can only predict tornadoes a few minutes before they occur.
• Both can destroy windows and roofs on buildings.	

"WIND" 457

TRY IT **Practice Words from "Wind"**

Students will answer questions to demonstrate their understanding of the vocabulary words from the reading.

WRAP-UP

Question About Text Structures

Students will answer a question to show that they understand the text structure an author chooses to use.

Handwriting

Students should gather their handwriting materials and begin where they left off. Remind students to form letters carefully and correctly.

TIP Set a timer to help students stay focused during handwriting practice.

“Wind” Wrap-Up

Lesson Overview

ACTIVITY	ACTIVITY TITLE	TIME	ONLINE/OFFLINE
GET READY	Introduction to “Wind” Wrap-Up	**1** minute	
	Spelling List 20 Activity Bank	**10** minutes	
	Read and Record	**15** minutes	
TRY IT	Write About the Weather **LEARNING COACH CHECK-IN**	**38** minutes	
	Review “Wind”	**20** minutes	
QUIZ	“Wind”	**15** minutes	
WRAP-UP	More Language Arts Practice	**15** minutes	
	Handwriting	**6** minutes	

Advance Preparation

Gather students’ completed Spelling List 20 Pretest activity page from “Wind.” Students will refer to this page during Get Ready: Spelling List 20 Activity Bank.

MATERIALS

Supplied

- *K12 World: Weather, Weather Everywhere*
- *Summit English Language Arts 3 Activity Book*
  - Spelling List 20 Activity Bank
  - Write About the Weather
- handwriting workbook

Also Needed

- completed Spelling List 20 Pretest activity page from “Wind”

Lesson Goals

- Practice all spelling words offline.
- Read aloud to practice fluency.
- Write a three-paragraph essay.
- Review what you learned.
- Take a reading quiz.
- Develop letter formation fluency.

GET READY

Introduction to "Wind" Wrap-Up

Students will read the lesson goals.

Spelling List 20 Activity Bank

Students will practice all spelling words from the workshop by completing Spelling List 20 Activity Bank from *Summit English Language Arts 3 Activity Book*. Make sure students have their completed Spelling List 20 Pretest activity page from "Wind" to refer to during this activity.

Remind students to pay special attention to words they spelled incorrectly on the Spelling Pretest.

GET READY
"Wind" Wrap-Up

Spelling List 20 Activity Bank

Circle any words in the box that you did not spell correctly on your pretest. Choose one activity to do with your circled words. Do as much of the activity as you can in the time given.

Did you spell all the words on the pretest correctly? Do the one activity with as many spelling words as you can.

bravely	delightful	hopeful	lonely	strangely
careful	fairness	joyful	peaceful	suddenly
dampness	faithful	kindness	quickly	totally
darkness	finally			

Spelling Activity Choices

Create a Crossword

1. Write one of your spelling words going down in the center of the grid.

"WIND" WRAP-UP 459

2. Write another spelling word going across that shares a letter with the first word. See how many words you can connect.

Example:

			p			
		k	i	s	s	e	s
	d		n			
r	o	c	k	s		
	g					
	s					

Word Search Puzzle

1. Draw a box on the grid. The box should be large enough to hold your spelling words.
2. Fill in the grid with your spelling words. Write them across, up and down, and diagonally. You can write them forward and backward.
3. Fill in the rest of the box with random letters.
4. Ask someone to find and circle your words in the puzzle.

460 "WIND" WRAP-UP

Complete the activity that you chose.

My chosen activity: ____________

Students should use this page to complete all steps in their chosen activity.

"WIND" WRAP-UP 461

Read and Record

Good readers read quickly, smoothly, and with expression. This is called *fluency*. Students will record themselves reading aloud. They will listen to their recording and think about how quick, smooth, and expressive they sound.

TIP Encourage students to rerecord as needed.

TRY IT

Write About the Weather

Students will complete Write About the Weather in *Summit English Language Arts 3 Activity Book*. Students will be able to choose the weather topic they write about. Encourage students to find an appropriate topic: one for which they can pose a question and use details in an article from *K12 World: Weather, Weather Everywhere* to compose the answer.

LEARNING COACH CHECK-IN This activity page contains an open-ended question, so it's important that you review students' responses. Give students feedback, using the sample answer provided to guide you.

TRY IT

"Wind" Wrap-Up

Write About the Weather

Flip through *K12 World: Weather, Weather Everywhere*. Choose a topic from the magazine that you'd like to write about.

Answers will vary.

What topic will you write about?

the water cycle

Read the writing prompt.

Prompt: **Write a three-paragraph essay using question-and-answer organization structure.**

- Paragraph 1: Ask a question, and explain why you are asking that question.
- Paragraph 2: Answer the question, using details.
- Paragraph 3: Conclude your essay.

Respond to the writing prompt.

When rain falls from the sky, where does it go? Water is one of our most precious resources. It's important to know what happens to it after it falls.

Rain is part of the water cycle. Rain is what falls when clouds get heavy and it is warm outside. This step is called precipitation. After rain falls, the water is collected and stored. Some of the places it is stored are oceans, rivers, and lakes. Sometimes, people collect rain to water plants.

There are other steps in the water cycle. Collection is the step that happens right after precipitation.

"WIND" WRAP-UP 463 · 464 "WIND" WRAP-UP · "WIND" WRAP-UP 465

Review "Wind"

Students will answer questions to review what they have learned about question-and-answer text structure, compare-and-contrast text structure, and identifying the main idea and supporting details in a text.

QUIZ

"Wind"

Students will complete the "Wind" quiz.

WRAP-UP

More Language Arts Practice

Students will practice skills according to their individual needs.

Handwriting

Students should gather their handwriting materials and begin where they left off. Remind students to form letters carefully and correctly.

TIP Set a timer to help students stay focused during handwriting practice.

"Storm Chasers"

Lesson Overview

ACTIVITY	ACTIVITY TITLE	TIME	ONLINE/OFFLINE
GET READY	Introduction to "Storm Chasers"	**1** minute	online
	Spelling List 20 Review Game	**10** minutes	online
	Before You Read "Storm Chasers"	**10** minutes	online
READ	"Storm Chasers"	**20** minutes	offline
	Check-In: "Storm Chasers"	**5** minutes	online
LEARN AND TRY IT	Identifying Problem-and-Solution Text Structure	**12** minutes	online
	Identify Problem-and-Solution Text Structure	**7** minutes	online
	Describing Steps in a Process	**10** minutes	online
	Describe Steps in a Process	**5** minutes	online
	Apply: Sequence	**12** minutes	online
	Brainstorm Steps in a Process LEARNING COACH CHECK-IN	**10** minutes	offline
	Practice Words from "Storm Chasers"	**8** minutes	online
WRAP-UP	Question About Text Structure	**2** minutes	online
	Handwriting	**8** minutes	offline

Content Background

Students will learn about problem-and-solution organization in an informational text. They will also learn how to identify and describe steps in a process.

While some descriptions of processes use signal words such as *first*, *next*, *then*, and *last*, not all processes require that steps be completed in order. These signal words may not be included in processes in which steps can be completed in any order. In a way, it is like making a salad and baking a cake. When making a salad, the ingredients can be added in any order. When baking a cake, most often the ingredients have to be added in a specific order to achieve the best outcome.

MATERIALS

Supplied

- *K12 World: Weather, Weather Everywhere*
  - "Storm Chasers"
- *Summit English Language Arts 3 Activity Book*
  - Brainstorm Steps in a Process
- handwriting workbook

"Storm Chasers" Synopsis

"Storm Chasers" is a nonfiction article that relays information about people who follow storms for a living and the tools they use. Students will also learn how to stay safe in storms. The article concludes with a cartoon called "Tornado Chase." Students should feel free to read the cartoon as time permits; they will not be assessed on its content.

KEYWORDS

problem-solution structure – organizational pattern in which a problem is described, followed by descriptions of its solution or possible solutions

Lesson Goals

- Practice all spelling words online.
- Read "Storm Chasers."
- Identify and explain problem-and-solution text structure.
- Identify and describe steps in a process.
- Practice vocabulary words.
- Develop letter formation fluency.

GET READY

Introduction to "Storm Chasers"

Students will get a glimpse of what they will learn about in the lesson. They will also read the lesson goals and keywords. Have students select each keyword and preview its definition.

Spelling List 20 Review Game

Students will practice all spelling words from the workshop.

Before You Read "Storm Chasers"

Students will be introduced to some key vocabulary words that they will encounter in the upcoming reading.

READ

"Storm Chasers"

Students will read "Storm Chasers" in *K12 World: Weather, Weather Everywhere*.

NOTE The last part of this article includes a cartoon for students to read as they have time.

Check-In: "Storm Chasers"

Students will answer several questions to demonstrate their comprehension of "Storm Chasers."

LEARN AND TRY IT

LEARN Identifying Problem-and-Solution Text Structure

Students will learn how to identify when an author is using problem-and-solution structure to organize information in an article.

NOTE The online activity asks students to identify the overall main problem discussed in the text. Encourage students to think about the overall main idea, which is how to keep people safe in storms.

TRY IT Identify Problem-and-Solution Text Structure

Students will practice identifying problem and solutions in the text.

LEARN Describing Steps in a Process

Students will learn about steps in a process, including how to identify and explain steps. They will also learn the signal words associated with steps in a process.

TRY IT Describe Steps in a Process

Students will order steps in a process.

TRY IT Apply: Sequence

Students will apply to a new work what they've learned about organizing information in sequence.

TRY IT Brainstorm Steps in a Process

Students will complete Brainstorm Steps in a Process in *Summit English Language Arts 3 Activity Book*. Encourage students to reexamine the entire magazine to help choose a process to write about.

LEARNING COACH CHECK-IN This activity page contains an open-ended question, so it's important that you review students' responses. Give students feedback, using the sample answer provided to guide you.

NOTE Have students keep their completed activity page in a safe place so they can refer to it later.

TRY IT

"Storm Chasers"

Brainstorm Steps in a Process

Flip through *K12 World: Weather, Weather Everywhere*. Choose a process explained in one of the articles. Then, brainstorm the steps someone would go through to complete the process you chose. If the steps need to be completed in a certain order, number the steps.

Answers will vary.

Process I will write about:

predicting the weather

Steps to complete the process:

Steps to predict the weather:

1. Gather data about air pressure, wind flow, and temperature using tools like weather balloons and satellites.
2. Find data on precipitation using radar and Doppler radar.
3. Feed data into a supercomputer, which creates weather models.

"STORM CHASERS" 467

4. Use data and models to create forecast.
5. Look at data and models again to confirm or update forecast.

468 "STORM CHASERS"

TRY IT Practice Words from "Storm Chasers"

Students will answer questions to demonstrate their understanding of the vocabulary words from the reading.

WRAP-UP

Question About Text Structure

Students will answer a question to show that they understand the organizational structure used in a text.

Handwriting

Students should gather their handwriting materials and begin where they left off. Remind students to form letters carefully and correctly.

TIP Set a timer to help students stay focused during handwriting practice.

"Storm Chasers" Wrap-Up

Lesson Overview

ACTIVITY	ACTIVITY TITLE	TIME	ONLINE/OFFLINE
GET READY	Introduction to "Storm Chasers" Wrap-Up	**1** minute	
	Read and Record	**8** minutes	
TRY IT	Write About Steps in a Process LEARNING COACH CHECK-IN	**30** minutes	
	Review "Storm Chasers"	**20** minutes	
QUIZ	"Storm Chasers"	**30** minutes	
	Spelling List 20	**10** minutes	
WRAP-UP	More Language Arts Practice	**15** minutes	
	Handwriting	**6** minutes	

Advance Preparation

Gather students' completed Brainstorm Steps in a Process activity page from "Storm Chasers." Students will refer to this page during Try It: Write About Steps in a Process.

MATERIALS

Supplied

- *K12 World: Weather, Weather Everywhere*
- *Summit English Language Arts 3 Activity Book*
  - Write About Steps in a Process
- handwriting workbook

Also Needed

- completed Brainstorm Steps in a Process activity page from "Storm Chasers"

Lesson Goals

- Read aloud to practice fluency.
- Describe steps in a process.
- Review what you learned.
- Take a reading quiz.
- Take a spelling quiz.
- Develop letter formation fluency.

GET READY

Introduction to "Winter Storms" Wrap-Up

Students will read the lesson goals.

Read and Record

Good readers read quickly, smoothly, and with expression. This is called *fluency*. Students will record themselves reading aloud. They will listen to their recording and think about how quick, smooth, and expressive they sound.

TIP Encourage students to rerecord as needed.

TRY IT

Write About Steps in a Process

Students will complete Write About Steps in a Process in *Summit English Language Arts 3 Activity Book*. Make sure students have their completed Brainstorm Steps in a Process activity page from "Storm Chasers" to refer to during this activity.

LEARNING COACH CHECK-IN This activity page contains an open-ended question, so it's important that you review students' responses. Give students feedback, using the sample answer provided to guide you.

TRY IT

"Storm Chasers" Wrap-Up

Write About Steps in a Process

Read the writing prompt.

Answers will vary.

Prompt: **Write a three-paragraph essay that thoroughly explains the process you identified on the Brainstorm Steps in a Process activity page.**

- Paragraph 1: Write a short introduction to the process.
- Paragraph 2: Explain the steps in the process. Use signal words if they help explain the process.
- Paragraph 3: Write why the process is important.

Respond to the writing prompt.

Meteorologists follow certain steps in a process to predict the weather. Predicting the weather helps them create a forecast.

First, meteorologists use tools like weather satellites and balloons to gather data about air pressure, wind flow, and temperature. They also use regular radar and Doppler radar to find data on precipitations. Next, meteorologists feed the data they have gathered into a supercomputer. The supercomputer creates weather models. Then, meteorologists use they data they have and the models from the supercomputer to create a forecast. Finally, they look at the data and models again to confirm or update the forecast.

Forecasting the weather is a very important process. It's important to know what kind of weather is coming. That way, people can stay safe in storms like hurricanes and tornadoes.

"STORM CHASERS" WRAP-UP 469

470 "STORM CHASERS" WRAP-UP

If you would like, illustrate the process you are describing.

Students may illustrate the process they are describing.

"STORM CHASERS" WRAP-UP 471

Review "Storm Chasers"

Students will answer questions to review what they have learned about problem-and-solution text structure, steps in a process, and main idea and key details.

QUIZ

"Storm Chasers"

Students will complete the "Storm Chasers" quiz.

Spelling List 20

Students will complete the Spelling List 20 quiz.

WRAP-UP

More Language Arts Practice

Students will practice skills according to their individual needs.

Handwriting

Students should gather their handwriting materials and begin where they left off. Remind students to form letters carefully and correctly.

TIP Set a timer to help students stay focused during handwriting practice.

Meteorology Words

Lesson Overview

ACTIVITY	ACTIVITY TITLE	TIME	ONLINE/OFFLINE
GET READY	Introduction to Meteorology Words	1 minute	online
	Look Back at Content Words	4 minutes	online
LEARN AND TRY IT	Meteorology Words	10 minutes	online
	Practice Using Meteorology Words	10 minutes	online
	Apply: Meteorology Words LEARNING COACH CHECK-IN	15 minutes	offline
	Review Meteorology Words	15 minutes	online
QUIZ	Meteorology Words	15 minutes	online
WRAP-UP	More Language Arts Practice	15 minutes	online
	Go Write! Reasons to Write	15 minutes	offline
	Go Read!	20 minutes	online or offline

Content Backgrounds

Students will learn about content-specific vocabulary. They will learn that it is important to be able to use specific words when talking to others about the weather forecast, or meterology.

Advance Preparation

During the Go Read! activity, students will have the option of using the digital library. Allow extra time for students to make their reading selection, or have students make a selection before beginning the lesson.

MATERIALS

Supplied

- *Summit English Language Arts 3 Activity Book*
  - Apply: Meteorology Words
  - Go Write! Reasons to Write

Also Needed

- reading material for Go Read!

Lesson Goals

- Practice vocabulary words.
- Use weather-related content words.
- Take the Meteorology Words quiz.
- Freewrite about a topic to develop writing fluency and practice letter formation.
- Read independently to develop fluency.

KEYWORDS

content-specific word – a word that has to do with a certain job or activity

context clue – a word or phrase in a text that helps you figure out the meaning of an unknown word

GET READY

Introduction to Meteorology Words

Students will get a glimpse of what they will learn about in the lesson. They will also read the lesson goals and keywords. Have students select each keyword and preview its definition.

Look Back at Content Words

Students will practice the prerequisite skill of learning and using content-related vocabulary words.

LEARN AND TRY IT

LEARN Meteorology Words

Students will be introduced to the vocabulary words for the lesson. Then they will learn how to determine which meteorology word to use in several contexts.

TRY IT Practice Using Meteorology Words

Students will practice using meteorology words by selecting the correct word in a sentence and matching words with their definitions.

TRY IT Apply: Meteorology Words

Students will complete Apply: Meteorology Words in *Summit English Language Arts 3 Activity Book*. They will practice using context clues to determine the correct meteorology word to complete a sentence.

LEARNING COACH CHECK-IN Have students explain the context clues that helped them determine the correct word to complete each sentence.

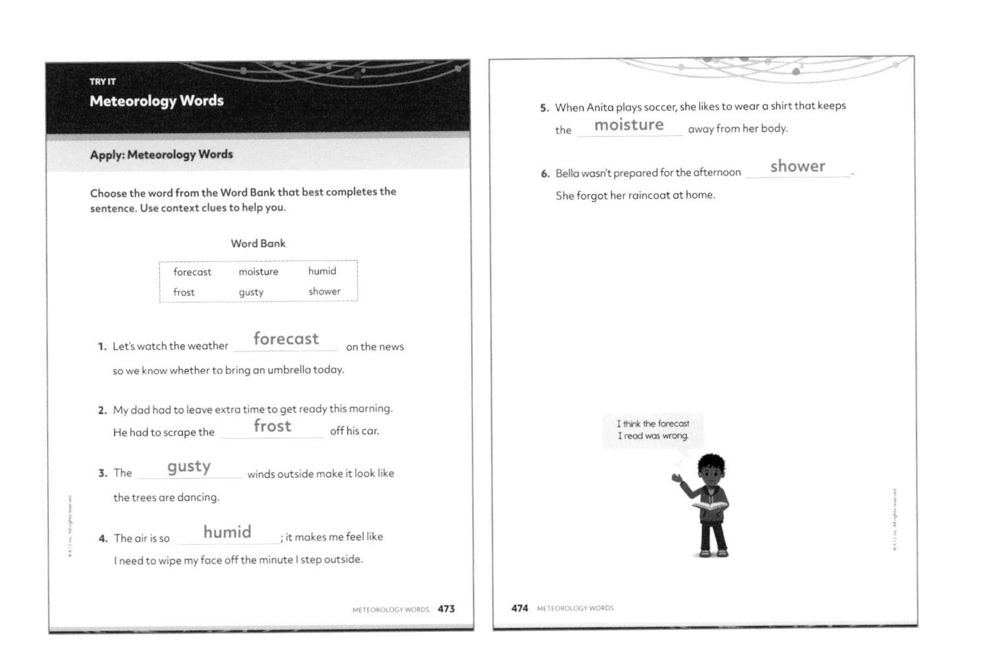
TRY IT

Meteorology Words

Apply: Meteorology Words

Choose the word from the Word Bank that best completes the sentence. Use context clues to help you.

Word Bank

forecast	moisture	humid
frost	gusty	shower

1. Let's watch the weather forecast on the news so we know whether to bring an umbrella today.
2. My dad had to leave extra time to get ready this morning. He had to scrape the frost off his car.
3. The gusty winds outside make it look like the trees are dancing.
4. The air is so humid; it makes me feel like I need to wipe my face off the minute I step outside.

METEOROLOGY WORDS 473

5. When Anita plays soccer, she likes to wear a shirt that keeps the moisture away from her body.
6. Bella wasn't prepared for the afternoon shower. She forgot her raincoat at home.

474 METEOROLOGY WORDS

TRY IT Review Meteorology Words

Students will answer questions to review what they have learned about meteorology words.

QUIZ

Meteorology Words

Students will complete the Meteorology Words quiz.

WRAP-UP

More Language Arts Practice

Students will practice skills according to their individual needs.

Go Write! Reasons to Write

Students will complete Go Write! Reasons to Write in *Summit English Language Arts 3 Activity Book*. They will have the option to either respond to a prompt or write about a topic of their choice.

NOTE This activity is intended to build writing fluency. Students should write for the entire allotted time.

SUPPORT If students have trouble writing for the allotted time, prompt them with questions. For example, *Can you tell me more about this? Why did you recently write an email, text, or letter to that person?*

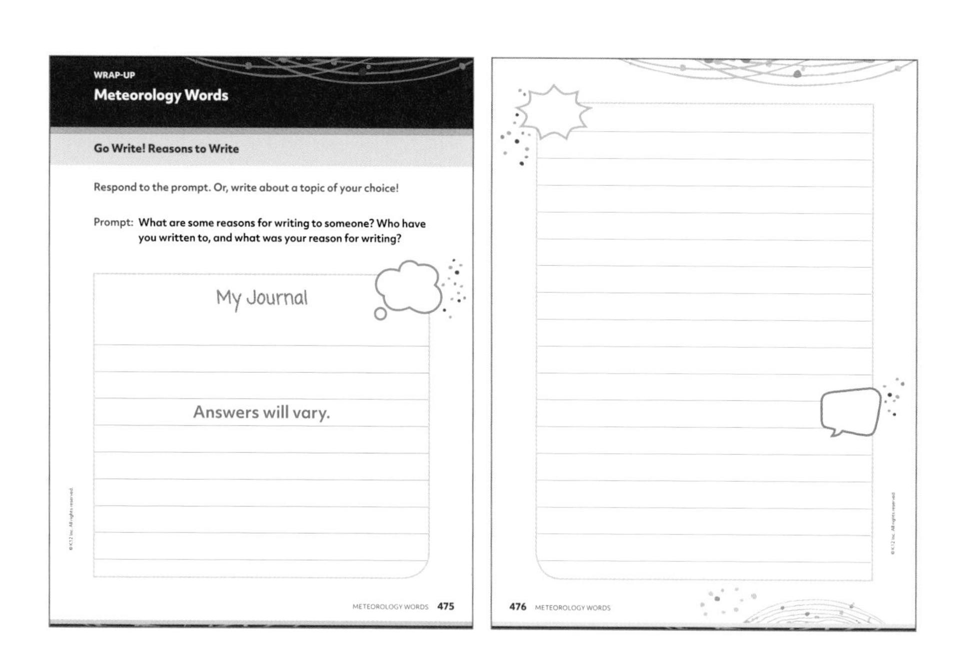
WRAP-UP

Meteorology Words

Go Write! Reasons to Write

Respond to the prompt. Or, write about a topic of your choice!

Prompt: **What are some reasons for writing to someone? Who have you written to, and what was your reason for writing?**

My Journal

Answers will vary.

METEOROLOGY WORDS 475

476 METEOROLOGY WORDS

Go Read!

Students will read for pleasure. They should choose a book or a magazine that interests them, or they may choose a selection from the digital library, linked in the online lesson.

- Have students read aloud a few paragraphs of their selection.
- Then have students read silently for the rest of the time.

SUPPORT Students should make no more than five errors in decoding when they read aloud a few paragraphs of their Go Read! selection. If students struggle or make more than five errors, they need to select a different (and easier) text for the Go Read! activity.

TIP Have students select something to read ahead of time to help them stay focused.

Poetry (A)

Lesson Overview

ACTIVITY	ACTIVITY TITLE	TIME	ONLINE/OFFLINE
GET READY	Introduction to Poetry (A)	**1** minute	online
	Spelling List 21 Pretest LEARNING COACH CHECK-IN	**10** minutes	online and offline
	Look Back at Rhythm and Rhyme	**4** minutes	online
	Before You Read "April Rain Song" and "The Raindrops' Ride"	**9** minutes	online
READ	"April Rain Song" and "The Raindrops' Ride"	**15** minutes	offline
	Check-In: "April Rain Song" and "The Raindrops' Ride"	**5** minutes	online
LEARN AND TRY IT	Identifying Stanzas and Making Inferences	**15** minutes	online
	Identify Stanzas and Make Inferences	**13** minutes	online
	Apply: Identify Stanzas	**10** minutes	online
	Write a Descriptive Poem LEARNING COACH CHECK-IN	**20** minutes	offline
	Practice Words from "April Rain Song" and "The Raindrops' Ride"	**8** minutes	online
WRAP-UP	Question About Stanzas	**2** minutes	online
	Handwriting	**8** minutes	offline

Content Background

Students will read two descriptive poems. Poems are made up of *stanzas*, or groups of lines. Generally, *poetry* is writing that is made up of lines or stanzas that often rhyme and follow a specific rhythm. Many nursery rhymes are poems:

> Jack and Jill
> Went up the hill
> To fetch a pail of water.
>
> Jack fell down
> And broke his crown
> And Jill came tumbling after.

This small poem contains two stanzas and rhymes, plus it has rhythm.

MATERIALS

Supplied

- *Summit English Language Arts 3 Expeditions in Reading*
  - "April Rain Song"
  - "The Raindrops' Ride"
- *Summit English Language Arts 3 Activity Book*
  - Spelling List 21 Pretest
  - Write a Descriptive Poem
- handwriting workbook

Students will learn about making inferences when reading poetry. An *inference* is a guess that readers make using the clues an author gives them in a piece of writing. In the nursery rhyme, for example, we don't know exactly why Jack and Jill were sent to fetch water. But, we can infer that someone sent them to do so.

Students will also learn about *sensory language*, or language that appeals to the five senses. Sensory language is a key part of descriptive writing, including descriptive poetry.

"April Rain Song" and "The Raindrops' Ride" Synopses

"April Rain Song" is a descriptive poem by Langston Hughes. In it, the speaker describes how the rain sounds and feels and what the rain does. In "The Raindrops' Ride," the speaker imagines that raindrops are on a journey in a cloud, falling to earth and being collected by a small brook.

Lesson Goals

- Take a spelling pretest.
- Read "April Rain Song" and "The Raindrops' Ride."
- Learn about stanzas and make inferences.
- Write a descriptive poem.
- Practice vocabulary words.
- Develop letter formation fluency.

KEYWORDS

inference – a guess that readers make using the clues an author gives them in a piece of writing

poem – a piece of poetry

poetry – writing that uses language, sound, and rhythm to make readers feel, experience, or imagine something

rhyme – the use of words that end with the same sounds; Example: *cat* and *hat* rhyme

rhythm – a regular pattern of sound and beats within a poem

sensory language – language that appeals to the five senses

stanza – a group of lines in a poem

GET READY

Introduction to Poetry (A)

Students will get a glimpse of what they will learn about in the lesson. They will also read the lesson goals and keywords. Have students select each keyword and preview its definition.

Spelling List 21 Pretest

Students will take a spelling pretest and learn a new spelling pattern.

LEARNING COACH CHECK-IN Have students turn to Spelling List 21 Pretest in *Summit English Language Arts 3 Activity Book* and open the online Spelling Pretest activity. Online, students will listen to the spelling word, type the word in the space indicated, and then check their answer. In the activity book, students will write the correct spelling of the word in the tables provided and

indicate with a ✓ or an ✗ if they spelled the word correctly or incorrectly online. Students will repeat this process with the remaining words.

As needed, help students with the interaction between the online activity and the activity book page until they become comfortable with what they need to do. As students practice their spelling words throughout the workshop, they should pay special attention to words they spelled incorrectly on the pretest.

This is the complete list of words students will be tested on.

Words with Prefixes		
dishonest	reconsider	underdog
disobey	reenter	underline
disown	reinstall	unfinished
displease	reissue	untie
disqualify	rethink	unwrap
disrespect	unbend	

NOTE Have students keep their completed activity page in a safe place so they can refer to it later.

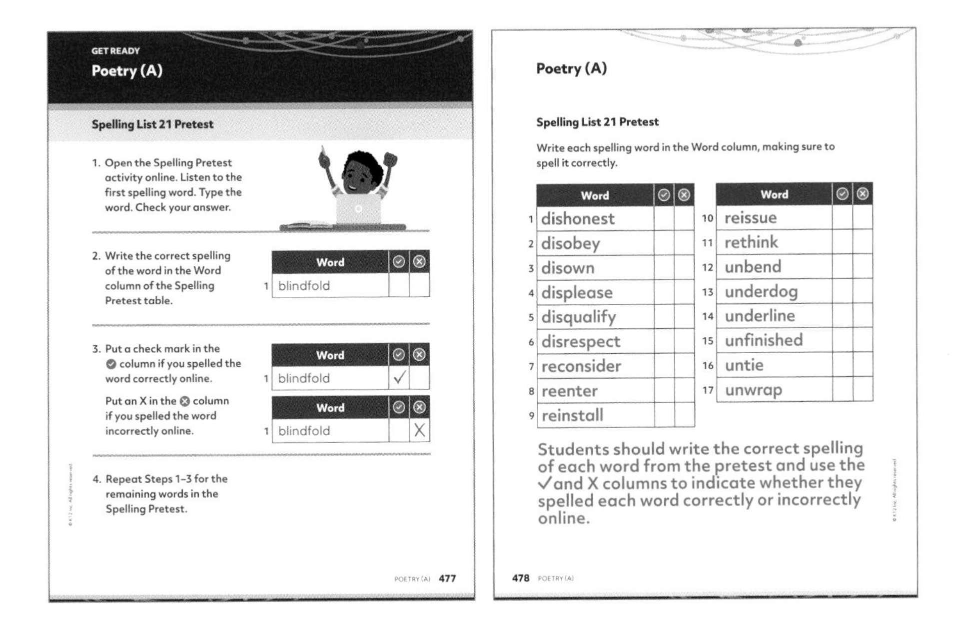

GET READY
Poetry (A)

Spelling List 21 Pretest

1. Open the Spelling Pretest activity online. Listen to the first spelling word. Type the word. Check your answer.
2. Write the correct spelling of the word in the Word column of the Spelling Pretest table.

	Word	✓	✗
1	blindfold		

3. Put a check mark in the ✓ column if you spelled the word correctly online.

	Word	✓	✗
1	blindfold	✓	

Put an X in the ✗ column if you spelled the word incorrectly online.

	Word	✓	✗
1	blindfold		X

4. Repeat Steps 1–3 for the remaining words in the Spelling Pretest.

POETRY (A) 477

Poetry (A)

Spelling List 21 Pretest

Write each spelling word in the Word column, making sure to spell it correctly.

	Word	✓	✗
1	dishonest		
2	disobey		
3	disown		
4	displease		
5	disqualify		
6	disrespect		
7	reconsider		
8	reenter		
9	reinstall		

	Word	✓	✗
10	reissue		
11	rethink		
12	unbend		
13	underdog		
14	underline		
15	unfinished		
16	untie		
17	unwrap		

Students should write the correct spelling of each word from the pretest and use the ✓ and X columns to indicate whether they spelled each word correctly or incorrectly online.

478 POETRY (A)

Look Back at Rhythm and Rhyme

Students will practice the prerequisite skill of identifying rhythm and rhyme in a poem.

TIP If students struggle with identifying rhythm, have them clap out the beats of the poem as they read it aloud.

Before You Read "April Rain Song" and "The Raindrops' Ride"

Students will be introduced to some key vocabulary words that they will encounter in the upcoming reading and learn some important background related to the reading.

READ

"April Rain Song" and "The Raindrops' Ride"

Students will read "April Rain Song" and "The Raindrops' Ride" in *Expeditions in Reading*.

Check-In: "April Rain Song" and "The Raindrops' Ride"

Students will answer several questions to demonstrate their comprehension of "April Rain Song" and "The Raindrops' Ride."

LEARN AND TRY IT

LEARN Identifying Stanzas and Making Inferences

Students will learn that poems are often divided into stanzas. They will also learn to use illustrations and images in poems to make inferences.

TRY IT Identify Stanzas and Make Inferences

Students will practice identifying stanzas in and making inferences about a poem.

TRY IT Apply: Identify Stanzas

Students will apply to a new work what they've learned about identifying stanzas in poetry.

TRY IT Write a Descriptive Poem

Students will complete Write a Descriptive Poem in *Summit English Language Arts 3 Activity Book*. Students should use the two poems they have read in this lesson as examples. The subject for their descriptive poem is completely up to them. They should choose something and write a poem that includes sensory language—language that appeals to the five senses.

TIP If students struggle with sensory language, find a picture online or choose an object nearby and help them brainstorm words to describe the picture or object. For example, use a piece of fruit. You can say, "What words would you use to describe this orange? How does it look? Feel? Smell? Taste?" These words can become the building blocks to a descriptive poem about an orange.

LEARNING COACH CHECK-IN This activity page contains an open-ended prompt, so it's important that you review students' responses. It is most important that students understand what a descriptive poem contains.

NOTE Have students keep their completed activity page in a safe place so they can refer to it later.

TRY IT

Poetry (A)

Write a Descriptive Poem

Read the writing prompt.

Prompt: **Write a descriptive poem about a person, place, object, idea, or feeling.**

- Decide who or what you would like to describe.
- Use sensory language.
- Use at least one type of figurative language, such as a simile.
- Use at least one sound pattern in your poem, such as rhyme.

Respond to the writing prompt.

Answers will vary. Students should write a poem in which they describe a person, place, object, idea, or feeling. They should use language that evokes visual imagery. They may choose to use other sensory imagery. The poem students write may or may not rhyme.

POETRY (A) 479

480 POETRY (A)

POETRY (A) 481

TRY IT **Practice Words from "April Rain Song" and "The Raindrops' Ride"**

Students will answer questions to demonstrate their understanding of the vocabulary words from the reading.

WRAP-UP

Question About Stanzas

Students will answer a question to show that they understand what a stanza is.

Handwriting

Students should gather their handwriting materials and begin where they left off. Remind students to form letters carefully and correctly.

TIP Set a timer to help students stay focused during handwriting practice.

Poetry (B)

Lesson Overview

ACTIVITY	ACTIVITY TITLE	TIME	ONLINE/OFFLINE
GET READY	Introduction to Poetry (B)	**1** minute	
	Spelling List 21 Activity Bank	**10** minutes	
	Recall "April Rain Song" and "The Raindrops' Ride"	**5** minutes	
	Before You Read "The Building of the Nest" and "The Secret"	**5** minutes	
READ	"The Building of the Nest" and "The Secret"	**15** minutes	
	Check-In: "The Building of the Nest" and "The Secret"	**5** minutes	
LEARN AND **TRY IT**	Exploring a Narrative Poem	**15** minutes	
	Explore a Narrative Poem	**15** minutes	
	Apply: Describe Stanzas	**10** minutes	
	Write a Narrative Poem LEARNING COACH CHECK-IN	**20** minutes	
	Practice Words from "The Building of the Nest" and "The Secret"	**8** minutes	
WRAP-UP	Question About Narrative Poems	**3** minutes	
	Handwriting	**8** minutes	

Content Background

Students will explore *narrative poems*, or poems that tell a story. A narrative poem contains a sequence of events just like a fictional story does. It has a beginning, middle, and end. Similar to other types of poetry, narrative poems also contain description and figurative language.

Description is language that tells how something looks, sounds, feels, tastes, or smells.

Figurative language compares one thing to something completely different. In "The Building of the Nest," for example, the poet uses a metaphor to compare the nest to a castle. The two things are completely different, but both provide safety and shelter for their inhabitants.

Advance Preparation

Gather students' completed Spelling List 21 Pretest activity page from Poetry (A). Students will refer to this page during Get Ready: Spelling List 21 Activity Bank.

"The Building of the Nest" and "The Secret" Synopses

"The Building of the Nest" and "The Secret" are both narrative poems. The stanzas in each poem build on one another. In "The Building of the Nest," the speaker in the poem observes a pair of robins building a nest for their eggs. They are careful to put the nest high in the trees. In "The Secret," the speaker in the poem notices that a robin has built a nest in a tree and has laid four eggs within it. The speaker is nervous that she will reveal the secret before the birds hatch.

Lesson Goals

- Practice all spelling words offline.
- Read "The Building of the Nest" and "The Secret."
- Explore narrative poems.
- Write a narrative poem.
- Practice vocabulary words.
- Develop letter formation fluency.

GET READY

Introduction to Poetry (B)

Students will get a glimpse of what they will learn about in the lesson. They will also read the lesson goals and keywords. Have students select each keyword and preview its definition.

Spelling List 21 Activity Bank

Students will practice all spelling words from the workshop by completing Spelling List 21 Activity Bank from *Summit English Language Arts 3 Activity Book*. Make sure students have their completed Spelling List 21 Pretest activity page from Poetry (A) to refer to during this activity.

Remind students to pay special attention to words they spelled incorrectly on the Spelling Pretest.

MATERIALS

Supplied

- *Summit English Language Arts 3 Expeditions in Reading*
  - "The Building of the Nest"
  - "The Secret"
- *Summit English Language Arts 3 Activity Book*
  - Spelling List 21 Activity Bank
  - Write a Narrative Poem
- handwriting workbook

Also Needed

- completed Spelling List 21 Pretest activity page from Poetry (A)

KEYWORDS

description – writing that uses words that show how something looks, sounds, feels, tastes, or smells; Example: The sky is a soft, powdery blue, and the golden sun feels warm on my face.

figurative language – words that describe something by comparing it to something completely different; figure of speech; Example: Rain fell in buckets and the streets looked like rivers.

narrative poem – a poem that tells a story

sequence of events – the order in which things happen in a story

speaker – the imaginary person who speaks the words of the poem, not the poet

stanza – a group of lines in a poem

GET READY

Poetry (B)

Spelling List 21 Activity Bank

Circle any words in the box that you did not spell correctly on your pretest. Choose one activity to do with your circled words. Do as much of the activity as you can in the time given.

Did you spell all the words on the pretest correctly? Do the one activity with as many spelling words as you can.

dishonest	disqualify	reinstall	unbend	unfinished
disobey	disrespect	reissue	underdog	untie
disown	reconsider	rethink	underline	unwrap
displease	reenter			

Spelling Activity Choices

Alphabetizing

1. In the left column, write your spelling words in alphabetical order.
2. Correct any spelling errors.

POETRY (B) 483

Vowel-Free Words

1. In the left column, write only the consonants in each of your spelling words. Put a dot where each vowel should be.
2. Spell each word aloud, stating which vowels should be in the places with dots.
3. In the right column, rewrite the entire spelling word.
4. Correct any spelling errors.

Rhymes

1. In the left column, write your spelling words.
2. In the right column, write a word that rhymes with each spelling word.
3. Correct any spelling errors.

Uppercase and Lowercase

1. In the left column, write each of your spelling words in all uppercase letters.
2. In the right column, write each of your spelling words in all lowercase letters.
3. Correct any spelling errors.

484 POETRY (B)

Complete the activity that you chose.

My chosen activity: ______

1. ______ ______
2. ______ ______
3. ______ ______
4. ______ ______
5. ______ ______
6. ______ ______
7. ______ ______
8. ______ ______
9. ______ ______
10. ______ ______
11. ______ ______
12. ______ ______
13. ______ ______
14. ______ ______
15. ______ ______
16. ______ ______
17. ______ ______

Students should use this page to complete all steps in their chosen activity.

POETRY (B) 485

Recall "April Rain Song" and "The Raindrops' Ride"

Students will answer some questions to review the reading that they have already completed.

Before You Read "The Building of the Nest" and "The Secret"

Students will be introduced to some key vocabulary words that they will encounter in the upcoming reading.

READ

"The Building of the Nest" and "The Secret"

Students will read "The Building of the Nest" and "The Secret" in *Expeditions in Reading*.

Check-In: "The Building of the Nest" and "The Secret"

Students will answer several questions to demonstrate their comprehension of "The Building of the Nest" and "The Secret."

LEARN AND TRY IT

LEARN Exploring a Narrative Poem

Students will learn about the characteristics of narrative poetry.

TRY IT Explore a Narrative Poem

Students will identify what makes a poem a narrative poem.

TRY IT Apply: Describe Stanzas

Students will apply to a new work what they've learned about identifying and describing stanzas.

TRY IT Write a Narrative Poem

Students will complete Write a Narrative Poem in *Summit English Language Arts 3 Activity Book*. In this activity, they will write a poem that tells a story. They should use description and at least one example of figurative language. Encourage students to write like a poet and choose the words they use carefully.

LEARNING COACH CHECK-IN This activity page contains an open-ended prompt, so it's important that you review students' responses.

NOTE Students do not have to tell a huge, long story in their poem. Even a small, short story has a beginning, middle, and end.

NOTE Have students keep their completed activity page in a safe place so they can refer to it later.

TRY IT
Poetry (B)

Write a Narrative Poem

Read the writing prompt.

Prompt: **Write a narrative poem, which is a poem that tells a story.**

- Decide on a story you would like to tell.
- Include a beginning, middle, and end.
- Include at least one character.
- Use sensory details and figurative language.
- Use at least one sound pattern in your poem, such as rhyme.

Answers will vary. Students should write a narrative poem in which they tell a story. They should use description and at least one example of figurative language. The poem students write may or may not rhyme.

POETRY (B) 487

488 POETRY (B)

POETRY (B) 489

TRY IT Practice Words from "The Building of the Nest" and "The Secret"

Students will answer questions to demonstrate their understanding of the vocabulary words from the reading.

WRAP-UP

Question About Narrative Poems

Students will answer a question to show that they understand the specific characteristics that describe a narrative poem.

Handwriting

Students should gather their handwriting materials and begin where they left off. Remind students to form letters carefully and correctly.

TIP Set a timer to help students stay focused during handwriting practice.

Poetry (C)

Lesson Overview

ACTIVITY	ACTIVITY TITLE	TIME	ONLINE/OFFLINE
GET READY	Introduction to Poetry (C)	**1** minute	online
	Spelling List 21 Review Game	**10** minutes	online
	Recall "The Building of the Nest" and "The Secret"	**5** minutes	online
	Before You Read "First Snow" and "Winter Jewels"	**5** minutes	online
READ	"First Snow" and "Winter Jewels"	**15** minutes	offline
	Check-In: "First Snow" and "Winter Jewels"	**5** minutes	online
LEARN AND TRY IT	Describing Poems	**15** minutes	online
	Describe Poems	**15** minutes	online
	Apply: Describe Plot in a Poem	**10** minutes	online
	Write or Expand a Poem LEARNING COACH CHECK-IN	**21** minutes	offline
	Practice Words from "First Snow" and "Winter Jewels"	**8** minutes	online
WRAP-UP	Question About Narrative Poems	**2** minutes	online
	Handwriting	**8** minutes	offline

Content Background

Students will learn about describing poems. They will learn how to draw inferences from poems. An *inference* is a guess that readers make using the clues the author gives them in a piece of writing. For example, the poet doesn't directly state that the maidens are trying to catch snowflakes in "Winter Jewels." Instead, the poet writes about diamonds. We can infer that she means snowflakes from the description and narrative story in the poem.

Students will also learn a bit about free verse. *Free verse* is a type of poetry that doesn't rhyme and does not have a regular rhythm. Free verse mimics an individual's normal speech patterns.

Advance Preparation

Gather students' completed Write a Descriptive Poem activity page from Poetry (A) and Write a Narrative Poem activity page from Poetry (B). Students will refer to these pages during Try It: Write or Expand a Poem.

"First Snow" and "Winter Jewels" Synopses

"First Snow" and "Winter Jewels" both describe winter scenes. In "First Snow," the speaker describes the scene out the window. "Winter Jewels" is a narrative poem that tells a small story of snow glittering in trees, maidens trying to catch snowflakes, and sunshine ultimately causing the snow to melt.

Lesson Goals

- Practice all spelling words online.
- Read "First Snow" and "Winter Jewels."
- Determine types of poems, inferences about poems, and figurative language within poems.
- Write a poem.
- Practice vocabulary words.
- Develop letter formation fluency.

MATERIALS

Supplied

- *Summit English Language Arts 3 Expeditions in Reading*
  - "First Snow"
  - "Winter Jewels"
- *Summit English Language Arts 3 Activity Book*
  - Write or Expand a Poem
- handwriting workbook

Also Needed

- completed Write a Descriptive Poem activity page from Poetry (A)
- completed Write a Narrative Poem activity page from Poetry (B)

KEYWORDS

figurative language – words that describe something by comparing it to something completely different; figure of speech; Example: Rain fell in buckets and the streets looked like rivers.

free verse – poetry whose rhythm follows natural speech patterns and does not rely on regular rhyme or meter

inference – a guess that readers make using the clues that an author gives them in a piece of writing

narrative poem – a poem that tells a story

stanza – a group of lines in a poem

GET READY

Introduction to Poetry (C)

Students will get a glimpse of what they will learn about in the lesson. They will also read the lesson goals and keywords. Have students select each keyword and preview its definition.

Spelling List 21 Review Game

Students will practice all spelling words from the workshop.

Recall "The Building of the Nest" and "The Secret"

Students will answer some questions to review the reading that they have already completed.

Before You Read "First Snow" and "Winter Jewels"

Students will be introduced to some key vocabulary words that they will encounter in the upcoming reading.

READ

"First Snow" and "Winter Jewels"

Students will read "First Snow" and "Winter Jewels" in *Expeditions in Reading*.

Check-In: "First Snow" and "Winter Jewels"

Students will answer several questions to demonstrate their comprehension of "First Snow" and "Winter Jewels."

LEARN AND TRY IT

LEARN Describing Poems

Students will look closely at two poems and describe the type of poems they are, examples of figurative language they contain, and inferences they can draw from them.

NOTE The narrative element of some short poems builds by line instead of by stanza. Encourage students to recognize how the story is revealed line by line in "Winter Jewels."

TRY IT Describe Poems

Students will describe poems, including their type and the figurative language contained within them. They will also describe inferences they can draw from the poems and the way the stanzas work together in poems.

TRY IT Apply: Describe Plot in a Poem

Students will apply to a new work what they've learned about describing plot and sequence of events in a poem.

TRY IT Write or Expand a Poem

Students will complete Write or Expand a Poem in *Summit English Language Arts 3 Activity Book*. Students may choose to write a third poem in a style they choose, or they may expand one of the poems they've already written. Make sure students have their completed Write a Descriptive Poem activity page from Poetry (A) and Write a Narrative Poem activity page from Poetry (B) to refer to during this activity.

LEARNING COACH CHECK-IN This activity page contains an open-ended prompt, so it's important that you review students' responses. Remind students of the characteristics of descriptive and narrative poetry.

NOTE Have students keep their completed activity page in a safe place so they can refer to it later.

TRY IT

Poetry (C)

Write or Expand a Poem

Read the writing prompt.

Prompt: **Write another narrative or descriptive poem. Or, expand one of the poems you wrote to make it longer.**

Respond to the writing prompt.

Answers will vary. Students should write a new descriptive poem in which they describe a person, place, object, idea, or feeling; write a new narrative poem in which they tell a story; or expand one of the poems they previously wrote to make it longer. They should use description and at least one example of figurative language. The poem students write may or may not rhyme.

POETRY (C) 491

492 POETRY (C)

POETRY (C) 493

TRY IT Practice Words from "First Snow" and "Winter Jewels"

Students will answer questions to demonstrate their understanding of the vocabulary words from the reading.

WRAP-UP

Question About Narrative Poems

Students will answer a question to show that they understand the characteristics of narrative poems.

Handwriting

Students should gather their handwriting materials and begin where they left off. Remind students to form letters carefully and correctly.

TIP Set a timer to help students stay focused during handwriting practice.

Poetry Wrap-Up

Lesson Overview

ACTIVITY	ACTIVITY TITLE	TIME	ONLINE/OFFLINE
GET READY	Introduction to Poetry Wrap-Up	**1** minute	online
	Read and Record	**8** minutes	online
TRY IT	Revise and Publish a Poem LEARNING COACH CHECK-IN	**30** minutes	offline
	Review Poetry	**20** minutes	online
QUIZ	Poetry	**15** minutes	online
	Spelling List 21	**10** minutes	online
WRAP-UP	More Language Arts Practice	**15** minutes	online
	Handwriting	**6** minutes	offline

Advance Preparation

Gather students' completed Write a Descriptive Poem activity page from Poetry (A), Write a Narrative Poem activity page from Poetry (B), and Write or Expand a Poem activity page from Poetry (C). Students will refer to these pages during Try It: Revise and Publish a Poem.

Lesson Goals

- Read aloud to practice fluency.
- Review what you learned.
- Take a reading quiz.
- Take a spelling quiz.
- Develop letter formation fluency.

MATERIALS

Supplied

- *Summit English Language Arts 3 Expeditions in Reading*
- *Summit English Language Arts 3 Activity Book*
  - Revise and Publish a Poem
- handwriting workbook

Also Needed

- completed Write a Descriptive Poem activity page from Poetry (A)
- completed Write a Narrative Poem activity page from Poetry (B)
- completed Write or Expand a Poem activity page from Poetry (C)

GET READY

Introduction to Poetry Wrap-Up

Students will read the lesson goals.

Read and Record

Good readers read quickly, smoothly, and with expression. This is called *fluency*. Students will record themselves reading aloud. They will listen to their recording and think about how quick, smooth, and expressive they sound.

TIP Encourage students to rerecord as needed.

TRY IT

Review and Publish a Poem

Students will complete Review and Publish a Poem in *Summit English Language Arts 3 Activity Book*. They should look over the poems they've written in this workshop and choose one to revise and publish.

LEARNING COACH CHECK-IN This activity page contains a checklist. Help students ask themselves each question on the checklist and make revisions directly to their chosen poem. Be sure to discuss both strengths and areas for improvement to their poem.

TIP Students may wish to put their revised and published poem in a safe place. They can use it on a future read and record if they choose.

OPTIONAL Students may illustrate their poem. If students wish, they can illustrate their poem through a medium other than drawing.

TRY IT

Poetry Wrap-Up

Revise and Publish a Poem

Reread the poems that you wrote. Choose one poem to revise. Use the appropriate checklist to revise your poem. Mark your revisions on your poem. Students should check off each item as they make necessary changes to their poem.

Checklist for Revising a Descriptive Poem

- ☐ Did I describe a person, place, object, idea, or feeling?
- ☐ Did I include figurative language to create a picture in readers' minds?
- ☐ Did I include sensory details?
- ☐ Did I use any sound elements, such as rhyme?

Checklist for Revising a Narrative Poem

- ☐ Did I include a clear beginning, middle, and end?
- ☐ Did I include figurative language to create a picture in readers' minds?
- ☐ Did I include sensory details?
- ☐ Did I use any sound elements, such as rhyme?

POETRY WRAP-UP 495

Write or type a clean copy of your poem. Include an illustration if you wish.

Answers will vary. Students should write or type a clean copy of their descriptive or narrative poem.

496 POETRY WRAP-UP

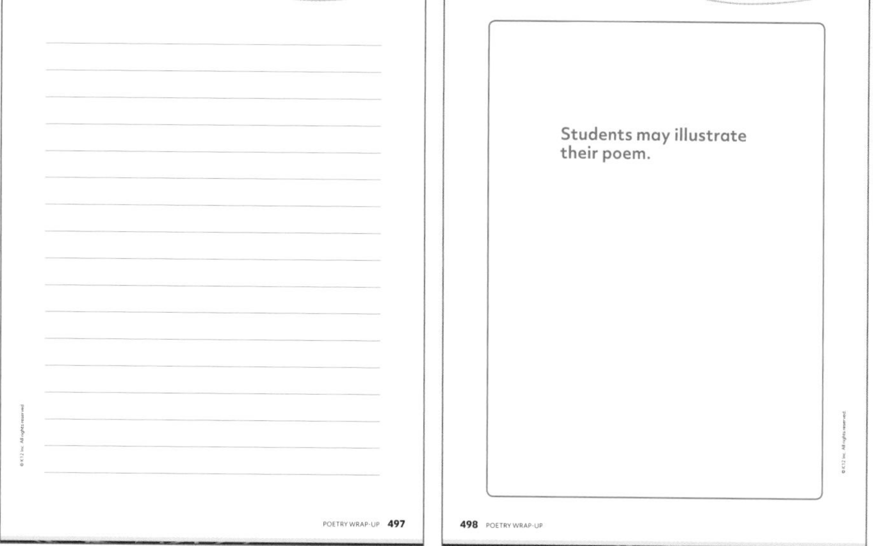

Poetry Review

Students will answer questions to review what they have learned about descriptive and narrative poems, how stanzas build on one another to tell a story, and drawing inferences.

QUIZ

Poetry

Students will complete the Poetry quiz.

Spelling List 21

Students will complete the Spelling List 21 quiz.

WRAP-UP

More Language Arts Practice

Students will practice skills according to their individual needs.

Handwriting

Students should gather their handwriting materials and begin where they left off. Remind students to form letters carefully and correctly.

TIP Set a timer to help students stay focused during handwriting practice.

Opinion Writing: Revising

Lesson Overview

ACTIVITY	ACTIVITY TITLE	TIME	ONLINE/OFFLINE
GET READY	Introduction to Opinion Writing: Revising	**1** minute	online
	Look Back at a Model Persuasive Essay	**10** minutes	online
LEARN AND TRY IT	Revising a Persuasive Essay	**20** minutes	online
	Revise Your Persuasive Essay **LEARNING COACH CHECK-IN**	**55** minutes	offline
WRAP-UP	Question About Revising a Persuasive Essay	**2** minutes	online
	Handwriting	**8** minutes	offline
	Go Read!	**24** minutes	online or offline

Content Background

Students will continue working on their **persuasive essay** about a way to improve their city, town, or neighborhood. In this lesson, students will **revise** their draft in order to use it as the body of a **business letter.**

Writing Process

In the revising step of the writing process, writers look back at their work and find ways to improve it. They focus on their ideas and organization, not on punctuation, grammar, and so on.

To revise their persuasive essay, students will use a checklist. The checklist focuses on ideas (*Does my introduction state my opinion clearly?*) and organization (*Do I need to put any ideas in a new paragraph?*).

During revision, students should think about their audience and purpose. For this assignment, their audience will be the person to whom they address their business letter. Their purpose is to persuade that person to agree with the opinion that they present. All revisions should be made with the audience and purpose in mind.

Students may not understand the difference between revising and proofreading. When revising, writers focus on large issues, such as the

MATERIALS

Supplied

- *Summit English Language Arts 3 Activity Book*
  - Revise Your Persuasive Essay
- Persuasive Essay: Revision Feedback Sheet (printout)
- Persuasive Essay Instructions (printout)
- handwriting workbook

Also Needed

- folder in which students are storing persuasive essay writing assignment pages
- reading material for Go Read!

development and grouping of ideas. When proofreading, writers fix errors in grammar, usage, and mechanics, such as spelling or punctuation mistakes. Encourage students to focus on revising during this lesson. In the next lesson, students will proofread their persuasive essay and business letter parts.

KEYWORDS

business letter – a letter written to an organization or a person at a business

persuasive essay – an essay in which the writer tries to convince readers to agree with a stance on an issue

revising – the step of the writing process for reviewing and fixing ideas and organization

Advance Preparation

Gather the folder that students are using to store the activity pages related to their persuasive essay. The folder should contain the following:

- Model Persuasive Essay activity page from Opinion Writing: Prewriting (A)
- Students' completed Brainstorm for Your Persuasive Essay activity page from Opinion Writing: Prewriting (A)
- Students' completed Plan Your Persuasive Essay activity page from Opinion Writing: Prewriting (B)
- Students' completed draft from Opinion Writing: Drafting (B)
- Model Business Letter activity page from Opinion Writing: Drafting (C)
- Students' completed Turn Your Persuasive Essay into a Business Letter activity page from Opinion Writing: Drafting (C)

Prior to the Revise Your Persuasive Essay activity in this lesson, read students' draft and complete the Persuasive Essay: Revision Feedback Sheet.

During the Go Read! activity, students will have the option of using the digital library. Allow extra time for students to make their reading selection, or have students make a selection before beginning the lesson.

Lesson Goals

- Use a checklist to revise your persuasive essay.
- Develop letter formation fluency.
- Read independently to develop fluency.

GET READY

Introduction to Opinion Writing: Revising

Students will get a glimpse of what they will learn about in the lesson. They will also read the lesson goals and keywords. Have students select each keyword and preview its definition.

Look Back at a Model Persuasive Essay

Students will review the key elements of an effective persuasive essay.

LEARN AND TRY IT

LEARN Revising a Persuasive Essay

Through a guided activity, students will explore how a student revises a persuasive essay that will become the body of a business letter.

TRY IT Revise Your Persuasive Essay

Students will revise their persuasive essay using Revise Your Persuasive Essay in *Summit English Language Arts 3 Activity Book*, which is a revising checklist. They will need their completed persuasive essay draft from Opinion Writing: Drafting (B).

LEARNING COACH CHECK-IN Guide students through the revision process.

1. Gather and use the Persuasive Essay: Revision Feedback Sheet that you filled out to guide a discussion with students.
   - Tell students the strengths of their essay. Provide positive comments about the opinion statement, supporting reasons, organization, or other elements that you enjoyed.
   - Walk through your feedback with students. As you discuss the feedback, encourage students to actively revise their draft in response. Reassure students that it's okay to remove or move around ideas and sentences. Students should revise their draft directly on the drafting page, using the lines they left blank.
2. Have students review their draft once independently, using the revising checklist from the activity book.
   - For students having difficulty recognizing areas they should revise, suggest a revision, and think aloud to model your revising. For example: *I am not sure how this reason connects to your opinion. What transition could you add to the beginning of the sentence to make that clearer?*
3. Make sure students store their revised draft in the folder they are using to organize their writing assignment pages.

TIP Remind students to focus on the checklist questions. Emphasize that they should not worry about spelling, punctuation, grammar, and so on.

NOTE If you or students wish, you can download and print another copy of the Persuasive Essay Instructions online.

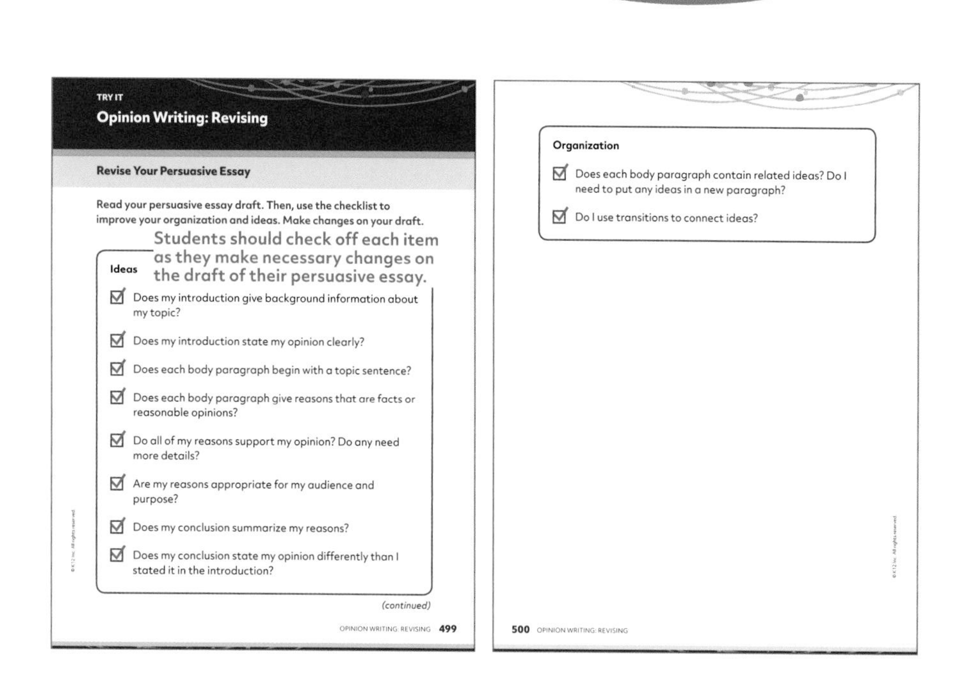
TRY IT
Opinion Writing: Revising

Revise Your Persuasive Essay

Read your persuasive essay draft. Then, use the checklist to improve your organization and ideas. Make changes on your draft.

Students should check off each item as they make necessary changes on the draft of their persuasive essay.

Ideas

- ☑ Does my introduction give background information about my topic?
- ☑ Does my introduction state my opinion clearly?
- ☑ Does each body paragraph begin with a topic sentence?
- ☑ Does each body paragraph give reasons that are facts or reasonable opinions?
- ☑ Do all of my reasons support my opinion? Do any need more details?
- ☑ Are my reasons appropriate for my audience and purpose?
- ☑ Does my conclusion summarize my reasons?
- ☑ Does my conclusion state my opinion differently than I stated it in the introduction?

(continued)

OPINION WRITING: REVISING 499

Organization

- ☑ Does each body paragraph contain related ideas? Do I need to put any ideas in a new paragraph?
- ☑ Do I use transitions to connect ideas?

500 OPINION WRITING: REVISING

WRAP-UP

Question About Revising a Persuasive Essay

Students will answer a question to show that they understand a key revision skill.

Handwriting

Students should gather their handwriting materials and begin where they left off. Remind students to form letters carefully and correctly.

TIP Set a timer to help students stay focused during handwriting practice.

Go Read!

Students will read for pleasure. They should choose a book or a magazine that interests them, or they may choose a selection from the digital library, linked in the online lesson.

- Have students read aloud a few paragraphs of their selection.
- Then have students read silently for the rest of the time.

SUPPORT Students should make no more than five errors in decoding when they read aloud a few paragraphs of their Go Read! selection. If students struggle or make more than five errors, they need to select a different (and easier) text for the Go Read! activity.

TIP Have students select something to read ahead of time to help them stay focused.

Opinion Writing: Proofreading

Lesson Overview

ACTIVITY	ACTIVITY TITLE	TIME	ONLINE/OFFLINE
GET READY	Introduction to Opinion Writing: Proofreading	**1** minute	
	Look Back at Verbs, Adjectives, and Adverbs	**10** minutes	
LEARN AND **TRY IT**	Proofreading a Persuasive Essay and Business Letter Parts	**20** minutes	
	Proofread Your Persuasive Essay and Business Letter Parts **LEARNING COACH CHECK-IN**	**55** minutes	
WRAP-UP	Question About Proofreading a Business Letter	**2** minutes	
	Handwriting	**8** minutes	
	Go Read!	**24** minutes	or

Content Background

Students will continue working on their **persuasive essay** about a way to improve their city, town, or neighborhood, which they will use as the body of a **business letter**. In this lesson, students will **proofread** their revised essay draft as well as proofread the business letter parts (heading, inside address, and so on) that they drafted earlier.

Writing Process

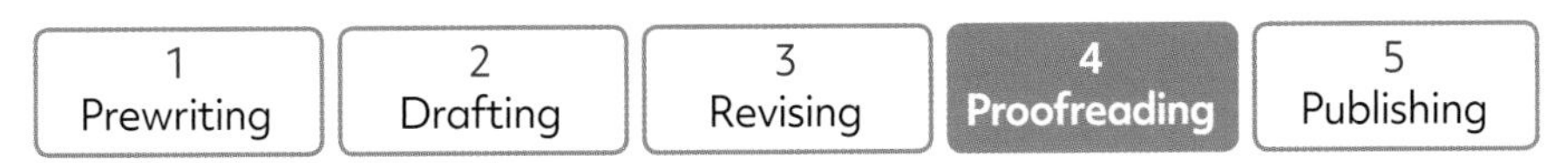

To proofread their persuasive essay and business letter parts, students will use a checklist. The checklist focuses on grammar and usage (*Are all sentences complete and correct?*) and mechanics (*Did I put a comma between the city and state in each address?*).

Proofreading is often thought of as a hunt for errors. But that's not completely accurate. During proofreading, writers evaluate whether the way they use words, capitalization, punctuation, and sentence structure makes their writing as clear as possible. Sometimes, that means fixing a clear error, like a misspelled word. Other times, that means combining two sentences or using a different verb in a sentence.

Proofreading is sometimes called *editing*.

MATERIALS

Supplied

- *Summit English Language Arts 3 Activity Book*
  - Proofread Your Persuasive Essay and Business Letter Parts
- Persuasive Essay and Business Letter Parts: Proofreading Feedback Sheet (printout)
- Persuasive Essay Instructions (printout)
- handwriting workbook

Also Needed

- folder in which students are storing persuasive essay writing assignment pages
- reading material for Go Read!

Advance Preparation

Gather the folder that students are using to store the activity pages related to their persuasive essay. The folder should contain the following:

- Model Persuasive Essay activity page from Opinion Writing: Prewriting (A)
- Students' completed Brainstorm for Your Persuasive Essay activity page from Opinion Writing: Prewriting (A)
- Students' completed Plan Your Persuasive Essay activity page from Opinion Writing: Prewriting (B)
- Model Business Letter activity page from Opinion Writing: Drafting (C)
- Students' completed Turn Your Persuasive Essay into a Business Letter activity page from Opinion Writing: Drafting (C)
- Students' revised draft from Opinion Writing: Revising

Prior to the Proofread Your Persuasive Essay and Business Letter Parts activity in this lesson, read students' draft and complete Persuasive Essay and Business Letter Parts: Proofreading Feedback Sheet.

During the Go Read! activity, students will have the option of using the digital library. Allow extra time for students to make their reading selection, or have students make a selection before beginning the lesson.

KEYWORDS

business letter – a letter written to an organization or a person at a business

persuasive essay – an essay in which the writer tries to convince readers to agree with a stance on an issue

proofreading – the step of the writing process for checking and fixing errors in grammar, punctuation, capitalization, and spelling

Lesson Goals

- Use a checklist to proofread your persuasive essay and business letter parts.
- Develop letter formation fluency.
- Read independently to develop fluency.

GET READY

Introduction to Opinion Writing: Proofreading

Students will get a glimpse of what they will learn about in the lesson. They will also read the lesson goals and keywords. Have students select each keyword and preview its definition.

Look Back at Verbs, Adjectives, and Adverbs

Students will practice forming and using verbs, adjectives, and adverbs, including comparative and superlative adjectives and adverbs. These are key skills that students will use as they proofread their research report.

LEARN AND TRY IT

LEARN Proofreading a Persuasive Essay and Business Letter Parts

Through a guided activity, students will explore how a student proofreads a persuasive essay with the intention of using it as the body of a business letter.

TRY IT Proofread Your Persuasive Essay and Business Letter Parts

Students will proofread their persuasive essay and business letter parts using Proofread Your Persuasive Essay and Business Letter Parts in *Summit English Language Arts 3 Activity Book*, which is a proofreading checklist. They will need their revised persuasive essay from Opinion Writing: Revising and their completed Turn Your Persuasive Essay into a Business Letter activity page from Opinion Writing: Drafting (C).

LEARNING COACH CHECK-IN Guide students through the proofreading process.

1. Have students read their essay draft aloud, listening for blatant errors such as missing words and incomplete sentences. As students catch errors, have them fix the errors on their draft, using the lines they left blank.
2. Have students review their essay draft and business letter parts, using the proofreading checklist from the activity book. They can refer to the Model Business Letter for a correct model for capitalization and punctuation of the business letter parts.
3. Review with students your comments on the Persuasive Essay and Business Letter Parts: Proofreading Feedback Sheet. Praise students for the improvements they made, and guide students to recognize any other critical improvements.
   - It is important that you don't edit students' reports for them, but it's appropriate to guide students with observations and questions. For example, *Your audience is the mayor. Is there a more formal word you could use instead of this slang word?*
4. Have students store their edited draft and activity page in the folder they are using to organize their writing assignment pages.

OPTIONAL Have students exchange revised essays with a peer and use the proofreading checklist from the activity book to proofread each other's essays.

NOTE If you or students wish, you can download and print another copy of the Persuasive Essay Instructions online.

TRY IT

Opinion Writing: Proofreading

Proofread Your Persuasive Essay

Read your revised persuasive essay draft and Turn Your Persuasive Essay into a Business Letter activity page. Then, use the checklist to improve your grammar, usage, and mechanics. Make changes on your revised draft and activity page.

Grammar and Usage

- ☑ Are all sentences complete and correct?
- ☑ Is there a variety of sentence types and lengths?
- ☑ Did I form and use verbs correctly?
- ☑ Did I use adjectives and adverbs correctly? Did I choose strong adjectives and adverbs?
- ☑ Is my language appropriate for my audience?
- ☑ Are there any missing or extra words?

(continued)

Students should check off each item as they make necessary changes on the draft of their persuasive essay and Turn Your Persuasive Essay into a Business Letter activity page.

Mechanics

- ☑ Is every word spelled correctly?
- ☑ Does every sentence begin with a capital letter and end with correct punctuation?
- ☑ Did I put a comma between the city and state in each address?
- ☑ Did I follow the correct format for all parts of a business letter?

WRAP-UP

Question About Proofreading a Business Letter

Students will answer a question to show that they understand a key proofreading skill.

Handwriting

Students should gather their handwriting materials and begin where they left off. Remind students to form letters carefully and correctly.

TIP Set a timer to help students stay focused during handwriting practice.

Go Read!

Students will read for pleasure. They should choose a book or a magazine that interests them, or they may choose a selection from the digital library, linked in the online lesson.

- Have students read aloud a few paragraphs of their selection.
- Then have students read silently for the rest of the time.

SUPPORT Students should make no more than five errors in decoding when they read aloud a few paragraphs of their Go Read! selection. If students struggle or make more than five errors, they need to select a different (and easier) text for the Go Read! activity.

TIP Have students select something to read ahead of time to help them stay focused.

Opinion Writing: Publishing

Lesson Overview

ACTIVITY	ACTIVITY TITLE	TIME	ONLINE/OFFLINE
GET READY	Introduction to Opinion Writing: Publishing	**1** minute	online
LEARN AND **TRY IT**	Publishing a Business Letter	**10** minutes	online
	Publish Your Business Letter **LEARNING COACH CHECK-IN**	**60** minutes	online
WRAP-UP	Turn In Your Business Letter	**1** minute	online
	More Language Arts Practice	**20** minutes	online
	Handwriting	**8** minutes	offline
	Go Read!	**20** minutes	online or offline

Content Background

Students will publish their **persuasive essay** about a way to improve their city, town, or neighborhood as a **business letter**. Then they will submit their completed business letter to their teacher.

Writing Process

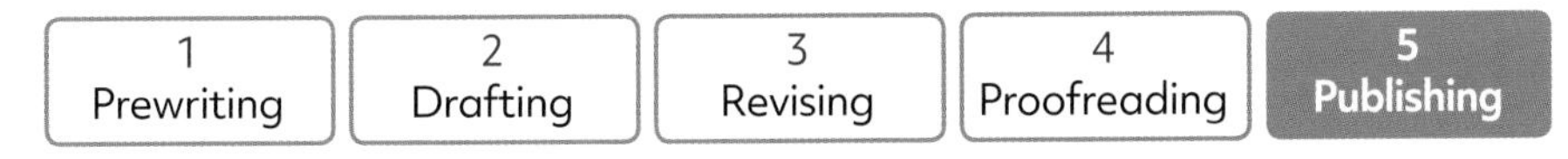

Students must type their clean copy. They will complete an activity to review basic word-processing skills as well as skills they will need to format their business letter. In particular, the paragraphs and other parts of a business letter are not indented; instead, there is a space between each paragraph. The Model Business Letter activity page reflects the formatting conventions that students should follow.

MATERIALS

Supplied

- *Summit English Language Arts 3 Activity Book*
  - Publish Your Business Letter
- handwriting workbook

Also Needed

- folder in which students are storing persuasive essay writing assignment pages
- reading material for Go Read!

Advance Preparation

Gather the folder that students are using to store the activity pages related to their persuasive essay. The folder should contain the following:

- Model Persuasive Essay activity page from Opinion Writing: Prewriting (A)
- Students' completed Brainstorm for Your Persuasive Essay activity page from Opinion Writing: Prewriting (A)

- Students' completed Plan Your Persuasive Essay activity page from Opinion Writing: Prewriting (B)
- Model Business Letter activity page from Opinion Writing: Drafting (C)
- Students' revised and edited draft from Opinion Writing: Proofreading
- Students' edited Turn Your Persuasive Essay into a Business Letter activity page from Opinion Writing: Proofreading

During the Go Read! activity, students will have the option of using the digital library. Allow extra time for students to make their reading selection, or have students make a selection before beginning the lesson.

KEYWORDS

business letter – a letter written to an organization or a person at a business

persuasive essay – an essay in which the writer tries to convince readers to agree with a stance on an issue

publishing – the step of the writing process for making a clean copy of the piece and sharing it

Lesson Goals

- Make a clean copy of your business letter.
- Submit your business letter to your teacher.
- Develop letter formation fluency.
- Read independently to develop fluency.

GET READY

Introduction to Opinion Writing: Publishing

Students will get a glimpse of what they will learn about in the lesson. They will also read the lesson goals and keywords. Have students select each keyword and preview its definition.

LEARN AND TRY IT

LEARN Publishing a Business Letter

Students will learn how to take their persuasive essay draft and their business letter parts and put them together to create a business letter. They will also review basic keyboarding skills, and they will learn things to keep in mind when typing a business letter.

TRY IT Publish Your Business Letter

Students will create a final copy of their business letter by following the directions on the Publish Your Business Letter activity page in *Summit English Language Arts 3 Activity Book*. Students should gather their revised and edited draft and their edited Turn Your Persuasive Essay into a Business Letter activity page. They should type a clean copy of their business letter that incorporates all of the changes they made in the workshop.

NOTE Students must type their clean copy.

TIP Have students refer to the Model Business Letter activity page as a model for formatting.

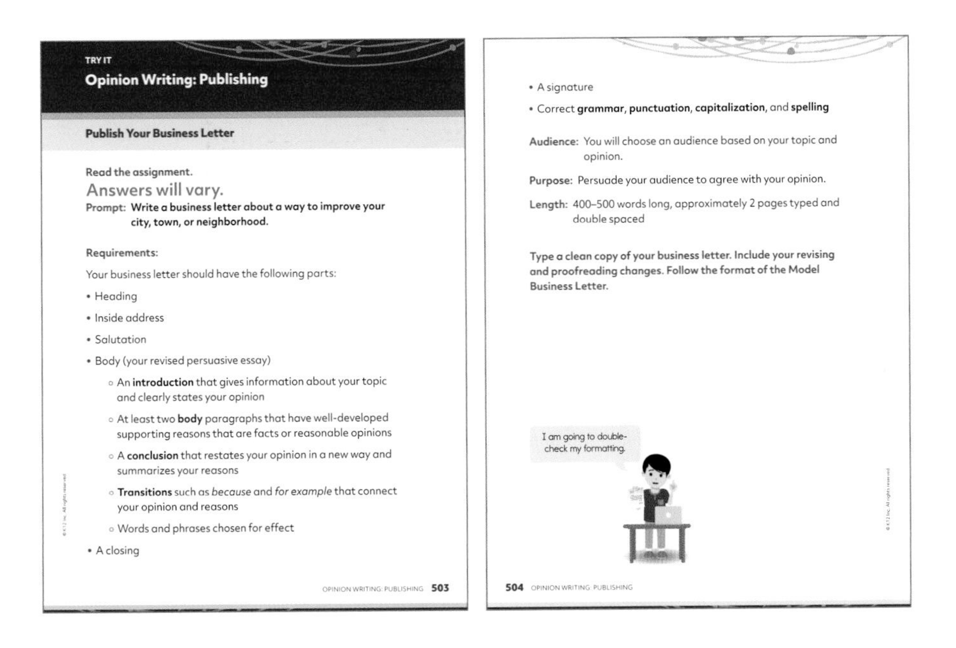

TRY IT

Opinion Writing: Publishing

Publish Your Business Letter

Read the assignment.

Answers will vary.

Prompt: **Write a business letter about a way to improve your city, town, or neighborhood.**

Requirements:

Your business letter should have the following parts:

- Heading
- Inside address
- Salutation
- Body (your revised persuasive essay)
  - An **introduction** that gives information about your topic and clearly states your opinion
  - At least two **body** paragraphs that have well-developed supporting reasons that are facts or reasonable opinions
  - A **conclusion** that restates your opinion in a new way and summarizes your reasons
  - **Transitions** such as *because* and *for example* that connect your opinion and reasons
  - Words and phrases chosen for effect
- A closing

OPINION WRITING: PUBLISHING 503

- A signature
- Correct **grammar**, **punctuation**, **capitalization**, and **spelling**

Audience: You will choose an audience based on your topic and opinion.

Purpose: Persuade your audience to agree with your opinion.

Length: 400–500 words long, approximately 2 pages typed and double spaced

Type a clean copy of your business letter. Include your revising and proofreading changes. Follow the format of the Model Business Letter.

504 OPINION WRITING: PUBLISHING

WRAP-UP

Turn In Your Business Letter

Students will submit their writing assignment to their teacher.

More Language Arts Practice

Students will practice skills according to their individual needs.

Handwriting

Students should gather their handwriting materials and begin where they left off. Remind students to form letters carefully and correctly.

TIP Set a timer to help students stay focused during handwriting practice.

Go Read!

Students will read for pleasure. They should choose a book or a magazine that interests them, or they may choose a selection from the digital library, linked in the online lesson.

- Have students read aloud a few paragraphs of their selection.
- Then have students read silently for the rest of the time.

SUPPORT Students should make no more than five errors in decoding when they read aloud a few paragraphs of their Go Read! selection. If students struggle or make more than five errors, they need to select a different (and easier) text for the Go Read! activity.

TIP Have students select something to read ahead of time to help them stay focused.

Big Ideas: Respond to a Prompt

Lesson Overview

Big Ideas lessons provide students the opportunity to further apply the knowledge acquired and skills learned throughout the unit workshops. Each Big Ideas lesson consists of these parts:

1. **Cumulative Review:** Students keep their skills fresh by reviewing prior content.
2. **Preview:** Students practice answering the types of questions they will commonly find on standardized tests.
3. **Synthesis:** Students complete an assignment that allows them to connect and apply what they have learned. Synthesis assignments vary throughout the course.

   In the Synthesis portion of this Big Ideas lesson, students will respond to an essay prompt based on reading selections. To respond meaningfully, students will need to use their own ideas as well as examples from the readings. Students' writing will be assessed in four categories: purpose and content; structure and organization; language and word choice; and grammar, usage, and mechanics.

   LEARNING COACH CHECK-IN This is a graded assessment. Make sure students complete, review, and submit the assignment to their teacher.

All materials needed for this lesson are linked online and not provided in the activity book.

MATERIALS

Supplied

- Respond to a Prompt (printout)

Choice Reading Project

Suffixes

Lesson Overview

ACTIVITY	ACTIVITY TITLE	TIME	ONLINE/OFFLINE
GET READY	Introduction to Suffixes	**2** minutes	online
	Look Back at Roots and Base Words	**4** minutes	online
LEARN AND TRY IT	Suffixes	**10** minutes	online
	Practice Using Suffixes	**10** minutes	online
	Apply: Suffixes LEARNING COACH CHECK-IN	**15** minutes	offline
	Review Suffixes	**15** minutes	online
QUIZ	Suffixes	**15** minutes	online
WRAP-UP	More Language Arts Practice	**19** minutes	online
	Go Write! Speak to a Group	**15** minutes	offline
	Go Read!	**15** minutes	online or offline

Content Background

Students will learn that a suffix can be attached to the end of a root or base word to create a new word with a new meaning. A *suffix* is a word part with its own meaning. For example, *–less* is a suffix that means "without." When it is attached to the end of the base word *home*, it forms *homeless*, which means "without a home." Students will learn the meanings of some of the more common suffixes: *–ly*, *–ness*, *–less*, *–ish*, *–er/or*, and *–ful*. Knowing the meaning of suffixes can help students figure out the meanings of new words and determine the words that fit the context of a text.

Advance Preparation

During the Go Read! activity, students will have the option of using the digital library. Allow extra time for students to make their reading selection, or have students make a selection before beginning the lesson.

MATERIALS

Supplied

- *Summit English Language Arts 3 Activity Book*
  - Apply: Suffixes
  - Go Write! Speak to a Group

Also Needed

- reading material for Go Read!

Lesson Goals

- Practice vocabulary words.
- Identify and determine the meaning of suffixes.
- Use suffixes to determine the meanings of words.
- Take the Suffixes quiz.
- Freewrite about a topic to develop writing fluency and practice letter formation.
- Read independently to develop fluency.

KEYWORDS

root – a word part with a special meaning to which prefixes and suffixes can be added; Example: *spec* is a root that means "see"

suffix – a word part added to the end of a base word or root that changes the meaning or part of speech of a word

GET READY

Introduction to Suffixes

After a quick introductory activity, students will read the lesson goals and keywords. Have students select each keyword and preview its definition.

Look Back at Roots and Base Words

Students will practice the prerequisite skill of identifying and determining the meaning of roots and base words.

LEARN AND TRY IT

LEARN Suffixes

Students will be introduced to the vocabulary words for the lesson. Then they will learn how to use words they know and context clues to figure out the meanings of suffixes and words formed with suffixes.

TRY IT Practice Using Suffixes

Students will practice determining the meaning of suffixes and using context clues to determine the suffix needed to correctly form a new word.

TRY IT Apply: Suffixes

Students will complete Apply: Suffixes in *Summit English Language Arts 3 Activity Book*. They will practice forming words with suffixes and using those words in sentences.

LEARNING COACH CHECK-IN This activity page contains open-ended questions, so it's important that you review students' responses. Give students feedback, using the sample answers provided to guide you.

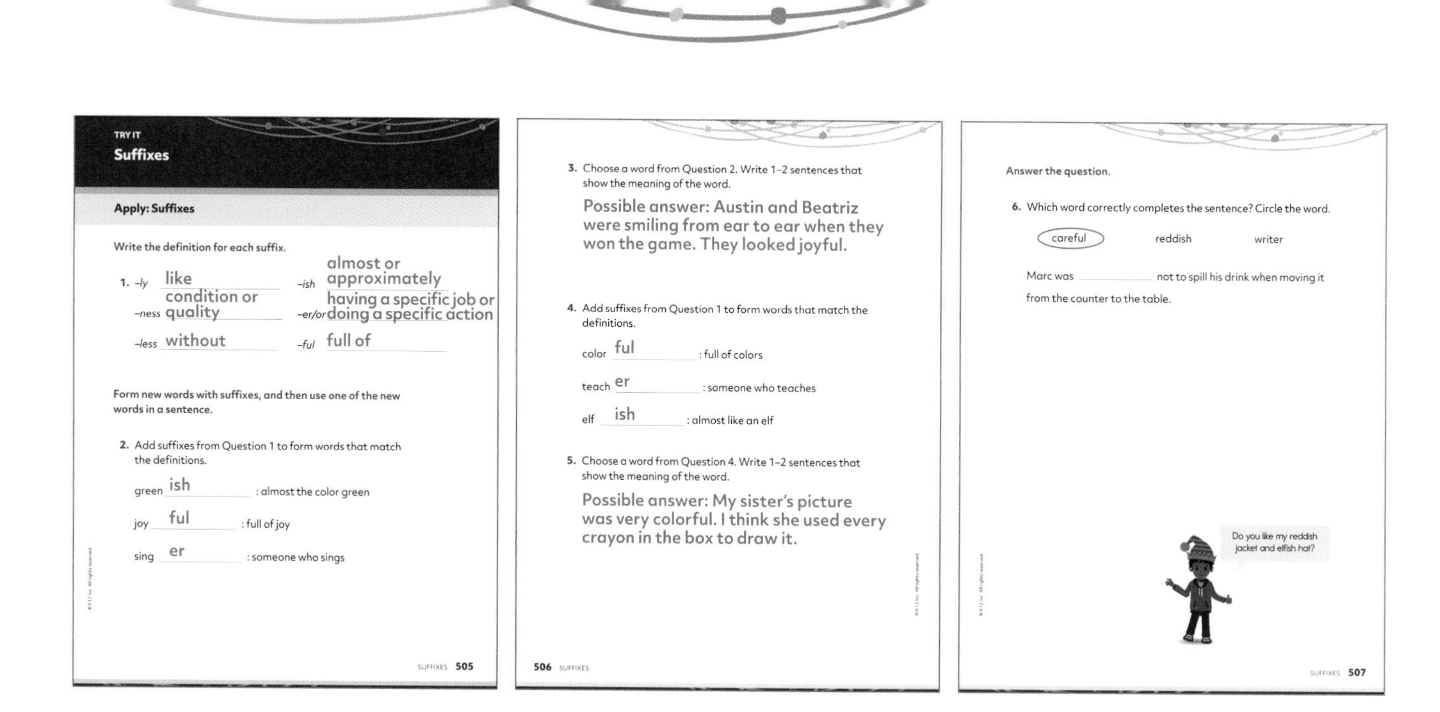
TRY IT
Suffixes

Apply: Suffixes

Write the definition for each suffix.

1. –ly like
–ish almost or approximately
–ness condition or quality
–er/or having a specific job or doing a specific action
–less without
–ful full of

Form new words with suffixes, and then use one of the new words in a sentence.

2. Add suffixes from Question 1 to form words that match the definitions.

green ish : almost the color green

joy ful : full of joy

sing er : someone who sings

SUFFIXES 505

3. Choose a word from Question 2. Write 1–2 sentences that show the meaning of the word.

Possible answer: Austin and Beatriz were smiling from ear to ear when they won the game. They looked joyful.

4. Add suffixes from Question 1 to form words that match the definitions.

color ful : full of colors

teach er : someone who teaches

elf ish : almost like an elf

5. Choose a word from Question 4. Write 1–2 sentences that show the meaning of the word.

Possible answer: My sister's picture was very colorful. I think she used every crayon in the box to draw it.

506 SUFFIXES

Answer the question.

6. Which word correctly completes the sentence? Circle the word.

careful reddish writer

Marc was ________ not to spill his drink when moving it from the counter to the table.

SUFFIXES 507

TRY IT **Review Suffixes**

Students will answer questions to review what they have learned about identifying and determining the meaning of suffixes.

QUIZ

Suffixes

Students will complete the Suffixes quiz.

WRAP-UP

More Language Arts Practice

Students will practice skills according to their individual needs.

Go Write! Speak to a Group

Students will complete Go Write! Speak to a Group in *Summit English Language Arts 3 Activity Book*. They will have the option to either respond to a prompt or write about a topic of their choice.

NOTE This activity is intended to build writing fluency. Students should write for the entire allotted time.

SUPPORT If students have trouble writing for the allotted time, prompt them with questions. For example, *Can you tell me more about this? Why do you feel this way?*

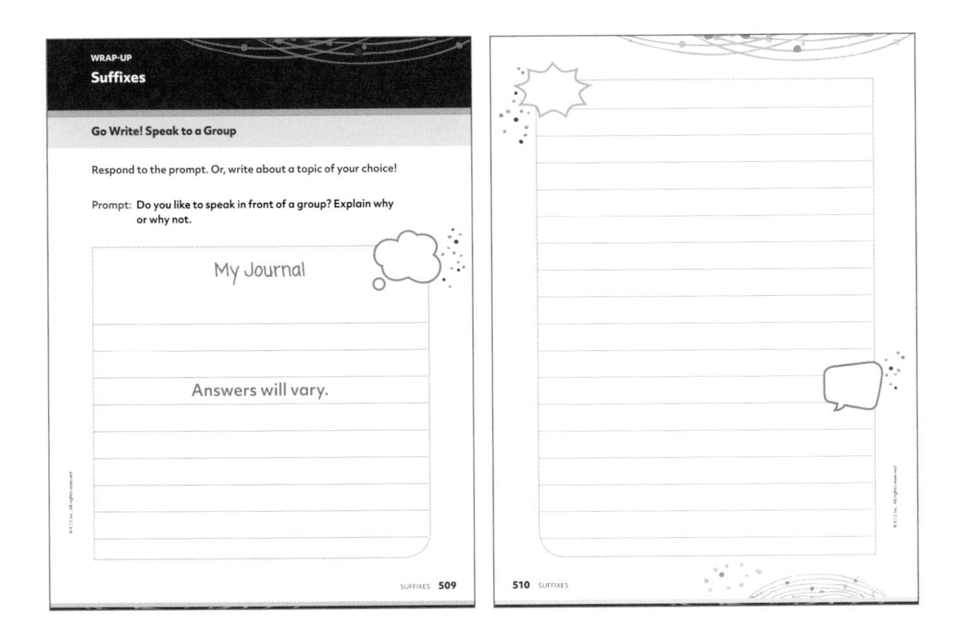
WRAP-UP

Suffixes

Go Write! Speak to a Group

Respond to the prompt. Or, write about a topic of your choice!

Prompt: Do you like to speak in front of a group? Explain why or why not.

My Journal

Answers will vary.

SUFFIXES 509

510 SUFFIXES

Go Read!

Students will read for pleasure. They should choose a book or a magazine that interests them, or they may choose a selection from the digital library, linked in the online lesson.

- Have students read aloud a few paragraphs of their selection.
- Then have students read silently for the rest of the time.

SUPPORT Students should make no more than five errors in decoding when they read aloud a few paragraphs of their Go Read! selection. If students struggle or make more than five errors, they need to select a different (and easier) text for the Go Read! activity.

TIP Have students select something to read ahead of time to help them stay focused.

Presentation Skills (A)

Lesson Overview

ACTIVITY	ACTIVITY TITLE	TIME	ONLINE/OFFLINE
GET READY	Introduction to Presentation Skills (A)	**1** minute	
	Look Back at Pronouns	**10** minutes	
LEARN AND **TRY IT**	Pronouns	**15** minutes	
	Use Pronouns	**15** minutes	
	Listening for the Main Idea and Details	**15** minutes	
	Listen for the Main Idea and Details	**15** minutes	
	Add the Perfect Picture **LEARNING COACH CHECK-IN**	**20** minutes	and
WRAP-UP	Questions About Pronouns and Main Idea	**4** minutes	
	Handwriting	**8** minutes	
	Go Read!	**17** minutes	or

Content Background

Students will explore speaking and listening skills, also called presentation skills. This lesson focuses on listening skills. Specifically, students will learn how to identify the main idea and supporting details of an oral presentation.

Additionally, students will learn that media, such as pictures or music, can enhance or distract from an oral presentation. Effective media directly relates to the main idea or an important supporting detail of the presentation.

Grammar, Usage, and Mechanics Students will learn about pronouns. A *pronoun* is a word that takes the place of one or more nouns in a sentence.

A *personal pronoun* takes the place of a subject or an object in a sentence.

Point of View	Singular Pronouns	Plural Pronouns
first person	I, me	we, us
second person	you	you
third person	he, she, him, her, it	they, them

MATERIALS

Supplied

- *Summit English Language Arts 3 Activity Book*
  - Add the Perfect Picture
- handwriting workbook

Also Needed

- reading material for Go Read!

A *possessive pronoun* shows ownership.

Point of View	Singular Pronouns	Plural Pronouns
first person	my, mine	our, ours
second person	your, yours	your, yours
third person	his, her, hers, its	their, theirs

A *reflexive pronoun* ends in *–self* or *–selves* and refers back to the subject.

Point of View	Singular Pronouns	Plural Pronouns
first person	myself	ourselves
second person	yourself	yourselves
third person	himself, herself, itself	themselves

NOTE Language changes over time. Many dictionaries and style manuals have recently adjusted their guidance on the use of the pronouns *they*, *their*, *them*, and *themselves* with singular antecedents. In the following sentence, the pronoun *their* agrees with the singular antecedent *Everyone*:

Example: Everyone said **their** name.

The pronouns *they*, *their*, *them*, and *themselves* have also been adopted by individuals with nonbinary gender identities. In the following sentence, the pronoun *they* agrees with the subject *instructor*:

Example: The **instructor** said that **they** played baseball as a teenager.

This course teaches that the traditionally singular pronouns agree with singular antecedents like *everyone*. But, through the idea that language evolves, the course also notes *their* can correctly be used with singular antecedents. (**Everyone** said **their** name.)

K12 curriculum affirms the use of the singular *they* for reasons of gender identity.

Advance Preparation

During the Go Read! activity, students will have the option of using the digital library. Allow extra time for students to make their reading selection, or have students make a selection before beginning the lesson.

KEYWORDS

main idea – the most important point the author makes; it may be stated or unstated

pronoun – a word that takes the place of one or more nouns

supporting detail – a detail that gives more information about a main idea

Lesson Goals

- Explain how a pronoun is used in a sentence.
- Identify the main idea and supporting details of a presentation.
- Choose a picture that supports the ideas in a presentation.
- Develop letter formation fluency.
- Read independently to develop fluency.

GET READY

Introduction to Presentation Skills (A)

Students will get a glimpse of what they will learn about in the lesson. They will also read the lesson goals and keywords. Have students select each keyword and preview its definition.

Look Back at Pronouns

Students will practice the prerequisite skill of identifying pronouns.

LEARN AND TRY IT

LEARN Pronouns

Students will learn what pronouns are and how they are used in sentences.

TIP To help students remember that pronouns replace nouns in sentences, point out to students that the word *pronoun* contains the word *noun*.

TRY IT Use Pronouns

Students will practice determining the function of pronouns. They will also practice using pronouns in sentences. They will receive feedback on their answers.

LEARN Listening for the Main Idea and Details

Students will listen to a text read aloud. Then they will learn how to identify the main idea and supporting details of that presentation. They will also learn that media can effectively support the main idea or supporting details of a presentation.

TRY IT Listen for the Main Idea and Details

Students will listen to a text read aloud and answer questions about its main idea and supporting details. They will receive feedback on their answers.

TRY IT Add the Perfect Picture

Students will complete Add the Perfect Picture in *Summit English Language Arts 3 Activity Book*.

TIP If students wish, they may use art supplies to create their "perfect pictures."

LEARNING COACH CHECK-IN This activity page contains open-ended questions, so it's important that you review students' responses. Give students feedback, using the sample answers provided to guide you.

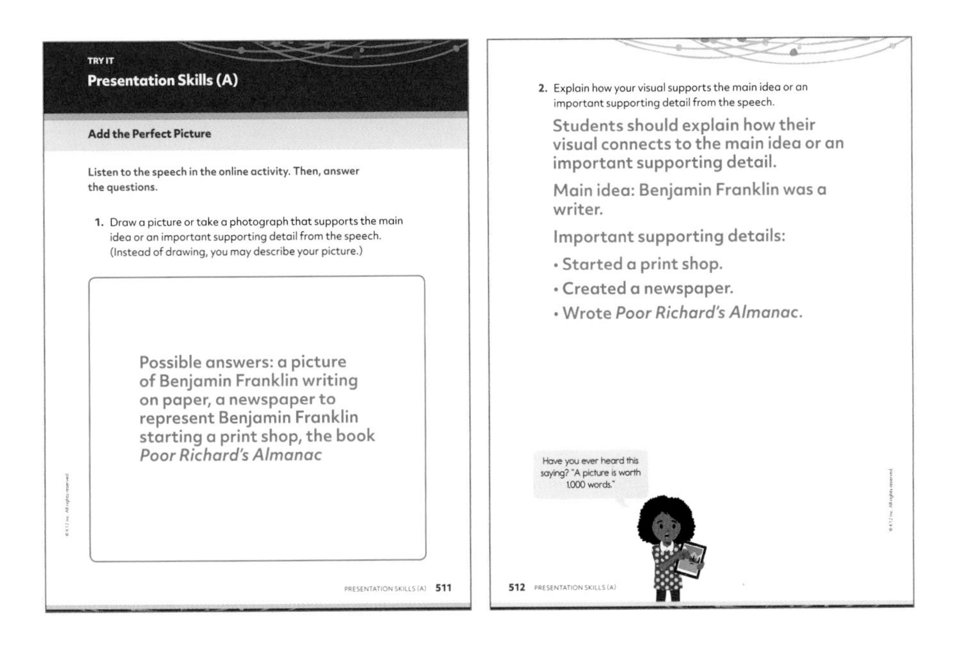

TRY IT

Presentation Skills (A)

Add the Perfect Picture

Listen to the speech in the online activity. Then, answer the questions.

1. Draw a picture or take a photograph that supports the main idea or an important supporting detail from the speech. (Instead of drawing, you may describe your picture.)

Possible answers: a picture of Benjamin Franklin writing on paper, a newspaper to represent Benjamin Franklin starting a print shop, the book *Poor Richard's Almanac*

PRESENTATION SKILLS (A) 511

2. Explain how your visual supports the main idea or an important supporting detail from the speech.

Students should explain how their visual connects to the main idea or an important supporting detail.

Main idea: Benjamin Franklin was a writer.

Important supporting details:

- Started a print shop.
- Created a newspaper.
- Wrote *Poor Richard's Almanac*.

512 PRESENTATION SKILLS (A)

WRAP-UP

Questions About Pronouns and Main Idea

Students will answer questions to show that they understand how a pronoun functions in a sentence and how to identify the main idea and supporting details of a text read aloud.

Handwriting

Students should gather their handwriting materials and begin where they left off. Remind students to form letters carefully and correctly.

TIP Set a timer to help students stay focused during handwriting practice.

Go Read!

Students will read for pleasure. They should choose a book or a magazine that interests them, or they may choose a selection from the digital library, linked in the online lesson.

- Have students read aloud a few paragraphs of their selection.
- Then have students read silently for the rest of the time.

SUPPORT Students should make no more than five errors in decoding when they read aloud a few paragraphs of their Go Read! selection. If students struggle or make more than five errors, they need to select a different (and easier) text for the Go Read! activity.

TIP Have students select something to read ahead of time to help them stay focused.

Presentation Skills (B)

Lesson Overview

ACTIVITY	ACTIVITY TITLE	TIME	ONLINE/OFFLINE
GET READY	Introduction to Presentation Skills (B)	**1** minute	
LEARN AND **TRY IT**	Pronoun-Antecedent Agreement	**10** minutes	
	Use Pronoun-Antecedent Agreement	**15** minutes	
	Listening for Strong Speaking Skills	**15** minutes	
	Listen for Strong Speaking Skills	**10** minutes	
	Read a Poem Aloud **LEARNING COACH CHECK-IN**	**30** minutes	and
WRAP-UP	Questions About Agreement and Speaking Skills	**4** minutes	
	Handwriting	**8** minutes	
	Go Read!	**27** minutes	or

Content Background

Students will continue to learn about presentation skills. In this lesson, they will focus on skills related to the mechanics of speaking: speaking at an understandable pace and speaking clearly. *Pace* refers to how quickly or slowly someone speaks. *Clarity* refers to correct pronunciation of words, as well as speaking at an appropriate volume.

To practice the presentation skills they learn in this lesson, students will record themselves reading aloud a poem. They will listen to their recording and critique their pace and clarity.

Grammar, Usage, and Mechanics Students will learn about pronoun-antecedent agreement. An *antecedent* is the word that a pronoun points back to. A pronoun and its antecedent must agree in number and gender.

Examples: **Jim** ate **his** pizza in one bite.

Lisa thought that was gross, so **she** left the table.

The other **children** covered **their** eyes.

MATERIALS

Supplied

- *Summit English Language Arts 3 Activity Book*
  - Read a Poem Aloud
- handwriting workbook

Also Needed

- reading material for Go Read!

Advance Preparation

During the Go Read! activity, students will have the option of using the digital library. Allow extra time for students to make their reading selection, or have students make a selection before beginning the lesson.

KEYWORDS

antecedent – the noun or pronoun that a pronoun points back to

clarity – the quality of being easy to understand

pace – the speed, and the change of speeds, of a speaker's delivery

pronoun – a word that takes the place of one or more nouns

Lesson Goals

- Use correct pronoun-antecedent agreement.
- Analyze a speaker's pace and clarity.
- Read aloud a passage with appropriate pace and clarity.
- Develop letter formation fluency.
- Read independently to develop fluency.

GET READY

Introduction to Presentation Skills (B)

Students will get a glimpse of what they will learn about in the lesson. They will also read the lesson goals and keywords. Have students select each keyword and preview its definition.

LEARN AND TRY IT

LEARN Pronoun-Antecedent Agreement

Students will learn that a pronoun must agree with its antecedent both in number and gender.

TIP Point out that the possessive pronouns *its*, *your*, and *their* all have homophones that are contractions (*it's*, *you're*, and *they're*). Have students use each word (the possessive pronouns and the contractions) in a sentence.

TRY IT Use Pronoun-Antecedent Agreement

Students will answer questions about pronoun-antecedent agreement. They will receive feedback on their answers.

LEARN Listening for Strong Speaking Skills

Students will learn what it means to speak clearly and at an understandable pace. They will also learn about using appropriate volume and speaking with feeling.

TRY IT Listen for Strong Speaking Skills

Students will answer questions about speaking clearly and at an understandable pace. They will receive feedback on their answers.

TRY IT Read a Poem Aloud

Students will complete Read a Poem Aloud in *Summit English Language Arts 3 Activity Book*.

NOTE Students will record themselves reading aloud a poem using an online recording tool. Then they will listen to their recording, think about improvements they can make, and read and record the poem again. Ensure that students have access to a computer while completing the activity.

LEARNING COACH CHECK-IN Encourage students to read aloud the poem to you before recording it. Assist students with decoding words that they read incorrectly before they record. Give students feedback, using Question 2 on the activity page as a guide.

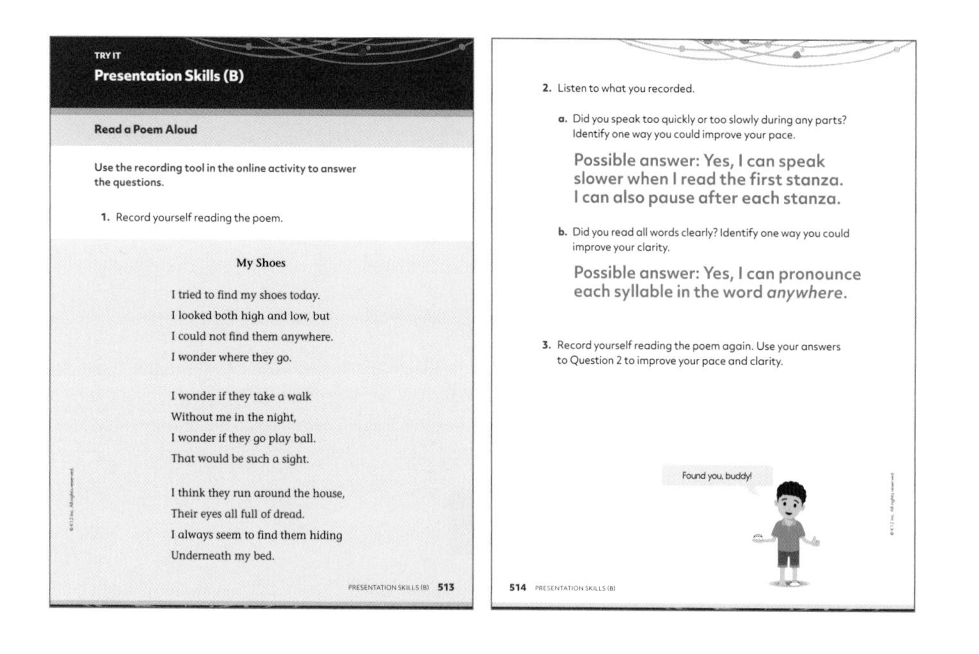

TRY IT
Presentation Skills (B)

Read a Poem Aloud

Use the recording tool in the online activity to answer the questions.

1. Record yourself reading the poem.

My Shoes

I tried to find my shoes today.
I looked both high and low, but
I could not find them anywhere.
I wonder where they go.

I wonder if they take a walk
Without me in the night,
I wonder if they go play ball.
That would be such a sight.

I think they run around the house,
Their eyes all full of dread.
I always seem to find them hiding
Underneath my bed.

PRESENTATION SKILLS (B) 513

2. Listen to what you recorded.
   a. Did you speak too quickly or too slowly during any parts? Identify one way you could improve your pace.
   Possible answer: Yes, I can speak slower when I read the first stanza. I can also pause after each stanza.
   b. Did you read all words clearly? Identify one way you could improve your clarity.
   Possible answer: Yes, I can pronounce each syllable in the word *anywhere*.
3. Record yourself reading the poem again. Use your answers to Question 2 to improve your pace and clarity.

514 PRESENTATION SKILLS (B)

WRAP-UP

Questions About Agreement and Speaking Skills

Students will answer questions to show that they understand pronoun-antecedent agreement and how to speak with appropriate pace and clarity.

Handwriting

Students should gather their handwriting materials and begin where they left off. Remind students to form letters carefully and correctly.

TIP Set a timer to help students stay focused during handwriting practice.

Go Read!

Students will read for pleasure. They should choose a book or a magazine that interests them, or they may choose a selection from the digital library, linked in the online lesson.

- Have students read aloud a few paragraphs of their selection.
- Then have students read silently for the rest of the time.

SUPPORT Students should make no more than five errors in decoding when they read aloud a few paragraphs of their Go Read! selection. If students struggle or make more than five errors, they need to select a different (and easier) text for the Go Read! activity.

TIP Have students select something to read ahead of time to help them stay focused.

Presentation Skills Wrap-Up

Lesson Overview

ACTIVITY	ACTIVITY TITLE	TIME	ONLINE/OFFLINE
GET READY	Introduction to Presentation Skills Wrap-Up	**1** minute	online
TRY IT	Use Presentation Skills LEARNING COACH CHECK-IN	**25** minutes	online and offline
	Review Pronouns	**20** minutes	online
QUIZ	Pronouns and Presentation Skills	**30** minutes	online
WRAP-UP	More Language Arts Practice	**16** minutes	online
	Handwriting	**8** minutes	offline
	Go Read!	**20** minutes	online or offline

Advance Preparation

During the Go Read! activity, students will have the option of using the digital library. Allow extra time for students to make their reading selection, or have students make a selection before beginning the lesson.

MATERIALS

Supplied

- *Summit English Language Arts 3 Activity Book*
  - Use Presentation Skills
- handwriting workbook

Also Needed

- reading material for Go Read!

Lesson Goals

- Review presentation skills by responding to a speaking prompt.
- Review pronouns.
- Take a quiz on pronouns and presentation skills.
- Develop letter formation fluency.
- Read independently to develop fluency.

GET READY

Introduction to Presentation Skills Wrap-Up

Students will read the lesson goals.

TRY IT

Use Presentation Skills

Students will complete Use Presentation Skills in *Summit English Language Arts 3 Activity Book*.

NOTE This activity involves planning a short speech, recording that speech using the online recording tool, and then listening to the speech and answering reflection questions. Ensure that students have access to a computer while completing the activity.

LEARNING COACH CHECK-IN Encourage students to present their speech to you. Give them feedback about their speaking pace and clarity. State what you believe are the main idea and supporting details in their speech and discuss how you knew. Point out places where students used descriptive language well.

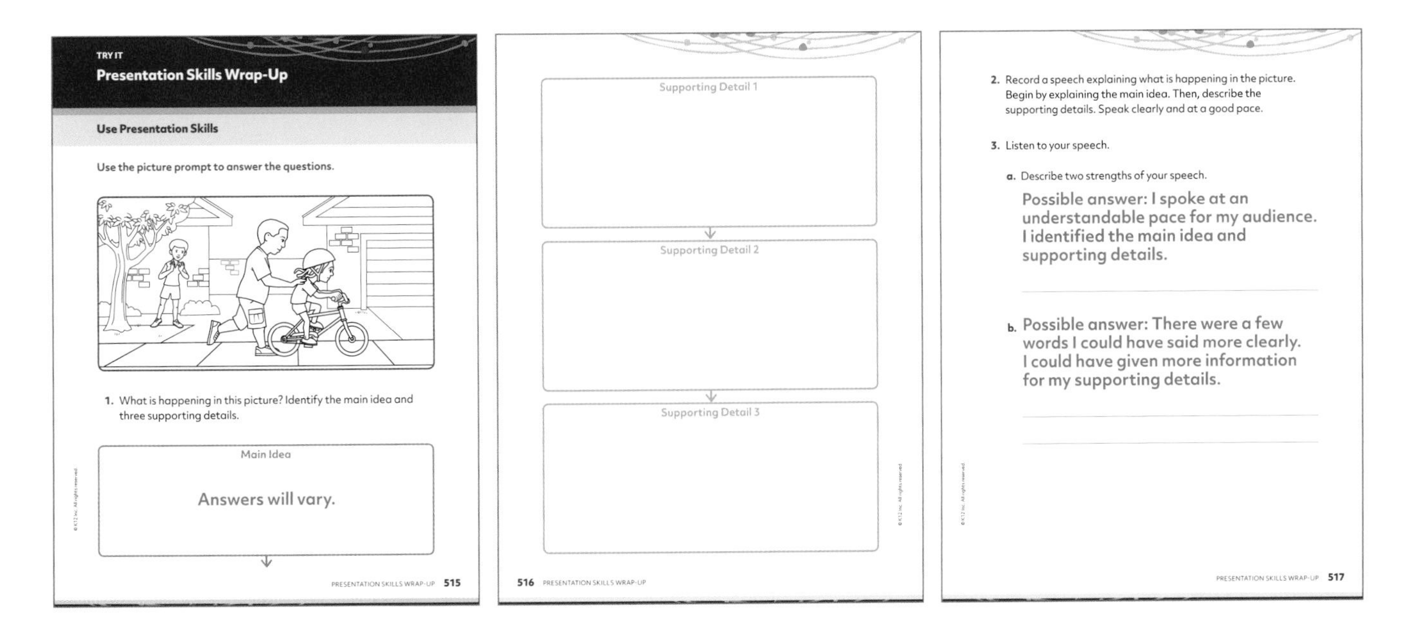

TRY IT

Presentation Skills Wrap-Up

Use Presentation Skills

Use the picture prompt to answer the questions.

1. What is happening in this picture? Identify the main idea and three supporting details.

Main Idea

Answers will vary.

PRESENTATION SKILLS WRAP-UP 515

Supporting Detail 1

Supporting Detail 2

Supporting Detail 3

516 PRESENTATION SKILLS WRAP-UP

2. Record a speech explaining what is happening in the picture. Begin by explaining the main idea. Then, describe the supporting details. Speak clearly and at a good pace.

3. Listen to your speech.

   a. Describe two strengths of your speech.

   Possible answer: I spoke at an understandable pace for my audience. I identified the main idea and supporting details.

   b. Possible answer: There were a few words I could have said more clearly. I could have given more information for my supporting details.

PRESENTATION SKILLS WRAP-UP 517

Review Pronouns

Students will answer questions to review what they have learned about pronouns.

QUIZ

Pronouns and Presentation Skills

Students will complete the Pronouns and Presentation Skills quiz.

WRAP-UP

More Language Arts Practice

Students will practice skills according to their individual needs.

Handwriting

Students should gather their handwriting materials and begin where they left off. Remind students to form letters carefully and correctly.

TIP Set a timer to help students stay focused during handwriting practice.

Go Read!

Students will read for pleasure. They should choose a book or a magazine that interests them, or they may choose a selection from the digital library, linked in the online lesson.

- Have students read aloud a few paragraphs of their selection.
- Then have students read silently for the rest of the time.

SUPPORT Students should make no more than five errors in decoding when they read aloud a few paragraphs of their Go Read! selection. If students struggle or make more than five errors, they need to select a different (and easier) text for the Go Read! activity.

TIP Have students select something to read ahead of time to help them stay focused.

Choice Reading Project

Workshop Overview

This unique reading workshop is designed to build students' comprehension and critical-thinking skills as they read a work or works of their choice and complete a related project. Research indicates that opportunities for choice enhance student performance and motivate readers.

Students will select a project and corresponding book or books from a bank of options. One project requires you to acquire a book on your own. The other project option uses a book or books available in the digital library linked in the online lesson. Discuss the choices with students to help ensure that they select an option that interests them. To help students make a choice, the online lessons include synopses of the books and descriptions of the related projects.

Given that students will encounter different lesson content depending on which project they choose, other than the standard Spelling and Handwriting activities (described below), detailed activity descriptions for each lesson of this workshop are not provided in this lesson guide. However, regardless of what students choose, the overall structure of the workshop is the same:

1. Select a project.
2. Complete Spelling activities.
3. Read chosen book(s), and complete project work.
4. Complete Handwriting activities.
5. Submit the project.

All materials needed for the choice project are linked online and not provided in the activity book.

Advance Preparation

If students select a project that requires acquiring a book on your own, you will need to acquire the book before students begin the workshop.

MATERIALS

Supplied
- project packet (printout)

Also Needed
- students' chosen book(s)

Choice Reading Project: Spelling and Handwriting

Lesson Overview

WORKSHOP LESSON	ACTIVITY	ACTIVITY TITLE	TIME	ONLINE/OFFLINE
CHOICE READING PROJECT (A)	**GET READY**	Spelling List 22 Pretest **LEARNING COACH CHECK-IN**	**10** minutes	and
	WRAP-UP	Handwriting	**8** minutes	
CHOICE READING PROJECT (B)	**GET READY**	Spelling List 22 Activity Bank	**10** minutes	
	WRAP-UP	Handwriting	**8** minutes	
CHOICE READING PROJECT (C)	**GET READY**	Spelling List 22 Practice	**10** minutes	
	WRAP-UP	Handwriting	**8** minutes	
CHOICE READING PROJECT (D)	**GET READY**	Spelling List 22 Review Game	**10** minutes	
	WRAP-UP	Handwriting	**8** minutes	
CHOICE READING PROJECT (E)	**QUIZ**	Spelling List 22	**10** minutes	
	WRAP-UP	Handwriting	**8** minutes	
CHOICE READING PROJECT (F)	**GET READY**	Spelling List 23 Pretest **LEARNING COACH CHECK-IN**	**10** minutes	and
	WRAP-UP	Handwriting	**8** minutes	
CHOICE READING PROJECT (G)	**GET READY**	Spelling List 23 Activity Bank	**10** minutes	
	WRAP-UP	Handwriting	**8** minutes	
CHOICE READING PROJECT (H)	**GET READY**	Spelling List 23 Practice	**10** minutes	
	WRAP-UP	Handwriting	**8** minutes	
CHOICE READING PROJECT (I)	**GET READY**	Spelling List 23 Review Game	**10** minutes	
	WRAP-UP	Handwriting	**8** minutes	
CHOICE READING PROJECT WRAP-UP	**QUIZ**	Spelling List 23	**10** minutes	
	WRAP-UP	Handwriting	**8** minutes	

Choice Reading Project (A)

GET READY

Spelling List 22 Pretest

Students will take a spelling pretest and learn a new spelling pattern.

LEARNING COACH CHECK-IN Have students turn to Spelling List 22 Pretest in *Summit English Language Arts 3 Activity Book* and open the online Spelling Pretest activity. Online, students will listen to the spelling word, type the word in the space indicated, and then check their answer. In the activity book, students will write the correct spelling of the word in the tables provided and indicate with a ✓ or an ✗ if they spelled the word correctly or incorrectly online. Students will repeat this process with the remaining words.

As needed, help students with the interaction between the online activity and the activity book page until they become comfortable with what they need to do. As students practice their spelling words throughout the workshop, they should pay special attention to words they spelled incorrectly on the pretest.

This is the complete list of words students will be tested on.

Words with /j/ Sound		
badge	gorge	large
edge	huge	ledge
energy	jellyfish	oxygen
garage	jolly	ranger
gelatin	judge	ridge
general	juice	stage
giant	jungle	strange

NOTE Have students keep their completed activity page in a safe place so they can refer to it later.

MATERIALS

Supplied

- *Summit English Language Arts 3 Activity Book*
  - Spelling List 22 Pretest
- handwriting workbook

GET READY

Choice Reading Project (A)

Spelling List 22 Pretest

1. Open the Spelling Pretest activity online. Listen to the first spelling word. Type the word. Check your answer.
2. Write the correct spelling of the word in the Word column of the Spelling Pretest table.

	Word	✓	⊗
1	blindfold		

3. Put a check mark in the ✓ column if you spelled the word correctly online.

	Word	✓	⊗
1	blindfold	✓	

Put an X in the ⊗ column if you spelled the word incorrectly online.

	Word	✓	⊗
1	blindfold		X

4. Repeat Steps 1–3 for the remaining words in the Spelling Pretest.

CHOICE READING PROJECT (A) 519

Choice Reading Project (A)

Spelling List 22 Pretest

Write each spelling word in the Word column, making sure to spell it correctly.

	Word	✓	⊗
1	badge		
2	edge		
3	energy		
4	garage		
5	gelatin		
6	general		
7	giant		
8	gorge		
9	huge		
10	jellyfish		
11	jolly		

	Word	✓	⊗
12	judge		
13	juice		
14	jungle		
15	large		
16	ledge		
17	oxygen		
18	ranger		
19	ridge		
20	stage		
21	strange		

Students should write the correct spelling of each word from the pretest and use the ✓and X columns to indicate whether they spelled each word correctly or incorrectly online.

520 CHOICE READING PROJECT (A)

WRAP-UP

Handwriting

Students should gather their handwriting materials and begin where they left off. Remind students to form letters carefully and correctly.

TIP Set a timer to help students stay focused during handwriting practice.

Choice Reading Project (B)

GET READY

Spelling List 22 Activity Bank

Students will practice all spelling words from Spelling List 22 by completing Spelling List 22 Activity Bank from *Summit English Language Arts 3 Activity Book*. Make sure students have their completed Spelling List 22 Pretest activity page from Choice Reading Project (A) to refer to during this activity.

Remind students to pay special attention to words they spelled incorrectly on the Spelling Pretest.

MATERIALS

Supplied

- *Summit English Language Arts 3 Activity Book*
    - Spelling List 22 Activity Bank
- handwriting workbook

Also Needed

- completed Spelling List 22 Pretest from Choice Reading Project (A)

GET READY

Choice Reading Project (B)

Spelling List 22 Activity Bank

Circle any words in the box that you did not spell correctly on the pretest. Choose one activity to do with your circled words. Do as much of the activity as you can in the time given.

Did you spell all the words on the pretest correctly? Do the one activity with as many spelling words as you can.

badge	general	jellyfish	jungle	ranger
edge	giant	jolly	large	ridge
energy	gorge	judge	ledge	stage
garage	huge	juice	oxygen	strange
gelatin				

Spelling Activity Choices

Silly Sentences

1. Write a silly sentence for each of your spelling words.
2. Underline the spelling word in each sentence.
   Example: The dog was driving a car.
3. Correct any spelling errors.

CHOICE READING PROJECT (B) 521

Spelling Story

1. Write a very short story using each of your spelling words.
2. Underline the spelling words in the story.
3. Correct any spelling errors.

Riddle Me This

1. Write a riddle for each of your spelling words.
   Example: "I have a trunk, but it's not on my car."
2. Write the answer, which is your word, for each riddle.
   Example: Answer: elephant
3. Correct any spelling errors.

RunOnWord

1. Gather some crayons, colored pencils, or markers. Use a different color to write each of your spelling words. Write the words end to end as one long word.
   Example: dogcatbirdfishturtle
2. Rewrite the words correctly and with proper spacing.
3. Correct any spelling errors.

522 CHOICE READING PROJECT (B)

Complete the activity that you chose.

My chosen activity: ______________

Students should use this page to complete all steps in their chosen activity.

CHOICE READING PROJECT (B) 523

WRAP-UP

Handwriting

Students should gather their handwriting materials and begin where they left off. Remind students to form letters carefully and correctly.

TIP Set a timer to help students stay focused during handwriting practice.

Choice Reading Project (C)

GET READY

Spelling List 22 Practice

Students will practice all spelling words from Spelling List 22.

SUPPORT Students may do an activity from Spelling List 22 Activity Bank instead of the online practice activity.

WRAP-UP

Handwriting

Students should gather their handwriting materials and begin where they left off. Remind students to form letters carefully and correctly.

TIP Set a timer to help students stay focused during handwriting practice.

MATERIALS

Supplied

- handwriting workbook

Choice Reading Project (D)

GET READY

Spelling Review Game

Students will practice all spelling words from Spelling List 22.

WRAP-UP

Handwriting

Students should gather their handwriting materials and begin where they left off. Remind students to form letters carefully and correctly.

TIP Set a timer to help students stay focused during handwriting practice.

MATERIALS

Supplied

- handwriting workbook

Choice Reading Project (E)

QUIZ

Spelling List 22

Students will complete the Spelling List 22 quiz.

WRAP-UP

Handwriting

Students should gather their handwriting materials and begin where they left off. Remind students to form letters carefully and correctly.

TIP Set a timer to help students stay focused during handwriting practice.

MATERIALS

Supplied

- handwriting workbook

Choice Reading Project (F)

GET READY

Spelling List 23 Pretest

Students will take a spelling pretest and learn a new spelling pattern.

LEARNING COACH CHECK-IN Have students turn to Spelling List 23 Pretest in *Summit English Language Arts 3 Activity Book* and open the online Spelling Pretest activity. Online, students will listen to the spelling word, type the word in the space indicated, and then check their answer. In the activity book, students will write the correct spelling of the word in the tables provided and indicate with a ✓ or an **x** if they spelled the word correctly or incorrectly online. Students will repeat this process with the remaining words.

As needed, help students with the interaction between the online activity and the activity book page until they become comfortable with what they need to do. As students practice their spelling words throughout the workshop, they should pay special attention to words they spelled incorrectly on the pretest.

This is the complete list of words students will be tested on.

Words with *–le* and *–el* Endings		
bagel	shovel	purple
camel	towel	scramble
damsel	example	settle
funnel	jingle	shuffle
grovel	little	single
marvel	middle	syllable
nickel	possible	uncle

NOTE Have students keep their completed activity page in a safe place so they can refer to it later.

MATERIALS

Supplied

- *Summit English Language Arts 3 Activity Book*
  - Spelling List 23 Pretest
- handwriting workbook

GET READY

Choice Reading Project (F)

Spelling List 23 Pretest

1. Open the Spelling Pretest activity online. Listen to the first spelling word. Type the word. Check your answer.

2. Write the correct spelling of the word in the Word column of the Spelling Pretest table.

	Word	✓	✗
1	blindfold		

3. Put a check mark in the ✓ column if you spelled the word correctly online.

	Word	✓	✗
1	blindfold	✓	

Put an X in the ✗ column if you spelled the word incorrectly online.

	Word	✓	✗
1	blindfold		X

4. Repeat Steps 1–3 for the remaining words in the Spelling Pretest.

Choice Reading Project (F)

Spelling List 23 Pretest

Write each spelling word in the Word column, making sure to spell it correctly.

	Word	✓	✗
1	bagel		
2	camel		
3	damsel		
4	funnel		
5	grovel		
6	marvel		
7	nickel		
8	shovel		
9	towel		
10	example		
11	jingle		

	Word	✓	✗
12	little		
13	middle		
14	possible		
15	purple		
16	scramble		
17	settle		
18	shuffle		
19	single		
20	syllable		
21	uncle		

Students should write the correct spelling of each word from the pretest and use the ✓and X columns to indicate whether they spelled each word correctly or incorrectly online.

WRAP-UP

Handwriting

Students should gather their handwriting materials and begin where they left off. Remind students to form letters carefully and correctly.

TIP Set a timer to help students stay focused during handwriting practice.

Choice Reading Project (G)

GET READY

Spelling List 23 Activity Bank

Students will practice all spelling words from Spelling List 23 by completing Spelling List 23 Activity Bank from *Summit English Language Arts 3 Activity Book*. Make sure students have their completed Spelling List 23 Pretest activity page from Choice Reading Project (F) to refer to during this activity.

Remind students to pay special attention to words they spelled incorrectly on the Spelling Pretest.

MATERIALS

Supplied

- *Summit English Language Arts 3 Activity Book*
  - Spelling List 23 Activity Bank
- handwriting workbook

Also Needed

- completed Spelling List 23 Pretest from Choice Reading Project (F)

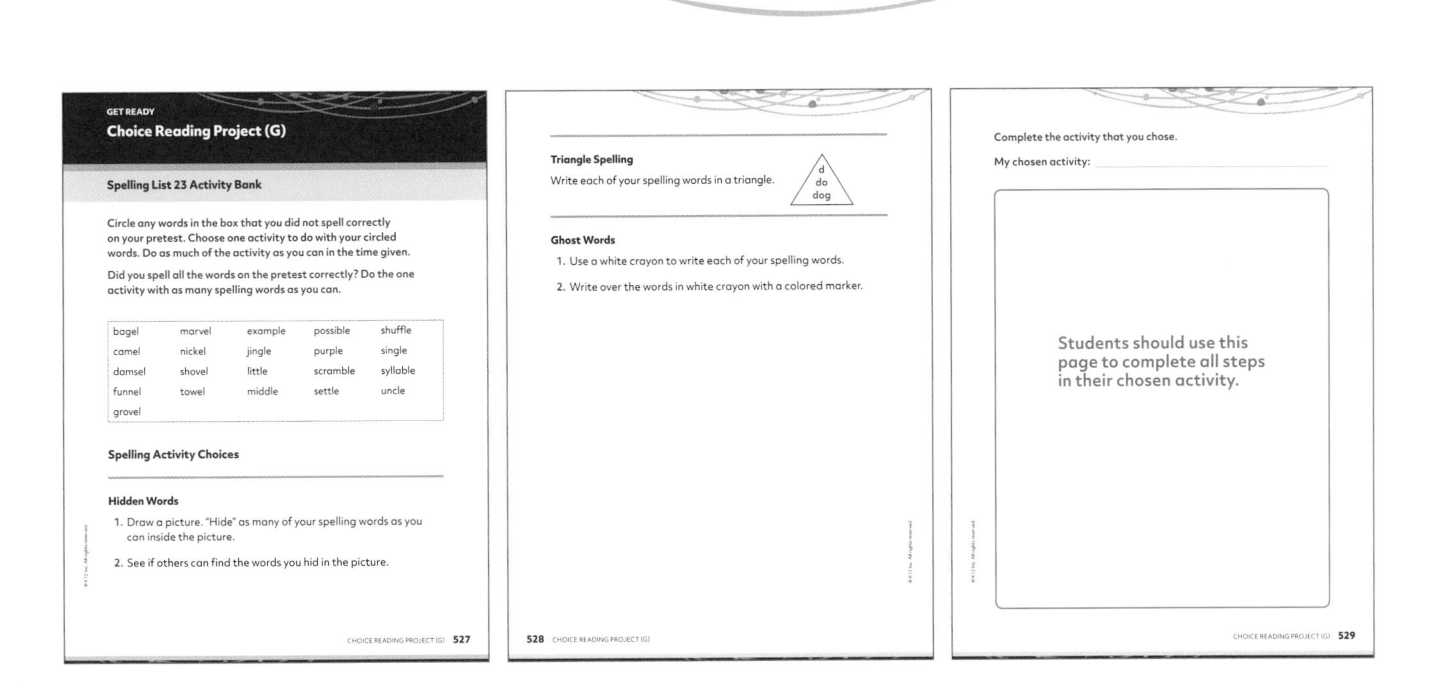

GET READY

Choice Reading Project (G)

Spelling List 23 Activity Bank

Circle any words in the box that you did not spell correctly on your pretest. Choose one activity to do with your circled words. Do as much of the activity as you can in the time given.

Did you spell all the words on the pretest correctly? Do the one activity with as many spelling words as you can.

bagel	marvel	example	possible	shuffle
camel	nickel	jingle	purple	single
damsel	shovel	little	scramble	syllable
funnel	towel	middle	settle	uncle
grovel				

Spelling Activity Choices

Hidden Words

1. Draw a picture. "Hide" as many of your spelling words as you can inside the picture.
2. See if others can find the words you hid in the picture.

CHOICE READING PROJECT (G) 527

Triangle Spelling

Write each of your spelling words in a triangle.

d
do
dog

Ghost Words

1. Use a white crayon to write each of your spelling words.
2. Write over the words in white crayon with a colored marker.

528 CHOICE READING PROJECT (G)

Complete the activity that you chose.

My chosen activity:

Students should use this page to complete all steps in their chosen activity.

CHOICE READING PROJECT (G) 529

WRAP-UP

Handwriting

Students should gather their handwriting materials and begin where they left off. Remind students to form letters carefully and correctly.

TIP Set a timer to help students stay focused during handwriting practice.

Choice Reading Project (H)

GET READY

Spelling List 23 Practice

Students will practice all spelling words from Spelling List 23.

OPTIONAL Students may do an activity from Spelling List 23 Activity Bank instead of the online practice activity.

WRAP-UP

Handwriting

Students should gather their handwriting materials and begin where they left off. Remind students to form letters carefully and correctly.

TIP Set a timer to help students stay focused during handwriting practice.

MATERIALS

Supplied

- handwriting workbook

Choice Reading Project (I)

GET READY

Spelling List 23 Review Game

Students will practice all spelling words from Spelling List 23.

WRAP-UP

Handwriting

Students should gather their handwriting materials and begin where they left off. Remind students to form letters carefully and correctly.

TIP Set a timer to help students stay focused during handwriting practice.

MATERIALS

Supplied

- handwriting workbook

Choice Reading Project Wrap-Up

QUIZ

Spelling List 23

Students will complete the Spelling List 23 quiz.

WRAP-UP

Handwriting

Students should gather their handwriting materials and begin where they left off. Remind students to form letters carefully and correctly.

TIP Set a timer to help students stay focused during handwriting practice.

MATERIALS

Supplied

- handwriting workbook

Big Ideas: Critical Skills Assignment

Lesson Overview

Big Ideas lessons provide students the opportunity to further apply the knowledge acquired and skills learned throughout the unit workshops. Each Big Ideas lesson consists of these parts:

1. **Cumulative Review:** Students keep their skills fresh by reviewing prior content.
2. **Preview:** Students practice answering the types of questions they will commonly find on standardized tests.
3. **Synthesis:** Students complete an assignment that allows them to connect and apply what they have learned. Synthesis assignments vary throughout the course.

   In the Synthesis portion of this Big Ideas lesson, students will read new selections. They will answer literal and inferential comprehension questions and complete writing questions that ask for short responses about the reading selections. Students should refer to the selections while answering the questions, because the questions emphasize using textual evidence. The questions call for students to demonstrate critical thinking, reading, and writing skills.

   LEARNING COACH CHECK-IN This is a graded assessment. Make sure students complete, review, and submit the assignment to their teacher.

All materials needed for this lesson are linked online and not provided in the activity book.

MATERIALS

Supplied

- Critical Skills Assignment (printout)

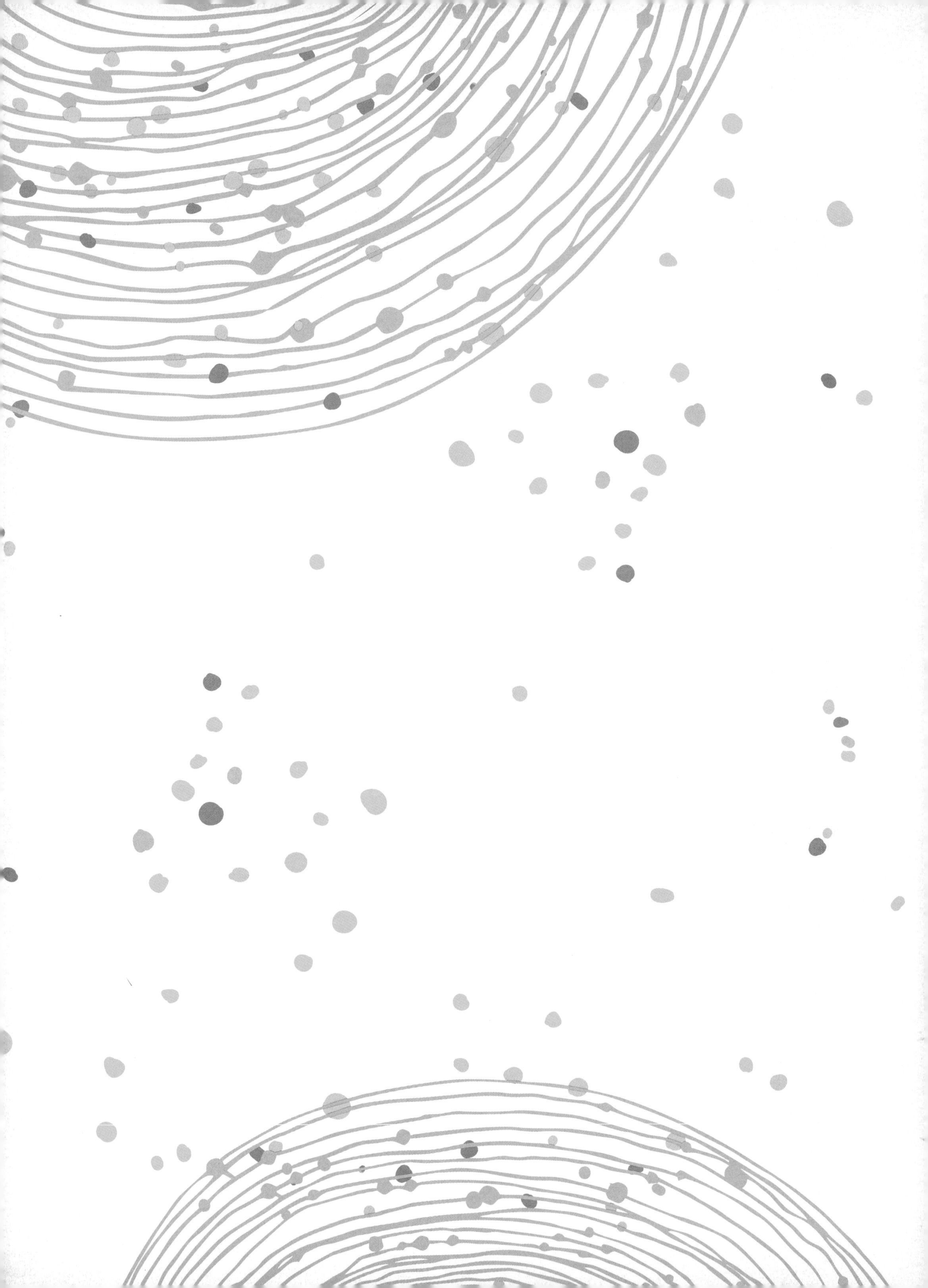

We the People

We the People (A)

Lesson Overview

ACTIVITY	ACTIVITY TITLE	TIME	ONLINE/OFFLINE
GET READY	Introduction to We the People (A)	**2** minutes	online
	Spelling List 24 Pretest **LEARNING COACH CHECK-IN**	**10** minutes	online and offline
	Before You Read *Michelle Obama: First Lady, Going Higher*	**10** minutes	online
READ	*Michelle Obama: First Lady, Going Higher*	**25** minutes	offline
	Check-In: *Michelle Obama: First Lady, Going Higher*	**5** minutes	online
LEARN AND TRY IT	Thinking Through Main Idea and Supporting Details	**10** minutes	online
	Think Through Main Idea and Supporting Details	**5** minutes	online
	Apply: Main Idea	**10** minutes	online
	Plan a Biography **LEARNING COACH CHECK-IN**	**25** minutes	offline
	Practice Words from *Michelle Obama: First Lady, Going Higher*	**8** minutes	online
WRAP-UP	Question About *Michelle Obama: First Lady, Going Higher*	**2** minutes	online
	Handwriting	**8** minutes	offline

Content Background

Students will learn about biographies and autobiographies. Both types of nonfiction are organized in *chronological order*, or time order. A *biography* is the story of someone's life, or part of someone's life, written by another person. An *autobiography* is similar, but there is one important difference: An autobiography is the story of someone's life written by that person.

For example, students will read *Michelle Obama: First Lady, Going Higher*. Shana Corey wrote this biography about Michelle Obama. You may wish to point out to students that Obama also has an autobiography, *Becoming*, in which she wrote her own story.

A Note About Potentially Sensitive Material

The author mentions Michelle Obama's father passing away due to the disease multiple sclerosis in this text.

MATERIALS

Supplied

- *Michelle Obama: First Lady, Going Higher* by Shana Corey
- *Summit English Language Arts 3 Activity Book*
  - Spelling List 24 Pretest
  - Plan a Biography
- handwriting workbook

Also Needed

- folder for organizing biography assignment pages

Advance Preparation

Gather a folder that students can use to keep all notes and activity pages related to their biography.

Michelle Obama: First Lady, Going Higher Synopsis

Michelle Obama: First Lady, Going Higher is a nonfiction text, a biography about former First Lady Michelle Obama by Shana Corey. Corey introduces Obama as the first African American First Lady in the United States and then explains her path to the job. Obama grew up as Michelle LaVaughn Robinson in Chicago and made her way to Princeton University and then to Harvard Law School, despite coming from a modest background. Her father passed away after a years-long struggle with multiple sclerosis. After his death, Obama left her job and decided to dedicate herself to helping others. At the same time, her husband, then Senator Barack Obama, was eyeing a run for the presidency. The book focuses on her role as First Lady: campaigning for her husband, starting initiatives to improve public health, and most important to her, being a mother to her children.

Lesson Goals

- Take a spelling pretest.
- Read *Michelle Obama: First Lady, Going Higher*.
- Determine the main idea of a text and the details that support the main idea.
- Plan a biography.
- Practice vocabulary words.
- Develop letter formation fluency.

KEYWORDS

autobiography – the story of a person's life written by that person

biography – the story of a person's life written by another person

chronological order – a way to organize that puts details in time order

main idea – the most important point the author makes; it may be stated or unstated

supporting detail – a detail that gives more information about a main idea

GET READY

Introduction to We the People (A)

After a quick introductory activity, students will read the lesson goals and keywords. Have students select each keyword and preview its definition.

Spelling List 24 Pretest

Students will take a spelling pretest and learn a new spelling pattern.

LEARNING COACH CHECK-IN Have students turn to Spelling List 24 Pretest in *Summit English Language Arts 3 Activity Book* and open the online Spelling Pretest activity. Online, students will listen to the spelling word, type the word in the space indicated, and then check their answer. In the activity book, students will write the correct spelling of the word in the tables provided and indicate with a ✓ or an ✗ if they spelled the word correctly or incorrectly online. Students will repeat this process with the remaining words.

As needed, help students with the interaction between the online activity and the activity book page until they become comfortable with what they need to do. As students practice their spelling words throughout the workshop, they should pay special attention to words they spelled incorrectly on the pretest.

This is the complete list of words students will be tested on.

Words with /aw/ Sound				
author	bought	fault	sauce	talk
automate	brought	laundry	saucer	taller
awful	chalk	lawsuit	saw	thought
ballpark	draw	mall	small	walk
because	falling	overhaul	stalk	withdraw

NOTE Have students keep their completed activity page in a safe place so they can refer to it later.

GET READY

We the People (A)

Spelling List 24 Pretest

1. Open the Spelling Pretest activity online. Listen to the first spelling word. Type the word. Check your answer.

2. Write the correct spelling of the word in the Word column of the Spelling Pretest table.

	Word	✓	✗
1	blindfold		

3. Put a check mark in the ✓ column if you spelled the word correctly online.

	Word	✓	✗
1	blindfold	✓	

Put an X in the ✗ column if you spelled the word incorrectly online.

	Word	✓	✗
1	blindfold		X

4. Repeat Steps 1–3 for the remaining words in the Spelling Pretest.

WE THE PEOPLE (A) 531

We the People (A)

Spelling List 24 Pretest

Write each spelling word in the Word column, making sure to spell it correctly.

	Word	✓	✗
1	author		
2	automate		
3	awful		
4	ballpark		
5	because		
6	bought		
7	brought		
8	chalk		
9	draw		
10	falling		
11	fault		
12	laundry		
13	lawsuit		

	Word	✓	✗
14	mall		
15	overhaul		
16	sauce		
17	saucer		
18	saw		
19	small		
20	stalk		
21	talk		
22	taller		
23	thought		
24	walk		
25	withdraw		

Students should write the correct spelling of each word from the pretest and use the ✓ and X columns to indicate whether they spelled each word correctly or incorrectly online.

532

Before You Read *Michelle Obama: First Lady, Going Higher*

Students will be introduced to some key vocabulary words that they will encounter in the upcoming reading and learn some important background related to the reading.

READ

Michelle Obama: First Lady, Going Higher

Students will read *Michelle Obama: First Lady, Going Higher* by Shana Corey.

Check-In: *Michelle Obama: First Lady, Going Higher*

Students will answer several questions to demonstrate their comprehension of *Michelle Obama: First Lady, Going Higher*.

LEARN AND TRY IT

LEARN Thinking Through Main Idea and Supporting Details

Students will think through and determine the main idea and supporting details in a text. They will then consider why it is important to ask questions of themselves as they are reading.

TRY IT Think Through the Main Idea and Supporting Details

Students will practice identifying the main idea and supporting details in a text.

TRY IT Apply: Main Idea

Students will apply to a new work what they've learned about determining the main idea of a text.

TRY IT Plan a Biography

Students will complete Plan a Biography in *Summit English Language Arts 3 Activity Book*. This activity does not require students to do research. They should choose someone they know well to focus on in their biography.

LEARNING COACH CHECK-IN This activity page contains open-ended questions, so it's important that you review students' responses. Give students feedback on their planning. Ensure that they've chosen enough events to cover to write three paragraphs, but not too many events.

NOTE Have students add their completed Plan a Biography activity page to the folder they are using to store their biography assignment pages.

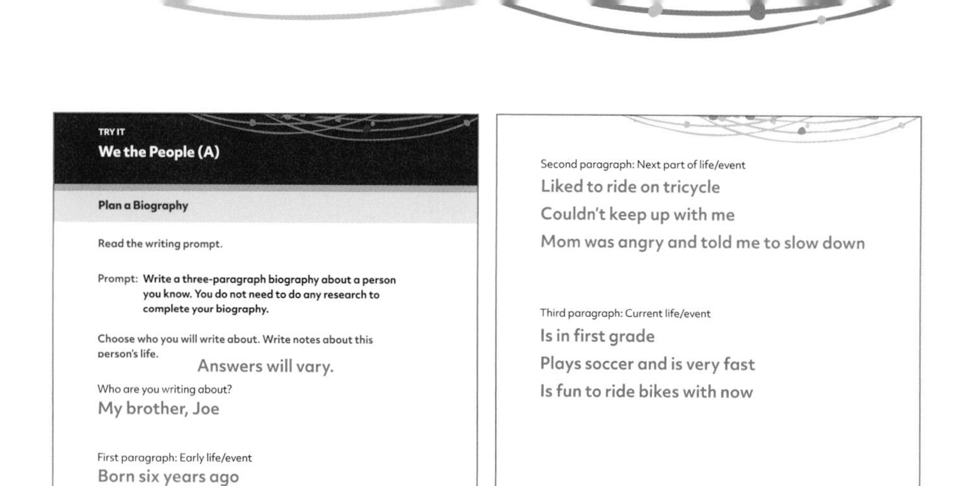
TRY IT
We the People (A)

Plan a Biography

Read the writing prompt.

Prompt: Write a three-paragraph biography about a person you know. You do not need to do any research to complete your biography.

Choose who you will write about. Write notes about this person's life.

Answers will vary.

Who are you writing about?
My brother, Joe

First paragraph: Early life/event
Born six years ago
Looked cute and happy
Cried all the time—Mom said it would stop

WE THE PEOPLE (A) 533

Second paragraph: Next part of life/event
Liked to ride on tricycle
Couldn't keep up with me
Mom was angry and told me to slow down

Third paragraph: Current life/event
Is in first grade
Plays soccer and is very fast
Is fun to ride bikes with now

I finished my planning.
Writing will be a breeze!

534 WE THE PEOPLE (A)

TRY IT **Practice Words from *Michelle Obama: First Lady, Going Higher***

Students will answer questions to demonstrate their understanding of the vocabulary words from the reading.

WRAP-UP

Question About *Michelle Obama: First Lady, Going Higher*

Students will answer a question to show that they understand *Michelle Obama: First Lady, Going Higher*.

Handwriting

Students should gather their handwriting materials and begin where they left off. Remind students to form letters carefully and correctly.

TIP Set a timer to help students stay focused during handwriting practice.

We the People (B)

Lesson Overview

ACTIVITY	ACTIVITY TITLE	TIME	ONLINE/OFFLINE
GET READY	Introduction to We the People (B)	**1** minute	
	Spelling List 24 Activity Bank	**10** minutes	
	Recall *Michelle Obama: First Lady, Going Higher*	**5** minutes	
	Before You Read *I Dissent!* Part 1	**10** minutes	
READ	*I Dissent!* Part 1	**26** minutes	
	Check-In: *I Dissent!* Part 1	**5** minutes	
LEARN AND **TRY IT**	Supporting the Main Idea	**10** minutes	
	Support the Main Idea	**5** minutes	
	Apply: Text-Based Evidence	**15** minutes	
	Draft a Biography LEARNING COACH CHECK-IN	**15** minutes	
	Practice Words from *I Dissent!* Part 1	**8** minutes	
WRAP-UP	Question About Idioms	**2** minutes	
	Handwriting	**8** minutes	

Content Background

Students will read the first half of a biography about Ruth Bader Ginsburg, a Supreme Court justice and champion of equal rights. They will review main idea and key details and will learn about idioms. An *idiom* is a group of words that does not actually mean what it says. "Raining cats and dogs" is an example of an idiom.

A Note About Potentially Sensitive Material

In *I Dissent! Ruth Bader Ginsburg Makes Her Mark*, students will read about the prejudice Ginsburg experienced as a child and young adult growing up Jewish in the United States. Additionally, they will learn that her mother, Celia, died just before Ruth graduated from high school.

Advance Preparation

Gather students' completed Spelling List 24 Pretest activity page from We the People (A). Students will refer to this page during Getting Ready: Spelling List 24 Activity Bank.

Gather the folder that students are using to store the activity pages related to their biography. The folder should contain the following:

- Students' completed Plan a Biography activity page from We the People (A)

I Dissent! Part 1 Synopsis

I Dissent! Ruth Bader Ginsburg Makes Her Mark is a biography about Ruth Bader Ginsburg, a Supreme Court justice. Ginsburg experienced prejudice and personal hardship as a child growing up in the 1940s and 1950s. Part 1 of the biography covers Ginsburg's childhood, during which time her mother set the foundation for Ginsburg's enduring beliefs: Women should be given opportunities equal to those of men, and it is okay to disagree with others. Readers follow Ginsburg's journey to high school and college, where she meets her future husband Marty. This part ends with the couple's decision to attend law school and the birth of their daughter.

Lesson Goals

- Practice all spelling words offline.
- Read *I Dissent!*
- Review main idea and key details and explore idioms.
- Draft a biography.
- Practice vocabulary words.
- Develop letter formation fluency.

MATERIALS

Supplied

- *I Dissent! Ruth Bader Ginsburg Makes Her Mark* by Debbie Levy
- *Summit English Language Arts 3 Activity Book*
  - Spelling List 24 Activity Bank
  - Draft a Biography
- handwriting workbook

Also Needed

- completed Spelling List 24 Pretest activity page from We the People (A)
- folder in which students are storing biography assignment pages

KEYWORDS

chronological order – a way to organize that puts details in time order

idiom – a group of words that does not actually mean what it says; Examples: raining cats and dogs, a month of Sundays

literal – exact or strict meaning

main idea – the most important point the author makes; it may be stated or unstated

supporting detail – a detail that gives more information about a main idea

GET READY

Introduction to We the People (B)

Students will get a glimpse of what they will learn about in the lesson. They will also read the lesson goals and keywords. Have students select each keyword and preview its definition.

Spelling List 24 Activity Bank

Students will practice all spelling words from the workshop by completing Spelling List 24 Activity Bank from *Summit English Language Arts 3 Activity Book*. Make sure students have their completed Spelling List 24 Pretest activity page from We the People (A) to refer to during this activity.

Remind students to pay special attention to words they spelled incorrectly on the Spelling Pretest.

GET READY

We the People (B)

Spelling List 24 Activity Bank

Circle any words in the box that you did not spell correctly on your pretest. Choose one activity to do with your circled words. Do as much of the activity as you can in the time given.

Did you spell all the words on the pretest correctly? Do the one activity with as many spelling words as you can.

author	bought	fault	sauce	talk
automate	brought	laundry	saucer	taller
awful	chalk	lawsuit	saw	thought
ballpark	draw	mall	small	walk
because	falling	overhaul	stalk	withdraw

Spelling Activity Choices

Create a Crossword

1. Write one of your spelling words going down in the center of the grid.

2. Write another spelling word going across that shares a letter with the first word. See how many words you can connect.

Example:

				p			
			k	i	s	s	e	s
	d			n			
r	o	c	k	s			
	g						
	s						

Word Search Puzzle

1. Draw a box on the grid. The box should be large enough to hold your spelling words.
2. Fill in the grid with your spelling words. Write them across, up and down, and diagonally. You can write them forward and backward.
3. Fill in the rest of the box with random letters.
4. Ask someone to find and circle your words in the puzzle.

Complete the activity that you chose.

My chosen activity: ______

Students should use this page to complete all steps in their chosen activity.

Recall *Michelle Obama: First Lady, Going Higher*

Students will answer some questions to review the reading that they have already completed.

Before You Read *I Dissent!* Part 1

Students will be introduced to some key vocabulary words that they will encounter in the upcoming reading, learn some important historical background related to the reading, and answer questions to help them set a purpose for their reading.

READ

I Dissent! Part 1

Students will read Part 1 of *I Dissent! Ruth Bader Ginsburg Makes Her Mark* by Debbie Levy. The should read through Ruth and Marty's marriage and the birth of their daughter.

Check-In: *I Dissent!* Part 1

Students will answer several questions to demonstrate their comprehension of Part 1 of *I Dissent! Ruth Bader Ginsburg Makes Her Mark*.

LEARN AND TRY IT

LEARN Supporting the Main Idea

Students will review the concepts of main idea and key details in a passage. They will also learn about nonliteral language, or idioms.

TRY IT Support the Main Idea

Students will practice identifying and supporting the main idea in a passage. They will also identify idioms.

TRY IT Apply: Text-Based Evidence

Students will apply to a new work what they've learned about using text-based evidence to support a main idea.

TRY IT Draft a Biography

Students will complete Draft a Biography in *Summit English Language Arts 3 Activity Book*. They should use their completed Plan a Biography activity page from We the People (A) to help them write the draft. As students are drafting, they should add an idiom somewhere into their draft.

LEARNING COACH CHECK-IN This activity page contains open-ended questions, so it's important that you review students' responses. Give students feedback, using the sample answers provided to guide you.

SUPPORT If students having difficulty coming up with an idiom, you may wish to consult a list of idioms online for some ideas.

NOTE Have students add their completed Draft a Biograph activity page to the folder they are using to store their biography assignment pages.

TRY IT

We the People (B)

Draft a Biography

Read the writing prompt.

Prompt: **Write a three-paragraph biography about a person you know.**

- Write the events in chronological order.
- To make your writing more interesting, use an idiom somewhere in your draft.

Respond to the writing prompt. Use your prewriting work to help you.

Answers will vary. Students should include an idiom in their writing. In this example, the writer uses "once in a blue moon" and "every cloud has a silver lining."

My brother Joe was born six years ago, when I was four. People said he was cute and was always happy. I remember him crying all the time. My mom said he would stop crying when he learned how to talk and ask for what he wanted.

When Joe was three, he loved riding his tricycle. Well, he liked trying to ride it. He wasn't very good at it. We rode with my mom to the playground at the end of the street. He could only keep up with me once in a blue moon. My mom told me that he would get stronger and better if he practiced. She said I should help him by slowing down.

Now, Joe is in first grade. He rides a bike, and he is very fast! He can keep up with me. He also plays soccer and runs faster than I do. It is fun to play with him in the park now. Having a younger brother wasn't easy, but I've learned that every cloud has a silver lining.

WE THE PEOPLE (B) 539

540 WE THE PEOPLE (B)

TRY IT Practice Words from *I Dissent!* Part 1

Students will answer questions to demonstrate their understanding of the vocabulary words from the reading.

WRAP-UP

Question About Idioms

Students will answer a question to show that they understand what an idiom is.

Handwriting

Students should gather their handwriting materials and begin where they left off. Remind students to form letters carefully and correctly.

TIP Set a timer to help students stay focused during handwriting practice.

We the People (C)

Lesson Overview

ACTIVITY	ACTIVITY TITLE	TIME	ONLINE/OFFLINE
GET READY	Introduction to We the People (C)	**1** minute	online
	Spelling List 24 Practice	**10** minutes	online
	Recall *I Dissent!* Part 1	**5** minutes	online
	Before You Read *I Dissent!* Part 2	**10** minutes	online
READ	*I Dissent!* Part 2	**25** minutes	offline
	Check-In: *I Dissent!* Part 2	**5** minutes	online
LEARN AND TRY IT	Supporting the Main Idea with Illustrations	**10** minutes	online
	Support the Main Idea with Illustrations	**6** minutes	online
	Apply: Key Details	**15** minutes	online
	Revise and Publish a Biography LEARNING COACH CHECK-IN	**15** minutes	offline
	Practice Words from *I Dissent!* Part 2	**8** minutes	online
WRAP-UP	Question About Key Details	**2** minutes	online
	Handwriting	**8** minutes	offline

Content Background

Students will finish reading *I Dissent! Ruth Bader Ginsburg Makes Her Mark.* They will learn that illustrations can act as supporting details in explaining the main idea of a text. The illustrations in this text strongly underscore the main idea. The illustrator calls out specific words and ideas and puts them in bold, colored print to highlight their importance to Ruth Bader Ginsburg's biography.

Advance Preparation

Gather the folder that students are using to store the activity pages related to their biography. The folder should contain the following:

- Students' completed Plan a Biography activity page from We the People (A)
- Students' completed Draft a Biography activity page from We the People (B)

MATERIALS

Supplied

- *I Dissent! Ruth Bader Ginsburg Makes Her Mark* by Debbie Levy
- *Summit English Language Arts 3 Activity Book*
  - Revise and Publish a Biography
- handwriting workbook

Also Needed

- folder in which students are storing biography assignment pages

I Dissent! Part 2 Synopsis

The second half of *I Dissent! Ruth Bader Ginsburg Makes Her Mark* covers Ginsburg's career, including her time in law school, her difficulty in finding a job after graduation, and her eventual hiring and work as a law professor. The book covers the first time she argued a case before the Supreme Court, her appointment as a federal judge, and her appointment to the Supreme Court. Throughout her career, Ginsburg argued for equality for all people.

KEYWORDS

illustration – a drawing

main idea – the most important point the author makes; it may be stated or unstated

supporting detail – a detail that gives more information about a main idea

Lesson Goals

- Practice all spelling words online.
- Read *I Dissent!*
- Describe how illustrations support the main idea of a text.
- Revise and publish a biography.
- Practice vocabulary words.
- Develop letter formation fluency.

GET READY

Introduction to We the People (C)

Students will get a glimpse of what they will learn about in the lesson. They will also read the lesson goals and keywords. Have students select each keyword and preview its definition.

Spelling List 24 Practice

Students will practice all spelling words from the workshop.

OPTIONAL Students may do an activity from Spelling List 24 Activity Bank instead of the online practice activity.

Recall *I Dissent!* Part 1

Students will answer some questions to review the reading that they have already completed.

Before You Read *I Dissent!* Part 2

Students will be introduced to some key vocabulary words that they will encounter in the upcoming reading and learn some important background related to the reading.

READ

I Dissent! Part 2

Students will read Part 2 of *I Dissent! Ruth Bader Ginsburg Makes Her Mark* by Debbie Levy. They should start on the page with the words "She resisted."

NOTE Students are not required to read the back matter in the book. However, with assistance, reading these pages provides opportunities for additional learning about Ginsburg. The back matter contains a more robust biography, photographs, information about Supreme Court cases, and a select bibliography for further exploration.

Check-In: *I Dissent!* Part 2

Students will answer several questions to demonstrate their comprehension of Part 2 of *I Dissent! Ruth Bader Ginsburg Makes Her Mark*.

LEARN AND TRY IT

LEARN Supporting the Main Idea with Illustrations

Students will learn that illustrations and key details support the main idea of a text.

TRY IT Support the Main Idea with Illustrations

Students will explain how illustrations and key details support the main idea.

TRY IT Apply: Key Details

Students will apply to a new work what they've learned about using key details to support main ideas.

TRY IT Revise and Publish a Biography

Students will complete Revise and Publish a Biography in *Summit English Language Arts 3 Activity Book*. They should have their completed Draft a Biography activity page to refer to as they work.

LEARNING COACH CHECK-IN This activity page contains a checklist of questions for students to use as they review the draft of their biography. Encourage students to read their draft slowly and ensure that they can check every box. If they wish, they can illustrate the subject of their biography in the space provided.

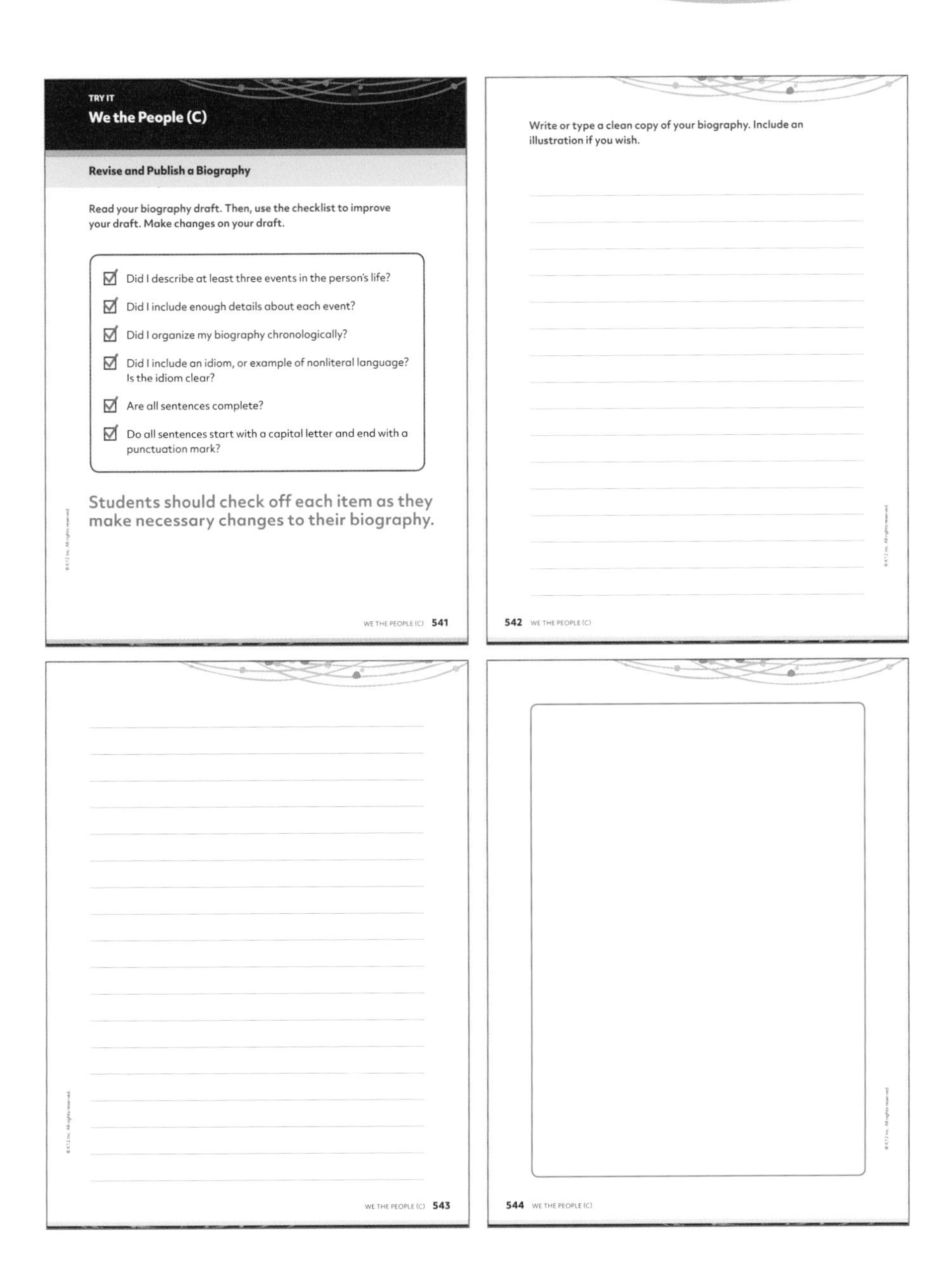

TRY IT

We the People (C)

Revise and Publish a Biography

Read your biography draft. Then, use the checklist to improve your draft. Make changes on your draft.

- ☑ Did I describe at least three events in the person's life?
- ☑ Did I include enough details about each event?
- ☑ Did I organize my biography chronologically?
- ☑ Did I include an idiom, or example of nonliteral language? Is the idiom clear?
- ☑ Are all sentences complete?
- ☑ Do all sentences start with a capital letter and end with a punctuation mark?

Students should check off each item as they make necessary changes to their biography.

WE THE PEOPLE (C) 541

Write or type a clean copy of your biography. Include an illustration if you wish.

542 WE THE PEOPLE (C)

WE THE PEOPLE (C) 543

544 WE THE PEOPLE (C)

TRY IT Practice Words from *I Dissent!* Part 2

Students will answer questions to demonstrate their understanding of the vocabulary words from the reading.

WRAP-UP

Question About Key Details

Students will answer a question to show that they understand how key details support a main idea.

Handwriting

Students should gather their handwriting materials and begin where they left off. Remind students to form letters carefully and correctly.

TIP Set a timer to help students stay focused during handwriting practice.

We the People (D)

Lesson Overview

ACTIVITY	ACTIVITY TITLE	TIME	ONLINE/OFFLINE
GET READY	Introduction to We the People (D)	1 minute	online
	Spelling List 24 More Practice	10 minutes	online
	Recall *I Dissent!* Part 2	10 minutes	online
READ	Review *Michelle Obama* and *I Dissent!*	19 minutes	offline
LEARN AND TRY IT	Compare and Contrast Autobiography and Biography	20 minutes	online
	Compare and Contrast Biographies	10 minutes	online
	Write About Biographies LEARNING COACH CHECK-IN	40 minutes	offline
WRAP-UP	Question About Autobiographies and Biographies	2 minutes	online
	Handwriting	8 minutes	offline

Content Background

Students will spend some time reviewing the two biographies they have read. Then they will read a student's autobiography and compare and contrast all three texts.

To *compare* means "to explain how two or more things are alike." To *contrast* means "to explain how two or more things are different."

One way that biographies and autobiographies differ is the point of view from which they are written. A *biography* is a story of someone's life written by another person; an *autobiography* is a story of someone's life written by that person. The points of view are different based on who is writing.

MATERIALS

Supplied

- *Michelle Obama: First Lady, Going Higher* by Shana Corey
- *I Dissent! Ruth Bader Ginsburg Makes Her Mark* by Debbie Levy
- *Summit English Language Arts 3 Activity Book*
  - Write About Biographies
- handwriting workbook

Lesson Goals

- Practice all spelling words online.
- Review *Michelle Obama: First Lady, Going Higher* and *I Dissent!*
- Compare and contrast autobiography and biography.
- Compare and contrast two biographies.
- Write about biographies.
- Develop letter formation fluency.

KEYWORDS

autobiography – the story of a person's life written by that person

biography – the story of a person's life written by another person

compare – to explain how two or more things are alike

contrast – to explain how two or more things are different

point of view – who is telling the story

GET READY

Introduction to We the People (D)

Students will get a glimpse of what they will learn about in the lesson. They will also read the lesson goals and keywords. Have students select each keyword and preview its definition.

Spelling List 24 More Practice

Students will practice all spelling words from the workshop.

OPTIONAL Students may do an activity from Spelling List 24 Activity Bank instead of the online practice activity.

Recall *I Dissent!* Part 2

Students will answer some questions to review the reading that they have already completed.

READ

Review *Michelle Obama* and *I Dissent!*

Students will review *Michelle Obama: First Lady, Going Higher* by Shana Corey and *I Dissent! Ruth Bader Ginsburg Makes Her Mark* by Debbie Levy.

NOTE Students should not reread the texts from cover to cover. They should skim the texts by flipping through them. They should look at the pictures and scan the words on the pages to remind themselves of the main ideas in each text.

LEARN AND TRY IT

LEARN Compare and Contrast Autobiography and Biography

Students will learn about the similarities and differences between autobiographies and biographies. They will also begin to compare and contrast the two biographies they have read in this workshop.

TRY IT Compare and Contrast Biographies

Students will identify the ways in which the Ginsburgs and the Obamas are alike and different.

TRY IT Write About Biographies

Students will complete Write About Biographies in *Summit English Language Arts 3 Activity Book*. On these activity pages, students will reflect on ways that Michelle Obama and Ruth Bader Ginsburg are similar and different. They will also think about the format of the two biographies they have read and which one they prefer.

LEARNING COACH CHECK-IN This activity page contains open-ended questions, so it's important that you review students' responses. Give students feedback, using the sample answers provided to guide you.

TRY IT

We the People (D)

Write About Biographies

Possible answers are shown.

Compare and contrast *Michelle Obama: First Lady, Going Higher* and *I Dissent! Ruth Bader Ginsburg Makes Her Mark.* Find three ways the biographies are alike and three ways they are different. Record your ideas on the T chart.

Alike	Different
• Mrs. Obama and Justice Ginsburg are both lawyers. • Mrs. Obama and Justice Ginsburg are both mothers. • Mrs. Obama and Justice Ginsburg both care about all people being treated equally. • Mrs. Obama and Justice Ginsburg both lost a parent when they were just becoming adults. • Mrs. Obama and Justice Ginsburg found ways to do what they wanted to do, even when it was difficult.	• Justice Ginsburg is a Supreme Court justice. • Mrs. Obama is a First Lady of the United States. • When Justice Ginsburg disagrees, she writes a dissent. • When Mrs. Obama disagrees, she gives a speech or creates a program. • Justice Ginsburg was treated unfairly because she is a woman, a mother, and Jewish. • Mrs. Obama was treated unfairly because she is African American.

545

Answer the questions in complete sentences.

1. Think about the format of the two biographies you read. Describe the format of each book.

   Possible answer: *Michelle Obama: First Lady, Going Higher* looks like many chapter books I have read. The words are easy to understand. The pictures illustrate the actions that take place in the book. The pages are equally divided between words and pictures. *I Dissent!* is more like a picture book. There are more pictures than words on a page. Words sometimes make up part of the pictures in the book.

2. Which format did you like better? Why?

   Answers will vary.

546 WE THE PEOPLE (D)

3. Do you think you're like Mrs. Obama or Justice Ginsburg in any way? If so, how?

   Answers will vary.

I have to choose a favorite? Impossible!

WE THE PEOPLE (D) 547

WRAP-UP

Question About Autobiographies and Biographies

Students will answer a question to show that they understand a key difference between autobiographies and biographies.

Handwriting

Students should gather their handwriting materials and begin where they left off. Remind students to form letters carefully and correctly.

TIP Set a timer to help students stay focused during handwriting practice.

We the People (E)

Lesson Overview

ACTIVITY	ACTIVITY TITLE	TIME	ONLINE/OFFLINE
GET READY	Introduction to We the People (E)	**1** minute	online
	Spelling List 24 Review Game	**10** minutes	online
	Before You Read Ben's Guide to the U.S. Government	**10** minutes	online
LEARN AND TRY IT	Learn About Website Features	**20** minutes	online
	Practice Using Website Features	**10** minutes	online
	Finding Main Idea and Key Details Online	**20** minutes	online
	Find Main Idea and Key Details Online	**10** minutes	online
	Apply: Finding Main Idea and Key Details	**14** minutes	online
	Complete a Scavenger Hunt LEARNING COACH CHECK-IN	**15** minutes	online and offline
WRAP-UP	Question About Website Features	**2** minutes	online
	Handwriting	**8** minutes	offline

Content Background

Students will be guided through an exploration of Ben's Guide to the U.S. Government, a website about the government of the United States (linked in the online activity). They will learn about basic features of websites, such as the address and navigation bars, web pages, and hyperlinks. They will also learn that websites have features similar to those found in nonfiction books, like glossaries. They will learn that reading text on a website is very similar to reading a nonfiction book—they will find main ideas and supporting details in both. Students will also complete a scavenger hunt through the website to practice their navigation skills.

MATERIALS

Supplied

- *Summit English Language Arts 3 Activity Book*
  - Complete a Scavenger Hunt
- handwriting workbook

Lesson Goals

- Practice all spelling words online.
- Explore and use interactive website features.
- Determine the main idea and key details on a web page.
- Complete a scavenger hunt to find specific information on a website.
- Develop letter formation fluency.

KEYWORDS

context clue – a word or phrase in a text that helps you figure out the meaning of an unknown word

hyperlink – a word or words in an online text that you can select; a hyperlink is usually blue and underlined

URL – the Internet address of a website; stands for uniform resource locator

website – place on the Internet devoted to a specific organization, group, or individual

GET READY

Introduction to We the People (E)

Students will get a glimpse of what they will learn about in the lesson. They will also read the lesson goals and keywords. Have students select each keyword and preview its definition.

Spelling List 24 Review Game

Students will practice all spelling words from the workshop.

Before You Read Ben's Guide to the U.S. Government

Students will learn some important background related to the reading and answer a question to help them set a purpose for their reading.

LEARN AND TRY IT

LEARN Learn About Website Features

Students will learn about the interactive features on a website.

TRY IT Practice Using Website Features

Students will practice using interactive features on a website.

LEARN Finding Main Idea and Key Details Online

Students will learn about finding the main idea and key details in online text.

TRY IT Find Main Idea and Key Details Online

Students will practice finding the main idea and key details in online text.

TRY IT Apply: Finding Main Idea and Key Details

Students will apply to a new work what they've learned about finding the main idea and supporting details in online text.

TRY IT Complete a Scavenger Hunt

Students will complete Complete a Scavenger Hunt in *Summit English Language Arts 3 Activity Book*. This activity page requires students to hunt for specific facts on topics on the Ben's Guide to the U.S. Government website, which is linked in the online activity.

LEARNING COACH CHECK-IN This activity page contains 10 questions that come from different pages on the website. If students are unable to figure out which section of the website to explore based on the question, you may suggest and help them use the search feature at the top of the web page to locate the information they need.

TRY IT

We the People (E)

Complete a Scavenger Hunt

Connect to the Ben's Guide to the U.S. Government website. Select Apprentice Level Learning Adventures. Answer the questions in complete sentences. Use the search bar if you need help finding something.

1. Who gave the Statue of Liberty to the American people?
   The people of France gave the Statue of Liberty to the American people.
2. Why was the Pledge of Allegiance written?
   The Pledge of Allegiance was written to mark the 400th anniversary of the arrival of Christopher Columbus.
3. Which branch of government makes laws?
   The legislative branch of government makes laws.
4. What is a bill?
   A bill is a rough draft of a law.

WE THE PEOPLE (E) 549

5. How old do you have to be to vote in an election in the United States?
   You have to be 18 years or older to vote in a U.S. election.
6. Which city houses the Liberty Bell?
   Philadelphia, Pennsylvania, houses the Liberty Bell.
7. What are two powers the federal government has that state governments do **not** have?
   Answers will vary. The federal government can make money, declare war, manage relationships with foreign countries, and oversee trade between the states and with other countries.
8. How many times has the U.S. Constitution been changed?
   The U.S. Constitution has been changed 27 times.
9. Where would you go if you wanted to see the original Emancipation Proclamation in person?
   You would go to the National Archives in Washington, D.C., to see the original Emancipation Proclamation in person.
10. What does GPO currently stand for?
    GPO currently stands for the Government Publishing Office.

550 WE THE PEOPLE (E)

WRAP-UP

Question About Website Features

Students will answer a question to show that they understand features they will find on a website.

Handwriting

Students should gather their handwriting materials and begin where they left off. Remind students to form letters carefully and correctly.

TIP Set a timer to help students stay focused during handwriting practice.

We the People Wrap-Up

Lesson Overview

ACTIVITY	ACTIVITY TITLE	TIME	ONLINE/OFFLINE
GET READY	Introduction to We the People Wrap-Up	**1** minute	online
	Read and Record	**8** minutes	online
TRY IT	Compare and Contrast Information Sources LEARNING COACH CHECK-IN	**30** minutes	offline
	Review We the People	**20** minutes	online
QUIZ	We the People	**30** minutes	online
	Spelling List 24	**10** minutes	online
WRAP-UP	More Language Arts Practice	**13** minutes	online
	Handwriting	**8** minutes	offline

Lesson Goals

- Read aloud to practice fluency.
- Compare and contrast people and events.
- Review what you learned.
- Take a reading quiz.
- Take a spelling quiz.
- Develop letter formation fluency.

MATERIALS

Supplied

- *Michelle Obama: First Lady, Going Higher* by Shana Corey
- *I Dissent! Ruth Bader Ginsburg Makes Her Mark* by Debbie Levy
- *Summit English Language Arts 3 Activity Book*
  - Compare and Contrast Information Sources
- handwriting workbook

GET READY

Introduction to We the People Wrap-Up

Students will read the lesson goals.

Read and Record

Good readers read quickly, smoothly, and with expression. This is called *fluency*. Students will record themselves reading aloud. They will listen to their recording and think about how quick, smooth, and expressive they sound.

TIP Encourage students to rerecord as needed.

TRY IT

Compare and Contrast Information Sources

Students will complete Compare and Contrast Information Sources in *Summit English Language Arts 3 Activity Book*. They will reflect on the similarities and differences between nonfiction books and online sources of information.

LEARNING COACH CHECK-IN This activity page contains open-ended questions, so it's important that you review students' responses. Give students feedback, using the sample answers provided to guide you.

TRY IT

We the People Wrap-Up

Compare and Contrast Information Sources

Answer the questions in complete sentences.

1. You have read biographies in books and looked at information on a website. How are the sources of information alike?
   Answer will vary. Students should write something about the similarities between the books and the website, such as both were about real people, contained facts, provided information about people who have made a difference in U.S. history, and so on.
2. How are the sources of information different?
   Answer will vary. Students should write something about the differences between the books and the website, such as we read books from the beginning to the end, but we don't examine websites in a given or specific order. They may also note that the biographies they read told stories of people's lives, while the website provided information about the government, not just Benjamin Franklin's life. Finally, they may note that certain features, such as hyperlinks, only occur online.

WE THE PEOPLE WRAP-UP 551

3. Which type of source did you prefer? Why? Use details from the source(s) to explain your answer.
   Answer will vary. Students may write that they prefer the website because they do not have to explore it from start to finish since they can use hyperlinks to move around. They may also enjoy the idea of playing games to learn more about a topic. Students may write that they prefer the books because it feels like reading a story and that they would rather work through a source from start to finish.

552 WE THE PEOPLE WRAP-UP

Review We the People

Students will answer questions to review what they have learned about determining the main idea and supporting details in nonfiction texts and on web pages, using information from illustrations, and describing features on websites.

QUIZ

We the People

Students will complete the We the People quiz.

Spelling List 24

Students will complete the Spelling List 24 quiz.

WRAP-UP

More Language Arts Practice

Students will practice skills according to their individual needs.

Handwriting

Students should gather their handwriting materials and begin where they left off. Remind students to form letters carefully and correctly.

TIP Set a timer to help students stay focused during handwriting practice.

Judiciary Words

Lesson Overview

ACTIVITY	ACTIVITY TITLE	TIME	ONLINE/OFFLINE
GET READY	Introduction to Judiciary Words	1 minute	online
	Look Back at Content-Area Vocabulary	4 minutes	online
LEARN AND TRY IT	Judiciary Words	10 minutes	online
	Practice Using Judiciary Words	10 minutes	online
	Apply: Judiciary Words LEARNING COACH CHECK-IN	15 minutes	offline
	Review Judiciary Words	15 minutes	online
QUIZ	Judiciary Words	15 minutes	online
WRAP-UP	More Language Arts Practice	15 minutes	online
	Go Write! Who Is Your Hero?	15 minutes	offline
	Go Read!	20 minutes	online or offline

Content Backgrounds

Students will learn words that are used when reading, writing, and talking about the law. They will use context clues to help determine the definitions of these words.

Advance Preparation

During the Go Read! activity, students will have the option of using the digital library. Allow extra time for students to make their reading selection, or have students make a selection before beginning the lesson.

MATERIALS

Supplied

- *Summit English Language Arts 3 Activity Book*
  - Apply: Judiciary Words
  - Go Write! Who Is Your Hero?

Also Needed

- reading material for Go Read!

Lesson Goals

- Practice vocabulary words.
- Use words related to the law and the judicial system.
- Take the Judiciary Words quiz.
- Freewrite about a topic to develop writing fluency and practice letter formation.
- Read independently to develop fluency.

KEYWORDS

content-specific word – a word that has to do with a certain job or activity

context clue – a word or phrase in a text that helps you figure out the meaning of an unknown word

GET READY

Introduction to Judiciary Words

Students will get a glimpse of what they will learn about in the lesson. They will also read the lesson goals and keywords. Have students select each keyword and preview its definition.

Look Back at Content-Area Vocabulary

Students will practice the prerequisite skill of learning and using content-area vocabulary in context.

LEARN AND TRY IT

LEARN Judiciary Words

Students will be introduced to the vocabulary words for the lesson. Then they will learn which judiciary word to use in a given context.

TRY IT Practice Using Judiciary Words

Students will practice using judiciary words by selecting the correct word in a sentence and matching words with their definitions.

TRY IT Apply: Judiciary Words

Students will complete Apply: Judiciary Words in *Summit English Language Arts 3 Activity Book*.

LEARNING COACH CHECK-IN This activity page contains open-ended questions, so it's important that you review students' responses. Give students feedback, using the sample answers provided to guide you.

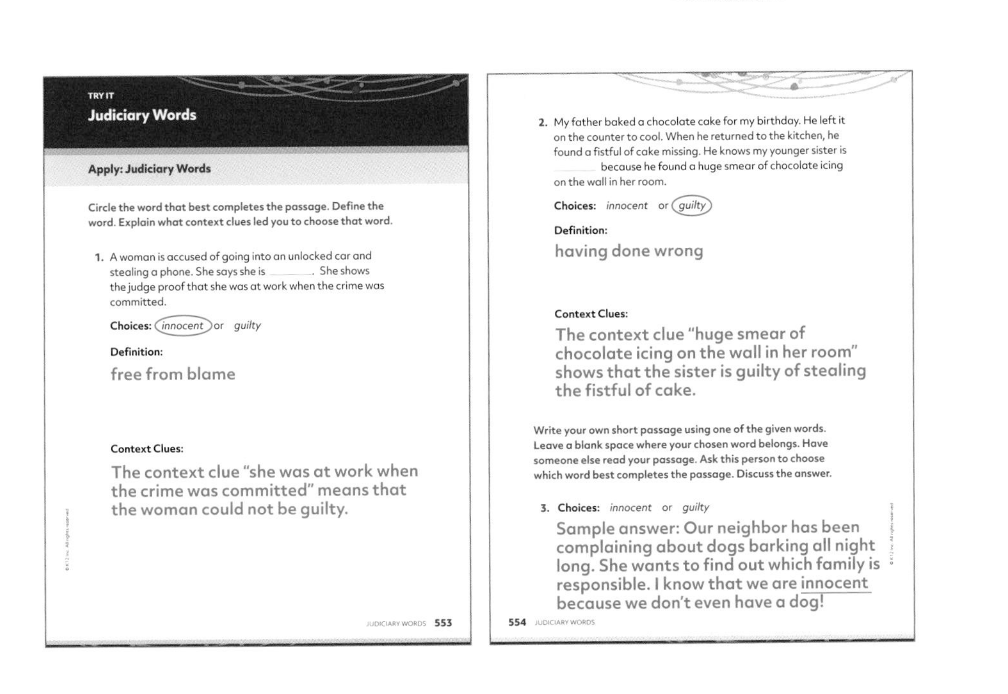

TRY IT
Judiciary Words

Apply: Judiciary Words

Circle the word that best completes the passage. Define the word. Explain what context clues led you to choose that word.

1. A woman is accused of going into an unlocked car and stealing a phone. She says she is ______. She shows the judge proof that she was at work when the crime was committed.

   Choices: *innocent* or *guilty*

   Definition:
   free from blame

   Context Clues:
   The context clue "she was at work when the crime was committed" means that the woman could not be guilty.

JUDICIARY WORDS 553

2. My father baked a chocolate cake for my birthday. He left it on the counter to cool. When he returned to the kitchen, he found a fistful of cake missing. He knows my younger sister is ______ because he found a huge smear of chocolate icing on the wall in her room.

   Choices: *innocent* or *guilty*

   Definition:
   having done wrong

   Context Clues:
   The context clue "huge smear of chocolate icing on the wall in her room" shows that the sister is guilty of stealing the fistful of cake.

Write your own short passage using one of the given words. Leave a blank space where your chosen word belongs. Have someone else read your passage. Ask this person to choose which word best completes the passage. Discuss the answer.

3. **Choices:** *innocent* or *guilty*
   Sample answer: Our neighbor has been complaining about dogs barking all night long. She wants to find out which family is responsible. I know that we are innocent because we don't even have a dog!

554 JUDICIARY WORDS

TRY IT Review Judiciary Words

Students will answer questions to review what they have learned about judiciary words.

QUIZ

Judiciary Words

Students will complete the Judiciary Words quiz.

WRAP-UP

More Language Arts Practice

Students will practice skills according to their individual needs.

Go Write! Who Is Your Hero?

Students will complete Go Write! Who Is Your Hero? in *Summit English Language Arts 3 Activity Book*. They will have the option to either respond to a prompt or write about a topic of their choice.

NOTE This activity is intended to build writing fluency. Students should write for the entire allotted time.

SUPPORT If students have trouble writing for the allotted time, prompt them with questions. For example, *Can you tell me more about this person?*

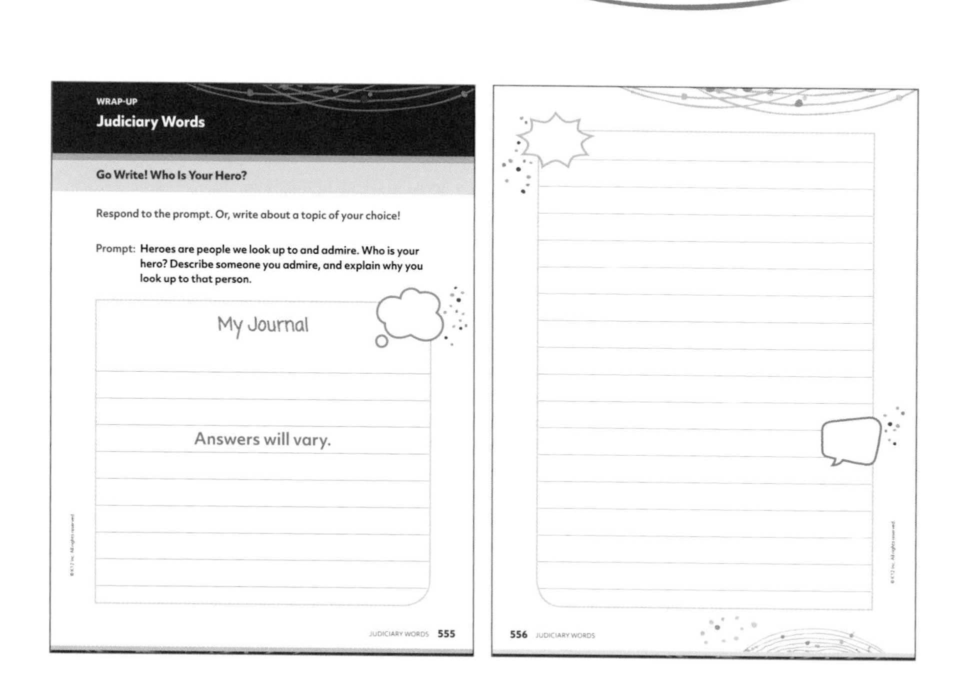
WRAP-UP
Judiciary Words

Go Write! Who Is Your Hero?

Respond to the prompt. Or, write about a topic of your choice!

Prompt: **Heroes are people we look up to and admire. Who is your hero? Describe someone you admire, and explain why you look up to that person.**

My Journal

Answers will vary.

JUDICIARY WORDS 555

556 JUDICIARY WORDS

Go Read!

Students will read for pleasure. They should choose a book or a magazine that interests them, or they may choose a selection from the digital library, linked in the online lesson.

- Have students read aloud a few paragraphs of their selection.
- Then have students read silently for the rest of the time.

SUPPORT Students should make no more than five errors in decoding when they read aloud a few paragraphs of their Go Read! selection. If students struggle or make more than five errors, they need to select a different (and easier) text for the Go Read! activity.

TIP Have students select something to read ahead of time to help them stay focused.

Presentation: Brainstorming

Lesson Overview

ACTIVITY	ACTIVITY TITLE	TIME	ONLINE/OFFLINE
GET READY	Introduction to Presentation: Brainstorming	**1** minute	
	Spelling List 25 Pretest **LEARNING COACH CHECK-IN**	**10** minutes	and
	Editing Practice: Riddle	**10** minutes	
LEARN AND **TRY IT**	Explore a Model Oral History Presentation	**15** minutes	
	Respond to a Model Oral History Presentation	**10** minutes	
	Brainstorm for an Oral History Presentation	**10** minutes	
	Brainstorm for Your Oral History Presentation **LEARNING COACH CHECK-IN**	**30** minutes	
WRAP-UP	Question About Oral History Presentations	**2** minutes	
	Handwriting	**8** minutes	
	Go Read!	**24** minutes	or

Content Background

Students will begin working on an **oral history presentation**. *Oral history* is a research method that involves interviewing people about past events and preserving those interviews. The assignment that students will complete is inspired by this research method. Students will learn about the importance of interviewing as a research method, conduct an interview, and then deliver a speech that retells an important story that they learned during their interview.

They will complete the oral history presentation over the course of several lessons by following the writing process.

Writing Process

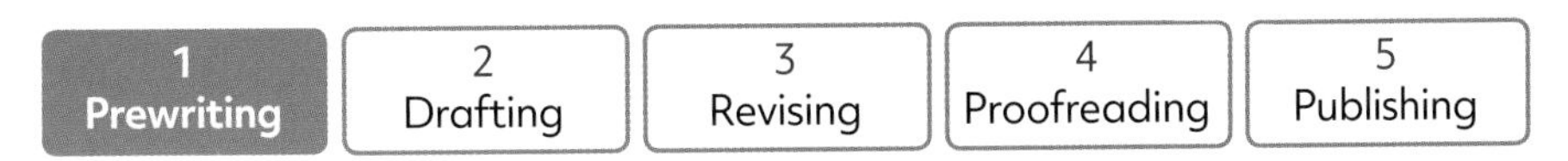

In this lesson, students will brainstorm and choose an interview subject.

MATERIALS

Supplied

- *Summit English Language Arts 3 Activity Book*
  - Spelling List 25 Pretest
  - Brainstorm for Your Oral History Presentation
- Oral History Presentation Instructions (printout)
- handwriting workbook

Also Needed

- folder for storing presentation assignment pages
- reading material for Go Read!

Advance Preparation

Gather a folder that students can use to keep all notes and activity pages related to their presentation.

During the Go Read! activity, students will have the option of using the digital library. Allow extra time for students to make their reading selection, or have students make a selection before beginning the lesson.

KEYWORDS

brainstorming – before writing, a way for the writer to come up with ideas

presentation – an oral report, usually with visuals

Lesson Goals

- Take a spelling pretest.
- Practice grammar skills by editing a short passage.
- Explore a model oral history presentation.
- Brainstorm and choose a person to interview.
- Develop letter formation fluency.
- Read independently to develop fluency.

GET READY

Introduction to Presentation: Brainstorming

Students will get a glimpse of what they will learn about in the lesson. They will also read the lesson goals and keywords. Have students select each keyword and preview its definition.

Spelling List 25 Pretest

Students will take a spelling pretest and learn a new spelling pattern.

LEARNING COACH CHECK-IN Have students turn to Spelling List 25 Pretest in *Summit English Language Arts 3 Activity Book* and open the online Spelling Pretest activity. Online, students will listen to the spelling word, type the word in the space indicated, and then check their answer. In the activity book, students will write the correct spelling of the word in the tables provided and indicate with a ✓ or an ✗ if they spelled the word correctly or incorrectly online. Students will repeat this process with the remaining words.

As needed, help students with the interaction between the online activity and the activity book page until they become comfortable with what they need to do. As students practice their spelling words throughout the workshop, they should pay special attention to words they spelled incorrectly on the pretest.

This is the complete list of words students will be tested on.

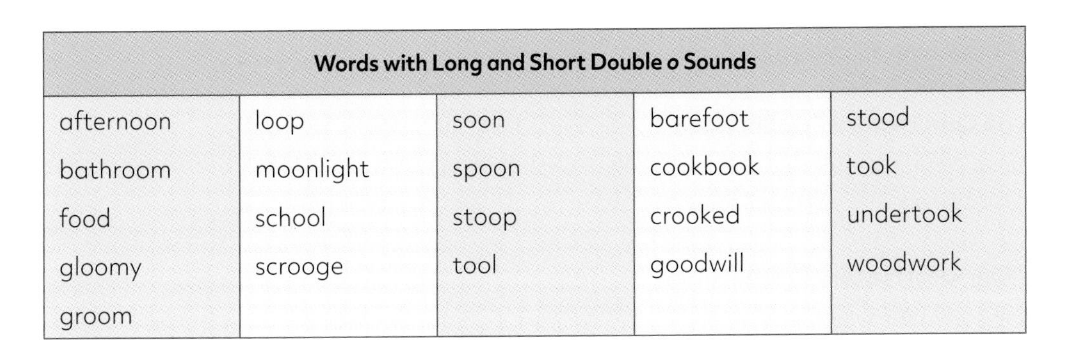

Words with Long and Short Double *o* Sounds				
afternoon	loop	soon	barefoot	stood
bathroom	moonlight	spoon	cookbook	took
food	school	stoop	crooked	undertook
gloomy	scrooge	tool	goodwill	woodwork
groom				

NOTE Have students keep their completed activity page in a safe place so they can refer to it later.

GET READY

Presentation: Brainstorming

Spelling List 25 Pretest

1. Open the Spelling Pretest activity online. Listen to the first spelling word. Type the word. Check your answer.
2. Write the correct spelling of the word in the Word column of the Spelling Pretest table.

	Word	✓	✗
1	blindfold		

3. Put a check mark in the ✓ column if you spelled the word correctly online.

	Word	✓	✗
1	blindfold	✓	

Put an X in the ✗ column if you spelled the word incorrectly online.

	Word	✓	✗
1	blindfold		X

4. Repeat Steps 1–3 for the remaining words in the Spelling Pretest.

PRESENTATION: BRAINSTORMING 557

Presentation: Brainstorming

Spelling List 25 Pretest

Write each spelling word in the Word column, making sure to spell it correctly.

	Word	✓	✗
1	afternoon		
2	bathroom		
3	food		
4	gloomy		
5	groom		
6	loop		
7	moonlight		
8	school		
9	scrooge		
10	soon		
11	spoon		

	Word	✓	✗
12	stoop		
13	tool		
14	barefoot		
15	cookbook		
16	crooked		
17	goodwill		
18	stood		
19	took		
20	undertook		
21	woodwork		

Students should write the correct spelling of each word from the pretest and use the ✓and X columns to indicate whether they spelled each word correctly or incorrectly online.

558 PRESENTATION: BRAINSTORMING

Editing Practice: Riddle

Students will edit a short passage to practice applying grammar skills.

LEARN AND TRY IT

LEARN Explore a Model Oral History Presentation

Students will be introduced to their assignment, which is to interview someone and tell an important story from that person's life. To help them better understand the assignment, students will explore a model oral history presentation and learn about the elements that make it successful.

TRY IT Respond to a Model Oral History Presentation

Students will answer questions to check and expand their understanding of the key elements of the model oral history presentation.

LEARN Brainstorm for an Oral History Presentation

Students will investigate how a student chooses whom to interview for an oral history presentation.

TRY IT Brainstorm for Your Oral History Presentation

Students will complete Brainstorm for Your Oral History Presentation in *Summit English Language Arts 3 Activity Book*.

LEARNING COACH CHECK-IN Assist students as needed as they complete this activity. Help them brainstorm different people in their lives that they could interview.

NOTE Have students add their completed Brainstorm for Your Oral History Presentation activity page to the folder they are using to store their presentation assignment pages.

TRY IT

Presentation: Brainstorming

Brainstorm for Your Oral History Presentation

Read the assignment. You will complete the assignment in steps over multiple lessons.

Prompt: **Interview someone who means a lot to you. Tell an important story that you learned from interviewing that person.**

Requirements:

Your oral history presentation should include the following:

- A **hook** that relates to your main idea and captures your audience's attention
- A story from a person's life that has a clear **beginning**, **middle**, and **end**
- Accurate facts and details gathered from an interview
- Descriptive language
- A piece of media (picture, song, chart) that relates to the story you are telling

Be sure to do the following:

- Speak clearly and at an appropriate pace.
- Use correct grammar.

Audience: Your teacher, peers, and Learning Coach

Purpose: Help others learn about the world by retelling an important experience in someone's life.

Length: $2\frac{1}{2}$–4 minutes

Brainstorm and choose someone to interview for your oral history presentation.

Answers will vary.

1. Think about people in your life. Create a list or a web of people you may want to interview.

2. Read over the names you brainstormed.
   a. Cross off any names of people who may be hard to interview in person or on video.
   b. Think about each remaining person you listed.
      - Has anyone lived through an interesting event or time period?
      - Has anyone experienced something that you have not?
      - Might anyone have a story that you want to share?
   c. Circle the person whom you think would be the most interesting to interview.

I will interview ____________________

Not all stories make the news. I can't wait to tell an important story.

WRAP-UP

Question About Oral History Presentations

Students will answer a question to show that they understand how to brainstorm for an oral history presentation.

Handwriting

Students should gather their handwriting materials and begin where they left off. Remind students to form letters carefully and correctly.

TIP Set a timer to help students stay focused during handwriting practice.

Go Read!

Students will read for pleasure. They should choose a book or a magazine that interests them, or they may choose a selection from the digital library, linked in the online lesson.

- Have students read aloud a few paragraphs of their selection.
- Then have students read silently for the rest of the time.

SUPPORT Students should make no more than five errors in decoding when they read aloud a few paragraphs of their Go Read! selection. If students struggle or make more than five errors, they need to select a different (and easier) text for the Go Read! activity.

TIP Have students select something to read ahead of time to help them stay focused.

Presentation: Research (A)

Lesson Overview

ACTIVITY	ACTIVITY TITLE	TIME	ONLINE/OFFLINE
GET READY	Introduction to Presentation: Research (A)	**1** minute	
	Spelling List 25 Activity Bank	**10** minutes	
	Editing Practice: Riddle	**10** minutes	
LEARN AND TRY IT	Primary Research	**15** minutes	
	Make a Research Plan LEARNING COACH CHECK-IN	**50** minutes	
WRAP-UP	Question About Making a Research Plan	**2** minutes	
	Handwriting	**8** minutes	
	Go Read!	**24** minutes	or

Content Background

Students will continue working on their **oral history presentation**. They will complete the assignment over the course of several lessons by following the writing process.

Writing Process

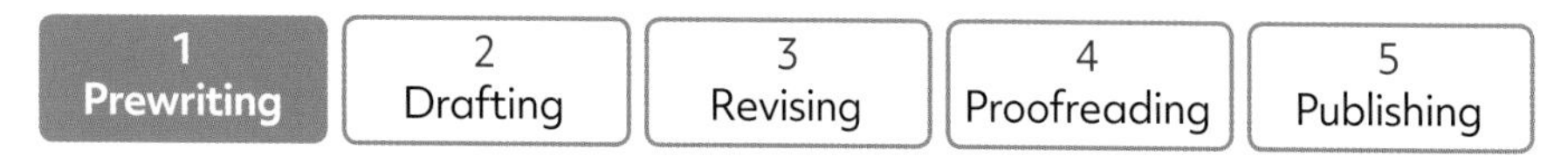

In this lesson, students will continue the prewriting phase by making a plan to conduct **primary research**. *Secondary research* is research done by reviewing the research of others. Websites, books, and videos are all sources of secondary research. In contrast, *primary research* is research that people themselves conduct. Methods of primary research include interviews, surveys, and observation. Students will use interviewing as their method of primary research.

MATERIALS

Supplied

- *Summit English Language Arts 3 Activity Book*
  - Spelling List 25 Activity Bank
  - Make a Research Plan
- Oral History Presentation Instructions (printout)
- handwriting workbook

Also Needed

- completed Spelling List 25 Pretest activity page from Presentation: Brainstorming
- folder in which students are storing presentation assignment pages
- reading material for Go Read!

Advance Preparation

Gather students' completed Spelling List 25 Pretest activity page from Presentation: Brainstorming. Students will refer to this page during Get Ready: Spelling List 25 Activity Bank.

Gather the folder that students are using to store the activity pages related to their presentation. The folder should contain the following:

- Students' completed Brainstorm for Your Oral History Presentation activity page from Presentation: Brainstorming

During the Go Read! activity, students will have the option of using the digital library. Allow extra time for students to make their reading selection, or have students make a selection before beginning the lesson.

KEYWORDS

interview (v.) – to ask someone questions to gather information

primary source – a record made by a person who saw or took part in an event or who lived at the time

research (n.) – a careful search for information about a subject

Lesson Goals

- Practice spelling words offline.
- Practice grammar skills by editing a short passage.
- Make a research plan.
- Develop letter formation fluency.
- Read independently to develop fluency.

GET READY

Introduction to Presentation: Research (A)

Students will get a glimpse of what they will learn about in the lesson. They will also read the lesson goals and keywords. Have students select each keyword and preview its definition.

Spelling List 25 Activity Bank

Students will practice all spelling words from the workshop by completing Spelling List 25 Activity Bank from *Summit English Language Arts 3 Activity Book*. Make sure students have their completed Spelling List 25 Pretest activity page from Presentation: Brainstorming to refer to during this activity.

Remind students to pay special attention to words they spelled incorrectly on the Spelling Pretest.

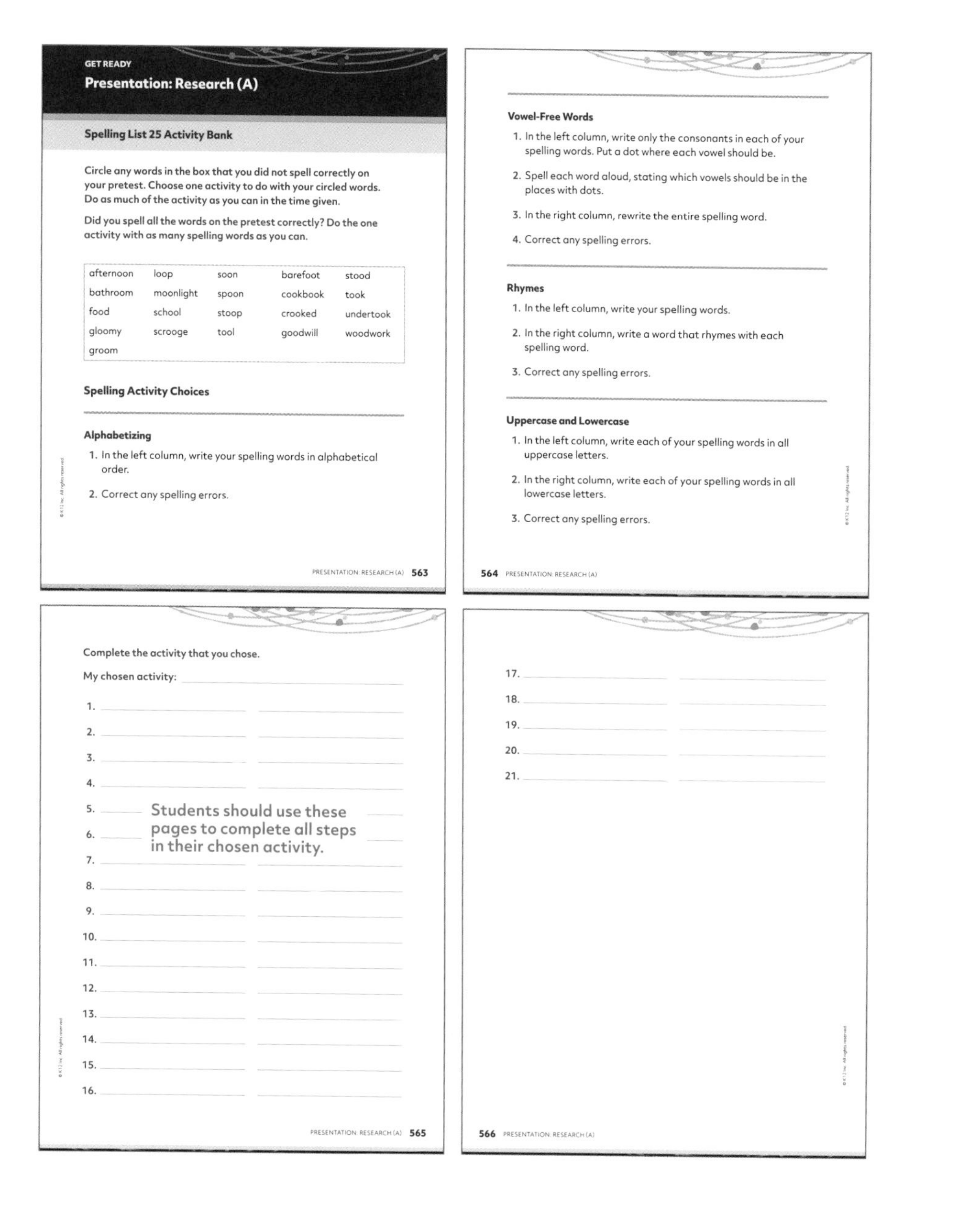

GET READY

Presentation: Research (A)

Spelling List 25 Activity Bank

Circle any words in the box that you did not spell correctly on your pretest. Choose one activity to do with your circled words. Do as much of the activity as you can in the time given.

Did you spell all the words on the pretest correctly? Do the one activity with as many spelling words as you can.

afternoon	loop	soon	barefoot	stood
bathroom	moonlight	spoon	cookbook	took
food	school	stoop	crooked	undertook
gloomy	scrooge	tool	goodwill	woodwork
groom				

Spelling Activity Choices

Alphabetizing

1. In the left column, write your spelling words in alphabetical order.
2. Correct any spelling errors.

PRESENTATION: RESEARCH (A) 563

Vowel-Free Words

1. In the left column, write only the consonants in each of your spelling words. Put a dot where each vowel should be.
2. Spell each word aloud, stating which vowels should be in the places with dots.
3. In the right column, rewrite the entire spelling word.
4. Correct any spelling errors.

Rhymes

1. In the left column, write your spelling words.
2. In the right column, write a word that rhymes with each spelling word.
3. Correct any spelling errors.

Uppercase and Lowercase

1. In the left column, write each of your spelling words in all uppercase letters.
2. In the right column, write each of your spelling words in all lowercase letters.
3. Correct any spelling errors.

564 PRESENTATION: RESEARCH (A)

Complete the activity that you chose.

My chosen activity: ______

1. ______ ______
2. ______ ______
3. ______ ______
4. ______ ______
5. ______ ______
6. ______ ______
7. ______ ______
8. ______ ______
9. ______ ______
10. ______ ______
11. ______ ______
12. ______ ______
13. ______ ______
14. ______ ______
15. ______ ______
16. ______ ______

Students should use these pages to complete all steps in their chosen activity.

PRESENTATION: RESEARCH (A) 565

17. ______ ______
18. ______ ______
19. ______ ______
20. ______ ______
21. ______ ______

566 PRESENTATION: RESEARCH (A)

Editing Practice: Riddle

Students will edit a short passage to practice applying grammar skills.

LEARN AND TRY IT

LEARN Primary Research

Students will learn about primary research and how it differs from secondary research. They will explore one method of primary research in particular: interviewing. They will also learn how to write effective interview questions.

TRY IT Make a Research Plan

Students will start Make a Research Plan in *Summit English Language Arts 3 Activity Book*.

LEARNING COACH CHECK-IN Assist students as needed to help them focus their interview questions on the story they are hoping to tell for their oral history presentation.

SUPPORT Students may struggle writing open-ended questions. Try role-playing with students. Have them ask you a question as if you were the interview subject, and model how you would answer. Discuss ways they could revise the question to make it more effective.

NOTE If you or students wish, you can download and print another copy of the Oral History Presentation Instructions online. Have students add their in-progress Make a Research Plan activity page to the folder they are using to store their presentation assignment pages.

TRY IT

Presentation: Research (A)

Make a Research Plan

Fill in the basic information about your interviewee. If you are unsure of anything, fill it out during the interview.

Answers will vary.

Full name of interviewee: ______

Age: ______ Year born: ______

Place of birth: ______

Place of current residence: ______

PRESENTATION: RESEARCH (A) 567

Write 8–10 interview questions. Use the boxes to record notes during the interview.

1. ______

2. ______

568 PRESENTATION: RESEARCH (A)

3. ______

4. ______

PRESENTATION: RESEARCH (A) 569

5. ______

6. ______

570 PRESENTATION: RESEARCH (A)

7. ______

8. ______

PRESENTATION: RESEARCH (A) 571

9. ______

10. ______

572 PRESENTATION: RESEARCH (A)

WRAP-UP

Question About Making a Research Plan

Students will answer a question to show that they understand how to make a research plan.

Handwriting

Students should gather their handwriting materials and begin where they left off. Remind students to form letters carefully and correctly.

TIP Set a timer to help students stay focused during handwriting practice.

Go Read!

Students will read for pleasure. They should choose a book or a magazine that interests them, or they may choose a selection from the digital library, linked in the online lesson.

- Have students read aloud a few paragraphs of their selection.
- Then have students read silently for the rest of the time.

SUPPORT Students should make no more than five errors in decoding when they read aloud a few paragraphs of their Go Read! selection. If students struggle or make more than five errors, they need to select a different (and easier) text for the Go Read! activity.

TIP Have students select something to read ahead of time to help them stay focused.

Presentation: Research (B)

Lesson Overview

ACTIVITY	ACTIVITY TITLE	TIME	ONLINE/OFFLINE
GET READY	Introduction to Presentation: Research (B)	**1** minute	
	Spelling List 25 Practice	**10** minutes	
	Editing Practice: Riddle	**10** minutes	
LEARN AND TRY IT	Interviews	**10** minutes	
	Conduct Interviews **LEARNING COACH CHECK-IN**	**55** minutes	
WRAP-UP	Question About Interviews	**2** minutes	
	Handwriting	**8** minutes	
	Go Read!	**24** minutes	or

Content Background

Students will continue working on their **oral history presentation**. They will complete the assignment over the course of several lessons by following the writing process.

Writing Process

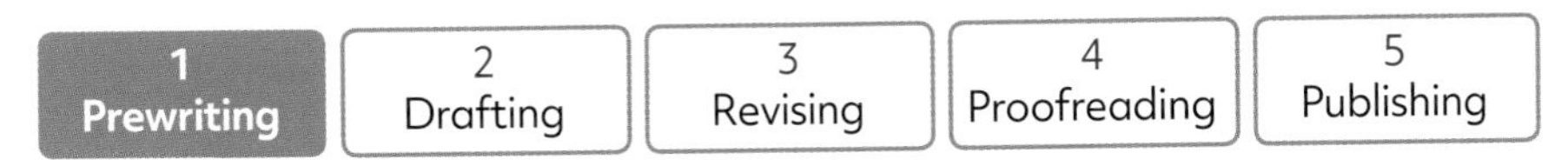

In this lesson, students will learn interviewing skills such as listening respectfully, asking follow-up questions, and taking good notes. They will then conduct an interview.

MATERIALS

Supplied

- Oral History Presentation Instructions (printout)
- handwriting workbook

Also Needed

- folder in which students are storing presentation assignment pages
- reading material for Go Read!

Advance Preparation

Gather the folder that students are using to store the activity pages related to their presentation. The folder should contain the following:

- Students' completed Brainstorm for Your Oral History Presentation activity page from Presentation: Brainstorming
- Students' in-progress Make a Research Plan activity page from Presentation: Research (A)

During the Conduct Interviews activity, students will need to conduct an interview either in person or via a call (phone or video). Ensure that students have scheduled the interview ahead of time.

During the Go Read! activity, students will have the option of using the digital library. Allow extra time for students to make their reading selection, or have students make a selection before beginning the lesson.

Lesson Goals

- Practice spelling words online.
- Practice grammar skills by editing a short passage.
- Conduct an interview.
- Develop letter formation fluency.
- Read independently to develop fluency.

GET READY

Introduction to Presentation: Research (B)

Students will get a glimpse of what they will learn about in the lesson. They will also read the lesson goals.

Spelling List 25 Practice

Students will practice all spelling words from the workshop.

OPTIONAL Students may do an activity from Spelling List 25 Activity Bank instead of the online practice activity.

Editing Practice: Riddle

Students will edit a short passage to practice applying grammar skills.

LEARN AND TRY IT

LEARN Interviews

Students will learn how to conduct an interview. Skills they will learn include scheduling an interview, taking notes, asking follow-up questions, and ending the interview.

TRY IT Conduct Interviews

Students will conduct an interview either in person or via a call (phone or video). They will use the interview questions they wrote on the Make a Research Plan activity page from Presentation: Research (A). They will record their notes on the activity page during the interview.

LEARNING COACH CHECK-IN Students need to conduct an interview to complete this activity. Supervise students during the interview.

NOTE If you or students wish, you can download and print another copy of the Oral History Presentation Instructions online. Have students add their completed Make a Research Plan activity page to the folder they are using to store their presentation assignment pages.

TRY IT

Presentation: Research (A)

Make a Research Plan

Fill in the basic information about your interviewee. If you are unsure of anything, fill it out during the interview.

Answers will vary.

Full name of interviewee: ______

Age: ______ Year born: ______

Place of birth: ______

Place of current residence: ______

PRESENTATION: RESEARCH (A) 567

Write 8–10 interview questions. Use the boxes to record notes during the interview.

1. ______

2. ______

568 PRESENTATION: RESEARCH (A)

3. ______

4. ______

PRESENTATION: RESEARCH (A) 569

5. ______

6. ______

570 PRESENTATION: RESEARCH (A)

7. ______

8. ______

PRESENTATION: RESEARCH (A) 571

9. ______

10. ______

572 PRESENTATION: RESEARCH (A)

WRAP-UP

Question About Interviews

Students will answer a question to show that they understand how to conduct an interview.

Handwriting

Students should gather their handwriting materials and begin where they left off. Remind students to form letters carefully and correctly.

TIP Set a timer to help students stay focused during handwriting practice.

Go Read!

Students will read for pleasure. They should choose a book or a magazine that interests them, or they may choose a selection from the digital library, linked in the online lesson.

- Have students read aloud a few paragraphs of their selection.
- Then have students read silently for the rest of the time.

SUPPORT Students should make no more than five errors in decoding when they read aloud a few paragraphs of their Go Read! selection. If students struggle or make more than five errors, they need to select a different (and easier) text for the Go Read! activity.

TIP Have students select something to read ahead of time to help them stay focused.

Presentation: Planning (A)

Lesson Overview

ACTIVITY	ACTIVITY TITLE	TIME	ONLINE/OFFLINE
GET READY	Introduction to Presentation: Planning (A)	**1** minute	
	Spelling List 25 Review Game	**10** minutes	
	Editing Practice: Riddle	**10** minutes	
LEARN AND TRY IT	Organize an Oral History Presentation	**10** minutes	
	Organize Your Oral History Presentation LEARNING COACH CHECK-IN	**55** minutes	
WRAP-UP	Question About Organizing a Presentation	**2** minutes	
	Handwriting	**8** minutes	
	Go Read!	**24** minutes	or

Content Background

Students will continue working on their **oral history presentation**. They will complete the assignment over the course of several lessons by following the writing process.

Writing Process

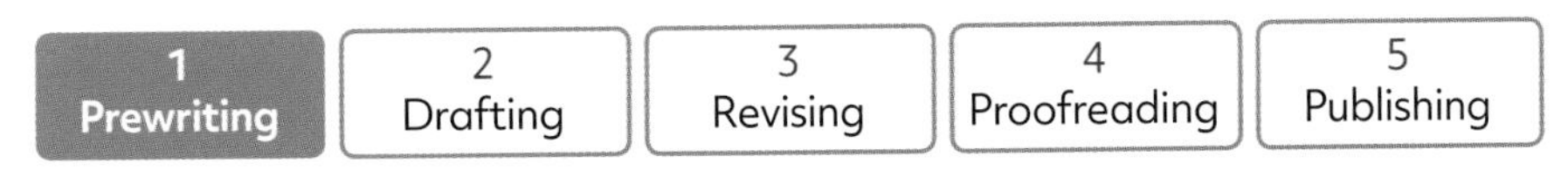

In this lesson, students will organize the notes that they took during their interview. Since students are ultimately telling a story based on what they learned in their interview, they will organize their notes chronologically, or in time order.

MATERIALS

Supplied

- *Summit English Language Arts 3 Activity Book*
  - Organize Your Oral History Presentation
- Oral History Presentation Instructions (printout)
- handwriting workbook

Also Needed

- folder in which students are storing presentation assignment pages
- reading material for Go Read!

Advance Preparation

Gather the folder that students are using to store the activity pages related to their presentation. The folder should contain the following:

- Students' completed Brainstorm for Your Oral History Presentation activity page from Presentation: Brainstorming

- Students' completed Make a Research Plan activity page from Presentation: Research (B)

During the Go Read! activity, students will have the option of using the digital library. Allow extra time for students to make their reading selection, or have students make a selection before beginning the lesson.

Lesson Goals

- Practice spelling words online.
- Practice grammar skills by editing a short passage.
- Organize your interview notes.
- Develop letter formation fluency.
- Read independently to develop fluency.

GET READY

Introduction to Presentation: Planning (A)

Students will get a glimpse of what they will learn about in the lesson. They will also read the lesson goals.

Spelling List 25 Review Game

Students will practice all spelling words from the workshop.

Editing Practice: Riddle

Students will edit a short passage to practice applying grammar skills.

LEARN AND TRY IT

LEARN Organize an Oral History Presentation

Students will learn how to organize notes from an interview. Since students will be using the information they gathered to tell a story, they will learn about organizing the notes chronologically. Additionally, students will learn about distinguishing relevant information from irrelevant information.

TRY IT Organize Your Oral History Presentation

Students will complete Organize Your Oral History Presentation in *Summit English Language Arts 3 Activity Book*. They will need the notes from the interview they conducted to complete this activity.

LEARNING COACH CHECK-IN Check in with students to make sure they are focusing on relevant details.

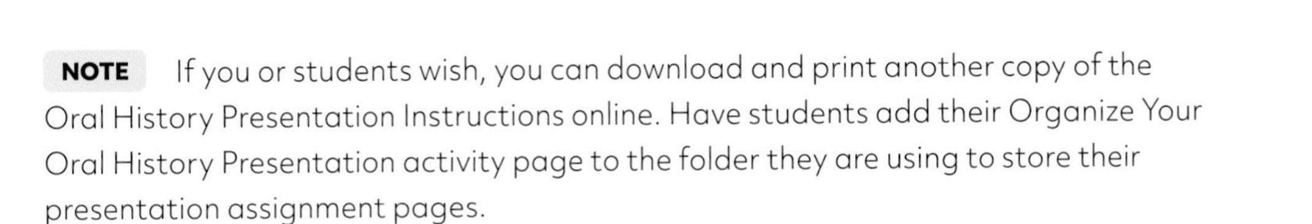

NOTE If you or students wish, you can download and print another copy of the Oral History Presentation Instructions online. Have students add their Organize Your Oral History Presentation activity page to the folder they are using to store their presentation assignment pages.

TRY IT

Presentation: Planning (A)

Organize Your Oral History Presentation

You want to tell a story with a beginning, middle, and end. To do that, you need to organize your interview notes. Use your interview notes to complete the graphic organizer. In each box:

- Write 1–2 sentences to summarize that part of the story.
- Write important facts and details from your interview.

Beginning

Summary:

Interview Notes:

Answers will vary. Students should include only relevant details. Facts and details should be accurate and should be obtained from students' interview notes.

Middle

Summary:

Interview Notes:

End

Summary:

Interview Notes:

WRAP-UP

Question About Organizing a Presentation

Students will answer a question to show that they understand how to organize research notes for a presentation.

Handwriting

Students should gather their handwriting materials and begin where they left off. Remind students to form letters carefully and correctly.

TIP Set a timer to help students stay focused during handwriting practice.

Go Read!

Students will read for pleasure. They should choose a book or a magazine that interests them, or they may choose a selection from the digital library, linked in the online lesson.

- Have students read aloud a few paragraphs of their selection.
- Then have students read silently for the rest of the time.

SUPPORT Students should make no more than five errors in decoding when they read aloud a few paragraphs of their Go Read! selection. If students struggle or make more than five errors, they need to select a different (and easier) text for the Go Read! activity.

TIP Have students select something to read ahead of time to help them stay focused.

Presentation: Planning (B)

Lesson Overview

ACTIVITY	ACTIVITY TITLE	TIME	ONLINE/OFFLINE
GET READY	Introduction to Presentation: Planning (B)	**1** minute	
	Editing Practice: Riddle	**10** minutes	
LEARN AND TRY IT	Create Note Cards	**10** minutes	
	Create Note Cards for Your Presentation **LEARNING COACH CHECK-IN**	**45** minutes	
QUIZ	Spelling List 25	**10** minutes	
WRAP-UP	More Language Arts Practice	**16** minutes	
	Handwriting	**8** minutes	
	Go Read!	**20** minutes	or

Content Background

Students will continue working on their **oral history presentation**. They will complete the assignment over the course of several lessons by following the writing process.

Writing Process

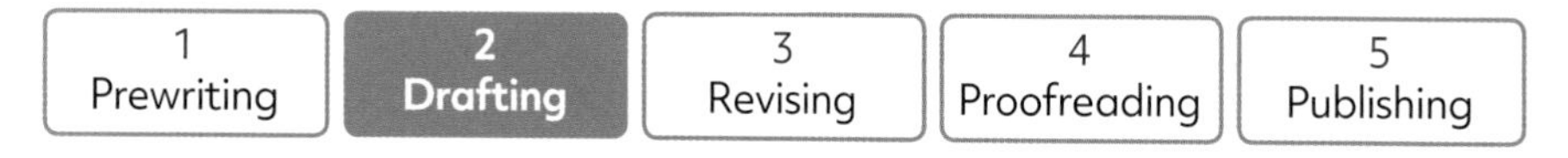

In this lesson, students will use their interview notes to create note cards for their presentation. This can be thought of as drafting, or writing, their presentation. As they create their note cards, they will focus on using descriptive language as appropriate.

MATERIALS

Supplied

- *Summit English Language Arts 3 Activity Book*
  - Create Note Cards for Your Presentation
- Oral History Presentation Instructions (printout)
- handwriting workbook

Also Needed

- folder in which students are storing presentation assignment pages
- index cards (20)
- reading material for Go Read!

Advance Preparation

Gather the folder that students are using to store the activity pages related to their presentation. The folder should contain the following:

- Students' completed Brainstorm for Your Oral History Presentation activity page from Presentation: Brainstorming
- Students' completed Make a Research Plan activity page from Presentation: Research (B)

- Students' completed Organize Your Oral History Presentation activity page from Presentation: Planning (A)

During the Go Read! activity, students will have the option of using the digital library. Allow extra time for students to make their reading selection, or have students make a selection before beginning the lesson.

Lesson Goals

- Practice grammar skills by editing a short passage.
- Write note cards for your oral history presentation.
- Take a spelling quiz.
- Develop letter formation fluency.
- Read independently to develop fluency.

GET READY

Introduction to Presentation: Planning (B)

Students will get a glimpse of what they will learn about in the lesson. They will also read the lesson goals.

Editing Practice: Riddle

Students will edit a short passage to practice applying grammar skills.

LEARN AND TRY IT

LEARN Create Note Cards

Students will learn how to create note cards that they can use to give a presentation. They will also learn that descriptive language enhances a presentation.

TRY IT Create Note Cards for Your Presentation

Students will use their completed Organize Your Oral History Presentation activity page from Presentation: Planning (A) to create notes cards that they can use to give their presentation. They will need approximately 20 index cards on which to take notes.

Have students turn to Create Note Cards for Your Presentation in *Summit English Language Arts 3 Activity Book* and follow the directions to create their note cards.

LEARNING COACH CHECK-IN Review students' note cards. Point out places where students could add transitions and description.

NOTE If you or students wish, you can download and print another copy of the Oral History Presentation Instructions online. Have students add their note cards to the folder they are using to store their presentation assignment pages.

TRY IT

Presentation: Planning (B)

Create Note Cards for Your Presentation

Follow the instructions to make note cards for your presentation.

1. Gather index cards. Label the first card "Hook" and number it "1."

Hook ①

2. Write your hook on that card. Use large, neat handwriting. Use more cards for your hook if you need to. Label the cards "2" and so on.
3. Label the next card "Beginning" and number it with the next number in order. Then, begin telling your story! Use your notes from the Beginning box on your Organize Your Oral History Presentation activity page. Add transitions and descriptive language. Use as many cards as you need.
4. Repeat Step 3 for the middle and end of your story.

PRESENTATION: PLANNING (B) **575**

QUIZ

Spelling List 25

Students will complete the Spelling List 25 quiz.

WRAP-UP

More Language Arts Practice

Students will practice skills according to their individual needs.

Handwriting

Students should gather their handwriting materials and begin where they left off. Remind students to form letters carefully and correctly.

TIP Set a timer to help students stay focused during handwriting practice.

Go Read!

Students will read for pleasure. They should choose a book or a magazine that interests them, or they may choose a selection from the digital library, linked in the online lesson.

- Have students read aloud a few paragraphs of their selection.
- Then have students read silently for the rest of the time.

SUPPORT Students should make no more than five errors in decoding when they read aloud a few paragraphs of their Go Read! selection. If students struggle or make more than five errors, they need to select a different (and easier) text for the Go Read! activity.

TIP Have students select something to read ahead of time to help them stay focused.

Big Ideas: Mini-Project

Lesson Overview

Big Ideas lessons provide students the opportunity to further apply the knowledge acquired and skills learned throughout the unit workshops. Each Big Ideas lesson consists of these parts:

1. **Cumulative Review:** Students keep their skills fresh by reviewing prior content.
2. **Preview:** Students practice answering the types of questions they will commonly find on standardized tests.
3. **Synthesis:** Students complete an assignment that allows them to connect and apply what they have learned. Synthesis assignments vary throughout the course.

   In the Synthesis portion of this Big Ideas lesson, students will complete a small creative project that ties together concepts and skills they have encountered across workshops. These small projects are designed to deepen students' understanding of those concepts and skills.

   LEARNING COACH CHECK-IN Make sure students complete, review, and submit the assignment to their teacher.

All materials needed for this lesson are linked online and not provided in the activity book.

MATERIALS

Supplied

- Mini-Project Instructions (printout)

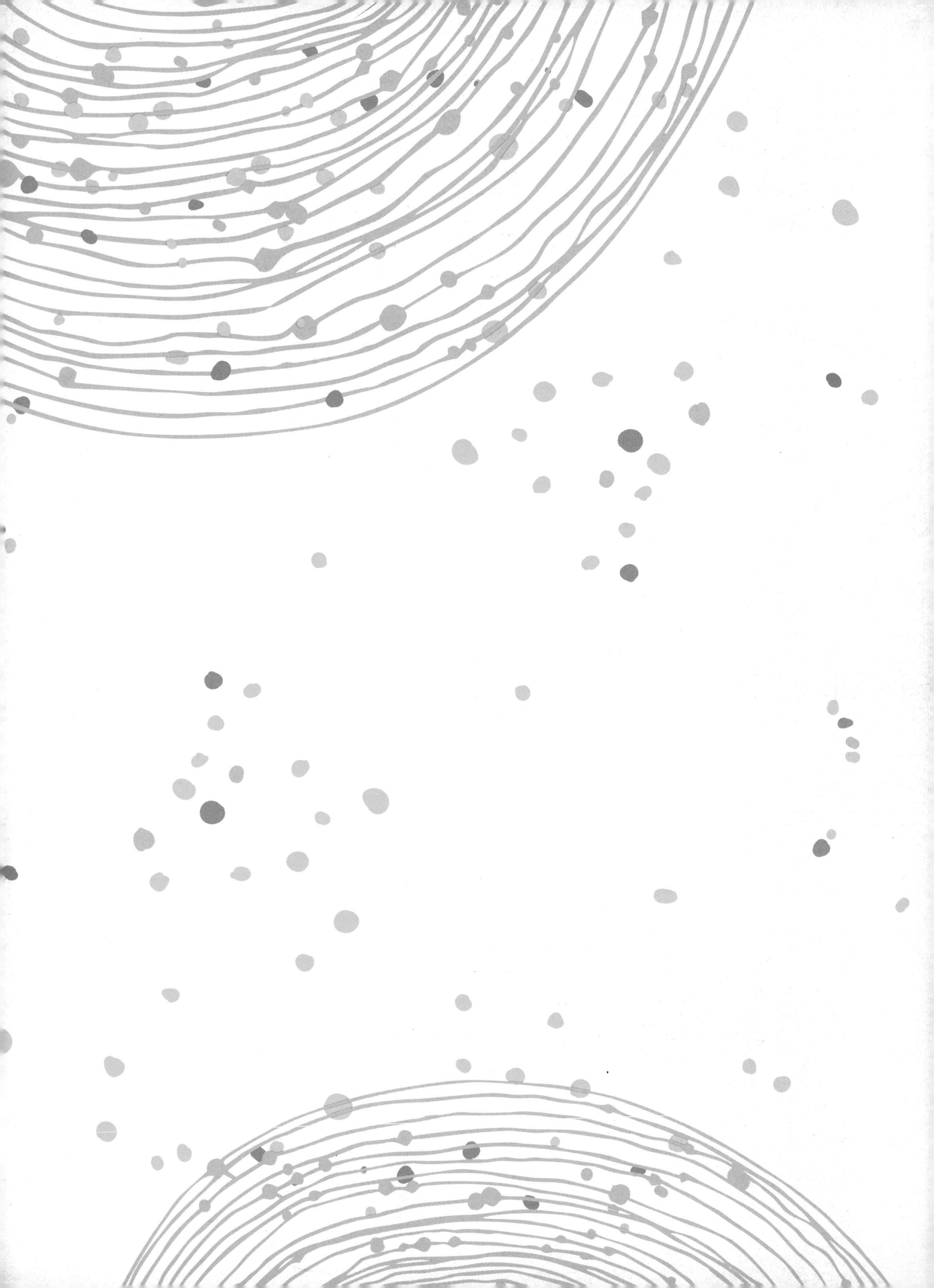

Lessons Learned

Presentation: Media

Lesson Overview

ACTIVITY	ACTIVITY TITLE	TIME	ONLINE/OFFLINE
GET READY	Introduction to Presentation: Media	**2** minutes	online
	Look Back at Media in a Presentation	**15** minutes	online
LEARN AND TRY IT	Choosing Media for an Oral History Presentation	**10** minutes	online
	Choose Media for Your Oral History Presentation LEARNING COACH CHECK-IN	**60** minutes	offline
WRAP-UP	Question About Choosing Media	**2** minutes	online
	Handwriting	**8** minutes	offline
	Go Read!	**24** minutes	online or offline

Content Background

Students will continue working on their **oral history presentation**. They will complete the assignment over the course of several lessons by following the writing process. In this lesson, students will choose a piece of media to show or play during their presentation.

Writing Process

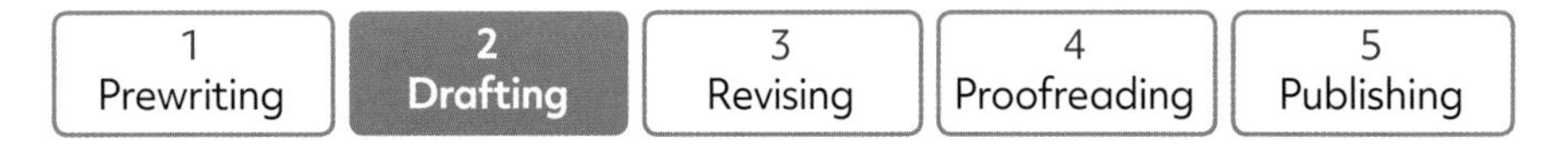

Effective media directly relates to the main idea or an important supporting detail of a presentation. To choose effective media, students will identify the main idea and supporting details of their presentation. Media may include pictures, photographs, videos, songs, or other displays.

Copyright law is complicated and beyond the scope of this course. If students choose media that is produced by others, such as a song or an image that they find online, **ensure that students do not publish a video of their completed presentation online**. That includes sharing the presentation on a personal or family website or on social media. Students should share their presentation with their teacher and classmates only.

MATERIALS

Supplied

- *Summit English Language Arts 3 Activity Book*
  - Choose Media for Your Oral History Presentation
- handwriting workbook

Also Needed

- folder in which students are storing presentation assignment pages
- completed note cards from Presentation: Planning (B)
- reading material for Go Read!

KEYWORDS

media – ways to express ideas, such as pictures, photographs, videos, and songs

Advance Preparation

Gather the folder that students are using to store the activity pages related to their presentation. The folder should contain the following:

- Students' completed Brainstorm for Your Oral History Presentation activity page from Presentation: Brainstorming
- Students' completed Make a Research Plan activity page from Presentation: Research (B)
- Students' completed Organize Your Oral History Presentation activity page from Presentation: Planning (A)

Gather students' completed note cards from Presentation: Planning (B). Students will refer to these note cards during Try it: Choose Media for Your Oral History Presentation.

During the Go Read! activity, students will have the option of using the digital library. Allow extra time for students to make their reading selection, or have students make a selection before beginning the lesson.

Lesson Goals

- Choose media for your presentation.
- Develop letter formation fluency.
- Read independently to develop fluency.

GET READY

Introduction to Presentation: Media

After a quick introductory activity, students will read the lesson goals and keywords. Have students select the keyword and preview its definition.

Look Back at Media in a Presentation

Students will review how to listen for the main idea and supporting details of a speech. Being able to identify the main idea and supporting details of a speech is prerequisite to choosing appropriate media for a speech.

LEARN AND TRY IT

LEARN Choosing Media for an Oral History Presentation

Students will learn how to choose media that supports the main idea or important supporting details of a presentation. Additionally, they will learn what types of media they may choose to use in their oral history presentation.

TRY IT **Choose Media for Your Oral History Presentation**

Students will complete Choose Media for Your Oral History Presentation in *Summit English Language Arts 3 Activity Book*. They will need their presentation note cards as they complete this activity.

LEARNING COACH CHECK-IN This activity page contains several steps that help students narrow down what kind of media they would like to use in their presentation. After determining what kind of media they would like to use, students will find or create it. Guide students toward a media choice that they can find or create in the time provided for this activity.

NOTE Students will find or create the media for their presentation during this activity. Ensure that students have the supplies they need, such as drawing materials.

NOTE If you or students wish, you can download and print another copy of the Oral History Presentation Instructions online. Have students add their media to the folder they are using to store their presentation assignment pages (if possible).

TRY IT

Presentation: Media

Choose Media for Your Oral History Presentation

Answer the questions to choose media for your presentation.

1. What is the main idea of your oral history presentation? Think about what message you want your audience to remember most.

   Answers will vary. Students' response should identify the main point or purpose of their oral history presentation.

2. List three details that support your main idea.

   a. Answers will vary. Details should be examples or facts related to the main idea.

   b.

   c.

3. List three ideas for media that connect with your main idea or supporting details. Examples of media are photographs, drawings, videos, music, objects, and maps. For each idea, explain how it supports your presentation.

Media Idea	How It Supports My Presentation
	Answers will vary.

4. Find or create the media that you will use in your presentation. Students should find or create the media they will use in their presentation.
5. At what point in your presentation will you show or play the media? Why?

   Answers will vary. Students should identify when in their presentation it makes the most sense to share their media. For example, media may help the audience understand something complex or show what something or someone looked like.

6. Find the note card for your presentation that matches your answer to Question 5. Make a note on that card that will remind you to show or play your media.

   Students should make a note on the appropriate card.

WRAP-UP

Question About Choosing Media

Students will answer a question to show that they understand how to effectively choose media for a presentation.

Handwriting

Students should gather their handwriting materials and begin where they left off. Remind students to form letters carefully and correctly.

TIP Set a timer to help students stay focused during handwriting practice.

Go Read!

Students will read for pleasure. They should choose a book or a magazine that interests them, or they may choose a selection from the digital library, linked in the online lesson.

- Have students read aloud a few paragraphs of their selection.
- Then have students read silently for the rest of the time.

SUPPORT Students should make no more than five errors in decoding when they read aloud a few paragraphs of their Go Read! selection. If students struggle or make more than five errors, they need to select a different (and easier) text for the Go Read! activity.

TIP Have students select something to read ahead of time to help them stay focused.

Presentation: Practice

Lesson Overview

ACTIVITY	ACTIVITY TITLE	TIME	ONLINE/OFFLINE
GET READY	Introduction to Presentation: Practice	**1** minute	online
	Look Back at Pronouns and Conventions	**10** minutes	online
LEARN AND **TRY IT**	Practicing an Oral History Presentation	**15** minutes	online
	Practice Your Oral History Presentation **LEARNING COACH CHECK-IN**	**60** minutes	online and offline
WRAP-UP	Question About Delivering a Presentation	**2** minutes	online
	Handwriting	**8** minutes	offline
	Go Read!	**24** minutes	online or offline

Content Background

Students will continue working on their **oral history presentation**. They will complete the assignment over the course of several lessons by following the writing process. In this lesson, students will practice delivering their presentation.

To fine-tune their presentation, students will use a checklist. The checklist focuses on the following:

- Ideas (*Did I use descriptive language? Are there words that could be stronger?*)
- Grammar (*Did I use correct grammar? For example, did I use pronouns correctly?*)
- Media (*Could my audience see or hear my media?*)
- Presentation skills (*Did I speak too loudly or too quietly?*)

Students will have the opportunity to make any necessary revisions before delivering their final oral history presentation in the next lesson.

MATERIALS

Supplied

- *Summit English Language Arts 3 Activity Book*
  - Practice Your Oral History Presentation
- Oral History Presentation: Feedback Sheet
- handwriting workbook

Also Needed

- folder in which students are storing presentation assignment pages
- completed note cards from Presentation: Media
- completed media from Presentation: Media
- reading material for Go Read!

Advance Preparation

Gather the folder that students are using to store the activity pages related to their presentation. The folder should contain the following:

- Students' completed Brainstorm for Your Oral History Presentation activity page from Presentation: Brainstorming
- Students' completed Make a Research Plan activity page from Presentation: Research (B)
- Students' completed Organize Your Oral History Presentation activity page from Presentation: Planning (A)

Gather students' completed note cards and their completed media from Presentation: Media. Students will use the note cards and media during Try it: Practice Your Oral History Presentation.

During the Go Read! activity, students will have the option of using the digital library. Allow extra time for students to make their reading selection, or have students make a selection before beginning the lesson.

KEYWORDS

clarity – the quality of being easy to understand

media – ways to express ideas, such as pictures, photographs, videos, and songs

pace – the speed, and the change of speeds, of a speaker's delivery

Lesson Goals

- Practice delivering your oral history presentation.
- Use a checklist to improve your presentation.
- Develop letter formation fluency.
- Read independently to develop fluency.

GET READY

Introduction to Presentation: Practice

Students will get a glimpse of what they will learn about in the lesson. They will also read the lesson goals and keywords. Have students select each keyword and preview its definition.

Look Back at Pronouns and Conventions

Students will practice using pronouns correctly and following conventions of spoken English. They will draw upon these skills as they fine-tune their presentation.

TIP Proper grammar is just as important in speech as it is in writing.

LEARN AND TRY IT

LEARN Practicing an Oral History Presentation

Students will learn how to effectively deliver their oral history presentation. They will learn how to use a checklist to reflect on and improve their presentation before delivering it to an audience.

TRY IT Practice Your Oral History Presentation

Students will complete Practice Your Oral History Presentation in *Summit English Language Arts 3 Activity Book*. They will need their presentation note cards as well as their presentation media to complete this activity.

NOTE Students should record themselves practicing their presentation. After recording themselves, they should listen to their presentation and use their checklist to identify ways they can improve it. Then students should practice again.

TIP Record a video of students' presentation and have students watch it. This will allow students to reflect on presentation skills like posture and eye contact, as well as allow them to see how they displayed their media (if their media is visual).

LEARNING COACH CHECK-IN Have students practice their presentation for you. Give students feedback, using the Oral History Presentation: Feedback Sheet that you filled out to guide a discussion with students. Focus on telling students what they did well, but also share as a few ways they could improve. For example, *I like the way you said your concluding sentence slowly and clearly. Next time you deliver your presentation, try speaking your beginning sentences with the same clarity and pace.*

NOTE If you or students wish, you can download and print another copy of the Oral History Presentation Instructions online.

TRY IT
Presentation: Practice

Practice Your Oral History Presentation

Use the recording tool in the online activity to record your presentation. Then, use the checklist to improve your ideas, media usage, grammar, and presentation skills. Practice multiple times.

Ideas
- ☑ Did I begin with a hook?
- ☑ Did I tell the story from beginning to end?
- ☑ Did I use descriptive language? Are there words that could be stronger?

Media
- ☑ Did I present my media at the right time?
- ☑ Could my audience see or hear my media?

Grammar
- ☑ Did I use correct grammar? For example, did I use pronouns correctly?

Students should check off each item after they make any necessary changes to their presentation.

PRESENTATION: PRACTICE 581

Presentation Skills
- ☑ Was my pace appropriate? Are there times I spoke too quickly or too slowly?
- ☑ Did I speak too loudly or too quietly?
- ☑ Did I speak clearly?
- ☑ Did I look at my audience?
- ☑ Was I comfortable presenting the information?

It was helpful to record myself!

582 PRESENTATION: PRACTICE

WRAP-UP

Question About Delivering a Presentation

Students will answer a question to show that they understand how to effectively deliver an oral history presentation.

Handwriting

Students should gather their handwriting materials and begin where they left off. Remind students to form letters carefully and correctly.

TIP Set a timer to help students stay focused during handwriting practice.

Go Read!

Students will read for pleasure. They should choose a book or a magazine that interests them, or they may choose a selection from the digital library, linked in the online lesson.

- Have students read aloud a few paragraphs of their selection.
- Then have students read silently for the rest of the time.

SUPPORT Students should make no more than five errors in decoding when they read aloud a few paragraphs of their Go Read! selection. If students struggle or make more than five errors, they need to select a different (and easier) text for the Go Read! activity.

TIP Have students select something to read ahead of time to help them stay focused.

Presentation: Deliver

Lesson Overview

ACTIVITY	ACTIVITY TITLE	TIME	ONLINE/OFFLINE
GET READY	Introduction to Presentation: Deliver	**1** minute	online
TRY IT	Practice Your Oral History Presentation	**50** minutes	online and offline
	Deliver Your Oral History Presentation LEARNING COACH CHECK-IN	**15** minutes	offline
WRAP-UP	Turn In Your Oral History Presentation	**1** minute	online
	More Language Arts Practice	**20** minutes	online
	Handwriting	**8** minutes	offline
	Go Read!	**25** minutes	online or offline

Content Background

Students will share their **oral history presentation** with their Learning Coach. They will also have the option to share their presentation with their peers. Finally, they will submit their presentation to their teacher.

Writing Process

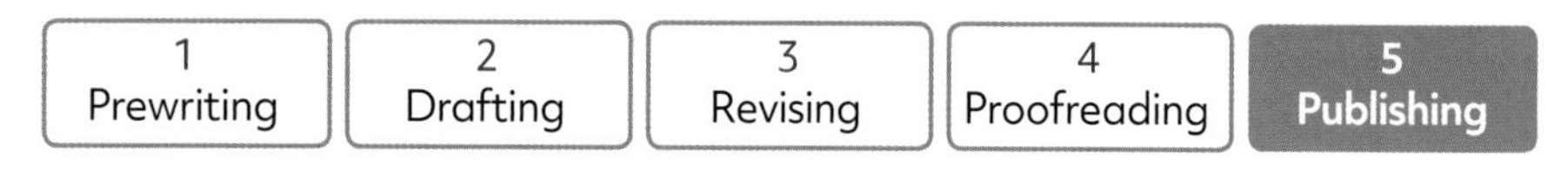

Advance Preparation

Gather the folder that students are using to store the activity pages related to their presentation. The folder should contain the following:

- Students' completed Brainstorm for Your Oral History Presentation activity page from Presentation: Brainstorming
- Students' completed Make a Research Plan activity page from Presentation: Research (B)
- Students' completed Organize Your Oral History Presentation activity page from Presentation: Planning (A)

MATERIALS

Supplied

- handwriting workbook

Also Needed

- folder in which students are storing presentation assignment pages
- completed note cards from Presentation: Practice
- completed media from Presentation: Media
- reading material for Go Read!

Gather students' final note cards and their media. Students will use the note cards and media throughout the lesson.

During the Go Read! activity, students will have the option of using the digital library. Allow extra time for students to make their reading selection, or have students make a selection before beginning the lesson.

Lesson Goals

- Deliver your oral history presentation to your Learning Coach.
- Submit your presentation to your teacher.
- Develop letter formation fluency.
- Read independently to develop fluency.

GET READY

Introduction to Presentation: Deliver

Students will get a glimpse of what they will learn about in the lesson. They will also read the lesson goals.

TRY IT

Practice Your Oral History Presentation

Students should use this time to practice their presentation. They should focus on presenting smoothly without relying too heavily on their note cards. They will have the option of recording themselves using the online recording tool if that is helpful to them as they practice.

OPTIONAL Have students deliver their presentation to a peer and ask for feedback.

NOTE If you or students wish, you can download and print another copy of the Oral History Presentation Instructions online.

Deliver Your Oral History Presentation

Students will present their oral history presentation to their Learning Coach.

LEARNING COACH CHECK-IN Watch students deliver their oral history presentation. After they finish, give specific praise and ask thoughtful questions. For example, *That picture of your aunt in her cap and gown really connected to the details you shared. What other types of media did you consider using?*

WRAP-UP

Turn In Your Your Oral History Presentation

Students will submit their presentation to their teacher.

More Language Arts Practice

Students will practice skills according to their individual needs.

Handwriting

Students should gather their handwriting materials and begin where they left off. Remind students to form letters carefully and correctly.

TIP Set a timer to help students stay focused during handwriting practice.

Go Read!

Students will read for pleasure. They should choose a book or a magazine that interests them, or they may choose a selection from the digital library, linked in the online lesson.

- Have students read aloud a few paragraphs of their selection.
- Then have students read silently for the rest of the time.

SUPPORT Students should make no more than five errors in decoding when they read aloud a few paragraphs of their Go Read! selection. If students struggle or make more than five errors, they need to select a different (and easier) text for the Go Read! activity.

TIP Have students select something to read ahead of time to help them stay focused.

"Squirrel and Spider"

Lesson Overview

ACTIVITY	ACTIVITY TITLE	TIME	ONLINE/OFFLINE
GET READY	Introduction to "Squirrel and Spider"	**1** minute	online
	Spelling List 26 Pretest **LEARNING COACH CHECK-IN**	**10** minutes	online and offline
	Before You Read "Squirrel and Spider"	**5** minutes	online
READ	"Squirrel and Spider"	**25** minutes	offline
	Check-In: "Squirrel and Spider"	**5** minutes	online
LEARN AND TRY IT	Explaining Sequence of Events	**11** minutes	online
	Explain Sequence of Events	**10** minutes	online
	Apply: Sequence of Events	**15** minutes	online
	Plan a Retelling of a Story **LEARNING COACH CHECK-IN**	**20** minutes	offline
	Practice Words from "Squirrel and Spider"	**8** minutes	online
WRAP-UP	Question About Character Action and Sequence of Events	**2** minutes	online
	Handwriting	**8** minutes	offline

Content Background

Students will read a short story that teaches a lesson. They will examine the story's sequence of events. The *sequence of events* is what happens in the story. They will also determine how characters' actions in the story influence the sequence of events.

MATERIALS

Supplied

- *Summit English Language Arts 3 Expeditions in Reading*
  - "Squirrel and Spider"
- *Summit English Language Arts 3 Activity Book*
  - Spelling List 26 Pretest
  - Plan a Retelling of a Story
- handwriting workbook

"Squirrel and Spider" Synopsis

Squirrel plants a field of grain. He does not build a road to his farm since he can use the tops of trees to travel. Spider, who is tricky, sees the lack of road and assumes that he can claim the grain for himself. He cuts down and takes Squirrel's grain but gets caught in a storm. During the storm, Crow sees the grain and takes it away. The lesson of the story is to treat people how you would like to be treated.

KEYWORDS

moral – the lesson of a story, particularly a fable

sequence of events – the order in which things happen in a story

Lesson Goals

- Take a spelling pretest.
- Read "Squirrel and Spider."
- Determine the sequence of events in a story and how characters' actions affect the sequence of events.
- Plan a retelling of a story.
- Practice vocabulary words.
- Develop letter formation fluency.

GET READY

Introduction to "Squirrel and Spider"

Students will get a glimpse of what they will learn about in the lesson. They will also read the lesson goals and keywords. Have students select each keyword and preview its definition.

Spelling List 26 Pretest

Students will take a spelling pretest and learn a new spelling pattern.

LEARNING COACH CHECK-IN Have students turn to Spelling List 26 Pretest in *Summit English Language Arts 3 Activity Book* and open the online Spelling Pretest activity. Online, students will listen to the spelling word, type the word in the space indicated, and then check their answer. In the activity book, students will write the correct spelling of the word in the tables provided and indicate with a ✓ or an ✗ if they spelled the word correctly or incorrectly online. Students will repeat this process with the remaining words. As needed, help students with the interaction between the online activity and the activity book page until they become comfortable with what they need to do. As students practice their spelling words throughout the workshop, they should pay special attention to words they spelled incorrectly on the pretest.

This is the complete list of words students will be tested on.

Words with Suffix *–ed*		
addressed	dimmed	printed
behaved	discovered	reached
believed	joined	repeated
blinked	lifted	scrubbed
clapped	needed	talented
dashed	prepared	

NOTE Have students keep their completed activity page in a safe place so they can refer to it later.

GET READY
"Squirrel and Spider"

Spelling List 26 Pretest

1. Open the Spelling Pretest activity online. Listen to the first spelling word. Type the word. Check your answer.
2. Write the correct spelling of the word in the Word column of the Spelling Pretest table.

	Word	✓	✗
1	blindfold		

3. Put a check mark in the ✓ column if you spelled the word correctly online.

	Word	✓	✗
1	blindfold	✓	

Put an X in the ✗ column if you spelled the word incorrectly online.

	Word	✓	✗
1	blindfold		X

4. Repeat Steps 1–3 for the remaining words in the Spelling Pretest.

"SQUIRREL AND SPIDER" 583

"Squirrel and Spider"

Spelling List 26 Pretest

Write each spelling word in the Word column, making sure to spell it correctly.

	Word	✓	✗		Word	✓	✗
1	addressed			10	lifted		
2	behaved			11	needed		
3	believed			12	prepared		
4	blinked			13	printed		
5	clapped			14	reached		
6	dashed			15	repeated		
7	dimmed			16	scrubbed		
8	discovered			17	talented		
9	joined						

Students should write the correct spelling of each word from the pretest and use the ✓and X columns to indicate whether they spelled each word correctly or incorrectly online.

584 "SQUIRREL AND SPIDER"

Before You Read "Squirrel and Spider"

Students will be introduced to some key vocabulary words that they will encounter in the upcoming reading and learn some important historical background related to the reading.

READ

"Squirrel and Spider"

Students will read "Squirrel and Spider" in *Expeditions in Reading*.

Check-In: "Squirrel and Spider"

Students will answer several questions to demonstrate their comprehension of "Squirrel and Spider."

LEARN AND TRY IT

LEARN Explaining Sequence of Events

Students will learn about sequence of events in a story and how characters' actions cause events to happen.

TRY IT Explain Sequence of Events

Students will put events in sequence and will determine how characters' actions affect the sequence of events in a story.

TRY IT Apply: Sequence of Events

Students will apply to a new work what they've learned about the sequence of events in a text.

TRY IT Plan a Retelling of a Story

Students will complete Plan a Retelling of a Story in *Summit English Language Arts 3 Activity Book*. Students will list the events of "Squirrel and Spider" in order. Then, they will identify the lesson the story teaches. Students will use the information they record on this page to retell the story in paragraph form in another lesson.

LEARNING COACH CHECK-IN This activity page contains open-ended questions, so it's important that you review students' responses. Give students feedback, using the sample answers provided to guide you.

TIP Students do not have to use complete sentences when they are listing the events of the story.

NOTE Have students keep their completed activity page in a safe place so they can refer to it later.

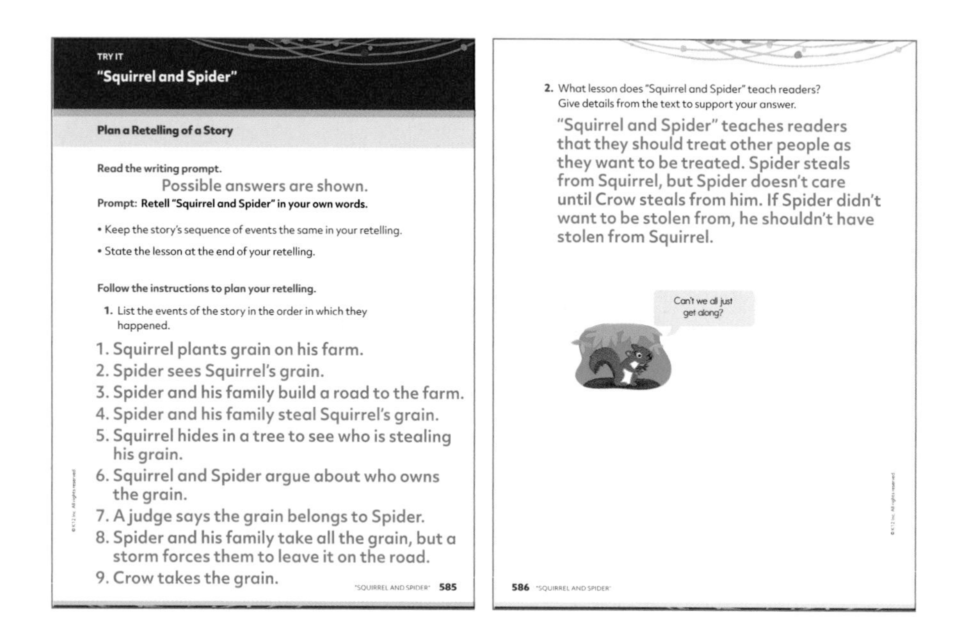

TRY IT

"Squirrel and Spider"

Plan a Retelling of a Story

Read the writing prompt.

Possible answers are shown.

Prompt: **Retell "Squirrel and Spider" in your own words.**

- Keep the story's sequence of events the same in your retelling.
- State the lesson at the end of your retelling.

Follow the instructions to plan your retelling.

1. List the events of the story in the order in which they happened.

1. Squirrel plants grain on his farm.
2. Spider sees Squirrel's grain.
3. Spider and his family build a road to the farm.
4. Spider and his family steal Squirrel's grain.
5. Squirrel hides in a tree to see who is stealing his grain.
6. Squirrel and Spider argue about who owns the grain.
7. A judge says the grain belongs to Spider.
8. Spider and his family take all the grain, but a storm forces them to leave it on the road.
9. Crow takes the grain.

"SQUIRREL AND SPIDER" 585

2. What lesson does "Squirrel and Spider" teach readers? Give details from the text to support your answer.

"Squirrel and Spider" teaches readers that they should treat other people as they want to be treated. Spider steals from Squirrel, but Spider doesn't care until Crow steals from him. If Spider didn't want to be stolen from, he shouldn't have stolen from Squirrel.

586 "SQUIRREL AND SPIDER"

TRY IT Practice Words from "Squirrel and Spider"

Students will answer questions to demonstrate their understanding of the vocabulary words from the reading.

WRAP-UP

Question About Character Actions and Sequence of Events

Students will answer a question to show that they understand how a character's actions influence the sequence of events in a story.

Handwriting

Students should gather their handwriting materials and begin where they left off. Remind students to form letters carefully and correctly.

TIP Set a timer to help students stay focused during handwriting practice.

"Squirrel and Spider" Wrap-Up

Lesson Overview

ACTIVITY	ACTIVITY TITLE	TIME	ONLINE/OFFLINE
GET READY	Introduction to "Squirrel and Spider" Wrap-Up	**1** minute	online
	Spelling List 26 Activity Bank	**10** minutes	offline
	Read and Record	**8** minutes	online
TRY IT	Retell a Story LEARNING COACH CHECK-IN	**33** minutes	offline
	Review "Squirrel and Spider"	**20** minutes	online
QUIZ	"Squirrel and Spider"	**20** minutes	online
WRAP-UP	More Language Arts Practice	**9** minutes	online
	Handwriting	**8** minutes	offline

Advance Preparation

Gather students' completed Spelling List 26 Pretest activity page from "Squirrel and Spider." Students will refer to this page during Get Ready: Spelling List 26 Activity Bank.

Gather students' completed Plan a Retelling of a Story activity page from "Squirrel and Spider." Students will refer to this page during Try It: Retell a Story.

MATERIALS

Supplied

- *Summit English Language Arts 3 Expeditions in Reading*
- *Summit English Language Arts 3 Activity Book*
  - Spelling List 26 Activity Bank
  - Retell a Story
- handwriting workbook

Also Needed

- completed Spelling List 26 Pretest activity page from "Squirrel and Spider"
- completed Plan a Retelling of a Story activity page from "Squirrel and Spider"

Lesson Goals

- Practice all spelling words offline.
- Read aloud to practice fluency.
- Retell a story in writing.
- Review what you learned.
- Take a reading quiz.
- Develop letter formation fluency.

GET READY

Introduction to "Squirrel and Spider" Wrap-Up

Students will read the lesson goals.

Spelling List 26 Activity Bank

Students will practice all spelling words from the workshop by completing Spelling List 26 Activity Bank from *Summit English Language Arts 3 Activity Book*. Make sure students have their completed Spelling List 26 Pretest activity page from "Squirrel and Spider" to refer to during this activity.

Remind students to pay special attention to words they spelled incorrectly on the Spelling Pretest.

GET READY

"Squirrel and Spider" Wrap-Up

Spelling List 26 Activity Bank

Circle any words in the box that you did not spell correctly on the pretest. Choose one activity to do with your circled words. Do as much of the activity as you can in the time given.

Did you spell all the words on the pretest correctly? Do the one activity with as many spelling words as you can.

addressed	clapped	joined	prepared	repeated
behaved	dashed	lifted	printed	scrubbed
believed	dimmed	needed	reached	talented
blinked	discovered			

Spelling Activity Choices

Silly Sentences

1. Write a silly sentence for each of your spelling words.
2. Underline the spelling word in each sentence.
   Example: The dog was driving a car.
3. Correct any spelling errors.

"SQUIRREL AND SPIDER" WRAP-UP 587

Spelling Story

1. Write a very short story using each of your spelling words.
2. Underline the spelling words in the story.
3. Correct any spelling errors.

Riddle Me This

1. Write a riddle for each of your spelling words.
   Example: "I have a trunk, but it's not on my car."
2. Write the answer, which is your word, for each riddle.
   Example: Answer: elephant
3. Correct any spelling errors.

RunOnWord

1. Gather some crayons, colored pencils, or markers. Use a different color to write each of your spelling words. Write the words end to end as one long word.
   Example: dogcatbirdfishturtle
2. Rewrite the words correctly and with proper spacing.
3. Correct any spelling errors.

588 "SQUIRREL AND SPIDER" WRAP-UP

Complete the activity that you chose.

My chosen activity: ______

Students should use this page to complete all steps in their chosen activity.

"SQUIRREL AND SPIDER" WRAP-UP 589

Read and Record

Good readers read quickly, smoothly, and with expression. This is called *fluency*. Students will record themselves reading aloud. They will listen to their recording and think about how quick, smooth, and expressive they sound.

TIP Encourage students to rerecord as needed.

TRY IT

Retell a Story

Students will complete Retell a Story in *Summit English Language Arts 3 Activity Book*. They should use their notes from Plan a Retelling of a Story activity page from "Squirrel and Spider" to keep the events of the story in order as they write.

LEARNING COACH CHECK-IN This activity page contains open-ended questions, so it's important that you review students' responses.

TRY IT

"Squirrel and Spider" Wrap-Up

Retell a Story

Read the writing prompt.

Prompt: **Retell "Squirrel and Spider" in your own words.**

- Keep the story's sequence of events the same in your retelling.
- State the lesson at the end of your retelling.

Respond to the writing prompt. Use your work on the Plan a Retelling of a Story activity page to help you.

Answers will vary. Students' response should follow the sequence of events from the story and include the lesson learned from the story.

"SQUIRREL AND SPIDER" WRAP-UP 591

592 "SQUIRREL AND SPIDER" WRAP-UP

Review "Squirrel and Spider"

Students will answer questions to review what they have learned about lessons and supporting details in stories, sequence of events, and how characters' actions influence the sequence of events in stories.

QUIZ

"Squirrel and Spider"

Students will complete the "Squirrel and Spider" quiz.

WRAP-UP

More Language Arts Practice

Students will practice skills according to their individual needs.

Handwriting

Students should gather their handwriting materials and begin where they left off. Remind students to form letters carefully and correctly.

TIP Set a timer to help students stay focused during handwriting practice.

"The Stone-Cutter"

Lesson Overview

ACTIVITY	ACTIVITY TITLE	TIME	ONLINE/OFFLINE
GET READY	Introduction to "The Stone-Cutter"	**1** minute	online
	Spelling List 26 Review Game	**10** minutes	online
	Before You Read "The Stone-Cutter"	**15** minutes	online
READ	"The Stone-Cutter"	**25** minutes	offline
	Check-In: "The Stone-Cutter"	**5** minutes	online
LEARN AND TRY IT	Identifying Plot and Character Feelings	**10** minutes	online
	Identify Plot and Character Feelings	**10** minutes	online
	Apply: Key Details	**14** minutes	online
	Plan a Story LEARNING COACH CHECK-IN	**10** minutes	offline
	Practice Words from "The Stone-Cutter"	**10** minutes	online
WRAP-UP	Question About Plot	**2** minutes	online
	Handwriting	**8** minutes	offline

Content Background

Students will read a short story and then identify the moral, the main character's feelings, and the ways in which the main character's feelings influence the plot. *Plot* is another word for what happens in a story, or the sequence of events. The *moral* of a story is the lesson that is taught by the events in the story.

Just as characters' actions often influence the plot or sequence of events, so too can characters' feelings. If a character feels a certain way, she may make a specific choice that affects what happens in the story. For example, Little Red Riding Hood is often portrayed as curious. She wants to know what the forest is like beyond the path to her grandmother's home. Her curiosity influences the events in the story. It leads her to stray from the path to Grandmother's—and into the path of the wolf.

MATERIALS

Supplied

- *Summit English Language Arts 3 Expeditions in Reading*
  - "The Stone-Cutter"
- *Summit English Language Arts 3 Activity Book*
  - Plan a Story
- handwriting workbook

"The Stone-Cutter" Synopsis

In this short story, a child named Taro dreams of working with the rest of the men in his village as a stone-cutter. As an adult, he becomes a stone-cutter, but he is quickly disillusioned with the job. He asks the spirit of the mountain to turn him into a series of different things: a rich man, a prince, the sun, a cloud, and eventually, a stone. At every turn, he wants to be powerful, and he perceives that every successive thing is more powerful than the previous thing. At the end, he asks the spirit of the mountain to turn him back into a stone-cutter. The moral of the story is to be happy with what you have.

KEYWORDS

moral – the lesson of a story, particularly a fable

plot – what happens in a story; the sequence of events

Lesson Goals

- Practice all spelling words online.
- Read "The Stone-Cutter."
- Identify plot events, characters' feelings, and how the two are connected.
- Plan a short story about a character.
- Practice vocabulary words.
- Develop letter formation fluency.

GET READY

Introduction to "The Stone-Cutter"

Students will get a glimpse of what they will learn about in the lesson. They will also read the lesson goals and keywords. Have students select each keyword and preview its definition.

Spelling List 26 Review Game

Students will practice all spelling words from the workshop.

Before You Read "The Stone-Cutter"

Students will be introduced to some key vocabulary words that they will encounter in the upcoming reading.

READ

"The Stone-Cutter"

Students will read "The Stone-Cutter" in *Expeditions in Reading*.

Check-In: "The Stone-Cutter"

Students will answer several questions to demonstrate their comprehension of "The Stone-Cutter."

LEARN AND TRY IT

LEARN Identifying Plot and Character Feelings

Students will learn that characters' feelings often influence the plot, or sequence of events, in a story.

TRY IT Identify Plot and Character Feelings

Students will practice identifying a character's feelings and how those feelings influence the plot of a story.

TRY IT Apply: Key Details

Students will apply to a new work what they've learned about using key details to support the main idea or moral of a story.

TRY IT Plan a Story

Students will complete Plan a Story in *Summit English Language Arts 3 Activity Book*. Students will answer questions to plan out a character's story that they will write in a subsequent lesson.

LEARNING COACH CHECK-IN This activity page contains open-ended questions, so it's important that you review students' responses. If needed, help students brainstorm the parts of their character's story, as well as how the character feels during the story.

TIP Remind students that they do not have to write in complete sentences when planning the story.

NOTE Have students keep their completed activity page in a safe place so they can refer to it later.

TRY IT
"The Stone-Cutter"

Plan a Story

Read the writing prompt.

Answers will vary.

Prompt: **Write a short story about a character. Include the following:**

- The name and a description of your main character
- The problem your character faces
- The events of the story
- How your character solves the problem
- How your character feels during the story
- The lesson your character learns in the story

Answer the questions to plan your story.

1. Who is your main character? Give your character a name, and describe him or her.

"THE STONE-CUTTER" 593

2. What problem does your main character face in the story?

3. What happens in the story?

594 "THE STONE-CUTTER"

4. How does your main character solve the problem?

5. What emotions does your main character feel during the story?

"THE STONE-CUTTER" 595

6. What lesson does your main character learn?

596 "THE STONE-CUTTER"

TRY IT Practice Words from "The Stone-Cutter"

Students will answer questions to demonstrate their understanding of the vocabulary words from the reading.

WRAP-UP

Question About Plot

Students will answer a question to show that they understand how characters influence the sequence of events in a story.

Handwriting

Students should gather their handwriting materials and begin where they left off. Remind students to form letters carefully and correctly.

TIP Set a timer to help students stay focused during handwriting practice.

"The Stone-Cutter" Wrap-Up

Lesson Overview

ACTIVITY	ACTIVITY TITLE	TIME	ONLINE/OFFLINE
GET READY	Introduction to "The Stone-Cutter" Wrap-Up	**1** minute	online
	Read and Record	**20** minutes	online
TRY IT	Write a Story LEARNING COACH CHECK-IN	**30** minutes	offline
	Review "The Stone-Cutter"	**10** minutes	online
QUIZ	"The Stone-Cutter"	**20** minutes	online
	Spelling List 26	**10** minutes	online
WRAP-UP	More Language Arts Practice	**19** minutes	online
	Handwriting	**10** minutes	offline

Advance Preparation

Gather students' completed Plan a Story activity page from "The Stone-Cutter." Students will refer to this page during Try It: Write a Story.

Lesson Goals

- Read aloud to practice fluency.
- Write a short story about a character.
- Review what you learned.
- Take a reading quiz.
- Take a spelling quiz.
- Develop letter formation fluency.

MATERIALS

Supplied

- *Summit English Language Arts 3 Expeditions in Reading*
- *Summit English Language Arts 3 Activity Book*
  - Write a Story
- handwriting workbook

Also Needed

- completed Plan a Story activity page from "The Stone-Cutter"

GET READY

Introduction to "The Stone-Cutter" Wrap-Up

Students will read the lesson goals.

Read and Record

Good readers read quickly, smoothly, and with expression. This is called *fluency*. Students will record themselves reading aloud. They will listen to their recording and think about how quick, smooth, and expressive they sound.

TIP Encourage students to rerecord as needed.

TRY IT

Write a Story

Students will complete Write a Story in *Summit English Language Arts 3 Activity Book*. They should use their completed Plan a Story activity page as a guide for writing their short story.

LEARNING COACH CHECK-IN This activity page contains an open-ended prompt, so it's important that you review students' responses. Students should be sure to include the emotions that their character feels during the different parts of the story. Encourage students to think about how the character's actions and feelings affect what happens next in their story.

TRY IT

"The Stone-Cutter" Wrap-Up

Write a Story

Read the writing prompt.

Prompt: **Write a short story about a character. Include the following:**

- The name and a description of your main character
- The problem your character faces
- The events of the story
- How your character solves the problem
- How your character feels during the story
- The lesson your character learns in the story

Respond to the writing prompt. Use your work on the Plan a Story activity page to help you.

Answers will vary. Students' response should include:

- A character facing a problem
- A description of how the character feels about the problem
- A description of events that help the character solve the problem
- The lesson the character learns from the problem and/or solution

"THE STONE-CUTTER" WRAP-UP 597

598 "THE STONE-CUTTER" WRAP-UP

"THE STONE-CUTTER" WRAP-UP 599

600 "THE STONE-CUTTER" WRAP-UP

Review "The Stone-Cutter"

Students will answer questions to review what they have learned about lessons and morals in a story, plot and sequence of events, and how characters' actions and feelings affect the sequence of events in a story.

QUIZ

"The Stone-Cutter"

Students will complete the "The Stone-Cutter" quiz.

Spelling List 26

Students will complete the Spelling List 26 quiz.

WRAP-UP

More Language Arts Practice

Students will practice skills according to their individual needs.

Handwriting

Students should gather their handwriting materials and begin where they left off. Remind students to form letters carefully and correctly.

TIP Set a timer to help students stay focused during handwriting practice.

Vocabulary in Everyday Life

Lesson Overview

ACTIVITY	ACTIVITY TITLE	TIME	ONLINE/OFFLINE
GET READY	Introduction to Vocabulary in Everyday Life	1 minute	online
	Look Back at Real-Life Connections	4 minutes	online
LEARN AND TRY IT	Vocabulary in Everyday Life	10 minutes	online
	Practice Using Vocabulary in Everyday Life	10 minutes	online
	Apply: Vocabulary in Everyday Life LEARNING COACH CHECK-IN	15 minutes	offline
	Review Vocabulary in Everyday Life	15 minutes	online
QUIZ	Vocabulary in Everyday Life	15 minutes	online
WRAP-UP	More Language Arts Practice	19 minutes	online
	Go Write! A Finished Project	15 minutes	offline
	Go Read!	16 minutes	online or offline

Content Background

Students will learn the difference between general words and specific words. General words lack description and precision, but convey an idea nonetheless. Specific words indicate a higher level of thought and result in clearer communication. Everyday communication is improved by using specific words.

General: I'm hungry.

Specific: My stomach is rumbling because I am ravenous.

Students will learn that using specific words helps them be more effective in their communication.

MATERIALS

Supplied

- *Summit English Language Arts 3 Activity Book*
  - Apply: Vocabulary in Everyday Life
  - Go Write! A Finished Project

Also Needed

- reading material for Go Read!

Advance Preparation

During the Go Read! activity, students will have the option of using the digital library. Allow extra time for students to make their reading selection, or have students make a selection before beginning the lesson.

Lesson Goals

- Practice vocabulary words.
- Identify real-life connections between words and how they are used.
- Use everyday vocabulary in context.
- Take the Vocabulary in Everyday Life quiz.
- Freewrite about a topic to develop writing fluency and practice letter formation.
- Read independently to develop fluency.

GET READY

Introduction to Vocabulary in Everyday Life

Students will get a glimpse of what they will learn about in the lesson. They will also read the lesson goals.

Look Back at Real-Life Connections

Students will practice the prerequisite skill of using appropriate vocabulary for real-life context.

LEARN AND TRY IT

LEARN Vocabulary in Everyday Life

Students will be introduced to the vocabulary words for the lesson. Then they will review how to use context clues to determine the meanings of new words.

TRY IT Practice Using Vocabulary in Everyday Life

Students will use specific words in context and match vocabulary words to their meanings.

TRY IT Apply: Vocabulary in Everyday Life

Students will complete Apply: Vocabulary in Everyday Life in *Summit English Language Arts 3 Activity Book*.

LEARNING COACH CHECK-IN This activity page contains open-ended questions, so it's important that you review students' responses. Give students feedback, using the sample answers provided to guide you.

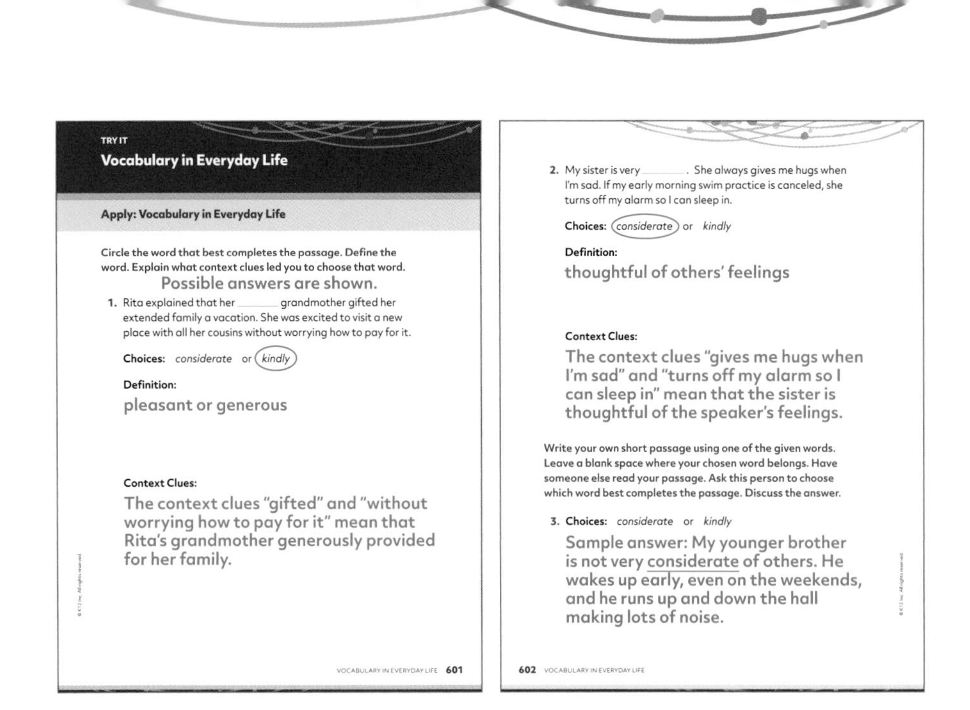

TRY IT

Vocabulary in Everyday Life

Apply: Vocabulary in Everyday Life

Circle the word that best completes the passage. Define the word. Explain what context clues led you to choose that word.

Possible answers are shown.

1. Rita explained that her ______ grandmother gifted her extended family a vacation. She was excited to visit a new place with all her cousins without worrying how to pay for it.

   Choices: *considerate* or *kindly* (circled)

   Definition:
   pleasant or generous

   Context Clues:
   The context clues "gifted" and "without worrying how to pay for it" mean that Rita's grandmother generously provided for her family.

VOCABULARY IN EVERYDAY LIFE 601

2. My sister is very ______. She always gives me hugs when I'm sad. If my early morning swim practice is canceled, she turns off my alarm so I can sleep in.

   Choices: *considerate* (circled) or *kindly*

   Definition:
   thoughtful of others' feelings

   Context Clues:
   The context clues "gives me hugs when I'm sad" and "turns off my alarm so I can sleep in" mean that the sister is thoughtful of the speaker's feelings.

Write your own short passage using one of the given words. Leave a blank space where your chosen word belongs. Have someone else read your passage. Ask this person to choose which word best completes the passage. Discuss the answer.

3. **Choices:** *considerate* or *kindly*

   Sample answer: My younger brother is not very considerate of others. He wakes up early, even on the weekends, and he runs up and down the hall making lots of noise.

602 VOCABULARY IN EVERYDAY LIFE

TRY IT Review Vocabulary in Everyday Life

Students will answer questions to review what they have learned about using specific words to describe people.

QUIZ

Vocabulary in Everyday Life

Students will complete the Vocabulary in Everyday Life quiz.

WRAP-UP

More Language Arts Practice

Students will practice skills according to their individual needs.

Go Write! A Finished Project

Students will complete Go Write! A Finished Project in *Summit English Language Arts 3 Activity Book*. They will have the option to either respond to a prompt or write about a topic of their choice.

NOTE This activity is intended to build writing fluency. Students should write for the entire allotted time.

SUPPORT If students have trouble writing for the allotted time, prompt them with questions. For example, *Can you tell me more about this?*

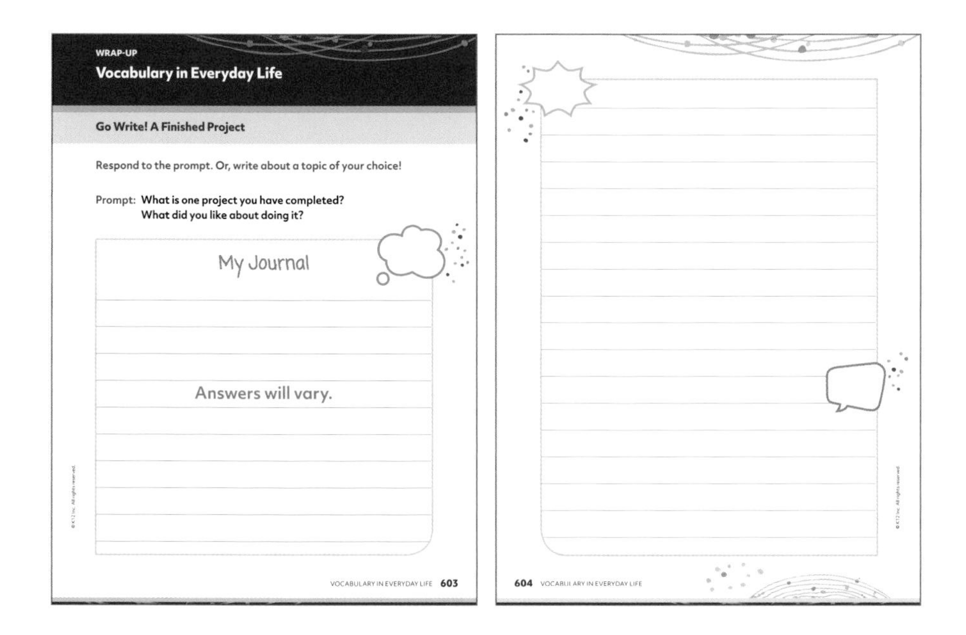
WRAP-UP

Vocabulary in Everyday Life

Go Write! A Finished Project

Respond to the prompt. Or, write about a topic of your choice!

Prompt: What is one project you have completed? What did you like about doing it?

My Journal

Answers will vary.

VOCABULARY IN EVERYDAY LIFE 603

604 VOCABULARY IN EVERYDAY LIFE

Go Read!

Students will read for pleasure. They should choose a book or a magazine that interests them, or they may choose a selection from the digital library, linked in the online lesson.

- Have students read aloud a few paragraphs of their selection.
- Then have students read silently for the rest of the time.

SUPPORT Students should make no more than five errors in decoding when they read aloud a few paragraphs of their Go Read! selection. If students struggle or make more than five errors, they need to select a different (and easier) text for the Go Read! activity.

TIP Have students select something to read ahead of time to help them stay focused.

"The Bundle of Sticks"

Lesson Overview

ACTIVITY	ACTIVITY TITLE	TIME	ONLINE/OFFLINE
GET READY	Introduction to "The Bundle of Sticks"	**1** minute	
	Spelling List 27 Pretest **LEARNING COACH CHECK-IN**	**10** minutes	and
	Before You Read "The Bundle of Sticks"	**4** minutes	
READ	"The Bundle of Sticks"	**15** minutes	
	Check-In: "The Bundle of Sticks"	**5** minutes	
LEARN AND **TRY IT**	Identifying Metaphors and Lessons	**10** minutes	
	Identify Metaphors and Lessons	**8** minutes	
	Looking at Point of View	**5** minutes	
	Look at Point of View	**2** minutes	
	Apply: Theme	**15** minutes	
	Plan an Essay with a Metaphor **LEARNING COACH CHECK-IN**	**25** minutes	
	Practice Words from "The Bundle of Sticks"	**8** minutes	
WRAP-UP	Question About Figurative Language	**2** minutes	
	Handwriting	**10** minutes	

Content Background

Students will learn about *figurative language*, or words that describe something by comparing it to something else. They will examine two types of figurative language:

A *simile* is a comparison of two unlike things using the words *like* or *as*.

Example: You are like sunshine.

A *metaphor* is a direct comparison of two unlike things without using the words *like* or *as*.

Example: You are my sunshine.

MATERIALS

Supplied

- *Summit English Language Arts 3 Expeditions in Reading*
  - "The Bundle of Sticks"
- *Summit English Language Arts 3 Activity Book*
  - Spelling List 27 Pretest
  - Plan an Essay with a Metaphor
- handwriting notebook

Students will also be introduced to the idea of first-person point of view and third-person point of view. When a story is written in first-person point of view, it is written by someone *inside* the story. When a story is written in third-person point of view, it is written by someone *outside* the story.

When writing a story in first person, authors use the pronouns *I*, *me*, *we*, and so on. When writing a story in third person, authors use the pronouns *he*, *she*, *they*, and so on.

"The Bundle of Sticks" Synopsis

In this short story, a man observes that his sons are always fighting. He uses sticks to teach his sons a lesson. Individually, each stick can be broken, but when they are gathered in a bundle, they are strong and cannot be broken. The lesson of the story is that when the sons are united and stand together, they are strong. The sticks serve as a metaphor for the sons.

Lesson Goals

- Take a spelling pretest.
- Read "The Bundle of Sticks."
- Identify metaphors in short stories and how they support lessons and themes.
- Plan to write an essay with a metaphor.
- Practice vocabulary words.
- Develop letter formation fluency.

KEYWORDS

figurative language – words that describe something by comparing it to something completely different; figure of speech; Example: Rain fell in buckets and the streets looked like rivers.

first-person point of view – the telling of a story by a character in that story, using pronouns such as *I*, *me*, and *we*

metaphor – a figure of speech that compares two unlike things, without using the word *like* or *as*; Example: The cat's eyes were emeralds shining in the night.

sequence of events – the order in which things happen in a story

simile – a comparison between two things using the word *like* or *as*; Example: I didn't hear him come in because he was as quiet as a mouse.

theme – the author's message or big idea

third-person point of view – the telling of a story by someone outside of the action, using the third-person pronouns *he*, *she*, and *they*

GET READY

Introduction to "The Bundle of Sticks"

Students will get a glimpse of what they will learn about in the lesson. They will also read the lesson goals and keywords. Have students select each keyword and preview its definition.

Spelling List 27 Pretest

Students will take a spelling pretest and learn a new spelling pattern.

LEARNING COACH CHECK-IN Have students turn to Spelling List 27 Pretest in *Summit English Language Arts 3 Activity Book* and open the online Spelling Pretest activity. Online, students will listen to the spelling word, type the word in the space indicated, and then check their answer. In the activity book, students will write the correct spelling of the word in the tables provided and indicate with a ✓ or an ✗ if they spelled the word correctly or incorrectly online. Students will repeat this process with the remaining words.

As needed, help students with the interaction between the online activity and the activity book page until they become comfortable with what they need to do. As students practice their spelling words throughout the workshop, they should pay special attention to words they spelled incorrectly on the pretest.

This is the complete list of words students will be tested on.

Words with Silent Letters		
autumn	highlight	subtle
bright	knee	thumb
column	knife	wrap
crumb	knit	wrist
doubt	know	wrong
flight	lamb	

NOTE Have students keep their completed activity page in a safe place so they can refer to it later.

GET READY

"The Bundle of Sticks"

Spelling List 27 Pretest

1. Open the Spelling Pretest activity online. Listen to the first spelling word. Type the word. Check your answer.

2. Write the correct spelling of the word in the Word column of the Spelling Pretest table.

	Word	✓	✗
1	blindfold		

3. Put a check mark in the ✓ column if you spelled the word correctly online.

	Word	✓	✗
1	blindfold	✓	

Put an X in the ✗ column if you spelled the word incorrectly online.

	Word	✓	✗
1	blindfold		X

4. Repeat Steps 1–3 for the remaining words in the Spelling Pretest.

"THE BUNDLE OF STICKS" 605

"The Bundle of Sticks"

Spelling List 27 Pretest

Write each spelling word in the Word column, making sure to spell it correctly.

	Word	✓	✗
1	autumn		
2	bright		
3	column		
4	crumb		
5	doubt		
6	flight		
7	highlight		
8	knee		
9	knife		

	Word	✓	✗
10	knit		
11	know		
12	lamb		
13	subtle		
14	thumb		
15	wrap		
16	wrist		
17	wrong		

Students should write the correct spelling of each word from the pretest and use the ✓and X columns to indicate whether they spelled each word correctly or incorrectly online.

606 "THE BUNDLE OF STICKS"

Before You Read "The Bundle of Sticks"

Students will be introduced to some key vocabulary words that they will encounter in the upcoming reading.

READ

"The Bundle of Sticks"

Students will read "The Bundle of Sticks" in *Expeditions in Reading*.

NOTE The story students will read is an extended metaphor, which means that the entire story is a metaphor. They will not learn the phrase "extended metaphor." They will instead learn that it is possible for a metaphor to encompass an entire story or poem.

Check-In: "The Bundle of Sticks"

Students will answer several questions to demonstrate their comprehension of "The Bundle of Sticks."

LEARN AND TRY IT

LEARN Identifying Metaphors and Lessons

Students will learn what a metaphor is, how the story they are reading is a big metaphor, and how metaphors can illustrate theme.

TRY IT Identify Metaphors and Lessons

Students will practice identifying metaphors and themes in a story.

LEARN Looking at Point of View

Students will learn the difference between first-person point of view and third-person point of view.

TRY IT Look at Point of View

Students will practice identifying which pronouns are used in first-person point of view and third-person point of view.

TRY IT Apply: Theme

Students will apply to a new work what they've learned about determining and supporting theme in a text.

TRY IT Plan an Essay with a Metaphor

Students will complete Plan an Essay with a Metaphor in *Summit English Language Arts 3 Activity Book*. For this assignment, students will plan out an essay that explains a time in their lives when they learned the lesson, "We are stronger together." Students need to include a metaphor in their essay.

LEARNING COACH CHECK-IN This activity page contains open-ended questions, so it's important that you review students' responses. If students struggle to think of a metaphor, prompt them by asking them to fill in the blank: *Strength is a* ______.

NOTE Have students keep their completed activity page in a safe place so they can refer to it later.

TRY IT
"The Bundle of Sticks"

Plan an Essay with a Metaphor

Read the writing prompt.

Answers will vary.

Prompt: **When in your life have you learned the lesson, "We are stonger together"? Write an essay about that time.**

- Use details to explain how you learned the lesson.
- Include a metaphor in your essay.

Answer the questions to plan your essay.

1. How did you learn the lesson, "We are stronger together"?

"THE BUNDLE OF STICKS" 607

2. Write a metaphor that you can include in your essay. Think of something that only becomes strong when there is a lot of it. For example, sticks aren't very strong unless many of them are bundled together.

608 "THE BUNDLE OF STICKS"

TRY IT Practice Words from "The Bundle of Sticks"

Students will answer questions to demonstrate their understanding of the vocabulary words from the reading.

WRAP-UP

Question About Figurative Language

Students will answer a question to show that they understand what a metaphor is.

Handwriting

Students should gather their handwriting materials and begin where they left off. Remind students to form letters carefully and correctly.

TIP Set a timer to help students stay focused during handwriting practice.

"The Bundle of Sticks" Wrap-Up

Lesson Overview

ACTIVITY	ACTIVITY TITLE	TIME	ONLINE/OFFLINE
GET READY	Introduction to "The Bundle of Sticks" Wrap-Up	**1** minute	online
	Spelling List 27 Activity Bank	**10** minutes	offline
	Read and Record	**19** minutes	online
TRY IT	Write an Essay with a Metaphor LEARNING COACH CHECK-IN	**30** minutes	offline
	Review "The Bundle of Sticks"	**15** minutes	online
QUIZ	"The Bundle of Sticks"	**20** minutes	online
WRAP-UP	More Language Arts Practice	**15** minutes	online
	Handwriting	**10** minutes	offline

Advance Preparation

Gather students' completed Spelling List 27 Pretest activity page from "The Bundle of Sticks." Students will refer to this page during Get Ready: Spelling List 27 Activity Bank.

Gather students' completed Plan an Essay with a Metaphor activity page from "The Bundle of Sticks." Students will refer to this page during Try It: Write an Essay with a Metaphor.

Lesson Goals

- Practice all spelling words offline.
- Read aloud to practice fluency.
- Write an essay with a metaphor.
- Review what you learned.
- Take a reading quiz.
- Develop letter formation fluency.

MATERIALS

Supplied

- *Summit English Language Arts 3 Expeditions in Reading*
- *Summit English Language Arts 3 Activity Book*
  - Spelling List 27 Activity Bank
  - Write an Essay with a Metaphor
- handwriting workbook

Also Needed

- completed Spelling List 27 Pretest activity page from "The Bundle of Sticks"
- completed Plan an Essay with a Metaphor activity page from "The Bundle of Sticks"

GET READY

Introduction to "The Bundle of Sticks" Wrap-Up

Students will read the lesson goals.

Spelling List 27 Activity Bank

Students will practice all spelling words from the workshop by completing Spelling List 27 Activity Bank from *Summit English Language Arts 3 Activity Book*. Make sure students have their completed Spelling List 27 Pretest activity page from "The Bundle of Sticks" to refer to during this activity.

Remind students to pay special attention to words they spelled incorrectly on the Spelling Pretest.

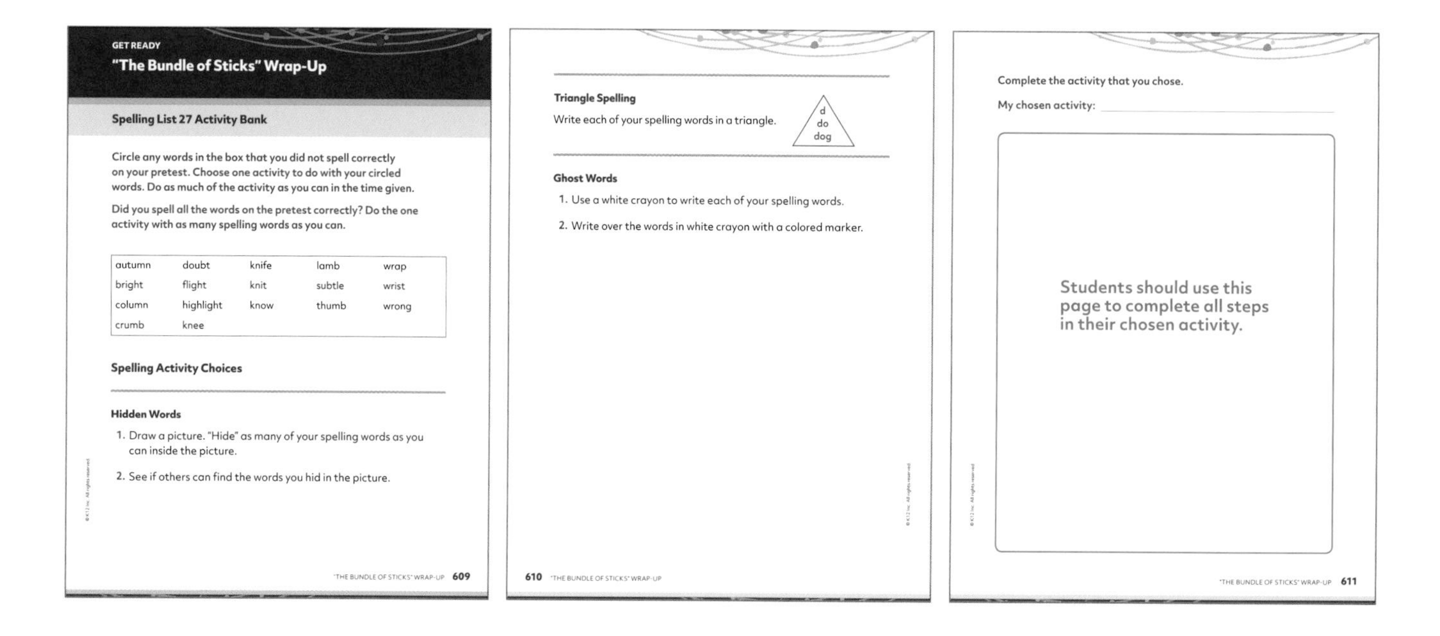

GET READY

"The Bundle of Sticks" Wrap-Up

Spelling List 27 Activity Bank

Circle any words in the box that you did not spell correctly on your pretest. Choose one activity to do with your circled words. Do as much of the activity as you can in the time given.

Did you spell all the words on the pretest correctly? Do the one activity with as many spelling words as you can.

autumn	doubt	knife	lamb	wrap
bright	flight	knit	subtle	wrist
column	highlight	know	thumb	wrong
crumb	knee			

Spelling Activity Choices

Hidden Words

1. Draw a picture. "Hide" as many of your spelling words as you can inside the picture.
2. See if others can find the words you hid in the picture.

"THE BUNDLE OF STICKS" WRAP-UP 609

Triangle Spelling

Write each of your spelling words in a triangle.

d
do
dog

Ghost Words

1. Use a white crayon to write each of your spelling words.
2. Write over the words in white crayon with a colored marker.

610 "THE BUNDLE OF STICKS" WRAP-UP

Complete the activity that you chose.

My chosen activity: ______

Students should use this page to complete all steps in their chosen activity.

"THE BUNDLE OF STICKS" WRAP-UP 611

Read and Record

Good readers read quickly, smoothly, and with expression. This is called *fluency*. Students will record themselves reading aloud. They will listen to their recording and think about how quick, smooth, and expressive they sound.

TIP Encourage students to rerecord as needed.

TRY IT

Write an Essay with a Metaphor

Students will complete Write an Essay with a Metaphor in *Summit English Language Arts 3 Activity Book*. They should use their completed Plan an Essay with a Metaphor activity page to write about a time they learned the lesson, "We are stronger together." They should also include a metaphor in their essay.

LEARNING COACH CHECK-IN This activity page contains an open-ended prompt, so it's important that you review students' essays.

TRY IT

"The Bundle of Sticks" Wrap-Up

Write an Essay with a Metaphor

Read the writing prompt.

Prompt: **When in your life have you learned the lesson, "We are stronger together"? Write an essay about that time.**

- Use details to explain how you learned the lesson.
- Include a metaphor in your essay.

Respond to the writing prompt. Use your work on the Plan an Essay with a Metaphor activity page to help you.

Answers will vary. Students' response should be an explanation of a time they learned the lesson, "We are stronger together," and include a metaphor.

"THE BUNDLE OF STICKS" WRAP-UP 613

614 "THE BUNDLE OF STICKS" WRAP-UP

Review "The Bundle of Sticks"

Students will answer questions to review what they have learned about describing sequence of events, determining the theme of a story, and explaining how the theme of a story is supported by key details.

QUIZ

"The Bundle of Sticks"

Students will complete the "The Bundle of Sticks" quiz.

WRAP-UP

More Language Arts Practice

Students will practice skills according to their individual needs.

Handwriting

Students should gather their handwriting materials and begin where they left off. Remind students to form letters carefully and correctly.

TIP Set a timer to help students stay focused during handwriting practice.

"The Necklace of Truth"

Lesson Overview

ACTIVITY	ACTIVITY TITLE	TIME	ONLINE/OFFLINE
GET READY	Introduction to "The Necklace of Truth"	**1** minute	
	Spelling List 27 Review Game	**10** minutes	
	Before You Read "The Necklace of Truth"	**5** minutes	
READ	"The Necklace of Truth"	**20** minutes	
	Check-In: "The Necklace of Truth"	**5** minutes	
LEARN AND **TRY IT**	Describing Setting and Characters in a Play	**10** minutes	
	Describe Setting and Characters in a Play	**10** minutes	
	Apply: Character's Feelings	**15** minutes	
	Plan a Play **LEARNING COACH CHECK-IN**	**24** minutes	
	Practice Words from "The Necklace of Truth"	**8** minutes	
WRAP-UP	Question About Parts of a Play	**2** minutes	
	Handwriting	**10** minutes	

Content Background

Students will read a play. They will explore a few differences between a play and a story written in prose. The play they will read is one act and is divided into scenes. A *scene* is the subdivision of an act of a play that happens at a fixed time and place.

Students will learn that unlike stories, which often have narrative text providing information like the setting and how characters feel, plays use different conventions to communicate that same information. Writers use stage directions to communicate the setting in a play. Stage directions, which appear in italics in a play, are not said aloud when a play is performed.

Writers also rely on characters' dialogue to give readers (and audiences) hints about when and where a play takes place. Characters' dialogue also helps readers and audiences understand how characters feel in a given scene.

MATERIALS

Supplied

- *Summit English Language Arts 3 Expeditions in Reading*
  - "The Necklace of Truth"
- *Summit English Language Arts 3 Activity Book*
  - Plan a Play
- handwriting workbook

"The Necklace of Truth" Synopsis

A girl named Pearl lives in England and is a terrible liar. Pearl's parents take her to see the wizard Merlin, who is rumored to have a cure for lying. Merlin gives Pearl a necklace with a diamond clasp and tells her not to take it off. Whenever Pearl tells a lie, the necklace changes. Pearls realizes just how often she lies and how much it hurts her to do so. She learns her lesson and does not lie anymore. At the end of the play, Merlin returns to Pearl and takes the necklace back, telling her that another child needs it.

Lesson Goals

- Practice all spelling words online.
- Read "The Necklace of Truth."
- Describe setting and characters' emotions in plays.
- Plan to write a scene in a play.
- Practice vocabulary words.
- Develop letter formation fluency.

KEYWORDS

dialogue – the words that characters say in a written work

drama – another word for *play*

scene – a part of an act of a play that happens at a fixed time and place

setting – where and when a story takes place

stage directions – instructions in a play that tell the actors what to do

theme – the author's message or big idea

GET READY

Introduction to "The Necklace of Truth"

Students will get a glimpse of what they will learn about in the lesson. They will also read the lesson goals and keywords. Have students select each keyword and preview its definition.

Spelling List 27 Review Game

Students will practice all spelling words from the workshop.

Before You Read "The Necklace of Truth"

Students will be introduced to some key vocabulary words that they will encounter in the upcoming reading.

READ

"The Necklace of Truth"

Students will read "The Necklace of Truth" in *Expeditions in Reading*.

Check-In: "The Necklace of Truth"

Students will answer several questions to demonstrate their comprehension of "The Necklace of Truth."

LEARN AND TRY IT

LEARN Describing Setting and Characters in a Play

Students will learn that writers use stage directions and dialogue to communicate the setting and characters' emotions in a play.

TRY IT Describe Setting and Characters in a Play

Students will describe scenes, how scenes build on one another, setting, and characters' emotions in a play.

TRY IT Apply: Character's Feelings

Students will apply to a new work what they've learned about determining a character's feelings in a text.

TRY IT Plan a Play

Students will complete Plan a Play in *Summit English Language Arts 3 Activity Book*. They will answer questions to help them brainstorm ideas for a play that teaches a lesson to an audience. They should choose or invent characters, a setting for the action, the problem a character faces, how the problem is resolved, and what lesson the play teaches.

LEARNING COACH CHECK-IN This activity page contains open-ended questions, so it's important that you review students' responses. Students will write a scene from the play they plan in another lesson. They will not be asked to write the entire play.

NOTE Have students keep their completed activity page in a safe place so they can refer to it later.

TRY IT
"The Necklace of Truth"

Plan a Play

Read the writing prompt.

Answers will vary.

Prompt: Write stage directions and dialogue for a scene from a play.

Answer the questions to plan your play. (You will plan the full play, but you will only write a scene.)

1. What is the name of your play?

2. What is the setting of your play?

3. What lesson will your play teach?

"THE NECKLACE OF TRUTH" 615

4. Who are the characters in your play? Write a sentence to describe each one.

5. What problem are the characters in your play trying to solve?

6. What happens in each scene?

Scene 1

616 "THE NECKLACE OF TRUTH"

Scene 2

Scene 3

"THE NECKLACE OF TRUTH" 617

7. How do the characters solve the problem?

8. How do the characters feel while they are trying to solve the problem?

I'm looking for actors for my play. Want to try out?

Director

618 "THE NECKLACE OF TRUTH"

TRY IT Practice Words from "The Necklace of Truth"

Students will answer questions to demonstrate their understanding of the vocabulary words from the reading.

WRAP-UP

Question About Parts of a Play

Students will answer a question to show that they understand what the parts of a play are called.

Handwriting

Students should gather their handwriting materials and begin where they left off. Remind students to form letters carefully and correctly.

TIP Set a timer to help students stay focused during handwriting practice.

"The Necklace of Truth" Wrap-Up

Lesson Overview

ACTIVITY	ACTIVITY TITLE	TIME	ONLINE/OFFLINE
GET READY	Introduction to "The Necklace of Truth" Wrap-Up	**1** minute	online
	Read and Record	**20** minutes	online
TRY IT	Write a Scene LEARNING COACH CHECK-IN	**20** minutes	offline
	Review "The Necklace of Truth"	**20** minutes	online
QUIZ	"The Necklace of Truth"	**25** minutes	online
	Spelling List 27	**10** minutes	online
WRAP-UP	More Language Arts Practice	**16** minutes	online
	Handwriting	**8** minutes	offline

Advance Preparation

Gather students' completed Plan a Play activity page from "The Necklace of Truth." Students will refer to this page during Try It: Write a Scene.

MATERIALS

Supplied

- *Summit English Language Arts 3 Expeditions in Reading*
- *Summit English Language Arts 3 Activity Book*
  - Write a Scene
- handwriting workbook

Also Needed

- completed Plan a Play activity page from "The Necklace of Truth"

Lesson Goals

- Read aloud to practice fluency.
- Write a scene from a play.
- Review what you learned.
- Take a reading quiz.
- Take a spelling quiz.
- Develop letter formation fluency.

GET READY

Introduction to "The Necklace of Truth" Wrap-Up

Students will read the lesson goals.

Read and Record

Good readers read quickly, smoothly, and with expression. This is called *fluency*. Students will record themselves reading aloud. They will listen to their recording and think about how quick, smooth, and expressive they sound.

TIP Encourage students to rerecord as needed.

TRY IT

Write a Scene

Students will complete Write a Scene in *Summit English Language Arts 3 Activity Book*. Students should choose one scene from their brainstorming in the Plan a Play activity page to develop. They should include a few stage directions in the beginning, and they should write the dialogue between their characters. Students should follow the format of the model scene included in the activity book.

LEARNING COACH CHECK-IN This activity page contains an open-ended prompt, so it's important that you review students' response. Read students' scene; remind them that dialogue in a scene has to work hard. It has to reveal setting and characters' emotions in a scene.

NOTE Students do not need to write out the entire play they brainstormed in the Plan a Play activity page.

TRY IT

"The Necklace of Truth" Wrap-Up

Write a Scene

Read the writing prompt.

Prompt: **Write stage directions and dialogue for a scene of a play.**

Respond to the prompt. Use your work on the Plan a Play activity page to help you. Follow the format of this model scene.

The Magic Cookie Jar

Scene 2

SAM and MAX are sitting at the kitchen table with the magic cookie jar between them.

SAM: Where did Sophie go?

MAX: She said she had to help a friend with some math homework. (*MAX eyes the cookie jar*) I want some more cookies.

SAM: Me too! Do you remember the magic words that Sophie said to get cookies?

MAX: I think so. Wasn't it something like "Chocolate, sugar, oatmeal and spice, three little cookies would be so nice?"

SAM: It worked! I wonder what would happen if we asked for 10 cookies?

MAX: Let's try it. Chocolate, sugar, oatmeal and spice, 10 little cookies would be so nice. *(Ten cookies appear in the jar. MAX and SAM eat them. Then, 10 more appear.)*

SAM: I'm getting full. I don't know how many more cookies I can eat.

MAX: Ugh. My stomach is starting to hurt. How do we stop the cookies from coming?

SAM: I don't know! Do you remember?

MAX: No. I was trying to wrestle you off the couch. I didn't hear what Aunt Peg said!

SAM: Oh no! What are we going to do with all these cookies?

Answers will vary. Students' response should include stage directions and dialogue for a scene from a play.

"THE NECKLACE OF TRUTH" WRAP-UP 621

622 "THE NECKLACE OF TRUTH" WRAP-UP

Review "The Necklace of Truth"

Students will answer questions to review what they have learned about parts of a play and setting, theme, and characters' feelings in a play.

QUIZ

"The Necklace of Truth"

Students will complete the "The Necklace of Truth" quiz.

Spelling List 27

Students will complete the Spelling List 27 quiz.

WRAP-UP

More Language Arts Practice

Students will practice skills according to their individual needs.

Handwriting

Students should gather their handwriting materials and begin where they left off. Remind students to form letters carefully and correctly.

Set a timer to help students stay focused during handwriting practice.

Big Ideas: Respond to a Prompt

Lesson Overview

Big Ideas lessons provide students the opportunity to further apply the knowledge acquired and skills learned throughout the unit workshops. Each Big Ideas lesson consists of these parts:

1. **Cumulative Review:** Students keep their skills fresh by reviewing prior content.
2. **Preview:** Students practice answering the types of questions they will commonly find on standardized tests.
3. **Synthesis:** Students complete an assignment that allows them to connect and apply what they have learned. Synthesis assignments vary throughout the course.

   In the Synthesis portion of this Big Ideas lesson, students will respond to an essay prompt based on reading selections. To respond meaningfully, students will need to use their own ideas as well as examples from the readings. Students' writing will be assessed in four categories: purpose and content; structure and organization; language and word choice; and grammar, usage, and mechanics.

   LEARNING COACH CHECK-IN This is a graded assessment. Make sure students complete, review, and submit the assignment to their teacher.

All materials needed for this lesson are linked online and not provided in the activity book.

MATERIALS

Supplied

- Respond to a Prompt (printout)

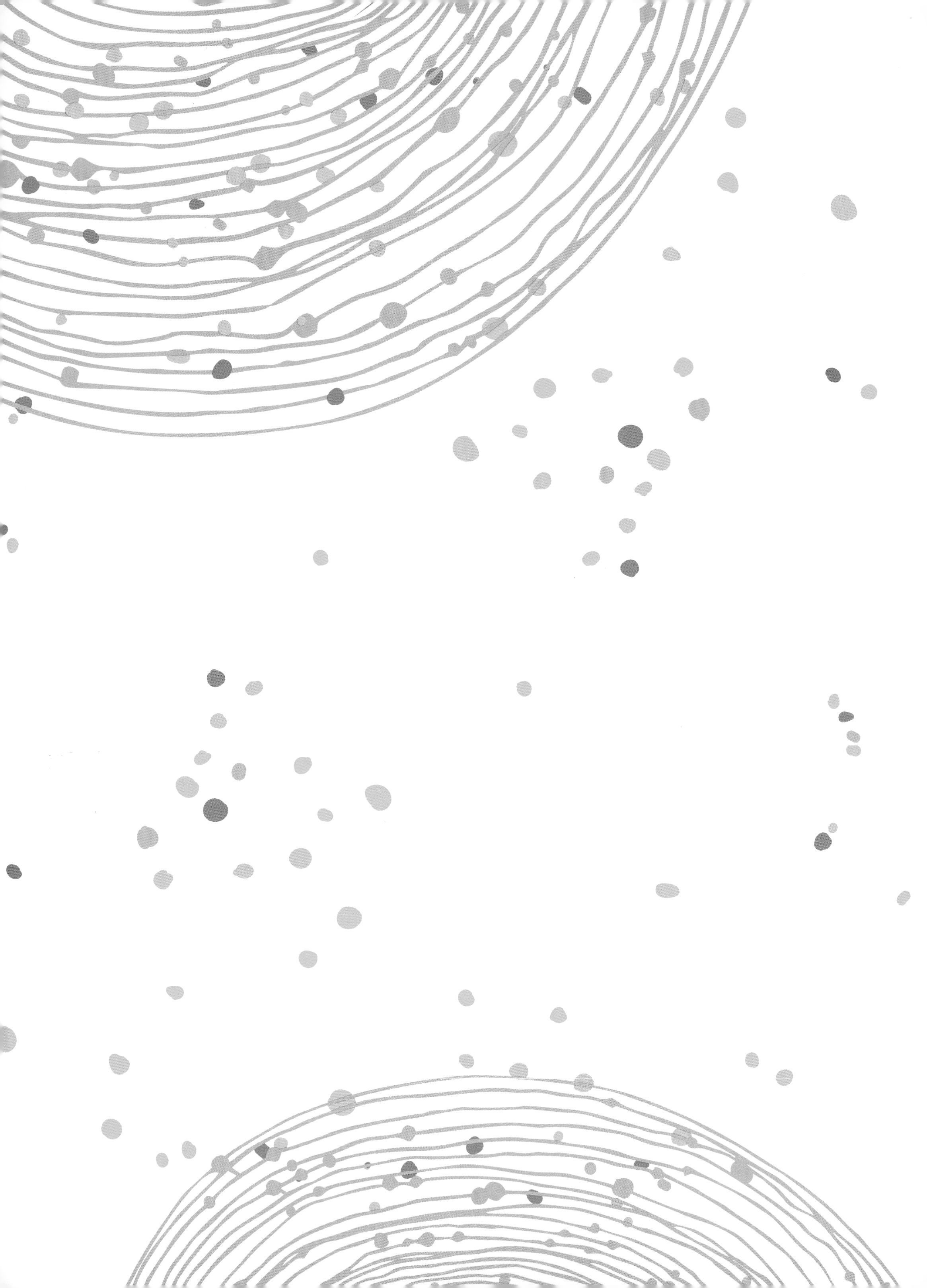